Toward Understanding
the
New Testament

TOWARD UNDERSTANDING
THE
NEW TESTAMENT

OBERT C. TANNER
LEWIS M. ROGERS
STERLING M. McMURRIN

Signature Books
Salt Lake City
1990

© 1990 by Signature Books, Inc.
Signature Books is a registered trademark of Signature Books, Inc.
All rights reserved.
Printed in the United States of America.

Except as permitted under the Copyright Act of 1976, no part of this publication may be reproduced or distributed in any form or by any means or stored in a database or retrieval system without prior written permission of the publisher.

∞ The paper in this book is acid free and meets the standards for permanence and durability established by the Committee on Production Guidelines for Book Longevity of the Council on Library Resources.

On the jacket: The name 'Jesus' written in Hebrew on an early ossuary.

LIBRARY OF CONGRESS CATALOGING-IN-PUBLICATION DATA

Tanner, Obert C. (Obert Clark), 1904–
    Toward understanding the New Testament/Obert C. Tanner, Lewis M. Rogers, Sterling M. McMurrin.
    p. cm.
    Bibliography: p.
    Includes index.
    ISBN 0-941214-76-1: $19.95
    1. Bible. N.T. — Introductions. 2. Bible. N.T. — Criticism, interpretation, etc. I. Rogers, Lewis M., 1918– .
II. McMurrin, Sterling M. III. Title.
BS2330.2.T36   1990
225.7 — dc19   88-22730
                                                                                 CIP

To those resolute scholars
past and present
whose commitment to reason and knowledge
has brought us closer to
an understanding of the New Testament

Contents

PREFACE ix

PART I JESUS IN THE GOSPELS 1

    1. The Early Years 3
    2. The Sources 30
    3. The Proclamation of the Kingdom 53
    4. The Sermons, Miracles, and Parables 78
    5. The Calling and Discipleship 106
    6. The Question of Jesus' Identity 133
    7. Jesus and the Messianic Consciousness 152
    8. On the Way to Jerusalem 174
    9. Last Days in Jerusalem 195
    10. The Passion and the Resurrection 214
    11. Jesus in the Gospel of John 252

PART II PAUL, PAULISM, AND THE EARLY CHURCH 277

    12. Paul and His Letters 279
    13. The Theology of Paul 316
    14. The Tradition of Paul 342
    15. The Tradition of John 362
    16. The Jewish Christian Tradition 385
    17. The Formation of the New Testament Canon 400

POSTSCRIPT 423

APPENDICES 424

    I. Important Versions of the Bible 424
    II. Historical Events from the Exodus to the New Testament 427
    III. An Early Christian Chronology 429
    IV. Major Non-Canonical Christian Writings, 95–430 CE 431

SELECTED READINGS 433

INDEX 447

Preface

In 1932 Professor Tanner published *New Testament Studies*, a text which was revised in 1935 as *The New Testament Speaks*. Several decades later, after numerous reprintings, Tanner considered publishing another revised, updated version. He invited his colleagues Rogers and McMurrin to join him in this venture. But rather than a conventional revision of *The New Testament Speaks*, we have produced a volume which is directed to a much larger audience and which introduces the reader to many of the problems that still trouble students of the New Testament.

Needless to say, anyone interested in a serious study of the New Testament owes an immeasurable debt to the great nineteenth-century and early twentieth-century students of the Bible, those who laid the foundations for the scholarly study of both the Old and New Testaments, and to the historians of the intertestamental period and the first centuries of the Common Era who have made the world of Jesus and the early Christians known as it was never known before. Our debt is not only for the vast knowledge that has accrued because of their work but also for the canons of historiography, the techniques of linguistic analysis, and the literary and historical modes of explanation and interpretation that have issued from the work of such scholars as Strauss, Baur, Ritschl, Pfleiderer, Schürer, Weiss, and Harnack.

But where once Harnack's treatment of Paul and the origins of Christianity and Schweitzer's eschatological exegesis seemed like the summit of scholarly study of Jesus, Paul, and the early church, these have proved to be temporary plateaus in a climb which has no end. Even Schürer's monumental studies on Jewish culture at the time of Jesus, while of immense and permanent value, have been surpassed by new insights and increased knowledge through the work of both Jewish and Christian historians and archaeologists.

Our own century has yielded a more bounteous harvest of scholarly work on the New Testament than could have been anticipated in 1900, and since the Second World War the extent of research and the output of valuable studies have increased at an incredible rate. The names are legion of those exegetes, linguists, historians, and archaeologists whose analytical skills have turned up new knowledge, new problems, and new historical perspectives, new explanatory theses, and new theological and philosophical interpretations—such names as Bultmann, Barth, Baeck, Sandmel, Davies, Finkelstein, Barrett, Bornkamm, Jonas, Herford, Daube, Jeremias, Werner, Dodd, Daniélou, Albright, and Yadin.

The large outpouring of scholarly work in recent decades indicates a great increase of interest not only in the historical context of Christian beginnings but also in the character of both Palestinian and Diaspora Judaism at the time of the destruction of the Second Temple to the completion of the Talmuds. This interest extends not only to the political, economic, and ideational backgrounds of the rise of the church and of the character of sectarian and Rabbinical Judaism but also to the entire spectrum of philosophical, moral, and religious ideas that pervaded the eastern Roman world at that time. The fortunate discoveries of the Nag Hammadi codices and the Qumran scrolls have not only provided increased knowledge but, together with the impressive work over recent decades by biblical archaeologists, have been a powerful stimulus to linguistic, literary, and historical research.

The result has been an important extension of our knowledge not only of Jewish and early Christian beliefs and practices but of the general character of the hellenistic culture of the period of Jesus and the primitive Christians. Light has been thrown on the possible relationship to Christian beginnings of Essenism, Pharisaism, Greek philosophic thought, Gnosticism, the Rabbinical religion, and even the eastern Mediterranean mystery religions.

In our research and writing we have been influenced by the powerful thrust of eschatology which Schweitzer gave to the interpretation of the Gospels and Paul, as well as his treatment of the mysticism of Paul. And the impact of the form criticism in the treatment of the Gospels that issued especially from the work of

Weiss will be evident, as well as the more recent demythologizing of the entire New Testament associated especially with Bultmann. But we are sensitive to the problems occasioned by changing scholarly fashions and the somewhat tentative character of even well-supported theses, and our writing has been tempered accordingly.

We agree with those historians who hold the now common view that the Gospels have seriously distorted the picture of Judaism at the time of Jesus, especially of the Pharisees and his relation to them, as well as the relation of the earliest Palestinian Christians to the Jewish religion generally. We have given much attention to this matter, describing the relations of Christians and Jews at a later time when the Gospels were written.

We have analyzed in some detail the several types of New Testament literature representative of the Pauline and Johannine as well as the Jewish or Petrine forms of the early religion. Here we have described the differences as well as continuities and commonalities of these early faiths. And, of course, we have given attention to the gnostic and hellenistic influences on the New Testament books, especially the Fourth Gospel and, to a lesser degree, the theology of Paul.

The path from the Galilean Jesus of the synoptic Gospels to the risen Savior God of Paul and the pre-existent Christ of the Fourth Gospel is both intriguing and difficult. We have attempted the perhaps impossible task of engaging the reader in some involvement with a broad spectrum of insights from leading scholars, while at the same time preserving the substance of the narrative tradition that has been the historical foundation of the Christian religion.

We are skeptical of the possibility of any definitive account of the events of Jesus' ministry or the substance and meaning of his teachings. But while recognizing the innumerable disputes among historians and Bible scholars, we have tried to identify what contemporary scholarship generally regards as the most reliable traditions about what happened in the beginning of the Christian movement.

We have assumed that the typical reader will already have some acquaintance with the New Testament. All biblical references are to the Revised Standard Version, which enjoys an unsurpassed reputation among scholars as an English version of the

Bible and Apocrypha. We have used this version with the permission of the Division of Christian Education of the National Council of the Churches of Christ in the United States of America.

We represent different viewpoints relative to specific interpretations of New Testament data, but in general we are in fundamental agreement. Especially, we agree in our effort to avoid any influence from religious or theological predisposition in our treatment of the historical materials, and we have made a serious attempt to understand both Jesus and Paul as living persons to be treated as belonging to their own time and place and circumstance. We do not describe or interpret them in terms of events or prophecies that lie in their past, or religious attitudes and beliefs that belong to their future. Both the writers of the New Testament and many of its interpreters have been victims of such bias. While recognizing that total objectivity in historical study is not possible, we have made a strenuous effort to free our study of the New Testament from the distortions that sometimes result from religious or non-religious belief.

This attitude should not be taken as a failure to recognize the piety of the writers of the Gospels, the great intellect and spirituality of the Apostle Paul, or his remarkable impact on subsequent history. And certainly our naturalistic disposition in the reading of the Gospels does not in the least diminish our reverence for Jesus and our appreciation for his spiritual and moral message and influence, or our respect for the religious tradition that issued from his life and death.

We are greatly indebted to Stan Larson for his careful reading of both the text and the notes. Denice Bowman and Dionne Williams have exhibited exceptional talent in preparing the manuscript, and Jacqueline Jacobsen has given valuable assistance in many ways. Donald M. Henriksen has enhanced the volume with his fine design and typography, and Trudy McMurrin has brought editorial expertise to the final reading of the proofs.

University of Utah, 1990   OBERT C. TANNER
LEWIS M. ROGERS
STERLING M. MCMURRIN

Part I

JESUS IN THE GOSPELS

CHAPTER 1

The Early Years

When Jesus was born in Palestine, Herod the Great was ending his long reign as king of the Jews and Caesar Augustus was the first emperor of Rome. Following a century of independence under the Jewish Hasmonean dynasty, the conquest of Jerusalem in 63 BCE by the pro-consul Gnaeus Pompey had made Palestine a part of the Roman Empire.

Jesus was born at least 1,250 years after Moses led the Hebrew tribes from Egypt to Canaan, 1,000 years after the coronation of King David, 700 years after the Prophet Isaiah, and almost 600 years after the destruction of Solomon's temple by the Babylonian king Nebuchadnezzar. For over seven centuries Israel had been under the yoke successively of Assyria, Babylonia, Persia, the Greek empires of Alexander the Great and Egypt and Syria, and finally, after a century of precarious independence, the overwhelming power of Rome.

The center of Jewish religious and cultural life was Jerusalem. The Temple, which had been rebuilt in the sixth century BCE as a modest structure after the return of the Jews from Babylon, had been enlarged by Herod to become one of the most impressive monuments in the entire Roman world. There, in the presence of Palestinian Jews and Jewish pilgrims from the numerous lands of the Diaspora, the priests daily performed the elaborate sacrificial rites required by the already ancient ceremonial law.

However, where there were adequate concentrations of Jews outside of Jerusalem, the local synagogues were the centers of religious worship and education. In the synagogues they learned the teaching of the prophets and the traditions of the Law, which had been handed down with meticulous care over many generations. The prophetic religious and moral precepts and the requirements of the Law had been kept alive through the centuries by a continued study of the sacred books, which were the foundations of Jewish religion and culture, the Law (Torah) and the Prophets.[1]

THE ACCOUNTS OF JESUS' BIRTH

Bethlehem, in the hills of Judea a few miles south of Jerusalem, has traditionally been considered the birthplace of Jesus. It is an ancient place, celebrated in the Old Testament as the city of David the King. According to Hebrew tradition, Rachel, the mother of Joseph, was buried on the way to Bethlehem.[a] Ruth, the ancestress of David and Jesus, came to Bethlehem from Moab.[b] And David, who became Israel's most illustrious king, was reared in Bethlehem[c] over a thousand years before the birth of Jesus.

According to Matthew 2:19, Jesus was born before the death of Herod the Great.[2] Since Herod died ca. 4 BCE, many historians accept that year as the date of Jesus' birth. Luke, on the other hand, suggests that the birth occurred the year of the Syrian governor Quirinius' census, which is believed by some to have been 6 CE. According to Luke 2:1f., the emperor Augustus decreed that a census be taken throughout the Roman world. Because he was of the "house and lineage of David," Joseph, who presumably lived in Nazareth, returned with Mary to his native city of Bethlehem to register for the census.

Early Christian tradition identified a cave or grotto in Bethlehem as the place where Jesus was born, and in the fourth century the Roman emperor Constantine built the Church of the Nativity

[a] Gn 35:19f. [b] Ru 1:19. [c] 1 Sm 17:12, 15.

[1] The title Old Testament was given to the collection of Hebrew-Jewish sacred writings by the early Christians, who regarded them as scripture. The Jewish name for the Old Testament is *Tanak*, which is derived from three Hebrew consonants T N K. Each letter represents one of the three major divisions of the Hebrew canon: T=Torah (Word or Revelation), N=Nebi'im (Prophets), and K=Kethubim (Writings). In Jesus' time only Torah and Prophets had been firmly established as sacred scripture.

[2] According to Oscar Cullmann, "In the earliest period the Christians not only accepted the fact that the date of the birth of Jesus is unknown; they felt besides no need to celebrate Christ's coming down to earth at all. The primitive Church was far more interested in Christ's death and resurrection than in his incarnation." Oscar Cullmann, *The Early Church, Studies in Early Christian History and Theology*, ed. A. J. B. Higgins, abridged ed. (Philadelphia, 1966), 23.

over this grotto. In the sixth century, the emperor Justinian rebuilt the church, and a good portion of the structure has survived. It is by many believed to be the oldest Christian church.

Luke's account of the birth of Jesus, which for centuries has been the heart of Christian lore and tradition, expressed the expectancy that prevailed among the common Jewish people of Palestine whose longing for their nation's redemption increased as their lives became more difficult under Roman rule. The hope that God would deliver Israel from bondage was already generations old, and the expectation of the coming of the day of redemption became even more intense with every disappointment and failure. That expectation, found especially in the later prophets and expressed with increasing strength in the apocalyptic and pseudepigraphic literature produced after the close of the Old Testament, reached its intensity in the period from Jesus' birth through the first century. The Jewish hope was for the redemption of the nation, of human history, and the world. This hope was to become in Christianity a faith in the redemption of the individual human soul.

The gospel stories of the nativity are far more than simply narratives of Jesus' birth or even expressions of the Jewish messianic expectations. Although their authors may have had access to earlier written accounts and certainly were acquainted with the existing oral traditions, the Gospels of Matthew and Luke, where the nativity stories appear, were not written until many years after the crucifixion of Jesus. By then the Christian communities, which came into existence following the crucifixion and the events of Pentecost, were in the process of formulating the foundations of their religious faith.

It is justifiable to believe that the faith of the church communities from which the Gospels of Luke and Matthew came was incorporated into the accounts of the nativity as well as into what are sometimes called the prologues of Matthew and Luke. The prologues include the annunciation of the births of John and Jesus, the presentation of the infant Jesus in the Temple, the visit of the Magi, and the flight to Egypt. These accounts are early

Christian reflections upon Jesus which proclaim him to be the source and heart of the new Christian faith.

The story of Jesus' birth is well known — the crowded inn, the stable and manger, the visit of the shepherds, and the appearance of the angel. Quite apart from the question of their literal truth, the account of these events has a permanent place in Christian tradition, poetry, and worship. As E. Titus has written:

> Whatever weight may be given them as historical documents, the stories [of Jesus' birth] are impressive monuments to the faith of the church. The person of Jesus had so impressed men that they could not account for his origin in ordinary terms. We must remember that the stories were written in the light of a knowledge of his magnificent life.[3]

Luke's prologue details the announcement of the birth of John the Baptist. John's father, Zechariah, was a priest, and his mother, Elizabeth, was a kinswoman of Mary, the mother of Jesus. Zechariah and Elizabeth were old and childless. According to Luke, an angel of the Lord appeared to Zechariah in the Temple while he was burning incense on the altar and foretold the birth of his son, to be called John.[d]

Luke records that six months after the visit to Zechariah, the angel Gabriel appeared to Mary. In contrast to the impressive surroundings in the Temple before the Holy Sanctuary where he appeared to Zechariah, the angel appeared to Mary in Nazareth, a small town in the hills of Galilee. It was here that Mary received the angel's salutation: "Hail, O favored one, the Lord is with you!"[e][4]

According to both Luke and Matthew, Mary was betrothed to Joseph at the time of the angel's appearance to her.[f] Betrothal was in Jewish practice as solemn as marriage itself, requiring a divorce for separation.[5] Joseph considered dissolving his betrothal,

---

[d] Lk 1:5–25. [e] Lk 1:28. [f] Mt 1:18; Lk 1:27.

[3] E. Titus, *Essentials of New Testament Study* (New York, 1958), 49.

[4] Luke provided the only account of these two predictions — the birth of John and the birth of Jesus.

[5] The ancient Hebrew law governing the violation of a betrothed virgin was set forth in Deuteronomy 22:23–27.

The Early Years

which could be done by public trial or by private agreement attested by a written document signed in the presence of witnesses. But according to Matthew, an angel appeared in a dream and counseled that he should not fear to take Mary as a wife for she would bear a son who would "save his people from their sins." [g]

The Song of Mary, recorded in Luke 1:46–55, has been known since the third century CE as "The Magnificat," the first word in the Latin translation. This song of praise is included in the ritual of several Christian churches. The words of Mary, similar in expression and thought to several passages in the Old Testament,[6] begin, "My soul magnifies the Lord, and my spirit rejoices in God my Savior, . . . For behold, henceforth all generations will call me blessed; for he who is mighty has done great things for me, and holy is his name."

When the son of Elizabeth was born and given the name John, Zechariah, according to Luke,[h] uttered a song-prophecy, recited in the ritual of the Christian church from the early centuries. Known as "The Benedictus," from the first word in the Latin translation, the language and thought of this song are also tied to Old Testament scripture and express the hopes of the Jewish nation for a Messiah: "Blessed be the Lord God of Israel, for he has visited and redeemed his people, and has raised up a horn of salvation for us in the house of his servant David." [i] [7]

THE GENEALOGIES OF JESUS

In both Luke and Matthew, the genealogy of Jesus is traced through Joseph back to David and Abraham.[8] However, the two

[g] Mt 1:19–21. [h] Lk 1:68–79. [i] Lk 1:68f.

[6] Compare Luke 1:39–55 with the story of Eli, Hannah's Prayer, and the birth of Samuel in 1 Samuel 2:1–10; also see Psalms 89, 103, 107; Micah 7:18–20; Isaiah 41:8–13.

[7] There are indications in the Gospels that John the Baptist had a substantial following and his disciples proclaimed him to be the Messiah. It has been suggested that Zechariah's prophecy stated in Luke 1:67–79 was originally part of a messianic tradition about John. A baptist sect may have existed in Ephesus after the death of John. This is suggested in Acts 18:24–19:7 where "about twelve" of John's disciples were converted to Christianity.

[8] Many of the names appearing in the genealogies of Matthew and Luke appear in 1 Chronicles 2–8. For a comparison of the two genealogies, see Raymond E. Brown, *The Birth of the Messiah* (New York, 1979), 84–94.

genealogies are quite different in detail. Matthew's gospel introduces "Jesus Christ, the son of David, the son of Abraham" [j] and begins with Abraham, the traditional common ancestor of the Hebrews who received the promise made in Genesis 12:3, "By you all the families of the earth shall bless themselves."

In the Gospel of Luke the genealogy is written in reverse order, beginning with Jesus and going back to Adam.[k] The genealogy also appears later in Luke where it is appended to the story of Jesus' baptism. Another difference is that Matthew traces the ancestry of Jesus through Solomon,[l] a son of David, and Luke traces it through Nathan, another son of David.[m] [9]

Some scholars have held that Matthew's genealogy is that of Joseph, Luke's that of Mary. It is more probable that the difference depends upon the point of view of the two evangelists. Apparently Matthew wrote his Gospel for Judean Jewish Christians and desired to show Jesus as a descendant of David, the one through whom the promise was to be fulfilled. This supported his claim that Jesus was the Messiah. Luke, on the other hand, apparently wrote especially for gentile Christians. His concern was to describe Jesus' relationship to man as universal, and therefore he traced the genealogy back to Adam, the biblical first man and father of the human race.

The story in Matthew of the wise men from the East visiting Mary, bringing gifts, and worshipping her child[n] has inspired much fiction, poetry, and painting. It is a story of great charm which, by virtue of its brevity, lack of detail, and legendary character, leaves much to the imagination. Matthew's account makes no attempt to identify the wise men who followed the star, who they were, how many, or where they came from. The description "from the East" suggests Mesopotamia or Persia, and the term "wise men" suggests they were astrologers or priests.[10] Astrology,

---

[j] Mt 1:1. [k] Lk 3:23–38. [l] Mt 1:6f. [m] Lk 3:31. [n] Mt 2:1–12.

[9] Nathan and Solomon are named in 1 Chronicles 3:5 as sons of Bathshua, or Bathsheba.

[10] The term *magai*, formerly interpreted as "wise men," is now more often understood as "astrologers." One of the second century church fathers, Ignatius of Antioch, in his letter to the Ephesians, seems to have assumed that Matthew meant "magicians," those who could interpret the signs in the heavens. The Letter of

The Early Years

a very ancient art in the East, was closely involved with both religion and science. There were then as now different interpretations of the star motif — that the stars determine the course of history or that every human being has a star in heaven which holds the secret of his destiny and watches over him wherever he goes.[11]

Matthew's tale of the adoration of the wise men with their costly gifts is in marked contrast to Luke's account of the shepherds coming from the nearby hills. The gifts of gold, incense, and myrrh, which followed the Eastern custom of giving impressive gifts on the occasion of audiences with a prince or monarch, point up Matthew's apparent interest in stressing the royalty of Jesus' birth and his messianic calling.[12]

The story of Herod's massacre of the infants which appears only in the Gospel of Matthew demonstrates Matthew's consistent effort to reinforce the belief among Jewish Christians that Jesus fulfilled biblical prophecy.º According to Matthew's account, an angel instructed Joseph to take the child and his mother to Egypt to escape Herod's anger. They remained there until Herod died. "This," says Matthew, "was to fulfil what the Lord had spoken by the prophet, 'Out of Egypt have I called my son.' "ᵖ The prophet of the passage is Hosea, but Hosea, it seems, did not intend the passage as a prophecy. There the "son" refers to the children of Israel, and the alleged prophecy reminds Israel of her

---

º Mt 2:13–23.   ᵖ Mt 2:15.

Ignatius to the Ephesians 19:2–3 in Cyril C. Richardson, ed. and trans., *Early Christian Fathers*, Vol. I of the *Library of Christian Classics*, ed. John Baillie, et al. (Philadelphia, 1953), 93.

[11] Accounts are not uncommon in which the whole universe attends the birth of religious heroes, as in the case of the Buddha and Muhammed. In some accounts the miracle is accompanied by a star or brilliant light. "Now at the moment when the future Buddha made himself incarnate in his mother's womb, . . . an immeasurable light appeared. The blind received their sight, as if from very longing to hold this his glory. The deaf heard the noise. The dumb spake one with another. The crooked became straight. The lame walked." C. H. Hamilton, ed., *Buddhism, A Religion of Infinite Compassion* (New York, 1952), 3.

[12] The traditional Christmas story is a synthesis of several elements from Matthew and Luke. The wise men from the East, the star, and the flight into Egypt and return following the death of Herod are features of Matthew's account. The appearance of angels, the shepherds in the field, and the manger are from Luke.

deliverance from Egyptian bondage: "When Israel was a child, I loved him, and out of Egypt I called my son." q

It is a common view that Matthew's Gospel was written especially for Jewish Christians. Certainly it is strongly oriented to readers of Jewish background. The story of the flight to Egypt is typical of the general theme of the book, which is that much Old Testament prophecy finds fulfillment in Jesus and his gospel. The authenticity of the story about the massacre of the young male children in the region of Bethlehem, which appears only in Matthew, is also questionable. However, Matthew's report is not inconsistent with the known character and crimes of Herod.[13] Herod was a highly competent but excessively cruel and amoral administrator who was committed to any course of action that promised to enhance and preserve his power.

Luke's account, which makes no mention of a journey to Egypt, follows the presentation in the Temple with these words: "And when they had performed everything according to the law of the Lord, they returned into Galilee, to their own city, Nazareth." r Matthew reports, however, that Joseph intended returning to Judea, but when he learned that following Herod's death his son Archelaüs reigned in Judea, "he withdrew to the district of Galilee." And Matthew continues, Jesus "dwelt in a city called Nazareth, that what was spoken by the prophets might be fulfilled, 'He shall be called a Nazarene.' " s [14]

Jesus was born and reared in a Jewish family. Apparently, his parents were believing, practicing Jews, and there is every evidence that throughout his own life Jesus also was a devout Jew in both belief and practice. The name "Jesus," not uncommon in that day, is a shortened Greek form of the Hebrew name Jeshua or Joshua, which means "the Lord saves." In this instance the

---

q Hos 11:1.   r Lk 2:39.   s Mt 2:22f.

[13] Many scholars regard the entire story of Herod's threat, the flight to and return from Egypt, and the massacre of the infants as a literary creation by Matthew intended to show Jesus as the Messiah fulfilling Old Testament prophecy.

[14] The source of this prophecy is problematic. Some have suggested Isaiah 11:1 as a possibility, but the Hebrew text of Isaiah is not sufficiently clear to establish this point. See Brown, *The Birth of the Messiah*, 207–13.

The Early Years

name had uncommon significance, for according to Luke's account here was one who had come to save his people.

All the rituals and ceremonies that were customary with Jewish children were no doubt a part of the infancy and childhood of Jesus. Luke indicates that when Jesus was eight days old he was circumcised, the custom among the Hebrews from earliest times. Forty days later came the ceremonial purification, a ritual related to the belief that the firstborn male child belonged to God and must be redeemed by offering a sacrifice in the Temple.[t][15] Leviticus 12:8 decreed that mothers who could not afford to sacrifice a lamb might substitute a pair of turtledoves or two young pigeons. The fact that Mary brought for the sacrifice only "a pair of turtle doves" indicates that Joseph and Mary were probably of modest means. In his account of the presentation of Jesus in the Temple, Luke introduced Simeon and the prophetess Anna, described as devout Jews looking for the consolation and redemption of the children of Israel.[u] These two, according to Luke, believed that the infant Jesus was to be the instrument of that redemption.

THE EARLY YEARS OF JESUS

Aside from its association with the youth and early manhood of Jesus, Nazareth is of little importance in Jewish literature. But for Christians, Nazareth has always been a celebrated place. Here, according to Luke, the angel Gabriel appeared to Mary; here also Joseph and his family made their home. Most important of all, apparently this was the home of Jesus during most of his life.

Perhaps Nazareth rather than Bethlehem was the place of Jesus' birth. Some scholars argue that to strengthen Jesus' connections with royalty in the Davidic line and thereby support their claim that Jesus was the long-awaited Messiah, the early Christian writers placed his birth in Bethlehem, because an ancient tradition

---

[t] Lk 2:21–40. [u] Lk 2:25, 36–38.

[15] According to Luke, Mary was considered "unclean" for seven days after giving birth and expected to remain in isolation for another thirty-three days — hence, a total of forty days in Bethlehem. The biblical basis for this is found in Leviticus 12:2–4.

decreed that the Messiah would come from the City of David. Crucial to this argument is the claim of some historians that the account of the Roman census given in Luke 2:1–3, which occasioned the journey of Joseph and Mary to Bethlehem, has no historical base and that the census of the Syrian governor Quirinius in 6 CE should be discounted. The Cambridge historian Michael Grant has argued, largely based on passages in the Gospel of John, especially 1:46 and 7:41–42, that Jesus was born in Galilee, probably in Nazareth.[16]

A traveler approaching Nazareth from almost any direction will come upon it very suddenly, for it is situated in a basin of hills. An observer standing today on the west rim of the highest hill just south of Nazareth confronts a spectacular view. To the east is the Jordan Valley with the plateau of Transjordan (Jordan) beyond. To the south is the Plain of Esdraelon and the mounds of Beth-Shean, Tabor, Gilboa, and Meggido. To the west in the distance, paralleling the plain all the way to the Mediterranean, runs the Mount Carmel mountain ridge.

The world in which Jesus lived was peopled not only with peasants but with religious leaders and scholars, traders, travelers, and Roman soldiers. Not far from Nazareth the major trade routes connected the sea coast with the interior of Syria and the vast trans-Jordan country. Greek culture had spread throughout Palestine, especially in the cities, and impressive Greek temples and Roman theatres and stadia were conspicuous in many large cities.

Only four miles northwest of Nazareth was Sepphoris, a city of some importance.[17] Here, when Jesus was about ten years old, Judas the Galilean led a desperate revolt against Roman control. For decades Galilee, whose people had a fierce love of indepen-

---

[16] Michael Grant, *Jesus: An Historian's Review of the Gospels* (New York, 1977), 72f. The Gospel of Mark seems to identify Jesus with Nazareth. See Mk 1:9, 24; 10:47; 14:67; 16:6.

[17] Sepphoris, today only an archaeological site, played a rather prominent role in early Jewish history. It was established as a military fortress in the time of Alexander Jannaeus (103–76 BCE) and continued to serve as a military post during the reign of Herod the Great. It was made the capital of Galilee during the rule of Gabinius, the Roman proconsul of Syria from 57 to 55 BCE, who established it as one of the five administrative centers in Palestine.

The Early Years

dence, had been a major center of sedition against the Romans. To crush Judas' rebellion, the Romans burned the city, sold the inhabitants into slavery, and crucified two thousand men who were suspected of participating in the uprising.[18] Jesus may have viewed this terrible scene. In any event, it is unlikely that his boyhood in Nazareth was entirely peaceful. The atmosphere of Galilee was charged with revolt against the hated yoke of the Romans. Nazareth was off the main routes of travel and commerce, but Palestine as a whole was busy and sustained a large population. It was the crossroads for major segments of the ancient world, alive with commercial, intellectual, military, and political activities.

The Gospels indicate that Jesus was one of a family of five brothers and at least two sisters. However, only his brothers' names are given: James, Joses (or Joseph), Judas, and Simon.[v] [19] It is usually assumed that Joseph, their father, belonged to the working class of the community. A typical Jewish home in Jesus' time followed a careful schedule of religious law and custom. Prayer would have been offered at meal times. A boy was taught to observe the Sabbath and give thanks at the first glimpse of the rising sun. A metal box containing the opening words of the *Shema* was placed above or at the upper side of the door of the house, to be touched on coming in or going out. "Hear, O Israel: The Lord our God is one Lord." [w]

In the Sabbath service at the synagogue, a boy would attend to the reading of the Law and listen to the interpretation of excerpts from the Law and the Prophets by an elder of the congregation. Aramaic Semitic, a dialect closely related to Hebrew, was the commonly spoken language of Palestine and the surrounding region and was undoubtedly the language Jesus spoke. The home and the synagogue school provided education in the foundations of

---

[v] Mk 6:3. [w] Dt 6:4f.

[18] It has been assumed by some scholars that this is the Judas and the rebellion against Quirinius' census in ca. 6 CE which is described by Gamaliel to the council in Acts 5:37. See J. W. Packer, *Acts of the Apostles* (Cambridge, 1966), 47. A more detailed account is provided by Josephus, who traces the origins of the Zealots to this uprising. Flavius Josephus, *Antiquities of the Jews*, Book XVII, Chap. X, Sec. 10 and Book XVIII, Chap. I, Sec. 6.

[19] Compare Mk 6:3 with Mt 13:55f., also with Lk 4:22, and Jn 1:45; 6:42.

Jewish religion, including some knowledge of language and an acquaintance with the sacred texts of the scriptures.

During his ministry Jesus often alluded to the world of his youth. He knew what it was to come home hungry and ask for bread[x] and eggs and fish.[y] He saw his mother grinding at the mill[z] and putting leaven in the meal.[a] Like his brothers, he gave his clothes hard wear and learned what happened when patches were sewn on clothes already worn.[b] In his parables he told of lost coins, of candles, bushels, beds, moths, rust, and the typical things a boy would experience in a rural community.

At six years of age Jesus was probably sent to school in the synagogue. Here he was taught to read and write. In the beginning concentration was on learning to read and write Hebrew, the language of the sacred literature. Sitting cross-legged on the floor in a circle about the teacher, the class learned their letters and memorized long passages from the Five Books of the Torah, the Pentateuch. Jesus would also have learned the history and traditions of his people. The stories of Abraham, Joseph, Moses, David, Elijah and the prophets, and especially the heroism of the Maccabees were no doubt familiar to every Jewish boy of his day.

Luke recorded the only incident concerning Jesus' youth reported in the canonical Gospels. At the time of the Passover, faithful Jews made the pilgrimage to Jerusalem, many from cities far beyond the borders of Palestine.[20] All male Jews were expected to attend the major religious festivals. The visit to Jerusalem reported by Luke probably had a special significance for Jesus and his parents, for at age thirteen a Jewish boy became *Bar Mitzvah*, "a son of the commandment." [21] Jesus was twelve years old and thus was nearing the time for accepting the obligations of the Law and being received into the religious community.

The incident of being lost on perhaps his first visit to a large city was the occasion for Luke to point up the uniqueness of

[x] Mt 7:9. [y] Mt 7:10; Lk 11:11f. [z] Lk 17:35. [a] Mt 13:33. [b] Mk 2:21.

[20] In the "period of the Second Temple approximately one million pilgrims from all over the country, as well as the Diaspora, made the journey on feast days three times a year." See Menashe Har-El, "Jerusalem and Judea: Roads and Fortifications" in *Biblical Archaeologist* Vol. 44 (1981), No. 1: 13.

[21] See Abraham Cohen, *Everyman's Talmud* (New York, 1975), 73, n. 1.

The Early Years

Jesus — his early sense of his destiny. Jesus' parents "found him in the temple, sitting among the teachers, listening to them and asking them questions." For Luke, Jesus was an exceptional child for "all who heard him were amazed at his understanding and his answers." [22] Here in Luke appear the earliest words of Jesus: "How is it that you sought me? Did you not know that I must be in my Father's house?" [c]

Luke's account is brief, yet his words eloquently describe his commitment to Jesus as the Son of God. However, these verses also indicate that Jesus lived a normal life, that he "gained" or "increased' in wisdom and in stature. For approximately eighteen years following the incident in the Temple, Jesus may have worked as a wood craftsman in Nazareth. No incident from these years is recorded. That there is no further mention of Joseph in the Gospels has suggested to some that he may have died before Jesus began his ministry.[23] If this were the case, it might explain why Jesus remained so long in Nazareth. As eldest son, he may have assumed responsibility for the care of his mother and brothers and sisters. Although we have no record of a single incident from the important adolescent and early adult years of Jesus' life, still we can be reasonably certain that they had a powerful impact upon his thought and character.

In Nazareth people probably knew one another rather intimately: the joys of a wedding, the welcome of a newborn babe, the sorrows of a funeral, the problems of the poor and oppressed. Jesus would have known those engaged in farming, fishing, building, carpentry, household work, and commerce. In the nearby city of Sepphoris were political officials, religious sects, teachers, and

---

[c] Lk 2:46f., 49.

[22] In the period from the second to the seventh century CE several gospels and other Christian documents were written, some available now only in fragments, which are not included in the New Testament canon: the Gospels of James, Nicodemus, the Hebrews, the Ebionites, the Egyptians, and Peter, and probably the most important of all, the Gospel of Thomas. A major concern of some of these gospels was to heighten the miraculous in the early life of Jesus. They say in effect that the power Jesus possessed by virtue of his divinity was clearly evident throughout his life, from infancy to his death and resurrection. In them Jesus was a wonder child.

[23] Mark speaks of Jesus' mother and brothers and sisters but not of his father (Mk 3:31f.; 6:3). Joseph nowhere appears in the account of Jesus' ministry.

Roman soldiers. Jesus no doubt experienced the common problems generated by the demands of morality and ceremonial law — proper observance of the Sabbath and proper relations with family and neighbors. He probably heard and perhaps engaged in discussions on such subjects as marriage, divorce, poverty, war, and debt. People close to him suffered anxiety, injustice, fear, pain, death, and mourning. He learned by experience the virtue of mercy and love, developed a respect for women, and no doubt found pleasure in the company of children. His experiences in the marketplace at Sepphoris, in his home at Nazareth, in the shop, and in the hills as well as in the synagogue increased his knowledge and matured his judgment and brought him an understanding of his people, the vicissitudes of their past, and their current anxieties, hopes, and expectations.

PALESTINE UNDER GREEK RULE

Palestine forms a land-bridge connecting Africa to the continents of Asia and Europe. For thousands of years it has been a route of commerce and conquest for the great civilizations which developed in Asia Minor, Egypt, and Mesopotamia.[24] From earliest times this land, known before the Hebrew occupation as Canaan, was an oasis for invading tribes; for the biblical Hebrews, it was a promised land, the land of "milk and honey."

The invasion of Canaan by Joshua and the Hebrew tribes was accomplished by both conquest and infiltration. Other Semitic peoples, including Amorites, Canaanites, Hurrians or Horites, and Hittites had settled in Canaan long before the coming of the Hebrews. The Amorites (Amurru), for example, were a semi-nomadic people from the West who overran most of Mesopotamia about 1728 BCE and established the First Babylonian dynasty, whose greatest monarch was Hammurabi. The Amorites were the dominant people of the Canaanite population before the Hebrew conquest and settlement.

[24] The term "Palestine" was derived from "Philistine," the name that designated the invaders of the coastland whose conquests were contemporaneous with the Hebrew conquest of the highlands of Canaan.

The Early Years

The succession of invasions of Canaan had a profound and lasting impact on its inhabitants. Through the centuries the people were captured, deported, destroyed, and enslaved. The endurance of the Hebrew people on this narrow strip between sea and desert, the survival of their culture and the lasting integrity of their religion in the midst of powerful forces that influenced but failed to assimilate them fully, is one of the wonders of history. The great empires which successively conquered, ruled, and exploited them, Assyria, Babylonia, Persia, Greece, and finally Rome, failed to remove them from the stage of history but rather seemed to strengthen them in their resolution, endurance, and hope. The explanation of this remarkable strength must be found in their religion with its powerful moral commitment.

The years following the conquest and settlement of Canaan and the establishment of the Davidic monarchy were crowded with important historical events. In the century following the end of the Old Testament period of Hebrew history — after the Assyrian, Babylonian, and Persian conquests — the center of power shifted westward. Beginning at 333 BCE, the Macedonian king, Alexander the Great, invaded Asia Minor, Palestine, and Egypt and moved eastward across Mesopotamia as far as India. Conquering the immense Persian Empire, he made himself master of the Eastern Mediterranean world and most of the Middle East.

While war was usually for conquest and economic exploitation, Alexander had other purposes as well. He was remarkably successful in his swift military campaigns and in establishing his authority over his conquered territories, but in the view of many historians, his interests were broader than simply conquest and rule. He was committed to extending the "civilizing" influence of Greek culture throughout his conquered domain.

The ancient world was indelibly affected both culturally and politically by the Alexandrian conquests. Palestine was not immune to these influences during its subjection to Greek rule, from 332 to 167 BCE. In general the Greeks were tolerant of the religious beliefs of other peoples, and under their rule the Jews were permitted to practice their religion in accordance with the established forms and traditions. But the eventual use throughout the eastern Mediterranean world of the Greek language and spread of hellenic literature and thought had a profound and permanent impact on the ancient world generally. Although the empire created by Alexander endured for a brief time only, the hellenic culture survived and is even today the chief foundation of occidental science, philosophy, and art.

However, at least one segment of Alexander's empire did not accept Greek culture without severe protest — Judea. While some Jewish groups, motivated by economic and political considerations, favored conformity rather than resistance to foreign ideas and practices, others condemned hellenization as a deadly menace to their religion. They were committed to the belief that only strict observance of the Jewish Law and tradition could insure the purity of religion and thereby fulfill their covenant with God. The issue of hellenization came to a climax in 168 BCE with the revolt of the Maccabees.

Alexander died in 323 BCE at the early age of thirty-two, but the cultural movement he began did not perish with him. After his death and following a two-decade struggle for power among his surviving generals, his empire was divided among three of the victors. Two of the resulting dynasties would eventually rule Palestine — the Ptolemaic and Seleucid. For a century Palestine was mainly under the rule of the Ptolemies, the Greek rulers of Egypt. The Ptolemies exacted tribute from the Jews but granted them considerable political autonomy and religious freedom. During their reign from at least 301 BCE to the Roman conquest, large numbers of Jews settled in Alexandria in Egypt. Founded by Alexander the Great at the mouth of the Nile, Alexandria was to become the chief cultural center of the Greek world, the Athens of the hellenistic era. Here the Jews were under strong hellenic influences and many of them, while retaining their traditional religion, became prominent and influential among the Egyptian Greeks. It was in Egypt during the reign of the Ptolemies that the sacred Jewish books were translated from the Hebrew into Greek, the so-called Septuagint.[25] By this time, around the middle of the

---

[25] The Septuagint, the Seventy (LXX), translated from Hebrew into Greek in Egypt ca. 250 BCE, became the bible of the early Greek-speaking Christian church.

third century BCE, great numbers of Diaspora Jews scattered throughout the Mediterranean world were unable to speak and read Hebrew, but the Greek language, the Koine, was familiar to them. With the Septuagint they were able to read the sacred texts of their religious tradition.

Following the death of Alexander, Palestine was under constant contention between the Syrian Seleucids and the Egyptian Ptolemies, both of them Greek kingdoms. In 198 BCE Palestine was finally wrested from Egypt by the Seleucids, whose capital was Antioch. The Syrian Greek king, Antiochus III the Great, ruled a vast empire that reached from the Mediterranean across Syria and Persia. His son, Antiochus IV, is of central interest in the history of the Jews because he forced the issues which led to the Maccabean rebellion and Jewish independence.

Antiochus IV, who assumed the epithet "Epiphanes," "the manifest (God)," attempted a general cultural as well as political unification of his domain, apparently in a desperate effort to save the declining empire from disintegration. In 168 BCE, after the Jews resisted his efforts, he proscribed their religion and forced violations of crucial elements of the Jewish Law. Many influential Jews were already hellenized and favored the adoption of Greek thought, manners, and morals, but Antiochus pushed his demands to the extreme by declaring circumcision and Sabbath observance capital offenses and by commanding that sacrifices be offered to Zeus rather than the Hebrew God. For the Jews submission to these demands was blasphemy, and though some acceded rather freely to the Syrian requirements, many submitted only through fear of the dreadful consequences that would fall upon Judah if they resisted. Antiochus pillaged the Temple of its treasures and desecrated it with pagan altars and the sacrifice of swine.

THE MACCABEAN REVOLT AND HASMONEAN DYNASTY

Those who stood firm against Graeco-Syrian rule and its atrocities perhaps inevitably united in revolt when effective leadership emerged. That leadership and the rebellion came when an old priest, Mattathias, in the village of Modein, refused to sacrifice swine to Zeus and killed a Jew who attempted under Syrian orders to make the sacrifice in his stead. He also killed the attending Syrian official. After this dramatic and crucial encounter, Mattathias fled with his sons and a few followers to the mountains. Here his ranks increased from the conservative segments of the population until he had the strength to carry on guerrilla warfare. The war was carried on not only against the Syrian Greeks but also against those Jews who accommodated Syrian demands and refused to join the revolt. Mattathias died in 166 BCE when the rebellion was just beginning, but his son, Judas, called Maccabaeus or the "Hammerer," and later his other sons Jonathan and Simon, each in turn, led the revolt to eventual success.[26] The temple area in Jerusalem was finally taken on the twenty-fifth of Kislev (approximately December) 165 BCE, and the Temple was rededicated.[27] By 141 BCE, for the first time since the conquests by Assyria and Babylon in the eighth and sixth centuries, Palestine had the firm status of an independent Jewish state. Its independence was recognized by Rome, which by this time had become an influential power. Descendants of the Maccabees became the hereditary monarchs of Judea and ruled until a generation before the time of Jesus.

PALESTINE UNDER ROME AND THE HERODS

The Maccabean princes, the Hasmoneans, were for the most part competent rulers, but they were not universally popular. In the beginning of the rebellion, the sons of Mattathias were motivated by religious ideals, and large numbers of the common people supported them. But when their successors in the Hasmonean dynasty became more concerned with satisfying their personal and political ambitions as kings, queens, and high priests, popular support weakened. In 63 BCE the Roman general and pro-consul Pompey, then headquartered in Damascus, brought the Romans directly into Jewish history. Two Hasmonean princes, Hyrcanus II

---

[26] For a detailed account of the Maccabean war, see 1 Maccabees, 1–10, and 2 Maccabees 5–15, and Josephus, *Antiquities*, XII, 5–9.

[27] The rededication of the Temple has been celebrated since by the Feast of Hanukkah. A legend connected with the rededication, that fuel for the lamps sufficient for only one day burned for eight days, is responsible for the celebration being called the Feast of Lights.

and Aristobulus II, were struggling over the throne at Jerusalem. A civil war ensued, and each of the contenders sent a delegation to Pompey seeking Roman support. However, a party of the common people also sent representatives to Damascus to petition Pompey to remove both princes and place the nation under the jurisdiction of a high priest. This conflict provided the occasion for Roman intervention, and Pompey took both princes into custody. Aristobulus later fled to Jerusalem to defend his claim. Pompey then marched on Jerusalem and, after a siege of three months, occupied the city, including the temple area. He then executed thousands of Jerusalem's inhabitants, exiled Aristobulus and his family to Rome, and appointed Hyrcanus II as high priest and titular ruler under Roman jurisdiction and with the support of a Roman garrison. After a century of precarious independence, Judea had become subject to Rome.

The history of Palestine from the Roman conquest until Herod became king is an account of continual political intrigue and discontent. Following the defeat of Pompey by Julius Caesar, an Idumean, called Antipater, who had been the chief administrator under Hyrcanus, was appointed governor of Judea. In 40 BCE through the intervention of the Roman statesman Marc Antony, Antipater's younger son Herod, who had demonstrated impressive political ability as governor of Galilee, was appointed by the Roman senate to be king over the Jews. It was three years, however, before Herod actually established control of the land. He reigned over Palestine until his death, probably in 4 BCE. According to the nativity stories in the Gospel of Matthew, it was during the closing years of Herod's reign that Jesus was born.

Herod the Great was in many respects an exceptionally efficient and successful ruler. He possessed unusual administrative capabilities and was able to please Rome while at the same time keeping the peace in Palestine. When Antony was defeated at Actium by Octavianus, who became the first Roman emperor, Augustus, Herod successfully shifted his allegiance to the victor and received strong support from him. Although only partly Jewish by birth, Herod was Jewish in his religion. However, he lived and ruled like a Roman and brought to Judea, especially through his great construction projects, a large element of Roman culture and civilization.[28] He had an efficient system of taxation and committed much of the income to his building program which reached beyond Palestine and took the larger part of a century to complete.[29] The reconstructed and enlarged temple in Jerusalem was one of the great structures of the Roman empire.[30]

However, Herod was excessively cruel. He murdered one of his wives and two of his own sons, Alexander and Aristobulus. Despite his public works and maintenance of peace and order, he was generally feared and hated by his Jewish subjects.[31] This was especially true during the later years of his life. The Gospel of Matthew exhibits his cruelty in the story of the slaying of the infants of Bethlehem.[32]

After the death of Herod the Great, ca. 4 BCE, the administration of the kingdom was divided by the Romans among three of his sons, Herod Archelaus, Herod Antipas, and Herod Philip. Archelaus was made ethnarch of Judea, Samaria, and Idumea. He was a failure as an administrator and after ten years of misrule

[28] The extent of Herod's assimilation to Roman culture is clearly evident. His three-tiered palace at Masada and his palace at the Herodium, for example, are Roman in style and architecture. Marble pillars and Roman baths have been discovered in both fortresses. Herod's greatest feat of construction was the coastal seaport city of Caesarea Maritima, which became the Roman capital of Palestine.

[29] In addition to reconstructing the Temple Mount, Herod built a beautiful palace for himself in Jerusalem, and to protect it, he constructed a barracks for his own guard with connecting ramparts and three towers, known today as the Citadel.

[30] Herod constructed an earthen and stone platform around the Temple Mount, and in order to contain the platform on the rather steep slope, he built a massive retaining wall on the western, southern, and eastern borders. All that remains today of the Second Temple is a portion of the western retaining wall, which is a place of pilgrimage for Jews from all over the world. The Temple Mount itself is now crowned by two Muslim structures, the Dome of the Rock and the Mosque of al-Aksa, built following the capture of Jerusalem by the caliph Omar in 637 CE.

[31] Herod's fear of revolt from within his own kingdom and his anxiety over the possible usurpation of his power by his chief competitor for Roman favor, Cleopatra, the last of the Greek Ptolemies of Egypt, compelled him to establish and supply several fortresses. Among these were the fortresses at Masada and Machaerus near the Dead Sea, which he reconstructed and garrisoned, and the Herodium located about seven miles southeast of Jerusalem, which he constructed.

[32] Josephus recorded that shortly before his death Herod commanded "that one out of every family should be slain," presumably to guarantee that there would be mourning at the time of his own death. This plot was apparently frustrated by Archelaus, Herod's son and successor in Judea. *Antiquities*, XVII, VI, 6.

was deposed by the emperor Augustus in 6 CE. Matthew indicated the feeling of the Jews toward Herod Archelaus when he stated that Joseph feared to return from Egypt to Bethlehem because of Archelaus and, therefore, returned to Galilee.[d] After the removal of Archelaus, Judea, Samaria, and Idumea were placed directly under Roman rule through a prefect and later a procurator, who was in charge of troops, taxation, and the administration of justice. The procurators were responsible to the Roman governors of the province of Syria, whose capital was Antioch. Pontius Pilate, the best known of the procurators because he was in office at the time of Jesus' execution, had his headquarters in Caesarea, the Roman city built by Herod the Great. However, he kept a garrison in Jerusalem to maintain the peace and was usually in Jerusalem at the time of the Passover and other important feasts.

Herod Antipas was given jurisdiction over Galilee and Perea, which he ruled under Roman control until 39 CE. Antipas also appears to have been an incompetent ruler and, like Archelaus, was disliked by the Jews. He is mentioned in the Gospels in connection with the imprisonment and execution of John the Baptist. He was in Jerusalem at the time of the trial of Jesus, and Jesus was brought before him presumably because Jesus was from Galilee.

According to Josephus, Herod Philip was the most able of the three brothers. He was given control of a large area northeast of Galilee, establishing Caesarea Philippi as his capital.[33] The Gospels record that on several occasions Jesus retired to Philip's territory when he felt unsafe in Judea and Galilee. Philip died in 34 CE.

JEWISH RELIGION IN THE TIME OF JESUS

The Jewish religion already had a long and involved history by the time of Jesus, beginning with the early Hebrew patriarchs and particularly with Moses, the Exodus, and with the giving of the Law and the Sinai covenant. These were important features

[d] Mt 2:22.

[33] Philip rebuilt the ancient city of Paneas and renamed it Caesarea Philippi. It is mentioned several times in the Gospels.

of Israel's heroic age when beliefs about Israel's God were emerging from the tribal religion. Israel's moral and religious insights and values and its social and political ideals had their roots in this age, the age when faith in God's promise of an ultimate, triumphant destiny was born.

The remarkable strength and integrity of the Jewish community, evidenced throughout history from as early as the Babylonian captivity, are no doubt due in large part to the role religion played in the life of the people. The ancient Hebrew tribes were bound together as a religious, social, and political community by a covenant. This covenant was based upon law, traditionally believed to have been revealed by God, which elicited from the people a remarkably strong religious commitment and a profound sense of moral duty. Israel's socio-religious life at the time of Jesus centered around this divine-human covenant, the Law (Torah), the Temple and its sacrificial cult, and the synagogue. Within these institutions, constantly strengthened and protected by the priests and sages, the group and individual religious and moral duties were defined and mandated. The great Hebrew prophets of the eighth, seventh, and sixth centuries BCE had been powerful critics, moral and religious teachers, and creators of the Jewish monotheism with its profound ethical commitments. The prophets' attacks were leveled especially at the idolatry and moral practices of their non-Hebrew enemies, practices that constantly threatened the integrity of Yahweh worship, and against the religious and political leaders of Israel and Judah who were unfaithful to the tenets of that worship. They demanded recognition and adherence to the spirit of the Mosaic covenant and Law. The prophetic religion was, with the Torah, the substance of the ethical-religious heritage of Judaism in Jesus' day.

From its construction by Solomon in the tenth century and its reconstruction in the sixth century BCE after the Babylonian captivity, the Temple in Jerusalem was the central religious shrine. Jewish worship related especially to the sacrificial rituals was centered there until the Temple's destruction by the Romans in 70 CE. The high priest, who during the Roman period was appointed by the Roman government, exerted considerable control over the people. The importance of the Temple in the religious life of Judea gave pre-eminence to Jerusalem and centralized the political and economic life of the Jews, strengthening the power of the priesthood. But in Jesus' time there was another center of religion in addition to the home and the Temple — the synagogue. While the Temple with its sacrificial ritual dated from the reign of Solomon, the synagogue was a much later development, probably beginning some time after the Babylonian captivity when the exiled Jews were permitted by the Persians to return to Jerusalem.[34] It has been said that whatever place is set aside for religious worship, wherever Jews "put up an Ark containing the Torah-scroll, source and symbol of the Tradition, there is a synagogue."[35] In the time of Jesus, as today, the synagogue served three primary functions, all non-sacrificial: as a "house of prayer"; as "a house of study," a school of Judaism; and as a gathering place of the people, the congregation. The heart of the synagogue service in Jesus' time was, as it is today, the reading of the Torah. The Gospels mention synagogues at Nazareth and Capernaum. Some historians hold that as early as the Babylonian captivity, when Jews could no longer "go up to the Temple," the synagogue served as a meeting place, a house of prayer. Originally, the Greek term "synagogue" referred to the *congregation* or gathering rather than to the *place* of assembly.[36]

The Torah as a literary document is traditionally composed of parchment sheets sewn together as a scroll and rolled around two spindles. It is a collection of five books, the pentateuch or the traditional books of Moses, which give a continuous narrative of events from the Creation to the death of Moses. But the substance of the Torah is more than simply the epic story of the Hebrews. Within the framework of the narrative, an impressive code of

---

[34] Although precise dating of the origin of the synagogue is obscure, it is generally assumed to have been in the period of the Second Temple. Psalms 74:8, which reports that "they burned all the meeting places of God in the land," may be the earliest extant literary reference to the synagogue.

[35] M. Steinberg, *Basic Judaism* (New York, 1975), 150.

[36] For a historical account of the Temple and synagogue and the Messianic movement, see Leo Baeck, "The Pharisees," in *The Pharisees and Other Essays* (New York, 1966).

religious and social legislation is set forth in great detail with instruction on such matters as the observance of the holy days, moral conduct, and the ceremonial law. The ethic of the Torah is based upon the Hebrew experience of God — of what he has done for Israel and what he requires of his people.

THE ORAL LAW

Even in ancient times the written Torah was not the whole of the Torah. Prophets, poets, and sages carried it on orally — not as "Torah in letter" but as "Torah in Spirit."[37] The latter is Torah-tradition, the Oral Law, the application of the Teaching. In Jesus' time, according to Josephus, the Pharisees advocated both the written and oral Torah, while the Sadducees were committed only to the written Torah. The Torah provided the requirements for daily living upon which the promise of blessings was predicated. Rules of proper conduct were sometimes extremely complex and required adaptations to the changing circumstances of personal and social life. Consider, for instance, the regulations governing the observance of the Sabbath. The Law of Moses set forth in Exodus prohibited work on the Sabbath. But the question inevitably arose, what is work? This question led to others, until many and detailed prescriptions and prohibitions governing Sabbath behavior were added. How far can a man walk on the Sabbath and not sin? The commandment was not explicit, but in former days it was permitted to walk a distance of 3,000 feet to the ark and return. In this way one mile became acceptable as a Sabbath's journey, while going farther was a sin. No fires were to be kindled, and no food cooked or prepared on the Sabbath. The disciples of Jesus were criticized for walking through a cornfield on the Sabbath and eating kernels of corn on the way. The First Book of the Maccabees,[e] a remarkable historical work composed before the time of Jesus, describes the massacre of Jews who refused to defend themselves against the Seleucid Greeks on

---

[e] 1 Mc 2:32–38.

[37] According to Steinberg, "everything which has its roots in the Torah-Book, which is consistent with its outlook, which draws forth its implications, and which realizes its potentialities," is Torah. Steinberg, *Basic Judaism*, 22.

The Early Years

the Sabbath. They sacrificed their lives rather than profane the Sabbath.

Genuinely pious Jews were as conscientious in the observance of the ceremonial and dietary law as in honoring the Sabbath. The Torah-tradition, for instance, prescribed the kinds of food which could and could not be eaten, how the food was to be prepared, and the kinds of dishes from which it could be eaten.[38] Pots and kettles were to be washed in a certain fashion before being used, and one's hands had to be ceremonially cleansed before eating.

The legalism that from ancient times was a prominent feature of Judaism has always interested historians and students of comparative religions. Critics have insisted that a religion so fully grounded in law lacks the higher qualities of morality and spirituality that are found in religions whose foundations are more subjective, with morality judged more by motive and faith and where grace rather than obedience to law is the essential for salvation. This criticism both oversimplifies and distorts Jewish legalism. Certainly the cause and justification of the Hebraic-Judaic legalism are complex and difficult to assess, but the value of rigorous adherence to the Mosaic Law as necessary to the survival of both the Jewish religion and the Jewish community should be entirely obvious to those acquainted with the history of occidental culture.

The critical question for Jewish leaders long before the time of Jesus was: How can we live and survive as a holy people under the religious, political, and cultural pressures that constantly besiege us from every side? Here was a small nation with a distinctive religion and way of life struggling to maintain its integrity and security against the almost insurmountable obstacles generated by its relations with the great empires that successively surrounded and dominated it. The survival of the Jews and Judaism depended on the strength of religious and moral commitment and on an indomitable hope. But without question that survival was contingent upon the imperative of the Law, the insistence on a me-

---

[38] In Book II of *Against Apion*, Josephus gave an account of the Mosaic law and its meaning for the Jewish people of his time.

ticulous observance of God's commands. The Law was a "fence" that protected Israel from assimilation to foreign culture.[39]

THE COVENANT AND THE MESSIANIC HOPE

While in the time of Jesus the behavior of conscientious practicing Jews was regulated to a marked degree by the Law, the heart of their religion was the promise and hope of the covenant. A powerful factor in that hope was the expectation of the messianic era. This eschatological movement apparently produced a variety of Jewish sects in Palestine, one of which, the Essenes, has been associated in recent years with the "Dead Sea Scrolls" discovered in 1947 near Qumran in the Judean wilderness. Christianity also arose as an eschatological Jewish sect. It was a popular belief that despite the evil in the world, especially the oppression suffered by the Jewish nation, God would eventually establish his Kingdom on earth. God would send his agent, a person anointed and appointed to the task of delivering Jerusalem and the nation from the oppressor, a messiah who would overthrow the foes of his people, restore their independence and freedom, and fulfill his covenant.

The covenant went beyond the imperfections of historical kingdoms, promising the realization of God's ideal Kingdom. These two themes merged in prophetic and poetic expressions with notions of a Messiah-agent who should serve and suffer, and of a "Son of man" who should come in the clouds with power at the end of the age. In Jesus' time there was no single form of messianic expectation commonly held by all Jews. However, hope for liberation from Roman rule gave strong support to the expectation of a political, Davidic messiah. The reign of David was the golden age whose memory was a perpetual inspiration for faith in the future.

Every promising Jewish leader was watched with care, with deep concern by the established authorities, and with anticipation by those who longed for deliverance. Judas Maccabaeus was thought by some to be the promised Messiah and, indeed, he

---

[39] Leo Baeck's *The Essence of Judaism* (New York, 1948) eloquently expounds the importance of the Law. Baeck's *Christianity and Judaism* (New York, 1958) is a study of the basic differences between Judaism and Christianity.

proved to be a deliverer. But his later life did not bear out this hope. There were many others who were thought by one faction or another to be the anointed of God.[40] One of the most popular was Simon bar Kokhba (Koseba) who led the ill-fated Jewish uprising against the Romans during the reign of Hadrian, from CE 132 to 135. Even the great Rabbi Akiba hailed this military leader as the Messiah and called him the "son of the star," Bar Kokhba. But the revolt ended in total failure and the death of the leader.[41]

Several different conceptions of messiah are found in the Old Testament, particularly in the Jewish apocryphal and pseudepigraphical literature written shortly before and after the time of Jesus. Probably the oldest was that of king-prophet-priest designated (anointed) by God for a specific task. Other conceptions included a king of the lineage of David and Solomon; a priestly messiah, usually from the tribe of Levi (this conception emerged in the period of the Maccabees, second century BCE); the "Son of man," a superhuman figure described in Daniel (7:9–12) who would descend in power at the end of the age to carry out the final phases of God's work; and the servant in Isaiah,[f] who through his suffering would bring the nations to "see" God's purpose in the world.

Messianic beliefs were current among the typically pious common people of Judea and Galilee when John, who was to be known as the Baptist, began preaching at the river Jordan. With the forthrightness of the Old Testament prophets, John boldly declared his message: "Repent, for the kingdom of heaven is at hand."[g] Crowds flocked to the Jordan to learn more of this great preacher from the wilderness. A largely poor and despairing people gathered to hear what hope he could give for the coming of God's kingdom.

[f] Is 43, 49, 50, 52f. [g] Mt 3:2.

[40] Joseph Klausner has pointed out that not all types of messiah were personal and that the Jewish expectation "was never pictured as 'a kingdom not of this world.'" J. Klausner, *The Messianic Idea in Israel*, trans. W. F. Stinespring (London, 1956), 10. Also, according to the Jewish historian Robert Seltzer, "Despite the rabbinic reformation of the turn of the century, messianic agitation in Judea and the diaspora led to further Jewish revolts." R. M. Seltzer, *Jewish People, Jewish Thought* (New York, 1980), 247–49.

[41] For an account of recent archaeological "digs" relating to the Bar Kokhba revolt, see Yigael Yadin, *Bar Kokhba* (New York, 1971).

CHAPTER 2

The Sources

Reliable knowledge of Jesus, his life and teaching, is limited. The years of his adolescence and young manhood are shrouded in silence, and his active ministry of not over two or three years is treated only briefly in the Gospels. There are only four short accounts of Jesus' ministry, and these record what people thought of him as well as what he did and taught. Beyond the narrative of his teachings and actions nothing is known of his personality, physical appearance, or bearing that might account for the remarkable charismatic power which he held over his disciples and the masses who at one time followed him.[1]

So far as is known, Jesus left no written statements of any kind, and the only instance of him writing is related in the story of the adultress (John 7:53–8:11), where twice he writes on the ground with his finger. There is no definite evidence that any of his disciples kept an account of his actions or teachings during his lifetime. It was the common practice in Jesus' time and place for disciples to memorize the words of their most revered teachers, but apparently it was not customary to make a written record of them. How, then, were Jesus' words and actions preserved in the Christian tradition? What was the origin of the Gospels, the New Testament documents that account for his birth, ministry, death, and resurrection?[2]

[1] Any attempt to understand the New Testament must take into account the differences between modern historiography and the character of ancient recording, writing, and publishing, both Hellenistic and Jewish. Martin Herzel's essay, "The Sources of the History of Earliest Christianity in the Context of Ancient Historiography and Biography," chapter 1 of *Acts and the History of Earliest Christianity* (Philadelphia, 1979), is informative on the subject.

[2] Since all four Gospels concentrate on the last thirty to thirty-five days of Jesus' life, they obviously were written not primarily as biographies or "lives" of Jesus but rather as accounts of his trial, death, and resurrection.

The Sources

Paul's first epistle to the Thessalonians is quite generally regarded as the earliest of the books of the New Testament and the earliest of the extant Christian writings. It is usually dated approximately 50–51 CE, written from Corinth. But neither here nor elsewhere in his known letters did Paul provide information about Jesus as a person who lived and taught in Galilee and Judea. Paul's primary interest was in Christ as the risen saviour, not in Jesus as a human person. Except for references to the crucifixion and resurrection, he made little mention of Jesus.

The Gospel of Mark is considered by most scholars to be the earliest existing account of Jesus' ministry. It was written thirty-five to forty years after his death. No doubt by this time most of those personally acquainted with him were dead. A generation had passed and firsthand information was no longer available. It is probable, however, that some written accounts of the teachings and actions of Jesus were in circulation among the Christians even before Mark wrote his Gospel. These early materials have not been preserved in their original form, but some fragments of them were probably incorporated into the Gospels. No doubt it was largely these first writings and even more the oral traditions or memorized sayings that provided the basic information on the life and teachings of Jesus set forth in the Gospels.

THE SYNOPTIC PROBLEM

The first three Gospels, Matthew, Mark, and Luke, are generally known as the "synoptic Gospels," a reference to their similarities and evidences of common sources. Indeed, these three evangelists not only frequently give the same account of an incident or discourse but often record it in the very same words. However, the three are not identical, for each Gospel contains material not found in the other two. The question of why they are almost identical in some passages yet different in others is the "synoptic problem," which has occupied much of the attention of New Testament scholars.

In the judgment of most competent scholars, Matthew and Luke borrowed much of their material from Mark, the earliest of the Gospels.³ But both Matthew and Luke are longer than Mark, and Matthew and Luke agree on a considerable amount of material not found in Mark. The fact that Matthew and Luke include common material that is not in Mark suggests that they had access to another common source. This source is referred to as "Q."⁴ In addition to these two main sources, Mark and "Q," Matthew apparently had access to material which neither Luke nor Mark possessed, and Luke had additional material not found in either Matthew or Mark.

The following diagram of the four-document thesis was developed by the New Testament scholar B. H. Streeter. The symbols "M" and "L" represent segments of early tradition found only in Matthew or only in Luke.

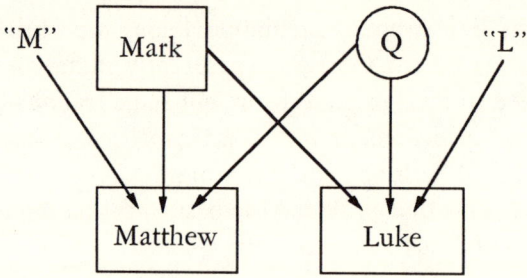

---

³ It has been estimated that approximately ninety percent of Mark is included in Matthew's Gospel; Luke includes about sixty percent of Mark. In many instances parallel passages in Matthew and Luke differ in arrangement from Mark and from each other. The arrangement and sequence of events and teachings apparently were closely related to the purposes of each evangelist.

Burton H. Throckmorton, ed., *Gospel Parallels: A Synopsis of the First Three Gospels* (Nashville and New York, 1979) and Kurt Aland, ed., *Synopsis of the Four Gospels: Greek-English Edition* (Stuttgart, 1972) are valuable tools for comparing the Synoptics.

⁴ "Q" probably refers to the German term, *Quelle*, meaning source. Although no copy of such a document exists, most scholars believe that it was a "saying source" probably written in Greek ca. 50 CE which explains the eschatological materials common to Matthew and Luke but not found in Mark. It is thought to have been produced possibly on the basis of late Jewish wisdom literature in an early Christian community in which charismatic prophets and prophecy were empha-

The Sources

This thesis considers Mark and "Q" to be the primary basis for Matthew and Luke, with "M" and "L" as possible additional sources drawn from different versions of the oral tradition.

Another hypothesis recently adopted by some scholars in an effort to overcome difficulties posed by the four-document thesis holds that Matthew was the earliest Gospel and that Luke and Mark relied upon Matthew as a basic source. According to this view, Mark was the latest of the three synoptics; Mark had access to both Luke and Matthew as the basis of his composition. Although none of the hypotheses thus far advanced fully resolves the synoptic problem, some variation of the four-document theory, with the Gospel of Mark as the earliest source, seems to offer the most adequate explanation. This hypothesis provides the clearest resolution of the synoptic problem, fitting together more of the pieces of the puzzle of their historical-literary relationship than any competing hypothesis.[5]

The recognition in the late nineteenth century of the basic differences between the Jesus of the Synoptics and the highly spiritualized Christ of the Gospel of John, the Fourth Gospel, was an

---

sized. "Q" materials concentrate on the expectation of the coming end and judgment: warnings and a sense of urgency about the end, woes, and conflict; the promise that God's Kingdom will come soon, and the radical nature of discipleship in that Kingdom. See Richard A. Edwards, *A Theology of Q: Eschatology, Prophecy, and Wisdom* (Philadelphia, 1976). Howard C. Kee, *Jesus in History*, 2d ed. (New York, 1977) presents a description and analysis of "Q."

[5] For a detailed analysis of the four-document hypothesis, see Burnett H. Streeter, *The Four Gospels: A Study of Origins* (New York, 1924). William R. Farmer, in *The Synoptic Problem* (New York, 1961), and others present the arguments in support of Matthew as the earliest of the synoptic Gospels. See Joseph B. Tyson, *The New Testament and Early Christianity* (New York, 1984), 153–58, and Robert M. Grant, *A Historical Introduction to the New Testament* (New York, 1963), 105–18. The view that Matthew was the earliest gospel seems to raise many more questions about the relationship of the three gospels than it resolves. If Matthew were earlier than Mark, why, for example, would Mark deliberately omit such significant materials as the birth stories, the Sermon on the Mount from Matthew, and the famous parables from the Gospel of Luke? Why, indeed, should Mark have taken such a harsh view of the disciples who deserted Jesus at his arrest, especially Peter, when he could have adopted the resolution of this problem provided by Matthew and Luke in which Peter is reinstated as the leading transitional figure in the history of the early church? Why did Mark not follow the lead of Matthew and Luke in proclaiming that there was to be an interim time of the church before the end of the age and the second coming of Jesus?

important step in the critical understanding of the Gospels.[6] It is a common opinion among scholars today that there was much greater diversity in belief and practice among the several Christian churches than had earlier been supposed. Equally important, it is now held that not only the individual writers of the Gospels but perhaps even more the various early churches were responsible for both the form and substance of the Christian tradition — or more correctly, the Christian traditions.

The theological-apologetic character of all four canonical Gospels is now widely acknowledged. Moreover, the essential difference in character between John and the Synoptics, so long taken for granted, is being seriously challenged. But the argument is not that John has been shown to be authentic history and is therefore more like Matthew, Mark, and Luke but rather that the Synoptics are more like John. Each of the four Gospels is regarded essentially as a faith account; each was written not as a biography but rather as an interpretation of Jesus and his teachings intended to express the faith of a particular Christian community.

The synoptic Gospels were evidently written in response to the experiences and problems of several Christian communities of the eastern Mediterranean in the last decades of the first century. Accordingly, they may be regarded as essentially trustworthy in recording the traditions about Jesus — what he said and what he did — but it should be remembered that the writers of these Gospels were not eyewitnesses. It appears that Matthew and Luke, using the Markan frame, arranged their materials, as Mark had done before them, to emphasize matters that were of special interest or concern to their respective churches.[7]

---

[6] Albert Schweitzer, *The Mystery of the Kingdom of God*, trans. Walter Lowrie (London, 1925) and Johannes Weiss, *Jesus' Proclamation of the Kingdom of God*, trans. and ed. R. H. Hiers and D. L. Holland (Philadelphia, 1971), were among those most responsible for this new assessment of the Gospels.

[7] This view is shared by an increasing number of scholars. "The Gospels were not written as historical records but as witnesses of the faith. The material they contained was handed down for the benefit of the Christian church, was formulated with the needs of the church in view." W. C. van Unnik, "Luke-Acts, A Storm Center in Contemporary Scholarship," in Leander E. Keck and J. Louis Martyn, eds., *Studies in Luke-Acts* (Philadelphia, 1980), 19.

THE SYNOPTIC GOSPELS

In 66 CE, during the reign of the emperor Nero, the Jews launched a major military revolt against Rome, a rebellion induced by an uprising of the Zealots of Galilee. Four years followed in which those who joined the rebellion fought against three legions under the leadership of the Roman general Vespasian. Declared emperor in 69 CE, Vespasian returned to Rome and left the leadership of the army to his son Titus, who conducted a siege of Jerusalem. The city fell and was destroyed in 70 CE. The Roman victory was greatly facilitated by internal strife among the city's Jewish factions. The Temple was desecrated and destroyed and thousands were put to the sword or taken into slavery.[8]

When Jerusalem fell, the last effective stronghold of the Jews was eliminated. However, it required three more years for the Romans to capture the remaining Jewish fortresses. Defended by Jewish forces, these strongholds, particularly the Herodium, Machaerus, and Masada, which had been fortified by Herod the Great, were difficult to conquer. Masada, occupied by Galilean Zealots, was the last to fall, in April 73 CE. When the Romans finally breached the wall atop the great rock of Masada, they found that except for two women and several children all the defenders had committed suicide, apparently in one last desperate protest against Rome.[9]

---

[8] Detailed knowledge of the Jewish rebellion and the destruction of Jerusalem in 70 CE comes largely from Josephus, *The Jewish War*. Books V–VI are concerned with the dramatic siege and fall of Jerusalem. Titus succeeded his father as emperor in 79 CE. Josephus was born in Jerusalem ca. 37 or 38 CE. He became a Pharisee at the age of nineteen. Later he was involved in the war against Rome, holding an important command in Galilee. After the fall of Jotapata in 67 CE, he was imprisoned by the Romans but won the favor of the Roman generals Vespasian and his son Titus and was released. Eventually he was sent to Rome where, adopting the name Flavius, the family name of Vespasian and Titus, he lived under protection of the Roman emperors and devoted himself to study and writing. His two major works, *The Jewish War* and *The Antiquities of the Jews*, are major sources of information on the Jews and Judaism in the Greek and Roman periods.

[9] The account of the siege and conquest of the fortress of Masada is found in Josephus, *The Jewish War*, Book VII, chapters VIII–IX. Josephus' account of the Roman assaults on Herodium and Machaerus are in Book VII, chapter VI. For a modern account of the siege of Masada, see Yigael Yadin, *Masada: Herod's Fortress and the Zealots' Last Stand*, trans. Moshe Pearlman (London, 1966). Professor Yadin led the expedition which excavated Masada in 1963–65.

Although the war had been terrible in its destruction of human life and property, the defeat inflicted by the Roman legions was not the end of Judaism; rather it was the beginning of a new era in Jewish history. The Romans made no attempt to exterminate the entire Jewish population of Palestine. They continued to recognize Judaism as a lawful religion, even granting the Jews exemption from the commonly required veneration of the emperor, a practice that violated their intense commitment to monotheism. With the conquest and destruction the Sadducees and Essenes disappeared as far as political or religious importance was concerned, but a strong spiritual revival of Judaism led by Pharisaic sages and scribes was soon underway. The sages began in earnest their central task of grounding Judaism on the Torah and the Oral Law. They defined the Jewish canon of scripture, provided a more precise form for daily prayers, and transferred to the home, synagogue, and Sanhedrin some of the rituals connected with the Temple. They continued the pilgrim festivals and preserved the religious calendar and some rituals, including the Passover seder and the blowing of the ram's horn (the shofar) on the New Year. Within two decades after the destruction of the Temple, the rabbis were clearly the official leaders of the Jewish community.[10] The major impact on Judaism caused by the war with Rome was the ascendancy of Torah religion. The rabbis, with their scholarly approach to morals and religion, gained strength in influence and leadership while the power of the priests and Sadducees declined. The synagogue prayer, worship, and study of the Torah replaced the sacrificial cult of the Temple as the center of the religion.

The Jewish-Roman war culminating in the destruction of Jerusalem probably provided the historical setting for the writing of the synoptic Gospels. All three Gospels seem to have been composed in the early postwar period, which was a time of reconstruction for both Judaism and Christianity. Apparently a considerable number of Christians had been drawn into the confrontation with Rome by the religious-patriotic fervor of the Jewish Zealots and by their own Christian prophets. These prophets professed to have

---

[10] For a detailed account of these developments within Judaism, see R. M. Seltzer, *Jewish People, Jewish Thought* (New York, 1980), 243 ff.

apocalyptic visitations promising Christ's imminent return as the messianic agent predicted in the Book of Daniel. The war was a disaster for Jews and Christians, producing devastation and chaos, but for both it was also a decisive turning point — the end of an era, of the "old way." Jewish and Christian survival was at stake. It was critical that both reconstitute and reconstruct their cultural and economic foundations.

Throughout the period from the destruction of the Temple to the first decade of the second century, the Christians lived in close proximity to the Jews. The dialogue and dispute between them continued, and the earlier tensions which had existed from Paul's day mounted with increasing bitterness and hostility.[11] For Christians reconstruction entailed: (1) a meaningful explanation of the disastrous war for those who in time might become disillusioned by the delay of the Parousia, that is, the second coming or return of Christ; (2) a more accurate perspective on Christianity's historical relations with Judaism, which included correcting and appropriating certain Hebrew-Jewish ideas and ideals, such as "covenant," "Israel," and "messiah," found in the Old Testament and in currently popular Jewish writings; and (3) a correction of some of the earlier Jewish Christian claims about Jesus as the Messiah.[12] Finally (4), Jesus' early connections with the movement of John the Baptist had never been fully explained, and the failure of some of the Apostles to understand Jesus' true identity and purpose required clarification.

The synoptic Gospels were apparently written to support this reconstruction. Each Gospel contributed to the orientation of Christianity upon a new foundation — the foundation of Jesus as the Christ. As a consequence of the efforts of the evangelists, Christianity became a religion in its own right. Although intimately tied to Judaism and grounded in biblical prophecy and promise, it transcended its own Jewish roots and went beyond the tradition of the Hebrew bible.

[11] The tensions between Jews and Christians and between Jewish Christians and gentile Christians are reported in Acts 1–15 and in Paul's letter to the Galatians.

[12] Jaroslav Pelikan uses the expression "correction-and-fulfillment" in his description of the church's quest for a tradition in *The Christian Tradition*, Vol. 1: *The Emergence of the Catholic Tradition, 100–600* (Chicago, 1971), 15.

Place and time seem to be of secondary importance to the Gospel writers. These are subordinate to their objectives and purposes. Mark makes reference to two geographical divisions — Galilee and Jerusalem. This format is followed by Matthew and Luke. Geographical considerations in the Gospel of John differ most radically from the Synoptics; John reports Jesus traveling between Galilee and Jerusalem several times for the celebration of the Passover, presumably to show Jesus in direct confrontation with Jewish officials and institutions throughout his ministry.

Matthew and Luke have similar chronologies, presumably based upon Mark's Gospel. They begin with Jesus' ministry in Galilee, near Capernaum and the northern end of the Sea of Galilee. The arrest and subsequent execution of John the Baptist followed by the feeding of the five thousand, the confession at Caesarea Philippi, the transfiguration, and Jesus' decision to go to Jerusalem are important elements of the synoptic story and are crucial to the structure of all three Gospels. These events set the stage for Jesus' entry into Jerusalem, his visits to the Temple, his Temple discourses, the growing opposition and conspiracy which led to his arrest, his trials, and his death on the cross. The three synoptic chronologies are similar in their treatment of these and other major events. However, they differ somewhat in their arrangement and the contexts they provide for Jesus' teachings and parables and his miracles of healing and exorcism.

Mark

The dates of the composition of the Synoptics are impossible to determine and can at best only be estimated. Many scholars believe that Mark was written about the time of the siege and destruction of Jerusalem by the Romans, ca. 65–70 CE. The authorship of Mark is questionable, but it is sometimes attributed to John Mark who is mentioned in Acts as a missionary companion of Paul. An early Christian author, Papias of Hierapolis in Phrygia who died about 155 CE, states that Mark acted as an interpreter for Peter when he was in Rome. According to this view, Mark did not personally listen to Jesus preach but recorded what Peter remembered of Jesus.[13] Contemporary scholars, however, are skeptical of this interpretation in part because of Mark's critical attitude toward Peter. Both Luke and Matthew are more positive than Mark in their estimate of Peter's loyalty and integrity as a disciple.

One quite obvious objective of the Gospel of Mark is to show that during his ministry Jesus predicted events connected with the destruction of Jerusalem. According to Mark, this destruction was an essential part of the drama of salvation in which Jesus played a decisive role as the Son of man. Mark believed the institutions of Judaism — the Temple and city — had been rejected by God. In Mark the confession, transfiguration, and entry into Jerusalem were closely followed by events which revealed Jesus' intention to break with Judaism — the episode of the fig tree and the cleansing of the Temple.[a] Viewed as a unit, these events show the development of a major theme in Mark's Gospel — that although Jerusalem was the center of religion and the seat of the ancient traditions and promises, it had become an arena of opposition and hostility.[14] For Mark, Jesus' act of cleansing the Temple had significance beyond the obvious condemnation of commercialism. It meant the coming of the end of the Temple and Judaism as the means of fulfilling Abraham's promise. Like the fig tree the Temple was barren, which meant that the religious institutions historically related to Jerusalem had been rejected.[b]

[a] Mk 11:12–19. [b] Mk 11:20–25; 13:28–32.

[13] Justin Martyr (ca. 100–165 CE), relying on the account of Papias, refers to the Gospel of Mark as the memoirs of Peter. Also, see comment by Clement of Alexandria in Eusebius' *Ecclesiastical History*, Vol. 14 in A. Roberts and J. Donaldson, eds., *The Ante-Nicene Fathers*. Vol. II *Fathers of the Second Century* (Michigan, 1956), 580: "Peter having preached the word publicly at Rome, and by the Spirit proclaimed the gospel. Those who were present, who were numerous, entreated Mark inasmuch as he had attended him from an earlier period and remembered what had been said, to write down what had been spoken. . . ."

[14] This view of Mark in general follows the interpretation suggested by W. Kelber in *The Kingdom in Mark*. Kelber interprets several events — crossing the sea, exorcising, healing — as having symbolic meaning which the disciples failed to discern. Indeed, Kelber identifies a "voyage" pattern in Mark which he maintains has a symbolic meaning — that Jesus intended to break with Judaism. Werner H. Kelber, *The Kingdom in Mark: A New Place and a New Time* (Philadelphia, 1974), 50ff.

Jesus' statements to his disciples on the Mount of Olives, following his predictions about the Temple, are referred to as the synoptic apocalypse or the "Little Apocalypse."[c] Here Mark presents Jesus' comments in the form of a sermon which is crucial to the structure and purpose of his Gospel. Jesus' apocalyptic sermon is integrally related to the events which prompted Mark to write his Gospel in the first place — the Jewish rebellion against the Romans and the destruction of Jerusalem. It reveals Mark's belief, and perhaps the beliefs of those for whom he wrote, that those events were the beginning of the end of the age. In his judgment the end was to come soon, for Jesus himself had forecast that end in his discourse as he sat with his disciples opposite the Temple on the Mount of Olives. For Mark the destruction marked the dissolution of the Jewish-Christian fellowship in Jerusalem. This fellowship was led by several of Jesus' disciples who remained in Jerusalem after Jesus' death, inspirited by their experience of the resurrection. Peter was the most prominent in their leadership, but among them were members of Jesus' family, notably his brother James, who later became known as James the Just, and John, presumably one of the original disciples. There were also charismatic prophets who proclaimed that Jesus would return with power as the resurrected Messiah to overthrow Roman rule and establish the Kingdom of God in Jerusalem.

In Mark's Gospel, Jesus warned against false prophets who would mistakenly identify the precise time and place of the Parousia. Also, Mark held that not only Peter and the family of Jesus but also other early disciples failed to understand Jesus' purposes. Some of them had denied him and at his arrest "they all forsook him, and fled."[d] Mark's case against Peter is evident, for instance, in the accounts of the confession at Caesarea Philippi.[e] In the confession Peter proclaimed Jesus as the Christ, but in response Jesus rebuked the disciples, charging them to tell no one concerning him. According to Mark's interpretation of these events, Peter was mistaken about Jesus' identity and his intention. In his description of the encounter between Jesus and Peter, Mark provides a redirection of Peter's statement and advances his own conception

[c] Mk 13:5–37. [d] Mk 14:50. [e] Mk 8:27–33.

of Jesus as the Son of man. His intention seems to be to correct Peter's conception of Jesus as a messiah of the Davidic type.

None of the passion-resurrection predictions which Mark regarded as authentic seems to have been fully understood by Jesus' disciples. They could not understand, or perhaps accept, his forewarning of his coming death. It was Mark's view that Jesus as the Messiah should suffer, die, and be resurrected to return in glory as the apocalyptic Son of man. Peter and the other disciples seemed bound to a traditional Jewish conviction that the Messiah-Son of David would rise up, overthrow Israel's enemies, and restore the Kingdom. According to Mark, the disciples did not grasp Jesus' true identity; they were not able to accept his role as the Son of man who was to suffer and die in Jerusalem. For them such an end would be a scandalous failure.

At a time of such despair for the primitive Christian community of Jerusalem, suffering the overwhelming power of Rome, Mark's message was one of renewed hope. The disastrous consequences of the war for the Jewish Christians of Jerusalem did not mean the extinction of all faith in the coming of the Kingdom. Mark did not abandon the expectation of Jesus' return, but it was his view that the promise was to be fulfilled in Galilee, which Jesus himself had named as the new gathering place.

Matthew

The Gospel of Matthew was probably written sometime between 80 and 90 CE. Its primary objective was to proclaim Jesus as the Messiah whose coming was prophesied in the Old Testament and to acclaim him as the one like Moses whose word came from God as law. Some scholars hold that the structure of this Gospel follows the model of the Pentateuch, the Five Books of Moses. It includes five collections of Jesus' "sayings" or teachings[15] described as follows:

Chaps. 5– 7 . . . . The Sermon on the Mount

Chap. 10   . . . . Instructions to the apostles

Chap. 13   . . . . Parables about the coming of the Kingdom

---

[15] See John C. Fenton, *The Gospel of St. Matthew* (Baltimore, 1963), 14f.

Chap. 18 ....Life in the Kingdom — and in the church

Chaps. 23–25....Warnings and woes, requirements in the Kingdom — charity and mercy

In Matthew's view, the Christian church was the repository of Jesus' teaching, which was to be the basis of a new standard and a new covenant. The Sermon on the Mount and the address to the Apostles are the best known of the Matthean discourses. The material used by Matthew in these sermons is also scattered throughout Luke's Gospel. In all probability the various themes of these sermons were presented by Jesus on several different occasions during his ministry.

Both Jews and Christians suffered critical losses in the war with Rome. Most Jewish Christians either fled Jerusalem or were killed in the siege.[16] Of the Jewish groups known today — the Sadducees, Zealots, Essenes, and Pharisees — only the Pharisees survived the disaster with enough strength and integrity to continue as an influential force in Judaism. The Pharisees had been moving away from the concept of Israel as a political entity toward the ideal of Judaism as a religion independent of any political-nationalist institution or body. The destruction, therefore, did not affect them as it did the Sadducees, whose life and collective function were centered in Jerusalem and the Temple cult. The influence of the synagogue was already established, and, most important, the Pharisees' commitment to the Oral Law enabled them to adjust their loyalty to the old tradition to the new conditions which confronted them following the destruction. Despite the severe consequences of the war, they were able not only to continue to minister to the religious and moral life of Israel but even to strengthen their influence. A Sanhedrin, the supreme council and tribunal, was established at Jamnia (Javneh) near the Mediterranean coast soon after 70 CE. This council exercised central

---

[16] Apparently many of the Jewish Christians left Jerusalem just prior to the siege, taking refuge in Pella to the north across the Jordan. Some eventually returned to Jerusalem; others remained in the upper Galilee. In any event, the Jewish war and subsequent events seem to have accentuated the estrangement of the Jewish Christians from the community of Jews.

religious authority in Judaism as well as civil and criminal jurisdiction within the new limits set by Roman rule.[17]

The primary task of the rabbis and the synagogue in this postwar period was teaching and perpetuating the oral Torah and achieving a successful transition from a religion centered in the temple cult to one grounded in moral and spiritual principles and practiced independently of priestly authority. The result was the building up of traditional usages, opinions, and commentaries into a formal system of directives relating the Law to life. The method employed by the great rabbis in teaching Torah independently of the scripture was known as mishnah, teaching by repetition. From their efforts issued a body of written material, the Mishnah, which related the Law to concrete, living experience and was to become the foundation of the Talmud, the sacred literature that has informed the life of Israel down to the present day.

The author of Matthew related the Christian tradition about Jesus to the life of the Christian church in his day. This entailed, among other things, a new understanding of the concept of Israel. Similar attempts to transform the traditional idea of Israel are found in Paul's writings, especially Galatians and Romans, and also in the anonymous epistle to the Hebrews. In fact, references to the Christian church as the "New Israel" became commonplace in the literature of the early church fathers. Matthew based his thesis on the idea that Jesus was the new Lawgiver to Israel with the Sermon on the Mount as a central element of his Gospel. Here the New Word, the teaching or revelation from God, supersedes the old, the Mosaic revelation. The instructional form attributed to Jesus in the Sermon, "You have heard that it was said to the men of old. . . . But I say to you," [f] clearly established Jesus' teaching as the new foundation of the religion. The requirements for discipleship, one of the chief concerns of the church in Matthew's day, are spelled out in considerable detail.

---

[f] Mt 5:21f., 27f., 33f., 38f., 43f.

[17] In this period the term *rabbi* came into general use as the designation of a sage. The sages at Jamnia summarized the teachings of the earlier schools of the great rabbis Hillel and Shammai. In approximately 90 CE they completed the official canonization of the Jewish scriptures. See Seltzer, *Jewish People, Jewish Thought*, 247.

In the account of the Transfiguration in Matthew,[g] the acceptance by the church of the sacred scripture of the Jews is dramatically affirmed. The circumstances described by Matthew are almost identical with those of Moses' epiphany recorded in Exodus.[h] The profound meaning of this overwhelming event for Matthew seems clear — the divine glory only partially revealed in the Old Way to Moses, Elijah, and the prophets was revealed in full in Jesus, who ushered in the New Way. Here the will of God intervenes in human history. Matthew obviously had searched the Old Testament and the traditions about Jesus for confirmation of the belief that the Jews would reject Jesus as the Messiah. He believed that in reprisal God would reject the Jewish religion and continue his revelation through a faithful remnant, the Christian church, which Matthew now represented.

For Matthew, Jesus' teaching is to be understood by the church as the New Law and Revelation. Jesus is the Way and his Word is the foundation of the living church. The principles of discipleship in the interim period of the church are found in Jesus' New Law, not in the temple cultus nor in Pharisaism or the rabbinic commentaries on the Law.[18]

Luke

Many authorities place the composition of the Gospel of Luke at approximately the time of the writing of Matthew's Gospel, perhaps as early as 80 CE. It is commonly held, moreover, that the work which begins as Luke's Gospel continues as the Acts of the Apostles. The link between the two is the reference to Theophilus, which appears in both documents.[19] It has been claimed that Luke

---

[g] Mt 17:1–8. [h] Ex 24:16–18.

[18] According to N. Perrin, "The gospel of Matthew is the first book in the New Testament. . . . It is very much a 'church book,' written specifically to meet the needs of the church as a developing organization. . . . It provided a basis on which the church could build its life." Norman Perrin, *The New Testament, An Introduction* (New York, 1974), 169.

[19] In Luke 1:3, "It seemed good to me also, . . . to write an orderly account for you, most excellent Theophilus," and in Acts 1:1, "In the first book, O Theophilus, I have dealt with all that Jesus began to do and teach."

was a traveling companion of Paul. However, the case against this claim is compelling.[20]

The Gospel of Luke was written to proclaim Christianity as a universal religion. In Luke the worldwide import of Jesus' ministry was emphasized. In the genealogies, for example, Luke traced Jesus' lineage back to Adam, apparently to announce that Jesus' message is for all mankind. In keeping with his universalistic conception of Christianity, he stressed the fact that Jesus was concerned for the despised Samaritans and other non-Jewish peoples. Clearly when this Gospel was written, Christianity was in the process of overcoming its limiting parochial ties to Judaism and becoming a religion for all humankind.

A special section (Lk. 9:51–18:14), probably taken from an early teaching source, was inserted by Luke into the narrative framework which he adopted from Mark. This material, which sometimes has parallels in Matthew and sometimes is unique among the Gospels, reveals important clues disclosing the purpose of Luke's Gospel. It includes the parables of the Good Samaritan, the Friend at Midnight, the Prodigal Son, and the Unjust Steward. It also gives an account of events not recorded in either Mark or Matthew — the sending out of Seventy and the healing of ten lepers. In addition there are in Luke teaching materials that parallel Matthew's Sermon on the Mount — the Lord's Prayer and Jesus' comments on the nature of Christian discipleship, on the need to share, and on the need to transcend fear and anxiety. Luke provides the setting and arrangement and portrays Jesus as an example of service and stewardship. In Luke 4:16–19, for ex-

---

[20] Irenaeus (ca. 140–202 CE), the Muratorian Canon (ca. 200 CE), Clement of Alexandria (150–215 CE), Tertullian (150–220 CE), Origen (184–254 CE), and Jerome (347–420 CE) all assume that Luke was the companion and colleague of Paul and the author of both Luke and Acts. However, it is difficult to reconcile the inconsistencies between Paul's letters and Luke's account of Paul in the Acts of the Apostles. It would appear that the author of Luke/Acts did not actually know Paul firsthand, but in Acts he placed him centrally in the development of early Christianity. Paul's letters are not mentioned in Acts. This problem and others are discussed in Leander E. Keck and J. Louis Martyn, eds., *Studies in Luke-Acts* (Philadelphia, 1980). For a detailed analysis of Luke's theology, see Hans Conzelmann, *The Theology of St. Luke*, trans. G. Buswell (New York, 1961).

ample, the image of the suffering servant from Second Isaiah[1] sets the stage for presenting Jesus as the supreme exemplar.

Another of Luke's aims was to present Jesus as the unique figure in the history of God's affairs among men. For this purpose Luke's Gospel involves three time frames: the past, from Adam to John the Baptist; the meridian of time, which is the period of Jesus' ministry; and the period of the church, the interim period before the second coming of Jesus and the end of the age.[21] Luke's treatment of the events recorded in Acts frequently glosses over the sharp divisions and controversies which existed in the early church. For example, the bitterness of the struggle between Paul and the Judaizers, clearly evident in Paul's letters, is smoothed over and minimized in Acts.[22] Jesus, Luke contends, was in full control of the events of his ministry from beginning to end. The suggestion of human doubt and bewilderment in Gethsemane recorded in Matthew and even more clearly in Mark are deleted or modified in Luke's Gospel. According to Luke, Jesus suffers as a God-Man who knows what is to come. He approaches the cross triumphantly with no doubts about the meaning and necessity of his death. In Luke's Gospel, Jesus utters no cry from the cross as he does in Matthew and Mark, "Why hast thou forsaken me?"[j]

It seems to have been Luke's purpose to shape and bring into a unified account all of the known primary sources about Jesus, including certain elements of the tradition about Paul. This would provide the Christian community of his day with a trustworthy assurance of Jesus' unique status and place in the drama of salvation and ensure faith in the church's indispensable role in that drama.

Luke's most immediate and practical concern was to uproot false expectations about the nearness of "The Day" as it was proclaimed by false prophets among the Christians. Jesus is represented by him as warning his disciples against any such interpreta-

---

[1] Is 61:1f. [j] Mt 27:46; Mk 15:34.

[21] For a discussion of the three stages in Luke's reconstruction of salvation history, see Conzelmann, *Theology of St. Luke*, 202–206.

[22] Paul's harsh words against the "Judaizers" are found in his letter to the Galatians, especially in 2:14; 5:7, 12.

tion. "You will desire to see one of the days of the Son of man, and you will not see it. . . . Do not go, do not follow them." [k] Luke's strategy involved an interpretation of the delay in the timing of the Second Coming. He introduced new chronological considerations — events which must precede the End — including the idea of "the times of the Gentiles" [l] which he claimed must be fulfilled "before the day when the Son of man returns." In place of the imminent eschatology of Paul that prevailed in the church before the Jewish-Roman war, Luke allowed for a passage of time before the Parousia, a position the church in the postwar period found more acceptable.

The power of the Spirit is central in the Gospel of Luke as it is in Paul and in John, the Fourth Gospel. For Luke, as for Paul, that power rests upon the church. The church set the limits within which the Spirit operates. According to Luke, the Spirit was present in all of the crucial events in the life of Jesus and of the church. After Jesus' baptism and while he was praying, the Holy Spirit descended upon him. Afterward "Jesus, full of the Holy Spirit" returned from the Jordan. Then, "Jesus returned in the power of the Spirit into Galilee," where his ministry began.[m] In the end, after his death and resurrection, Jesus appeared to his disciples in Jerusalem and said "I send the promise of my Father upon you; but stay in the city, until you are clothed with power from on high." [n] Luke's anticipation of the fulfillment of the promise comes to fruition in the Acts of the Apostles at Pentecost when the Spirit returns and remains in the church. It was the power of the Holy Spirit, according to Acts, which brought such phenomenal missionary success to Christianity in the gentile world of the first century.

Luke's Gospel probably contributed importantly to the stabilization of the institutional forms of the early church. It introduced several important changes in belief and practice which became the norms for Christian life. Luke's vision of Christianity as the major force in world history, involving his reinterpretation of the Parousia and his doctrine of the Spirit, contributed to the unity and integrity of the church necessary to its survival.

[k] Lk 17:22f. [l] Lk 17:24, 30; 21:8–24. [m] Lk 3:21f.; 4:1, 14f. [n] Lk 24:49.

THE FOURTH GOSPEL

Even an approximate dating of the composition of the Fourth Gospel, the Gospel of John, is difficult, if not impossible. It has often been assigned to the last decade of the first century, but some scholars argue that it was written later, in the first or second decade of the second century. However, a date of approximately 100 CE seems required by the discovery in Egypt of an early papyrus known as Papyrus 52, which dates from the first half of the second century. The Gospel itself claims that "the disciple whom Jesus loved" was its author,° but it does not name him. Early Christian authors, Papias and Irenaeus, attributed the Gospel to John, the son of Zebedee, or to another John called the "Elder," but the question of authorship is still controversial among the most competent contemporary scholars. Some are of the opinion that at least two authors, perhaps three, were involved in writing the book. The theology set forth in the Gospel may represent the views of a group or a community rather than simply of the author or authors.[23]

It is generally held, on ancient authority, that the Fourth Gospel was composed in Ephesus, in modern Turkey, but there is no definite evidence for this. It was no doubt written in Greek, but with definite Aramaic linguistic influence. Although not essentially a narrative of events, it exhibits a rather pronounced knowledge of Palestinian geography.

Many scholars assume that the author of John may have used the synoptic Gospels, especially Mark and Luke, as primary sources for his book. But basic differences from the Synoptics exist. For example, few events prior to the triumphal entry into Jerusalem a few days before the crucifixion are found in both John and the

---

° Jn 21:20–24.

[23] See Perrin, *New Testament*, p. 249f. for a discussion of the Johannine School. On the problem of the authorship of John, see William D. Davies, *Invitation to the New Testament* (New York, 1969), chap. 30; Rudolf Bultmann, *Theology of the New Testament*, trans. Kendrick Grobel, Vol. II (New York, 1955), chap. I; Charles H. Dodd, *The Interpretation of the Fourth Gospel* (Cambridge, 1963), appendix; Raymond E. Brown, Joseph A. Fitzmyer, and Roland E. Murphy, eds., *The Jerome Biblical Commentary* (Englewood Cliffs, New Jersey, 1968), Vol. II, 414ff.; Charles M. Laymon, ed., *The Interpreter's One-Volume Commentary on the Bible* (Nashville and New York, 1971), 707ff.

The Sources

Synoptics. The Synoptics tell of Jesus doing most of his work in Galilee and relate only one final visit to Jerusalem. In John, however, a major portion of Jesus' ministry takes place in Jerusalem. Also, according to the synoptic account, the ministry of Jesus lasted no longer than one year, but according to John it extended over approximately three years.

John has no parables. In this Gospel, which has more symbolism than the Synoptics, Jesus teaches by discourse, dogmatic sermons, and occasional diatribes. Other differences from the Synoptics relate to John's arrangement of events and his addition of material. For example, in John, the cleansing of the Temple took place at the beginning of Jesus' ministry, while the Synoptics place that incident near the end of the ministry. And John's Gospel includes four major miracles not found in the Synoptics — turning water into wine at Cana,[p] healing the impotent man at Bethzatha,[q] giving sight to the blind man at the pool of Siloam,[r] and raising Lazarus of Bethany.[s]

Also, John omits several matters of major importance reported in the Synoptics. Although some of these when taken by themselves seem relatively insignificant, when viewed together they indicate a dramatic difference in John's perspective and purpose. For example, in John there is no genealogy of Jesus, no birth story, no temptation of Jesus, no transfiguration, no institution of the Lord's Supper, no agony at Gethsemane, and no cry from the cross. In the opinion of some scholars, most of these omissions were deliberate. They were not included in John's Gospel because they did not coincide with the author's view of Jesus and with the purpose of his Gospel. The Fourth Gospel was not intended as a supplement to the Synoptics but rather as a complete transformation of the proclamation about Jesus the Christ.[24] As Professors Colwell and Titus have pointed out, John's primary concern was not with the life and history of the man Jesus but with

> the timeless, universal spiritual values which men had experienced in him. . . . The world of meaning and value which Jesus conveyed

[p] Jn 2:1–11. [q] Jn 5:2–9. [r] Jn 9:1–7. [s] Jn 11:1–44.

[24] For an analysis of similarities and differences between John and the Synoptics, see Ernest C. Colwell and Eric L. Titus, *The Gospel of the Spirit* (New York, 1953), 30–41.

transcended his own physical body even as it transcends time and place. In this Gospel the *essential fact* of the Jesus of history becomes the content of the Christ of faith. . . . this is the Gospel of the Spirit.[25]

John's own statement seems to confirm this conclusion: "These are written that you may believe that Jesus is the Christ, the Son of God, and that believing you may have life in his name." [t]

NON-BIBLICAL SOURCES

Non-Christian Writers

Besides the four Gospels, there are other valuable early sources of information about Jesus and his followers. Some were written by non-Christians. The Roman historian Cornelius Tacitus, writing about 115 CE, for instance, described events in Rome when he was young. Referring to Nero's execution of great numbers of "the people commonly called Christians," he explained that "they derived their name and origin from one Christus, who in the reign of Tiberius had suffered death by the sentence of the procurator Pontius Pilate." A contemporary of Tacitus, Seutonius (65–135 CE), referred to the banishment of Jewish Christians from Rome by the Emperor Claudius about 52 CE. Pliny the Younger, the Roman governor in Asia Minor, wrote to the emperor Trajan in 112 CE asking his advice on dealing with the Christians, who were increasing in numbers so rapidly that the heathen temples were almost deserted.

The most famous and controversial passage concerning Jesus in early non-Christian literature appears in *The Antiquities of the Jews*, by the first-century Jewish historian Flavius Josephus. In this passage Jesus is referred to as "Christ" and includes the statement "Now, there was about this time Jesus, a wise man, if it be lawful to call him a man, for he was a doer of wonderful works." Though this passage was known to the historian Eusebius (ca. 260–340 CE), most competent scholars regard its present form as in whole or part a Christian interpolation. In all probability,

---

[t] Jn 20:31.

[25] Ibid., 21f.

The Sources

Josephus, who was a Pharisee, would not have treated Jesus in such a brief and casual manner if he had actually referred to him as Christ. A second reference to Jesus appears near the end of the *Antiquities* in a comment on Jesus' brother James. Here Josephus refers to Jesus "who was called Christ." Most scholars have been inclined to believe that this passage is authentic.[26]

Though adding little to the information about Jesus, these non-Christian sources at least tend to confirm his historicity. They corroborate the New Testament account that Jesus was crucified during the reign of Tiberius Caesar and that his followers, called Christians, increased in such numbers as to constitute a problem for Rome.

Christian Writers

There are extant, of course, many writings by the Christian fathers of the second and third centuries, scholars as well as churchmen. The fathers used the Gospels as scripture, quoting freely from them to edify and instruct their congregations. The earliest of these, Clement, Bishop of Rome, wrote his first letter near the close of the first century, about 96 CE. Ignatius of Antioch, who wrote seven surviving letters, 98–117 CE, was personally acquainted with the early setting of the Christian church. His letters, touching nearly all matters of Christ's ministry and the early church, were collected after his death. Polycarp, writing in Smyrna about 110–117 CE, claims to have known John and mentions the letters of Paul. The "Shepherd of Hermas," written in Rome probably some time before 150 CE, was included as scripture in the earliest collections of Christian literature. It included discussions of very early Christian doctrines.

Clearly a rich variety of literary documents was produced in the first and second centuries of the Christian era. Many letters,

---

[26] A valuable analysis of the Josephus passages as well as the references in Tacitus, Suetonius, and Pliny the Younger is found in Joseph Klausner, *Jesus of Nazareth*, trans. Herbert Danby (New York, 1925), Book I, Sec. II. Also in Book I, Sec. I, Klausner analyzes early references to Jesus and the Christians in Jewish sources, the Talmud and Midrash. He also considers the treatment afforded the ancient references to Jesus by modern Jewish and Christian historians. Klausner regards the first Josephus statements in *Antiquities* as authentic in part — in their basic references to Jesus as a wise man — but having a later Christian interpolation. He considers the second reference to be entirely authentic.

theological tracts and sermons, and apocryphal and apologetic treatises dealing with folklore, legends, and miracle stories were written defending Christianity against its challengers. Together, they constitute an important library about life in the early church and its tradition about Jesus.[27]

---

[27] Several English language editions of these writings are available. A convenient recent edition which includes work by Clement, Ignatius, Polycarp, and others is Cyril C. Richardson, ed. and trans., *Early Christian Fathers*, Vol. 1 of *The Library of Christian Classics* (Philadelphia, 1953).

CHAPTER 3

The Proclamation of the Kingdom

Except in the Gospel of Luke, John the Baptist first appears in the biblical narrative already in the full tide of his public ministry. The infancy stories in Luke are followed by the simple statement, "And the child grew and became strong in spirit, and he was in the wilderness till the day of his manifestation to Israel." [a] There is no record of Jesus' youth and young manhood. According to Luke's account, John was six months older than Jesus, and their mothers, Elizabeth and Mary, were related. Some writers have assumed, therefore, that Jesus and John knew each other as children, but on the matter of their relationship there is no reliable corroboration of Luke's account.[1]

THE MESSAGE OF THE BAPTIST

The Baptist's warning, "Repent, for the kingdom of heaven is at hand," [b] undoubtedly caused great excitement, for many would have known of the prophecy of Malachi, "Behold, I will send you Elijah the prophet before the great and terrible day of the Lord comes." [c] [2] Was this Elijah now returned as the prophets of old had promised? Or, could John be the Messiah himself? Throngs of people traveled to the Jordan to see John and listen to his prophetic warning. The time of judgment, he cried, is now at hand. Those who believed in John's message were baptized by

---

[a] Lk 1:80. [b] Mt 3:2. [c] Mal 4:5.

[1] According to the Fourth Gospel, the Baptist did not know Jesus: "I myself did not know him" (Jn 1:31, 33). The Baptist's question put to Jesus at the time of John's imprisonment in Luke 7:20, "Are you he who is to come, or shall we look for another?" seems strange in view of Luke's claim that they were related (Lk 1:36f.).

[2] Matthew consistently employs the expression "kingdom of heaven"; Mark and Luke use the phrase "kingdom of God."

[53]

him in the Jordan. His message demanded Israel's repentance as preparation for the new age.[d]

With unyielding determination, the Baptist declared: "Bear fruit that befits repentance, and do not presume to say to yourselves,' We have Abraham as our father.'"[e] John leveled his charge particularly against the Pharisees and Sadducees for presuming a privileged position because of their claim that they were descendants of Abraham. He warned them that a repentant attitude, not "good" ancestry, was the chief requirement for God's Kingdom.

Mark presents the briefest of the four Gospel "accounts" of the Baptist's ministry. In one verse he describes John's work, the substance of his message, and the meaning of his baptism.[f][3] But an important factor in all of the Gospels was the declaration that John was preparing the way for one who was "mightier" than he. "I baptize you with water for repentance, but he who is coming after me . . . will baptize you with the Holy Spirit and with fire."[g][4] This ascetic, desert preacher with his camel hair garment seems to have had the charisma of the Prophet Elijah, for crowds came to see and hear him and even the Sadducees and Pharisees paid attention to him.

The real importance of John was probably underestimated by both early Christian and Jewish writers. He is remembered in the Gospels primarily for baptizing Jesus and for setting the stage as the forerunner of the Messiah. But John deserves consideration in his own right as a religious figure of power and influence quite independent of Jesus, for he launched a messianic movement in Israel of considerable importance.[5] There is reason to believe that

---

[d] Mt 3:11; Mk 1:4; Lk 3:3. [e] Mt 3:8f. [f] Mk 1:4. [g] Mt 3:11.

[3] Neither the Gospel of John nor Mark provides an account of Jesus' birth. Mark's Gospel, "good news" or "tidings," begins with the active ministry of Jesus following a brief account of the Baptist.

[4] Matthew (3:11) seems to attach special importance to his wording "for repentance." This suggests that for him John's baptism "with water" was preliminary to and inferior to Jesus' baptism "with the Holy Spirit."

[5] The passage on the Baptist in the *Antiquities of Josephus*, which is generally regarded as authentic, testifies to the historic importance of John's movement.

> Now, some of the Jews thought that the destruction of Herod's army came from God, and that very justly, as a punishment for what he did against John, that was called the *Baptist*; for Herod slew him, who was a good man, and com-

the followers of Jesus may have played down the full importance of John in that movement.

In some respects John resembled the Essenes of the Qumran community. Like them he rejected the ecclesiastical establishment in Jerusalem and lived a more or less ascetic life in the desert. And like the Essenes he lived in hope and anticipation of the End of the Age and the coming of God's Kingdom. These parallels between John and the Essenes have led some scholars to the conclusion that John was a member of the Essene sect.[6] However, expectation of the last or final judgment and even of the return to Moses and the Sinai covenant before the End, was not peculiar to the Essenes. Such beliefs were strong among the masses in Judea as well as Galilee, where a tradition about prophecy and prophets relating to the coming of the Kingdom persisted from an early period.

John commanded a substantial following in the time of Jesus, and his revival apparently continued for some time after his death. John's disciples may have been rivals of the early Jewish Christians in Galilee before the writing of the Gospels. The earliest Christian writers knew of Jesus' baptism by John and were faced with the task of accounting for that fact and accommodating it to the traditions about Jesus. In the Gospel accounts this was done by subordinating John to Jesus, even though Jesus had gone to hear John's message and had submitted to his baptism.

> manded the Jews to exercise virtue, both as to righteousness towards one another, and piety towards God, and so to come to baptism; for that the washing [with water] would be acceptable to him, if they made use of it, not in order to the putting away, [or the remission] of some sins [only], but for the purification of the body: supposing still that the soul was thoroughly purified beforehand by righteousness. Now, when [many] others came to crowd about him, for they were greatly moved [or pleased] by hearing his words, Herod, who feared lest the great influence John had over the people might put it into his power and inclination to raise a rebellion, (for they seemed ready to do anything he should advise,) thought it best, by putting him to death, to prevent any mischief he might cause, and not bring himself into difficulties, by sparing a man who might make him repent of it when it should be too late. (Book XVIII, chap. V, para 2)

[6] For a detailed discussion of John and the Qumran community, which apparently produced the Dead Sea Scrolls, see W. H. Brownlee, "John the Baptist in the New Light of Ancient Scrolls," in Kristen Stendahl, ed., *The Scrolls and the New Testament* (New York, 1957), 33–53.

JEWISH BAPTISM

As a young man, Jesus was no doubt acquainted with stories about the failures, frustrations, and hopes of his nation. Like every practicing Jew, he was concerned for his people and revered the Hebrew-Jewish tradition. But like John, he clearly saw that the Mosaic tradition was being violated. When he heard of John's proclamation, he knew that the nation must unite under its ancient covenant and prepare for the coming of God's Kingdom. John's proclamation must have sounded to Jesus "like a bell striking the decisive hour." It is not known where in the Jordan Jesus was baptized, but today it is popularly believed to have been within a mile or two north of where the river flows into the Dead Sea. Another tradition places the baptism not far south of the Sea of Galilee.

Presumably, baptism[7] was connected with the ancient Hebrew rites of purification, which had their basis in Old Testament religious law. For most ancient people there was a close relationship between desecration, ritual purity, and the holiness of deity. For the early Hebrews, the ritual of sacrifice was the primary means of purification and consecration. However, washing or cleansing was an essential element of the sacrificial ceremonies.[8] Ritual cleansing was required for admission to the holy precinct of the Temple. Priests were required to wash before beginning the sacrifice and after leaving the Holy of Holies. Similar acts for purifying the body in preparation for one's participation in worship were, and are today, a standard procedure in many religions. There are numerous instances in the Old and New Testaments of lepers and other persons stricken with diseases and infirmities cleansing themselves in accordance with ritual law. At a later time proselytes to Judaism, after being circumcised, were baptized, apparently to wash away the defilements of idolatry. Such baptisms

---

[7] The Greek term for baptize means literally "to dip, plunge." See Henry G. Liddell and Robert Scott, *A Greek-English Lexicon*, 9th ed. (Oxford, 1940), 305f.

[8] Many of the laws on ritual purity are to be found in Leviticus, Numbers, and Exodus. Laws of purification and atonement in Leviticus (11–16) are combined with the laws of holiness (Lv 17–26) and are referred to as the Holiness Code. See the classic work of Alfred Edersheim, *The Temple: Its Ministry and Services*, reprinted in 1982, for a treatment of Jewish ritual at the time of Jesus.

were usually self-administered. The candidate immersed himself in the presence of two persons standing nearby who recited portions of the Law.[9]

It seems evident from excavations in Israel at Qumran and Masada that the ritual bath had become a feature of Jewish practice in the first century BCE and was connected with the synagogue. The discovery of several pools for ritual baths (*mikve*) among the ruins at Qumran indicates the significance of ablutions for the Essene sect. References in the scroll texts support this conclusion. From the Essene point of view, Jewish society generally had been desecrated by a corrupt and impure priesthood. Therefore, all initiates to the Essene community were required to undergo two years of probation and ceremonial cleansing for purification.[10]

THE BAPTISM OF JESUS

The synoptic Gospels vary somewhat in their accounts of Jesus' baptism. Mark, who views the work of John the Baptist as the beginning of the Christian movement, assumes a close connection between John and Jesus. Matthew records that when Jesus was baptized he "went up immediately from the water, and behold, the heavens were opened and he saw the Spirit of God descending like a dove, and alighting on him; and lo, a voice from heaven, saying, 'This is my beloved Son, with whom I am well pleased.' "[h] The heavens opening is a metaphor sometimes employed by New Testament writers to indicate a spiritual vision.

---

[h] Mt 3:16f.

[9] For a detailed examination of the place of washing and ritual cleansing in connection with the sacrifice, see Roland de Vaux, *Ancient Israel: Its Life and Institutions*, trans. John McHugh (New York, 1961), 461f. It is known from the Babylonian Talmud that converts were inducted into Judaism by baptism by immersion as well as circumcision. In cases of religious revival, as with John's preaching, baptism by immersion was sometimes practiced by the Jews as a public confession of faith. See David Daube, *The New Testament and Rabbinic Judaism* (London, 1956), chap. V.

[10] In his account of the archaeological work at Masada in 1963–65, Yigael Yadin describes the discovery of two ritual baths on the rock of Masada. An account of the examination of the baths by rabbis who were experts in the Law governing the requirement, size, and volume of the *mikve* is given in Yadin's *Masada, Herod's Fortress and the Zealots' Last Stand*, trans. Moshe Pearlman (London, 1966), 164–67.

In Acts 7:56, for example, the vision of Stephen is introduced with this same metaphor.[11]

According to Matthew, the Baptist would have prevented Jesus from accepting baptism. Why should Jesus submit to baptism of repentance? John said, "I need to be baptized by you, and do you come to me?"[i] In Matthew's view, the sinlessness and superiority of Jesus were at once apparent to John. Jesus' answer to John's question was, "Let it be so now; for thus it is fitting for us to fulfil all righteousness."[12] Matthew's interpretation of this matter was adopted by many early Christians and eventually became the generally accepted view of the Christian church.

The content of the Baptist's preaching as reported in Luke is probably from Luke's special source, "L." It has a focus different from that of the other synoptists. Luke's primary concern was not the baptism by water at John's hands but rather the descent of the Holy Spirit upon Jesus. This occurred after the baptism had taken place as Jesus was praying. Luke says, "The heaven was opened, and the Holy Spirit descended upon him in bodily form, as a dove. . . ."[j] [13] This is in accord with his account of John's earlier promise that one mightier than he would come to baptize "with the Holy Spirit and with fire."[k] In this account, Luke apparently

---

[i] Mt 3:14–16. [j] Lk 3:21f. [k] Lk 3:16.

[11] In the account of baptism by the apostles in Acts 8:14–18, the coming of the Spirit follows prayer and the "laying on of hands." In Luke's Gospel, most of the major events in Jesus' ministry include accounts of Jesus praying: at his baptism (3:21); choosing the Twelve (6:12f.); the confession at Caesarea Philippi (9:18); the Transfiguration (9:28f.); at Golgotha (23:34); and at the moment of his death (23:46).

[12] The query by John about Jesus' need for baptism and Jesus' reply are found only in Matthew (3:14f.). Presumably this is Matthew's resolution of the dilemma posed by the accepted fact of Jesus' baptism at the hands of John. When the early church began to interpret baptism as relating to repentance for personal sins, the Christians, who regarded Christ as sinless, faced the problem of why he was baptized by John.

[13] The dove motif is presented in all four accounts. That the dove symbolized in the Gospels the coming of the Spirit seems appropriate, as it was already a religious symbol in Hebrew literature. In the Genesis story of the flood, the dove was a symbol of the reconciliation of man to God. In the later rabbinical writings, as among the early Christians, the dove was a symbol of the spirit or the Holy Spirit.

intended to establish the superiority of Jesus and his baptism of the Spirit over John's water baptism.

In the Fourth Gospel, as in Luke, John's baptism merely provided the occasion for Jesus' baptism of the Spirit. Here the Baptist's role is clearly delineated. He is not the Christ. He is not Elijah. And he is not the prophet to come.[1] His single function in the Fourth Gospel was to bear witness that God's Spirit had descended upon and remained with Jesus, that Jesus was the Son of God.

John's converts were not gentile proselytes being initiated into Judaism. They were already Jews, as were the disciples of Jesus and those who were converted by Jesus' disciples. What, then, did baptism mean for John and those whom he baptized? Perhaps the baptism of John was a variation from the more traditional Jewish practice of washing or cleansing for purification. Although the Baptist was preaching repentance, it was not repentance from individual, personal sins. John's baptism probably did not mean redemption from personal sin nor was it for the forgiveness of sins; it was for ablution not absolution. While repentance for the forgiveness of personal sin was in all likelihood a belief of the Christian churches at an early date, in John's time repentance was a "return" of Israel to its covenants with God. Undoubtedly, eschatology is the key to an understanding of this matter. For many Jews, as for the Jewish Essenes at Qumran, the new age of the Kingdom of God was about to begin.

One of the most prominent features of the Qumran community was its eschatology, its doctrine of the End of the Age. The abundance of apocalyptic expressions from texts found in the caves attests to this fact.[14] Apocalyptic literature expressing a strong sense of group destiny and explaining the historical crises in Jewish life gave the Essenes both inspiration and direction. According to their scripture "The War of the Sons of Light and

---

[1] Jn 1:20f.

[14] The pseudepigrapha has traditionally included pseudonymous and anonymous Jewish writings produced between ca. 200 BCE and ca. 200 CE. They usually purport to have been written by illustrious figures from Jewish history who lived long before they were actually composed.

the Sons of Darkness," they believed that the End was imminent, that during the final stage of history a mighty battle would be fought between the forces of good and evil, and that ultimately this world and Satan's domain would be destroyed. But, on the positive side, as recorded in the Essene Book of Hymns, this would also be a time of renewal. The world labors at a new birth and all things will be renewed.[15]

In the Essene communities, baptism symbolized the candidates' intentions to surrender themselves completely to the belief of the coming end of the era and to totally commit themselves to preparing for and bringing in the Kingdom. There can be little doubt that Jesus' decision to submit to John's baptism had a similarly profound meaning for both the Baptist and Jesus.

Jesus' convictions regarding himself may have been greatly affected by the preaching of John. Perhaps in his baptism by John, intimations of his own role and destiny began to emerge. If this was the case, his baptism was surely a decisive turning point in his life. Although it is doubtful that Jesus had a clear conception of mission at an earlier age, at his baptism he seems to have reached a climax in his commitment. He may even have identified his own mission with that of John. He identified himself with the hopes and expectations of the Jewish people, and his baptism seems to have been a consecration of his life to their cause.

THE TEMPTATION IN THE WILDERNESS

According to the synoptic accounts, after his baptism Jesus went alone into the wilderness of Judea. Mark says, "The Spirit immediately drove him out into the wilderness."[m][16] Between Jerusalem and the low Jordan Valley stretches a strip of arid, barren country about thirty-five miles long and fifteen miles wide.

---

[m] Mk 1:12.

[15] See Theodor H. Gaster's introduction, notes, and text of the "Book of Hymns," or "Psalms of Thanksgiving," in *The Dead Sea Scriptures*, 3rd ed. (New York, 1976), 144–216.

[16] Mark's interpretation of the Spirit driving Jesus into the wilderness conforms to accounts of the Spirit coming with great power upon Old Testament heroes, kings, and prophets — Saul, David, Samuel, and Elijah (1 Sm 10:6–10; 16:13f.; 19:20–24; 2 Kgs 2:15f.).

The Proclamation of the Kingdom 61

This is an area of steep, mountainous cliffs and rocky gorges — the Judean desert. Little vegetation grows on the stony surface of this rough country and few trails cross it. In the Old Testament it is called "Jeshimon," meaning devastation or waste.

Following his baptism Jesus quite naturally would have sought solitude to reflect on the meaning of his experience and its import for his life and labors. In a sense the temptation was a sequel to the baptism. Jesus must have been deeply concerned with the alternatives before him. Many centuries earlier, when confronted with crises of their destiny, the prophets of Israel had retired to this same desolate mountainous area, the wilderness of Judea. And it was there that David sought refuge from the wrath of King Saul. Now, according to Matthew, as Jesus pondered his task, he experienced an intense inward spiritual struggle.

There are various interpretations of the temptation story. It was commonly believed by the New Testament writers that demons or evil spirits were real entities whose power could be observed in the natural world. The devil, a powerful demon, was the chief tempter. The earth was a place of supernatural activity as well as of natural, everyday events. Whether the account of the temptation was intended to be taken literally or as a parable-like representation of the inner world of moral and spiritual struggle is difficult to determine.[17] Whether accepted literally or not, the story of Jesus' temptation is designed to exhibit the demonic power that forces profound moral choices, decisions that must be made whatever the risks. "And he fasted forty days and forty nights, and afterward he was hungry. And the tempter came and said to him, 'If you are the Son of God, command these stones to become loaves of bread.' "[n]

Various scholars of the New Testament have suggested that for the synoptists the focus of the temptation was on three strategies:[18] (1) Meet the immediate and material needs of the people

---

[n] Mt 4:2f.

[17] See R. Bultmann's discussion of the Christian proclamation about Christ and the problem of mythology in his *Jesus Christ and Mythology* (New York, 1958).

[18] Matthew and Luke provide most of the details. The Gospel writers unquestionably regarded Jesus as the Messiah and the Son of God. From the perspective

first; (2) employ miracles and public display as a strategy for winning popular support, and (3) generate public enthusiasm through a nationalistic interpretation of the proclamation of the Kingdom. Any one or any combination of these might have meant almost immediate success for Jesus in enlisting widespread and enthusiastic support.

Why not administer to the basic material needs of the people? Did not God provide food for Israel in the Exodus? Was not the Messiah expected to prepare a great banquet?[19] Yet, there is a precedent in the Mosaic tradition for a contrary view. During the Exodus, God allowed Israel to become hungry; then he fed them on manna to teach them that man cannot live on bread alone. God cared for them; nevertheless, he tested and disciplined them to see whether or not they would keep the commandments.º Jesus, according to Matthew, exercised self-restraint and resisted the temptation to exploit his opportunities for personal or political ends. Referring to Deuteronomy, he replied to the tempter, "Man shall not live by bread alone, but by every word that proceeds from the mouth of God." ᵖ

Then the temptation from the pinnacle or parapet of the Temple: "If you are the Son of God, throw yourself down." ᑫ This "temptation," taken literally, might well have been intended by Matthew as a shortcut to the achievement of Jesus' purposes. The masses would quickly acclaim him the Messiah if he performed a miracle such as being saved by angels when he fell from the pinnacle of the Temple. As in the time of the Exodus there was a longing among the people to know whether God was in their midst. In their view no harm could come to God's anointed. Therefore, let him throw himself down and challenge deity to prove the truth of his claim. On the other hand, would rejection of such an act mean that he should never ask God for the special protection

º Dt 8:2–6. ᵖ Mt 4:4. ᑫ Mt 4:6.

---

of the Christian Church of their time, what Jesus did and said bore witness to the truth of their claim of his Messiahship and sonship.

[19] This is suggested in Isaiah's expression of hope for the deliverance and restoration of Judah (Is 25:6–8).

which the scriptures had promised? Again, the answer came from Deuteronomy, "You shall not tempt the Lord your God." [20]

"Again, the devil took him to a very high mountain, and showed him all the kingdoms of the world and the glory of them; and he said to him, 'All these I will give you, if you will fall down and worship me.' " [r] There was, of course, much popular support for the idea that the Messiah would be a powerful leader. Jesus was surely acquainted with the anti-Roman Zealots of Galilee, who expected the Messiah to lead a war of liberation against Rome and restore the Davidic empire. But he did not yield: "Begone, Satan! for it is written, 'You shall worship the Lord your God and him only shall you serve.' " [s] His response, based on passages from Deuteronomy 6:13, was similar to his rebuke of Peter later at Caesarea Philippi, when Peter apparently refused to accept Jesus' decision to go to Jerusalem to suffer and be killed at the hands of his opponents.[t] In both instances Jesus was apparently refusing to identify himself as a Davidic Messiah.

THE PROCLAMATION OF THE KINGDOM

According to the Synoptics, Jesus began his ministry at the time of John's imprisonment. In view of John's fate, he probably was aware that he faced serious risks in proclaiming his message of the Kingdom. Nevertheless, he persisted in carrying the message of the Kingdom of God to the people. He called Israel to repentance and promised the joy of deliverance in the new Kingdom. "Now after John was arrested, Jesus came into Galilee, preaching the gospel of God, and saying, 'The time is fulfilled, and the kingdom of God is at hand; repent, and believe in the gospel.' " [u]

With this dramatic proclamation, Jesus entered upon a task which thereafter claimed his total commitment and energy. The Kingdom of God or Kingdom of Heaven is the focus and sub-

---

[r] Mt 4:8f. [s] Mt 4:10. [t] Mt 16:23; Mk 8:33. [u] Mk 1:14f.

[20] This has an apparent reference to Deuteronomy 6:16: "You shall not put the Lord your God to the test, as you tested him at Massah." Exodus 17:7 reads, "And he [Moses] called the name of the place Massah and Meribah, because of the fault-finding of the children of Israel, and because they put the Lord to the proof by saying, 'Is the Lord among us or not?' "

stance of all his teaching. His parables began "The kingdom of Heaven is like." And in the Sermon on the Mount, he required of true disciples that they "seek first his kingdom and his righteousness." References to the "Kingdom of God" in Luke are synonymous with the "Kingdom of Heaven" in Matthew. Nothing in the Gospels is more authentic as a teaching of Jesus than the proclamation of the coming of the Kingdom. To the very end he spoke confidently of it. Indeed, the most revolutionary elements of his entire message were centered in this pronouncement.

Among the problems encountered in the New Testament none is more difficult to treat than Jesus' meaning of the "Kingdom." Obviously from the Gospel writers' points of view, Jesus had no use for the power, the pomp, and the obeisance commonly associated with kings and kingdoms. According to the Gospel of John, the followers of Jesus at one time "were about to come and take him by force to make him king." To escape them he "withdrew . . . to the mountain by himself." [v] It is understandable that the Jews would commonly refer to God as King because they thought of him as a divine and absolute lawgiver. God was the author of the moral law which was the foundation of their religious beliefs and their social institutions. The Old Testament does not employ the expression "Kingdom of God," but it does make reference to the "Lord's Kingdom." This appears not to be a reference to a place of actual rule but rather an expression to convey the idea of the supremacy of God and his moral law. Such references are found for instance in the 103rd and 145th Psalms.

Jesus' conception of the Kingdom as represented by the Gospel writers is not always clear. Their interpretations vary from a view of the Kingdom as a future event to one already present. This is perhaps due in part to the different views among early Christians at the time of the writing of the Gospels. Some accepted the common Jewish notion that the Kingdom would be a political entity in this world. Others believed it would be God's realm in the hereafter. Clear identification of the Kingdom with the church was apparently not made before Augustine, 354–430 CE. Perhaps

---

[v] Jn 6:15.

The Proclamation of the Kingdom 65

what Jesus intended is best expressed in the prayer in the sixth chapter of Matthew: "Thy kingdom come. Thy will be done, On earth as it is in heaven." [w] The establishment of God's rule on earth had long been the hope of Israel. Now, according to the Gospel writers, the day of deliverance had dawned; the time of waiting was over. God's Kingdom was near; it was at the door.[21]

GALILEE

It was fitting that Jesus began his ministry in the Galilee.[22] In Old Testament times, the Galilee and the Plains of Esdraelon southward, including Mount Gilboa, Bet She'an, and Mount Carmel, were places of great activity. Heroic scenes in Israel's history were enacted here. At Mount Carmel, Elijah made his great stand against the priests of Baal.[x] Near Mount Tabor, Deborah rallied the forces of Israel against the tyrant Sisera.[y] At Mount Gilboa, Saul and Jonathan lost their lives in a crucial battle with the Philistines.[z] There in the north are the Lebanon Mountains and Mount Hermon. The eastern boundary is provided by the Jordan or Rift Valley and the Sea of Galilee. The "Upper" and "Lower" Galilee are separated by the rugged Meron mountain range, of which Mount Meron is a prominent feature. The Phoenician coast forms the western boundary. On the south the Lower Galilee drops off into the Plain of Esdraelon, today referred to as the Yizreel Valley.

The Sea of Galilee, a prominent feature of this area, has been known by various names: "Sea of Tiberias" in the Gospel of John,[a] and "lake of Gennesaret" in Luke.[b] In the Old Testament it is referred to as "Chinnereth" and in modern Hebrew

---

[w] Mt 6:10.   [x] 1 Kgs 18:17–46.   [y] Jgs 4:1–5:31.   [z] 1 Sm 31:1–13.
[a] Jn 6:1; 21:1.   [b] Lk 5:1.

[21] Jesus was talking to Palestinian Jews who were steeped in apocalyptic imagery and confident that God would deliver them. The Age to Come, the new age, would suddenly and spectacularly appear. Morton S. Enslin, *The Prophet from Nazareth* (New York, 1968), 71.

[22] The term "Galilee" is thought by some to have referred originally to a small circuit or ring of cities in the northern area of Palestine. Solomon gave King Hiram of Tyre these cities in payment for materials and services in the building of the Temple. More likely "Galilee" derived from the several prominent round-shaped hills which dominate this northern region.

as "Kinneret," which means harp, possibly so named because of its shape.²³

The Galileans engaged in manufacturing and fishing and were active in commerce, but the majority were laborers on the land. During the ministry of Jesus, Galilee was one of the districts ruled by Herod Antipas under Roman dominion. According to Josephus, who was governor of Galilee a few years after the time of Jesus and who was sometimes given to exaggeration in his histories, Galilee was thickly populated and had 204 cities and villages when the revolt against the Romans broke out in 66 CE. Many of the larger towns were fortified. It was within this limited area, only fifty miles in length from north to south and from twenty-five to thirty miles east to west, that Jesus pursued most of his active ministry.

In the time of Jesus and even earlier, the Galilean dialect was distinct, marriage customs were different from those of Judea, and the Galilean system of coinage and weight varied from that of Judea.²⁴ Galilee had been so often the focal point of periodic uprisings against Roman rule that for many Judeans the name "Galilean" meant "rebel." Josephus, for example, refers to the Zealots from Galilee as "robbers." In general, the Galileans were considered by the Judeans to be uncouth and uncultured. They were sometimes regarded as pagans.

That Jesus was a Galilean Jew probably contributed to the opposition against him. The Judeans who held power and influence in Jerusalem were not disposed to favor Galileans. The Galileans shared a northern religious tradition founded on Moses and the Exodus-Sinai covenant. This tradition continued through the major preliterary prophets, Samuel, Elijah, and Elisha. This apparently was the covenant which, according to Joshua 24, was renewed at Shechem in the period of the conquest of Canaan. But, Judean Jews and those in positions of leadership, the Pharisees

---

²³ The Sea of Galilee is approximately 695 feet below the level of the Mediterranean. It is approximately 14 miles long from north to south, 7 miles in width, and averages about 150 feet in depth. Capernaum, where Jesus centered his activities in Galilee, was located on the northwest shore.

²⁴ In his account of Peter's denial of Jesus, Matthew reports that one of the bystanders said to Peter, "your accent betrays you" as a Galilean (Mt 26:73).

and the Temple officials, who usually were Sadducees, shared a David-Zion covenant. In the time of the monarchy this southern tradition superseded the earlier Exodus-Sinai covenant. The royal covenant was based on the claim that David and his dynasty were elected by God to rule Israel in perpetuity and that Jerusalem had been designated by God as Zion, the place of God's central sanctuary.[25] These differences may explain in part the scorn, resentments, and condemnations directed at Galileans by Judean Jews that are expressed in the insult, "Can anything good come out of Nazareth?" [c]

Although Palestine was a small area, between Galilee and Judea there were important cultural differences. Variations can be found today, for instance, in art forms, decorative elements, and symbols in synagogues and other ruins. A conservative tendency seems to have characterized the synagogues of the Upper Galilee, including preferences for the Hebrew and Aramaic languages for inscriptions rather than the Greek language so widely employed in southern Galilee. It has been suggested that the rugged terrain in the north and in the Golan accounts for these variations, since it is probable that many of those who settled in the northern mountainous regions did so to protect themselves from Graeco-Roman cultural influences and to take refuge from the Roman imperial administration which was very effective and oppressive in the south. This was especially true following the destruction of Jerusalem in 70 CE.

JESUS AND JUDAISM

From the beginning there were dramatic events in Jesus' ministry. He preached and was rejected in Nazareth. He preached in the synagogue at Capernaum. He performed exorcisms and healings. And he accepted into his presence sinners who did not fully observe the religious law and publicans, the despised tax collectors. As a consequence he soon became not only well known

[c] Jn 1:46.

[25] For a detailed discussion of the history of these religious traditions, northern and southern, see Bernard W. Anderson, *Understanding the Old Testament*, 3rd ed. (Englewood Cliffs, New Jersey, 1975), 267f., 518–21.

but notorious. As his fame grew, opposition to him from the Jewish political-religious establishment became more intense. A most dramatic moment in Jesus' early ministry occurred when on his return to Nazareth following his baptism, he announced in the synagogue that in his own person the prophecy of Isaiah was fulfilled, that the time of the Lord was at hand. The incident is given in the Gospel of Luke. According to the custom, which continues to this day in the more conservative synagogues,

> he stood up to read; and there was given to him the book of the prophet Isaiah. He opened the book and found the place where it was written, "The Spirit of the Lord is upon me, because he has anointed me to preach good news to the poor. He has sent me to proclaim release to the captives and recovering of sight to the blind, to set at liberty those who are oppressed, to proclaim the acceptable year of the Lord." [d]

This account from Luke is evidence that Jesus was a practicing Jew who attended synagogue services and participated in the reading of the scriptures. This is a most important index to the character of his religion, the meaning of his teachings, and the understanding of Palestinian Christianity. The passage which he read from Chapter 61 of Isaiah undoubtedly referred to the deliverance of Israel from bondage in Babylonia. However, the Jews of Jesus' day, tying the biblical prophecies to their own time and condition, regarded it as presaging the coming of the Kingdom.[26] For Luke the Isaiah verses were clearly a prophecy encapsulating the whole purpose of Jesus' ministry.

Understandably, Jesus chose Nazareth where he would be among friends and acquaintances as the place to proclaim this message. But when he said, "Today this scripture has been fulfilled in your hearing," [e] it surely produced shock in those who knew him and his family. Some were understandably puzzled: "Is not this Joseph's son?" [f] He must have sensed the opposition

---

[d] Lk 4:16–19.   [e] Lk 4:21.   [f] Lk 4:22.

[26] The statement from Isaiah 61:1f.; 58:6 cited in Luke's Gospel is not mentioned in either Matthew or Mark.

among them.²⁷ Indeed in Luke's Gospel, he is represented as knowing their very thoughts. "Doubtless," he said, "you will quote to me this proverb, 'Physician, heal yourself.' " ᵍ He was aware of the low esteem sometimes accorded the Hebrew prophets in the past, as indicated in the aphorism that no prophet is accepted in his own country.ʰ According to Luke, Jesus pointed out that God cares for the needy and forsaken of all nations. He cited the examples of the prophet Elijah, who helped a widow living beyond the borders of the Jewish nation,ⁱ and Elisha, who healed Naaman the leper, a Syrian.ʲ Jesus' assertion that God might bless Gentiles even in preference to the people of Israel, and his apparent readiness to set aside the people of his own town while he ministered to others, aroused some in the synagogue to violence.²⁸ But according to Luke he escaped with apparent ease. In Luke's view Jesus' message of the establishment of God's Kingdom was now proclaimed, and his ministry was formally begun.²⁹

It is impossible to overstate the importance of the fact that Jesus was a believing, practicing Jew. Notwithstanding his liberal interpretations of some Jewish principles and his conflict with some Jewish religious leaders, especially the Sadducees, he was a devout Jew. Even though the Gospels were written many years after Jesus' crucifixion and during the early period of the Christian church, they were written by and for those closely tied to Jewish

---

ᵍ Lk 4:23.   ʰ Lk 4:24.   ⁱ 1 Kgs 17:1–24.   ʲ 2 Kgs 5:1–14.

²⁷ Matthew and Mark record that, "they took offense at him" (Mt 13:57, Mk 6:3). Also, Matthew reports that Jesus "did not do many mighty works there, because of their unbelief" (Mt 13:58). The fact that in Mark, Jesus is referred to as "the Son of Mary" (Mk 6:3) and Joseph is not mentioned suggests either that Joseph died while Jesus was a young man or that the earliest Gospel retains a tradition that knows of no father for Jesus. In Luke, however, Jesus is referred to as Joseph's son (Lk 4:22). Four brothers are named in Matthew and Mark, and the fact that sisters are mentioned indicates that Jesus was a member of a family of at least seven children (Mt 13:55f.; Mk 6:3).

²⁸ In Luke all major crises seem to have been fully anticipated, and Jesus is described as having full control of events from the beginning to the end of his ministry.

²⁹ Luke's account places the event at Nazareth soon after Jesus' baptism, the temptation, and his first preaching tour in Galilee. Mark and Matthew place the rejection at Nazareth later in the sequence of events. This fact has given rise to the claim of some that there were two rejections at Nazareth. The evidence seems to favor two versions of a single event.

tradition, culture, religion, morality, and worship. It is clear from such accounts as that of Jesus reading from the sacred books in the synagogue at Nazareth that his later followers regarded him in the light of Jewish customs and practice. Knowing him intimately, as many of the people in Nazareth no doubt did, they were understandably puzzled and deeply concerned by his authoritative pronouncements. To them he was just one of their townsmen. His mother and brothers and sisters were known to them. He perhaps seemed arrogant and presumptuous in his synagogue pronouncements, no doubt calling for repentance and announcing the establishment of the Kingdom. Had Jesus come from some other country, they might have respected his views and believed in him. But here in the place where he was reared and known from childhood, they could not believe him.

THE FIRST DISCIPLES

Following his baptism and the temptation, Jesus made Capernaum on the north shore of the Sea of Galilee the center of his activities. No doubt there were several reasons for his interest in Capernaum. It was an important cosmopolitan center, partly Jewish in population but supporting many nationalities. Here Greeks from the nearby cities of Decapolis and bedouins from the desert mingled with Romans in the military, on civil assignment, or as commercial travelers. Capernaum was an important link between Damascus and the Galilee and south to Jerusalem. It was a center for commercial and military traffic between the East and the Mediterranean.[30] Matthew regarded it as significant that Jesus located his headquarters there.[31] He may have considered it an indication of Jesus' intention to extend his ministry beyond the boundaries of

---

[30] In the New Testament and in Josephus the name of Capernaum is more frequently written as *Capharnaum*. The original Hebrew name *Kfar Nahum* means the village of Nahum. In Jesus' time Capharnaum extended for some distance along the narrow shoreline, confined between the hills and the sea. For details, see Stanislau Loffreda, *A Visit to Capharnaum* (Jerusalem, 1981).

[31] Capernaum was the location of Peter's and Andrew's home; here Jesus healed Peter's mother-in-law of a fever (Mk 1:29–31). According to the Gospels, several other important events occurred here: Jesus taught in the synagogue at Capernaum, healed a man with an unclean spirit (Mk 1:21–28), and cured a servant of a Roman centurion (Lk 7:1–10).

Israel. Matthew quoted a prophecy of Isaiah[k] as meaning, apparently, that the very lands which had been invaded by the Assyrians and Syrians and had suffered greatly from the enemies of Israel and Judah would be the first to enjoy the multiple blessings which would accompany the coming of the Kingdom.[32]

The account of the calling of the four disciples by the Sea of Galilee set forth in Mark, 1:16–20, indicates they were not from the poorest economic class. Simon and his brother Andrew and James and John were all fishermen. Zebedee, the father of James and John, may have owned the boat and nets. Also, it may be concluded from the mention of hired laborers that these men were engaged in a prosperous fishing enterprise. The details of the story in Matthew and Mark are similar. Luke, however, gives the account of the so-called "miraculous catch" of fish which led to the conversion of Peter, James, and John. They were astonished at their catch, which they attributed to Jesus' supernatural power.[33]

In Mark's account, the four accompanied Jesus to Capernaum. On the Sabbath he taught in the synagogue "as one who had authority, and not as the scribes."[l] He exorcised an unclean spirit from a man in the synagogue, and his fame spread throughout the region. The reference to "authority" suggests Jesus spoke from his own wisdom, insight, and experience. He did not speak like a scholar, tracing the genealogy of scholarly opinions and relying on past precedents in interpreting the sacred texts. Perhaps he adduced no argument to support his pronouncements, for the Gospel writers portray Jesus as possessing a unique insight into universal truths and moral principles. In Mark's view Jesus, recognized by the unclean spirit as "the Holy One of God,"[m] was himself the final

---

[k] Is 9:1f. [l] Mk 1:21–28. [m] Mk 1:24.

[32] In Matthew the pattern of future events is established early in Jesus' ministry. Matthew's account differs from Mark and Luke in that according to Matthew, Jesus left Nazareth and "dwelt in Capernaum by the sea, in the territory of Zebulun and Naphtali" (Mt 4:12f.). This account, in accordance with Matthew's predisposition to relate Jesus to earlier prophecy, fulfilled scripture. The move to Capernaum was probably to inaugurate Jesus' ministry to the gentiles, i.e., "the people who sat in darkness" (Mt 4:16/Is 9:2).

[33] John reports an earlier meeting in Bethany between Jesus and Andrew and his brother Simon Peter in connection with the Baptist's testimony about Jesus (Jn 1:35–42).

authority for his teaching. The authoritative character of his pronouncements apparently had an astonishing effect on his listeners.

MATTHEW THE PUBLICAN

The synoptics agree that following the healing of the paralytic, Jesus called to discipleship the tax collector named Matthew in the Gospel of Matthew and referred to as Levi in Mark and Luke. Thereafter, according to the synoptic writers, both tax collectors and sinners "sat at table" with him and his disciples.[n] [34]

In the Latin version the Greek for "tax collector" is translated as "publicanus," hence our English word publican. Matthew may have collected customs for goods shipped across the Sea of Galilee, or as some scholars conjecture, he may have been given taxing responsibility for the caravan route leading into Capernaum from Syria. The phrases "publicans and sinners" and "publicans and harlots" were expressions which clearly indicated the contempt with which people regarded Jews who collected tax for the Roman government. It was bad enough for a gentile to collect the imperial taxes, but a Jew engaged in this occupation was regarded with special suspicion because his vocation provided him with ample opportunities for graft and corruption. Moreover, the tax collector's work brought him into contact with the gentiles, who were outside the Law.

But Jesus looked upon Matthew differently. "Follow me" was his brief command. This incident is a vivid example of the evangelist's view that Jesus extended his circle of disciples even to those who were held in low esteem. Matthew, the tax-gatherer, leaving the security and possibly even the wealth of his position, "rose, and followed him."

POPULAR ACCEPTANCE OF JESUS

When Matthew prepared a public dinner, perhaps in honor of his master, the opposition of the Pharisees was aroused. In their opinion, Jesus cared too much for social outcasts and too little for

[n] Mt 9:9–13; Mk 2:13–17; Lk 5:27–32.

[34] In the opinion of most scholars, Matthew the disciple was not the author of the Gospel known as Matthew.

Jewish tradition. The dinner with sinners and tax collectors was a public disgrace. The laws and rituals regarding the preparation and eating of food were violated. The "sinners" with whom Jesus associated probably were those who did not observe the Law, especially the dietary and ceremonial prescriptions associated with eating. It appears that these sinners were sometimes persons who did not know or fully understand the requirements of the Law or whose circumstances made it difficult or impossible to keep its requirements.

The scribes who belonged to the Pharisaic party put the question to the four disciples: "Why does your teacher eat with tax collectors and sinners?" ° The whole situation presented an opportunity for misunderstanding. Hearing their expressed resentment of his behavior, Jesus answered, "Those who are well have no need of a physician." Then, perhaps with some indignation that these men of religious profession should so completely misunderstand the humanitarian purpose of the gathering, Jesus said, "Go and learn what this means." He quoted an important pronouncement from Hosea, "I desire mercy, and not sacrifice," insisting that God values mercy and acts of service to those in need above the ceremonial forms of religious worship.[35] The occasion demanded courage, for Jesus had challenged the religious authorities who assumed it was their religious and moral duty to shun persons whom they regarded as sinful.[36]

The local officials and religious leaders would be understandably concerned and no doubt deeply disturbed by the activities of one who commanded such a following as Jesus had generated. Jesus' actions and teachings were neither authorized nor controlled by them. But according to the Gospel accounts, he did not write or in any way encourage publicity. Nor did he court confrontation with the religious leaders. In Matthew, for instance, Jesus on one

---

° Mt 9:11.

[35] See Mt 9:13. Matthew seems to have added this reference to Hosea 6:6 to show that Jesus' teaching on mercy was consistent with the teachings of the Hebrew prophets.

[36] Each of the synoptic writers mentions that Jesus' intention was not to call "the righteous, but sinners to repentance" (Lk 5:32). See parallels in Mt 9:13 and Mk 2:17, which omit the phrase "to repentance."

occasion withdrew from the vicinity of Capernaum to avoid conflict with the Pharisees. The conflict was threatened as a consequence of his defending healing on the Sabbath.[p]

It is apparent from the accounts in all three Synoptics that great popularity came to Jesus early in his ministry. The news of his preaching of the Kingdom and his exorcisms and healing spread rapidly. Many came to see and hear him from nearby Galilean cities, from Judea and Jerusalem, from Idumea south of the Dead Sea, and from the gentile cities of Tyre and Sidon on the Mediterranean coast.[q] Some were merely curious; others wanted to be healed or to witness miracles. But perhaps most came to hear Jesus' words about the Kingdom. The gospel of the coming of the Kingdom was "good news" for the oppressed and underprivileged. This was the burden of Jesus' message, and it was this promise and expectation that became the foundation of the Christian movement.

EXORCISM

There was a prevailing fear among many people that a person could be possessed by actual, living demons who could then direct his will and dominate his life. Moreover, it was believed that evil spirits were the cause of sickness and disease. Such phenomena had been reported among the early Hebrews, as in the case of the "evil spirit from God" which tormented King Saul.[r] It is clear from the New Testament that this belief was also common among the Christians of the primitive church. Mark 1:23–26, 32–34 refers to the many healings and exorcisms which Jesus performed. According to Mark, God and his angels were engaged in a cosmic struggle against Satan and his hosts. Jesus as the Messiah had entered human history at a critical juncture when Satan's kingdom had almost prevailed. Mark held that one of Jesus' primary objectives in preparing for the coming of God's Kingdom was to weaken Satan's dominion by exorcising evil spirits.[37]

[p] Mt 12:1–14f. See Mk 3:6f. [q] Mk 3:7f. [r] Is 16:14–16, 23; 18:10; 19:9.

[37] For a more detailed analysis of the belief in demon possession in early Christianity, see Shirley J. Case, *Experience with the Supernatural in Early Christian Times* (New York, 1929).

The Proclamation of the Kingdom

It is possible that the spread of Jesus' fame throughout Galilee was due as much to his success as an exorcist in casting out demons as to his success in healing the sick. If the account in Luke 4:39 of the healing of Peter's mother-in-law is taken literally, Jesus regarded some forms of sickness as due to evil spirits, for it says that he "rebuked the fever." It is difficult for modern readers of the Gospels to adjust their thinking to the fact that Jesus, his disciples, and the Gospel writers believed literally in demons and demon possession. But these accounts must be read in terms of the practices and beliefs of the place and time when they were written. It would seriously distort Jesus and his teachings to modernize him by placing him within the culture of the twentieth century.[38]

THE MIRACLES

The problem of miracles, which will be treated later in more detail, is difficult and perhaps cannot be discussed with full satisfaction in an age of science and scientific intelligence. However, in the case of miracles of healing, the influence of the mind on the physical body offers some explanation. Although the miracles reported in the Gospels are often described as interruptions of natural processes, in some cases they may be regarded as natural processes that were not understood in Jesus' day. Moreover, the problem of miracles in the New Testament cannot be divorced from

---

H. C. Kee holds the view that the portrayal of conflict with the demonic in "Q" and Mark "is an essential factor in the fulfillment of God's redemptive purpose through Jesus." Howard C. Kee, *Jesus in History*, 2nd ed. (New York, 1977), 98. *Jesus the Magician*, by Morton Smith (San Francisco, 1978), is an account of the view of Jesus held by his enemies and the opposers of Christianity. It gives an extensive treatment of demonology and Jesus' exorcisms. Jeffrey Burton Russell, *The Devil: Perceptions of Evil from Antiquity to Primitive Christianity* (Ithaca, New York, 1977) and *Satan: The Early Christian Tradition* (Ithaca, New York, 1981), are informative studies on early conceptions of the sources of evil.

[38] The error of modernizing Jesus is the subject of Albert Schweitzer's influential *The Quest of the Historical Jesus*, trans. W. Montgomery (New York, 1906). See also the work of Rudolf Bultmann, whose basic interest has been the eschatological framework of Jesus and the early church. Rudolf Bultmann, *Theology of the New Testament*, trans. Kendrick Grobel, Vol. 1 (New York, 1951).

the analysis of myth and its prevalence in the Jewish eschatology of Jesus' time.[39]

That the disciples often failed "to see," that is, to grasp Jesus' meaning and intention, is a frequent theme in the Gospel of Mark. As recorded in Mark 1:35–38, this apparent failure to understand appeared early in the ministry. When Jesus went to a "lonely place" for prayer, his disciples followed him to persuade him to continue to administer to the people of Capernaum. He reminded his disciples of the urgency of his ministry by saying that those in other towns and cities must hear his word. So, "he went throughout all Galilee, preaching in their synagogues and casting out demons."[s][40]

The account of Jesus healing the leper, given in Mark 1:40–45, has always intrigued those interested in the miracle stories.[41] In ancient time leprosy was one of the most dreaded diseases, for it was believed that once the disease was contracted, the afflicted person was doomed to a slow and horrible death. Even more tragic, lepers were shunned by everyone because of the fear of contamination and because they were ceremonially unclean.[t] The law regarding leprosy in Leviticus was explicit: "The leper who has the disease shall wear torn clothes and let the hair of his head hang loose, and he shall cover his upper lip and cry, 'Unclean, unclean.' He shall remain unclean as long as he has the disease; he is unclean; he shall dwell alone in a habitation outside the camp."[u][42] But the leper in the story disregarded these regula-

[s] Mk 1:39. [t] Lv 13, 14. [u] Lv 13:45f.

[39] The Bultmann concept of demythologizing the New Testament with its three-storied conception of the universe contributed importantly to the enthusiasm for biblical study over the last several decades. See Bultmann, *Jesus Christ and Mythology*.

[40] Luke is even more explicit than Mark (1:35–39) about Jesus' motivation to reach other people, "for I was sent for this purpose." Also, according to Luke (4:42f.), the people, not the disciples, attempted to detain Jesus, "The people sought him . . . and would have kept him from leaving them."

[41] The parallels of this account of healing occur at the end of the Sermon on the Mount (Mt 8:1–4) and at Luke 5:12–16.

[42] "Leprosy" is a biblical term apparently employed to refer to a variety of skin diseases. The distinction between clean and unclean was primarily a religious distinction, although it probably had some connection with early tribal codes of hygiene. In ancient Israel only the priest could declare a leper clean; only he could make atonement for the leper, which was essential for his return to normal life in the community. Leviticus 14:1–32 describes the extensive ritual of cleansing.

The Proclamation of the Kingdom

tions. His hope led him to desperate action — "If you will, you can make me clean." And Jesus, "moved with pity, . . . stretched out his hand and touched him," and when he said the words "be clean" the leper was healed. Jesus' adherence to Leviticus 14 is evident in this account when he tells the healed man to show himself to the priest.

When Jesus came again to Capernaum his fame had spread and crowds were attracted to him. The account of Jesus' healing a paralytic at this time is given in some detail in Mark.[v] The words, "When Jesus saw their faith," refer to the four men and the paralytic whom they lowered through the roof because of the crowded room. His statement, "My son, your sins are forgiven," inevitably produced shock in the listeners. To heal the sick was one thing, but only God could forgive a person of his sins. There were evidences of hostility among those present, and the scribes who witnessed the event raised the serious question, "Who can forgive sins but God alone?" Then Jesus, sensing their reservations about him, posed the question: "Which is easier, to say to the paralytic, 'Your sins are forgiven,' or to say, 'Rise, take up your pallet and walk'?" Jesus' identity and authority are prominent themes in Mark, and in this instance he makes it clear that Jesus is the Son of man and that he has the authority to forgive sins.[43]

---

[v] Mk 2:1–12.

[43] See Mk 2:3–12. For Mark the true nature of Jesus required no explanation; events themselves clearly revealed his identity and those who were present should have known at once who he was.

CHAPTER 4

The Sermons, Miracles, and Parables

The traditions about Jesus handed down in oral or written form were concerned mainly with what he did and said. They were accounts of his miracles, exorcisms, sermons, and especially his proclamation of the Kingdom of God. That he was regarded as a moral teacher of supreme sensitivity and religious wisdom is obvious. As the Messiah he was seen by Paul and the early church not as a Davidic deliverer of the nation but rather as the divine savior through whom God grants salvation to the individual human soul.

For Christians generally, Jesus as supreme teacher and Christ as savior are one and the same person, human and divine. These conceptions, however different, are not incompatible. Yet especially in early Christianity, major theological controversies arose relating to the divine-human question. The Apostle Paul, like most theologians until recent times, gave virtually no attention to the life and teachings of Jesus. He was interested almost exclusively in Christ as the agent of salvation. Modern scholars, on the other hand, have been concerned more with Jesus as a person who walked in the pathways of Galilee and Judea, associated with people of diverse social station and religious and political views, who comforted the oppressed and suffering, and, above all, expounded on moral and spiritual matters with an impact that is beyond estimate.

THE SERMON ON THE MOUNT

The Sermon on the Mount set forth in chapters 5, 6, and 7 of Matthew is the fullest and most effective presentation of Jesus' teachings. It is usually regarded as a single sermon given at one time to his disciples and followers, presumably on a Galilee hill-

The Sermons, Miracles, and Parables

side. The Sermon on the Plain, recorded in chapter 6 of Luke, is similar to the Sermon on the Mount. It is often identified with the Sermon on the Mount, although it contains only about one-fourth of the material found in Matthew. However, scattered through later chapters in Luke are approximately thirty-five verses that correspond to statements found in Matthew's account of the Sermon.[1]

In common with many other New Testament students, Joachim Jeremias holds that Matthew's account of the Sermon on the Mount is a compilation of smaller collections of originally isolated sayings of Jesus. Each collection is a sermon-like summary of Jesus' teachings or at least an expression of a theme found in those teachings.[2] According to Jeremias, it can be assumed that each teaching relates to Jesus' proclamation about the Kingdom of God and the promise of sonship in that Kingdom.

Matthew placed the Sermon on a mountain or hillside. Ancient tradition has identified the place of the Sermon in the hills of Galilee overlooking the sea from the northwest. But even if it was in fact a sermon delivered at a single time and place, which is highly unlikely, the precise location cannot be determined. In both Matthew and Luke the Sermon was addressed primarily to Jesus' disciples[a]; Luke refers to "a great crowd of his disciples."[b] However, both accounts indicate that many other people were present and heard Jesus' instruction.[3]

It seems reasonable to believe that the Sermon on the Mount was not intended by Matthew to be understood simply as a single sermon. Rather, it was the new Word from God, a revelation of

---

[a] Mt 5:1. [b] Lk 6:17.

[1] Luke's "Sermon on the Plain," 6:20–49, includes the Beatitudes (6:20–23), love of one's enemies (6:27–36), judging (6:37–42), tests of goodness (6:43–46), and the statement on hearers and doers of the word (6:47–49). Luke also includes an important feature in the introduction to the sermon — that following his night of prayer Jesus chose the twelve disciples and then delivered the sermon (6:12f., 17f.).

[2] Joachim Jeremias, *The Sermon on the Mount*, trans. Norman Perrin (Philadelphia, 1963).

[3] Luke reports that in addition to his disciples a "great multitude" came to hear Jesus "from all Judea and Jerusalem and the seacoast of Tyre and Sidon" (Lk 6:17). Matthew says at the end of the sermon that "the crowds were astonished at his teaching" (Mt 7:28).

the foundation of the New Covenant, the constitution of the Kingdom of Heaven. The expression "Kingdom of God" in Mark and Luke clearly includes reference to the historical kingdom of David and Solomon. It was the hope and expectation of many Jews that God's future kingdom would be a restoration of the ancient monarchy. However, in the Sermon on the Mount, Matthew's expression "Kingdom of Heaven" seems to contain a more abstract and transcendent conception of the Kingdom. For Matthew Jesus' sermon contains a new Torah teaching, a new standard of righteousness that is grounded in the Hebrew prophetic tradition rather than in rabbinic argument and commentary. For Matthew, the Kingdom is to be a restoration on the model of a heavenly kingdom in which the ideal of moral perfection is to be achieved, "as it is in heaven." Composing the Gospel at least forty years after Pentecost, the evangelist may have regarded the Christian church as the beginning of the earthly realization of that ideal.

For Matthew the Sermon was an instrument for teaching the Christians of his own day the requirements of discipleship by providing a prescription for a new Way. It was a call for saintliness in the lives of the followers of Jesus. The Sermon may have been set out by Matthew in a more formal way as the central portion of a manual or book of instruction intended for use in the church.[4] It begins with the Beatitudes, which in Matthew's formulation are somewhat abstract. Perhaps the original utterances of Jesus were more direct and life-centered, for he was teaching the "people of the land," among whom were the humble, the poor, and those who mourned and were despised. It was as though Jesus were saying, "Even though you are now discouraged and downtrodden, look up, be hopeful, for God's kingdom is coming!"[5]

THE BEATITUDES

The theme of the Beatitudes is happiness — not happiness defined as pleasure but as joy or blessedness. The word *blessed*,

---

[4] See note 17 in chapter 2.

[5] The parallel material in Luke (6:20f.), "you poor," "you that hunger now," "you that weep now," seems to some scholars to be closer to the real spirit of Jesus' teaching than the Matthean statements.

The Sermons, Miracles, and Parables

which appears in the King James Version and Revised Standard Version, is translated in the New English Bible as "how blest." That Jesus begins each of the Beatitudes with this word indicates his high expectations for life in the Kingdom. The Beatitudes are explained and elaborated in the remainder of the Sermon. According to J. C. Fenton, "They show who will enter the kingdom and share with God, under God, in the new order which is about to come." [6] They are directed at the powerless and those in despair, for they will eventually be first and blessed by God.

Since the English translation of the Beatitudes in the Revised Standard Version reproduces most of the familiar language of the Authorized or King James Version, there is perhaps something to be gained in meaning by reading the Beatitudes as translated by the New English Bible.[7]

> How blest are those who know their need of God;
>   the kingdom of Heaven is theirs.
> How blest are the sorrowful;
>   they shall find consolation.
> How blest are those of a gentle spirit;
>   they shall have the earth for their possession.
> How blest are those who hunger and thirst to see right prevail;
>   they shall be satisfied.
> How blest are those who show mercy;
>   mercy shall be shown to them.
> How blest are those whose hearts are pure;
>   they shall see God.
> How blest are the peacemakers;
>   God shall call them his sons.
> How blest are those who have suffered persecution for
>   the cause of right;
>   the kingdom of Heaven is theirs.
> How blest you are, when you suffer insults and persecution and every kind of calumny for my sake. Accept it with gladness and exultation, for you have a rich reward in heaven; in the same way they persecuted the prophets before you.

[6] John C. Fenton, *The Gospel of St. Matthew* (London, 1963), 82.

[7] *The New English Bible with the Apocrypha* (New York, 1970).

It may be appropriate to attempt an approximation of the early church's understanding of these Beatitudes and their proper meaning in the lives of Christian disciples:

"How blest are those who know their need of God." The qualities of character required for discipleship in the Kingdom are the opposite of conceit, boastfulness, and self-righteousness; true disciples are persons of genuine humility; their worth is not measured in terms of worldly merit or position. In God's Kingdom, common human judgments about goodness and merit will be reversed; the usual assessments of worth based upon position, wealth, or world achievement must be abandoned when the ultimate values of the future Kingdom are considered.

"How blest are the sorrowful." Sorrow follows from the remorse one feels, not only for his own personal wrongs but even more for the wrong course Israel has taken. To mourn is to sorrow for one's lack and for one's need, to experience heartfelt repentance. The promise is to those who feel such sorrow; they will be comforted and strengthened when the Kingdom comes.

"How blest are those of a gentle spirit." The meek, the unassuming and unpretentious are worthy of the Kingdom. Those whose strength is within, in contrast with those whose status rests on pride of race and privilege or the arrogance of learning or power, will inherit the Kingdom.

"How blest are those who hunger and thirst to see right prevail." Jesus' conception of the good was in positive rather than negative terms. For him the good person was not one who merely refrains from violating the social conventions and rules but rather one who is active and courageous in seeking to establish the Kingdom of Heaven. "Hunger and thirst" are powerful metaphors for expressing intense commitment.

"How blest are those who show mercy." Happy are they who are compassionate toward others, who forgive others. This does not mean merely to pity them or to befriend them from a sense of duty or obligation. It is to know emptiness or need from one's own experience and to have sympathy and compassion for others who feel that need.

The Sermons, Miracles, and Parables

"How blest are those whose hearts are pure." The expressions "clean heart" and "pure in heart" are found in several of the most popular Old Testament Psalms:

> Who shall ascend the hill of the Lord?
> And who shall stand in his holy place?
> He who has clean hands and a pure heart,
> who does not lift up his soul to what is false,
> and does not swear deceitfully.[c] [8]

In Hebrew psychology, the heart represents the center of life. It is the seat of personal will and commitment. The "pure in heart" refers to those of genuine integrity who persevere with patience, trusting in the promise of God, and are committed to repentance and virtue. They will see God in the age to come.

"How blest are the peacemakers." Peacemakers are those who attempt to create a community in which understanding and love prevail. The phrase "be sons of" appears in another passage in the Sermon: "Love your enemies . . . so that you may be sons of your Father who is in heaven." [d]

"How blest are those who have suffered persecution for the cause of right." This Beatitude should be read with verses 11 and 12, "How blest you are, when you suffer insults and persecution and every kind of calumny for my sake. Accept it with gladness and exultation, for you have a rich reward in heaven." "Persecution for the cause of right" here means persecution on Jesus' account for allegiance to the Kingdom of Heaven. This final Beatitude requires that a disciple completely and unreservedly, with whole heart and soul, commit himself to the cause which Jesus proclaims. Prophets before them were persecuted, says Matthew, for allegiance to God, and the promise is great for those who are faithful to their commitment to righteousness. Some ancient writers as well as modern historians have held that many early Christians possessed a martyr complex which exacerbated the persecutions against them and even contributed to their deaths.

[c] Ps 24:3f. [d] Mt 5:44f.
[8] See also Ps 51:10 and 73:1.

THE MORAL ADMONITIONS: OLD AND NEW

The Sermon on the Mount continues from Matthew 5:13 through chapters 6 and 7 with an impressive summary of Jesus' moral and religious teachings set forth with remarkable effectiveness. The teachings were usually in a pattern of metaphor and parable that embodied basic principles in concrete and familiar reality. The admonitions of Jesus to his disciples are too well known to warrant extensive comment. "You are the salt of the earth; . . . You are the light of the world. A city set on a hill cannot be hid." [e] The disciples are reminded that salt can lose its savor.[9]

"Think not that I have come to abolish the law and the prophets." [f] The Law, the so-called books of Moses, the Pentateuch, was considered God's word by every faithful Jew of Jesus' time; the Prophets were the prophetic books written by or about the prophets of the eighth, seventh, and sixth centuries BCE, who were powerful advocates of social justice and righteousness.[10] Jesus did not intend to reject the injunctions of the books of the Torah or the admonitions of the Prophets. According to Matthew, Jesus would complete the Law and the Prophets. He would not abolish the old foundation but would build upon and perfect it. When the child becomes a man, the child is no more. But the child is not destroyed; he is fulfilled in the man. For Matthew, Jesus' word was the foundation or standard of the new covenant for a new Israel.

"Unless your righteousness exceeds that of the scribes and Pharisees, you will never enter the kingdom of heaven." [g] Instead of the formalism that sometimes characterized the ceremonial and

---

[e] Mt 5:13f.   [f] Mt 5:17.   [g] Mt 5:20.

[9] Water and light are frequently used by the Gospel writers, especially John, as symbols of Jesus' life-giving power. In Matthew's view these admonitions probably mean that Israel had lost its savor, which could not be restored. The Christian church is the new Israel.

[10] The portion of the Jewish Canon known as the Nebiim (Prophets) is comprised of the Former Prophets, the books of Joshua, Judges, 1 and 2 Samuel, 1 and 2 Kings, and the Latter Prophets, Isaiah, Jeremiah, Ezekiel, and the Twelve minor prophets. The canonical books were all in existence and highly honored in Jesus' day, but the canon was not officially and finally settled until the rabbinical Synod of Jamnia (Jabneh) about 90 CE.

The Sermons, Miracles, and Parables

moral requirements of the Jewish Law, Jesus insisted on a sincere pursuit of righteousness, or uprightness, as a requirement for the Kingdom. It is not enough to know the Law and demand its formal observance; the more difficult course of pursuing the personal virtues described in the Sermon on the Mount is essential for acceptance by God.

The formula "You have heard that it was said to the men of old . . . But I say to you," expresses the principles of the "new" righteousness in contrast to the old commands. Jesus' new word is made binding upon the disciples of the new covenant.[11] The new morality is a morality of inwardness and motive as well as of overt action. On the question of murder, Jesus said, "You have heard that it was said to the men of old, 'You shall not kill'; . . . But I say to you that every one who is angry with his brother shall be liable to judgment." [h]

Under the narrow interpretation of the old Law it was held that there was no guilt until the overt act of murder was committed. But for Jesus the act itself was the end of the guilt, not the beginning of it. Anger or hostility is the beginning of murder, and one who feels anger or the hatred it may generate toward another is in danger of judgment.[12] But one who throws insults at one of his fellows or calls him a fool to demean him as a person is even more liable.[13] For Jesus, the obligation to be reconciled with one's "brother" takes precedence over one's duties to worship

---

[h] Mt 5:21f.

[11] It is commonly assumed that the expression in Matthew (5:21f., 27f., 33f., 38f., 43f.), "You have heard," refers to the teachings of the past, presumably time-honored teachings that were accepted in Jesus' time by the official guardians of the moral law. However, David Daube holds that this may be simply a narrow, literalistic understanding of the Law to which Jesus is objecting in Matthew. In Daube's interpretation, "You have heard" might be read as "You have literally understood" or "You might understand literally." David Daube, *The New Testament and Rabbinic Judaism* (London, 1956), 55–62.

[12] Jesus' teachings emphasizing motive and intention are not unique to Judaism. For example Rabbi Eliezer (ca. 90 CE) is reported to have said, "He who hates his neighbour, lo he belongs to the shedders of blood." Quoted from Fenton, *Matthew*, 87.

[13] The King James Version preserves the term "Raca" in the text of Matthew (5:22). The Aramaic term "Raca" probably meant something like "stupid" or "empty-head."

at the Temple. The worship of God must be with a clear conscience; if a person is out of harmony with man, he is out of harmony with God.

Concerning adultery, Jesus' standard, says Matthew,[i] was stricter than the written law. Just as with anger, lust is the motive underlying and preceding an immoral act, an aggression against another person. "If your right eye causes you to sin, pluck it out and throw it away." In these verses, by the use of forceful, hyperbolic illustrations, Jesus insisted upon the importance of personal integrity.

On the subject of divorce,[j] the parallels in Mark 10:11–12 and in Luke 16:18 say straightforwardly that "whoever divorces his wife and marries another, commits adultery." Only in Matthew is there the exception "on the ground of unchastity." It is possible that the exception in Matthew represents an early church interpretation of Jesus in support of its own rules or practice on divorce at the time the Gospel was written.[14] In any case, according to Matthew, Jesus is pointing up the higher standard implicit in the Law which was to take effect when God's Kingdom comes. In that ideal realm, the worth of both persons would be held in such high esteem that divorce would be out of the question.

Jesus saw the folly of the custom of putting one's self under oath as a guarantee of truth. "But I say to you, Do not swear at all."[k] False witness or lying cannot be prevented by merely requiring or giving an oath. One who is false at heart will lie if the pressure is sufficiently strong. Jesus clearly wanted the speech of his disciples to be simple, direct, free from oaths.[15] Only the habit of truth and honesty can ensure the integrity of one's word.

"An eye for an eye" had been the old Law, and presumably it was intended to set some limits upon the primitive instinct to

---

[i] Mt 5:27–30. [j] Mt 5:31f.; 19:3–12. [k] Mt 5:33–37.

[14] J. C. Fenton suggests that "the permission to allow divorce in certain circumstances seems to be one example of the use of this authority [Mt 16:19; 18:18] by the early Church; cf. 1 Cor. 7:12ff., 25ff., where Paul . . . distinguishes clearly and explicitly between his *opinion* and the Lord's *command*." Fenton, *Matthew*, 90.

[15] In the New English Bible Matthew 5:37 is translated, "Plain 'Yes' or 'No' is all you need to say; anything beyond that comes from the devil."

retaliate and punish more than the original hurt.[16] Jesus' instruction to turn the other cheek and love one's enemies was dramatically different; perhaps none of his moral teachings has occasioned more comment. He may not have been pointing out how to respond to an act of physical violence so much as to an insult — a piece of social insolence. Jesus' teaching was directed at those who suffer the scorn and contempt of the powerful and at those who would be disciples in the Kingdom to come. They must be capable of living above personal insult and injury.

"You have heard that it was said, 'You shall . . . hate your enemy.' "[l] The Jewish Law set forth in the Pentateuch does not enjoin hatred of enemies. Jesus seems to be opposing such attitudes, policies, and practices as are found, for instance, in the "Manual of Discipline" of the Qumran community. In this document, usually presumed to be a work of the Essenes, there is an injunction requiring both love and hatred: It is the duty of members "to love all that He has chosen and hate all that He has rejected. . . . to hate all the children of darkness."[17] According to Jesus, in the Kingdom of Heaven love will be the natural emotion of the pure in heart. This is not the love of natural affection that is experienced, for instance, in filial relationships, but love conceived in the Greek sense as *agape*, a god-like love. Also, the Sermon continues, "pray for those who persecute you, so that you may be sons of your Father who is in heaven." To be a disciple one must act as a true son of God. And God is impartial in his love — "he makes his sun rise on the evil and on the good. . . . And if you salute only your brethren, what more are you doing than others?"[m] Love is neither born of nor cultivated by what is received from others.

It is a common error to suppose because Jesus laid such great stress on love as the foundation of religion and morality, a foundation which has always been central to the meaning of

---

[l] Mt 5:43. [m] Mt 5:45, 47.

[16] "Then you shall give life for life, eye for eye, tooth for tooth, hand for hand, foot for foot, burn for burn, wound for wound, stripe for stripe" (Ex 21:23ff.). The same warning is found in Lv 24:19f. and in Dt 19:21.

[17] The Manual of Discipline, "Of the Commitment" (i, 1–15).

Christianity, that Christianity in this respect is different in principle from Judaism with its legal and rabbinical tradition. But the Old Testament itself enjoined love not only in the works of the Prophets, as is seen superbly in such writings as Hosea, but in the Law itself, which Jesus quoted when asked concerning the greatest of the commandments. Nor is it true, as some suppose, that the Jewish legal tradition interpreted love simply in terms of formalism and externals, even though in the Gospels Jesus directed his accusations especially against such narrow, literalistic, and legalistic religion and morals. But it is true that the meaning of love in the teachings of Jesus and in the Christian tradition assumed a somewhat new meaning and character as a quality of supernatural grace expressed especially by the term *agape*.[18]

"You, therefore, must be perfect, as your heavenly Father is perfect."[n] This is the summary of the new teaching begun in Matthew 5:17. The righteousness of the new covenant, according to the Sermon, must exceed the righteousness of those whose commitment to the externals of moral legislation and tradition blinds them to the full values of the very Law which they honor. In seeking a norm against which to measure human moral and spiritual possibilities, Jesus set a standard that reached toward and embraced the idea of perfection in God's own character.

THE NATURE AND MEANING OF THE MIRACLES

Nothing in the evangelists' accounts has generated more concern, produced more discussion, or elicited more controversy than the accounts of Jesus' miracles. In the main tradition of Christianity, they have generally been accepted as literally true. The more skeptical have rejected their historicity with varying explana-

[n] Mt 5:48.

[18] For the meaning of *agape* in the Christian religion, see especially the classic work by Anders Nygren, *Agape and Eros*, trans. Philip S. Watson (New York, 1969). For an analysis of the fundamental differences between Judaism and Christianity, see the work of the Jewish scholar Leo Baeck, *Judaism and Christianity*, trans. Walter Kaufmann (New York, 1958); Leo Baeck *The Essence of Judaism*, trans. Victor Grubenweiser and Leonard Pearl (New York, 1948); and Martin Buber, *Two Types of Faith*, trans. Norman P. Goldhawk (New York, 1961). See also Geza Vermes, *Jesus the Jew: A Historian's Reading of the Gospels* (New York, 1973).

tions for their inclusion in the Gospels. Those explanations have referred to the credulity, superstition, and mythical propensities of the early Christians and the Gospel writers, the attempts of the early church to celebrate the supernatural powers of Jesus to establish conclusively his messiahship and to place him in the line of the prophets as the harbinger of the Kingdom, the Son of God. The miracles have been variously treated as literal truths, myths, legends, allegories, and symbols.[19] A full consideration of the miracles, of course, includes not only those allegedly performed by Jesus but also the accounts of his miraculous birth, his resurrection, his appearances to the disciples, and his ascension.

The term "miracle" has been employed with various meanings, ranging from the unknown, uncommon, and misunderstood to the supernatural or the intervention of God in the processes of the natural order. Its most common meaning in theology is a sensible fact which is independent of, if not actually contrary to, natural law — an event produced by direct or supernatural power transcending the natural order.

It was commonplace for the Jews of Jesus' time to believe in miracles. Miracles are recorded in the Old Testament and in the intertestamental literature. The Talmud refers to miracles performed by rabbis at the time of Jesus. But the Gospel accounts feature miracles to a far greater extent than do the books of the Old Testament or, indeed, the non-Christian Jewish literature of the time of Jesus. That Jesus had miraculous powers was clearly a matter of utmost importance to the evangelists and, without

---

[19] For an interesting, exhaustive treatment of the problem of the miracles, see the early (1835) monumental work by David Friedrich Strauss, *Life of Jesus Critically Examined*, trans. George Eliot, ed. Peter C. Hodgson (Philadelphia, 1972). Strauss treated miracles primarily in terms of mythology. Like many others today, the contemporary British historian Michael Grant sees them from a naturalistic standpoint. For Grant, the miracle stories serve to symbolize and point up the establishment of the Kingdom. "Since, then, the Kingdom of God according to Jesus' conviction was not only about to be consummated in the immediate future but was already dawning by his own agency, the Gospels' claim that his miraculous actions conquered and reversed the processes of nature in the world and among human beings constituted an assertion that these deeds both prefigured the Kingdom's imminent consummation and symbolized and actually formed part of its current initial unfolding." Michael Grant, *Jesus, An Historian's Review of the Gospels* (New York, 1977), 44.

doubt, to the early Christians for whom they composed the Gospels. The miracles appear to have been considered necessary to the success of Jesus' ministry and quite surely were a foundation for the faith of his immediate disciples and the early church.[20]

The Gospel reports describe more than thirty miracles, and the early non-canonical Christian literature lists many more. The miracle accounts of the Gospels can be conveniently summarized under four headings: (1) exorcism, (2) healing, (3) control of nature, and (4) raising the dead.[21] Miracles appear in all four Gospels, but John records only seven.[22] However, the miracles described by John are especially impressive and seem to have been selected to exhibit the most spectacular supernatural power.

It is evident that not only the followers of Jesus but also many of his enemies believed in his miraculous powers. Nevertheless, according to the Gospel writers, many refused to accept the miracles as authentic. The question of whether or not the miraculous events as reported actually took place is not the only, nor necessarily the most important, issue for understanding the place of miracles in the New Testament. Of major interest are the evangelists' motives or purposes in relating them. There are reasons for thinking that they believed the healing miracles were not per-

---

[20] The Roman Catholic church enjoins its members to accept not only the miracles recorded in scripture but also the continuation of miracles to the present. Beatification and canonization, with few exceptions, have been associated with miracles. It is more characteristic of traditional Protestantism to accept simply the scriptural miracles, though miraculous claims are common today among evangelical Protestants.

[21] In his celebrated essay "Of Miracles," the Scottish philosopher David Hume provided skeptics with their classic maxim for assessing miracle claims: "No testimony is sufficient to establish a miracle, unless the testimony be of such a kind, that its falsehood would be more miraculous, than the fact which it endeavours to establish." David Hume, *An Enquiry Concerning Human Understanding* (New York, 1955), Sec. X, Pt. I. The Jewish historian Joseph Klausner divided the miracles of Jesus reported in the Gospels into five categories: (1) "Miracles due to a wish to fulfill some statement in the Old Testament or to imitate some Prophet"; (2) "Poetical descriptions which, in the minds of the disciples, were transformed into miracles"; (3) "Illusions"; (4) "Acts only apparently miraculous"; and (5) "The curing of numerous 'nerve-cases.'" Joseph Klausner, *Jesus of Nazareth*, trans. Herbert Danby (London, 1947), 267–70.

[22] Four of these miracles are unique to John's Gospel: changing water to wine at Cana (Jn 2:1–11), healing the impotent man at Beth-zatha (5:2–9), giving sight to the man born blind (9:1–12), and the raising of Lazarus (11:1–44).

formed simply, or primarily, out of concern for human suffering, notwithstanding Jesus' compassion. Some accounts make this clear. For the Gospel writers, whatever else their meaning, the miracles were demonstrations of superhuman power that testified to the calling of Jesus. They were signs of the imminent coming, if not indeed the actual presence, of the Kingdom.

In the Gospel of John, for example, miracles are understood as signs exhibiting Jesus' true identity and his power and glory, the source of which transcends the temporal order. The special feature of each miracle is a sign of some facet of Jesus' unique inner quality, which is Spirit. Changing water into wine, for example, is a disclosure of the power of the Spirit to transform life. The power of the Spirit to give sight is manifest in the healing of the blind man at Siloam. In this instance being able to "see" has special meaning for the believer. According to John, while for most persons "seeing" is limited to the physical, the true believer "sees" Jesus' true nature and glory and shares in his eternal life.

Mark's account of Jesus rebuking the storm is the prime example of a miracle exhibiting the control of nature.° According to Mark, as Jesus and the disciples crossed the Sea of Galilee, a storm arose. Although Jesus slept, the disciples believed the situation was desperate. They expressed their alarm with an emotional question: "Do you not care if we perish?" Jesus' calming the storm gave Mark an occasion to comment on the faith, as well as the lack of faith, of the disciples. And it was an occasion for Mark to again, as at other times, portray the disciples as men who failed to understand Jesus despite his teachings and demonstrations of power, or perhaps because of them. Even those who were closest to him, according to Mark, failed to grasp the true character of his message and the deeper meaning of his actions.

Jesus and the others landed in the country of the Gerasenes, on the east shore of the Sea of Galilee. In Jesus' time this region was the Decapolis, or ten allied, Greek speaking hellenistic cities, which included Gadara, Gerasa, and Damascus. The population of this region was predominantly of gentile birth and hellenistic culture.

° Mk 4:35–41.

According to Mark, after Jesus left the boat he was confronted by a demoniac living in a nearby cemetery, who apparently had become violent.[p] All attempts to restrain him had been unsuccessful. Jesus' authoritative command to the demons possessing the man: "Come out of the man, you unclean spirit!" restored him to normality. The demons then entered a herd of swine.

Some have held that this account of the healing was probably grafted to a local tradition of drowning swine stampeded by the ravings of a maniac. The Jews, of course, were forbidden to keep swine, which were regarded as unclean,[q] but this was predominantly gentile country. There can be little doubt that for Mark and the early church this event recorded a confrontation between two powers beyond the comprehension of ordinary men — the power of Satan and the power of Christ.

According to Mark the swine herdsmen fled and reported what had happened.[r] The villagers came and "saw the demoniac sitting there, clothed and in his right mind, . . . and they were afraid."[s] Fearing his strange power, they begged Jesus to leave their neighborhood. The grateful man who had been possessed went away as Jesus instructed him and told of the great thing that had happened to him. And, Mark concluded, "all men marveled."[23]

These two miracles, stilling the storm and healing the Gerasene demoniac, demonstrate, in Mark's view, Jesus' dominion over nature, man, and the demonic powers. They exhibit the power of God. They are supernatural miracles, signs that God's Kingdom is breaking in upon the world.

For the evangelists and the early church, Jesus' ability to restore life demonstrated conclusively his true nature. Those miracles build progressively in dramatic power from the story of Jairus's daughter near death to the widow's son being carried to his grave to the account in John's Gospel of the raising of Lazarus, who had been in the tomb four days. In these events the Christian proclamation

---

[p] Mk 5:2–13. [q] Lv 11:7f. [r] Mk 5:14–20. [s] Mk 5:15.

[23] Whereas in several of the miracles reported in Mark, Jesus charged those present to say nothing of them to others, here at Gerasa, in gentile territory — possibly the present village of Khersa on the eastern shore of the Sea of Galilee — he advised the healed demoniac to tell his friends what had happened (Mk 5:19f.).

The Sermons, Miracles, and Parables

about Jesus as the Messiah-Savior came to a dramatic climax — Jesus is the Resurrection and the Life.

The setting for the story of Jairus's daughter was probably the seashore near Capernaum. Here Jesus received the request of Jairus to heal his child. Jairus, who was an official at the synagogue, seems to have been a person of some wealth as well as a religious leader. In Mark's account and that of Luke the daughter of Jairus was still alive when her father came to Jesus, perhaps in a coma, but to heighten the dramatic effect, in Matthew's record the child is reported to have just died.[t] Apparently the mourners had already arrived at the house before Jairus returned. On such occasions even the poorest Jews would be expected to employ at least two flute players and a woman to lament. At Jairus's home were many mourners. Mark wrote that Jesus "allowed no one to follow him [to Jairus' house] except Peter and James and John the brother of James."[u]

The raising of Jairus' daughter was a dramatic event. "Why do you make a tumult and weep? The child is not dead but sleeping,"[v] Jesus exclaimed as he arrived. According to Mark, Jesus "said to her, 'Talitha cumi'; which means, 'Little girl, I say to you, arise.' And immediately the girl got up and walked."[w] Those present at the home were overcome with amazement. In Luke as in Mark, Jesus charged those present to say nothing of what had happened, but Matthew indicates that "the report of this went through all that district."[x]

The other instance in the Synoptics of Jesus' reviving the dead, or, in the case of Jairus' daughter, one who may have been in a coma, is the raising of the widow's son at Nain.[y] This miracle appears only in Luke. The funeral procession of the widow's son apparently was on its way to the tombs or burial caves outside the city. Jesus and his followers met the mourners at the city gate. It was a mournful scene; the widow was borne down by the weight of her loss. But the raising of her son was not only an act of compassion for a grieving mother; it was, in Luke's view, a sign of Jesus' authority and power.

[t] Mt 9:18. [u] Mk 5:37. [v] Mk 5:39. [w] Mk 5:41f. [x] Mt 9:26. [y] Lk 7:11–17.

Nain was a small village in southern Galilee, only a few miles south of Nazareth. The fact that this event occurred in Galilee, where in Old Testament times Elijah and Elisha imbued with the spirit and power of Yahweh led bands of prophets and worked great miracles, has special significance for Luke. The books of the Old Testament indicate that there were few prophets of note from the northern kingdom. Nevertheless, in the northern Hebrew tradition, Elijah and Elisha were among the most illustrious after Moses and Samuel. For Luke and Mark, Jesus stood within the prophetic tradition of the North. This meant that he performed the miracles which Elijah and Elisha performed. In this instance, he revived the widow's son, as Elijah revived the dead son of the widow of Zarephath[z] and Elisha raised up the dead son of the Shunammite woman.[a] As a silent reminder of the Elijah typology, the words "and he gave him to his mother" are from the Elijah story.[24] Luke was careful to establish continuity between the power of these two prophets to work their miracles and the power of the Spirit in Jesus to do the same.[25]

In the opinion of some Old Testament scholars, the story of Elijah's flight from Jezebel to Mount Sinai and his encounter with God in a cave[b] represents Elijah's return to Moses and to the source of Israel's faith.[26] For Luke and the early Christians, Jesus, like Elijah, represented a renewal of the faith. For them, Jesus provided the way to Moses and to a new life. And the people said, "A great prophet has arisen among us!" and "God has visited his people!"[c]

Following the account of the raising of Jairus's daughter and of the woman who had been ill for twelve years (a miracle within a miracle), Matthew recorded two accounts[d] of Jesus' extraordinary power — the healing of two blind men and the healing of

---

[z] 1 Kgs 17:8–24. [a] 2 Kgs 4:8–37. [b] 1 Kgs 19:1–14. [c] Lk 7:16. [d] Mt 9:27–34.

[24] Compare Lk 7:15 with 1 Kgs 17:23.

[25] The similarities between the report of Elisha's feeding the people with twenty barley loaves (2 Kgs 4:42–44) and the accounts of all four Gospels of Jesus feeding the five thousand lend support to this interpretation.

[26] See, for example, Bernard W. Anderson, *Understanding the Old Testament*, 3rd ed. (Englewood Cliffs, New Jersey, 1975), 255.

a dumb demoniac.²⁷ These miracles involve the restoration of the faculties of sight and speech, miracles which for Matthew may have fulfilled Isaiah's predictions: "Then the eyes of the blind shall be opened, and the ears of the deaf unstopped; then shall the lame man leap like a hart, and the tongue of the dumb sing for joy." ᵉ

Matthew saw in blindness a metaphor for unbelief. In a number of instances, according to Matthew, Jesus spoke of the Pharisees as blind: "Let them alone; they are blind guides." ᶠ Also, in Mark's Gospel, failure to see, to perceive or understand, seems to have been a problem among Jesus' own disciples: "Then are you also without understanding?" ᵍ Again in Mark, after the feeding of the four thousand, Jesus and his disciples were discussing the leaven of the Pharisees. They said, "We have no bread." Jesus said to them, "Why do you discuss the fact that you have no bread? Do you not yet perceive or understand? . . . Having eyes do you not see. . . . And do you not yet remember?" ʰ

THE PARABLES

A leading characteristic of Jesus' teaching was his use of parables, which brought his principles down to earth and usually enabled his hearers to gain a better grasp of his meaning. A parable is generally a short story based on natural things, events, and ordinary happenings in everyday life. It presents, in a graphic and animated way, an ideal or principle which has moral and spiritual meaning, and it becomes an inspiration and concrete guide in the task of making the common decisions which everyone must face.²⁸

In his lectures on the foundation of religion, the philosopher Alfred North Whitehead wrote perceptively about Jesus' teachings and his use of parables: "In the Sermon on the Mount, and in the

---

ᵉ Is 35:5f. ᶠ Mt 15:14. ᵍ Mk 7:18. ʰ Mk 8:16–18.

²⁷ The charge at Matthew 9:34 that Jesus exorcised demons by the prince of demons is continued by the Pharisees in Matthew 12:24.

²⁸ Charles H. Dodd describes the parable as a metaphor and simile "drawn from nature or common life." The parables, he says, "are perhaps the most characteristic element in the teaching of Jesus Christ as recorded in the Gospels. . . . Certainly there is no part of the Gospel record which has for the reader a clearer ring of authenticity." C. H. Dodd, *The Parables of the Kingdom* (New York, 1961), 1.

Parables, there is no reasoning about the facts. They are seen with immeasurable innocence." According to Whitehead, the reported sayings of Jesus are not formal, systematized statements expressed in a prescribed form or as a model. They are, he says, "descriptions of direct insight." The ideas are in Jesus' mind "as immediate pictures" which are drawn from life, expressed in metaphor, and not analyzed in terms of abstract or theoretical concepts.[29]

In the view of Joachim Jeremias the parables represent a "firm historical foundation"; they "are a fragment of the original rock of tradition." [30] But Jeremias holds that the parables have sometimes been incorrectly interpreted. From the beginning, church theologians, constantly seeking hidden meanings, applied allegorical interpretations to Jesus' parables, modifying and expanding them to meet the needs of the church in its own time and in the light of its current conditions. As a consequence, some of the parables have taken on a double historical meaning: what Jesus meant in his own historical setting, and what they came to mean in the continuing life of the church. The task of modern scholarship, then, is to get behind the allegorical interpretations of the early church to the life-situation of Jesus and recover the original form of the parables.[31]

Jesus' parables are pictures from his life. They take the reader back to Galilee in the first century CE. One may watch the housewife making bread or patching a worn garment. The reader may see the marketplace, walk through the field with the sower, or stand on the seashore observing the fishermen cast their nets. An analysis of a few of the parables is instructive.

Parable of the Sower

And he told them many things in parables, saying: "A sower went out to sow. And as he sowed, some seeds fell along the path, and the birds came and devoured them. Other seeds fell on rocky ground, where they had not much soil, and immediately they sprang up, since

---

[29] Alfred North Whitehead, *Religion in the Making* (New York, 1926), 56f.

[30] Joachim Jeremias, *The Parables of Jesus*, trans. S. H. Hooke, rev. ed. (New York, 1963), 11.

[31] Ibid., 12f.; 66–89.

they had no depth of soil, but when the sun rose they were scorched; and since they had no root they withered away. Other seeds fell upon thorns, and the thorns grew up and choked them. Other seeds fell on good soil and brought forth grain, some a hundredfold, some sixty, some thirty." [i]

The Parable of the Sower reflects the degree of rejection that the early Christians experienced. It points to the failure of some to accept Jesus and of others to understand him. But placed in the setting of the life of Jesus, it is a parable of encouragement, for God has made a beginning and apparent failures should not bring despair. There is good soil and God has promised to bring in the Kingdom, despite its rather feeble beginnings. What God has promised will surely come about.

In the opinion of Jeremias and others, the Christian church transformed this parable about the hopeful coming of the Kingdom at the end of the age into an allegory of warning to members of the Christian community to stand fast against worldliness in a time of persecution. The parable became an allegory of soil with the principal emphasis placed upon the kinds of soils (persons who hear the word). As the sower sows, his seeds fall into four different kinds of soils. Just as the harvest depends upon the kind of soil into which the seed is planted, so, according to the interpretation of the church, the teaching of Jesus will yield its fruits (noble character and a righteous world), depending upon the condition of the heart and mind of those who hear it. Jesus and all who seek to spread the truth are the "sowers." Furthermore, according to Matthew, "As for what was sown on good soil, this is he who hears the word and understands it; he indeed bears fruit, and yields, in one case a hundredfold." [j]

Parable of the Weeds

Another parable he put before them, saying, "The kingdom of heaven may be compared to a man who sowed good seed in his field; but while men were sleeping, his enemy came and sowed weeds among the wheat, and went away. So when the plants came up and bore grain, then the weeds appeared also. And the servants of the house-

---

[i] Mt 13:3–8. [j] Mt 13:23.

holder came and said to him, 'Sir, did you not sow good seed in your field? How then has it weeds?' He said to them, 'An enemy has done this.' The servants said to him, 'Then do you want us to go and gather them?' But he said, 'No; lest in gathering the weeds you root up the wheat along with them. Let both grow together until the harvest; and at harvest time I will tell the reapers, Gather the weeds first and bind them in bundles to be burned, but gather the wheat into my barn.' " [k]

Like the others, the Parable of the Weeds (Tares) among the Wheat was not intended as an abstract treatise or rule for church discipline. This is Matthew's replacement for the Markan parable of the Seed Growing Secretly. The parable is concerned with sensitivity to wrongdoing. Taken in its entirety it exhibits the delicate intermeshing of good and evil in human will and the difficulties and dangers in attempting to judge and separate them. "Let both [the weeds and wheat] grow together until the harvest" was Jesus' instruction. Here is a realistic treatment of the attempt made by many moral and religious enthusiasts who believe that separation from sinners is required for a righteous society. This separatist theme was especially pronounced among the Essenes who believed that the religious institutions in Jerusalem — priesthood, Temple, and the ceremonial calendar — had been defiled. They insisted that they alone were the "faithful remnant" spoken of by Isaiah through whom God's promise would be fulfilled. Many of them retired to the desert seeking separation and seclusion from sinners to establish the pure community of Israel and await the coming of the Messiah.

For Jesus, such a separating out of sinners for the purpose of purifying the community was a grievous error. In the early stages of preparing for the Kingdom, wheat and tares are much alike, as are the righteous and the sinners. Judging and excluding for the sake of purity would imperil the chosen who were concealed among them. "Let both grow together"; God is in control "until the harvest." The time of Judgment and of separation is imminent, but not yet; until that time repentance is possible.

[k] Mt 13:24–30.

Parable of the Seed Growing Secretly

And he said, "The kingdom of God is as if a man should scatter seed upon the ground, and should sleep and rise night and day, and the seed should sprout and grow, he knows not how. The earth produces of itself, first the blade, then the ear, then the full grain in the ear. But when the grain is ripe, at once he puts in the sickle, because the harvest has come." [l]

The Seed Growing Secretly, another parable of contrast, is found only in Mark and is the only Markan parable that is not copied by either Matthew or Luke. In this parable Jesus' disciples were told to observe how the earth and seed produce a harvest by means of the power which is within them. So it is with God's Kingdom. From an insignificant beginning, suddenly through God's power there is the triumphant emergence of the Kingdom. What is hidden in the seed will surely come to fruition in its own time. Just so, God's Kingdom will surely come in *its* own time and by its own power.

Parable of the Mustard Seed

Another parable he put before them, saying, "The kingdom of heaven is like a grain of mustard seed which a man took and sowed in his field; it is the smallest of all seeds, but when it has grown it is the greatest of shrubs and becomes a tree, so that the birds of the air come and make nests in its branches." [m]

The Parable of the Mustard Seed is one of several parables which focus on growth: the parables of the Tares, the Seed Growing Secretly, the Net, and the Leaven. Each begins with "The kingdom of God is like" or "It is as if." A mustard seed grows silently and naturally into a large sheltering plant. It is the least, the smallest, of seeds; yet, it becomes "the greatest of shrubs . . . so that the birds . . . come and make nests in its branches." Here Jesus' concern is probably to encourage and reassure his small company of disciples that the movement to which they were attached, with small beginnings, could yet become a transforming force. Perhaps the occasion was brought on by doubt and skepticism

---

[l] Mk 4:26–29.   [m] Mt 13:31f.

which he had sensed among some of his disciples. According to Jeremias, Jesus' encouraging response was, "With the same compelling certainty that causes a tall shrub to grow out of a minute grain of mustard-seed . . . will God's miraculous power cause my small band to swell into the mighty host of the people of God in the Messianic Age." [32]

According to Albert Schweitzer, it was Jesus' view that God is preparing a secret like one experiences in nature. The parables, he says, are signs of the secret. As the harvest follows from the sowing without any apparent explanation, so will the Kingdom come with great power, a consequence of moral renewal: "Repentance and moral renewal in prospect of the Kingdom of God are like a pressure which is exerted in order to compel its appearance. This movement had begun with the days of the Baptist." [33]

Parable of the Leaven

> He told them another parable. "The kingdom of heaven is like leaven which a woman took and hid in three measures of meal, till it was all leavened." [n]

The figures of leaven, the mustard seed, and the seed that silently germinates illustrate certain characteristics of the Kingdom. The parable of the mustard seed reveals the extensive growth of the Kingdom from a small beginning, and the figure of the leaven extends this meaning. There is no coercion from the outside; the power of fermentation and growth is within.[34]

---

[n] Mt 13:33.

[32] Jeremias, *Parables of Jesus*, 149. Jeremias, 146–60, classifies the Parables of the Mustard Seed, the Leaven, the Sower, the Patient Husbandman (the Seed Growing Secretly), the Unjust Judge, and the Man Asking for Help by Night as parables of the Great Assurance.

[33] Albert Schweitzer, *The Mystery of the Kingdom of God*, trans. Walter Lowrie (New York, 1964), 112.

[34] Dodd, *Parables of the Kingdom*, 63, 155, points out that the nearest parallel to the Parable of the Leaven in Matthew 13:33 and Luke 13:21 is to be found in Luke's puzzling statement, "the Kingdom of God is within you" (Lk 17:20f.). Dodd points out that two other possible translations are "is among you" or "is within your power." The RSV says "in the midst of you."

The parables of growth, in the view of C. H. Dodd, are commentaries on the actual situation during the ministry of Jesus. They are metaphors about the coming of the Kingdom of God in history. "They are not to be taken as implying a long process of development introduced by the ministry of Jesus and to be consummated by His second advent, though the Church later understood them in that sense." [35] In these parables, Jesus is teaching that the growth of the Kingdom of God would be natural and silent, yet transforming and complete, "till it was all leavened."

Parable of the Net

> Again, the kingdom of heaven is like a net which was thrown into the sea and gathered fish of every kind; when it was full, men drew it ashore and sat down and sorted the good into vessels but threw away the bad. So it will be at the close of the age. The angels will come out and separate the evil from the righteous, and throw them into the furnace of fire; there men will weep and gnash their teeth.[o]

The Parable of the Net, found only in Matthew, is a comparison to the Parable of the Tares. Both appear to have been made over by the church as allegorical descriptions of the last judgment. The original point of the parable as told by Jesus apparently was to impress upon his disciples the necessity for patience until the time for judgment, which would be determined by God. Prior to the time of selection, edible and non-edible fish were mixed.[36] Fishermen cannot discern what the net holds until precisely the right moment. In Jesus' view of the coming Kingdom that right moment had not yet come; therefore, the net must be cast widely. Also, as had been indicated earlier, Jesus applied the metaphor of catching fish to the call of his first disciples: "Follow me and I will make you fishers of men."[p]

Dodd suggests that there is a process of selection implicit in the metaphor of the net. The proclamation about the Kingdom

---

[o] Mt 13:47–50. [p] Mt 4:19.

[35] Dodd, *Parables of the Kingdom*, 155f.

[36] Some species of fish found in the Sea of Galilee have no scales and were therefore judged unclean according to Lv 11:9–12. See Jeremias, *Parables of Jesus*, 225f.

(like the net) is to all without distinction, but the appeal itself is selective in that it calls for an immediate decision, a judgment on the part of the hearer. Dodd says, "This selection *is* the divine judgment, though men pass it upon themselves by their ultimate attitude to the appeal." [37] According to this view, selection and judgment are not imposed upon people from the outside but emerge in the very process of deciding and believing.

Parables of the Treasure and the Pearl

The kingdom of heaven is like treasure hidden in a field, which a man found and covered up; then in his joy he goes and sells all that he has and buys that field. Again, the kingdom of heaven is like a merchant in search of fine pearls, who, on finding one pearl of great value, went and sold all that he had and bought it.[q]

The parables were apparently specific responses to particular situations of importance which Jesus encountered. Now and again someone plowing or digging in a field would accidentally discover buried items, and under Roman law the discoverer was allowed to keep one-half of the treasure's value. It is not the central point of the parable of the hidden treasure to consider the morality of the farmer's action in purchasing the field from an unsuspecting owner in order to gain the treasure. To press the question of the farmer's culpability would thwart the purpose and aim of the parable. Actually, these two parables make the same point: the Kingdom of God is the supreme treasure — worth more than all other possessions — the pearl without peer. The Kingdom of God is upon you. Decide for it now without hesitation.

The Parables as Secret Sayings

Then the disciples came and said to him, "Why do you speak to them in parables?" And he answered them, "To you it has been given to know the secrets of the kingdom of heaven, but to them it has not been given. . . . because seeing they do not see, and hearing they do not hear, nor do they understand." [r]

[q] Mt 13:44–46. [r] Mt 13:10–13.

[37] Dodd holds that the process of selection, a sifting among the disciples of Jesus, is shown in the Gospels: "A rich man comes . . . asking the way to life:

There is a persistent question of whether Jesus intended to obscure his meaning through the use of parables as puzzles, as Matthew and Mark seem to suggest, or as a means of enlightening listeners by drawing upon their experiences and personal resources. Matthew suggests that spiritual blindness was upon the Jews,[s] which, he says, is in fulfillment of Isaiah's prophecy, "Hear and hear, but do not understand." [t] Those who heard but received nothing from the parables fulfilled Isaiah's prophecy that they were not capable of understanding. However, those given to know the secrets of the Kingdom heard and understood. Mark's view is different. He says that Jesus spoke in parables for "those outside . . . so that they may indeed see but not perceive." [u]

There is some precedent for the interpretation of Jesus' use of parables as puzzles in *The Book of Enoch*, a collection of pseudepigraphic writings dating from the first or second century BCE.[38] "The Parable of Enoch" contains a similar notion of hiddenness; "And he took up his parable and said — Enoch a righteous man, whose eyes were opened by God, saw the vision of the Holy One in the heavens [which] the angels showed me, and from them I heard everything . . . but not for this generation, but for a remote one which is for to come." Albert Schweitzer held that the secrecy theme in the parables about the secret of the Kingdom of God is authentic to Jesus: How the mustard seed becomes the greatest of shrubs, according to Schweitzer, is the secret.[39]

However, many New Testament scholars believe that concealment is contrary to the spirit and purpose of Jesus' ministry as clearly indicated elsewhere in the synoptic Gospels. Dodd concluded that the idea that Jesus "desired not to be understood by the people in general, and therefore clothed His teaching in un-

---

[s] Mt 13:14f. [t] Is 6:9f. [u] Mk 4:11f.

he is tested by the call to abandon his riches, and fails (Mk 10:17–22). . . . Another is called to follow, but pleads for time to bury his father" (Mt 8:21). Dodd, *Parables of the Kingdom*, 151f.

[38] Robert H. Charles, *The Book of Enoch* (London, 1960), 31.

[39] Schweitzer, *The Mystery of the Kingdom of God*, 106–10.

intelligible forms, cannot be made credible on any reasonable reading of the Gospels." [40]

If Jesus' intention was to clarify lofty and somewhat abstract ideas about the Kingdom by means of concrete parables or stories, why is his meaning at times so elusive and susceptible to a variety of interpretations? J. C. Fenton has offered a plausible explanation of this predicament. "When Jesus used a parable," he wrote, "its meaning was probably clear to his audience from the context in which he used it — though his audience may not always have wanted to understand his meaning. What seems to have happened is: the parables were remembered without their context, new meanings were read into them, they were put to new uses in the life of the Church, and the original intention of the parables was forgotten. It was then thought that Jesus had used parables in order to hide his message, and sayings of Jesus from another context were used to express this attitude." [41]

The extent to which the practice developed of putting Jesus' sayings "to new use" in the life of the church may be seen in the non-canonical Gospel of Thomas. The Gospel of Thomas, which was translated from the original Greek into Coptic, is a collection of parable-like materials, sayings, prophecies, and proverbs dating from about 150 CE. Its authorship is attributed to Didymos Judas Thomas, assumed by the Syrian Christian Church to have been the apostle and a twin brother of Jesus. The resemblance of this document to the synoptic Gospels, particularly to Matthew and Luke, is immediately evident to the reader. But Thomas is distinctly different. Thomas is a sayings source which assumes that secrecy was the most significant feature of Jesus' teachings. The Gospel begins with the announcement that "These are the secret sayings which the living Jesus spoke and which Didymos Judas Thomas wrote down." [42] Thomas promises that "whoever finds the inter-

---

[40] Dodd, *Parables of the Kingdom*, 4.

[41] Fenton, *Matthew*, 215f.

[42] "The Gospel of Thomas," *The Nag Hammadi Library in English*, trans. Members of the Coptic Gnostic Library Project, James M. Robinson, director (San Francisco, 1988), 126.

pretation of these sayings will not experience death." This esoteric document, which is concerned with both the origin and destiny of the individual, shows later Gnostic influence, but in much of its substance its source may have been related to a primary source of the Synoptics.

CHAPTER 5

The Calling and Discipleship

In Luke's Gospel the stories of the healing of the centurion's slave, the raising of the widow's son at Nain, the questioning about Jesus' messianic credentials by John the Baptist, and the anointing of Jesus by the sinful woman follow chronologically the Sermon on the Plain.[a][1] There is a question whether Luke attaches some special significance to the sequence of these seemingly random events. Are they simply early events in the Galilean ministry or is there a theme which joins the stories as a unit with the Sermon on the Plain? Some scholars assume that in Luke's view no single event or combination of circumstances shaped the course of Jesus' messianic program. They contend that following his sermon an inner power or necessity moved Jesus to visit the towns and villages of Galilee.[2] According to this view, Jesus' ministry was forecast by his statement in the synagogue at Nazareth: "The Spirit of the Lord is upon me. . . ." Then, at the conclusion of his reading, he said to those assembled, "Today this scripture has been fulfilled in your hearing."[b]

JESUS AND THE GENTILES

In Luke's account, when Jesus finished his sermon he went to Capernaum, where he was approached by a Roman centurion whose slave was near death from sickness.

> When he heard of Jesus, he sent to him elders of the Jews, asking him to come and heal his slave. And when they came to Jesus, they

[a] Lk 6:20–49. [b] Lk 4:18, 21.

[1] These same stories, except for the widow's son at Nain which appears only in Luke 7:11–17, are included in Matthew in a different context (Mt 8:5–13; 11:2–19; 26:6–13). Mark includes only the account of the woman anointing Jesus, which appears later in the context of his passion narrative (Mk 14:3–9).

[2] This is suggested, for instance, in George B. Caird, *The Gospel of St. Luke* (Baltimore, 1963), 116.

besought him earnestly, saying, "He is worthy to have you do this for him, for he loves our nation, and he built us our synagogue." c

The centurion was a Roman officer, the captain of a hundred men, who perhaps served under Herod Antipas. The Roman government provided military or police support for the Herods because the Jews, by agreement with Rome, were exempt from military service. The centurion may well have been one of the large number of gentiles who were called "godfearers," those who were not full Jewish proselytes but were nevertheless attracted to Judaism as a religion, especially its monotheism and strong moral teachings.

Matthew also recounted the incident, but earlier in his chronology of events. In this account, the centurion spoke directly to Jesus regarding his servant.d In Luke the centurion communicated through others, possibly to gain benefit from their intercession. Or perhaps the centurion had others plead his cause because of a sense of personal unworthiness. The centurion's deference to Jesus and his conviction of Jesus' power to heal demonstrated for Luke a supreme expression of faith. Jesus was impressed by this trust, saying to those present, "not even in Israel have I found such faith." e [3]

How is Jesus' acceptance of the faith of a gentile, and particularly a Roman officer, to be understood? Does this account, as it stands, accurately represent Jesus' intent to broaden the vision of the Kingdom to include gentiles. Or does it express a liberal attitude attributed to Jesus by Luke, whose Gospel expressed the more ecumenical Christian interests of later years. Some of those who hold this latter view regard the account as an effort by the early church to improve Roman-Christian relations and present Christianity as a universal religion.

JOHN'S INQUIRY

When John the Baptist's disciples advised him of Jesus' activities at Capernaum and Nain, John sent two of them to Jesus to

c Lk 7:3–5. d Mt 8:5–13. e Lk 7:9.

[3] A somewhat similar story of Jesus healing the son of a royal official at Capernaum is found in John 4:46–54.

ask, "Are you he who is to come, or shall we look for another?" [f] John had been imprisoned by Herod Antipas in the fortress of Machaerus in the mountains east of the Dead Sea. Luke attributed the imprisonment of John chiefly to his reproving Herod Antipas for marrying Herodias, the divorced wife of his half-brother Philip.[g] Under Levitical law this marriage was not legal because Philip was still living. The Jewish historian Josephus held that Antipas feared John because of the political implications of his preaching, which could conceivably lead his followers to acts of rebellion against the state.[4] Apparently, some liberty was granted to John in prison, for he seems to have been able to communicate with his followers. In response to the inquiry from John's disciples, Jesus did not present a lengthy statement or make any explicit claim. He said simply, "Go and tell John what you have seen and heard: the blind receive their sight, the lame walk, lepers are cleansed, and the deaf hear, the dead are raised up, the poor have good news preached to them." [h] In Luke's view these statements were a summary of the messianic program. Jesus' reply was a reminder to John of Jesus' fulfillment of the messianic predictions found in Isaiah.[5] Clearly, Jesus is identified as the Messiah by his deeds; for Luke, nothing could have been more convincing.

THE SCRIBES AND PHARISEES

Some Pharisees and scribes seem to have listened to the conversation between Jesus and John's disciples. Some of these no doubt regarded John as a religious fanatic. Historically, the scribes (*Soferim*) were the spiritual successors of the biblical Ezra, who

[f] Lk 7:19. [g] Lk 3:19f. [h] Lk 7:22.

[4] Machaerus was located on the Perea side of the Dead Sea, inland from the eastern shore. Herod Antipas was tetrarch of Perea as well as Galilee. See Josephus, *The Antiquities of the Jews*, Book XVIII, Chap. V, Sec. 2.

[5] Isaiah 29:18f.; 35:5f.; 61:1f. In the well-founded opinion of some scholars, the disciples of John regarded the Baptist himself as the Messiah. Cf., e.g., Michael Grant, *Jesus: An Historian's Review of the Gospels* (New York, 1977), 97: "Particular veneration was centred upon the Baptist; and he was unequivocally credited with Messianic status by his disciples. After he died, they pronounced him to have been raised from the dead, and the tradition of his Messiahship persisted for centuries. Later on, John's Gospel explicitly denied that the Baptist himself had ever claimed to be the Messiah." On this point see Jn 1:20f.

The Calling and Discipleship

lived in the fifth century BCE. Following Ezra's time, as the accepted teachers and interpreters of the Law, they were of major importance in adapting the strict requirements of Torah-religion to the daily life of the people.[6] In the Jewish view, all law — civic and criminal, social and economic — was founded upon Torah; hence, the scribes were engaged in an essentially religious task. Their activities were apparently often similar to those of the Pharisees, and some scribes were Pharisees.[i] The interest of the Pharisees and scribes in John the Baptist and Jesus is entirely understandable when one considers their importance in the religion and life of the Jews.

When Jesus praised John, saying there was no greater prophet than John, those who heard him, even the tax collectors, praised God, for they had already accepted John's baptism. But the Pharisees and scribes refused to accept the message of either John or Jesus. Jesus compared them to spoiled children whom nothing seemed to satisfy. For the Pharisees and scribes, John the Baptist was an overbearing fanatic and Jesus an overindulging socialite who associated with sinners. As one writer so aptly put it: they "found John too unsociable to be sane and Jesus too sociable to be moral."[7]

It is now generally recognized that the Gospel writers often described the Pharisees and scribes in prejudicial terms that distorted the true character of Jewish religious leadership. Moreover, the positive relation of Jesus to these leaders is commonly ignored or at least minimized. The Gospel of Mark, especially, calls favorable attention to the Pharisees and Luke gives an account of Jesus receiving and accepting an invitation to dine at home with a Pharisee, Simon.[j] There is convincing evidence that beyond participation in the synagogue service Jesus seems to have

---

[i] Mk 2:16; Acts 22:9.   [j] Lk 7:36–50.

[6] See Ellis Rivkin, *The Shaping of Jewish History* (New York, 1971), pp. 44–50, for a discussion of the history of the *Soferim*. Isidore Epstein has effectively described a major role of the Soferim or scribes as establishing rules called "fences," intended to prevent any "violation of the sacred enclosure of the Torah itself." Isidore Epstein, *Judaism; a Historical Presentation* (Baltimore, Maryland, 1959), 87.

[7] Caird, *Luke*, 112.

had friendly relationships with at least some Jewish religious leaders.

While Jesus was dining with the Pharisee at his table, an uninvited woman apparently well known in Capernaum as either a prostitute or an adulteress, joined the company. Jewish homes were opened on certain occasions to admit friends who wanted to talk as well as beggars who were in need. The host would ordinarily greet his guest with gestures of hospitality and furnish water to bathe his feet. Marked respect was shown to special guests by furnishing ointment for their heads. The uninvited woman provided these tokens for Jesus, signs of welcome which Simon the Pharisee had apparently neglected. She knelt before Jesus and as an act of respect and devotion anointed his feet with ointment. Sensing that Simon was disturbed that he would accept the ministrations of such a person, Jesus said to him, "I tell you, her sins, which are many, are forgiven, for she loved much." [k]

Simon flinched at this contact with the woman, blinded by his own rigid attitude toward sinners: "If this man were a prophet, he would have known who and what sort of woman this is." [l] According to Luke, Simon saw only a sinner; Jesus saw a person who, though judged to be a sinner, openly acknowledged her faithful devotion to his cause. She knew Jesus, and he perceived that although she had been a sinner her regeneration had already begun. "Your sins are forgiven." [8] That Jesus would presume to forgive the woman of her sins and announce that her sins were forgiven was unquestionably a shock to those present. Neither the prophets nor the rabbis had assumed the prerogative and authority for forgiving sins.

When Jesus completed his ministry in Capernaum, he made his way through Galilee proclaiming the coming of the Kingdom of God. According to Luke there were women among those who

---

[k] Lk 7:47.   [l] Lk 7:39.

[8] Caird's suggestion, at this point, seems to have merit — that the woman's love was not the basis of the forgiveness she had come to seek, "but the proof of a pardon she had come to acknowledge." (Ibid., 114f.) In his work *Jesus*, 83, Michael Grant says that Jesus and the woman "became the targets, of their host Simon's reproaches, which Jesus sought to silence on the grounds that she was showing emphatic loyalty, as she should, to the inaugurator of the Kingdom of God."

The Calling and Discipleship

accompanied him.ᵐ The Jewish women of that day were rarely allowed to participate in important affairs, yet Jesus not only included them in his company but apparently considered them essential to the establishment of the Kingdom.[9] As her name indicates, Mary called Magdalene, was from Magdala, a place on the west shore of the Sea of Galilee.[10] She was now giving her time and money in support of Jesus' cause, for she had been sick, according to Luke, possessed of evil spirits, and Jesus had cured her. Two other women mentioned by Luke, Susanna and Joanna, probably had property of their own. Joanna was the wife of a steward of Herod Antipas who no doubt occupied an important post in relation to Herod's estates.ⁿ The expenses of Jesus' expanding mission were no doubt being met by contributions.

Jesus' popularity and fame and the consequent opposition to him by some religious leaders were addressed by each of the synoptic writers. But the failure of even his closest disciples to "see" — to grasp his true nature and to realize fully the meaning of his message — is most evident in Mark. A large and excited crowd had gathered about Jesus. Some members of his own family thought Jesus had lost his mind and had become mentally irresponsible; apparently they mistook his zeal for God as some form of madness. Scribes from Jerusalem who were in the crowd accused him of casting out demons by the power of Beelzebul.[11] Jesus challenged this malicious charge, attempting to show by metaphoric parable how false it was. "How can Satan cast out Satan?" How can one who relieves the distressed, one who drives out the evil

---

ᵐ Lk 8:2f. ⁿ Lk 8:3.

[9] Somewhat in contrast to Mark and Matthew, Luke featured women in his account of Jesus' ministry. The women who received special attention by Luke seem to have had two things in common — each had been healed by Jesus and each brought resources and energy to support his ministry.

[10] There is no conclusive evidence to support the idea, sometimes advanced in the past and often now popularly accepted, that Mary of Magdala (Migdal) was the woman whom Jesus encountered in the house of Simon the Pharisee. Mary, or Miriam, was a common Jewish name. According to the Fourth Gospel she was the first to arrive at the empty tomb and the first to see and hear the risen Lord (Jn 20:1f., 11–18). In Mark, with Jesus' mother and other women, she brought the spices to anoint his body (Mk 16:1f.). And in the longer ending in Mark (16:9–20), Jesus appeared first to her.

[11] Beelzebul was a pagan god identified by the Jews with Satan.

spirits, be in league with Satan?º The doer cannot be separated from his works. "No one can enter a strong man's house and plunder his goods, unless he first binds the strong man." ᵖ Satan cannot prevail because his kingdom is divided against itself. Mark's picture of Jesus was of one who will bind and defeat Satan by rescuing those who are under his dominion.

Apparently Jesus' family heard of the crowds and the disturbance which he seemed to create. It must have been difficult, particularly for those closest to him, to understand why he opposed with such vigor the established traditions and authorities. Perhaps they feared that he was too ambitious for his own good. In any event, he was told that his mother and brothers were seeking him.[12] His response before the crowd, "Who are my mother and my brothers?" must have been both surprising and shocking to his listeners.ᑫ If authentic, this reply seems harsh and insensitive, and many Christian historians and theologians have attempted to soften it with varying interpretations of its meaning. To those who were with him, Jesus answered his own question, "Here are my mother and my brothers! Whoever does the will of God is my brother, and sister, and mother." ʳ This was a strong and direct statement that expressed his concept of the Kingdom of God; it affirmed that relationships within the Kingdom transcend familial ties.

Jesus' proclamation of the Kingdom dominated his entire ministry. The values associated with the Kingdom superseded those of the established social institutions of his time, not excepting even the values of family and intimate social experience. His message at this point seems to be not only unduly stern but almost indifferent to much that is commonly held to be of worth. Certainly it did not express the sentimentality which nineteenth-century romantics commonly ascribed to Jesus and which is even now a typical image of him.

º Mk 3:23.   ᵖ Mk 3:27.   ᑫ Mk 3:33.   ʳ Mk 3:34f.

[12] The New International Version of the Bible translates Mark 3:21 as, "When his family heard about this, they went to take charge of him, for they said, 'He is out of his mind.' " The accusation of insanity comes from his own relatives.

The Calling and Discipleship

Almost from the beginning Jesus' efforts were opposed and often misunderstood by those closest to him as well as by those from various prestigious religious and political groups. Most evident in the Gospel accounts is the opposition of the Pharisees, a powerful religious party whose historical roots may go back as far as the Babylonian Exile (586–38 BCE) when many Israelites were totally isolated from the destroyed Temple and their native land. Most historians, however, date the beginnings of the Pharisees as a definable religious movement from a later era. Pharisaism was given impetus by the scribal movement begun by Ezra in the early period of the Second Temple (ca. 445 BCE) and was continued by the Pietists of the Maccabean period.[13] The name "Pharisee" was probably derived from the Hebrew term *parush*, meaning "separated." It was applied to this group, presumably, because they separated themselves from the masses for the sake of holiness or purity. These separatists became the sages of their day. They were men skilled in law and jurisprudence who, according to Josephus, had reputations as "exact exponents of the law."[14]

All Jewish parties, religious or political, accepted Torah as the basis of belief and practice, but they differed in their interpretation of Torah. For the Sadducees, the scripture without further commentary or elaboration was considered the full basis of orthodoxy. The Pharisees, on the other hand, attempted to keep the Law effectively adapted to the changing circumstances of

---

[13] The Pharisaic movement was apparently related to the Hasidim, the pious ones, who were primarily responsible for the Maccabean revolt in 168 BCE. Through dedicated determination, the Hasidim attempted to preserve the Jewish faith in its purity. See the accounts of the revolt in Epstein, *Judaism*, 92f.; in Victor Tcherikover, *Hellenistic Civilization and the Jews* (New York, 1970), Part I; and in Martin Hengel, *Judaism and Hellenism*, trans. John Bowden (London, 1974).

[14] For varying accounts of the origin, beliefs, and activities of the Pharisees and Sadducees see R. Travers Herford, *The Pharisees* (Boston, 1962); Robert M. Seltzer, *Jewish People, Jewish Thought: The Jewish Experience in History* (New York, 1980); Rivkin, *Shaping of Jewish History*, Chaps. III, IV; Louis Finkelstein, *The Pharisees*, 3rd ed. (Philadelphia, 1962); and Leo Baeck, *The Pharisees and Other Essays* (New York, 1947). Baeck opposes the common practice of describing the Pharisees as a party, referring to them rather as a "movement." The Pharisees figured prominently in political controversy during the Hasmonean dynasty, especially during the reigns of John Hyrcanus (135–105 BCE), Alexander Jannaeus (103–76 BCE), and Alexandra (76–67 BCE). See e.g., Josephus, *Antiquities*, Book XIII, Chaps. XI, XVI.

Jewish life. They regarded the oral or unwritten tradition which interpreted the written Torah as a necessary and living supplement to the written Law. As a consequence, for them Torah-tradition, or the Oral Law, came to have equal status with the Written Law.[15]

The Pharisees did not oppose the temple cultus in principle, but for them it did not have the central importance in Jewish religion that it had for the Sadducees. And the Pharisees did not consider royal or priestly power or political struggle against Roman domination essential to the Jewish religion. For the Pharisees, establishing and preserving Torah as the foundation of Jewish life was primary. The Pharisees became the dominant religious influence among the Jews, especially after the Jewish-Roman war, 66–70 CE, and their tradition became the chief force in conserving and strengthening the Jewish religion until modern times.[16] The Jewish rabbinate today is the inheritor of the Pharisaic religion and tradition.

THE SADDUCEES

The origin of the Sadducees is less certain than that of the Pharisees.[17] The Sadducees considered themselves "old believers,"

---

[15] As Leo Baeck points out, the Oral Law "is a development of the presuppositions implicit in the Bible." Torah was not regarded as final and finished, but, he says, it was "a force constantly renewing itself," each age searching "in it for what is most relevant and peculiar to itself." The direct outcome of this process was the Talmud, a large collection of written opinions by the rabbis directed to the practical application of the Law. Its beginning was largely the work and inspiration of Rabbi Judah, called the Prince (ca. 135–217 CE). Leo Baeck, *The Essence of Judaism* (New York, 1961), 23–25.

[16] See Rivkin's *Shaping of Jewish History: A Decisive Mutation*, Chap. III, "The Pharisaic Revolution," for an analysis of the development of Pharisaism and its revolutionary contribution to Jewish and western history.

[17] The name "Sadducee" may have been derived from the Hebrew name *Zadok*, a priest of David and Solomon. In Ezekiel 40:46; 44:15; 48:11, priests in Jerusalem are referred to as "sons of Zadok."

For details on the origins of the Sadducees and Pharisees, and their differences, see F. F. Bruce, *New Testament History* (New York, 1972), 69–81. Also, I. Epstein's comments on the Second Hebrew Commonwealth, in *Judaism*, 95–110. Ancient sources on the Pharisees, Sadducees, and Essenes are Josephus, *Antiquities*, Book XIII, Chap. V, Sec. 9, and *Wars of the Jews*, Book II, Chap. VIII, Sec. 2–14. The Jewish philosopher Philo of Alexandria (c. 20 BCE–54 CE) described the three "sects."

The Calling and Discipleship

probably referring to their rejection of doctrines which they assumed originated with the Persian Zoroastrians: resurrection of the body, angels, demons, and judgment after death. However, their political role was more important historically than their doctrine. Although relatively few in number, the Sadducees had served as counselors and supporters of the Hasmonean rulers and were on comparatively good terms with the Romans. As a result, at the time of Jesus they were the most influential and powerful men in the land, especially in Judea and Jerusalem. The Sadducees were the Temple and aristocratic party. They more or less controlled the Temple and its cult and were powerful in the Sanhedrin. Being of the priestly, wealthy, and politically influential group, their interests were best served by cordial relations with foreigners. They encouraged Greek culture and were more willing than the Pharisees to accept and cultivate association and dealings with Greeks, Romans, and other foreigners. However, the Pharisees were the chief protectors of the faith, and their influence dominated much of the intellectual and religious culture of the Jews at the time of Jesus. Their power was mainly through the synagogues and their commitment to education and scholarly pursuits as well as through the general esteem of the Jewish people which they enjoyed.

ESSENES AND ZEALOTS

There were, of course, other important religious groups, communities, and movements within Judaism whose concerns, judged on the basis of the Gospel texts, were not entirely incompatible with those of Jesus. The Essenes, for example, were a separatist religious fellowship who believed that the Law, the sacred calendar, and the Temple rituals had been corrupted by the Jerusalem priesthood. This religious brotherhood regarded themselves as the "faithful remnant" of Isaiah who would eventually save Israel. It was their duty, they believed, to preserve the ancient covenant and thereby guarantee the continuation of God's guidance and support for the nation. In accord with these beliefs, some of which were held in closest secrecy, many if not most of the Essenes literally separated themselves from other Jewish communities. As

Moses of old, they fled into the desert to prepare for the imminent end of the age. In their social life they were ascetic and communal; ritual baths, daily ritual communal meals, formal prayers, and recitation of their scriptures were features of their communal brotherhood.[18]

Another group, the Zealots, has often been regarded as radical and fanatic in its zeal. However, it would be a mistake to assume that the so-called Zealots were motivated only by nationalistic or political aims. Their patriotism was supported by a fervent devotion to Torah.[19] They were intensely committed to resistance against Roman domination and defilement because they believed Israel's integrity as a covenant people was at stake. In this respect the Zealots differed from Pharisees and Sadducees, both of whom in general favored maintaining peace with Rome. The Pharisees held that Israel's future was guaranteed by God's promise and not by violence or political power. The Sadducees feared that agitation would upset the practical compromises with Rome, on which their prosperity depended, and would eventually lead to the elimination of the Jewish state and religion altogether.

Some New Testament scholars hold the view that an uprising led by Judas against the census required by Sulpicius Quirinius, legate of Syria (ca. 6 CE), accounts for the origin of the Zealots as a distinct religious-political party.[20] However, their spiritual

---

[18] Most Jewish and Christian scholars hold that the Qumran community associated with the Dead Sea Scrolls was one of several Essene colonies. See Frank Cross, Jr., *The Ancient Library of Qumran and Modern Biblical Studies* (New York, 1958); Theodor H. Gaster, *The Dead Sea Scriptures*, 3rd ed. (New York, 1976); and Millar Burrows, *The Dead Sea Scrolls* (New York, 1955), and *More Light on the Dead Sea Scrolls* (New York, 1958).

[19] Josephus held a negative view of the Zealots. He regarded them as extremists or fanatics largely responsible for precipitating the disastrous Jewish-Roman war of 66–70 CE. The evidence from Masada, which was defended by Zealots for many months following the destruction of Jerusalem in 70 CE, indicates that the defenders were pious Jews who, under the most difficult conditions, persisted in following the strict injunctions of Torah.

[20] Quirinius's census is probably the one alluded to by Gamaliel in Acts 5:37: "After him Judas the Galilean arose in the days of the census and drew away some of the people after him; he also perished, and all who followed him were scattered." The census may have been taken in order to determine how much tribute the Romans could exact from the people. Paying such taxes was considered by Zealots as well as other devout Jews as treasonous, since, in their view, God alone

The Calling and Discipleship

heritage is thought to date back to Phinehas and Elijah. Phinehas, grandson of Aaron, showed his zeal for his God by overthrowing Israelite worship of the Baal of Peor.[s] Elijah likewise fought against Jezebel and Phoenician baalism.[t] [21]

These parties or sects constituted only a part of the total Jewish community. By far the most numerous were the common people, those referred to as "the people of the land," Am-ha-aretz.[22] They were spoken of by Jesus as the "sheep without a shepherd."[u] It was to these people that Jesus directed most of his attention. They in turn were the most responsive to his proclamation of the new age.

The Jewish scholar R. Seltzer has called attention to rabbinic traditions of the first century which mention Pharisaic brotherhoods constituting what scholars refer to as "table-fellowship groups." These groups adhered to a uniform law concerning Jewish food and ate their meals in common, probably accompanied by prayers and learned discussions. In his description of the varieties of Judaism in the late Second Temple period, Seltzer includes the Essenes as an example of a table-fellowship.[23] The table-fellowship may have an important bearing on the beginnings of the Christian community, which is identified as a brotherhood participating in a common meal with prayer and the reading and discussion of sacred texts.

GROWING OPPOSITION AND THE CALLING OF THE TWELVE

The term *apostle* means literally "one who is sent." It appears only once in Matthew (10:2) and once in Mark (6:30), where

---

[s] Nm 25:1–13. [t] 1 Kgs 18:17–46. [u] Mt 9:36; Mk 6:34.

was Israel's monarch. In his *Antiquities*, Book XVIII, Chap. I, Sec. 6, Josephus refers to a "Judas the Galilean" as "the author of the fourth sect of Jewish philosophy."

[21] For an account of the origin of the Zealots, see Bruce, *New Testament History*, 93–100.

[22] *Am-ha-aretz* originally referred to the Israelite people, as differentiated from the special Jewish parties and priesthood. In time it was used to refer to the unlearned in contrast to the rabbis and students who received formal training in the Law.

[23] Seltzer, *Jewish People, Jewish Thought*, 218, 220f.

the meaning seems to be "missionary," referring to the mission the Twelve had just completed. The term appears more often in Luke, where it probably carries the more generalized meaning of "messenger," "witness," or "delegate" — one who has a formal commission relating to the new church.

A succinct account of the calling of the Twelve Apostles appears in the Gospel of Luke.

> In these days he went out to the mountain to pray; and all night he continued in prayer to God. And when it was day, he called his disciples, and chose from them twelve, whom he named apostles; Simon, whom he named Peter, and Andrew his brother, and James and John, and Philip, and Bartholomew, and Matthew, and Thomas, and James the son of Alphaeus, and Simon who was called the Zealot, and Judas the son of James, and Judas Iscariot, who became a traitor.[v]

Luke is the only gospel which claims that Jesus himself used the term "apostle." This passage incidentally calls attention to a special feature of Luke's Gospel — Jesus praying before making his most critical decisions. Although many had associated themselves with Jesus as his disciples, he now "appointed twelve, to be with him, and to be sent out to preach."[w][24] Jesus' appointment of the Twelve is thought by some to have been a response to the growing hostility of the Pharisees. Mark's account of the calling follows a series of confrontations with Pharisees on questions regarding fasting and the sabbath. Luke's account of this opposition seems to mark the inauguration of the new Israel, the Twelve corresponding to the Twelve Tribes of Israel. For Luke they formed a nucleus in preparation for the coming Kingdom of God.[x][25] Luke developed this theme further in the Acts of the Apostles.

---

[v] Lk 6:12–16.   [w] Mk 3:14.   [x] Lk 22:28–30.

[24] Parallel lists of the Twelve are found in Mark 3:14–19; Luke 6:13–16 (Acts 1:13); and Matthew 10:1–4. Matthew's list is similar to that of Mark; Luke's departure from the Markan account is more pronounced, since he drops Thaddaeus and inserts Judas the son of James. B. G. Caird holds that at the time the Gospels were written there was no certainty about the identity of the Twelve, that with one or two exceptions little attention was given them as individuals. In Caird's opinion, in the early church (at least the Christian community which Luke represents) the number twelve was more important than the individual names. Caird, *Luke*, 100f.

[25] According to Caird, "In the early Church there were more apostles than twelve (I Cor. 15:7; Gal. 1:1, 19; Acts 14:14; Rom. 16:7), and it was only towards

The Calling and Discipleship

Whatever Luke's explanations, however, it seems most likely that growing opposition from Jewish officials was a major factor in Jesus' calling of the Twelve. According to Mark, "after John was arrested, Jesus came into Galilee preaching the gospel of God." [y] Under the pressure of John's arrest and imprisonment, Jesus realized the need to share the responsibility for the future of the movement among his most loyal followers. His own personal future, like that of John the Baptist, was at risk.

As has already been noted, at the calling of Levi (or Matthew), the Scribes began to reproach Jesus for eating with sinners and tax collectors.[z] Soon after, Jesus' disciples were observed violating the fast. According to Matthew's account, it was John's disciples who registered the complaint, "your disciples do not fast." Jesus' declaration that "No one sews a piece of unshrunk cloth on an old garment," "no one puts new wine into old wineskins," indicates that for him the old way was no longer adequate.[a]

Further confrontations centered on Jesus' comments about the institution of the sabbath. His disciples were seen plucking the heads of grain on the sabbath day. According to the Jewish tradition such behavior was unlawful. In response to the Pharisees' complaint, Jesus pointed to the very notable example of David, who during an emergency entered the house of God and took bread which was not lawful for any but a priest to eat.[b] With this precedent as his defense, Jesus declared, "The sabbath was made for man, not man for the sabbath." [c] The expression "the Son of man" in this context is to be understood as referring to "mortal man" or simply "man" and not to a supernatural agent of God as in later Christian interpretations. According to Mark Jesus' teaching was that man himself is lord of the sabbath.

Matthew adds an interesting comment to the David story when he records that Jesus asked, "have you not read in the law how on the sabbath the priests in the temple profane the sabbath, and are guiltless? I tell you, something greater than the temple

[y] Mk 1:1–14. [z] Mk 2:13–17. [a] Mk 2:18–22. [b] 1 Sm 21:4–6. [c] Mk 2:27f.

---

the end of the first century that the name was restricted to the twelve (Rev. 21:14)." Caird, *Luke*, 100.

is here."[d] The expression "something greater is here" is based upon a quotation from the prophet Hosea, "I desire mercy, and not sacrifice."[e] In both accounts, Mark and Matthew, the point is clear that Jesus required virtue and mercy over the rules and regulations of institutional religion.

A similar point is made in the episode about Jesus attending the synagogue. The Pharisees asked him if he would heal a person on the sabbath. Jesus' rejoinder, "Is it lawful on the sabbath to do good ... to save life or to kill?" and his restoration of the man's hand angered the Pharisees. According to Mark, they immediately went out and conspired with the Herodians to destroy Jesus.[f]

There are considerable variations among the several lists of apostles: Bartholomew is included in the Synoptics but does not appear in the Gospel of John. Nathanael is an important member of the Twelve in John but is not included in the synoptic Gospels; the Gospel of Matthew adds the description "the tax collector" to the name of the disciple Matthew. Matthew and Mark read "Simon the Cananaean"; the parallel passage in Luke reads "Simon who was called the Zealot." Other references to the disciples in the synoptic Gospels show some interesting differences: In Mark 2:14, Levi is presumed to be the tax collector. Also in Mark, Levi is referred to as "the son of Alphaeus." "Judas the son of James"[g] does not appear in the lists of Mark and Matthew. Apparently in Luke Thaddaeus has been replaced by this Judas. Some early texts of Matthew 10:3 read "Lebbaeus" or "Lebbaeus called Thaddaeus" or "Thaddaeus called Lebbaeus" instead of Thaddaeus.

Much of the traditional characterization of the twelve disciples depends upon the Gospel of John. According to John, Simon was surnamed "Cephas," which means Rock; also, it is reported that his father's name was John.[h] [26] When called to be a disciple, Simon Peter was a fisherman with his brother Andrew. In the Christian tradition Peter is pictured as rough and impetuous, with despondency sometimes following confidence. It was only later

[d] Mt 12:5-7. [e] Hos 6:6. [f] Mk 3:1-6. [g] Lk 6:16. [h] Jn 1:42.

[26] The Greek "Peter" and the Aramaic "Cephas" both mean "rock."

The Calling and Discipleship

that he achieved the firmness of character commonly ascribed to him. According to tradition Peter was martyred in Rome, probably about 64 CE during the reign of Nero.

Andrew was a brother of Peter and also a fisherman by trade. He and Peter were together when they were promised: "Follow me and I will make you become fishers of men." [i] Before this time Andrew had been a disciple of John the Baptist. The Fourth Gospel records that Andrew first met Jesus at Bethsaida, where, after hearing Jesus and being convinced that he was the Messiah, he told Peter of his great discovery.[27] The tradition that Andrew suffered a martyr's death is generally considered unreliable.

James and John are referred to as the sons of Zebedee. They were also fishermen on the Sea of Galilee, apparently in partnership with Peter and Andrew. These two brothers, says Mark, were "surnamed Boanerges, that is, sons of thunder." [j] This characterization suggests strength, impulsiveness, and ambition. The three, Peter, James, and John, were leading figures in many of the Gospel stories. This James was not Jesus' brother, whom, according to Eusebius, the Jews referred to as James the Just, and who is generally regarded as having been the first leader of the infant church in Jerusalem.[28]

Philip was from Bethsaida.[k] No doubt he was a fisherman like his fellow apostles from that place. He seems to have been an especially close friend of Andrew and, according to the Gospel of John, was one of those who had come to hear John the Baptist. Nathanael, according to the Gospel of John, came from "Cana in Galilee." [l] It was Nathanael who doubted whether anything good could come out of Nazareth. And it was of Nathanael that Jesus declared, "Behold, an Israelite indeed, in whom is not guile!" [m] Thomas is remembered for his scepticism about Jesus' resurrec-

---

[i] Mk 1:17. [j] Mk 3:17. [k] Jn 1:44. [l] Jn 21:2. [m] Jn 1:47.

[27] The details about Andrew being a disciple of John the Baptist (Jn 1:40) and his report to Peter about Jesus are supplied by the Fourth Gospel (Jn 1:35–42) and are not found in the synoptic accounts.

[28] Regarding Jesus' brothers, see Mt 12:46, 13:55; Mk 6:3; Jn 7:3; Acts 1:14; and 1 Cor 9:5. James, the brother of Jesus, was probably converted after the resurrection. He is mentioned in Acts 12:17, 15:13, 21:18, and in Gal 1:19; 2:9, 12.

tion. According to the Fourth Gospel, Thomas failed to grasp the meaning of Jesus' mission.[n]

The Gospels give little information about James, "the son of Alphaeus," sometimes called James the Little, or about Simon, referred to in Luke as "the Zealot." [o] [29] By process of elimination, it seems that Judas, "the son of James," may be the person called Thaddaeus in Matthew and Mark. In any event, it is reported in John that at one time this Judas asked the question: "Lord, how is it that you will manifest yourself to us, and not to the world?" [p] The other Judas — Judas Iscariot — perhaps the only one of the Twelve who was a Judean, is remembered for his role in the arrest of Jesus. However, little else is known about him except for his suicide. Some scholars assume that the name "Iscariot" was used by Gospel writers to distinguish him from the other Judas, the son of James.

As Jesus went among the towns and villages in Galilee, he was moved to compassion by the condition of the people. Their lives, according to Matthew and Mark, were desperate. Their society was economically and politically unstable. Some were burdened with guilt, presumably because they were not living strictly by traditional ceremonial laws. Some violated the moral codes. Many, including the despised publicans, were ostracized by the people. Large numbers of people were plagued with anxieties that were the consequence of personal and social failure or with fears engendered by common superstitions regarding evil spirits. Like the Roman authorities in Judea, the Herodian princes in Galilee and the other districts apparently had little or no concern for the plight of the common people. Nor were the leaders of the synagogues able to provide the leadership necessary to establish general confidence and peace of mind. Conditions of deprivation, anxiety, and unrest were part of the social milieu in which Jesus gave his instructions to the Twelve. Moreover, the Jews did not

[n] Jn 20:24–29.   [o] Lk 6:15.   [p] Jn 14:22.

[29] Professor O. Cullmann has suggested that several of Jesus' disciples may have been Zealots: Peter, Judas, and possibly the brothers James and John, as well as Simon. Oscar Cullmann, *The State in the New Testament* (New York, 1956), 15–18.

The Calling and Discipleship

have a unified society, and Judaism was not a simple, unified religion but a conglomerate of parties and sects.

INSTRUCTIONS TO THE TWELVE

> When he saw the crowds, he had compassion for them, because they were harassed and helpless, like sheep without a shepherd. . . .
> And he called to him his twelve disciples and gave them authority over unclean spirits, to cast them out, and to heal every disease and every infirmity. . . .
> These twelve Jesus sent out, charging them, "Go nowhere among the Gentiles, and enter no town of the Samaritans, but go rather to the lost sheep of the house of Israel. And preach as you go, saying, 'The kingdom of heaven is at hand.' " [q] [30]

Jesus' instruction to the disciples not to go among the Gentiles or the Samaritans raises interesting and difficult questions for modern Christians. Christians today are accustomed to a strong ecumenical quality in their religion and commonly regard Jesus as one having an interest in the well-being and salvation of everyone, regardless of race or creed. Possibly the parochialism in Matthew's account reflects the intense Judaic sentiment of the early Jerusalem church. This sentiment is found elsewhere in the Gospels, especially in Mark. In the last chapter of Matthew, there appears the final instruction of Jesus to his disciples following the resurrection, "Go therefore and make disciples of all nations." [r] This late indication of universalism may have expressed a new attitude entering the post-resurrection Christian community with the establishment of the gentile mission.[31] When the Gospel of Matthew was written, the church had already been established among the gentiles. There may, of course, have been a practical motive in Jesus' early instruction, as it may have been important to plan his activities step by step, moving from one objective to an-

[q] Mt 9:36; 10:1, 5–7.   [r] Mt 28:19.

[30] The reference to the "lost sheep of the house of Israel" is reminiscent of the shepherd theme in the Old Testament. For examples, see Nm 27:15–17; 1 Kgs 22:17; and Zec 10:2f.

[31] It seems likely that in 10:5f. Matthew was using an older tradition in which Jesus is interpreted as restricting his ministry to the House of Israel.

other. Or Matthew may have interpreted the injunction to avoid the gentiles as referring to the interim period prior to the establishment of the church.

In Matthew's Gospel, Jesus is represented as demanding an ascetic discipline in his disciples as they pursued their ministry. They were to "take no gold, nor silver, nor copper" in their belts. Here Matthew seems to understand that Jesus is setting the rule for the church's later ministry. The disciples were not allowed to accept money for the services they rendered. Their clothing was to be plain, and only the necessities for survival were to be taken along.[s]

The disciples were instructed to proclaim the message of the Kingdom in as many towns and villages as would receive them. They were to bless those who were receptive, but a harsh judgment was made against those who rejected the message. Jesus' instruction to "shake off the dust" and his comparison of those who rejected the message to those in Sodom and Gomorrah should be understood as following his rigorous conception of the expected Kingdom. There is a sense of urgency and finality in his proclamation — *Now* is the moment of decision; the Kingdom is upon you! The judgment may be upon you if you disbelieve. Jesus' exhortation to his disciples was not only an expression of critical urgency but a warning of the dangers of discipleship as well. "Behold, I send you out as sheep in the midst of wolves; so be wise as serpents and innocent as doves."[t]

THE CONDITIONS OF DISCIPLESHIP

It is evident that to be a disciple of Jesus in proclaiming the message meant not only sharing the promises and blessings of the Kingdom to come, but also a share in the hardships and the risks of preparing the way. The disciples must be ready to cope with violence, cruelty, and treachery, for everything possible would be done to oppose them. John the Baptist was even now confined within prison walls not knowing what to expect, and his disciples feared for their future.

[s] Mt 10:9f. [t] Mt 10:16.

The Calling and Discipleship

In Matthew's view, Christian disciples in his own day should not expect less hardship than that endured by their leader, but "he who endures to the end will be saved." [u] That Jesus early anticipated serious troubles, quite possibly his own death, appears evident. But he exhorted the Twelve to follow his own fearless confession.[v] He trusted that God was in control and would bring in the Kingdom. According to Matthew, anyone who fails to "take his cross" and follow Jesus will be unworthy of him when the Kingdom comes.[w] [32] In a passage that has caused considerable consternation to the followers of the Prince of Peace, Jesus said, "Do not think that I have come to bring peace on earth; I have not come to bring peace, but a sword." [x]

The conditions of discipleship were rigorous. Commitment to Jesus and his purposes meant giving up everything, even one's own life and family if necessary. "He who loves father or mother more than me is not worthy of me." [y] [33] The threat of persecution should not deter the disciples. They must expect resistance, since the Word would not bring peace but strife and contention, even within families. Such woes, Matthew implies, were predicted of the messianic age by the prophet Micah: "For the son treats the father with contempt, the daughter rises up against her mother, the daughter-in-law against her mother-in-law; a man's enemies are the men of his own house." [z] If Matthew's account reliably reports Jesus' actual admonition regarding family relationships and acceptance of him and his message, his statement probably reflected Jesus' experience with his own family, his mother and brothers. He had been misunderstood and rejected by some in his own family; those who followed him might well expect a similar rejection, according to Matthew.

"He who receives you receives me." [a] With this point, Matthew's intention seems clear: to proclaim Jesus himself as the

---

[u] Mt 10:22. [v] Mt 10:32f. [w] Mt 10:38. [x] Mt 10:34. [y] Mt 10:37. [z] Mi 7:6. [a] Mt 10:40.

[32] Matthew 10:38 is the earliest reference to the cross in Matthew's Gospel.

[33] Perhaps the severity of the demands and expectations Jesus placed upon his disciples may be explained in part by his belief that the coming of the Kingdom was imminent: "You will not have gone through all the towns of Israel, before the Son of man comes" (Mt 10:23).

model for Christian discipleship. Matthew extended the anticipation of strife and persecution experienced by Jesus to his own day and beyond. For Matthew it was not only the original Twelve who were commissioned, but all true Christian disciples.[34]

Perhaps no passage in religious literature has received more attention than Jesus' statement to his disciples that "He who finds his life will lose it, and he who loses his life for my sake will find it."[b] It has, of course, been lifted from its context of instruction to the disciples and generalized as a principle expressing the highest ideal of moral selflessness. Perhaps more than any other saying attributed to Jesus, this statement has epitomized the heart of Christian ethics.

JOURNEY TO PHOENICIA

Early in his ministry Jesus left Galilee and went to the gentile country of Tyre and Sidon, one of the few instances recorded in the Gospels of Jesus going entirely outside of what can be regarded as "Jewish" territory. The Gospels of Matthew, Mark, and John do not totally agree on this matter, and certain details are difficult to correlate. For example, in Mark Jesus repeatedly requests that his identity be kept hidden: "tell no one." This attitude of secrecy seems to contradict his usual openness. Both Mark and Matthew refer to the journey to Tyre and Sidon as a "withdrawal."

Was this an attempt to escape from real or imagined enemies in Galilee, or was it a desire to avoid the crowds and be alone with the Twelve? Or, as Luke seems to suggest, did the journey to Tyre beyond the borders of Palestine signal an intended ministry to the gentiles and indicate that the gospel was not exclusively for the Jews? Scholars do not agree on this question. The withdrawal was probably occasioned by the execution of John the Baptist and the growing hostility toward Jesus exhibited by Herod Antipas, his loyal supporters the Herodians, and by some Pharisees and other religious leaders. Also to be considered is the people's misunder-

---

[b] Mt 10:39.

[34] At the close of Matthew's Gospel the original commission to proclaim the Kingdom only to Israel (10:5f.) is extended to "all nations" (Mt 28:19).

standing of Jesus' messianic role reported in the Gospel of John that prompted them to attempt to proclaim him king.[35]

The two Phoenician cities of Tyre and Sidon were located outside the domain of the Herods in the Roman province of Syria, which accounts for the reference in Mark to a "Syro-Phoenician" woman. For many centuries Tyre and Sidon, today in modern Lebanon, had been important seaports and commercial centers. The strength of Tyre was dramatically demonstrated in 332 BCE by its impressive resistance to the invading forces of Alexander the Great. Phoenician ships had sailed as far north as England and completely around the continent of Africa. Hundreds of years earlier, the Hebrew prophet Isaiah had pronounced his oracle against Tyre and Sidon.[c][36]

Despite his desire for secrecy, Jesus' fame had apparently spread beyond the borders of Galilee. His presence could not be kept hidden. His answer to the Syro-Phoenician woman who sought his help for her daughter, whom she believed to be possessed by an "unclean spirit," seems unduly severe and out of character for one who often demonstrated compassion. His response to her entreaty, "Let the children first be fed, for it is not right to take the children's bread and throw it to the dogs," [d] will probably always be a matter of dispute. Did he really intend to exclude gentiles from his public ministry? Certainly he went among them, but whether or not he intended to include them in the Kingdom or to extend to them his teachings and healing ministry is unclear.[37]

There is a close connection between Jesus' earlier debate with the Pharisees concerning what defiles a person and the conclusion

---

[c] Is 23:1–18. [d] Mk 7:27.

[35] This view is followed by M. Goguel in *The Life of Jesus*, trans. Olive Wyon (New York, 1949), 376f., 397–99, and, among contemporary historians, by Grant, *Jesus*, 128–33.

[36] Also, see Lk 10:13f. Isaiah denounced Tyre as a harlot, a city of pride "whose merchants were princes, whose traders were the honored of the earth" (Is 23:8f., 17).

[37] Mt 9:9–13; 11:19. The "sinners" with whom Jesus ate were probably, for the most part, persons who did not observe the ritual law associated with washing or the preparation of food.

of this account of the Syro-Phoenician woman — " 'O woman, great is your faith!' . . . And her daughter was healed instantly." [e] Jesus' position on what defiles and what is shown as righteousness in this account may perhaps be taken as a repudiation of the strict Pharisaic separatism and exclusivist practices.

For Matthew and Mark, such details clearly anticipate a more universal standard of righteousness. At any rate, universalist elements were present in the early church, which regarded its inclusiveness as consonant with the spirit of Jesus' conception of the Kingdom.

JOURNEY TO DECAPOLIS

There was a road from Sidon across the Lebanon mountains to Damascus. Possibly Jesus followed this road on his journey to the Decapolis. Turning southward from the Damascus way, they entered "the region of the Decapolis." [f] The country was Greek in name, in religion, culture, civil practice, and architecture. From the time of Alexander's invasion over three hundred years earlier, Greek cities with their "Greek" colonists and hellenistic culture had increased in number throughout the eastern Mediterranean world. To resist invasion from the south and east, ten Greek cities east of Galilee and Samaria had formed a league known as the Decapolis. The league included Gadara, Scythopolis, Pella, Gerasa, and Philadelphia. Into this land of Greek culture, learning, and practice, Jesus and his disciples came with their Jewish traditions and expectations.

Matthew describes in general terms what Jesus did in the Decapolis. They brought to him "the lame, the maimed, the blind, the dumb, and many others, and they put them at his feet, and he healed them." [g] Mark tells of one incident in detail — of the deaf man with a speech impediment. Jesus put his fingers into the man's ears, spat, perhaps on his finger, touched the man's tongue, and he was healed, regaining his hearing and ability to speak plainly. Then, according to Mark, Jesus "charged them to tell no one . . . . And they were astonished beyond measure." [h]

[e] Mt 15:28. [f] Mk 7:31. [g] Mt 15:30. [h] Mk 7:36f.

The Calling and Discipleship

This account of this miracle involves more than Jesus' word or command and makes no mention of the role of faith in the healing. Here, as in most of Jesus' miracles, there was actual contact, but of an unusual nature. Saliva was often regarded as having curative properties.[38] The Jewish scholar Geza Vermes has called attention to the "simplicity" of Jesus' cures, not only in matters involving exorcism, but also in healing the sick, lame, and blind. Was Jesus a professional exorcist of the type described by the ancient rabbis, asks Vermes. His reply:

> He is said to have cast out many devils, but no rite is mentioned in connection with these achievements. In fact, compared with the esotericism of other methods, his own, as depicted in the Gospels, is simplicity itself. Even in regard to healing, the closest he came to the Noachic, Solomonic and Essene type of cure was when he touched the sick with his own saliva, a substance generally thought to be medicinal.[39]

Following his return to Capernaum, Jesus was involved in controversy over the relation of the religious community to the state, always a serious problem for the Jews. Matthew's account of the Temple tax collectors inquiring whether Jesus was willing to pay the tax may have resulted from the early church's relation to Jewish Temple authorities or Roman bureaucracy.[1] In accordance with Exodus, every male Jew above twenty years of age was taxed one-half shekel each year to support the Temple.[40] Apparently after the destruction of Jerusalem in 70 CE Roman authorities continued to collect this tax, but to support a temple to Jupiter, which the Romans had constructed on the Temple site. Matthew's Gospel probably was produced at this time, when the early Palestinian Christians faced the difficult problem of their political loyalties. This gives meaning to Jesus' statement to Peter that they were free of this obligation but should pay the tax rather than "give offense."

---

[1] Mt 17:24–27.

[38] Mark 8:23–25 describes the healing of a blind man where the healing involves Jesus spitting on the man's eyes.

[39] Geza Vermes, *Jesus the Jew* (Philadelphia, 1981), 65.

[40] It is likely that the tax was based on Ex 30:13f.

Such sound counsel could avoid serious trouble. In several places in the Gospels, Jesus is represented as allowing no compromise with evil. On one occasion, for instance, he said, "Every tree that does not bear good fruit is cut down and thrown into the fire." ʲ Yet in this instance he advises compromise to avoid offense.

DISCIPLESHIP IN THE KINGDOM

A dispute had arisen among the disciples of Jesus concerning who among them was the greatest. Apparently they still relished the view that Jesus would fulfill their expectations in a temporal way — that he would establish an earthly kingdom. Their dispute arose from the question of who should receive the highest positions of honor in the Kingdom. The disciples apparently tried to conceal their dispute from Jesus and kept an embarrassed silence when he questioned them. His response to their controversy is well known, "If any one would be first, he must be last of all and servant of all." ᵏ

On this occasion Jesus tried to correct the disciples' mistaken views about discipleship. He showed the folly of competing with one another for social status, implying that worldly credentials are not the standard for membership in the Kingdom. In order to be clearly understood, he admonished them to receive the Kingdom of Heaven as a child.ˡ A child has no worldly status, owns no property, and can claim no prestigious title. The disciples should receive the Kingdom with joy and gratitude as a gift from God.

In the same spirit of concern about priority, John complained to Jesus that a man who was not "following us" was casting out demons in Jesus' name. Jesus replied that one who is "not against us is for us." ᵐ For Jesus there were no tests of authority, no established channels which confined God's activity.[41]

It is clear that some of the sayings of Jesus, which were no doubt directed to his disciples, were employed by the writers of the

---

ʲ Mt 7:19. ᵏ Mk 9:35. ˡ Mt 18:3. ᵐ Mk 9:40.

[41] Caird in *Luke*, 135f., held that here Jesus was consistent with his general statements on other occasions when he was questioned about credentials. His response seems to have been that conformity with formal tests or going through "proper channels" was not required. The word one speaks and the works one does for the Kingdom of God are self-authenticating; no other credentials are required.

The Calling and Discipleship

Gospels to instruct the members of the early Christian community in general on their proper relations with one another.[42] A series of these instructions appears in Matthew. Of special interest are the warnings not to cause one of the "little ones" to perish, the discourse on reconciliation, and the Parable of the Unmerciful Servant on the virtue of forgiveness and mercy.[n] The "little ones" referred to in Matthew are generally considered to be the members of the early church. Those who lead them astray, causing them "to stumble," incur the wrath of judgment.

The question "Who is the greatest in the kingdom of heaven?" introduces a theme which was of great concern to the church in Matthew's day — namely, that the life one leads as a disciple determines whether or not he will be received in the future Kingdom. A faithful disciple will care for his brother; those who sin are to be approached with tenderness, but if they are obstinate, even before witnesses, they are to be brought before the church.

Peter's question, "Lord, how often shall my brother sin against me, and I forgive him?"[o] raised the question of forgiveness by the individual person. If the church may reject its unrepentant members, shall individuals also refuse them forgiveness? Jesus' response, "seventy times seven," meant that forgiveness was a constant requirement, not to be measured by any formula.

In the Parable of the Unmerciful Servant, a servant whose master forgave him a debt of thousands refused to forgive a very small debt owed to him by another.[43] The central meaning of the parable is clear — to refuse forgiveness to another is a moral wrong which may prevent God's forgiveness of the unforgiving.

---

[n] Mt 18:1–35. [o] Mt 18:21.

[42] Chapter 18 of Matthew contains the fourth of five teaching sections. In 19:1, the evangelist returns to the narrative with the formula, "Now when Jesus had finished these sayings." J. C. Fenton holds the view that in this section Matthew uses the Tradition (what Jesus said) in order to instruct Christians in his day about life within the church. J. C. Fenton, *The Gospel of St. Matthew* (Baltimore, 1963), 289f.

[43] This parable is found only in Matthew, 18:23–35, presumably included at this point as a conclusion for his teaching collection. J. Jeremias contends that this is a parable about the last judgment which Matthew employs as an exhortation and a warning to the church. J. Jeremias, *The Parables of Jesus*, rev. ed. (New York, 1963), 210–13.

Jesus had taught this before — "if you do not forgive men their trespasses, neither will your Father forgive your trespasses," [p] and "forgive us our debts, as we also have forgiven our debtors." [q] Jesus repeated this theme again at the end of Matthew 18.[r] God's gift of forgiveness, which is beyond any measure of merit, will be rescinded if one does not sincerely and wholeheartedly forgive others.

[p] Mt 6:15.　[q] Mt 6:12.　[r] Mt 18:35.

CHAPTER 6

The Question of Jesus' Identity

The imprisonment and subsequent execution of John the Baptist was a crucial factor in the ministry of Jesus. It probably affected not only his movements and those of his disciples over the ensuing period but also his concept of himself and his mission. It is reasonable to assume, moreover, that John's death influenced Jesus' own expectation of death, which was to play such an important role in the calling of his disciples and his instructions to them.

EXECUTION OF THE BAPTIST

The well-known account of John's execution is given by Mark.[a] The "King Herod" referred to by Mark was Herod Antipas, the son of Herod the Great. In condemning Herod's unlawful relation to Herodias, the former wife of Herod's brother Philip, tetrarch of the territory northeast of Galilee from 4 BCE to 34 CE, John showed the same courage that apparently characterized all his preaching. Herod's main reason for the imprisonment of John, however, may have been his fear that John, who seems to have had a considerable following, might incite a rebellion. This, at least, was the opinion of Josephus, who recorded John's imprisonment and execution[1] but made no mention of Herodias's daughter and the events recorded in Mark immediately leading to John's death.[2]

---

[a] Mk 6:14–29.

[1] For Josephus's statement on the Baptist, see note 5 in Chapter 3.

[2] Matthew's account of the execution of John the Baptist follows Mark but adds that after John's disciples buried him, they "went and told Jesus" (14:12). Luke mentions the execution (9:7–9) but does not give the events leading to John's death. John's execution is not reported in the Fourth Gospel.

The question of Jesus' relationship to the Baptist is a matter of primary concern to the Gospel writers, who attempted to establish Jesus' superiority to John and insisted on his independence of the Johannine movement. The Lukan infancy narrative, for example, and the accounts of Jesus' baptism, particularly in John's Gospel and in Matthew, clearly set Jesus apart from John and subordinate the Baptist to him. However, notwithstanding this apologetic strategy of the Gospels, the Baptist must be acknowledged as an important historical figure in Palestine quite apart from Jesus and his ministry. It is not improbable that at the baptism, Jesus identified himself as a follower of John, and that following the Baptist's arrest and imprisonment he became the chief inspiration and leader of the eschatological movement which John had initiated.

FEEDING THE FIVE THOUSAND

Major events in Jesus' ministry from this time forward — the feeding of the five thousand, the confession at Philippi, and the Transfiguration — can be best understood against the backdrop of John's imprisonment and death. These events gave Jesus a sense of urgency about his own future, prompting the question about his status as John's successor and bearer of the Elijah mantle: "But who do you say that I am?" [b]

The traditions about Jesus feeding the crowds, recorded in Mark 6:30–44 and Matthew 14:13–21, and the reports of incidents preceding and following this event are puzzling. Mark and Matthew both record two miraculous occasions of feeding large numbers of people with a few loaves and fishes, first the five thousand and later the four thousand.[c] The second "feeding" is not included in Luke's or John's account. Those New Testament historians who regard the accounts in Mark and Matthew as two versions of a single event are probably correct.[3] Also, the occasion for the feeding of the five thousand is described differently by the Gospel writers. In Mark and Luke the feeding follows the return of the apostles from their missionary journeys when they withdrew

---

[b] Mk 8:29. [c] Mt 14:13–21; 15:32–39; Mk 6:32–44; 8:1–10.

[3] Francis W. Beare, *The Gospel According to Matthew: A Commentary* (Oxford, 1981), 328, 347.

The Question of Jesus' Identity

to find seclusion and rest.[d] Matthew, however, connected this event with the arrest and execution of John the Baptist: "Now when Jesus heard this [the execution of John], he withdrew."

In Matthew's account, Jesus withdrew across the lake presumably to be outside the jurisdiction of Herod Antipas, who had executed John.[e] A crowd gathered as Jesus came ashore. However, this was not the usual gathering of the curious and of those who came for healing or exorcism, but more likely a gathering of John's disciples and others aroused by the death of the Baptist, including people strongly opposed to Rome. A serious confrontation with Herod seemed inevitable.

The Fourth Gospel places this event near the Passover[f] and suggests that in feeding the multitude Jesus may have intended a feast or banquet celebrating the coming of God's Kingdom. In any case this was a critical juncture in Jesus' ministry, for according to the Fourth Gospel, Jesus proclaimed openly his identity as the Messiah and God's son. Apparently the hope for a messiah who would be a national leader, a hope strong among the Galileans, was capturing the imagination of Jesus' followers. But he resisted the effort to make him king.[4]

> When the people saw the sign which he had done [the feeding of the multitude], they said, "This is indeed the prophet who is to come into the world!"
> Perceiving then that they were about to come and take him by force to make him king, Jesus withdrew to the mountain by himself.[g]

Later, according to John's account, Jesus returned to Capernaum. There he elaborated on the meaning of the sign given at the feeding, that he was the bread of life sent from God. John recorded that many of the disciples were offended by the apparent literalness of Jesus' teaching about eating his flesh and many withdrew from his company.[h]

---

[d] Mk 6:30f.; Lk 9:10. [e] Mt 14:13. [f] Jn 6:4. [g] Jn 6:14f. [h] Jn 6:60f., 66f.

[4] M. Goguel holds the view common among scholars that "The refusal of Jesus to accept the title of king, and to use the force supplied by his followers, coupled with the supernatural power which God would give him to overthrow the Tetrarch, led to the immediate collapse of his influence over the masses." Maurice Goguel, *The Life of Jesus*, trans. Olive Wyon (New York, 1949), 377.

The strong sacramental flavor of the Johannine account is less evident in the synoptic Gospels. Nevertheless, the Feeding of the Five Thousand (or four thousand) has great significance for the Synoptics, not simply as a miracle of feeding a great throng from five loaves and two fish but even more as a sign of Jesus' purpose to usher in the Kingdom of God. In the synoptic presentations it seems intended as a symbol of the messianic banquet.[5] In fact, in all four Gospels this story is laden with symbolism and is later related to the Last Supper. In the Gospel of John, Israel's eating manna in the desert is interpreted as foreshadowing Jesus as the bread from heaven.[i]

Apparently by the time John wrote his Gospel, probably not earlier than the end of the first century, the feeding of the multitude had been invested by the Christian community with sacramental meaning. However, some other meaning seems intended by the synoptic accounts. Mark points out that Jesus had compassion on the great throng because they were like sheep without a shepherd.[j] But there is more here than a story of Jesus' compassion, for when the disciples, realizing the lateness of the hour, requested that Jesus send the people to nearby villages to obtain food, Jesus answered, "You give them something to eat."[k] This was unexpected. Apparently, Jesus anticipated the time soon to come when he would be arrested and executed just as John had been. Then the disciples must assume leadership of "the flock." But they did not fully understand Jesus' metaphor about the loaves and the twelve baskets left over which apparently symbolized the apostles' responsibilities that would follow upon Jesus' death.

---

[i] Jn 6:31–35, 47–51, 58. [j] Mk 6:34. [k] Mk 6:37.

[5] The feeding of the five thousand at Mark 6:40 and Luke 9:14 is reminiscent of the ordering of the multitude in hundreds and fifties during the Exodus (Ex 18:21–23). Also it bears resemblance to the story of Elisha's feeding the hundred in 2 Kings 4:42–44.

M. Goguel says, "The idea of this [Messianic] Feast was so widespread in the Judaism of that day that it is quite natural to think that Jesus may have had it in mind when he invited the multitude, to whom he had just been speaking about the kingdom of God, to sit down to this meal. To him also the distribution of the loaves was a symbol of the Messianic Feast." Goguel, *Life of Jesus*, 368f. Also, see A. Schweitzer, *The Mystery of the Kingdom of God*, trans. W. Lowrie (New York, 1964), 171f.

The Question of Jesus' Identity

They were unable "to see" beyond what was immediately before them — the temporal realities of hunger and bread. Later Jesus' meaning would become more apparent in his discourse on leaven.

The event of Jesus walking on the water, one of the so-called "nature" miracles which supposedly defy natural law, may well have been an illusion or hallucination experienced by one or more of his exhausted disciples as they struggled with their boat. For in Jesus' time there was no understanding of natural law describing the regularity of nature.

> And in the fourth watch of the night he came to them, walking on the sea. But when the disciples saw him walking on the sea, they were terrified, saying, "It is a ghost!" And they cried out for fear. But immediately he spoke to them, saying, "Take heart, it is I; have no fear." [l]

This entire episode is omitted from Luke, but for Matthew and Mark the event had significance beyond simply describing Jesus' miraculous power over nature. Its main value in Matthew comes from the confession of those in the boat: "Truly you are the Son of God." [m] [6] However, in Mark the event does not lead to a confession. On the contrary, the disciples do not understand its meaning. Mark's view must be understood in connection with other crucial events and sayings of Jesus: the feeding of the five thousand, the discourse on leaven, and the Transfiguration. All of these events have to do with the disclosure of Jesus' identity and, in Mark's view, the failure of the disciples to discern his true nature and role as the Messiah. Mark reported that when Jesus came to them and got into the boat, the wind ceased. "And," he continues, "they were utterly astounded, for they did not understand about the loaves, but their hearts were hardened." [n] References to "the loaves" could only refer to the five loaves which fed the crowd. Apparently, for Mark, what the disciples could not grasp about the miracle of the loaves was the identity and real significance of Jesus — that he was not merely the Jewish Messiah

---

[l] Mt 14:25–27. [m] Mt 14:33. [n] Mk 6:51f.

[6] The confession and the report of Peter's attempt to walk on the sea appear only in Matthew.

but also the Son of man and Son of God who must suffer and die and be raised up. This motif is continued by Mark and the other synoptic evangelists in Jesus' discourse on leaven.

JESUS AND THE LAW

Gennesaret lies at the northwestern shore of the Sea of Galilee between the sea and high rolling hills. This well-populated, fertile area near Capernaum was a trade center and the base of Jesus' Galilean ministry. Perhaps the news of Jesus' teachings had preceded him and his disciples, for the people's enthusiasm was high. They flocked to him bringing their sick to the marketplaces where they might touch even the fringe of his robe.º [7]

Here Jesus encountered a group of Pharisees and scribes from Jerusalem. They asked him why his disciples did not live according to the tradition of the elders but ate with defiled hands.ᵖ Jesus had become well known in Galilee. He had attracted much attention and apparently was a subject of discussion wherever he went. He was accepted mainly by the common people, who found hope and consolation in his teachings of the Kingdom. But the religious leaders were often opposed to him. The fact that the Pharisees and scribes who came to confer with Jesus were from Jerusalem suggests that they may have been an official delegation sent to investigate him.[8] Their complaint that Jesus' disciples failed to respect the established ceremonial practices was serious for those who strictly observed the Law and tradition. Jesus' reply to the question with a counterquestion followed a pattern of argumentation common in rabbinic controversy. "And why do you transgress the commandment of God for the sake of your tradition?" ᑫ

As has been indicated, the tradition of the elders to which the Pharisees and Jesus referred was the extension of the Mosaic Law

---

º Mk 6:56. ᵖ Mk 7:5. ᑫ Mt 15:3.

[7] The "fringe of his garment" probably refers to tassels at the four corners of a cloak — specified in Nm 15:37–39 and Dt 22:12 — which were intended to remind the devotee of the commandments of God.

[8] Matthew 15:1 specifies that the Pharisees and scribes came from Jerusalem. The parallel passage in Mark (7:1) seems to indicate that only the scribes were from Jerusalem; a similar description of Jerusalem scribes is found at Mark 3:22.

sometimes called the Oral Law, a legal tradition that had issued from the practical necessity of adapting the written Mosaic Law to the growing complexities of everyday life. For the Pharisees and the scribes, who by common consent were responsible for interpreting the Law, the oral tradition was a body of religious and moral principles second in importance only to the Written Law, the Torah. According to Josephus, the Sadducees were strong defenders of the Written Law but, unlike the Pharisees, were not adherents to the oral tradition.[9]

Among the rules and observances of the oral tradition was a ceremony for the washing of hands before eating. Observing the tradition of the elders in this instance was more than a matter of sanitary regulation; it was a religious duty. Torah required ceremonial observances for many kinds of defilement.[r] Moreover, through the years the elders had added rules to protect the Law against defilement just as a fence protects property.[10] As they explained it, one might be defiled and break the Law without knowing it, such as unconsciously or unavoidably touching a Samaritan in the marketplace.

Jesus' countercharge against the Pharisees raised the question as to what it is that defiles a person. His answer was that nothing going into a person's mouth can defile him. In his response Jesus referred to one of the ten commandments, "Honor your father and your mother,"[s] then added, addressing the Pharisees and scribes, "But you say, 'If anyone tells his father or his mother, What you would have gained from me is given to God, he need not honor his father.'"[t] With these words Jesus condemned a tradition which permitted a person by means of a vow to keep his property from being used for the relief of his parents. This was in his view a manipulation of the law of God.[11] When the disciples reported

---

[r] Lv 14:15–20. [s] Ex 20:12. [t] Mt 15:5.

[9] *Antiquities*, Book XIII, Chap. X, Sec. 6.

[10] Leo Baeck, *The Essence of Judaism* (New York: Schocken Books, 1961), 23.

[11] "Corban" (Mk 7:11) was a declaration that one's property was to be given to the Temple. Under this provision a clever or unprincipled person might retain the use of his property for his lifetime without assuming any obligation to his parents as required under the fifth commandment.

to Jesus that the Pharisees were offended by his teaching, he cautioned them against the Pharisees, calling them blind guides: "And if a blind man leads a blind man, both will fall into a pit." [u]

Peter's request, reported by Matthew, that Jesus explain the parable implied that although the Pharisees seemed to understand Jesus' points about blindness and what defiles, the disciples did not.[v] Mark's account is explicit at this point when Jesus said to them, "Then are you also without understanding? Do you not see that whatever goes into a man from outside cannot defile him, ... What comes out of a man is what defiles a man." [w]

The Gospels, especially Matthew, often give a distorted picture of the Pharisaic religion. It is unfortunate that in the Gospels most of the references to the Pharisees occur in accounts of Jesus' conflict with them. Since the Gospels were written during a period of conflict with Jewish authorities, they reflect the attitudes of the Christians of the time in which they were written. Much that was basic in Jesus' religious and moral teachings was acceptable to the Pharisees. Some of the Pharisees were intensely legalistic, as is evident from the Gospel accounts. However, others were more liberal in their teachings and quite unlike those pictured in the New Testament in conflict with Jesus. Jesus was not opposed to the Law, and his teachings on the whole were consonant with the basic Pharisaic doctrines. Like the great teacher Hillel, a Pharisee who was his near contemporary (ca. BCE 60–CE 10), Jesus stressed the spirit rather than the letter of the Law.

A more balanced account of the Pharisaic religion is provided by R. Travers Herford:

> The Pharisees are commonly regarded as the opponents of Jesus, the men who had reduced Judaism to such a condition that Christianity was the reaction by which the free prophetic spirit was liberated from the bondage of the Law. Historical justice is thought to be satisfied by remembering against them the stinging gibe — "Scribes and Pharisees, hypocrites." Yet, however natural this view may be, it is obviously inadequate and superficial. It takes no account of the reasons why the Pharisees were what they were, nor of the process by which they became such, nor of the fact that being what they were they have

[u] Mt 15:14. [v] Mt 15:12–16. [w] Mk 7:18–20.

The Question of Jesus' Identity

continued to order their lives by the same principles of religion and morality down to the present day. Nor does it take account of the consideration that if the Pharisees had been in their real nature and characters such as they are usually depicted, and Pharisaism the organised hypocrisy commonly supposed, such continued existence and unfailing vitality would have been impossible.[12]

THE DISCIPLES' BLINDNESS

According to Matthew, Jesus crossed by boat to the west side of the Sea of Galilee to the locality known as Magadan, which probably included Magdala. Then he was accosted by a group of Pharisees and Sadducees who had come to test him, requesting a sign from heaven — a Semitic idiom for a sign from God. But Jesus was distressed by their skeptical attitude and preoccupation with signs as proof. He complained that although they were able to discern the weather from the appearance of the sky, they could not interpret the signs of the times. His reply was, "An evil and adulterous generation seeks for a sign, but no sign shall be given to it except the sign of Jonah."[x] In Matthew, the sign of Jonah may be a reference to the burial and resurrection of Jesus. The expression "sign of Jonah" does not appear in Mark's Gospel. Mark reports that Jesus simply refused to give them a sign.[y] On another occasion Luke provides a possible explanation for Jesus' refusal — Jesus would present no sign except that which Jonah offered the men of Nineveh, namely, a call to repentance.[z] As the Assyrians of Nineveh had recognized God's demand in Jonah's call to repentance, so the Jews should recognize the authenticity of Jesus' proclamation. And since they were blind to this sign, it was unlikely that another more spectacular sign would convince them.[13]

At this point, according to Mark and Matthew, Jesus left for the other side of the sea and on the way the disciples discovered they had forgotten to bring bread.[a] Disturbed by their failure to grasp the full meaning of his comments about bread, Jesus rebuked

---

[x] Mt 16:4. [y] Mk 8:12. [z] Lk 11:29–32. [a] Mt 16:5; Mk 8:14.

[12] Robert Travers Herford, *The Pharisees* (Boston, 1962), 11f. See also Louis Finkelstein, *The Pharisees*, 3rd ed., 2 vols. (Philadelphia, 1962).

[13] This is suggested in G. B. Caird, *The Gospel of St. Luke* (Baltimore, 1963), 156.

them for their lack of discernment. "Take heed and beware of the leaven of the Pharisees and Sadducees." [b][14] Presumably the meaning of "leaven" here is the teaching of the Pharisees and Sadducees. The Sadducees had compromised teachings of the Jewish religion, especially in regard to Roman and hellenistic culture, in an effort to retain their status and control of the central religious establishment in Jerusalem. In Matthew the term "leaven" is used in Jesus' attack on the skepticism of the Pharisees about the Kingdom of God — their doubts about the coming of the Kingdom as a historical reality, and their doubt that God's anointed, the Messiah, would bring the Kingdom. Matthew regarded their disbelief as evidence of perversity. In his account of Jesus' discourse against the Pharisees, Luke explicitly referred to the leaven of the Pharisees, "which is hypocrisy." [c] Leaven or yeast works quietly from within. Often its presence is not known until it has transformed the "whole lump." [d] In either case Jesus' statement apparently meant that the skepticism of the Pharisees might work silently and insidiously among his disciples and be unnoticed until it dampened or killed their commitments and hopes.

In both Matthew and Mark, the disciples are represented as entirely missing the point of Jesus' warning. Their response that "we have no bread" [e] indicates their blindness. According to Mark, Jesus, aware of his disciples' discussion about bread, pressed the point. "Are your hearts hardened? Having eyes do you not see? . . . And do you not remember?" [f] Clearly in Mark's view they have not seen and remembered the disclosure of Jesus' identity in the events of feeding the multitude and his walking on the sea. Apparently, for Mark the disciples continued to believe in traditional Jewish ways and not as the Christians believed in Mark's day that Jesus was the Messiah, the Son of God. But Mark left the matter without further explanation. According to Matthew, however, Jesus explained his cryptic remarks so that "they under-

---

[b] Mt 16:6. [c] Lk 11:37–12:1. [d] 1 Cor 5:6. [e] Mk 8:16. [f] Mk 8:17f.

[14] In Mark (8:15), Jesus' warning is against the leaven of the Pharisees and Herodians. This represents a strange alliance between the Pharisees, whose interests were essentially religious rather than political, and a political party, the supporters of Herod.

stood." Matthew repeatedly softened Mark's account of Jesus' harshness toward the disciples, especially Peter. For example, in Matthew's Gospel Jesus made certain that the disciples understood that in the reference to the leaven he was not speaking literally of bread but was referring rather to the teaching of the Pharisees and Sadducees.[g]

The entire program of seeing or not seeing, believing or not believing, is of central importance to the Gospel writers and to the early Christian church whose views they expressed. But the failure of the early disciples was a special problem for Mark, involved as he was in the difficulties caused by the Jewish-Roman War and the subsequent disaster for the Jews and Christians. For Matthew and Luke the problem was different. In their day (ca. CE 80–90) both Judaism and Christianity were engaged in reconstructing their respective religious communities. The Jewish and Christian communities lived in close proximity, making claims, engaging in apologetics, and leveling charges and countercharges. This probably explains in part why there are excessive denunciations of the Pharisees in Matthew. The problem of the disciples' failure to understand Jesus, of primary concern in the Gospel of Mark, was in Matthew secondary to the blindness and perversity of the Pharisees. For Matthew, the Pharisees had become the prime example of stubborn disbelief, the primary concern of the church in his day. Also both Matthew and Luke faced the need to preserve the integrity and unity of the Twelve in order to support an organizational structure for the church.

From the beginning of his ministry, Jesus drew to himself the poor and afflicted. In an account reported only in Mark, friends at Bethsaida brought a blind man to Jesus and urged him to touch the man, apparently in the belief that his actual touch would restore sight.[h] Taking the blind man by the hand, Jesus led him out of the village, spat on his eyes, and then touched them. That the blind man saw is of special import to Mark. "Do you see anything?" At first the man saw, but not clearly. "Then again he laid his hands upon his eyes; and he looked intently and was

[g] Mt 16:6, 11f. [h] Mk 8:22–26.

restored, and saw everything clearly." In an earlier and very similar report found only in Mark,[1] Jesus healed a man who was deaf and could not speak plainly. In each case Jesus took the afflicted person aside in private and thereafter enjoined him to avoid publicity. And both healings were effected by the use of saliva and by touching.[15]

Those scholars may be correct who believe Mark was hinting at more than literal blindness here, that there is a symbolic relationship between the blind man, only gradually coming to see clearly, and the intellectual and spiritual blindness of the disciples. Under this quite plausible interpretation, the "seeing" and "hearing" are miracles of discernment.

THE CONFESSION AT CAESAREA PHILIPPI

The district of Caesarea Philippi north of Galilee was named in honor of the Emperor Tiberias Caesar by the tetrarch Herod Philip. It was called Philippi to distinguish it from the important Mediterranean seaport Caesarea, the Roman capital of Judea, which had been founded in honor of Augustus by Herod the Great. From the Sea of Galilee the journey to this area up the lower slopes of Mount Hermon was a distance of perhaps twenty miles. This was gentile territory and apparently Jesus withdrew there to seek seclusion and to ponder the question of his leadership following the death of the Baptist. This was a critical time for Jesus. His acceptance by the people had reached its height. Many of his followers, according to the Gospel of John, would have rallied to his leadership in revolt against Rome, but Jesus refused to be identified with national leadership or as a messiah of rebellion.[16] At this critical point when the understanding and loyalty of his dis-

---

[1] Mk 7:31–36.

[15] Some commentators have regarded these two healings as intended to indicate the fulfillment of the Isaiah prophecy that

> In that day the deaf shall hear
> the words of a book,
> and out of their gloom and darkness
> the eyes of the blind shall see (Is 29:18).

[16] Joseph Klausner, *The Messianic Idea in Israel*, trans. W. F. Stinespring, 3rd ed. (New York, 1955), 7f.

The Question of Jesus' Identity

ciples were crucial to him, Jesus questioned them about his identity. Their reply that some believed him to be John the Baptist returned from heaven or Elijah or Jeremiah or "one of the prophets" perhaps came as no surprise. For there was a popular Jewish tradition that Elijah or Elijah's spirit would return at the end of the age, and Jesus may have already encountered the belief that he was that ancient prophet returned.

Apparently Jesus' pressing concern at this point was not so much how others regarded him as what he meant to his own most intimate disciples. How did they regard him? What was their conception of the meaning of his proclamation and role in restoring the Kingdom? According to Mark, Peter replied, "You are the Christ."[j] The term *Christ* is from the Greek word *Christos* which translates the Hebrew term *Messiah* or one anointed. The Hebrew term does not refer to a divine being. It gradually became an honorific title signifying one who was chosen as God's agent.[17] All three synoptists reported that Jesus enjoined the disciples to tell no one of their belief that he was the Messiah. Although in these gospel portraits he clearly regards himself as having a messianic mission to prepare the way for the Kingdom, it is not clear that he considered himself to be *the* Messiah.

The account of Peter's confession, which has played a large role in Christian history, appears in all three of the synoptic Gospels. But only Matthew contains Jesus' reply to Peter. "For flesh and blood has not revealed this to you, but my Father who is in heaven. And I tell you, you are Peter, and on this rock I will build my church, and the powers of death shall not prevail against it."[k][18] Thus, Matthew claims, full responsibility as leaders of a continuing earthly community was given to Peter and those few disciples. Again, those scholars are probably correct who believe

---

[j] Mk 8:29. [k] Mt 16:17–19.

[17] M. Goguel, in interpreting John 6:66–69, observes of Peter's confession that "while it appears to be a statement of belief in Jesus, [it] is really and mainly a declaration of personal attachment and loyalty. So at the very moment when Jesus is being pursued by Herod, and deserted by many of his disciples, Peter proclaims the undying attachment and loyalty of the Twelve." Goguel, *Life of Jesus*, 385.

[18] On the term "church" in Matthew, see Fenton, *Matthew*, 266 and Norman Perrin, *New Testament* (New York, 1974), 175–77.

that these verses simply expressed the beliefs of the later church, added to the briefer account of Mark in order to support the church's claim that Peter held the keys of ecclesiastical authority.[19] In Mark's Gospel there is no report of a blessing on Peter or suggestion of revelation or church authority.

At this point, just as his intimate disciples were finally grasping the fact of his messiahship, Jesus confronted them with the awful announcement that he must suffer and die. Both Mark and Matthew describe Jesus' effort to lead his disciples from the popular view of the Messiah as a kingly figure to his view that it was his destiny to suffer for his people. A growing hostility against him was clearly evident in his encounters with religious leaders, and opposition from civil officials seemed inevitable. It was clear to the Gospel authors, writing many years after the fact, that Jesus' mission must be consummated in Jerusalem. And it was equally clear that the consummation required his death. Matthew says, "From that time Jesus began to show his disciples that he must go to Jerusalem and suffer many things from the elders and chief priests and scribes, and be killed, and on the third day be raised."[l] For all three synoptists Jesus was the Son of man and this was the first prediction of his passion.[m] In Mark, Jesus clearly explained that the Son of man was to be killed and after three days rise again. And Mark added that Peter took Jesus and "began to rebuke him."[n] For Peter, as for any Jew who believed in the messianic promise, the belief that the Messiah would be killed was an utter impossibility. Peter, the most outspoken and vigorous of the Twelve, apparently hoped, as did the others, for a Jewish Messiah who was a patriot, a deliverer, a soldier, an empire builder — a greater David. Jesus' rebuke of Peter, "Get behind me, Satan!" was a rejection of Peter's view of the messianic role. Also, this rebuke would have countered typical Jewish messianic expecta-

---

[l] Mt 16:21. [m] Mk 8:31; Lk 9:22. [n] Mk 8:32f.

[19] According to M. S. Enslin, the passage "thou art Peter and upon this rock" is "a late addition to the earlier account given in Mark." Matthew's addition of Jesus' blessing and exaltation of Peter is seen by Enslin as protecting the "worthiness" of Peter's image in the church against possible misunderstanding of Jesus' rebuke in Mark 8:32f. Morton S. Enslin, *The Prophet from Nazareth* (New York, 1968), 165.

tions which, presumably, were still being promoted by some Christians when Mark's Gospel was written.

THE TRANSFIGURATION

According to the synoptic writers, Jesus' appointed role was to suffer and be killed. His way would not win favor or friends but rather would generate hostile and powerful enemies. The end for Jesus would not be acceptance but rather disbelief, rejection, and death. Discipleship in the immediate future would be exceedingly dangerous and would require total loyalty and self-denial: "If any man would come after me, let him deny himself and take up his cross and follow me," [20] and "whoever loses his life for my sake and the gospel's will save it." [o] [21] These were the terms and promises of discipleship in the time of the early church. The synoptists conclude this episode with Jesus' statement that there would be some remaining who would not taste death before the Kingdom of God had come with power.[p]

According to Luke, about eight days after Peter's confession Jesus went into the mountains to pray, taking with him Peter, John, and James.

> And as he was praying, the appearance of his countenance was altered, and his raiment became dazzling white. And behold, two men talked with him, Moses and Elijah, who appeared in glory . . . .[q] [22]

Matthew referred to the events on the mountain as a vision.[r] The occasion for this event, the Transfiguration, may have been the

---

[o] Mk 8:34f. [p] Mk 9:1; Lk 9:27; Mt 16:28. [q] Lk 9:29-31. [r] Mt 17:9.

[20] The reference to the "cross" in Mark and Matthew is probably a warning of possible martyrdom. It was no doubt a post-crucifixion usage of the term that entered into the language of the church. Some, however, have thought that it may have been a rather common metaphor referring to the burdens of discipleship.

[21] This is one of the most fully attested sayings in the Gospels. It is stated in at least six different places: Mt 10:39; 16:25; Mk 8:35; Lk 9:24; 17:33; and Jn 12:25.

[22] This story recalls the circumstances of Moses' epiphany at Mount Sinai. According to Exodus "the cloud covered it [Mount Sinai] six days" and "he called to Moses out of the midst of the cloud" (Ex 24:16), and "he [Moses] came down from the mountain" and "the skin of his face shone" (Ex 34:29f.). See the parallel accounts in Mt 17:1-8; Mk 9:2-8; and Lk 9:28-36.

fall agricultural festival, *Sukkot* (the Festival of Booths), which celebrated the harvesting of grapes and other crops. The custom of dwelling in temporary huts was a reminder of God's protection during the Hebrews' early experience in the desert.[23] Also one aspect of *Sukkot* was the expectation that invisible guests might appear — illustrious figures from the past such as the Hebrew patriarchs Abraham, Isaac, or Jacob.

Moses' position as founder of the Hebrew religion, the author of Torah, was acknowledged by all Jews. Elijah, as champion of the people in whom God's spirit was expressed most powerfully, was second in the tradition only to Moses. Elijah was a redemptive figure of major importance in popular Hebrew-Jewish lore. His return in power before "the great and terrible day of the Lord" was prophesied in Malachi 3:1 and 4:5. In the Jewish apocryphal book Ecclesiasticus (The Wisdom of Jesus, Son of Sirach), Elijah is portrayed as a prophet "like a fire" whose word "burned like a torch." This explanation of his great miracles is the dominant theme of Sirach 48:1–12. In the end, Elijah was "taken up by a whirlwind of fire, in a chariot with horses of fire," and it was predicted that he would come "at the appointed time with warnings . . . to reconcile father and son and to restore the tribes of Jacob." [24] According to popular tradition, both Moses and Elijah were translated and taken into heaven, which gave them special status among Hebrew-Jewish heroes.

To the accounts of the other evangelists, Luke added that at the Transfiguration Moses and Elijah spoke to Jesus about his departure, which was to occur at Jerusalem.[s] Jerusalem, the very center of the Jewish religion, was of special importance in Luke's Gospel. Luke held that it was God's plan that the new Israel was

---

[s] Lk 9:31.

[23] According to some Jewish scholars, in an early biblical calendar of events *Sukkot* marked the end of one year and the beginning of the next (Ex 23:16). Robert M. Seltzer, *Jewish People, Jewish Thought: The Jewish Experience in History* (New York, 1980), 74. For a description of Sukkot and other traditional services and feasts of the Jews, see Yaacov Vainstein, *The Cycle of the Jewish Year* (Jerusalem, 1953).

[24] Many of the miracles of the Old Testament are connected with the popular folklore of Elijah (1 Kgs 17–19; 2 Kgs 1:3–2:14).

to originate in Jerusalem with Jesus' rejection of the "old" institutions of Judaism which had been identified with that ancient city.

In keeping with Jewish tradition respecting *Sukkot*, which was a thanksgiving festival, Peter proposed making three booths, places of honor, for Jesus and the two guests.[25] Mark's explanation of Peter's proposal suggests that Peter's concept of Christ, perhaps representing the views of early Jewish-Christianity, was mistaken. Peter's conditioning in the "old way" led him to conclude that Jesus stood in the Hebrew-Jewish tradition with other great figures of the past. "Let us make three booths, one for you and one for Moses and one for Elijah." [t] [26]

Mark's comment that Peter "did not know what to say" is consistent with his rather negative assessment of Peter.[u] Luke replaces this with the phrase, "not knowing what he said," as though to indicate that Peter was entirely innocent of any misunderstanding about Jesus' unique and superior status.[v] Then a voice came out of a cloud which had covered them, saying, "This is my beloved Son; listen to him." [w] It is significant that the three Synoptics agree that after the voice was heard Moses and Elijah vanished and only Jesus remained. For the Gospel writers, says G. B. Caird, "There was no need for three tabernacles: the divine glory, imperfectly and partially revealed under the old dispensation, was now being gathered up in the sole person of this Jesus who had set his face to go to Jerusalem. He stood alone, and the cloud of the divine presence overshadowed him and his." [27]

According to Mark, as Jesus and his disciples descended the mountain, he charged them "to tell no one what they had seen,

[t] Mk 9:5. [u] Mk 9:6. [v] Lk 9:33. [w] Mk 9:7.

[25] The Sukkot festival requirement in Leviticus 23:39–43 that "all that are native in Israel shall dwell in booths" for seven days is claimed by some Jewish scholars to have been grafted to the historic occasion of the Exodus (Ex 12:37; 13:20). The biblical commandment to dwell in booths helped preserve the Israelite memory as nomads in the wilderness. See Zeev Meshel, "An Explanation of the Journeys of the Israelites in the Wilderness," *Biblical Archaeologist* 45 (1982), 1:19f.

[26] According to Deuteronomy 18:15–19, it was predicted that "God will raise up for you a prophet like me [Moses] from among you."

[27] Caird, *Luke*, 133.

until the Son of man should have risen from the dead." [x] At this point Mark commented that the disciples were questioning together what resurrection from the dead meant, and they asked Jesus why the scribes say "that first Elijah must come." [28] This is the occasion in Mark for Jesus to make a significant statement about Elijah. Elijah "does come first to restore all things . . . . But I tell you Elijah has come, and they did to him whatever they pleased." [y] Matthew underscored the fact that Elijah had already come but the people did not recognize him. Matthew concluded that the disciples understood that Jesus was speaking to them of John the Baptist.[z] Thus, Matthew explicitly identifies John the Baptist as the Elijah who had *already* come. This point is not sufficiently clear in the text of Mark, where one might suppose that Jesus played the Elijah role. However, it is clear in Matthew that it is the Baptist who is identified as Elijah and not Jesus. Matthew's reference to the Baptist may be seen simply as a strategy to support his contention that Jesus *is* the Christ and not a lesser figure such as John, who was to prepare for the coming of the Messiah.

In the Synoptics a central theme connects the confession at Philippi, the Transfiguration, Jesus' censure of the crowd following his healing of an epileptic boy, and the second prediction of his passion: the failure of understanding and belief and the power of positive belief. Prior to Jesus' return from the mountain, the father of an epileptic boy had asked Jesus' disciples to cast out the demon (or dumb spirit), but they were not able to do so.[a] Jesus anguished at their failure and lamented, "O faithless generation, how long am I to be with you?" Then the father petitioned Jesus, "If you can do anything, . . . help us." Jesus quickly responded, "All things are possible to him who believes." He then exorcised the evil spirit from the boy.[b]

After the events at Caesarea Philippi and at the Transfiguration, a sense of urgency apparently came upon Jesus. Mark re-

[x] Mk 9:9. [y] Mk 9:11–13. [z] Mt 17:13. [a] Mk 9:18. [b] Mk 9:19–26.

[28] "Elias," the Graecized name employed in the New Testament portion of the King James Version, is rendered "Elijah" in the Revised Standard Version, the New English Bible, and most modern translations.

ported that they passed through Galilee and "he would not have anyone know it." [c] [29] This was the occasion for Jesus' second prediction of his passion. He said of the Son of man that "they will kill him; and when he is killed, after three days he will rise." [d] Mark concluded the episode with another severe rebuke of the disciples because they did not understand Jesus' prediction and were afraid to ask him about it.[e] The failure to understand on the part of the disciples does not appear in Matthew's account. Clearly in his view, the disciples were distressed *because* they did, in fact, grasp the meaning of Jesus' declaration.[f] Luke attempted to soften Mark's conclusion about the disciples' failure with his explanation that the purport of Jesus' words was concealed from them, "that they should not perceive it." [g]

---

[c] Mk 9:30. [d] Mk 9:31; Mt 17:23. [e] Mk 9:32. [f] Mt 17:23. [g] Lk 9:45.

[29] The Gospel of John reports that "after this [Peter's confession] Jesus went about in Galilee; he would not go about in Judea, because the Jews sought to kill him" (Jn 7:1).

CHAPTER 7

Jesus and the Messianic Consciousness

Messianism as a belief and expectation played an important role in the Judaism of the first century CE, but it was by no means the most important theme of the religion or the most basic concern of the Jewish people. In all probability Jesus was more concerned with the coming of God's Kingdom than with messianic claims. He saw his primary mission as proclaiming the coming of the Kingdom and preparing the Jews for that eschatological event. Nevertheless, the question of his own messianic consciousness is basic to any understanding of him. That the Christian church has regarded him as the prophesied Messiah is obvious. But what were his beliefs and claims about himself and his authority?

THE MESSIANIC IMAGE

Did Jesus think of himself as the founder of a new religion? What was his belief regarding his relationship to God? Did he conceive of himself as the Messiah, the anointed of God, who was to re-establish the Davidic kingdom? Or did he believe that he was the "Son of man," who was to appear in the clouds of heaven according to the predictions of some apocalypticists? There are widely differing opinions on these matters, and most scholars agree that determining and understanding Jesus' concept of himself is one of the most difficult problems in New Testament analysis. According to the Gospels Jesus referred to himself as the Son of man. But did he regard himself as a prophet, as the Son of God, or as the Messiah?

At the outset it must be recognized that there is no simple solution to this problem. Some scholars approach the matter with preconceived theological commitments which affect their judgment.

Although full objectivity is impossible, treating an issue such as this demands a maximum of freedom from presuppositions and the predisposition of religious sentiment. It is, of course, common to think of Jesus as being fully aware of a divine nature and calling from his early youth — that suddenly, after the so-called silent years of preparation, he appeared in Galilee filled with the Spirit and promptly announced his messiahship, that he performed miracles and wonders to prove his claim and then proceeded to call all men to accept him. This simple theme, the product of centuries of piety, must be subjected to serious examination in any effort to establish an authentic picture of Jesus.

From its beginning, the Christian tradition has combined elements of both the religion *of* Jesus, the living person who walked the paths of Galilee and Judea, and the religion *about* Jesus, the resurrected Savior-Christ. In a relatively short time, Jesus the historical figure became the Christ of Christian faith. In consequence, it is difficult to distinguish the theological interpretations of many writers from the primary data — Jesus' actual religious life and teachings insofar as these can be discerned in the ancient documents through scholarly effort.

Two basic interests seem to have predominated in the early Christian communities. Certain groups collected those sayings of Jesus which expressed principally his ideals about morals and religion. This collection, probably at first simply an oral tradition, was apparently transmitted in written form rather early. Such a written recollection may have been accessible for much of the non-Markan material used by Matthew and Luke. Others, however, seem to have had a special interest in recalling the deeds rather than the teachings of Jesus. To them Jesus was more hero than prophet or teacher. His power over evil spirits, control of the forces of nature, possession of the Holy Spirit, and finally his resurrection demonstrated his divinely given powers and authority and was convincing evidence of God's approval. The image of Jesus portrayed by the Gospel writers obviously has a heroic coloring. Those who saw Jesus in this light were not interested in his personal religious biography except as it helped to establish him as a more worthy object of devotion. His words and deeds were selected and interpreted to substantiate their beliefs about him and to develop confidence in his role as the founder of their religious movement and church.

It was essential to the early Christian leaders that Jesus' authority be established in the Christian community. Since Jesus had been elevated by them to a position second only to God, attempts were made to find suitable titles indicative of his exalted status. Consequently, he was conceived as having authority, wisdom, and divine commission and support of an order far above that of Israel's greatest prophets.

Even the words of Jesus, according to the evangelists, had tremendous power. As a boy of twelve he amazed the learned men of the Temple.[a] During his temptation experience, he rebuked the power of Satan by the power and authority of his words.[b] When he spoke in the synagogue, his audience was astonished by his new teaching and his presumption of authority and they marveled at his words.[c] According to the Gospels, the evil spirits early recognized Jesus and his authority but were commanded by him not to disclose the secret of his identity and powers.[d] Also, in the synoptic view of Jesus, especially as set forth in Mark, the disciples were unable to grasp his full significance. However, for Mark, Matthew, and Luke no uncertainty was present in the mind of Jesus himself. Always he is represented as having full knowledge of his identity, his death, and his victorious resurrection.[e]

Accounts of miracles are another indication of the evangelistic belief in Jesus' authority and power. Descriptions of the confidence with which he calmed the sea and winds, his self-assurance as he walked upon the water or fed the five (or four) thousand,[f] and many of the accounts of less spectacular miracles, such as healing the sick and casting out evil spirits, were probably preserved if not actually generated to demonstrate the uniqueness of Jesus' authority and as evidence of his divine power. For the gentiles especially, these marvelous accounts greatly heightened the character of Jesus. Indeed, they were probably intended for use among the gentiles, for there the Christian movement was in serious com-

---

[a] Lk 2:46f. [b] Mt 4:4, 7, 10; Lk 4:4, 8, 12. [c] Mk 1:22, 27; Lk 4:22.
[d] Mk 1:24f.; 3:11f. [e] Mk 8:31f. [f] Mk 6:30–44; Mk 8:1–10.

petition with other religions that were grounded in various ways in the miraculous and in some cases had impressive similarities to Christianity.[1]

The synoptic Gospels, the principal sources on Jesus' life and teachings, were written by men looking back upon him and the scenes in Galilee from the perspective of early followers of Jesus after Pentecost and at the beginning of the church movement. The infant church was concerned with providing a firm foundation for the faith and with winning converts. Consequently, the Gospels probably express only part of what Jesus intended or what others thought about him during his lifetime. They reflect at best what the early, post-Easter Christian community believed about Jesus and his teachings.[2]

THE QUESTION OF PAROCHIALISM AND UNIVERSALISM

Many Christians still believe that Jesus intended to found a church apart from the synagogue, that his purpose was not simply to expound a new or revitalized message but to found a new religion. However, the record of the Gospels does not substantiate this view. As far as is known from the Gospels, the Temple, synagogue, and scriptures, the three basic religious institutions of Judaism in Jesus' time, were accepted by Jesus without question. This is a clear indication that he was a devout, practicing Jew. According to the Gospels, Jesus frequently attended the synagogues — "And he went throughout all Galilee, preaching in their synagogues."[g] According to Luke 4:16, Jesus regularly attended the synagogue on the Sabbath. There is no evidence that he opposed the practice of circumcision, a basic requirement of the Law. The reverence he had for the Temple is demonstrated most forc-

---

[g] Mk 1:39.

[1] For a sample of texts from Hellenistic, Roman, and Jewish religion and religious philosophy of the period of the beginning of Christianity, see C. K. Barrett, *The New Testament Background* (New York, 1961). Also, see R. Bultmann, *Primitive Christianity in Its Contemporary Setting*, trans. R. H. Fuller (New York, 1956), and F. F. Bruce, *Jesus and Christian Origins Outside the New Testament* (Grand Rapids, 1974).

[2] Morton Smith's *Jesus the Magician* (New York, 1978) is a fascinating scholarly account of negative, polemical attitudes toward Jesus in the ancient world.

ibly in that dramatic event which began his final ministry in Jerusalem.ʰ The Temple, in which the Jewish religion was centralized and which was the most sacred place of the Jews, had such profound meaning and value for Jesus that he objected violently to its being made a house of profit. He challenged the Temple authorities knowing full well the seriousness of his action and the dire consequences which might follow.

The Gospels show that Jesus had a typical Jewish reverence for the scriptures, the Old Testament. When a lawyer asked how he might inherit eternal life, Jesus answered, "What is written in the law? How do you read?" ⁱ Frequently when questioned, Jesus stated his answer in the form of a counterquestion or quoted directly from the Law or the Prophets. When asked, "Which commandment is the first of all?" Jesus quoted from Deuteronomy 6:4 and Leviticus 19:18.ʲ Though he was critical toward and sometimes in opposition to the religious tradition of his people, that tradition was sacred to him and central to his own religious life and purposes.

No one has expressed the character of Jesus as a believing, practicing Jew better than the influential Jewish scholar and leader Leo Baeck in *Judaism and Christianity*. As described in the old Gospel, Jesus was

> a man with noble features who lived in the land of the Jews in tense and excited times and helped and labored and suffered and died: a man out of the Jewish people who walked on Jewish paths with Jewish faith and hopes. His spirit was at home in the Holy Scriptures, and his imagination and thought were anchored there; and he proclaimed and taught the word of God because God had given it to him to hear and to preach . . . . In this old tradition we behold a man who is Jewish in every feature and trait of his character, manifesting in every particular what is pure and good in Judaism. This man could have developed as he came to be only on the soil of Judaism; and only on this soil, too, could he find his followers as they were. Here alone, in this Jewish sphere, in this Jewish atmosphere of trust and longing, could the man live his life and meet his death — a Jew among Jews. Jewish history and Jewish reflection may not pass him by nor ignore him.[3]

ʰ Mk 11:15–19. ⁱ Lk 10:26. ʲ Mk 12:28–31.

[3] Leo Baeck, *Judaism and Christianity*, trans. Walter Kaufmann (New York, 1958 and 1966). On Jesus' identification with the Jewish religion of his time, see

Another aspect of the question of Jesus' concept of himself pertains to the universal versus parochial quality of his teaching. Most Christians assume that Jesus' teachings were universal and ageless. But did he really intend to advocate what today is commonly understood as a universal religion? Was his message intended for all persons at all times, or simply for his Jewish contemporaries? The early Christians were bound to insist upon some kind of universalism as authentic to his teachings if for no other reason than to justify the existence of the gentile church. Probably Matthew had this in mind when he recorded Jesus' final great commission to his disciples: "Go therefore and make disciples of all nations." ᵏ But Jesus seems to have kept himself within the national boundaries of his own religion. There were exceptions, but these seem to have been accidental and not the result of any intentional missionary interest or message to the gentiles. Mark indicates that while in Tyre and Sidon, foreign cities, Jesus preferred not to be identified.ˡ Several of Jesus' sayings also confirm this view: "And in praying do not heap up empty phrases as the Gentiles do; for they think that they will be heard for their many words. Do not be like them." ᵐ It has already been noted that the missionary charge to the disciples recorded in Matthew 10:5f. seems to be consistent with Jesus' choice of his field of activity: "Go nowhere among the Gentiles, and enter no town of the Samaritans, but go rather to the lost sheep of the house of Israel." And probably even more significant was Jesus' reply to the request of the Syro-Phoenician woman, "Let the children first be fed, for it is not right to take the children's bread and throw it to the dogs." ⁿ

Some students of the New Testament have questioned the authenticity of this last harsh statement because it apparently contradicts the later commitment of the church to a universal Christianity. Certainly it conflicts seriously with the common conception

---

ᵏ Mt 28:19. ˡ Mk 7:24. ᵐ Mt 6:7f. ⁿ Mk 7:27.

also Joseph Klausner, *Jesus of Nazareth*, trans. H. Danby (New York, 1926); Samuel Sandmel, *Judaism and Christian Beginnings* (New York, 1978); Günther Bornkamm, *Jesus of Nazareth*, trans. Irene and Fraser McLusky (New York, 1960); Geza Vermes, *Jesus the Jew* (Philadelphia, 1973) and *Jesus and the World of Judaism* (Philadelphia, 1983); and Michael Grant, *Jesus* (New York, 1977).

of Jesus' humanity and compassion. That the statement is authentic, however, can hardly be doubted. Its authenticity is strongly supported by the fact that it was included by Mark in the Gospel account of the actions and sayings of Jesus despite its obvious opposition to the character of the early church. Notwithstanding the universal meaning and applicability of most of Jesus' moral and spiritual teachings, his own words show him as a somewhat parochial Jew of his own time fully absorbed in the task of proclaiming his message to his own people.

SON OF GOD

What is the meaning of the various terms employed by the evangelists as designations for Jesus — Son of God, Davidic Messiah, Suffering Servant, or Son of man? How should they be interpreted in reference to him? It is clear that for the Gospel writers Jesus was *the* Son of God; they call him the Son of God numerous times. Mark uses this expression in the beginning verse of his gospel, in the mouth of unclean spirits, and in the mouth of the Roman centurion after Jesus died on the cross.° Many of the relevant passages place strong emphasis upon the number of testimonies to Jesus' divine sonship, testimonies which were the chief ground for the claim of his divinity. However, a careful examination of such passages, especially those from Mark, indicates that many of them may not have originated in the Jewish milieu in which Jesus lived. The messianic concept implied by all three synoptic Gospels in their use of the appellation "Son of God" indicates that it was more Greek than Jewish in origin and reflected doctrinal developments well after the time of Jesus.

The expression "Son of God" was applied in Jewish literature to a righteous or favored individual whose life reflected a close proximity to the conception of God as a moral being. Of course, the idea that the "Son of God" was a divine being in the sense in which God was conceived as divine was blasphemous to the intensely monotheistic Jews. It seems unlikely that Jesus regarded himself as "the Son" in this sense.

° Mk 3:11; 5:7; 15:39.

That Jesus did not consider himself to have the divine status that is expressed by some Christian creeds is evident from several of his sayings. According to Mark's account, for example, as Jesus was setting out upon a journey, a man approached and asked him the question, "Good Teacher, what must I do to inherit eternal life?" Jesus' reply, "Why do you call me good? No one is good but God alone,"ᵖ clearly indicates his Jewish orthodoxy — that worship and service to God, and *him only*, in accordance with Deuteronomy 6:13f., was basic in his life.⁴ This view is further substantiated by the statement in Mark: "and whoever receives me, receives not me but him who sent me."ᑫ It is attested also by his prayer to the Father in the garden of Gethsemane.ʳ ⁵

SON OF DAVID

Some Jews of the first century CE assumed that the Messiah would be a descendant of David, the great king of their early national history. Jesus is purported on several occasions to have been acclaimed "son of David" by those who saw in him the fulfillment of their messianic and "golden age" hopes. These acclamations, however, are neither numerous nor strongly attested. The most definite reference is found in Mark's account of the healing of Bartimaeus.ˢ ⁶ Other instances in the Gospel of Matthew are probably from a later date and may reflect the position of the church in Matthew's day.ᵗ For example, Matthew's account of Jesus' entry into Jerusalem seems to be a description of a triumph with crowds gathered shouting "Hosanna to the Son of David!"ᵘ By contrast, Mark's account is more modest, and the specific Davidic acclaim is not so present.ᵛ But the clearest evidence that Jesus rejected the concept of the Messiah as the son of David appears later in a scriptural debate with the Pharisees: "How can

---

ᵖ Mk 10:17f. ᑫ Mk 9:37. ʳ Mk 14:36. ˢ Mk 10:47f. ᵗ Mt 9:27; 15:22. ᵘ Mt 21:9. ᵛ Mk 11:9f.

⁴ Luke and Mark essentially agree on this matter, but Matthew apparently modified his account in order to avoid contradiction between Jesus' statement and the early Christian concept of his divinity. Cf Lk 18:18f. and Mt 19:16f.

⁵ Cf. Mt 26:39 and Lk 22:42.

⁶ Cf. Mt 20:30f. and Lk 18:38f.

the scribes say that the Christ is the son of David? ... David himself calls him Lord; so how is he his son?"[w][7] To describe Jesus as David's son attributed David's military powers to him and suggested that he planned a military campaign against the oppressors of the Jews. This view, however, denies much of the tradition about Jesus — his rejection of political aspirations implied in the narrative of the temptations[x] and his sayings about service and turning the other cheek.[y] Had Jesus aspired to a leadership of force, he quite surely would have instructed his disciples differently; he would have sought public popularity and, like the Zealots, would have aroused his followers against the Romans. There seems to be little evidence, regardless of what others thought, that he identified himself as a son of David.

THE SUFFERING SERVANT

Another view, and one which seems to be increasingly popular among New Testament critics, is that which presents Jesus as the Messiah who saves by suffering. A concept of redemptive suffering for others was not new to the Jews in Jesus' time. It was familiar in Jewish thinking in connection with problems of the suffering of the righteous as attested, for instance, in the Book of Job, in Jeremiah, or in Deutero-Isaiah.[z] However, most Jewish scholars do not regard the Suffering Servant passages (Is. 40–55) as messianic or as pertaining to any individual. Rather, as in the case of Abraham, the servant is seen as representing the entire people of Israel. Although the covenant was in the form of a promise to Abraham, it was not a covenant with an individual or with a collection of different individuals over time but rather with an entire people. Also, according to this view, Deutero-Isaiah was not looking forward to a distant future time for the coming

---

[w] Mk 12:35, 37. [x] Mt 4:4–11. [y] Mt 5:39–42. [z] Is 42:1–4; 49:1–6; 52:13–53:12.

[7] Cf. Mt 22:41–46; Lk 20:41–44. This piece of rabbinic argumentation is based upon Psalm 110, which is attributed to David. The position taken by Jesus in this passage clashes directly with the correction of Matthew and the early church that Jesus claimed to be the Son of David. Had it not been regarded as authentic, the author probably would have either omitted it from his text or altered it to fit his general point of view.

of the Servant but to a time within his own historical perspective.⁸ Christians, of course, have traditionally regarded the Suffering Servant passages of Isaiah as referring prophetically to Jesus as the Messiah-redeemer of Israel. The Christian Messiah, the crucified Christ, was to be seen as meek, gentle, sinless, and afflicted and punished as the bearer of the guilt of the world, descriptions consonant with Deutero-Isaiah's conception of the Suffering Servant.

SON OF MAN

The Synoptists, presumably because of their Jewish orientation, interpreted Jesus' messianic role as advancing a revolutionary doctrine which even his intimate disciples found difficult if not impossible to understand. Jesus' role as suffering servant was combined with the eschatological Son of man who would come to power at the end of the age. Before the end, "the Son of man must suffer many things"; ᵃ "And how is it written of the Son of man, that he should suffer many things and be treated with contempt?"; ᵇ and "For the Son of man also came not to be served but to serve, and to give his life as a ransom for many." ᶜ One variation on this theme holds that on the final day Jesus would be taken away and hidden by God until the time when he would appear as the Son of man. Realizing the inevitability of his suffering, Jesus would have concluded that his hiding would be accomplished through his death and that he would conquer death before his return.⁹

The expression "Son of man" presents one of the most complicated elements of the question of Jesus' self-identification. The significance of the term is difficult to assess from its use in Jewish literature. That the Gospel writers were convinced of the impor-

---

ᵃ Mk 8:31. ᵇ Mk 9:12. ᶜ Mk 10:45.

⁸ For a discussion of the Servant passages in Deutero-Isaiah, see Bernard Anderson, *Understanding the Old Testament*, 3rd ed. (Englewood Cliffs, New Jersey, 1975), 456–70.

⁹ This is the view suggested by Rudolf Otto in *The Kingdom of God and The Son of Man* (London, 1938) and earlier with some additional variations by Albert Schweitzer in *The Mystery of the Kingdom of God* (New York, 1914).

tance of this designation for Jesus is clearly indicated by the persistence with which they record him referring to himself as the Son of man. There are more than sixty passages in the four canonical Gospels in which the expression "Son of man" appears. However, the term does not have the same meaning in each instance.[10] Which "Son of man" passages, if any, are authentic to Jesus? If he did in fact use the expression, how did he apply it to himself, or to others? And if referring to himself, did he simply mean "man" or "mortal man" as in Ezekiel, or did he allude to the future, as in the case of the apocalyptic figure portrayed in the Book of First Enoch. In Enoch, the Son of man is the Messiah who is to come.

The Christian use and meaning of the expression "Son of man" was probably influenced by First Enoch and the Old Testament Book of Daniel written probably in the second century BCE.

> I saw in the night visions,
> and behold, with the clouds of heaven
> there came one like a son of man.[d] [11]

Does this term "a son of man" refer to an individual messiah, or to the entire people of Israel as the messiah? The latter seems to be implied in the more complete context of Daniel 7:18, 22, 27, where the interpretation of Daniel's dream is given to him:

> The saints of the Most High shall receive the kingdom, and possess the kingdom for ever, . . . judgment was given for the saints of the Most High, and the time came when the saints received the kingdom. . . .

[d] Dan 7:13.

[10] The expression the Son of man was apparently not in general use in the early church. It does not appear in Paul's letters or in the general letters. This title seems to have been used sparingly by the early church fathers. Justin and Eusebius are notable exceptions. "The First Apology of Justin, The Martyr," in *Early Christian Fathers*, ed. C. C. Richardson (Philadelphia, 1953), 1:275; Eusebius, *Ecclesiastical History*, Book 2, Chap. 23.

[11] The setting for the Book of Daniel is the Babylonian exile (587–539 BCE). The visions of Daniel, purporting to come from this early date, predict future events in Israel's history. However, the book itself is considered by most competent scholars to have been composed several centuries later in the very difficult period of persecution under Syrian rule during the reign of Antiochus IV, Epiphanes.

> And the kingdom and the dominion
> and the greatness of the kingdoms
> under the whole heaven
> shall be given to the people of the
> saints of the Most High; . . .
> and all dominions shall serve
> and obey them.

Based upon the Hebrew text of Daniel, Joseph Klausner holds that this latter meaning was intended, that two documents, Deutero-Isaiah (Isaiah 40–66) and Daniel, had significantly altered the Jewish conception of messiah prior to the time of Jesus. In these two books, he maintains, the messiah is not one man, a person, from the house of David or from "any other royal line, but *the whole people Israel*." According to this view Israel itself is the servant-messiah, "a light of the Gentiles" and "the servant of the LORD," spoken of in Deutero-Isaiah.[12] However, the Greek text the Septuagint, which the early Christians adopted as their scripture, provides a different reading: "on the clouds of heaven came one like a son of man . . . and there was given him power . . . ." From the early Christian point of view, this text explicitly indicated that the Son of man was a particular individual, the "Elect One, who is to come." This is the interpretation popularized by certain Jewish writers in the First Book of Enoch and adopted by the synoptic writers.[13] As Klausner has indicated, only in the Gospels (Mt 24:15 and some manuscripts of Mk 13:14) is Daniel referred to as "the prophet." In the Septuagint, the Book of Daniel is included with the Prophets. In the traditional Jewish canon, Daniel is included with the Writings, the Hagiographa.

How then are the "Son of man" passages to be understood? Did Jesus use this term as a self-designation? How was the ex-

---

[12] J. Klausner, *The Messianic Idea in Israel*, trans. W. F. Stinespring (London, 1956), 241–43. This view is supported by the French scholar Charles Guignebert, *Jesus*, trans. S. H. Hooke (New York, 1956), 270–79.

[13] R. H. Charles has shown that early Christian literature followed the Son of man idea set forth in the Parable Section of First Enoch. Chapters xxxvii–lxxi are probably the basis for other ideas besides the Son of man — demonology, future messiah, judgment, and resurrection — which are presupposed by the authors of the Synoptic Gospels. See R. H. Charles, *The Book of Enoch* (London, 1960).

pression interpreted by the early church? First, there are a number of passages in which the title "Son of man" appears to have been used by the Gospel writers as an editorial addition. The expression "Son of man" was substituted for Jesus' self-designation "I." For example, in Mark 8:27 the simple question "Who do men say that I am?" is altered in the parallel text of Matthew to read "who do men say that the Son of man is?" [e] [14] In another instance the context of the passage suggests that Jesus may have been making a straightforward declaration about his eating and drinking, which is modified in Matthew and Luke to read "The Son of man came eating and drinking." [f] [15]

In addition to its use as a title, there are passages in the Synoptics in which "Son of man" may be used as a generic designation meaning simply "man" or "mortal man." The expression was understood in this way in the Book of Ezekiel when, according to the author, God addressed the prophet. "And he said to me, 'Son of man, stand upon your feet, and I will speak with you.' " [g] One passage in the Synoptics is Mark 2:27f., "The sabbath was made for man, not man for the sabbath; so the Son of man is lord even of the sabbath." [16] Jesus' meaning may be that man as mortal man is master of the sabbath — his point being, of course, that the well-being of persons takes precedence over sabbath observances. Another view is that Mark 2:28 represents the comment of Mark himself on the meaning of the episode for the Christian community.[17] A similar interpretation may be applied to Mark 2:10, "that the Son of man has authority on earth to forgive sins." [18] It

[e] Mt 16:13. [f] Mt 11:19; Lk 7:34. [g] Ez 2:1; 3:4, 17; 4:1.

[14] The parallel in Lk is 9:18. Cf. Mt 19:28 with Mk 10:29 and Mt 20:28 with Lk 22:27. There are some instances of editorial additions in Lk. and Mt. for which there are no parallel materials in Mark (cf. Lk 6:22 and Mt 5:11; Lk 12:8 and Mt 10:32). Also, Luke employs the title in some passages for which there are no parallels in either Matthew or Mark (Lk 18:8; 19:10; 21:36; 22:48; and 24:7).

[15] Other examples include Mt 8:20 and Lk 9:58. Also, compare Mt 12:32 and Lk 12:10 with Mk 3:28.

[16] Cf. Mt 12:8 and Lk 6:5.

[17] William L. Lane, *The Gospel According to Mark* (Grand Rapids, Michigan, 1974), 120.

[18] Cf. Mt 9:6 and Lk 5:24. In this connection, Mark employs the expression, "the sons of men" in 3:28.

has been suggested that Jesus did not intend to say that he forgave their sins but rather that "a man [i.e., anyone so called by God] may have power on earth to forgive sins." [19] Clearly the synoptic writers intended to reinforce Christian beliefs about Jesus as the Messiah-Son of man by making it appear that Jesus frequently and in a number of different contexts employed the expression "Son of man" to designate his own messianic claim.

The most important Son of man passages are those already alluded to in which Jesus is purported to have referred to himself as the Son of man — the one to suffer and be raised from the dead. These are the passages upon which the question of Jesus' messianic self-consciousness really depends.[20] For example, in his charge to the Twelve prior to sending them out, Jesus declared "you will not have gone through all the towns of Israel, before the Son of man comes." [h] Later, at Caesarea Philippi, Jesus announced to his disciples that the Son of man must suffer and be rejected. On these occasions, Matthew took for granted that the messianic claim ascribed to Jesus included his identification as "Son of man" and that as such he must go to Jerusalem and "suffer many things." [i] [21] Also, following the Transfiguration, according to Matthew and Mark, Jesus charged his disciples that they tell no one about the vision "until the Son of man is raised from the dead." [j] And at the Last Supper, Jesus proclaimed that the Son of man "is betrayed" and that "the Son of man goes as it is written of him." [k] [22]

There is no doubt that the evangelists, Matthew, Mark, and Luke, identified Jesus as the Son of man who was to go to Jerusalem to suffer and be rejected. Nevertheless, the question about Jesus' meaning in the use of the expression remains unclear, and

[h] Mt 10:23. [i] Mt 16:21. [j] Mt 17:9; Mk 9:9. [k] Mt 26:24.

[19] Barnabas Lindars, *Jesus Son of Man* (London, 1983), 102.

[20] Mk 8:31; 9:9, 31; 10:33f.; 14:21, 41 and Mt 10:23. Albert Schweitzer holds that these passages are authentic to Jesus and that "this designation [Son of man] must have been peculiarly apt as a rendering of his messianic consciousness." *Kingdom of God*, 190f.

[21] Cf. "Son of man" passages in Mt 16:13–23; Mk 8:27–33 and Lk 9:18–22.

[22] See Mk 14:21. Luke modified the statement to read, "For the Son of man goes as it has been determined" (Lk 22:22).

the best of New Testament scholars differ in their speculations and opinions on the subject.[23] Howard Kee's resolution seems to have considerable support. He has advanced the view that Jesus did announce the coming of the Son of man as part of his proclamation about the Kingdom of God but that he did not identify himself as that person. After Jesus' death, when the Christian communities were required to clarify and reconstitute the major doctrines of their faith, "they came to believe that Jesus was himself the Son of Man, whose coming . . . they still awaited," and this claim was inserted into the Christian Gospels.[24]

When all of the passages containing the expression "Son of man" are considered in the context of Jewish thought and discourse of the first century CE, it seems unlikely that Jesus designated himself as the messianic eschatological figure. It seems probable that he made some references to the phrase in an impersonal sense meaning "man" or that he had in mind another person — the Son of man who was to come on the clouds. For many Jews who accepted apocalyptic doctrine, a person as an intermediary was not essential for establishing God's Kingdom. God could bring the Kingdom if Israel was faithful in her role as a model before all nations. Here the Christian church significantly altered the common Jewish eschatological conception and adopted the view of Daniel and Enoch that God would send a person as his agent to accomplish this task. In the rapidly developing Christology of the early church, Jesus became that person.

---

[23] M. Goguel holds that at some point Jesus came to know "that he was called to be the Son of man," *The Life of Jesus* (New York, 1949), 578. Norman Perrin, on the other hand, maintains that "Jesus himself did not speak of the Son of man as eschatological judge at all . . . . All apocalyptic Son of man sayings," he says, "fail the test of the criteria for authenticity of sayings of Jesus," *The New Testament, An Introduction* (New York, 1974), 76f. In his work *Jesus* (p. 278), C. Guignebert maintains that, "even though Jesus may have employed the expression 'Son of Man,' there is not one passage to indicate that he used it as a special and characteristic designation of himself." "In short," he continues, "there is no use of it which cannot be interpreted in a way entirely different from the pseudo-Danielic 'Son of Man.'"

[24] H. C. Kee, *Jesus in History*, 2nd ed. (New York, 1977), 135. Kee's hypothesis follows the suggestions of H. E. Todt in *The Son of Man in the Synoptic Tradition* (Philadelphia, 1965), 222–83.

JESUS AS PROPHET

So far, three main points bearing on Jesus' identity come into focus. (1) For at least some Christians, perhaps many, the idea of "prophecy" meant vision-predictions of the future on the model provided by Jewish apocalyptic literature, Daniel and the Book of Enoch being primary examples. (2) In accepting the Old Testament as scripture, the early Christians adopted the Septuagint, a translation which supported their claim that the Messiah was to be an individual person whom they had identified as Jesus. (3) The Suffering Servant from Deutero-Isaiah (especially Isaiah 53) identified by Christians as Jesus, was joined in the Christian mind with Daniel's supernatural agent of salvation, the "Son of man," who was to come at the end of the age.

The Christian view of Jesus as Christ thus embraced several of the popular Jewish interpretations of "messiah": Son of David, Suffering Servant, and Son of man in the supernatural sense. All of these were eventually subsumed under the peculiarly Christian title, "Son of God." It appears, therefore, that the Gospel writers were themselves clear about Jesus' identity. In almost every account of miracles and occasions for teaching about the Kingdom, Jesus' special authority and status as Messiah (Christ), Son of man, Suffering Servant, and Son of God are proclaimed or strongly implied. According to the evangelists, even the demons understood the source of Jesus' power. But the question still remains — what did Jesus himself claim? What role did he envision for himself as he proclaimed the coming of God's Kingdom?

Did Jesus claim only to be a prophet — a *nabi* in the Hebrew-Jewish tradition? This is a common question, and the usual reaction to it by many Christians is confusion and frustration, because they misunderstand the full import and significance of the term "prophet." To a Jew of the first century CE, "prophet" was the highest office. A prophet stood next to God himself in importance and, for many Jews in Jesus' time, a "prophet" had more religious significance than any of the various messianic designations. A prophet was one who brought forth the word of God. Fortunately, some traces of what might have been Jesus' original claim as prophet remain in the Gospel texts. For example, in the story of Jesus' rejection at Nazareth, his prophetic role seems to have been assumed — "A prophet is not without honor, except in his own country, and among his own kin, and in his own house." [1] At the conclusion of Luke's Sermon on the Plain, after Jesus entered Capernaum and healed the centurion's slave[m] and raised the widow's son at Nain,[n] he was invited to the Pharisee's home to share a meal. After the prostitute anointed Jesus' feet, the Pharisee thought to himself, "If this man were a prophet, he would have known who and what sort of woman this is." [o] Why would the Pharisee wonder if Jesus was a prophet unless this was Jesus' claim or at least a claim made for him by his followers?

On the way through the district of Caesarea Philippi, Jesus "asked his disciples, 'Who do men say that I am?' And they told him, 'John the Baptist; and others say, Elijah; and others one of the prophets.'" [p] [25] When Jesus announced his resolve to go to Jerusalem, he is reported by Luke to have said, "Nevertheless I must go on my way . . . ; for it cannot be that a prophet should perish away from Jerusalem." [q] Matthew records that at a later time when he entered Jerusalem, all the city was stirred saying, " 'Who is this?' And the crowds said, 'This is the prophet Jesus from Nazareth of Galilee.' " [r] Also, after Jesus had been teaching in the Temple, when the chief priests and the Pharisees tried to arrest him, they "feared the multitudes, because they held him to be a prophet." [s]

In Luke's account, at Jesus' trial before the Jewish council some of those present, after hearing his responses, "mocked him and beat him; they also blindfolded him and asked him, 'Prophesy! Who is it that struck you?' " [t] [26] There would have been no reason for his adversaries to taunt Jesus in this way unless "prophet" and "prophecy" were a central part of his claim or the claim of others concerning him.

---

[1] Mk 6:4. [m] Lk 7:1–10. [n] Lk 7:11–17. [o] Lk 7:39. [p] Mk 8:27f. [q] Lk 13:33. [r] Mt 21:10f. [s] Mt 21:46. [t] Lk 22:63f.

[25] Mt 16:14 adds "Jeremiah" to those specified by Mark. Also, see Jn 4:19, "Sir, I perceive that you are a prophet."

[26] Cf. Mt 26:68; Mk 14:65. The parallel in Matthew lacks any reference to the blindfolding.

Finally, in Luke's report of the appearances of the risen Lord, Jesus approached two of "the apostles" on their way to Emmaus and asked what they were discussing. They answered, "Concerning Jesus of Nazareth, who was a prophet mighty in deed and word before God and all the people." [u]

But why in the Gospels does not Jesus by his own statements make his prophetic role more obvious? What socio-psychological forces operating at the time the Gospels were written account for this omission? One such factor is the evangelists' own views and confessions about Jesus as the Christ. For the Gospel writers, the Jewish concept of "prophet," important as it was, did not convey adequately the meaning and significance of Jesus. Consequently, other titles — Christ, Son of man, Son of God — were added. "Prophet" remained in the texts as an appendage, submerged among the seemingly more important confessional titles and for the most part overlooked and unexplained.

But if Jesus did regard himself as a prophet, what meaning did he attach to "prophet"? Many commentaries interpret Jesus as standing within the main stream of the Hebrew-Jewish tradition along side the great prophets of the eighth, seventh, and sixth centuries BCE — Amos, Hosea, Isaiah, Jeremiah, and Ezekiel. In the early period before the monarchy was established, prophets were assumed to be persons possessed by God's spirit to act and speak in his name. The Books of Samuel and Kings tell about "bands of prophets"; Samuel and Saul were also thought at times to have God's spirit and power to direct the people.[v] Moses, Samuel, Elijah, and Elisha, in the old Hebrew tradition, were spokesmen for the deity in a particularly active sense — they used their power to heal, control nature, and raise the dead.[w] Because they possessed God's spirit, they were pivotal figures in changing and shaping the historical-political events which determined the fate of Israel.

In Judea in Jesus' time it was common, at least among the leading Jewish parties, to believe that the day of prophets and prophecy in the ancient form had passed. This transformation had taken

[u] Lk 24:10, 19. [v] 1 Sm 10:5–13. [w] 1 Kgs 17:1–24.

place after the Exile as Hebrews returning to Palestine struggled with the difficult problems of reconstruction. They inherited several Yahwist traditions and institutions — prophets and prophecy, monarchy and priesthood. Each was considered to be authoritative and was accorded legitimacy, and each had its proponents and sponsors contending for control of the community. The prophetic authority, with its emphasis upon freedom and spontaneity after the model provided by Moses, Samuel, and Elijah, and later by Amos, Isaiah, and Jeremiah, was regarded by some to threaten anarchy. Defenders of the monarchy and of the priesthood maintained that institutional security was impossible so long as prophets such as Amos were allowed complete freedom to speak for God. The continuity of the religious, social community could not be guaranteed on the basis of such conduct. Subsequently, a new class of priests arose who claimed to be the descendants and heirs of Aaron. They succeeded in establishing the Pentateuch as the standard for Jewish faith and practice and in the process edited and shaped its content to legitimize their authority. Eventually, the Aaronides achieved full control over the Temple and its sacrificial cult.[27]

In Jesus' day prophets like Elijah or Amos were not expected to appear in Judea. The time for uncontrolled, unrestrained displays of God's word and power had come to an end. The divine word was incorporated in the Pentateuch to be interpreted by the scribes and other learned religious leaders within the control and restraints of the religious establishment. But it should be pointed out that competent scholars of both the Old and the New Testaments have become increasingly aware of differences among

---

[27] This view is proposed by Ellis Rivkin. "The problem," he says, "was prophetic authority . . . . If the worship of Yahweh was to endure, and a Yahwist community be established, then prophecy had to go. But how?" According to Rivkin, to establish national stability a major revolution took place within the Jewish community in Judea some time after 445 BCE. A priestly class, descendants of Aaron, was created to replace the priests of the tribe of Levi whose claim to authority was based on Deuteronomy. All power was eventually transferred to this Aaronide priest class, "its rights being grounded in immutable laws revealed by Yahweh to Moses on Mount Sinai, laws investing the Aaronides with absolute power." Ellis Rivkin, *The Shaping of Jewish History* (New York, 1971), 20f.; see especially chaps. 2 and 3.

the various traditions, North and South, between Galileans and Judeans.[28] Apparently, certain themes of the ancient Ephraimitic tradition were kept alive in the folklore of Galileans. One included the account of prophets who, when possessed by God's spirit, intervened in the social-political life of the nation. Elijah, for example, went to Mount Carmel and by the power of the Hebrew deity defeated the Phoenician baalim. When Jezebel threatened his life, he fled. In his solitude he recommitted himself to God and set out to reaffirm Israel's commitment to the Sinai-Mosaic Covenant and tradition.[x] As Elijah of old went up to Mount Carmel and with God's spirit and power turned the course of the nation around, so according to the Gospel writers, Jesus set out for Jerusalem to confront the religious officials who controlled the Temple and religious life in Judea. In the spirit of Elijah he would reform Israel's religion and restore her integrity as a Jewish nation on the foundation of a new standard in anticipation of God's Kingdom.

Moses and Elijah figure prominently in the Gospel narratives. Statements in Deuteronomy about the central position and status of Moses were well known to the evangelists. Moses as prophet-lawgiver is the prototype: "There has not arisen a prophet since in Israel like Moses."[y] According to Deuteronomy, Moses spoke to the Israelites of a future day when, "The Lord your God will

---

[x] 1 Kgs 18:1–46; 19:1–21. [y] Dt 34:10.

[28] It is the theory of several prominent Old Testament scholars that a new theology and a new covenant were inaugurated in the South during the reign of Solomon. According to this theory, the royal court of Solomon advanced a theology of King and Temple which claimed that God had elected Zion as the place of his sanctuary and promised that the House of David should rule there as long as they kept his covenant. In this connection, Psalm 78 is presented to show that the northern Israelites (the tribe of Ephraim) did not keep the covenant:

> He rejected the tent of Joseph,
>   he did not choose the tribe of Ephraim;
> but he chose the tribe of Judah,
>   Mount Zion, which he loves (Ps 78:67f.).

For a brief account of this view, see Anderson, *Understanding the Old Testament*, 351, 519–25. Rivalry between the northern tribes and the tribe of Judah may be seen in the account of Absalom's revolt (2 Sm 15:1–18:8). This rivalry, involving the preservation of different strains of the Hebrew-Jewish tradition, may have persisted between Galileans and Judean Jews into the time of Jesus.

raise up for you a prophet like me from among you, from your brethren — him you shall heed." [z]

In the confession at Caesarea Philippi, reference was made to the fact that some persons thought Jesus was "Elijah," [a] and in the synoptic accounts of the Transfiguration a short time later, Moses and Elijah appeared and talked with Jesus. Jesus' response to the disciples' inquiry about the coming of Elijah is based on a text from Malachi, "Behold, I will send you Elijah the prophet before the great and terrible day of the Lord comes." [b] Then, as already indicated, Jesus declared, "But I tell you that Elijah has come." [c] One might conclude from this Markan account that in the Transfiguration the spirit of Elijah, which in ancient times was passed on to Elisha,[d] had been transferred from Moses and Elijah to Jesus. Jesus was the one like Moses and the prophet Elijah to come with God's spirit and power to restore Israel.[29]

The "Spirit" is the leading theme in the Gospel concept of the prophets, especially in the Gospel of Luke. The Holy Spirit is said to have come upon Jesus at his baptism. Mark recorded that afterward the Spirit "drove him out into the wilderness." [e] Luke says that, full of the Holy Spirit Jesus "returned from the Jordan, and was led by the Spirit." [f] Luke continues that when Jesus was in Nazareth in the synagogue, he opened the Book of Isaiah[g] where it was written, "The Spirit of the Lord is upon me." [h] According to Luke, it was the Spirit which empowered the prophets that Jesus possessed in full measure during his life and was poured out upon the Christian church following his Ascension.[i]

According to Luke, as Jesus and his disciples were preparing to go up to Jerusalem, Jesus sent messengers ahead into the Samaritan villages "to make ready for him," but "the people would not receive him." [j] Learning of this, James and John proposed to Jesus that they bid fire come down from heaven and consume the offenders. The wording used in Luke alludes to the action of

[z] Dt 18:15. [a] Mt 16:14; Mk 8:28; Lk 9:19. [b] Mal 4:5. [c] Mk 9:13.
[d] 1 Kgs 19:19; 2 Kgs 2:8–15. [e] Mk 1:12. [f] Lk 4:1. [g] Is 61:1f. [h] Lk 4:17–19.
[i] Acts 2:32f. [j] Lk 9:52f.

[29] This interpretation connecting prophet, spirit, and Elijah with Jesus was suggested by M. S. Enslin in *The Prophet from Nazareth* (New York, 1961), 57–69.

Elijah in 2 Kings 1:10, 12, and significantly some scribes added the explanatory phrase "as Elijah did" to some texts of Luke 9:54. But Jesus rebuked them.[k] Again, some ancient texts of Luke add Jesus' explanation for the rebuke: "You do not know what manner of spirit you are of; for the Son of man came not to destroy men's lives but to save them." It is apparent that Luke's interest was not in the idea of Spirit as sheer power, as in the Elijah and Elisha stories, but in Spirit as the power to save.[30]

There is justification for holding that Jesus was a prophet in the northern tradition of Elijah and Hosea. Like them, he felt the presence of God's Spirit and power to restore, to reform, and to save Israel. But in many respects his teaching on discipleship, his declarations about the failure of insight among his opponents, and his criticism of Jewish leaders for promoting the forms and externals of religion to the neglect of the weightier matters — the moral virtues of justice and mercy — are similar to the themes emphasized by the classical Judaic prophets. In these respects Jesus clearly stood in the tradition of Amos, Micah, Hosea, Isaiah, and Jeremiah.

---

[k] Lk 9:55.

[30] One is reminded here of the Elisha story. As the prophet journeyed to Bethel some small boys jeered at him and "he cursed them in the name of the Lord. And two she-bears came out of the woods and tore forty-two of the boys" (2 Kgs 2:23f.).

CHAPTER 8

On the Way to Jerusalem

From passages in the Gospels of Matthew and Luke it is evident that Jesus intended to go to Jerusalem, where he expected to encounter severe opposition that would lead eventually to his death.[a] Some Pharisees warned Jesus to leave Galilee because Herod wanted to kill him. Jesus replied that he would go to Jerusalem, not because he feared Herod but, according to Luke, because "it cannot be that a prophet should perish away from Jerusalem."[b] And when the time came for the final proclamation of the Kingdom of God, Jesus went into Judea beyond the Jordan.[c] [1] For the evangelists, the events on the way to Jerusalem, the preaching and teaching about the Kingdom, sustained and reinforced the beliefs and practices of the early church at the time the Gospels were written. For Matthew especially, Jesus was the model for the true believer to follow. His teaching as he journeyed to Jerusalem to celebrate the Passover became a manual of instruction for Christian disciples seeking the Kingdom of Heaven.[2]

Luke's Gospel points to a time beyond the ministry of Jesus. It is a gospel of anticipation, a foreshadowing of what is to come in Luke's second volume, the Acts of the Apostles, his account of the beginning of the church after Jesus' death and resurrection. In Luke Jesus' ministry sets the stage for the Christian church, for the interim period before the End. According to Acts, at the Feast of Pentecost the Spirit came upon the early followers of Jesus and gave them the power to proclaim the gospel to all nations of the world.

[a] Mt 16:21. [b] Lk 13:33. [c] Mt 19:1f.

[1] See also Mk 10:1.

[2] Mt 19, 20.

Much of Luke's material on the meaning of discipleship in the Kingdom appears in a special section (9:51–18:14), which begins with Jesus' resolve to go to Jerusalem. Luke departs in 9:51 from the Markan format and follows a different tradition perhaps based on "Q" and his own source, sometimes referred to as "L." Some New Testament scholars hold the view that Luke's formula — on the "way to Jerusalem" [d] — is an artificial, literary structure. G. B. Caird, for example, is of the opinion that Luke's chronology is "full of topographical inconsistencies." Jesus started out from Galilee by the short route to Jerusalem through Samaria but arrived by the longer route through Jericho. On the way he appeared at the home of Martha and Mary in Bethany, a few miles from Jerusalem,[e] but later Luke locates Jesus on the borders of Samaria and Galilee.[f] [3] Whatever the order of events was historically, Luke's reconstruction of them, as Caird points out, preserves "the dramatic tension of his story by constant reminders of the crisis which lay ahead." [4] It also provides an account of the growing opposition to Jesus, his discourses on the end of the age, the costs of discipleship, and the meaning of alienation and acceptance in the coming Kingdom.[5]

[d] Lk 9:51; 13:22; 17:11.   [e] Lk 10:38; Jn 11:1.   [f] Lk 17:11.

[3] G. B. Caird, *The Gospel of St. Luke* (Baltimore, 1963), 139.

[4] Ibid.

[5] Many of the events and teachings treated in Luke's special section have parallels in Matthew, and some have parallels in Mark. Most of the parallel passages in Matthew appear earlier in his order of events: The Lord's Prayer, on seeking and finding, the Parable of the Lamp (Lk 11:1–36), and Jesus' comments about being anxious (Lk 12:22–34) and agreeing with one's accuser (Lk 12:57–59) appear in Matthew's collection, the Sermon on the Mount (Mt 5–7). Other parallels relate to Jesus' instruction to the Twelve (cf. Lk 10:1–16, 21f. with Mt 9:37f.; 10:7–16; 11:25–27) and to growing opposition to Jesus and his responses — on the Beelzebul controversy, the return of the evil spirit, the sign of Jonah (cf. Lk 11:14–23, 24–26, 29–32 with Mt 12:22–30, 38–42, 43–45), and Matthew's account of Jesus' ministry in the critical period following the Transfiguration and the first predictions of his passion. This includes Jesus' statements on the meaning of discipleship, on causing another to sin, on reproving another and forgiving, and on faith (cf. Lk 9:57–62; 14:25–35; 17:1–6 and Mt 8:19–22; 10:37f.; 18:6f., 15; 17:20). All of these passages appear earlier in the chronology of Matthew than in Luke.

Important parallels to Luke's special section also appear later in Matthew's Gospel: Jesus' confrontation with Jewish officials, the scribes and Pharisees (cf. Lk 11:37–12:1 and Mt 23:4, 6f., 13, 23, 25–27, 29–31, 34–36); his comments on

COMMITMENT TO THE KINGDOM

As Jesus and his disciples went toward Jerusalem they were approached by three men, each declaring his intention to become a disciple.[g] Jesus responded with dramatic statements about the urgency of the time and of the cost of total commitment: conflicts in loyalty will inevitably arise, and commitment to the Kingdom requires extreme personal sacrifices. Such commitment means the subordination of family ties and affections to discipleship, the loss of public approval, and great risks to personal security. To the first man Jesus said, "the Son of man has nowhere to lay his head"; to the second who wished first to go and bury his father, "Leave the dead to bury their own dead"; and to the last who desired to say farewell to his family, "No one who puts his hand to the plow and looks back is fit for the kingdom of God."[h] Matthew mentions only the first two claimants to discipleship and identifies the first as "a scribe," who addresses Jesus as "teacher."

LUKE'S PARABLES

The Unjust Steward

The Gospel of Luke introduces a number of parables into the account of the journey to Jerusalem that help readers better understand the message of Jesus. In the Parable of the Unjust Steward a rich man called his steward to account for wasting his goods and threatened to remove him from his office.[i] However, the rich man later commended his steward for the shrewd way in which he provided for himself in this crisis. Originally this was probably a parable of warning — that the impending disaster required vigorous and decisive action. The steward resolutely pursued his goal of providing for his own future. The lesson was drawn from this that the "sons of light," who may have been too passive about

---

[g] Lk 9:57. [h] Lk 9:57–62; Mt 8:19–22. [i] Lk 16:1–13.

---

the lawyer's question (cf. Lk 10:25–28 and Mt 22:34–40; also Mk 12:28–31) and on watchfulness and faithfulness (cf. Lk 12:35–46 and Mt 24:43–51); his lament over Jerusalem (cf. Lk 13:34f. and Mt 23:37–39); his Parable of the Banquet (cf. Lk 14:15–24 and Mt 22:1–10); and the description of the Day of the Son of man (cf. Lk 17:22–37 and Mt 24:26–28, 37–41).

the urgent needs of the time, should in their time of impending crisis emulate the zeal, the boldness, and the tenacity of the "sons of this world" (or worldly men, exemplified by the unjust steward).

The Servant's Wages

However, after the sense of urgency about the imminent end passed, the parable of the Servant's Wages was probably used by the church in Luke's day to teach the proper attitude of a Christian toward riches. Luke extended his interpretation of the parable to include a warning against divided loyalty — "no servant can serve two masters .... You cannot serve God and mammon" (riches).[j] The parable also attacked the Pharisees, who were "lovers of money" and interpreted their own prosperity as God's reward for righteous living.[k] The Parable of the Servant's Wages in 12:47f. and in 17:7–10 illustrated the same point — commitment to the Kingdom requires more than merely doing one's duty. More is expected of those to whom much is given. An employer does not thank his employee because he did only what was expected.[l]

The Rich Fool and the Great Banquet

In the Parable of the Rich Fool[m] Jesus warned against covetousness: a person's life does not consist in the abundance of possessions. And on humility[n] Jesus taught that a true disciple must be totally devoted to God and not choose places of honor or seek to exalt himself. A humble servant does not invite guests to his banquet whom he expects to return his invitation — his relatives, rich neighbors, or business associates — but rather those who are unable to repay — the poor, the maimed, and the blind.[o]

The Friend at Midnight and the Unjust Judge

Joachim Jeremias ties Luke's twin parables, The Friend at Midnight[p] and the Unjust Judge,[q] to the parables in both Mark and Matthew of the Mustard Seed, and Leaven, the Seed Growing Secretly, and the Sower. All assure believers of the coming

[j] Lk 16:13. [k] Lk 16:14f. [l] Lk 17:10. [m] Lk 12:13–21. [n] Lk 14:7–14.
[o] Lk 14:12–14, 15–24. [p] Lk 11:5–8. [q] Lk 18:1–8.

of God's Kingdom. These later parables, according to Jeremias, were occasioned by doubts arising among the followers of Jesus when he failed to elicit a satisfactory response from the people and their leaders. According to Jeremias, these parables exhibit confidence that God's hour is near and that the End is already implicit in the beginning as fruit is implicit in the seed.[6]

The point of the twin parables in Luke is not, as is often assumed, with the importunity of the petitioners — the friend and the persistent widow — but rather with the certainty and speed of God's vindication. If the friend and the persistent widow prevail, then surely God will hear and will respond. It is unthinkable that God who is just should refuse to fulfill his promise.

Sending the Seventy

This expectation of fulfilled promises was borne out in Luke's report of the sending of the seventy, or according to the earliest manuscripts, the seventy-two.[r] But the story, which is not found in the other Gospels, poses some problems. Is the account of the seventy a historical event from Luke's special source which was not available to the other evangelists? Or is it an editorial statement in which Luke intends to convey an important symbolic meaning? If the latter, what do the seventy or seventy-two symbolize? Caird suggests that the "seventy" may have been derived from the table of nations in Genesis Chapter 10 (said by the rabbis to have been seventy in number) and interpreted by Luke as a prophecy to be fulfilled among the seventy nations of the gentile world. More likely, he continues, it is based upon the seventy (or seventy-two, including Nadab and Abihu) elders appointed at Sinai to assist Moses, who went up with him to the Mountain.[s] According to Caird, Luke's deliberate symbolism establishes the Moses and Elijah theme.[7] In his account Luke presents Jesus as

---

[r] Lk 10:1–16. [s] Ex 24:1, 9.

[6] J. Jeremias, *The Parables of Jesus*, trans. S. H. Hooke, rev. ed. (New York, 1963), 146–60.

[7] Caird, *Luke*, 144. The language of Luke's drama of salvation involving the fall of Satan (10:17f.) is similar in some respects to the statement in John's Gospel, "Now is the judgment of this world, now shall the ruler of this world be cast out" (12:31).

one like Moses, sharing responsibility for the Kingdom with his seventy assistants, and as one like Elijah, possessing the spirit and power of Elijah to maintain continuity with the ancient Mosaic covenant.

The seventy returned with joy over the fact that even demons were subject to them. According to Luke, Jesus in response to their high expectations recounted to them his vision of the End in which Satan would fall as swiftly as lightning from heaven.[t] But, he cautioned them, although they had been given power, and Satan's dominion on the earth would surely collapse, the time of the End was still in the future. This Lukan theme reaches its climax with Jesus rejoicing in the Holy Spirit and with his prayers of gratitude that the vision of God's purpose, up until this point committed to him alone, would be shared with his disciples: "Blessed are the eyes which see what you see."[u]

Several of the parables in Luke's special section may originally have been directed at Jesus' opponents: The Good Samaritan, the Rich Fool, the Lost Sheep, the Lost Coin, the Prodigal Son, and the Rich Man and Lazarus.

The Good Samaritan

In Jesus' time, the Samaritans were excluded from normal association with the Jews, and a faithful Jew ordinarily would not accept a kindness from them. Yet in Luke's parable,[v] it is a Samaritan who is acclaimed by Jesus as righteous in contrast to a Levite and a priest who passed by on the other side of the road. The importance of this story is fully appreciated only if it is understood that the animosity between Jews and Samaritans was deep seated and long standing. The Samaritans were apparently descendants of colonists imported into Samaria by the Assyrians following their deportation of large numbers of the people of the northern Kingdom of Israel after Samaria, the capital city of Israel, fell to the Assyrians in 722 BCE.[w] The imported colonists intermarried with the remaining Hebrews of the Kingdom of Israel and were eventually assimilated into the Hebrew religion, but were

---

[t] Lk 10:17–20.　[u] Lk 10:23f.　[v] Lk 10:29–37.　[w] 2 Kgs 18:9–12.

never accepted as orthodox by the Jews of the later post-exilic period.

Luke connected the Parable of the Good Samaritan with his account of the lawyer's question. "Teacher, what shall I do to inherit eternal life?"[x] In response to Jesus' reply that the Law required one to love one's neighbor as one's self, the lawyer, according to Luke, in an effort to portray himself as righteous, asked Jesus "and who is my neighbor?"

The point of the parable turns on two details: that the robbers left their victim not dead but "half dead" and that the two principal characters other than the Samaritan—a priest and a Levite—were highly placed in the Jewish religion as functionaries of the Temple in Jerusalem. The love of God and one's neighbor, enjoined in Deuteronomy and Leviticus, was especially incumbent upon them. In the parable, both the priest and Levite passed by, perhaps because they assumed the stricken person to be dead and were concerned with the ban against touching the deceased and risking defilement. This suggests that in Luke's interpretation of the Jewish religion, concentration on purity and holiness had come to mean exclusiveness and separation. As a result the term "neighbor" had come to carry a limited sense of responsibility. It applied only to those who belonged to the same religious community and were committed to the same beliefs and practices. Others were regarded as not belonging, not neighbors in that sense, but as outsiders, and in some instances were regarded as sinners. The parable, interpreted for church use in Luke's day, is perhaps the most widely known of all Jesus' parables. It is remarkably effective in impressing listeners with the meaning of loving service by showing that it transcends institutional policy and rules and parochial prejudices. One's neighbor is any person who is in need and that person's need lays a claim upon the love and good will of others.

The Mary and Martha episode which appears in Luke 10:38–42 has been widely misunderstood.[8] Through the centuries, Chris-

---

[x] Lk 10:25–28.

[8] There are at least five variant readings of the text in which Jesus replies to Martha, "one thing is needful" (Lk 10:42), all of which appear to be later glosses probably intended to describe Mary as an example of the superior, contemplative life. Joseph A. Fitzmeyer, *The Gospel According to Luke* (New York, 1985), 894.

tian interpretations have focused upon Mary, the idealized spiritual person, rather than Martha, who is portrayed as worldly and materialistic. However, a close study of the Lukan text reveals that this story is a sequel to the Parable of the Good Samaritan and that Luke intended Martha to be the central figure. She was the hostess attending to all of the details required of her in that role. But, like so many well-meaning and ordinary people tending to their jobs, she had a somewhat pedestrian attitude toward life. She was preoccupied with the particulars of her daily tasks to the extent that all else was overlooked; she was "distracted with much serving." Like the priest and the Levite, she was lost, not as they were in the mesh of rules and regulations of the official religion, but rather in the details, the little chores, the routine of being a good housekeeper and hostess.

The Lost Sheep and Lost Coin

On another occasion when Jesus was teaching tax collectors and sinners, the Pharisees and scribes complained, "This man receives sinners and eats with them." [y] Jesus responded with the Parables of the Lost Sheep and of the Woman Who Lost a Coin.[z] These are parables on being lost and found. Who does not search for a lost sheep? Or a lost coin? According to Luke, Jesus announced that there is joy in heaven over one sinner who is reclaimed.

The Two Sons

This motif is further emphasized in the story of the Prodigal Son, which follows in the Lukan chronology and is one of the best known parables.[a] However, the commonly employed title, "Prodigal Son," does not adequately describe the story or express its central theme. The parable is about "a man who had *two sons*." One selfishly and recklessly chose to spend his inheritance in "loose living," and the other was the model of an obedient son. Yet in a calculating and subtle way he too was selfish. He chose to serve his father, possibly to earn a richer inheritance at his father's death.

[y] Lk 15:1f. [z] Lk 15:3–10. [a] Lk 15:11–32.

When the younger son's inheritance was spent, he was compelled to herd swine to survive. In his despair, he gained a new perspective on life; he repented and determined to return to his father's house as a hired servant. His father was overjoyed with his return and bestowed upon him all of the tokens of forgiveness — "the best robe . . . a ring on his hand, and shoes on his feet." A banquet was prepared for the reinstatement of this son who "was dead, and is alive again," who "was lost, and is found." Here the focus of the parable shifts from the younger to the elder son. Advised of his brother's return, he was resentful and refused to attend the celebration feast. He angrily complained to his father, "you never gave me a kid . . . . But when this son of yours came . . . you killed for him the fatted calf!" Observe the language which Luke so skillfully employs here — "this son of yours" not "my brother." Obviously, the elder son was thinking of that portion of the estate which he now stood to lose. The younger brother was getting more than was just, and his father was being unfair in his dealings with them. The father concludes the parable: "It was fitting to . . . be glad, for this your brother was dead, and is alive; he was lost, and is found."

The opponents of Jesus, according to Luke, are like the elder brother whose claim upon the inheritance was planned and calculated as in a business contract. They claim God's promises through adherence to customs; they had earned the rewards of God through righteousness. Yet they remain estranged from God because they ignore God's way with sinners, the way of restoration through mercy and forgiveness.

The Rich Man

Luke's assessment of the Jewish leaders, especially the Pharisees and Sadducees, is clearly visible in the Parable of the Rich Man and Lazarus.[b] This unnamed rich man is often referred to as Dives, the Latin for "rich." When the rich man, who feasted sumptuously every day, died, he went to Hades. When Lazarus,

[b] Lk 16:19–31.

who ate crumbs from the rich man's table in order to survive, died, he was taken by the angels to Abraham's bosom. In Hades the rich man saw Abraham far off and petitioned him for relief from his miserable plight. But Abraham pointed out to him that a "great chasm" had been "fixed" between them which neither he nor the rich man could cross. The rich man then appealed to Abraham that Lazarus be sent to warn his five brothers of their fate. But Abraham refused on the grounds that the evidence was clear and sufficient and signs or miracles would not convince those whose minds were already set and insensitive to the truth.

The rich man had taken his salvation for granted. His mind was closed to any claim other than that he was a descendant of Abraham. Moreover, he assumed he had fully carried out the rules for righteous living prescribed by the established religion. The point of the parable is that being a descendant or son of Abraham does not by itself guarantee one's salvation.

The Ten Lepers

This theme — that the failure of discernment led to insensitivity, then to a lack of humility, and finally to ingratitude and arrogance — was spelled out further in Luke's story of the Ten Lepers[c] and in the Parable of the Pharisee and the Tax Collector.[d] Jesus was passing between Samaria and Galilee on the journey to Jerusalem, and as he entered a village ten lepers approached and called to him from a distance. Jesus instructed them to show themselves to the priests. Then, Luke adds, "as they went they were cleansed." But only one, a Samaritan, turned back to express his gratitude to God. And Jesus asked, "Where are the nine? Was no one found to return and give praise to God except this foreigner?" It was not the priests who healed the lepers nor did Jesus claim credit for the miracle. Rather, he declared that their faith had cured them. Moreover, it is significant that for Luke, the Samaritan was the only one who realized that his healing was brought about through the loving mercy of God. He was not only cleansed from leprosy but transformed in spirit.

[c] Lk 17:11–19. [d] Lk 18:9–14.

The Pharisee and the Tax Collector

Jesus told the Parable of the Pharisee and the Publican to those "who trusted in themselves that they were righteous and despised others." [e] Two men went up into the Temple to pray, but the Pharisee stood apart and prayed, "God, I thank thee that I am not like other men." He had done all that was legally required — he fasted twice a week and paid a full tithe. But the tax collector, anxious about his wrongdoing and his standing in the sacred place, prayed, "God, be merciful to me a sinner!" And, Jesus said, "this man [the tax collector], went down to his house justified rather than the other."

Like the rich man, the nine lepers who were cleansed, the unworthy servants who were satisfied to do only what their duty required, and the elder son in the Parable of the Prodigal Son, the Pharisee took for granted his privileged status before God on the basis of his meticulous observance of the rules of formal religion. His piety and claim to righteousness as a son of Abraham rested upon the foundation of institutional religion. He had done all that was expected of him and was therefore secure in his belief that all was well between him and God.

THE IMMINENCE OF THE KINGDOM

When certain Pharisees asked Jesus when the Kingdom of God was coming, he replied, "The kingdom of God is in the midst of you." [f] The question of what Jesus meant by this statement has been a persistent problem in New Testament study. The phrase employs the Greek term *entos*, which can be translated as "in the midst of" or "within." There can be little doubt that Jesus as a Jew, albeit a Galilean Jew, held a popular eschatological view of the Kingdom: that its coming was imminent, probably within his lifetime. Indeed, this urgent faith may explain his determination in Jerusalem to confront the Jewish religious leaders in an effort to bring the nation to repentance and effect a restoration of commitment to the ancient Mosaic covenant. No doubt Jesus' original point, made in response to pharisaic skepticism about the literal-

---

[e] Lk 18:9. [f] Lk 17:21.

ness of his proclamation of the Kingdom, was that the seeds of its beginning were to be found in the commitment and integrity of the believers themselves. But the critical problem for Luke and for the followers of Jesus in Luke's day was Jesus' execution and the apparent failure of his promise that the Kingdom would come. Luke's interpretation of the declaration "the kingdom of God is in the midst of you" seems to address this problem. For Luke this was the capstone of Jesus' teaching. He joins it with Jesus' proclamation about the day of the Son of man.[g] Luke understood Jesus' proclamation as meaning that to be a disciple was to have a present vision of God's Kingdom, a vision which demanded a total commitment to God's will and to the practical ideals enjoined by the Jewish faith. Being "rich toward God" [h] and serving one's fellows are the meanings of the Kingdom which is already at work within you or "in the midst of you." Luke's interpretation provided the foundation upon which the early church faced the paradox of the crucified Christ and his promise of the Kingdom.

REJECTION OF JESUS

A more general problem relates to Jesus' rejection by Judean leaders, who supported the charges brought against him. No doubt the fact that Jesus was a Galilean Jew from a rural village, a village with no traditional credentials for leadership, is part of the explanation. That he appeared to be without formal schooling in the Torah, with little or no sophistication in the Jewish tradition, could have added to their opposition to him. And since Judeans regarded Galileans as outside the mainstream of Judaism, Jesus the Galilean could not readily be regarded as an authentic leader for the Jewish people — certainly not the Messiah. Most Judean Jews looked to the established parties and professions as the sources of religious authority and leadership. Finally, Galilee had a history of generating extremists and radicals whose actions threatened the stability of the Jewish state under Roman rule. The appearance of a charismatic Galilean such as Jesus in Jerusalem at the time of a great pilgrimage might agitate the Judean populace

[g] Lk 17:22–37. [h] Lk 12:21.

and would thereby generate concern among their leaders and Roman officials.

But it was not simply a problem of Galileans versus Judeans that generated the antagonism of the established authorities toward Jesus. Despite Jesus' essential agreement with the Pharisees on matters of religious belief and morality, Jesus went to Jerusalem as the leader of an apocalyptic religious movement. Both the Sadducees and Pharisees were in principle opposed to the popular apocalyptic religion which could destroy the status quo. The Pharisees were concerned primarily with religion and the Law and were somewhat indifferent to the cause of overthrowing Roman rule. The Sadducees prospered under their favorable status with Rome and their power in domestic affairs. Both opposed on theological and practical grounds the spirit and doctrine of the sporadic messianic movements that fired the imagination and enthusiasm of the masses and kept them in a state of unrest. With its strong eschatological bent, messianism was foreign to the rabbinical tradition that eventually produced the Talmud, and it was opposed as well to the social authoritarianism of the priests and Sadducees. Although Christianity had its birth within apocalyptic Judaism and this kind of religion was prominent in the literature of that period, apocalyptic religion was not in the main line of Jewish thought and belief at the time of Jesus, nor has apocalypticism been central to normative Judaism at any time in its history.[9]

Of course, when considering the opposition to Jesus it should not be forgotten that for the most part the New Testament has given only one side of the story — as seen by those who became Jesus' followers either in association with him or in the Christian communities a few decades later. Its authors wrote from a prejudiced and sometimes polemical viewpoint. The position of those who for one cause or another opposed him and the reasons for that opposition received short shrift at the hands of the Christian writers. And, as has been mentioned, the evangelists composed their books at a time of strong antagonism between the Jews and

---

[9] The distinguished historian of ancient Judaism, R. Travers Herford, has examined this matter with much thoroughness in his *Talmud and Apocrypha* (New York, 1971).

primitive Christians, an antagonism probably produced by political circumstances.[10]

JESUS ON MARRIAGE AND DIVORCE

The Gospel writers saw Jesus' teaching of the Law as more profound, penetrating, and persuasive than the tradition of the Pharisees. When the Pharisees challenged him, for instance, on the question of divorce, presumably to expose his ignorance of the Law and thereby make a case against him, Jesus replied with a careful exposition of the problem. "Is it lawful to divorce one's wife for any cause?"[i] was their question. Referring to the Genesis passages on the creation of man and woman and the institution of marriage, Jesus called on the authority of the Torah, saying that from the beginning God made male and female and that a man should leave his mother and father and be joined to his wife. He climaxed his statement by saying, "What therefore God has joined together, let not man put asunder."

Jesus' statement was regarded by some in the early church as a direct reproof to the Pharisees, who were considered to be so immersed in the oral tradition that they neglected the written Law. The clear intent of Jesus' answer was to insist that from the beginning marriage was an institution ordained by God.[j][11] The Pharisees pressed the issue further, asking why Moses commanded that a certificate of divorce be given to a wife. It was a clever question, for it would seem that Jesus was caught in either compromising the principle of marriage as given in Genesis or the law

---

[i] Mt 19:3–6. [j] Gn 1:27; 2:21–24.

[10] Morton Smith's *Jesus the Magician* (San Francisco, 1978) is a scholarly treatise on the opposition to Jesus which deserves the attention of anyone interested in a balanced view.

[11] At the time of Jesus, one school of thought, advanced by Rabbi Hillel, held the liberal view that a man might divorce his wife for no other cause than that he had found another woman more pleasing to him. The opposing rabbinical school, that of Shammai, taught that divorce was only justified when a wife was unfaithful. The more lenient position of Hillel seems to have prevailed in practice. For an extended discussion of Jesus' position on divorce in relation to the Law and the rabbinical teachings and its implications for the practice of polygamy as well as the ancient myth of the androgynous Adam, see David Daube, *The New Testament and Rabbinic Judaism* (London, 1956), 71–86.

of Moses set forth in Deuteronomy.^k But he avoided the trap by saying, "For your hardness of heart Moses allowed you to divorce your wives, but from the beginning it was not so."¹ In Deuteronomy the Law was adjusted to the conditions of the time. Here Moses was seen as regulating rather than prohibiting divorce. Jesus' final statement was a strong condemnation of unrestricted divorce. "Whoever divorces his wife, except for unchastity, and marries another, commits adultery." ^m 12

Jesus' teaching in Matthew about divorce is sometimes regarded as pertaining to the coming Kingdom.[13] The law of Moses might be interpreted to permit divorce — Moses may have allowed it — but how woefully that missed the point! In the Kingdom of Heaven which is to come, the original law joining a man and his wife would be restored. It is equally important that in his statement in Matthew Jesus is revealed as one greater than Moses. For after referring to Moses, he concludes "And I say to you . . ." [14]

The disciples, sensing the implication of the discussion, commented further that if such is the case, "it is not expedient to marry." According to Matthew, Jesus responded, "not all men can receive this saying, but only those to whom it is given." [15] The context of Matthew 19:10–12 suggests an argument for celibacy, for Jesus concluded his statement by identifying three categories of celibates — those impotent from birth, those "made eunuchs by men," and those who do not enter into marriage for the sake of the Kingdom. There is a question of whether these

---

^k Dt 24:1–4. ¹ Mt 19:8. ^m Mt 19:9.

[12] There are some variations among several of the Greek texts of Matthew 19:9. In one group of texts, it is rendered "except for unchastity, and marries another, commits adultery"; another group following the parallel at Matthew 5:32 reads, "except on the ground of unchastity, and marries another, makes her commit adultery." Since this exception is not found at Mark 10:11 and Luke 16:18, some scholars suggest that the exception, "for unchastity," may have been added by the church in Matthew's day. According to Matthew, the church had been given authority by Jesus to forbid or to allow divorce (16:19; 18:18).

[13] J. C. Fenton, *The Gospel of St. Matthew* (Baltimore, 1963), 307f.

[14] See Daube, *New Testament and Rabbinic Judaism*, 55–62, for a discussion of the "but I say unto you" passages in Matthew and in rabbinic literature.

[15] Not everyone is able to accept not marrying (celibacy) for the sake of the Kingdom. "He who is able to receive this, let him receive it" (Mt 19:12).

comments were authentic to Jesus. The seeming case for celibacy may represent the position of a faction of the early church rather than that of Jesus. The discussion on celibacy appears only in Matthew. In the parallel passage in Mark, Jesus simply said, "Whoever divorces his wife and marries another, commits adultery against her; and if she divorces her husband and marries another, she commits adultery." ⁿ He did not mention refraining from marriage.

TRUE DISCIPLESHIP

On several occasions Jesus had employed the image of a child to impress upon his followers the qualities required of a true disciple. Now the disciples rebuked those who brought their children to him, but Jesus took them in his arms and blessed them: "Let the children come to me, do not hinder them; for to such belongs the kingdom of God." ᵒ [16] Only those who have a childlike sense of need and dependence and are open and able to trust are ready for the Kingdom. "Whoever does not receive the kingdom of God like a child shall not enter it." ᵖ A true disciple does not rest his case upon his achievements or his status among men. He is like a child, unencumbered by the pride and prejudice which too often characterize those who give the appearance of piety. The Kingdom belongs to those who have trust and faith.

Few incidents in the accounts of the life of Jesus are better known than that of the man who came asking "What must I do to inherit eternal life?" ᵍ Luke describes the man as a "ruler" who was "very rich." ʳ He may have been an official of the synagogue or a member of the Sanhedrin. The young man's eagerness in seeking Jesus is vividly portrayed in Mark's account, which reports that the man ran up and knelt before him.

In addressing Jesus as "Good Teacher," the young man elicited a response which has occasioned considerable debate among Christian theologians about whether Jesus was confessing his own sin-

ⁿ Mk 10:11f. ᵒ Mk 10:14. ᵖ Mk 10:15. ᵍ Mk 10:17. ʳ Lk 18:18, 23.

[16] Mark 10:14 reports that Jesus was "indignant" with the disciples for their attitude, but Matthew and Luke have eliminated any mention of his anger (Mt 19:14; Lk 18:16).

fulness. "Why do you call me good? No one is good but God alone." ˢ ¹⁷ However, this remark can be seen simply as an indication of Jesus' own modesty and lack of spiritual pride. When the young man, who believed he had kept the commandments, heard Jesus' admonition that he sell all his possessions, give to the poor, and follow the master, he became gloomy and "went away sorrowful; for he had great possessions." ᵗ The central meaning of this incident should not be overlooked — the simple observance of the moral law without a full religious commitment that overrides all other attachments is not sufficient for discipleship. This principle figured prominently in the early church's struggle for survival.

The encounter with the rich young man set the stage for Jesus' statement, and the early church's position, on the matter of wealth and the Kingdom.¹⁸ The reference to a camel going through the eye of a needle is an instance of Jesus' employing a popular hyperbole to make the point entirely clear.ᵘ ¹⁹ On hearing the harsh judgment on the possession of wealth, the disciples, who so often failed to discern their master's teaching, asked, "Who then can be saved?" ᵛ They probably were under the common assumption, supported especially by passages from the Old Testament, that having extensive possessions or other prestigious credentials was a sign of divine approval. But in Jesus' view, as set forth in all

---

ˢ Mk 10:18. ᵗ Mk 10:22. ᵘ Mt 19:23f. ᵛ Mt 19:25.

¹⁷ Compare Mark 10:17f. with Matthew 19:16f. Matthew changes Mark's "Good Teacher, what must I do . . ." to "Teacher, what good deed must I do." Matthew also changes the question, "Why do you call me good?" to, "Why do you ask me about what is good?" Perhaps Matthew was concerned about Jesus rejecting the appellation of "good" for himself.

¹⁸ In Matthew and Mark, Jesus' continuing discourse on riches is directed to his disciples. In these two Gospels, Jesus' discussion with the rich young man seems to have set the stage for a more general discourse about how wealth estranges one from good and compromises one's loyalty. However, in Luke (18:24) Jesus addresses his comments to the wealthy ruler.

¹⁹ Many attempts have been made by Bible commentators to interpret this statement in a way that will qualify at least some wealthy persons for the Kingdom, for example, the suggestion that the "eye of the needle" was a small gate which, though difficult to negotiate, was not impossible. Such an explanation is probably not authentic to Jesus but reflects rather the typical Christian's reluctance to accept the severity of the judgment.

three Synoptics, a man's salvation is not under his own control. "With men," he said, "it is impossible, but not with God; for all things are possible with God." [w] [20] Here is an expression of the concept that eventually became such a powerful force in the Christian Church, that salvation is by God's grace and not through human effort alone.

When Peter said, "Lo, we have left everything and followed you. What then shall we have?" thinking no doubt of home and family and of nets and fishing, Jesus assured his disciples that those who followed him would "receive a hundredfold, and inherit eternal life." [x] Then he uttered the paradoxical statement, "But many that are first will be last, and the last first." [y] These words contain a warning — the rich, the powerful, and the pious who expect to come first will be last, and the meek, the outcasts, and sinners will be first in God's Kingdom. The values commonly established among men do not reflect the standards of the Kingdom; man's judgment is not God's judgment.

As Jesus and the disciples continued on their way toward Judea, he again attempted to make clear to his disciples that in Jerusalem he would face a confrontation with Jewish and Roman authorities which would lead to his death. The disciples experienced increasing tension, for Mark reported that they were afraid. However, their fear may have been more for themselves than for Jesus. As Mark pointed out on two earlier occasions, they did not understand his prediction that he would be delivered up, condemned, and put to death.[21] But despite their fears, Jesus' predictions about his death had so far apparently failed to destroy

---

[w] Mk 10:27. [x] Mt 19:27, 29. [y] 19:30.

[20] The theme of Deuteronomy, that if Israel would keep God's commandments she would be blessed, runs through the Old Testament books of history — Joshua, Judges, Samuel, and Kings. This principle was sometimes applied to individuals as well — as though their prosperity were a sign of God's favor and their poverty a sign of his disfavor due to their sins. This was one line of argument followed by the so-called "friends" of Job, 4:6–9; 8:2–7; 22:21–30.

[21] There are three explicit predictions of Jesus' passion (suffering) in Mark: at Caesarea Philippi (8:31), following the Transfiguration (9:30–32), and on the way to Jerusalem (10:33f.).

their hope and expectation for an immediate fulfillment of his promises.²²

As was indicated earlier, the disciples' lack of a clear understanding of Jesus' intentions and their inability to comprehend his meaning are prominent themes in the Gospel of Mark. At the miracles of the loaves and walking on the water, for example, they were utterly astounded, for they did not perceive the meaning of these events. Certainly, of growing concern to Jesus was the lack of awareness among his own disciples, their pride and ambition, and their apparent inability to understand clearly his purposes. These failures led finally to their deserting him at his Passion.

On the occasion of the confession at Caesarea Philippi, Peter had proclaimed Jesus as Messiah and then immediately presumed to correct him as if he were chastening a wayward child. In turn Peter was severely rebuked, "Get behind me, Satan!" ᶻ It is likely that Peter's vision and expectations were precisely those of his fellow countrymen who held the view that the messianic agent would use political and military power to overthrow Rome and restore Israel's prestige and glory as in ancient times. This common hope was almost native to Galileans. According to Mark and Matthew, Peter's understanding was at odds with Jesus' own expectation — that as the servant of all he would suffer and be put to death. But the zest for power and position which had infected all of his disciples finally came into the open. James and John, the sons of Zebedee, approached Jesus with the request that they be permitted to sit beside him in glory. According to Mark this request for high position in the Kingdom came directly from the disciples, but in Matthew, perhaps to soften the presumptuousness of the request, it is made by their mother.ᵃ Apparently the two brothers looked forward to the coming Kingdom as a place of grandeur and power.

"You do not know what you are asking," was Jesus' reply. Again his disciples failed to comprehend the relation of the King-

---

ᶻ Mk 8:33. ᵃ Mt 20:20.

[22] According to Luke, the meaning of Jesus' passion was hidden from the Twelve. "This saying [that he should be delivered up] was hid from them, and they did not grasp what was said" (Lk 18:34).

dom to suffering. "Are you able to drink the cup that I drink?" The cup symbolized the dramatic and tragic events to come.[23] "We are able," they replied. "And Jesus said to them, 'The cup that I drink you will drink; . . . but to sit at my right hand . . . is not mine to grant.' " [b]

According to Mark the other disciples were indignant at James and John, perhaps out of jealousy that these two might gain some advantage or possibly in disgust at the nature of their request. Jesus warned his disciples against becoming ambitious like the gentiles, whose chief aim was to gain power and the authority to command. "You know that those who are supposed to rule over the Gentiles lord it over them," he said, "and their great men exercise authority over them. But it shall not be so among you." [c] The Kingdom of God is to be different. There would be greatness, but greatness measured in terms of one's service to others. "Whoever would be great among you must be your servant." [d] According to Mark the "Son of man" was the supreme example of service. He came not to be served but to serve and "to give his life as a ransom for many." [e] [24] This was to become the key to the Christian concept of discipleship in the second century: "The Way" of a Christian is to serve even in the face of persecution and, if necessary, at the cost of one's own life.

Jesus and his disciples passed through Jericho on the way to Jerusalem. As they were leaving Jericho, Bartimaeus, a blind beggar, cried, "Jesus, Son of David, have mercy on me! . . . let me receive my sight." [f] Blindness was common in the ancient Middle East, and its victims often sat at the city gates to gain the attention and sympathy of those who might give them alms. This was

---

[b] Mk 10:38–40. [c] Mk 10:42f. [d] Mk 10:43. [e] Mk 10:45. [f] Mk 10:47, 51.

[23] Isaiah 51:22 contains an example of such usage of the cup motif from the Old Testament. Second Isaiah proclaims that God would comfort Zion: "Behold, I have taken from your hand the cup of staggering; the bowl of my wrath you shall drink no more."

[24] Luke emphasized the suffering servant theme but did not include Mark's mention of ransom. The term "ransom" appears nowhere else in the Gospels. However, the concept of Christ as a ransom for souls, a purchase price for souls, is found elsewhere in the New Testament, for example in Paul's letter to the Galatians and the first letter to the Corinthians. This is a matter of some importance in relation to the origin of the "ransom' doctrine of the atonement in early Christian thought.

especially true during the Passover season when the roads were crowded with travelers to Jerusalem. But there is more to this story than Jesus' healing a blind person. For the writer of Mark's Gospel, the healing expresses release from spiritual blindness through humility and faith. Luke and Mark are explicit in their accounts, " 'Go your way; your faith has made you well.' And immediately," says Mark, "he received his sight" and followed Jesus.[25]

According to Luke, when Jesus and his party passed through Jericho a man named Zacchaeus, a wealthy tax collector who was anxious to see Jesus but unable to get near him because of the crowds, climbed a tree in order to see him as he passed. As Jesus came near, he called to Zacchaeus "come down; for I must stay at your house today." Here Jesus is represented by Luke as ignoring social and religious prejudices by reaching out to a man who belonged to the despised class of publicans. Predictably, this friendly association of Jesus with Zacchaeus, who received him joyfully, aroused concern and censure from some in the crowd. For the Gospel reports that when they saw it they complained "He has gone in to be the guest of a man who is a sinner." [g]

Zacchaeus had shown his fitness for the Kingdom because he saw what the typically rich and powerful did not see — that integrity, humility born of the sense of need, and service to others must be placed ahead of temporal well-being and ambition for wealth. Jesus did not condemn Zacchaeus or criticize him for his vocation. Rather, he said, "Today salvation has come to this house, since he also is a son of Abraham. For the Son of man came to seek and to save the lost." [h]

---

[g] Lk 19:5, 7. [h] Lk 19:9f.

[25] Mark 10:52. In Matthew's account, 20:30–34, there are two blind men and neither is named. Also, Matthew adds that the blind men received their sight when he touched their eyes.

CHAPTER 9

Last Days in Jerusalem

Matthew described Jesus' entry into Jerusalem mounted on an ass as another fulfillment of Old Testament prophecy. In this instance it was Zechariah 9:9 and Isaiah 62:11, "Tell the daughter of Zion, Behold, your king is coming to you, humble, and mounted on an ass, and on a colt, the foal of an ass."[a][1] The entry, according to all four Gospels, was indeed triumphant. In Matthew's account crowds went before Jesus shouting hosannas and proclaimed him the Son of David, the prophet from Nazareth.[b] For Matthew, this was Jesus' public confession of his messiahship. Mark added, "Blessed is the kingdom of our father David that is coming!"[c] Perhaps for Mark Jesus' entry was not the public proclamation of the Messiah, as claimed by Matthew, but rather a declaration of the coming of God's Kingdom. The Gospel of John records that the crowds proclaimed Jesus king of Israel.[d]

Some scholars have held that Jesus may have entered Jerusalem on the occasion of the Passover, hoping to arouse the multitude to his support. It is well to recall, however, that according to Mark, Jesus was reluctant to disclose his identity even though some Galileans believed that he was the one like Moses who would deliver Israel from oppression.

THE CONFRONTATION IN THE TEMPLE

There is ample evidence in the Gospels that Jesus profoundly respected both the Temple and the synagogue. His attendance

---

[a] Mt 21:5. [b] Mt 21:9–11. [c] Mk 11:10. [d] Jn 12:12–14.

[1] Matthew stated that Jesus rode on "them" (21:7), that is, two animals. In this instance, Matthew's eagerness to fulfill the prophecy of Zechariah 9:9 with precise detail led to an awkward situation, for the passage from Zechariah referred to only one animal. The repetition of the theme, "on a colt, the foal of an ass," is an instance of Hebrew parallelism which Matthew apparently misunderstood as meaning two animals.

in the synagogue is recorded several times in the Gospels. Now his entry into Jerusalem brought him and his followers to the Temple. From the days of Jeremiah after the discovery of "the Book of the Law" in the Temple and the renewal of the Mosaic covenant which followed, the Israelites had concentrated their religious worship at a central shrine.[2] The historical and prophetic books of the Old Testament are replete with indications that centralization of religious rituals was strongly advocated by both secular and religious leaders. This centralization can now be seen as essential to the definition and integrity of the Hebrew faith. The ancient Temple of Solomon in Jerusalem, from the tenth century until its destruction by the Babylonians in 586 BCE, was the focal point of pilgrimage and worship of the Israelites. After their return from the Babylonian captivity in 538 BCE, the Jews erected a second but less impressive temple. Its construction extended probably from about 520 to 515 BCE. Herod the Great undertook a renovation and expansion of this "Second Temple" about 20 BCE. The new structure was unparalleled in Jewish history and was one of the great buildings of the Roman Empire. At the time of Jesus' ministry, the Temple and its outer buildings were still under construction. It was not completed until just before the Roman conquest of Jerusalem at the close of the Jewish rebellion in CE 70, when it was destroyed by fire.

In Mark's account, when Jesus entered Jerusalem he went first into the Temple and then went out to Bethany with the twelve.[e] The next day he entered the Temple again "and began to drive out those who sold and those who bought."[f] [3] Jesus said to them, "Is it not written, 'My house shall be called a house of prayer for

[e] Mk 11:11. [f] Mk 11:15.

[2] These events, reported in 2 Kings 22, took place during the reign of the young King Josiah (640–609 BCE). See Bernard Anderson, *Understanding the Old Testament*, 3rd ed. (Englewood Cliffs, New Jersey, 1975), 348–62, for a discussion and interpretation of the historical details.

[3] The Synoptics and John's Gospel differ with respect to the time of the so-called cleansing of the Temple. John placed this incident at the beginning of Jesus' ministry (2:12–22). However, Matthew, Mark, and Luke are in agreement that the cleansing of the Temple took place at the end (Mt 21:10–17; Mk 11:15–19; Lk 19:45–48).

all the nations?' But you have made it a den of robbers." [g] [4] John referred specifically to the sellers of oxen, sheep, and pigeons[h] and provided additional detail on Jesus' activity at the Temple. "And making a whip of cords, he drove them all, with the sheep and oxen, out of the temple; and he poured out the coins of the money-changers and overturned their tables." [i] [5] From John's account and from ancient descriptions of the Temple sacrificial rituals, it is evident that animals were brought to the Temple to be offered as sacrifices.[6] For the Jews who came to Jerusalem from the Diaspora as well as from Galilee and Judea to fulfill one of their most important religious duties, the sacrificial offering, the Temple market and the money-changers were a convenience, as well apparently as a source of income for the Temple establishment.

According to Mark, the strange case of Jesus cursing the fig tree occurred on the way from Bethany as he and his disciples journeyed to the Temple. This is a miracle unlike any others attributed to Jesus; Luke and John make no reference to it. "When he came to it, he found nothing but leaves. . . . And he said to it, 'May no one ever eat fruit from you again.'" [j] The report of the fig tree cursing was undoubtedly intended by Mark to convey a symbolic meaning. Otherwise, it seems quite senseless. In Mark three episodes stand together as a literary unit: cursing the fig tree, cleansing the Temple, and Jesus' discourse in the Temple. Jerusalem was the central shrine, the city of David, the seat of ancient traditions and promises, and, in Mark's view, the center of opposition and hostility to Jesus. For Mark, Jesus' act of cleansing the Temple and cursing the tree brought an end to the Temple and to

---

[g] Mk 11:17. [h] Jn 2:14. [i] Jn 2:15. [j] Mk 11:12–14.

[4] This phrasing in Mark was from Jeremiah's famous Temple sermon (7:1–15) in which the prophet predicted destruction of the Temple in his day because of the sins of Judah.

[5] "Money-changers" referred to the requirement that because all buying and selling in the Temple area was done in the currency of Tyre, other coins had to be changed. A fee of half-shekel was paid for the exchange.

[6] According to the Law (Lv 5:7; 12:8), either two "turtledoves or two young pigeons" were accepted as sacrifices for those who could not afford a lamb. A classic account of the Temple and its ritual is Alfred Edersheim's work *The Temple: Its Ministry and Services*, reprint (Grand Rapids, Michigan, 1982).

traditional Judaism as the means of fulfilling Abraham's promise.[r] Earlier, John the Baptist had warned Jewish religious leaders and officials against the complacency of the claim to "have Abraham as our father."[k] Descent from Abraham was not a guarantee of salvation in God's Kingdom.

Jesus' rejection of the Temple officials is reminiscent of the harsh words of the Prophet Jeremiah against the priests and prophets of his day who induced attitudes of arrogance and self-satisfaction among the people. "They dress my people's wound, but skin-deep only, with their saying, 'All is well.' All well? Nothing is well."[l] In his famous Temple sermon, Jeremiah rebuked the people for their complacency. "You keep saying 'This place is the temple of the Lord, the temple of the Lord, the temple of the Lord!' This catchword of yours is a lie; put no trust in it."[m] [s]

CONFLICT WITH THE OFFICIANTS

In his rebuke, according to the Synoptics, Jesus utilized the pronouncements of both Isaiah and Jeremiah. "For my house shall be called a house of prayer for all peoples,"[n] and "Has this house, which is called by my name, become a den of robbers in your eyes?"[o] Judaism had been expected to bear fruit for the Kingdom, but like the fig tree whose leaves held out only the promise of fruit, Judaism was barren. The next morning as they passed by, Mark reported that the fig tree had "withered away to its roots. And Peter remembered."[p] This was the occasion for Jesus to comment upon the essentials for life under the new Covenant after the rejection of Judaism — the necessity for belief without doubt, for fidelity, for prayer, and for forgiveness.[q] Thus, the Temple — as the fig tree — was judged sterile and unproductive.

[k] Mt 3:9; Lk 3:8. [l] Jer 8:11. [m] Jer 7:4. [n] Is 56:7. [o] Jer 7:11. [p] Mk 11:20f. [q] Mk 11:22–25.

[r] This interpretation of Mark follows Werner Kelber's perceptive analysis of Mark 11:1–13:37 in *Mark's Story of Jesus* (Philadelphia: Fortress Press, 1979), 57–66. In Mark's gospel the Temple-figtree episode dramatizes Jesus' final rejection of the Temple. See also N. Perrin, *The New Testament* (New York, 1974), 158.

[s] These two passages from Jeremiah (8:11 and 7:4) are from the New English Bible. The sharpness of Jeremiah's rebuke is most clearly shown in this translation.

For Mark, this meant that the old institutions connected with Jerusalem would be rejected as the foundation of the Kingdom of God which is to come.

Mark reported that when Jesus returned to the Temple, he was addressed by the chief priests, the scribes, and the elders.[r] Perhaps they were an official committee from the Sanhedrin. Mark said earlier that the chief priests and scribes heard about Jesus' performance the day before and that they sought a way to destroy him because of the influence of his teaching upon the masses.[s] The question, "By what authority are you doing these things?" no doubt referred to Jesus' actions in the Temple and to the fact that he did not have any formal rabbinical training. But he countered with a question about the authority of John's baptism. John had no formal credentials, for like Jesus he had not been authorized by any formal body such as the Sanhedrin. Yet John the Baptist was so popular that those who opposed him did not dare challenge him openly. According to Mark Jesus needed no further defense.[t]

By reporting verbal exchanges between Jesus and his opponents, Matthew apparently intended to illustrate the following points: (1) that Jesus was superior in wisdom and argument to the Sadducees and Pharisees; (2) that Jesus was the Messiah whose coming was predicted in the Old Testament; and (3) that the Jewish view of the Messiah was not adequate — Jesus, as the son of God, had status far beyond that envisioned in Jewish expectations.

Matthew records that certain of the Pharisees and some Herodians were sent to discredit Jesus before the people and their Roman rulers. Their attack was carefully and cleverly planned. Ordinarily, the Pharisees opposed the Herodians, but in this case Pharisees and Herodians joined in a common effort to entangle Jesus and destroy his credibility.[9] To dispel any suspicions the people might have, they offered, though in a rather superficial

---

[r] Mk 11:27f. [s] Mk 11:18, 28. [t] Mk 11:33.

[9] The Herodians were not a religious party as the Pharisees were. They were partisans of Herod's who favored collaboration with Rome. The Herodians supported taxation by Rome, for instance, which the Pharisees opposed.

way, their respect for him. "Teacher, we know that you are true, and teach the way of God truthfully." Then they asked, "Is it lawful to pay taxes to Caesar, or not?" [u] At first it appeared that their question could be easily answered "yes" or "no." However, Jesus was quick to see the trap. On the one hand, had he answered "no," the Herodians, the partisans of the Romans, would have charged him with treason for failing to support Roman rule. But, had he answered "yes," the common people would have charged him with insincerity or with being a traitor to the Jewish cause.

According to Matthew, Jesus perceived their intentions and offered a practical solution. "Show me the money for the tax." The coin bore the face and name familiar to all.[10] "Whose likeness and inscription is this?" Only one answer was possible: "Caesar's." Sovereignty belonged to Rome, and in Matthew's view Jesus was not involved in supporting those who favored the popular resistance movement against Rome. The carefully set trap failed to ensnare Jesus, who uttered the famous words, "Render therefore to Caesar the things that are Caesar's." He then pressed the issue further by pointing out to his questioners the all-important matter which they seemed to have forgotten — "Render . . . to God the things that are God's." According to Matthew, Jesus' antagonists marveled at his knowledge and skill and went away.[v]

In Jesus' time the Sadducees were the chief power in Judea, and in Jerusalem, with the priests and Levites, they controlled the Temple.[11] From the moment Jesus entered Jerusalem and opposed the Temple establishment, he was confronted with the power of this religious-political party. Apparently the Sadducees were the chief instigators of his arrest. But why is this fact not more obvious in the Gospel reports? Perhaps because in the period when the Gospels were composed, not earlier than the rebellion of 66–

---

[u] Mt 22:16f.   [v] Mt 22:19–22.

[10] The coin, a denarius, was stamped with the image of the Roman Emperor Tiberius (CE 14–37).

[11] Michael Grant in *Jesus, An Historian's Review of the Gospels* (New York, 1977), 146f., interprets the Parable of the Good Samaritan as intending to show Jesus' strong negative feelings toward priests and Levites.

70 CE, the Sadducees were no longer an important factor in Jewish-Christian relations. With the destruction of the Temple and the breakdown of centralized Jewish control, the priestly caste and the aristocratic Sadducees lost their traditional function and authority. The Pharisees assumed leadership among the Jews in the period of reconstruction following the Roman destruction. In that role they became the chief rivals of the primitive Jewish-Christian churches. The Gospels reflected the emerging influence of Pharisaic Judaism, the tension between the Christians and Pharisees, and the growing resentment among Christians toward Jews.

QUESTIONS OF MARRIAGE

Certain Sadducees approached Jesus with a test case based upon the law of Levirate marriage found in Deuteronomy 25:5–10, which states that a surviving brother should marry the older brother's widow and raise children in his name. They asked Jesus a question which was intended to show that on the basis of that "scripture" the doctrine of resurrection was absurd.[12]

> Teacher, Moses said, "If a man dies, having no children, his brother must marry the widow, and raise up children for his brother." Now there were seven brothers among us; the first married, and died, and having no children left his wife to his brother. So too the second and third, down to the seventh. After them all, the woman died. In the resurrection, therefore, to which of the seven will she be wife? For they all had her.[w]

The question was complicated and presented what seemed to be an impossible dilemma for those believing in both the Levirate commandment and the doctrine of resurrection, but Jesus did not turn it aside.[13] He showed the Sadducees how they were wrong

---

[w] Mt 22:24–28.

[12] The Sadducees kept the written Law but did not accept the oral tradition. Any beliefs not clearly established by the written Law were rejected. In this instance the Sadducees provided a test case intended to illustrate the absurdity of the doctrine of resurrection, which they did not accept. Resurrection of the body was an accepted Pharisaic belief.

[13] By the expression, "in the resurrection," the Sadducees, who did not believe in the resurrection, apparently meant, "If in fact there were to be a resurrection."

in the way they presented the question, "because you know neither the scriptures nor the power of God. For in the resurrection they neither marry nor are given in marriage, but are like angels in heaven." ˣ Here, in Matthew's version, Jesus proceeded with the precision and clarity of rabbinic argumentation to show from texts that the Sadducees were mistaken. They had not taken seriously God's power to raise up persons to a new life. Since there is no death, marrying and giving birth would make no sense.

THE GREAT COMMANDMENTS

Further, Jesus pointed out the implication of God's words to Moses in Exodus 3:6, "I am the God of Abraham, and the God of Isaac, and the God of Jacob." For Jesus this meant that "He is not God of the dead, but of the living." ʸ This passage, presumed to have been spoken to Moses long after the deaths of the patriarchs Abraham, Isaac, and Jacob, was cited by Jesus in support of the doctrine of resurrection. This interpretation was based upon the precise wording of the text which was accepted by orthodox Jews as the literal word of God. God's pronouncement, "I am the God of Abraham" (not "I was") established that Abraham and the other patriarchs were still alive.

Though some Jewish leaders and scholars opposed Jesus, they were not all hostile to him. Indeed, some apparently were impressed with the perceptive way in which he presented his arguments. According to Mark, when he observed that Jesus answered well, one scribe asked him the key question, "Which commandment is the first of all?" [14] Immediately Jesus responded as a practicing, believing Jew, by quoting from the Law, "Hear, O Israel: The Lord our God, the Lord is one; and you shall love the Lord your God with all your heart, and with all your soul, and with all your mind, and with all your strength." ᶻ [15]

ˣ Mt 22:29f. ʸ Mt 22:32. ᶻ Mk 12:28–30.

[14] Matthew represented this as another in a continuing series of tests, "And one of them [the Pharisees], a lawyer, asked him a question, to test him" (Mt 22:35f.).

[15] The Shema (Dt 6:4f.), expressed then as now the heart of the Jewish religion.

Last Days in Jerusalem

For Jesus, however, complete love of God required a commitment of love to others. Quoting Leviticus, he added, "The second is this, 'You shall love your neighbor as yourself.'"[a] These two verses, Deuteronomy 6:5 and Leviticus 19:18, contained Jesus' summation of the Law, but he was by no means the first to stress these principles as basic in religion. It is sometimes forgotten by Christians that Jesus was referring to well-known and commonly quoted passages from the Old Testament. Here he and the Pharisees were on common ground.[16] The scribe was favorably impressed with Jesus' teaching and replied, "You are right, Teacher; you have truly said that he is one . . . and to love one's neighbor as oneself, is much more than all whole burnt offerings and sacrifices."[b] The scribe had discerned a central principle in Jesus' teachings, that religion is more than ceremony. Jesus responded, "You are not far from the kingdom of God." And, according to Mark, after that no one dared to question him.[c]

At this point, according to Matthew, the Pharisees ceased to be the aggressors, and Jesus assumed the offensive. There was the common belief at that time that the Messiah to come would be the "son of David," and many assumed that he would be an aggressive political leader. Jesus asked the Pharisees a question, "What do you think of the Christ? Whose son is he?" They replied that he was "The son of David." Then Jesus asked them, "How is it then that David, inspired by the Spirit, calls him Lord saying, 'The Lord said to my Lord . . .' ? If David thus calls him Lord, how is he his son?"[d] The quote, "The Lord said to my Lord . . . ," is from Psalm 110, which, according to Matthew, was written by King David and implied that the Messiah is David's Lord. On the basis of this technical, scriptural analysis the Messiah, as David's Lord, could not be regarded merely as David's son. It seems that Matthew did not intend to deny that Jesus was a son of David but rather to affirm that his status as the Christ was infinitely superior to David or any descendant of David.

[a] Mk 12:31. [b] Mk 12:32f. [c] Mk 12:34. [d] Mt 22:42–45.

[16] A century later the great Rabbi Akiba (ca. CE 135) said that Leviticus 19:18 was the great principle in the Law.

THE PARABLES IN THE TEMPLE

The Parables of the Two Sons, the Wicked Tenants, and the Marriage Feast were given in the context of Jesus' discourse in the Temple, following his attack upon some of the Temple practices. Mark's and Luke's accounts are brief, but Matthew's account of these parables illustrates in some detail Jesus' confrontations with his antagonists.

The Two Sons

"What do you think? A man had two sons; and he went to the first and said, 'Son, go and work in the vineyard today.' And he answered, 'I will not'; but afterward he repented and went. And he went to the second and said the same; and he answered, 'I go, sir,' but did not go." [e] This parable is sometimes called the Parable of "the Test of Deeds." It raised the penetrating question: Which son *did* the will of his father? The chief priests and the elders answered, "The first." According to Matthew, those who presumed to be righteous, like the second son, failed to accept the way of the Baptist, but many of those whom they had called sinners, the tax collectors and harlots, were like the first of the two brothers and afterward repented and believed. Matthew's apparent purpose in this parable was to show Jesus as fulfilling the promise and his opponents as failing "to believe" and "to *do*" the will of God.

The Wicked Tenants

The Parable of the Wicked Tenants, who beat or killed the landowner's servants and son, is similar to an allegory found in the early apocryphal Gospel of Thomas. This story was apparently based upon the Song of the Vineyard in Isaiah.[f][17] For the Gospel of Matthew, the original parable was probably expanded and colored to fit the circumstances of the early church.[18] In Matthew's

---

[e] Mt 21:28–30. [f] Is 5:1–7.

[17] This is sometimes called the Parable of the Vineyard or Parable of the Wicked Tenants. It appears in Mt 21:33–46; Mk 12:1–12; and Lk 20:9–19.

[18] J. Jeremias suggests that the original of Mk. 12:9 was a simple story "of a single messenger repeatedly dismissed by the tenants." The original meaning, he says, was to vindicate "the offer of the gospel to the poor. You, it says, you tenants of the vineyard, you leaders of the people! you have opposed . . . God. Your cup is

Last Days in Jerusalem

version, the vineyard was Israel and the tenants were Israel's leaders. Matthew made it plain that the Pharisees failed to discern Jesus' identity and rejected him, and that Judaism in turn would be refused any future role in the Kingdom of God. The "kingdom of God will be taken away from you and given to a nation producing the fruits of it." [g] At this point the opponents of Jesus, realizing he was speaking of them, tried to arrest him, but fearing the multitudes who regarded him as a prophet, they failed to follow through with their attempt.

The Marriage Feast

The Parable of the Tenants is followed in Matthew[h] by the well-known Parable of the Marriage or Wedding Feast, but it occurs earlier in the gospel of Luke.[i] This parable is sometimes called the "rejected invitation." Jesus pointed out that those who were first expected to fulfill predictions of the Kingdom rejected the invitation to the feast and were themselves rejected. "They would not come . . . . they made light of it." Nevertheless, "The wedding is ready." Therefore the invitation was extended to others, those gathered from the streets, "both bad and good," and "the wedding hall was filled with guests." [j]

In the original parable Jesus may have meant to explain and justify his fellowship with "sinners" and tax collectors because Pharisees and others had steadfastly refused his invitation. However, Matthew expanded the meaning of the parable, applying it to his own time and to God's relations with the Jews. Because of their rebelliousness the Jews would be rejected and a new invitation would be offered to the gentiles.

According to some scholars, the account of the wedding garment, the story of the guest who was rejected because of improper dress,[k] was added to the original parable to show the gentiles of Matthew's day that not all of those who were invited would be chosen. "For many are called, but few are chosen." Luke added

[g] Mt 21:43. [h] Mt 22:1–14. [i] Lk 14:16–24. [j] Mt 22:2–10. [k] Mt 22:11–14.

full! Therefore shall the vineyard of God be given to 'others.' " J. Jeremias, *The Parables of Jesus*, rev. ed. (New York, 1963), 72, 76.

a special note that "none of those men who were invited shall taste my banquet."[1] Applied to the Christian church, this meant that there would be great disappointment among Christians who believed that membership in the church would secure special privileges. Membership in the Kingdom required faith and love, and the "stranger" and "accursed" who lived far off might prove more worthy than the so-called chosen ones.

CHARGES AGAINST THE PHARISEES

These parables, addressed by Jesus to the leaders who had confronted him, quite clearly expressed the attitude toward the Jewish establishment that prevailed in the Christian churches at the time of the writing of the synoptic Gospels. Jesus was represented, particularly in Matthew, as sternly opposed to the methods and practices of the scribes and Pharisees. His words according to Matthew were clear and cutting, "Woe to you, scribes and Pharisees, hypocrites!" The word "Woe" was used to pronounce a curse. The denunciation, "Woe to you," is repeated several times. Jesus accused the Pharisees of ostentation and hypocrisy.[m] Pharisees often used rules designed to protect persons against breaking the Law. However, sometimes the rules were so strict that from Jesus' point of view they appeared to "shut the kingdom of heaven against men."[n]

In the Gospel of Matthew, Jesus' charges against the Pharisees were severe. They made proselytes as zealous for minutiae as themselves.[o] They neglected the "weightier matters of the law, justice and mercy and faith," in their concern for their minute regulations — "You blind guides, straining out a gnat and swallowing a camel!"[p] They kept the external conventions and allowed the inward reality of righteousness to be compromised.[q] And they paid lip service to the memory of the great prophets while at the same time reinforcing the spirit of those who murdered the prophets.[r] Matthew 23 ends with Jesus' final rejection of the Jews and "their house," the Jewish religion. "O Jerusalem, Jerusalem, killing the prophets. . . . How often would I have gathered your chil-

---

[1] Lk 14:24.   [m] Mt 23:3, 5f.   [n] Mt 23:13.   [o] Mt 23:15.   [p] Mt 23:23f.   [q] Mt 23:27.
[r] Mt 23:29–32.

dren together . . . and you would not! Behold, your house is forsaken and desolate."ˢ The bitterness of this attack upon the Pharisees can be attributed at least in part to the personal attitudes of the anonymous author of Matthew and to the circumstances which prompted his writing. According to Norman Perrin "the diatribe against 'the scribes and Pharisees' in Matthew 23 does not reflect a conflict between Jesus and the scribes and Pharisees of his day," but the conflict fifty years later between Matthew and their descendants.[19]

Mark offers the reader a sharp contrast between what he saw as the false piety of the powerful and the genuine piety of the poor and under-privileged who, though they had almost nothing to offer, carried through in full faith with their religious obligations. Jesus and a few of his disciples sat down not far from the treasury in the court of the women. It was at the treasury that the people made free-will offerings to the Temple. He saw the rich as they placed large sums in the treasury. Then came the poor widow, a person without social status, who placed two copper coins in the treasury. Many had merely scraped the surface of their holdings, but this widow who had no surplus gave everything she owned. As Jesus said, she offered "her whole living."ᵗ

THE COMING OF THE END

Jesus' efforts to convince people of the coming of the Kingdom were drawing to a close. Standing on the Mount of Olives, he and his disciples could see Jerusalem, across the valley of the Kidron. It was a magnificent sight. Little wonder that these Galileans were impressed. With its white marble pillars and well-polished cedar wood, the Temple was a sacred shrine for all of them. But the disciples were awed by the structure itself, and one of them exclaimed, "Look, Teacher, what wonderful stones and what wonderful buildings!" Jesus' response to their exclamations was unexpected. "Do you see these great buildings? There will not be left here one stone upon another, that will not be thrown

---

ˢ Mt 23:37–39. ᵗ Mk 12:40–44.

[19] Perrin, *New Testament*, 171.

down." ᵘ For the disciples, steeped as they were in Jewish tradition, this seemed impossible. Then as "he sat on the Mount of Olives opposite the temple, Peter and James and John and Andrew asked him privately, 'Tell us, when will this be, and what will be the sign when these things are all to be accomplished?' " ᵛ [20] This question set the stage for Jesus' sermon on the End of the Age.

As it stands in the synoptic Gospels, this sermon is primarily a prediction by Jesus of events leading up to the end. But the account was written later, probably after the destruction of the Temple had taken place. There is a strong sense of urgency in the Gospels about the time of these final events. Yet the reader is cautioned again and again to be calm and not to be misled or to commit his expectations to any specific time.

Clearly, hopes were high in Jesus' time for the coming of God's Kingdom. The belief that God's agent, a descendant of David, would overthrow Roman rule and restore the ancient kingdom aroused great excitement among the masses. The early Christians in Jerusalem, who were Jewish in their religious and cultural background with Jewish expectations about the Messiah, obviously shared this hope and enthusiasm. No doubt many Jewish Christians after the death of Jesus became nationalistic in their views about Jesus' role as the Messiah and Son of man. Many probably joined the Jewish enthusiasts, Zealots and Essenes, in open resistance to Roman authority.

The apocalyptic doctrine, the belief in the imminent end of the age, lent fanatic zeal to the resistance movement. No doubt early Christian prophets, filled with the Spirit, aroused the passions of the Christian fellowship by proclaiming the End and the "coming" of Jesus in power. Christians and Jews were thus joined in a common but catastrophic venture. Jerusalem and the Temple were destroyed in 70 CE; the Jewish nationalist religious parties collapsed; and the Jerusalem Christians, the "Followers of the

---

ᵘ Mk 13:1f. ᵛ Mk 13:3f.

[20] Matthew's text reads somewhat differently. "The disciples came to him" and said, "What will be the sign of your coming [parousia] and of the close of the age?" (Mt 24:3). Matthew is the only Gospel to use the expression *coming* (parousia). See Mt 24:27, 37, 39.

Way," had either fled or were killed in the Roman seige and destruction of the city.²¹

With the disintegration of the early church in Jerusalem, new Christian centers were established outside of Palestine in the Mediterranean world. At this juncture an explanation of these catastrophic events from a Christian perspective was absolutely essential as the prerequisite for continuing with Jesus' proclamation about the coming of God's Kingdom. The Gospel of Mark provided this explanation. Mark looked back upon the events preceding the war and examined the tradition about Jesus for clues which would serve to explain the destruction in 70 CE. He found the clues he needed for his account in Jesus' teachings about the End of the Age. According to Mark's interpretation, Jesus predicted the very happenings which led to the devastation of Jerusalem by Rome. This was recorded by Mark in Jesus' sermon on the Mount of Olives (called the Little Apocalypse — Mark 13), which in Mark's chronology occurred immediately after Jesus predicted the destruction of the Temple.

Jesus' sermon began with warnings against being deceived and misled by false pretenders. "Take heed that no one leads you astray. Many will come in my name, saying, 'I am he!'" But before the end there will come wars and threats of war — nations in conflict — earthquakes, and famines. This, Mark claimed, is "but the beginning of the birth-pangs." The faithful will be taken before councils, synagogues, governors, and kings to bear witness, for, Mark continued, "the gospel must first be preached to all nations. And when they bring you to trial . . . do not be anxious . . . for it is not you who speak, but the Holy Spirit . . . . And you will be hated by all for my name's sake." ʷ ²²

ʷ Mk 13:5–13.

²¹ A later revolt occurred under the leadership of another messianic claimant, Bar-Kokhba, during the reign of the Emperor Hadrian. It came to a disastrous end at Bethar, Modern Bittir, in 135 CE, after three years of desperate fighting. Of the Jewish political or religious parties, only the Pharisees survived to carry on the Jewish tradition. For a scholarly treatment of the second revolt, see Yigael Yadin, *Bar-Kokhba* (New York, 1971).

²² That these were times of unrest and excitement is attested to in the Acts of the Apostles where Gamaliel warned his fellow council members against taking hasty

In Mark's version of the sermon, the climax will be reached at the moment of a great tribulation — when the "desolating sacrilege is set up where it ought not to be." Undoubtedly, this referred to the desecration of the Jerusalem Temple predicted in Daniel.[23] That Luke is clear about the meaning of Mark's cryptic comment, "Let the reader understand," seems evident from his observation, "But when you see Jerusalem surrounded by armies, then know that its desolation has come near." [x] Then Mark continued, "Let those who are in Judea flee to the mountains." [y] And at the peak of suffering and great confusion there will arise "false Christs and false prophets" to lead astray even the elect. After this catastrophic "tribulation, the sun will be darkened . . . and the stars will be falling from heaven, and the powers in the heavens will be shaken." [z] [24] Then, Mark continued, "They will see the Son of man coming in clouds with great power and glory. And then he will send out the angels, and gather his elect . . . from the ends of the earth." [a] [25]

Learn the lesson "from the fig tree," Jesus said. When its leaves appear everyone knows that summer, the time of fruition, is imminent. Then "know that he is near, at the very gates. . . . This generation will not pass away before all these things take place." [b] [26] Nevertheless, no one, not even "the Son" knows pre-

---

[x] Lk 21:20. [y] Mk 13:14. [z] Mk 13:22-25. [a] Mk 13:26f. [b] Mk 13:28-30.

action against various claimants — for example, Theudas and Judas, the Galilean (Acts 5:27-39). Matthew observed that "many false prophets will arise and lead many astray" (Mt 24:11).

[23] Mt 24:15 added, "desolating sacrilege spoken of by the prophet Daniel" and "standing in the holy place." Daniel predicted such catastrophic events in 9:27; 12:11.

[24] This is apparently an allusion to the Isaiah prophecies in Is. 13:10.

[25] Matthew and Luke included the observation that the coming of the Son of man will be sudden, like the gathering of vultures to a carcass. Also, his coming will not go unobserved. It will be like lightning from the east which "shines as far as the west" (Mt 24:27; Lk 17:24).

[26] The phrase "this generation" is controversial. Some interpreters have maintained that Jesus referred to the Jews or to "the human race in general." "It is more likely," says Professor Fenton, "that originally it meant the generation living at the time of Jesus." J. C. Fenton, *The Gospel of St. Matthew* (Baltimore, 1963), 391.

cisely the moment or the day. Only the Father knows the exact hour. Luke warned that the day will "come upon you suddenly like a snare." [c] And Mark, at the end of his account of the sermon, cautioned with great seriousness, "Watch therefore — for you do not know when the master . . . will come." Do not let him "find you asleep. And what I say to you I say to all: Watch." [d]

At this point, according to Mark, Jesus ended his apocalyptic sermon. Mark held that Jesus pointed to a new beginning outside of Judea, possibly in Galilee: "But after I am raised up, I will go before you to Galilee." [e] Mark retained the view that fulfillment of this promise is imminent, that Jesus would soon come in power as Lord and apocalyptic Son of man. Mark seems to have accepted a brief delay in the timetable, but Jesus promised to return, a promise to be fulfilled outside of Judea and Jerusalem, to bring about a new beginning for the faithful.

Matthew elaborated upon the uncertainty of the time of the end. For him the end was near, but not yet. Before the end there was to be a time for the building of the church, a time of preparation and of waiting with faith for the coming of the Son of man. In Matthew's Gospel, Jesus followed his predictions concerning the destruction of Jerusalem with three parables which warn about the need for watchfulness: the parables of the Ten Maidens, of the Talents, and of the Last Judgment.[27]

THE APOCALYPTIC PARABLES

The Ten Maidens

The Parable of the Ten Maidens is found only in Matthew.[f] Five of the maidens were wise, and five were foolish. The foolish took no oil for their lamps, but the wise took flasks of oil with their lamps. The foolish lacked foresight. Their preparation was incomplete. Their intentions on the surface seemed sufficient, but the whole effort lacked genuine integrity. The bridegroom did not come as the maidens expected; his coming was delayed, and "they all slumbered and slept." "But at midnight there was a cry,

---

[c] Lk 21:34. [d] Mk 13:35–37. [e] Mk 14:28. [f] Mt 25:1–13.

[27] Chapters 23–25 contain the last of Matthew's five teaching sections.

'Behold, the bridegroom! Come out to meet him.'" Nothing more could be done. They must go at once if they were to attend the wedding. In a last effort the foolish tried to rectify their carelessness. They went to buy oil, but while they were gone the marriage was held and "the door was shut."

The Talents

In the Parable of the Talents,[g] three servants were entrusted with different amounts — one five talents, another two, and the third only one talent. The two men who were given the five and two talents, through trust and some effort, doubled the amount that had been given them. The third lacked the courage to increase his talent but rather "dug in the ground and hid his master's money." When the master returned to settle accounts with his servants, the one who had received five talents and the one who received two were both rewarded with an enthusiastic and earnest "Well done, good and faithful servant; you have been faithful over a little, I will set you over much."

The point of the parable is to be found in the account of the man who received only one talent. "I was afraid, and I went and hid your talent in the ground," he explained. And the master responded, "I should have received what was my own with interest. So take the talent from him, and give it to him who has the ten talents."[h] This third servant who had hidden the talent probably expected praise for preserving what had been entrusted to him. But the situation required trust and risk. Because of his fear this servant risked nothing and earned nothing. According to the parable, timid and overcautious, even though scrupulous, behavior among disciples is tantamount to breach of trust. For Jesus, trust meant more than merely preserving the tradition intact; it meant making an all-out commitment to God and the Kingdom in spite of great risk to one's self.[28]

[g] Mt 25:14–30. [h] Mt 25:25–28.

[28] While this parable appears only in Matthew, a similar teaching is to be found earlier in Luke's special section (Lk 19:11–27). The two parables, the Pounds in Luke and the Talents in Matthew, are closely parallel. Also, the Gospel of the Hebrews, as reported in Eusebius' *Theophany*, contains a third variation of this parable. The term "talent" referred to a measure of weight. It later came to denote a specific sum of gold or silver (approximately $1,000).

The Last Judgment

The Parable of the Last Judgment, found only in Matthew,[i] is the last in the series of three having to do with watchfulness, with being ready, and with rewards and punishments at the end. It is explicit about what kind of life will be rewarded. "When the Son of man comes . . . before him will be gathered all the nations, and he will separate them . . . as a shepherd separates the sheep from the goats. . . . For I was hungry . . . thirsty . . . was a stranger . . . naked . . . sick . . . in prison and you came to me."[j] According to the Gospel of Matthew, Jesus had been building toward this conclusion: showing mercy toward the weak, poor, helpless, and childlike is a test of discipleship. This is a meaning of righteousness which extends beyond that of the scribes and Pharisees. The great failing of the Pharisees, according to Matthew, was that they "preach, but do not practice." They bind heavy burdens upon the backs of ordinary people, "but they themselves will not move them with their finger. . . . Truly, I say to you, as you did it not to one of the least of these, you did it not to me."[k]

This completed Matthew's account of the sermons of Jesus. From this point until the end of his Gospel, Matthew provided examples of how Jesus put his teaching into practice. Jesus himself was given as the model for disciples to follow; righteousness required that teaching be followed by commitment and action.

---

[i] Mt 25:31–46. [j] Mt 25:31f., 35f. [k] Mt 23:3f.; 25:45.

CHAPTER 10

The Passion and the Resurrection

From the beginning of the church, the Passion was crucial to the Christian doctrine of salvation.[1] It is understandable, therefore, that the Gospel accounts of the last events in Jesus' life were expanded and enriched as faith in his messiahship spread. Some details were probably modified to support the claim that these events fulfilled Old Testament prophecies about the coming Messiah. For example, the literary form of the reports of Jesus' pronouncements from the cross was probably influenced by several of the Psalms.[a]

THE PASSION NARRATIVES

Questions relating to the fact and manner of Jesus' death greatly troubled the early Christians: Why should the Messiah suffer and die? Who brought about his execution? Did he die because of Jewish persecution or were Rome and Roman officials responsible for his death? Why were his disciples not more valiant in his defense? How did Jesus conduct himself before his accusers? How did he answer charges brought against him? How did he finally meet his suffering and death? How should a Christian conduct himself in the face of similar persecution? The passion narratives were responses to these and related questions.

Behind the account of the last events of Jesus' life described in Mark 14 and 15 there may have been an earlier pre-Markan account consisting of at least the following elements: a conspiracy theme; a last meal, arrest, and trials before the Jewish council and Pilate; sentencing; the procession to Golgotha; and the crucifixion.

---

[a] Ps 22; 31:5; 38:11; 69:21.

[1] The account of Jesus' Passion includes the events from the Last Supper through the crucifixion and the empty tomb (Mt 26–28; Mk 14–16; Lk 22–24).

[214]

The Passion and the Resurrection

Variations among the four Gospels have led some scholars to conclude that there are really three different canonical forms of the narrative: Mark-Matthew, Luke, and John. Luke and John, although seeming to follow the same basic tradition, differ in important respects from the format of Mark-Matthew and perhaps had independent sources.[2]

Mark's account began with the dramatic, succinct statement that "It was now two days before the Passover and the feast of Unleavened Bread. And the chief priests and the scribes were seeking how to arrest him by stealth, and kill him."[b] Matthew added that Jesus predicted his own arrest and death and that at the Passover he would be "delivered up to be crucified."[c] Matthew recorded that while Jesus was still with his disciples, a council composed of the chief priests and the elders of the people was gathering at the court of Caiaphas. Matthew interpreted this gathering as a formal meeting of the council called in order to arrest Jesus. That the council was anxious to arrest him without risking a serious disturbance among the people suggests that Jesus probably had an appreciable following.

JUDAS

The chief priests were apparently uncertain as to the best time to take action against Jesus. Their problem was simplified, however, when one of the twelve, Judas Iscariot, who seemed to have grave doubts about the purposes or the direction of Jesus' ministry, stepped forward with his proposal to deliver Jesus to them. For this they paid Judas the generous sum of thirty pieces of silver.[d] All he needed thereafter was an opportunity to complete the bargain. Luke added that "Satan entered into Judas."[e] In Luke's view, this explained the betrayal.[3]

[b] Mk 14:1. [c] Mt 26:2–5. [d] Mt 26:14–16. [e] Lk 22:3–5.

[2] For a more complete account of this view, see E. W. Saunders, *Jesus in the Gospels* (Englewood Cliffs, 1967), 259–61.

[3] Similar references to Satan entering Judas are found in John's Gospel (Jn 13:2, 27). The view expressed in Luke 22:21–23 and John 13:21–30 that all was planned by God and known beforehand by Jesus, including his betrayal, exhibits the early church's treatment of the difficult problem of the crucifixion by placing it squarely within the purposes of God. John has Jesus satisfying what he

The problem of Judas' treachery is difficult and perplexing. What was his motive? The characterization of Judas as the tightfisted keeper and manager of the treasury and as a thief, a portrayal well known to Christians over the centuries, is based primarily upon the story in John's Gospel of the anointing of Jesus' feet by Mary.[f] According to John, Judas Iscariot said, "Why was this ointment not sold for three hundred denarii and given to the poor?" John added that Judas said this not because he cared for the poor "but because he was a thief" and that since Judas kept the "money box he used to take what was put into it."

Matthew's explanation supports the Christian claim that events involving Jesus fulfilled the prophecies and expectations of the Messiah. Matthew drew a parallel between Judas and the treasonous shepherd of Zechariah's allegory, "And they weighed out as my wages thirty shekels of silver."[g] But if Judas was actually the miserly, treacherous thief portrayed in the Gospels, why would he have accepted the risks of joining Jesus' company at all? And why would Jesus have chosen him as a special companion and disciple? How can Judas' final resolve to take his own life be explained? The Gospel accounts fail to answer these questions; rather, they tell more about the strong feelings of the evangelists toward Judas than about Judas' own character and motives.

The name "Iscariot" is used to distinguish Judas, the betrayer, from the other Judas, son of James, who was also a disciple of Jesus. Judas Iscariot was apparently a southerner, a Judean rather than a Galilean. He may have gone to Jerusalem expecting Jesus to confront Jewish officials and, based on the model of John the Baptist, bring them and the populace to repentance in preparation for the coming of God's Kingdom. This view assumes that Judas was devoted to Jesus and was loyal to his cause until a critical point. But as a Judean, his loyalty to traditional Judaism was deeper, and he could not betray it. Judas' commitment to the Jewish religion — to the way of Torah — is the crucial element of

---

[f] Jn 12:4–6. [g] Zec 11:7, 12–14.

regards as a prophecy in Psalm 41:9, "It is that the scripture may be fulfilled, 'He who ate my bread has lifted his heel against me' " (Jn 13:18).

this theory. It was not possible for Judas to depart in any fundamental way from Judaism, and Jesus seemed to be going beyond his original aim to reform and restore Israel according to the Mosaic Covenant. Specifically, Jesus' direct attack upon the Temple and its officials seemed to Judas to threaten the very integrity and foundation of Judaism itself. Also, the course Jesus was pursuing would inevitably bring him into confrontation with Roman power with disastrous consequences both for him and his followers and for the Jewish religious and civil establishment. On this theory, Judas betrayed Jesus in order to prevent such a disaster.

According to an alternative view, Judas had been a member of a company of Jewish radicals or revolutionaries such as the Zealots and had joined Jesus' band expecting that Jesus would play a political/military role in leading the populace in Jerusalem and Judea to overthrow the Romans and the privileged classes of Greeks and Syrians who had gained their prestige and power under Roman rule. When Jesus failed to satisfy these expectations, Judas became disillusioned and abandoned the entire venture. To prevent further disaster to himself and the Galilean disciples, he went to the Jewish officials intending to put an end to Jesus. Explanations such as these are at least as plausible as the accounts provided by the Gospel writers themselves. However, all attempts to explain Judas' actions, his motives and intentions are conjectures without much evidential support.[4]

THE LAST SUPPER

Jesus explicitly predicted that he would be betrayed at the so-called Last Supper which the disciples had prepared. "Truly, I say to you, one of you will betray me." In response to the excited questions of the disciples, Jesus replied, "It is one of the twelve, one who is dipping bread into the dish with me." [h] It is clear that

[h] Mk 14:18, 20.

[4] On the problem of the betrayal, see A. Schweitzer, *The Mystery of the Kingdom of God*, trans. Walter Lowrie (New York, 1964), 214–17, and M. S. Enslin, *The Prophet from Nazareth* (New York, 1968), 192f. Eric Titus maintains that "The group which attached itself to Jesus was not composed of neutral people with no real involvements in society. It is entirely possible that members of the Zealot group saw in him a leader for the realization of their hopes for national independence." *Essentials of New Testament Study* (New York, 1958), 65f.

Mark (followed by Matthew and Luke) intended this supper to be understood as the Passover meal, which occurs on the first day of the Unleavened Bread. Although John seems to have assumed that the event took place, he gave no account of it. In place of the Last Supper, John's Gospel included an account of Jesus washing the disciples' feet.[1][5] Because essential ingredients for the celebration of the Passover are not mentioned, and because John omits the event, some historians have concluded that the original account referred to a special meal shared by Jesus with his disciples that was later, for theological purposes, recast by Mark as a Passover meal. Understood in this way, the synoptic Gospels have interpreted this last meal as the celebration of the Jewish Passover to which Jesus attached a new meaning for the Gospel writers and for the early Christian church. Whatever the occasion, the last meal was the origin of the Christian celebration of the Lord's Supper.

According to Mark, during the meal Jesus took bread, blessed it, broke it, and gave it to the disciples, saying, "Take; this is my body." Then he took a cup, and when he had given thanks he gave it to them, saying, "This is my blood of the covenant, which is poured out for many."[j][6] Sharing a meal and breaking bread in a table-fellowship is an important motif in the Gospels. This theme occurs at the most critical times in Jesus' ministry — events connected with the feeding of the five thousand when he probably made his decision to go to Jerusalem and the Last Supper just after his confrontation at the Temple with the Jewish officials.[7]

[1] Jn 13:1–20. [j] Mk 14:22–24.

[5] For a detailed analysis of the similarities and differences between John and the synoptic Gospels on the matter of the Last Supper, see M. Goguel, *The Life of Jesus* (New York, 1949), 429–62.

[6] Some later manuscripts of Mark 14:24 and Matthew 26:28 add the word "new" before covenant, based on its presence at Luke 22:20.

[7] Sharing a meal often has symbolic meaning in ancient tradition. The sharing of a banquet among the gods is one of several characteristic marks of the seasonal myth — the ritual pattern found among ancient Greek, Egyptian, and Canaanite nature cults. The practice of partaking a meal in relation to covenant making is suggested in some texts from the Hebrew tradition (Gn 14:18; 31:54; Ex 24:11; and Ez 44:3). Also "the banquet at the end of days" is a common theme in apocalyptic and rabbinic literature, e.g., Syr. Apoc. Baruch XXIX 3–8; IV Ezra VI 52. See fn. 1 in Theodor H. Gaster's *Thespis* (New York, 1961), 234, also 93f., 311, for details.

For the Gospel writers and the early church whose attitudes and beliefs they expressed, the Last Supper had a sacramental meaning. For Jesus this was the final participation in the tablefellowship with his apostles. It was the last opportunity to break bread with his closest disciples and to recommit himself and them to their common goal, the realization of the Kingdom of God. Bread and wine were symbols of their common purpose. However, it was the *breaking* of the bread and the *drinking* of the wine as a company or fellowship and not the bread and wine in themselves which were truly significant. Jesus and his disciples were companions breaking bread together as a last expression of their shared commitment to the promise of a new Israel.[8]

The "cup" stands out dramatically in the passion events — in the Last Supper and at Gethsemane. It is especially prominent in the earliest manuscripts of Luke's Gospel.[k] "This cup which is poured out for you is the new covenant in my blood." This statement and the passage "Do this in remembrance of me" may have been borrowed by Luke from Paul's wording in 1 Corinthians 11:24f.[9] In Matthew and Mark the sense of immediacy and urgency associated with the idea of the promise is clear, "I shall not drink again of this fruit of the vine until that day when I drink it new with you in my Father's kingdom."[l]

GETHSEMANE

After eating and singing a hymn, Jesus and the disciples went outside the city walls to the Mount of Olives. Luke's account sug-

---

[k] Lk 22:19f. [l] Mt 26:29.

[8] It is of interest that the terms "companion" and "company" are from Latin *com* (together) plus *panis* (bread). Some interpreters have concluded that in the text of Mark the supper is the anticipation of the reunion of the disciples with Jesus in the Kingdom, perhaps of the messianic banquet. In John's Gospel and in the view of Christians of John's persuasion, Jesus himself is the bread of life. This means that for those who believe, Jesus *is* the Spirit and the Power which transform ordinary life into eternal life.

[9] This precise formula does not appear in some manuscripts of the Luke text. In ancient Israel the palm branch and the cup were employed as messianic symbols. For example, in some Old Testament documents, "the cup" represents both divine judgment as a cup of wrath and a "cup of salvation" (Jer 25:15–17; Ps 11:6; 75:8; 116:13). Coins dating from the Maccabean period show the cup which some scholars interpret as a symbol of messianic restoration.

gests that Jesus had gone on previous nights to the same place. They passed through one of the gates of the city wall, crossed the Kidron Valley, and ascended the slope of the Mount to a place called Gethsemane, meaning "oil press." The name apparently referred to a particular olive orchard in which an olive press was located.[m] [10] Jesus went to pray in this secluded spot and, presumably, to contemplate coming events.

Apparently Jesus had realized for some time that he and his intimate associates would be extremely vulnerable in Jerusalem. His preaching had aroused opposition from some Jewish officials, and Jerusalem was the seat of their power. Now he faced his greatest opposition — he had attacked the most holy of Jewish institutions, the Temple, and had challenged the authority and power of those who controlled the Temple, the priests and Levites, most of whom were Sadducees. His preaching against the city, "Your house is forsaken," [n] and against the Temple, "There will not be left here one stone," [o] could not go uncontested. Those who feared him most would surely seek to have him silenced.

On the way to Gethsemane, according to Mark and Matthew, Jesus said that his disciples would abandon him, "You will all fall away." [11] The denial motif is prominent in all four Gospels, with Peter as the central figure: "You will deny me three times." [p] [12] Perhaps these are predictions after the fact that were included by the Gospel authors in order to soften the defection of the disciples. It seems unlikely, for example, that the prediction found only in Luke[q] that Peter would turn again to strengthen his "brethren" is authentic to Jesus. Rather this may be an assessment of Peter by the early church after he had become a pillar of the faith. For the Gospel writers, especially Luke, the defection and Peter's

[m] Mt 26:36. [n] Mt 23:38. [o] Mt 24:2. [p] Mk 14:27, 30. [q] Lk 22:32.

[10] John recorded simply that Jesus "went forth with his disciples across the Kidron valley, where there was a garden" (Jn 18:1). Matthew, Mark, and Luke are in agreement that the place of betrayal and arrest was on the side or near the foot of the Mount of Olives.

[11] The statement in Mark 14:27, "I will strike the shepherd, and the sheep will be scattered," is a reference to Zechariah 13:7.

[12] On Peter's denial, compare accounts in Matthew and Mark with Luke 22:31–34 and John 13:36–38.

denials were integral to the divine purpose. This interpretation absolved the disciples from full responsibility for their behavior in abandoning Jesus in his last hours. Apologetics is a basic characteristic of the Gospels.

The familiar story of Jesus' prayer in the garden is a crucial element of the account of the Passion.

> And he took with him Peter and James and John, and began to be greatly distressed and troubled. And he said to them, "My soul is very sorrowful, even to death; remain here, and watch." And going a little farther, he fell on the ground and prayed that, if it were possible, the hour might pass from him. And he said, "Abba, Father, all things are possible to thee; remove this cup from me; yet not what I will, but what thou wilt." r 13

Even this late the temptation for Jesus to abandon his course may have been great. Was it really God's purpose to bring his mission to the climax of death? Would his disciples be able to see it through to the end? The intensity of the inner struggle and the great stress Jesus experienced are expressed in some later manuscripts of the Luke text by the report that "his sweat became like great drops of blood falling down upon the ground." s Jesus was alone at the moment of his greatest crisis, the moment of his supreme commitment to the cause of the Kingdom, for the disciples, wrapped in their cloaks, were sleeping. When he returned to them, he said to Peter, "Simon, are you asleep? Could you not watch one hour?" t

THE ARREST OF JESUS

While he was still speaking, Judas came leading a crowd, armed with swords and clubs, sent by the chief priests, the scribes, and the elders. Mark explains that "the betrayer had given them

---

r Mk 14:33–36.   s Lk 22:44.   t Mk 14:37.

13 In the Gospel of John there is no report of anguish about Jesus' impending death and no petition, as in the synoptics — "Remove this cup from me" (Mk 14:36; Lk 22:42; Mt 26:39). In John the cup appears in a different context — in connection with the arrest and Peter's impetuous act of resistance. Peter's apparent misunderstanding of these events provided the occasion for Jesus' response to Peter. "Shall I not drink the cup which the Father has given me?" (Jn 18:11). In this connection, see John 12:27–36.

a sign, saying, 'The one I shall kiss is the man.' " [u] [14] He kissed Jesus and as they seized him, one of his disciples drew his sword.[15] According to Matthew, Jesus reprimanded him, saying that those who take the sword will perish by the sword. "All this has taken place," he said, "that the scriptures of the prophets might be fulfilled." [v]

Surely Jesus was sufficiently well known in Jerusalem by this time that there was no need for Judas to identify him. It seems, rather, that the betrayal was disclosing Jesus' nightly refuge, for it was important to take him secretly away from the main body of his Galilean followers and other sympathizers in order to avoid a possible public disturbance. If he was arrested quietly, his intimate band could be scattered without a public demonstration. He was apprehended when, with a few disciples, he was otherwise alone, isolated, and most vulnerable. No doubt this was what the Jewish officials had bargained for. Jesus' comment, "Have you come out as against a robber, with swords and clubs to capture me? Day after day I was with you in the temple teaching, and you did not seize me," [w] confirms this interpretation. When Jesus yielded without a struggle, the disciples, surprised and no doubt frightened and in complete confusion, fled from the scene.[x] [16]

Here the record from Luke differs somewhat from that of Mark and Matthew. In Luke, when the disciples saw that Jesus was about to be seized, they asked if they should strike the armed men with their swords. Then one of them struck the slave of the high priest. When Jesus saw this, he sternly replied, "No more of

[u] Mk 14:44. [v] Mt 26:56. [w] Mk 14:48f. [x] Mk 14:48–50.

[14] Matthew, Luke, and John apparently add certain details to their accounts to enlarge and dramatize the events. Matthew explains that "a great crowd" came with Judas (Mt 26:47); Luke includes "officers of the temple" (Lk 22:52); and John records that Judas himself procured a band of Roman soldiers as well as officers from the chief priests and the Pharisees to accompany him and make the arrest (Jn 18:2f.).

[15] This disciple is identified in the Gospel of John as "Simon Peter" (Jn 18:10).

[16] Mark includes the account of a young man who apparently attempted to show his loyalty and remain with Jesus but was seized and only narrowly escaped (Mk 14:51f.) The identity of this individual is not indicated, but ancient tradition suggested John or James the Lord's brother, and modern commentators often suggest Mark himself. See Vincent Taylor, *The Gospel According to St. Mark*, 2nd ed. (New York, 1966), 562.

this!"ʸ This may be the dramatic conclusion of an earlier episode, reported only in Luke, involving Jesus' puzzling comments about the two swords.ᶻ In these passages Jesus reminded his disciples of their experience in Galilee when he sent them out among the people with no purse, bag, or sandals. He asked, "Did you lack anything?" and "they said, 'Nothing.'" Jesus' metaphor, intended as irony, "let him who has a purse take it . . . And let him who has no sword sell his mantle and buy one," was misunderstood and taken literally by his disciples, "Look, Lord, here are two swords." Once the disciples completely accepted their total dependence upon God and the generosity of the people. Now, when the tide of approval and popularity changed, they followed the way of violence and power. Then Jesus, apparently dismayed by their failure to understand correctly what had taken place, dismissed the subject, "It is enough." In Luke's view what they did not understand was that these happenings were much more than simply historical events. For Luke the betrayal, the arrest, and the trial leading to Jesus' death had cosmic import; behind the conspiracy against Jesus was the power of evil. According to Luke what Jesus understood and his disciples could not "see" was that all these events occurred in accordance with the divine plan. This is what Jesus meant when he said to the crowd accompanying Judas, "But this is your hour, and the power of darkness." ᵃ

The Gospel of John repeats the major Lukan theme, that the plot to betray Jesus was a supernatural, cosmic drama with Satan at the helm. But in the Fourth Gospel the particulars of the historical conflict involving the opposition from Sadducees, Pharisees, and Herodians have all but disappeared. Here the expression "the Jews" is used to represent the entire group of unbelievers who willfully and knowingly reject the Christ. John refers to "the Jews" as though Jesus was not one of them.ᵇ They are in open rebellion against "the Light," "the Truth," and "the Life," which is Christ. Thus, in John's Gospel the theme of opposition is extended — "the Jews" are perceived as pawns playing out roles directed by Satan and his demons to bring about Jesus' downfall. This stereotype became in time a central feature of the Passion Plays of the

ʸ Lk 22:49–51. ᶻ Lk 22:35–38. ᵃ Lk 22:53. ᵇ Jn 19:7, 12–14.

medieval Christian churches and contributed greatly to the anti-Semitism of the Christians.

JESUS BEFORE THE JEWISH AUTHORITIES

Jesus was taken to the private residence of the high priest, identified by Matthew as Caiaphas. He was probably held there until the early morning, when he was arraigned before the council.[17] The palace of Caiaphas contained an enclosed court, and here as Peter joined the servants of the high priest who were warming themselves by the flickering fire, he was identified as a disciple of Jesus.[c] According to Matthew, when Peter denied being with Jesus his accent betrayed him as a Galilean. Perhaps also his clothing made him a suspicious figure among the Judean servants. He denied his association with Jesus three times in the course of the night.[d] Following his third denial, the cock crowed. Luke tempered the words of Peter, omitting Peter's cursing himself as reported in Mark and Matthew, and added, "The Lord turned and looked at Peter. And Peter remembered . . . ."[e] This remembering is a significant feature of the synoptic interpretation of the last events, because it supported the tradition that the entire course of events accorded with the divine purpose.

Certain factors relating to the trials of Jesus have long been a matter of controversy among both Jewish and Christian scholars. All four Gospels record seven hearings or judicial proceedings, each of which is purported by one or more of the authors to have been a legal action. These proceedings cannot plausibly be harmonized into one chronological account. E. Saunders and others have pointed out that such an interpretation would require that the interval between Jesus' arrest and his crucifixion be lengthened by several days. Such delay would undermine the claims of the evangelists that everything was done hastily to avoid undue disturbance among the populace.[18] Although there is no ground for believing that the evangelists' narratives do not report essentially

[c] Mk 14:67.   [d] Mt 26:69–75.   [e] Lk 22:61.

[17] An account of an earlier preliminary hearing before Annas is found only in the Gospel of John (Jn 18:13–24).

[18] See E. W. Saunders, *Jesus in the Gospels*, 276–283.

authentic data, the confusing, complex composition of the Gospels is nowhere more evident than in the Passion stories. The Gospels were written not only to preserve the tradition about Jesus but also to strengthen the faith of the Christian community at a later period. They contain an overlay of early Christian beliefs about the last events in Jesus' life which provided direction for the church in the critical period of reconstruction after the Jewish-Roman war.

Mark and Matthew refer to Jesus' arraignment before the "whole council," apparently referring to the Sanhedrin, the supreme Jewish tribunal.[f] However, there is some question of whether Jesus was tried before this highest court or before some lesser assembly. Some scholars have concluded that the council indicated was not the religious Sanhedrin but rather a civil court presided over by the high priest and made up of members who were Sadducees.[19] R. M. Seltzer has pointed out that for the late Second Temple period it is unclear how much control the Sanhedrin had over provincial and local courts or what jurisdiction the Romans exercised in the Jewish court system.[20] Because of the lack of reliable knowledge in such matters, many problems relating to the trials have not been fully resolved and are matters of continuing debate.

In Luke's account, following his arrest Jesus was held for the remainder of the night at the high priest's home. Here the circumstances of Peter's denial were detailed and Luke reported that "the men who were holding Jesus mocked him and beat him." Then, Luke concluded, "When day came, the assembly of the elders . . . gathered together, both chief priests and scribes; and they led him away to their council."[g] Perhaps a preliminary interrogation was conducted by the high priest; however, it is doubtful that this interrogation constituted a formal trial before "the whole council"

[f] Mk 14:53, 55; Mt 26:57–59. [g] Lk 22:63, 66.

[19] See Solomon Zeitlin, *Who Crucified Jesus?*, 4th ed. (New York, 1964), 68–83.

[20] R. M. Seltzer, *Jewish People, Jewish Thought* (New York, 1980), 215. Also, see discussions of the status and authority of the Sanhedrin in Jesus' time in Samuel Sandmel, *Judaism and Christian Beginnings* (New York, 1978), 136–39, and Enslin, *Prophet from Nazareth*, 195–200.

as Matthew and Mark imply.[h] In these accounts the council appears determined that Jesus should die.[21] The pertinent question was how could his execution be brought about without creating a disturbance among the people. Many historians have concluded that the trial was illegal according to Jewish law because it was held at night and in secrecy. Others, however, have questioned the reliability of certain elements in the traditional accounts. The Jewish historian Joseph Klausner, for instance, held in his work *Jesus of Nazareth* that the so-called trial was a preliminary investigation only and legally could have been held at night. Moreover, Klausner doubted whether the Sadducean-dominated Sanhedrin recognized the rule prohibiting night trials. Also he questioned the report of Mark and Matthew that the "trial" was at night, since Luke placed it in the morning.[i] [22]

When the high priest asked Jesus for his answer to those who testified that he had said he would destroy the Temple, he made no reply. But according to Mark, when the high priest asked him, "Are you the Christ, the Son of the Blessed?" (Matthew reads "the Son of God"[j]), he replied either "you say that I am"[23] or "I am."[k] Then the high priest tore his mantle and, accusing Jesus of blasphemy, called for the council's decision. "And they all condemned him as deserving death."[l]

THE QUESTION OF JESUS' GUILT

In Matthew and Luke, and some manuscripts of Mark, Jesus' answer was indirect, "You have said so," and "If I tell you, you

---

[h] Mk 14:55; Mt 26:59. [i] Lk 22:66. [j] Mt 26:63. [k] Mk 14:61f. [l] Mk 14:63f.

[21] Mark reported that "the chief priests and the whole council sought testimony against Jesus to put him to death." Matthew added that they "sought false testimony" (Mk 14:55f.; Mt 26:59f.). Jewish law required that the accusors have at least two witnesses who agree before the prosecution could proceed. According to Matthew, many false witnesses came forward, and Mark said "their witness did not agree."

[22] See Joseph Klausner, *Jesus of Nazareth*, trans. H. Danby (New York, 1925), Seventh Book, chap. II.

[23] B. H. Streeter suggests that the reading "you say that I am," which is supported by important Greek and Armenian manuscripts, is the original text of Mark and helps explain the texts of Matthew and Luke. See *The Four Gospels* (London, 1930), 322.

will not believe" and "you say that I am."ᵐ Jesus' response was understood by the high priest and the council to be blasphemous, and he was promptly declared worthy of death. In all of this Jesus was perceived by the Gospel writers as entirely innocent of any charge of crime or blasphemy. He was described as the model for Christian martyrdom. In demeanor he was calm and poised, at peace with himself, accepting whatever consequences might result from his confession.[24]

Why were some Jewish officials so opposed to Jesus? With respect to much of his teachings and practices, Jesus was thoroughly Jewish. He went regularly to the synagogue, and during his last days in Jerusalem he taught in the Temple. He cited passages from the books of the Old Testament which clearly indicate that for him they were holy scripture. When, for example, he was asked which commandment came first, he responded as a devout Jew, quoting from the Shema and from Leviticus.ⁿ When, on another occasion, he was addressed as "Good Teacher," his response was prompt and direct, as if to correct a mistaken notion about himself: "Why do you call me good? No one is good but God alone." ᵒ

Would the claim to be the Messiah have constituted blasphemy under Jewish custom and law? There were other messianic figures in the first century, none of whom, so far as is known, was tried by Jewish courts for blasphemy.[25] Was the content of what he proclaimed and taught about the coming of God's Kingdom at issue? Did the problem lie in his eschatological pronouncements? From Jesus' time to the present Judaism has had the greatest tolerance for differences in belief; also apocalyptic books and themes

---

ᵐ Mk 14:62; Mt 26:64; Lk 22:67, 70. ⁿ Dt 6:4f.; Lv 19:18. ᵒ Mk 10:18.

[24] According to Klausner, it is unthinkable that the high priest who was a Sadducee would have asked Jesus whether he was the Son of God as reported in Matthew 26:63. See *Jesus of Nazareth*, 342. See Klausner also for a discussion of the Last Supper, trial, and crucifixion in relation to the Passover.

[25] It is doubtful that the Jews at this time would have regarded the claim to be the Messiah as blasphemous, as Mark reported. See Seltzer, *Jewish People, Jewish Thought*, 232, on this point. The Hebrew-Jewish meaning of the term "messiah" meant "one anointed by God as God's agent"; it did not mean what Christians claimed later, for example in the Gospel of John, that the Messiah (the Christ) was the Son of God. "Do you say of him whom the Father consecrated and sent into the world, 'You are blaspheming,' because I said, 'I am the Son of God' " (Jn 10:36).

were well known and very popular among some Jewish religious groups in Jesus' day. The movement associated with Jesus issued from the strong eschatological temper that prevailed among the Jews of the first century CE.

Jesus' actions were no doubt more disconcerting than his teachings. He went to Jerusalem followed by a band of Galileans. This alone would have threatened Judean and Roman officials. Whatever Jesus believed about his own identity, for some of his disciples he was a messianic figure like Elijah, heralding the coming of the messianic era, or was the Messiah himself. In the so-called cleansing of the Temple and in the statements about the destruction of the Temple with which he was charged, Jesus appeared to attack the most sacred institution in Judaism. But his attack was directed not at the Temple itself but at the power structure which managed the Temple, the priests and their attendants who controlled many facets of the civic and personal religious life of the people. This meant that Jesus' major opponents were the Sadducees, the most politically powerful group in Judea, whose interests coincided with those of Rome.[26] The Sadducees had the most to lose from an uprising against the Temple establishment or against Rome.

THE ROMAN TRIAL AND THE ARRAIGNMENT BEFORE HEROD

The Passion narratives place the responsibility for Jesus' conviction and death primarily on the Jewish authorities and more or less exonerate the Roman officials. This raises interesting questions concerning the relationship of the Christian churches to both Jews and Romans at the time the Gospels were composed. Pontius Pilate, who was of Spanish origin, had served in the Roman legions in the German campaigns. At the close of that war, he had led a dissolute life of pleasure at Rome. A royal marriage with Claudia, foster daughter of the Emperor Tiberius, secured him the position of procurator of Judea in 25 or 26 CE. The pro-

---

[26] This is essentially the view presented in M. Grant, *Jesus, An Historian's Review of the Gospels* (New York, 1977), 145–47. For other interpretations, see S. G. F. Brandon, *The Trial of Jesus of Nazareth* (New York, 1968), and Paul Winter, *On the Trial of Jesus* (Berlin, 1961).

curator of Judea had considerable power but was responsible to the Roman governor of Syria at Antioch. Philo, a Jewish contemporary at Alexandria, is said to have referred to Pilate as a man of harsh quality. Pilate's official residence was at Caesarea on the shore of the Mediterranean, the Roman capital city constructed by Herod the Great. However, he apparently went to Jerusalem during the holy days, perhaps for the purpose of preventing or containing any threatened uprising. It was probably at the fortress Antonia, remains of which can be seen even now near the Temple site, that Jesus was arraigned before Pilate when he was delivered by the council.

Luke's narrative provides the fullest account of the complaints against Jesus — that he perverted the nation and forbade the payment of tribute. "We found this man perverting our nation, and forbidding us to give tribute to Caesar, and saying that he himself is Christ a king." [p] In the eyes of a Roman official, of course, these were damaging charges and the worst was that Jesus claimed to be "Christ, a king." In the account of all four Gospels this claim was central to Pilate's examination of Jesus. The charge of blasphemy or other complaints relating entirely to the Jewish religion probably would have carried little weight with Pilate.

The contention that the Roman procurator was provoked into executing Jesus by Jewish religious leaders and officials is strongly supported in the Fourth Gospel. In this connection, John added to the account the accusation of the mob that if Pilate were to release Jesus, he would not be Caesar's friend.[q] According to John, Caiaphas and the high priests employed this threat to force Pilate to do their bidding. A message to Rome that Pilate was protecting an insurrectionist would undermine Pilate's apparently already precarious position as an official representative of Roman authority. In a key passage from John's Gospel, Pilate instructed the Jewish authorities to take Jesus and judge him by their own law. But they replied that it was not lawful for them to execute a person.[r] Whether the Jewish Sanhedrin was actually prevented from executing a person because of the restrictions placed upon it by Roman authority has been a matter of controversy among his-

[p] Lk 23:2. [q] Jn 19:12. [r] Jn 18:31.

torians. That the Sanhedrin was restricted in this way is challenged today by some scholars. Joseph Klausner, in *Jesus of Nazareth*, says, "We have seen that at that time the Jews could not pass sentence of death, at least not in a case affecting a Messiah, i.e., a political question." [27]

Some have argued that the passage regarding the restriction on Jewish authority, which is recorded only in John's Gospel, is historical on the ground that John had a historically reliable source not available to the synoptic writers. However, John's statement might simply reflect his bias against the Jews and in favor of the Romans. In any event, according to John, one charge would ensure Jesus' death — the charge of sedition. If the council could convince Pilate of the danger to Rome of the claims made for Jesus as a political messiah, it would have grounds for forcing the procurator's hand.

When Pilate asked Jesus whether he was the King of the Jews, Jesus responded, as reported by all three synoptics, "You have said so." [s] This might be interpreted as an affirmative reply. But clearly Jesus did not intend to become a political figure, a monarch on the model of David or the Hasmonean kings. In his reply to Pilate he may have meant that he did not make the claim but that Pilate had raised the question. According to Luke, when Pilate told the chief priests and the assembled people that he found no crime in Jesus, the chief priests "were urgent, saying, 'He stirs up the people, teaching throughout all Judea, from Galilee even to this place.'" [t]

Jesus was a Galilean and probably in some matters under the jurisdiction of Herod Antipas. According to Luke's Gospel, which contains the only report of this event,[u] when Pilate learned that Jesus was a Galilean he sent him to Herod, who was also in Jeru-

---

[s] Mt 27:11; Mk 15:2; Lk 23:3. [t] Lk 23:5. [u] Lk 23:6–12.

[27] Klausner expressed the following opinion on the arraignment before Pilate: "It is certain that the priests did not see in Jesus anything more than an ordinary rebel: they did not recognize his special spiritual nature; what they did they did, in all simplicity, in order to save the people from the cruel vengeance of Pilate, who was on the watch for some possible excuse to demonstrate the power of Rome and the nugatory nature of Jewish autonomy in any matter of political importance." *Jesus of Nazareth*, 345.

salem, probably for the Passover. Herod questioned Jesus at some length, but Jesus made no response. In Luke's account Herod and his attendants treated the entire matter lightly; they arrayed Jesus in "gorgeous apparel" to show their contempt of him and sent him back to Pilate.[28]

The authenticity of the account of the arraignment before Herod is subject to question. Some scholars have questioned whether the Roman procurator would have acknowledged Herod's jurisdiction in Jerusalem.[29] Moreover, Luke's account of the trial before and after the arraignment before Herod is continuous, as if the Herod episode were arbitrarily inserted. But why might Luke have modified the story in this way? How are his curious comments about Pilate and Herod becoming friends "that very day" to be understood?[v]

M. Goguel has suggested that the Herod story supports one of Luke's major beliefs, that all the powers of this world were set against Jesus. According to Luke-Acts such a state of affairs fulfilled Old Testament prophecy that "The kings of the earth set themselves in array, . . . against the Lord and against his Anointed."[w] Pilate and Herod were specifically referred to in Acts as the rulers "gathered together . . . against his Anointed." All of this was happening, in Luke's view, according to God's predestined plan.[x] Some have held that the reference to Jesus in this passage as "thy holy servant" relates to the Suffering Servant,[y] who was oppressed, was taken away without justice, and did not open his mouth.[30] Primitive Christians identified Jesus with Isaiah's Suffering Servant, establishing a tradition that has persisted to the present.

---

[v] Lk 23:12. [w] Acts 4:26. [x] Acts 4:27f. [y] Is 53:7ff.

[28] According to Matthew and Mark these events occurred in the Praetorium at the hands of Pilate's soldiers after Jesus had been sentenced (Mt 27:27–31; Mk 15:16–20).

[29] M. Goguel maintains that this incident cannot be historical. See Goguel, *Life of Jesus*, 515, n. 1.

[30] Luke's theme is based upon a quote from Psalm 2:1f. which the author of Luke-Acts assumed was written by King David. For a discussion of this point, see G. B. Caird, *The Gospel of St. Luke* (Baltimore, 1963), 247.

THE SENTENCE OF JESUS

According to Luke, neither Pilate nor Herod found Jesus' behavior deserving of death. Presumably he could then have been released. Pilate proposed to let him off with a flogging, apparently not hesitating to scourge an innocent man if it were politically expedient.[z] But the Gospels give another way out for Pilate. They represent Pilate as following a custom of releasing a prisoner at popular request at the Passover feast.[31] However, such a Passover custom is not known from other sources. Also the evidence is lacking to show conclusively that lesser Roman officials — legates or procurators — had the power to grant pardons or that they did so. On the other hand, all four Gospel writers agree on this matter, a fact which lends some credibility to their accounts.

The identification of Barabbas as a prisoner who might be released poses yet another problem. Though Barabbas is referred to in John as "a robber,"[a] the term can also refer to a guerrilla warrior.[32] In Mark and Luke he is a rebel imprisoned for insurrection and murder.[b] According to Luke an insurrection had been incited in the city.[c] Apparently Jesus and Barabbas had been imprisoned on similar charges — rebellion against established authority. Although the civil charges against the two may have been similar, even identical, the crowd is represented as demanding release for Barabbas and death for Jesus. According to Mark and Matthew, the chief priests and the elders had stirred the crowd into a mob, and Pilate knew this to be the case.[d] [33]

---

[z] Lk 23:16. [a] Jn 18:40. [b] Mk 15:7. [c] Lk 23:19. [d] Mk 15:10; Mt 27:18.

[31] That this was customary is not clear from the earliest Lukan text. However, a later addition to Luke 23:17 makes this point explicit, "Now he was obliged to release one man to them at the festival." This is in agreement with John 18:39, "But you have a custom that I should release one man for you at the Passover."

[32] Raymond E. Brown, *The Gospel According to John* (New York, 1970), 857.

[33] Envy can hardly be considered an adequate explanation of the motive of Jewish authorities. "The point of importance," according to M. S. Enslin, "is that none of the principals — Roman governor or Jewish authorities — had made a detailed or dispassionate 'study of the case.' It seemed to them all a dangerous plot — one of but many — and to be promptly suppressed." M. S. Enslin, *Prophet from Nazareth*, 206.

In some manuscripts of the Matthew text (27:16f.), Barabbas is identified more precisely by name as "Jesus Barabbas." [34] Because of this, some scholars have conjectured that Pilate's question was for the purpose of identifying the prisoner who was about to appear before him. It was intended for the lesser officials who had direct charge of such matters. Who was he about to examine and sentence — Jesus Barabbas (son of Abbas) or Jesus son of Joseph?[35]

Matthew added that when Pilate saw that he was gaining nothing and that a riot was beginning, he took water and washed his hands saying, "I am innocent of this man's blood; see to it yourselves." [e] A Roman official would not normally wash his hands on such an occasion. But this final dramatic gesture impressed upon Christian disciples in Matthew's day Pilate's complete innocence. Matthew added the comment, "His blood be on us and on our children!" [36] Then Pilate released Barabbas, and after having scourged Jesus turned him over to the soldiers to be crucified.[f]

The Gospel of John supplies some additional details. After the scourging Pilate would have released Jesus, but the Jewish prosecutors cried out, " 'Everyone who makes himself a king sets himself against Caesar . . . . We have no king but Caesar.' Then he handed him over to them to be crucified." [g]

THE CRUCIFIXION

The castle of Antonia or the Antonia Fortress was constructed on the northeastern corner of the Temple Mount by Herod the

---

[e] Mt 27:24. [f] Mt 27:25f. [g] Jn 19:12–16.

[34] Many scholars conclude that "Jesus Barabbas" is the original reading of Matthew 27:16f. F. W. Beare says, "It is not unnatural that scribes . . . should be offended that the notorious bandit should also bear the name of 'Jesus'; and that this feeling should bring about the dropping of the name. . . ." F. W. Beare, *The Gospel According to Matthew* (San Francisco, 1981), 529.

[35] Goguel suggests that the story about Jesus Barabbas became fused with the account of the trial of Jesus. *Life of Jesus*, 520.

[36] Matthew is the only source for the details of the dream of Pilate's wife and of Pilate washing his hands before the crowd. The Jewish custom of washing one's hands as a sign of innocence is found in Deuteronomy 21:6–9: "And all the elders . . . shall wash their hands . . . and they shall testify, 'Our hands did not shed this blood.' "

Great and named in honor of Mark Antony, the Roman official most instrumental in placing him on the Jewish throne. The Antonia was joined to the Temple compound by a staircase, and in Jesus' time its highest tower (approximately 115 feet high) dominated the Temple and the city. Some historians, following a statement of Josephus that Pilate did not inhabit the Antonia when in Jerusalem, have argued that the trial was held at the Herodian palace. But it is usually believed that the Praetorium, the place of the trial, was located in the Antonia.[37] It was in the Praetorium that, according to John 19:5, Pilate uttered the words which have become famous through the Latin vulgate, *Ecce Homo* or "Behold the man!"

On the western side of the Antonia Fortress was a tessellated stone pavement. This paved square was used in Roman times by the legionnaires for training, for parades, and for recreation. It may have been at this place that the soldiers stripped Jesus and placed a robe upon him, possibly a soldier's cloak. They made a crown to parody the emperor's crown and placed in his hand a reed as a sceptre of his authority. All of this was intended to mock Jesus for allegedly claiming to be the "King of the Jews."[h]

Under the Roman judicial system, sentences were carried out immediately. Jesus was dressed in his own clothing and led away to the place of execution. Crucifixion was a common mode of Roman punishment for the most serious crimes, but it was also used by other ancient people — Greeks, Phoenicians, and Persians.[38] In early Roman times crucifixion was considered so demeaning that it was used only for the execution of slaves.

In the earliest form of this execution, the victim was fastened not upon a cross but on a single post set upright in the ground, and left to die. The Roman cross was more elaborate, an upright post and a cross-beam to which the victim was either nailed or tied.

---

[h] Mk 15:17–19.

[37] It has been a popular belief since ca. 1200 CE that the Via Dolorosa, "Way of the Cross," began near the fortress.

[38] Josephus reported that at the time of the siege of Jerusalem the Romans crucified so many Jews that "there was not enough room for the crosses or enough crosses." *Jewish War*, V, 11, 1.

Apparently the Roman mode of execution was based on a deterrence theory of punishment — the more horrible and public the punishment, the fewer the crimes. Hence the victims were placed along the main highways or near the city wall, usually on a hill where they could be easily observed.

For sixteen centuries the Church of the Holy Sepulchre has been venerated by the pious as the place of Jesus' crucifixion and burial — Golgotha. Its location at the time of Jesus was probably outside the city walls; today it is inside the "old city" whose northern wall is of more recent origin. This church was first constructed by the Roman emperor Constantine in the early fourth century in the place identified by his mother, Helena, during her pilgrimage to Jerusalem. However, evidence in support of this and other locations identified by Helena, which have become traditional in Christianity, is at best inconclusive.[39] In more recent times Golgotha, the place of the skull, has been identified with a rocky prominence located outside of the ancient city of Jerusalem, north and east of the Damascus Gate.

Luke added an important detail relating to the crucifixion not included in the other Gospels. As the tragic procession wended its way through the narrow streets of Jerusalem, a number of women "bewailed and lamented him." Jesus' comment to them, "Do not weep for me, but weep for yourselves and for your children," was not intended by Luke as a rebuke. It was a warning prompted by Jesus' understanding of future events, specifically the impending fate of a nation blinded by an immoderate presumption of its own mission and powers.[i][40]

---

[i] Lk 23:27–29.

[39] The term "Golgotha" is from the Aramaic which means "skull." "Calvary," derived from the term "Calvaria" meaning "a bare skull," "a scalp without hair," "bald," is a translation of the Greek *kranion* (skull). For a competent analysis of the problem of the location of the execution, see Kathleen M. Kenyon's archaeological study *Jerusalem* (New York, 1967).

[40] Jesus' humanitarianism, his concern for women and recognition of their sensitiveness to human need, has sometimes been regarded as a special feature of the Gospel of Luke. H. Kee and others state that Luke's purpose was to place the story of Jesus in a larger historical context; the tradition about what Jesus did and taught is set in a "ministry" of cosmic significance. See Howard Kee, *Jesus in History* (New York, 1977), for an informative discussion of this interpretation of Luke.

Matthew wrote that when they crucified Jesus, "they offered him wine to drink, mingled with gall; but when he tasted it, he would not drink it."[41] This refusal seems to be a part of a Christological theme found in Mark and Matthew.[j] In this view the inordinate hostility of Jewish officials and the excessively brutal behavior of the Roman soldiers are explained in terms of the idea that the Messiah must suffer completely, as was predicted in Isaiah 53. Even the two who were crucified with him shared this hostility; they reviled him, as did observers and the chief priests and elders.[k] The tradition of the "good" bandit, who rebuked the other for his mockery of Jesus and declared Jesus' innocence of any crime is found only in Luke. Jesus said to him, "Truly, I say to you, today you will be with me in Paradise."[l]

The suffering of the victims could last for days. They were stripped of their clothing and left exposed to the elements. They suffered great pain from their cramped and unnatural positions and were consumed by a burning thirst and fever and often severe infection from which there was no release until death. In their excruciating suffering, the victims would often cry out in anguish or curse their executioners and others who were nearby. Luke finds special meaning in Jesus' remarkable composure. He may have seen this as a miracle; undoubtedly he intended Jesus' example of composure while suffering the most extreme pain to be a model for all Christian disciples.[42] In the early Church martyrdom became a seal of supreme piety.

"Father, forgive them; for they know not what they do."[m] This first utterance from the cross was recorded only in Luke. Soldiers watched to see that no one rescued Jesus in order to revive him. The clothes of the victim stripped from his body were part

---

[j] Mt 27:34; Mk 15:23. [k] Mt 27:38–44. [l] Lk 23:43. [m] Lk 23:34.

[41] Apparently it was a Jewish custom to give the condemned person wine containing the opiate frankincense to numb or to render him unconscious. Luke (23:36) mentioned the offering of sour wine or vinegar to Jesus while he was on the cross. In Luke's account the offering of wine seems to be part of the mockery by the soldiers. See Klausner, *Jesus of Nazareth*, 352.

[42] In one of the apocryphal gospels it is said that "he [Jesus] held his peace, as if he felt no pain." *Gospel of Peter*, 4:10–14, in W. Schneemelcher, *New Testament Apocrypha*, I, 184.

The Passion and the Resurrection

of their compensation. According to the Gospel of John, it was the outer cloak, his tunic "without seam, woven from top to bottom," for which they cast lots. This was all done, according to John, to fulfill the scripture, "They parted my garments among them, and for my clothing they cast lots." [n] [43]

In Roman usage, a statement of the charge against the condemned person was placed over him or hung about his neck. In the case of Jesus, the inscription of the charge read "The King of the Jews." [44] According to John, this inscription was dictated by Pilate as a final stroke of sarcasm against the Jews. When the chief priests objected, demanding that he change the wording on the placard, Pilate scornfully dismissed the matter, maintaining that what he had written should stand.[o]

"And when the sixth hour had come, there was darkness over the whole land until the ninth hour. And at the ninth hour Jesus cried with a loud voice, 'Eloi, Eloi, lama sabachthani?'" which Mark interpreted as "My God, my God, why hast thou forsaken me?" Apparently, some of the bystanders hearing Jesus thought that he was calling Elijah.[p]

THE SAYINGS FROM THE CROSS

The Gospel accounts with respect to Jesus' sayings from the cross vary considerably. Two sayings from Luke are not recorded in any of the other three Gospels, "Father, forgive them. . . ." and "into thy hands I commit my spirit!" [q] The cry, "My God, my God" appears in Mark and Matthew but not in Luke and John.[r] Some scholars have concluded that this most agonizing cry

---

[n] Jn 19:23f.   [o] Jn 19:22.   [p] Mk 15:33–36.   [q] Lk 23:34, 46.   [r] Mt 27:46; Mk 15:34.

[43] It was obviously very important to the Gospel writers, especially Matthew, that the various details of this most crucial of all events be regarded as fulfilling scripture — the garment that may not be torn, the casting of lots, the reviling by robbers, and the offering of wine. See Ps 22:18 and 69:21, and Ex 28:32. Joseph Klausner comments on the reported details of the crucifixion as claims for the fulfillment of prophecy in *Jesus of Nazareth*, 352. Klausner says of the statement "Father, forgive them . . .": "it comes fittingly from the mouth of Jesus — but not in such terrible circumstances."

[44] This simplest form of the inscription is found at Mark 15:26. The text of Matthew 27:37 reads, "This is Jesus the King of the Jews." Compare Luke 23:38 and John 19:19.

was omitted by Luke and John because it was not in accord with the authors' image of Jesus as divine. The fact that the wording of the cry is almost identical with Psalm 22:1 may have had special significance to the writers, especially Matthew. Matthew depicted Jesus' death as a voluntary surrender of his life to God's will; he "yielded up his spirit." ˢ Here Matthew is similar to the Gospel of John where Jesus, knowing that all was now finished, said "I thirst," merely to fulfill the scripture. And, John added, "A bowl full of vinegar stood there." Presumably, for John, offering vinegar or sour wine did not merely show that some mocked Jesus or that Jesus took the vinegar as a mild anesthetic, but symbolized Jesus having fulfilled all that was predicted of him. John recorded that when Jesus had received the vinegar, he said, "It is finished." ᵗ [45]

Notwithstanding differences in detail, the portraits of Jesus given in the Gospels have many features in common. They describe him as having complete control of himself through the Passion on the cross. When the drama of salvation had reached its climax, Jesus simply gave up his life.[46] The attention given to the Prophet Elijah in Mark and in Matthew underscored this theme of control over the moment of death. According to popular Jewish tradition, based on 2 Kings 2:9–12, Elijah did not die but was miraculously carried into heaven by a whirlwind. It was believed that he would return to aid those in distress.[47]

ˢ Mt 27:50. ᵗ Jn 19:28–30.

[45] John 19:28 indicates that Jesus "knowing that all was now finished," that all had come to its appointed end, said, to fulfill the scripture, "I thirst." Apparently at this juncture, Jesus exclaimed precisely what John believed Psalm 69:21 had predicted.

[46] See Lk 23:46 and Mt 27:50.

[47] Meyer Levin has described Elijah's prominence in the Jewish celebration of Passover: "We are told that Elijah the Prophet visits every house where a Seder is being held . . . Of all the Biblical Prophets, it is Elijah who became the kindly mediator between Heaven and Earth." According to Levin, it was believed that Elijah would return to help prepare mankind for the time of the coming of the Messiah. Through the centuries in times of suffering many Jews expressed their longing for peace and security, and they told tales of how Elijah would appear "if a Jew in great trouble or danger called out, 'Elijah! Help me!'" Meyer Levin *An Israel Haggadah for Passover* (New York, n.d.), 92–94.

For all four evangelists the Crucifixion was the supreme event, the historical foundation for the Christian doctrine of salvation. That this event was regarded as having cosmic import is clear from details found in Matthew and Luke — the Temple curtain was torn in two, an earthquake occurred, the "rocks were split," [u] [48] the "sun's light failed," [v] the tombs opened, "and many bodies of the saints . . . were raised." [w] The centurion who was in charge of the execution and others with him were filled with awe at what had taken place and said, "Truly this man was the Son of God!" [x] [49] In the Christian concept of redemption, this was the beginning of the end. Christ must die and initiate the way — the way of resurrection which would come at the end of time.

THE BURIAL

In ancient Palestine, especially among the rich, family tombs were not uncommon. Caves and openings offered a ready place for the burial of the poor, but the more affluent had tombs cut from solid limestone ledges. In the Gospel of John the burial place of Jesus is described as a garden.[y]

Joseph of Arimathea, a respected member of the council and a follower of Jesus, obtained permission from Pilate to secure the body of Jesus.[z] Luke made it clear that, although Joseph was a member of the council, Joseph had not consented to the actions against Jesus. After it had been prepared for burial according to custom, Jesus' body was laid in Joseph's new tomb and a stone was rolled across its entrance, sealing the opening.[50] The Gospel of

---

[u] Mt 27:51. [v] Lk 23:45. [w] Mt 27:52f. [x] Mk 15:39; Mt 27:54. [y] Jn 19:41.
[z] Mt 27:57–60.

[48] Certain other details were reported only in the Fourth Gospel — the nailing of Jesus to the cross (Jn 20:25), the breaking of the legs of the other two victims, the piercing of Jesus' side, and the gushing forth of blood and water (Jn 19:31–37). The reference to blood and water may have been intended to establish the humanness of Jesus in opposition to those in the early church who held that he was divine only and simply appeared to suffer.

[49] "The Son of God" can be translated as "a son of God" (Mt 27:54; Mk 15:39). In Luke the centurion said, "Certainly this man was innocent" (Lk 23:47).

[50] Many Jews at this time believed that corpses were unclean and should be removed before night, especially before the Jewish Sabbath, which begins at sun-

John added a few details to the story — that Nicodemus came bringing costly spices, myrrh, and aloes used in the burial of noblemen and kings and that he and Joseph laid Jesus in the tomb.[a] According to the synoptic writers, several women, including Mary Magdalene and the other Mary, were present at the burial in the sepulchre.[b] [51] The apostles had already fled.

THE RESURRECTION NARRATIVES

The Jewish Sabbath begins on Friday evening at sundown and ends on Saturday evening. Accordingly, by the Christian calendar it was Sunday morning when Mary Magdalene and Mary the mother of James and Salome went to the tomb with spices, probably fragrant oil, to anoint the body of Jesus. The Gospel stories vary at this point. The stone rolled across the opening of the tomb had been removed.[c] [52] In the tomb, by Mark's account, the women saw a young man in a white robe. He said to them, "Do not be amazed; you seek Jesus of Nazareth, who was crucified. He has risen, he is not here."[d] Mark did not explain how the stone was rolled away, but Matthew wrote that "there was a great earthquake; for an angel of the Lord descended from heaven and came and rolled back the stone, and sat upon it."[e] Although Mark spoke only of a young man dressed in a white robe, Matthew said it was an angel, while Luke wrote of two men dressed in dazzling apparel.[f] The Gospel writers agree that the events at the tomb filled the women with amazement and fear. It was beyond their

---

[a] Jn 19:39–42. [b] Mt 27:61. [c] Mk 16:4. [d] Mk 16:5f. [e] Mt 28:2. [f] Lk 24:4.

down. This was in accord with Jewish law: "And if a man . . . is put to death, and you hang him on a tree, his body shall not remain all night upon the tree, but you shall bury him the same day, for a hanged man is accursed by God" (Dt 21:22f.).

[51] Earlier in the accounts of the crucifixion there was mention of women standing "at a distance" (Lk 23:49) and women "looking on from afar" (Mk 15:40). The presence of the women "who had come with him from Galilee" was not noted until the event of the cross (Lk 23:55f.). Three women were mentioned — "Mary Magdalene and Mary the mother of James and Joseph, and [Salome] the mother of the sons of Zebedee" (Mt 27:56; Mk 15:40).

[52] A large, flat, circular stone approximately four feet in diameter and several inches thick which rolls in a groove to close the tomb may be seen today at the entrance of the Herodian family sepulchre in Jerusalem near the King David Hotel.

understanding and hence "trembling and astonishment," overpowered them and they fled.⁵³

In some ancient texts, Mark's Gospel ended with verse 8 of chapter 16, the statement that the women were afraid and said nothing of what they had seen and heard.ᵍ Nevertheless, because of grammatical problems, some scholars have concluded that the original Gospel probably did not end with verse 8. Moreover, the abruptness of that ending of Mark presents a problem, for here there is no resurrection appearance. It simply leaves the reader with the declaration of the young man sitting within the tomb, "He has risen. . . . he is going before you to Galilee."

But some ancient manuscripts of Mark have a longer endingʰ which contained all of the details that Christians of a later date would have expected. In this extended ending, which is commonly added to chapter 16 as verses 9 to 20, Mark's emphasis upon the lack of belief among the disciples is pronounced.ⁱ Jesus appeared "in another form" to two of the disciples. They reported this appearance to the others "but they did not believe them." ʲ Finally, Jesus appeared to the eleven themselves, and reproached them for their unbelief.ᵏ His final charge to the disciples featured the necessity for belief: "Go into all the world . . . . He who believes and is baptized will be saved." ˡ

Mark was written in the shadow of the Jewish-Roman war. The author anticipated the imminent End of the Age; apparently he did not write as Luke and Matthew did in anticipation of an extended interim period in which the church was to play a central role. According to Mark, in his apocalyptic sermon Jesus had repudiated the Jewish religion in its institutional forms. The Temple, with all its attendant officials, had been overturned in the Jewish rebellion as Jesus had predicted. Jerusalem itself, which had been the center of Jewish faith, was to be replaced. In Mark's view Galilee was to be the place for the gathering of the faithful and for the Son of man's return to inaugurate a new era. Presumably this would occur within Mark's generation. Later when

ᵍ Mk 16:8. ʰ Mk 16:9–20. ⁱ Mk 16:11. ʲ Mk 16:12f. ᵏ Mk 16:14. ˡ Mk 16:15f.

⁵³ For a discussion of problems associated with the resurrection narratives in the synoptic Gospels, see Norman Perrin, *The Resurrection* (Philadelphia, 1977).

the turmoil had passed and explanations were needed, it is probable that the longer ending of the Gospel was composed to justify beliefs circulated in the early Christian communities about the delay of the Second Coming.[54]

The Gospel of Matthew probably was written in the post war period some years later than Mark. The Christian fellowship still awaited the Parousia, the Second Coming, and as a consequence the people were trying to adjust their beliefs to the disappointing delay and to create a format for church life in the world. Peter and the disciples were pivotal figures in this adjustment. They provided the continuity needed by the church as the heads of the original company of Jesus' followers. Mark's harsh comments on their lack of belief and loyalty, their repeated failure "to see" and discern Jesus' true nature, were modified in Matthew. He described the disciples' failures as a necessary response to the requirement that Christ suffer as a solitary figure.

Two events, Jesus' meeting with the women following his resurrection and the bribing of the soldiers, were reported only by Matthew. When Jesus met the women they were on their way to report to the disciples. In Matthew's account this was the first appearance of the risen Lord. To Mark's abrupt ending, Matthew added, "They [the women] departed quickly . . . with fear and great joy, and ran to tell his disciples." Jesus met them, "And they came up and took hold of his feet and worshipped him. Then Jesus said to them, 'Do not be afraid; go and tell my brethren to go to Galilee, and there they will see me.' "[m]

At this point, according to Matthew, some of the guards posted at the sepulchre went into the city and reported to the chief priests what had happened. After the elders met to consider the situation, they paid the soldiers to say that Jesus' body was stolen at night by the disciples while they slept, a story that was widely disseminated among the Jews.[n]

[m] Mt 28:8–10. [n] Mt 28:11–15.

[54] In the longer ending of Mark, the author explained that Jesus appeared first to Mary Magdalene. Mark's point seems to be to show how obstinately the disciples held to their disbelief. When Mary told them she had seen Jesus they did not believe her. The problem of the ending of Mark's Gospel at 16:8 or 16:20 is treated in a note on pages 1238f. of *The New Oxford Annotated Bible* (New York, 1977). See also textual note "k" on page 1239, which is attached to Mark 16:20.

Earlier, in 27:62–66, Matthew reported that the chief priests were concerned about the security of the tomb lest the disciples steal the body of Jesus. According to Matthew, some recalled the statement of Jesus that he would rise again after three days. The Jewish authorities placed the official seal upon the door of the sepulchre and posted a guard. Under the Roman code, the guard presumably was to forfeit his life if the guarded person escaped or if the object being watched was lost or stolen. It is quite probable that Matthew's account of the guard and of the anxiety of the Jewish officials, reported only in his Gospel, exhibited his determination to defend the Christian claim of Jesus' resurrection against any opposing explanation of the disappearance of his body.

RESURRECTION APPEARANCES AND THE PAROUSIA

Parallels may be observed between Matthew, concerned with the problems of an emerging Christian church, and the Pharisees, who were confronted with the task of developing a new life for Judaism following the destruction of Jerusalem. For Matthew Jesus was the Word, the Revelation, as Torah was for Pharisaic Judaism. Matthew's Gospel, as the new revelation, contained the standard of faith, the basis of a new covenant. The content of this new "way" was set forth in the Sermon on the Mount.

For Matthew, then, Jesus' resurrection appearances provided a bridge between the infant church and its origin in Christ's commission to his apostles to "make disciples of all nations." ° For Matthew the end was not imminent; the Parousia was not denied or dismissed but rather postponed until after an interim period of the church in the world. According to the final chapter of Matthew, Jesus' religion was to extend beyond Judea and Galilee to the known world of the Roman Empire; no nation or people were to be excluded. Baptism was the symbol of their commitment to God to carry through with this bold program. And to the faithful, the church, Matthew added the promise that Jesus' spirit would never be absent from among them as a guiding influence even to the end of the age.ᴾ

° Mt 28:19.   ᴾ Mt 28:20.

The resurrection stories in the Gospel of Luke differ significantly from those of the other three Gospels. The setting in Luke is entirely in Judea, in and around Jerusalem, whereas in Mark and Matthew the focus is upon Galilee. Certain features of Luke's Gospel stand out — the role of the women in the discovery of the empty tomb, the disbelief of the disciples, and the report of Peter running to the tomb and wondering about its being empty. As the women stood by the tomb, two men nearby spoke to them, "Why do you seek the living among the dead? Remember how he told you, while he was still in Galilee, that the Son of man must be . . . crucified, and on the third day rise," and, says Luke, "they remembered his words." But when the women reported these things, the apostles did not believe them.[q] Some manuscripts of Luke include verse twelve as an extension to this account, "But Peter rose and ran to the tomb; stooping and looking in, he saw the linen cloths by themselves; and he went home wondering at what had happened." [r]

Of particular interest is the significance Luke seems to attach to "remembering" Jesus' words, a theme developed further in Luke's important story about the two disciples walking toward the village named Emmaus.[s] The resurrected Christ joined the two men, but they did not know him. Luke said, "their eyes were kept from recognizing him." The disciples assumed that he was a fellow traveler. On the way he asked them, "What is this conversation which you are holding?" Being surprised at his question, they answered,

> "Are you the only visitor to Jerusalem who does not know the things that have happened there in these days?" And he said to them, "What things?" And they said to him, "Concerning Jesus of Nazareth, who was a prophet mighty in deed and word before God and all the people . . . . But we had hoped that he was the one to redeem Israel. . . . Some women of our company amazed us. They were at the tomb . . . and did not find his body; and they came back saying that they had even seen a vision of angels, who said that he was alive." [t]

As they drew near the village, they invited the stranger to stay with them. Then, Luke related, toward evening "when he was at

[q] Lk 24:2–9. [r] Lk 24:12. [s] Lk 24:13–35. [t] Lk 24:18–23.

The Passion and the Resurrection

table with them," he "took the bread and blessed, and broke it, and gave it to them." At that moment "their eyes were opened and they recognized him." He then "vanished out of their sight." [u]

The account of the two men in the Emmaus story, who hoped Jesus would be the one to redeem Israel, is crucial to Luke's interpretation of the Passion and Resurrection. Despite Jesus' declarations about his suffering, the disciples did not fully understand his teaching of the meaning of redemption and how it was to be accomplished. According to Luke, Jews in Jesus' time, including many of his own disciples, could not possibly have understood that the Messiah should be brought to such an ignominious death as a common criminal.

This failure "to see" that the Christ must suffer came to the foreground of Luke's Gospel when Jesus chastized the two disciples, who represent all of those who failed to understand and to believe. "O foolish men, and slow of heart to believe all that the prophets have spoken! Was it not necessary that the Christ should suffer these things and enter into his glory?" [v] This theme was reemphasized shortly after the Emmaus incident, when he appeared to the eleven in Jerusalem. "These are my words which I spoke to you, while I was still with you, that everything written about me in the law of Moses and the prophets and the psalms must be fulfilled." [w] In Luke's day Christian leaders searched the Hebrew scriptures to demonstrate that Jesus fulfilled prophecy. For Luke there was no ambiguity or uncertainty about Jesus' identity or any doubt that the Messiah should suffer and die.

The two disciples returned to Jerusalem to the eleven and told them what had occurred on the way and how they recognized Jesus at the breaking of the bread. At that, according to Luke, the risen Christ appeared to them and they were frightened, thinking that they were seeing a spirit. Not until they examined his hands and feet and he had eaten before them were their minds opened to an understanding of the scriptures that Christ should die and rise from the dead.[x]

Luke closed his Gospel with the final instruction by Jesus that repentance and forgiveness of sins should be proclaimed to all

---

[u] Lk 24:30f. [v] Lk 24:25f. [w] Lk 24:44. [x] Lk 24:36–47.

nations in his name. In Luke's view, Jesus' mortal ministry — his death, resurrection, and ascension — completed the second phase of God's eternal plan. Preaching the Word to all nations in his name in the interim period before the Parousia is the final stage before the End of the Age. In the total scheme of things, each stage naturally succeeds the other. The age of the church and preaching the Word must begin where Jesus left off in his ministry. The disciples are witnesses who provide continuity from one phase to another. The promise of the Father was given them, but they were instructed to "stay in the city" until they were "clothed with power from on high." [55] Then in Bethany, Jesus blessed them and was "carried up into heaven." [y]

THE MEANING OF THE RESURRECTION

Luke corrected the imminent eschatology of both Mark and Paul and set the stage for overcoming the disbelief of the disciples and their failure in faith. For Luke the disciples stood as the pillars of the church; they functioned as a bridge with the past. In the Acts of the Apostles Peter filled the role of a crucial transitional figure. He was an essential link between Jesus and Paul, or between Jesus and his teachings and Pauline Christianity. It is probable that a form of Jewish Christianity had developed among Christian converts in Jerusalem claiming authoritative succession through the family of Jesus. In Luke-Acts this early claim for succession and continuity was rejected and replaced with Paul's doctrine of the Spirit. The Spirit, according to Acts, came upon the disciples at Pentecost.[z] This was the same Spirit by which Jesus was made known to the two at Emmaus in the breaking of the bread. So it was that breaking bread and sharing the Spirit became a means of remembering, seeing, believing, and understanding the meaning of scripture in the life of the Christian church.

For the Gospel writers the resurrection story is one of promises fulfilled. This is especially true in Luke's account, where the connection between the breaking of bread in the Emmaus incident and

[y] Lk 24:49–52. [z] Acts 2:1–4.

[55] Acts 2:1–4 tells of the coming of the Spirit on the "day of Pentecost" when the disciples were "all filled with the Holy Spirit."

the Last Supper is most evident. In the resurrection, the promise of a new covenant is fulfilled. At the Last Supper, Jesus had said, "Do this in remembrance of me," this is "the new covenant in my blood."[a] And at Emmaus they remembered. By the Spirit of Christ they grasped the meaning and significance of earlier events and words of Jesus which had been a puzzle to them. They understood, and at that moment the chasm between the disciples and Jesus was bridged. Thus the reconciliation implicit in the Last Supper became an accomplished fact through the coming of the Spirit of the risen Christ.

This interpretation suggests one way in which some Christians at the time of Luke's writing may have understood the Christian doctrine of resurrection. In the breaking of the bread, "their eyes were opened and they recognized him." "Did not our hearts burn within us . . . while he opened to us the scriptures?" Then they told what had happened, "how he was known to them in the breaking of the bread."[b] Does the story bear witness of a literal seeing of the person or of a feeling of the presence of the Christ? Perhaps, at that moment when all seemed lost and they were in despair, the Christ of faith became visible to them; there was a moment of insight, an awakening to a new beginning with a vision of the future and of a new life in the Spirit which is the Christ.

JESUS IN THE SYNOPTIC GOSPELS

The synoptic Gospels are accounts and interpretations of Jesus and his ministry setting forth his identity and meaning as Messiah (Christ) and the son of God. Written not less than a generation after the crucifixion of Jesus, they were based on the living oral tradition that began with those who knew him and was nourished by those who believed that he was their Savior. They probably were not intended primarily to simply record the facts of Jesus' life or even to transmit his teachings, but rather to confirm and advance the belief already established in the church that Jesus is the Christ and that those who believe in him are on the path to redemption.

Notwithstanding this central purpose of the synoptic Gospels, and their limitations as sources of accurate biographical data, com-

[a] Lk 22:19f. [b] Lk 24:31f., 35.

paratively little is known of Jesus and his teachings that does not come from Mark, Matthew, and Luke. These books provide the most reliable information about his purposes, his actions, his message, his conception of the Kingdom and what it means to be his disciple. Christian theology is to a considerable degree grounded in the writings of Paul and the Fourth Gospel, but Jesus as a living human being is known for the most part from the Synoptics.

A few early non-Christian references to Jesus were mentioned previously, but their value is limited to the evidence they present of his actual historicity. Despite his impressive description of Christ as Savior, which is the main ground of Christian theology, Paul appears to have had little interest in the historical Jesus and perhaps little knowledge of him. And the Gospel of John, though obviously involved with the biographical tradition about Jesus, adds little factual information to the Synoptics. Indeed, John sometimes seems to confuse the facts. The Fourth Gospel is a theological work devoted not to the knowledge and understanding of Jesus as a human being, but to celebrating the cosmic role of Christ as the logos, the creative and saving power of God. The so-called apocryphal gospels are important in understanding the early Christian movement, as they are an index into some aspects of primitive Christianity. But they provide little or no reliable information on the life and teachings of Jesus. As sources of biographical data they do not approach the value of Mark, Matthew, and Luke.

In the beginning, Jesus was drawn to John the Baptist and apparently was committed to John's mission to prepare Israel for the coming of God's Kingdom. After the imprisonment and execution of John, Jesus emerged as the new leader of this eschatological movement and as a powerful charismatic figure. That Jesus was initially a follower of John and after John's death assumed leadership of the movement is not commonly held. In *Jesus of Nazareth*, for instance, Günther Bornkamm explicitly states that "Jesus of course did not begin his own work as a disciple of John, and did not directly continue John's work," but neither Bornkamm nor other scholars who hold this view are very persuasive. In his *Jesus of Nazareth*, Joseph Klausner lays great stress on the importance of the Baptist's work as the foundation of Jesus' ministry.

In the moral substance of his message — the requirements of personal righteousness, moral accountability, and civil justice — Jesus stood with the ancient prophets — Amos, Hosea, Isaiah, and Jeremiah. Israel had failed for lack of knowledge and will, the failure of insight and discernment and steadfastness in observance of the Law. God will not accept the externals and forms of religion, tithes and sacrifices as substitutes for the moral substance of authentic religious faith, social justice, kindness, and mercy. These values were the very foundation of Israel's prophetic religion, the issue of a long history and tradition from the patriarchs to the Second Temple that will always remain as a supreme achievement of the human race. The steadfastness and confidence of Jesus' faith in God, in his justice and love, the faith that he cares for the underprivileged and powerless as a loving father cares for his child, the clarity and persuasiveness of Jesus' teachings about the Kingdom, that its coming is imminent and even present and that God is in control of all events, and finally his courage to the end in the face of persistent and dangerous opposition left an overwhelming impression on his followers. His charismatic person and his message of hope inspired the eventual creation of an eschatological community of followers, informing their beliefs about him and his identity, the moral and spiritual meaning of his acts and teachings, and, most important, his cosmic role in their salvation.

After a year of quite spectacular success preaching, teaching, and healing in and around Galilee, Jesus led his band to Jerusalem, to the seat of religious and political authority. It was probably his intention to proclaim there the coming of God's Kingdom and seek popular support for his cause. But he had forebodings of the coming tragedy. The officials in Jerusalem, both Jewish and Roman, saw him as a major threat to the peace. He was arrested secretly to avoid arousing the populace, charged with blasphemy, and turned over to the Roman authorities for criminal prosecution. They convicted him of sedition against the government and executed him.

In accompanying him to Jerusalem, Jesus' followers probably expected an uprising against Roman rule as evidence of God's approval of him and his message. But their hopes and expectations were totally frustrated. Shocked and overwhelmed by the turn of events, they fled; even the Twelve deserted him. Later after the trauma of the crucifixion the Twelve regained their composure and came together again. And on the occasion of their breaking bread together, as was their custom when Jesus was alive and with them, they were suddenly and, they believed, miraculously inspired by his presence. It became apparent to them that it was Jesus' profound faith in his mission, his resolute purpose to inaugurate God's Kingdom, which sustained him. Under the inspiration of his presence, they realized that their Lord was not dead, that he had risen, and that his spirit, God's spirit, the Spirit of Elijah which was present in him, would sustain them. This became the Christian proclamation: that Jesus had risen and that the Holy Spirit would abide with the apostles until they carried his proclamation to the ends of the earth.

The authors of the synoptic Gospels, Matthew, Mark, and Luke, are among the powerful forces in the Christian movement of the first century. If not the creators, they were the editors and shapers of the earliest surviving tradition about Jesus. Each of them was an author-editor in his own right, recording and interpreting the living tradition about Jesus in terms of the experience and beliefs of the church which he served.

In Mark, Christianity was given a new focal point — a rejection of Judaism in Jerusalem and the promise of returning to Galilee, where the initial drive for the Kingdom had begun. Mark made the emphasis upon the Spirit, already basic in the writings of Paul, crucial to Christian faith in Jesus' abiding presence, and he retained the eschatological belief, already in Paul's letters, that the end of the age was imminent.

Within a very few years after the composition of Mark, it was apparent that the delay of Jesus' triumphal return was a threat to the faith of those who believed that he was the Messiah. Some explanation of that delay was crucial to the survival of the community of his followers. Matthew and Luke provided that explanation: God had ordained a time for the church, an interim period before the end. It was God's plan that there should be a time of preparation and of the proclamation of the Word. This was the vision and rationale which enabled the Christian church to define its place in the course of contemporary events and to establish itself in the stream of history.

Matthew strengthened Christianity in its new foundation. For him, Jesus clearly was the long-awaited Messiah whose coming was prophesied in the Old Testament. Jesus was the new lawgiver, the new Moses, and his teachings, especially the Sermon on the Mount, were the new Word or Revelation from God which became the basis of the new covenant and the foundation of the church.

Luke set the Christian movement in the center of a cosmic frame, a divine plan woven into the history of the world with Jesus as the pivotal figure, the Messiah and Savior. In Luke, Christianity is proclaimed a universal religion, with the doctrine of the Spirit — which he may have taken from Paul — as a crucial element in that proclamation. In Luke, the Spirit explains God's power to change and save the world. In the Acts of the Apostles, the second part of Luke's work, the spirit which was in Jesus came again into the world at Pentecost, with the promise to sustain the church and to guarantee its success until the Second Coming and the end of the age. For Luke, the power of the Spirit rested not upon individual persons directly but through the church. This doctrine of the Spirit established the institution of the church as the center of Christian life and guaranteed its preservation and continuity until it emerged eventually as the church universal.

CHAPTER 11

Jesus in the Gospel of John

The Christian conception of Jesus as a divine Savior-Messiah is drawn to a considerable extent from the Fourth Gospel, the most theologically oriented of the Gospels. The Gospel of John both exhibits and expresses the profound resurrection faith which has informed and sustained the Christian church to the present time. Indeed, the entire Gospel is a meditation and discourse on the meaning of Jesus as the Christ, the author of salvation. It proclaims that Jesus is the Son of God, that he possesses in perfection all powers and virtues, the light, the truth, and the life. This conception, which was to become a moving force in historical Christianity, is presaged in the prologue of the Gospel and in the proclamations of John the Baptist.

THE LOGOS

The book opens with the dramatic declaration of the Logos, the Word, the pre-existent Christ: "In the beginning was the Word, and the Word was with God, and the Word was God. He was in the beginning with God; all things were made through him, and without him was not anything made that was made." [a] This somewhat enigmatic but arresting and powerful statement has had a determining impact on the development of Christian theology to the present time.

The concept of the Logos was well established in philosophic and religious thought in the Hellenistic world long before the Fourth Gospel was written. From as early as the pre-Socratic philosopher Heraclitus, the Logos idea has been employed in Greek thought to refer to the principle of Reason inherent in the universe. In both Plato and Aristotle and in the popular forms of

[a] Jn 1:1–3.

Stoicism, the Logos was the active governing force of the world, including that spark of divinity which dwelt in each person's soul and gave to each the faculty of reason. In his treatment of Greek philosophical terms, F. E. Peters has analyzed the use of the term "Logos" as "speech, account, reason, definition, rational faculty [and] proportion." [1]

Philo Judaeus, the foremost Jewish philosopher of antiquity and a contemporary of Jesus who attempted an accommodation of Platonic-Stoic philosophy to the Mosaic religious tradition of the Word of God, adapted the Logos to his Jewish thought. In Philo the Logos is the spiritual agency of the deity, the self-revelation, creative energy, and Divine Reason that is the elder Son of God. For Philo the Logos is not identical to the One God but is the instrument of creation. In John, in principle not unlike its application in Philo, the Logos idea is applied to Jesus as the Christ but with important modifications: the pre-existent Logos became flesh in the person of Jesus; he is the expression of God's life and energy in the world. "In him was life, and the life was the light of men. The light shines in the darkness, and the darkness has not overcome it." [b]

The terminology employed in the Logos christology of the Fourth Gospel, such terms as "life," "light," and "darkness," is an evidence of the prominent element of Gnosticism that prevailed in the religious culture from which the Johannine doctrines issued. The Logos idea was common in Gnosticism, a semi-mythological cosmology and metaphysics with Persian, Greek, Syrian, Jewish, and Christian ingredients, which by the close of the first century was a major influence in religion throughout the eastern Mediterranean world. It is now quite generally accepted by New Testament scholars that both Paul and the author of the Fourth Gospel were importantly influenced by Gnosticism.[2]

---

[b] Jn 1:4f.

[1] F. E. Peters, *Greek Philosophical Terms* (New York, 1967).

[2] See Helmut Koester, *History and Literature of Early Christianity*, vol. 2 (Berlin and New York, 1982), for a treatment of Gnosticism involving the Prologue passion hymn and other Christian writings. See Kurt Rudolph, *Gnosis*, trans. by R. M. Wilson (San Francisco, 1983), 305ff., for a treatment of Gnosticism in the "Johannine" writings and in early Christian thought.

That the Johannine Logos was related to the Greek philosophical Logos was widely accepted among early Christian apologists, some of whom were of the opinion that their Logos doctrine was evidence that some Greek thinkers were Christians even before the ministry of Christ.[3] Whether Philo was a direct influence on John in his use of the Logos concept has been a matter of considerable debate. In point of time, John could have had access to some of Philo's writings, but there is no convincing evidence of this. Perhaps the most impressive similarity between John and Philo is the idea that the Logos was a mediator between man and God, obviously a concept basic to Christian doctrine.

However, that John's Logos is primarily of Greek origin has been seriously challenged by some scholars who have found its provenance in the Hebraic tradition of the Wisdom literature, where "Wisdom" is sometimes an intermediary between man and God, or in the Mēmrā of the Aramaic Targums where Mēmrā or the Word of God performs divine creative functions.

John uses the term "Logos" only in the prologue and not in the main body of his text. Although the prologue hymn is in some respects foreign to other elements of the Fourth Gospel, it effectively serves the evangelist's purpose: to proclaim Jesus as the preexistent creator and divine redeemer whose glory is made manifest in the world.[4]

[3] Philo Judaeus lived from about 25 BCE to about 45 CE. *The Essential Philo*, ed. by Nahum N. Glatzer (New York, 1971), is an excellent selection of Philo's work. See also Erwin R. Goodenough, *An Introduction to Philo Judaeus* (Oxford, 1962), and Samuel Sandmel, *Philo of Alexandria, an Introduction* (New York and Oxford, 1979). H. A. Wolfson's *Philo: Foundations of Religious Philosophy in Judaism, Christianity, and Islam* 2 vols., 1947, is the major scholarly study of Philo's philosophy. See also his *The Philosophy of the Church Fathers*, vol. 1 (Cambridge, MA, 1956), for an analysis of the impact of Philo on Christian thought, including the theology of the Fourth Gospel. The extent, if any, of the influence of Philo on the New Testament cannot be clearly determined, but he greatly influenced the early development of Christian theology, especially through the Alexandrian theologians Clement and Origen.

[4] E. F. Scott and B. W. Bacon hold that John's christology rested philosophically upon the Logos concept found in the Prologue. See B. W. Bacon, *The Gospel of the Hellenists* (New York, 1933) for an expression of this view. See Rudolf Bultmann, *The Gospel of John: A Commentary*, trans. by G. R. Beasley-Murray, R. W. N. Hoare, and J. K. Riches (Philadelphia, 1971), 13–83, for an extended analysis of the Logos concept of the Prologue. See also C. K. Barrett, *The Gospel according to John*, 2nd ed. (London, 1978), 149–70.

THE SPIRIT

But it is the coming of the Spirit rather than the Logos concept which is the central and controlling theme of the Gospel of John. Clement of Alexandria, commenting on the Gospels in the late second century, wrote that John, "perceiving that what had reference to the body in the gospel of our Saviour, was sufficiently detailed, and being encouraged by his familiar friends, and urged by the spirit, he wrote a spiritual gospel." [5]

The Spirit, which descended upon Jesus at baptism, "remained on him" [c] throughout his ministry. By virtue of the Spirit, Jesus was God's revelation, the Messiah, the light and life of the world. The miracles that are unique to John's Gospel — changing water into wine, healing the blind man at Siloam, and raising Lazarus from the dead — are regarded by the author as signs exhibiting the special virtue and power of the Spirit in Jesus and identifying him as the Son of God. According to John, the same Spirit which abode with Jesus, which Jesus gave to his disciples, and which was finally extended to all believers at his death and resurrection, is the source of the Christian's life, of his power in the world and for salvation. " 'As the Father has sent me, even so I send you.' And when he had said this, he breathed on them, and said to them, 'Receive the Holy Spirit.' " [d]

Although the Fourth Gospel gives no direct account of the actual event, the baptism of Jesus is crucial for the Gospel's doctrine of the Spirit. Why Jesus was led to seek baptism from John is a matter of conjecture, but in the synoptic accounts both clearly were committed to the same religious principles and proclaimed the same message, "Repent, for the kingdom of heaven is at hand." [e] Whether Jesus and John had been in any way associated before Jesus came for baptism is not known, despite the annunciation story in Luke that their mothers were related. The baptism accounts in the four Gospels do not suggest prior acquaintance. All references to their contacts or communications indicate mutual respect and esteem and reflect the gospel authors' conceptions of

---

[c] Jn 1:32. [d] Jn 20:21f. [e] Mt 3:2; 4:17.

[5] Quoted by Eusebius, *Ecclesiastical History*, trans. by S. E. Parker, Bk. 6, Chap. 14.

their religious roles and messages, but there is no suggestion of close affiliation between them or even of full mutual understanding. Indeed, according to the Fourth Gospel, John the Baptist twice denied knowing Jesus, "I myself did not know him." [f] Moreover, there are some indications of a continuing rivalry among their disciples.

Although they were concerned that John was performing baptisms even though he had no official status in the religious establishment, those sent from the Pharisees to challenge and question him apparently did not seriously condemn him. "And this is the testimony of John, when the Jews sent priests and Levites from Jerusalem to ask him, 'Who are you?' He confessed, he did not deny, but confessed, 'I am not the Christ.' And they asked him, 'What then? Are you Elijah?' He said, 'I am not.' 'Are you the prophet?' And he answered, 'No.' . . . They asked him, 'Then why are you baptizing, if you are neither the Christ, nor Elijah, nor the prophet?' John answered them, 'I baptize with water; but among you stands one whom you did not know . . . .' " [g] Here, it would seem, John the evangelist is denying what Matthew, Mark, and Luke had affirmed earlier, namely, that the Baptist was "Elijah who is to come." [6] These denials indicate that such claims for the Baptist had been made and were known to the church in John the evangelist's day.[7]

Later on, according to the Gospel of John, a discussion arose between the disciples of John the Baptist and "a Jew" over purification, and, referring to Jesus, the Baptist's disciples spoke to John about the matter, "Rabbi, he . . . to whom you bore witness, here he is, baptizing, and all are going to him." [h] But in the evangelist's interpretation, the Baptist was not disturbed by this ap-

---

[f] Jn 1:31, 33.   [g] Jn 1:19–21, 25f.   [h] Jn 3:22–26.

[6] On this matter, see Mt 11:11–14; 17:10–13; Mk 9:12f.; cf. Luke in Acts 13:24f.

[7] It has been suggested that Luke's Gospel contains hints of the Baptist's messianic status. A portion of Luke's infancy narrative, for example, is thought by some scholars to have been borrowed from earlier Baptist literature proclaiming John as the Messiah (Lk 1:5–24, 57–80). Luke suggests the probability of such a claim in yet another passage, "As the people were in expectation, and all men questioned in their hearts concerning John, whether perhaps he were the Christ, John answered them all" (Lk 3:15f.).

parent threat to his own status. This is what the Baptist's followers should have expected, "You yourselves bear me witness, that I said, I am not the Christ, but I have been sent before him." [i] Thus in the Fourth Gospel John the Baptist stands to Jesus as a friend to the bridegroom: John's fame must decline; Jesus, because he is divine, "must increase." Jesus has the Spirit in full measure; he speaks of heavenly things: "He who comes from above is above all." [j]

The Baptist's denial that he was Elijah raises another question: if in the evangelist's view the Baptist was not Elijah, who then does the evangelist cast in that role and who is "the prophet" referring to? The Fourth Gospel seems to imply that Jesus is that person; in him is combined the power and status of Elijah and of the prophet spoken about in Deuteronomy 18:18 — "a prophet like you," meaning one like Moses.[8]

Spirit is the symbol by which the evangelist identifies the two personages — Elijah and Jesus.[9] Here, as in many ancient religions, Spirit provides the bridge between heaven and earth; it is the vehicle by means of which earthlings have access to the heavens. The Spirit descended upon Jesus at his baptism and Jesus thereby became the bridge between heaven and earth. His work, like that of Elijah, was a manifestation of great power. For John the Spirit, which is Christ, is light and truth as opposed to darkness and ignorance; it is warmth and life as opposed to cold and death; the Spirit is the Word, the Christ, the Son of God.

There has been a persistent question about the role of John the Baptist in the Fourth Gospel and the meaning of John's baptism, the baptism of water. Some scholars have argued that the baptism is to be understood primarily as a sign of the Baptist's recognition of Jesus' true identity and supreme status and that the

---

[i] Jn 3:28. [j] Jn 3:30f.

[8] Dt 18:18–22. Also see Acts 3:22, 7:37f.

[9] In the apocryphal book Ecclesiasticus, Elijah is referred to as a prophet of fire who performed many miracles. Three times he called down fire, and he "raised a corpse from death . . . by the word of the Most High." Elijah was "taken up by a whirlwind of fire, in a chariot with horses of fire." He is to come, "at the appointed time . . . to calm the wrath of God . . . [and] to turn the heart of the father to the son, and to restore the tribes of Jacob" (48:3–10).

evangelist did not attach further meaning to the rite. It was important to the early Christians, of course, to establish an acceptable concept of the relationship between Jesus and the Baptist, but a far more important meaning of the baptism was no doubt intended by the evangelist. For him the baptism was the occasion for Jesus to receive the Spirit.

> The next day he saw Jesus coming toward him, and said, "Behold, the Lamb of God, who takes away the sin of the world! This is he of whom I said, 'After me comes a man who ranks before me, for he was before me.' I myself did not know him; but for this I came baptizing with water, that he might be revealed to Israel." And John bore witness, "I saw the Spirit descend as a dove from heaven, and it remained on him. I myself did not know him; but he who sent me to baptize with water said to me, 'He on whom you see the Spirit descend and remain, this is he who baptizes with the Holy Spirit.' And I have seen and have borne witness that this is the Son of God." [k]

The Gospels attribute divinity to Jesus in several ways. In Matthew and Luke the accounts of his supernatural birth confirm his divine nature, but according to Mark, as interpreted by some scholars, Jesus is adopted as God's son at his baptism: "Thou art my beloved Son." [l] In the Fourth Gospel Jesus' unique nature is accounted for by the coming of the Spirit at his baptism. This event is the ground of the Johannine incarnation Christology. In the descent of the Spirit, which "remained on him," [m] Jesus becomes the Christ, the Son of God and Savior of the world.[10] Thus in the Fourth Gospel, the supremacy of Jesus and of Jesus' baptism of the Spirit is clearly asserted. In this Gospel, baptism of water is insufficient. Baptism of the Spirit which comes from above and "is above all" [n] supersedes the way of the Baptist.

---

[k] Jn 1:29–34. [l] Mk 1:11. [m] Jn 1:32. [n] Jn 3:31.

[10] John does not seem to question the natural birth of Jesus or the fact that he was born in Nazareth; " 'We have found him . . . Jesus of Nazareth, the Son of Joseph.' Nathanael said to him [Philip], 'Can anything good come out of Nazareth?' " (Jn 1:45f.). See Thomas Sheehan, *The First Coming* (New York, 1986), 192–205, for an interesting simplified treatment of the growth of christology from the early Jewish Christian concept of the Son of Man at the Parousia to the later gentile Christian doctrine of the pre-existent Christ.

THE MIRACLES AND SIGNS

Miracle stories appear in all four canonical Gospels. The purpose of these accounts of the miracles is not simply to picture Jesus as a wonderworker who has compassion for the sick and afflicted, but also to provide evidence of his power and authority. In the Synoptics the miracles mark the promise of the coming Kingdom. Miracles have a special meaning in John's interpretation of Jesus. They are signs of his divine nature and of the meaning of his message, signs of his glory, of the actual presence of the power of God. The first twelve chapters of John are sometimes referred to as the Book of Signs, an account of miracles which signify Jesus as the revelation of God.

According to John, Jesus' ministry began with a miracle. In the synoptic accounts, at the beginning of his ministry Jesus said to the brothers Simon (who is called Peter) and Andrew fishing in the Sea of Galilee, "Follow me." And he "called" the brothers James and John the sons of Zebedee, also fishermen, and "immediately they left their boat and their father, and followed him." º But in John Jesus appears as a powerful charismatic personality who miraculously draws persons to him. Here Jesus did not "call" the disciples; they came to him without invitation as if they had discerned that he was the master whom they should follow, and Jesus' knowledge of them is cited by the evangelist as an evidence of his divinity. He knew them before they came to him.ᵖ Significantly these first disciples came from among the followers of John the Baptist — Andrew and an un-named disciple.[11] Andrew found his brother Simon Peter and broke the exciting news, "We have found the Messiah." ᵍ The following day Jesus went to Galilee where Philip and Nathanael joined his band. Nathanael recognized him as the Son of God, the King of Israel.ʳ

The miracle of changing the water to wine at the Cana wedding feast is given only in the Fourth Gospel. "This, the first of his signs," says John, "Jesus did at Cana in Galilee, and manifested his glory; and his disciples believed in him." ˢ In John's

---

º Mt 4:18–22; Mk 1:16–20.   ᵖ Jn 1:47–50.   ᵍ Jn 1:41.   ʳ Jn 1:49.   ˢ Jn 2:11.

[11] There may have been some competition between Jesus and John, and rivalry among their disciples may have continued for some time.

Gospel then, Jesus' first public act was to give a sign, the miracle of the wine, which introduces the higher quality of life which Jesus brings into the world. In John's view, Jesus' spiritual nature transcends the temporal order, and changing the water into wine, a foreshadowing of the coming of the Spirit, represents the power of the Spirit to transform life. As water is transformed miraculously into "good wine," ᵗ so through the power of the Spirit, ordinary life may be transformed into a higher spiritual quality.[12]

In three important episodes, John contrasts Jesus' emphasis upon the spiritual dimension of religion with what he regarded as the temporal, external concerns of "the Jews": the confrontation on the occasion of the cleansing of the Temple,ᵘ the interview with Nicodemus the Pharisee,ᵛ and the discourse to the Samaritan women on the spiritual meaning of water.ʷ

Statements in the Gospel of John about Jesus' visits to Jerusalem at Passover are the basis of estimates that Jesus' ministry was at least three years in length. In the Synoptics the recorded events occupy approximately one year. Other differences in chronology exist between the synoptic and the Johannine Gospels. Moreover, in the Synoptics Jesus' ministry takes place primarily in Galilee, but in John he makes several visits to Jerusalem for the celebration of the Passover. This focus upon Jesus in Jerusalem and upon the Jews and Judaism in Judea rather than upon Galilee suggests to some scholars that the format of the Fourth Gospel may have been motivated by the Christian opposition to the Jews which was strong after the fall of Jerusalem in 70 CE. Apparently the majority of Christians were not active in the revolt against Rome and thereafter wanted to separate themselves from the defeated Jews in the eyes of the Romans.

In John, the "cleansing" of the Temple occurred during Jesus' visit to Jerusalem soon after his baptism, whereas in the Synoptics it took place just prior to his arrest and crucifixion. When his

---

ᵗ Jn 2:10. ᵘ Jn 2:13–15. ᵛ Jn 3:1–21. ʷ Jn 4:5–30.

[12] Some Christian theologians have applied the symbolism represented in this miracle directly to the relationship of Judaism to Christianity. Through the Spirit, which is Christ, Judaism is to be transformed and superseded by the religion of Christ. Such an interpretation is a reading of later Christian theology back into the primary sources, a not uncommon practice.

action in the Temple was challenged by those who said, "What sign have you to show us for doing this?" Jesus answered, "Destroy this temple, and in three days I will raise it up." But, misunderstanding Jesus' meaning, his audience replied in literal terms, "It has taken forty-six years to build this temple." According to John, Jesus "spoke of the temple of his body." [x] For John, the more significant meanings, that Jesus is the temple which will be raised up and that the sign of his authority as Messiah is his resurrection, are summarized later in Jesus' debate with the Pharisees: "When you have lifted up the Son of man, then you will know that I am he." [y]

Nicodemus is described by John as a Pharisee and "a ruler of the Jews." Perhaps John meant that Nicodemus was a member of the Jewish Sanhedrin, the supreme tribunal of the Jewish nation. In any event, Nicodemus, a man apparently of high rank, came to see Jesus at night. "Rabbi," he said, "we know that you are a teacher come from God; for no one can do these signs that you do, unless God is with him." Jesus answered, "Unless one is born anew, he cannot see the kingdom of God." [z] But, according to John, Nicodemus' understanding of Jesus, like that of the others, was limited and inadequate, for he perceived only the temporal, physical meaning of Jesus' pronouncement and missed its symbolic, spiritual meaning. "How can a man be born when he is old?" [a] he asked.

According to John, from the very outset of his ministry in Jerusalem, Jesus made no compromise with current popular Jewish notions about the Kingdom of God. Nicodemus, who for John represents all official Judaism, was bound up with the temporal concerns of his people. He was presumably an authority on rites and rules for salvation, but his thinking was limited to the physical dimension of this world. In the discourses in John, Jesus moves from the mundane and the physical toward higher spiritual levels of meaning. Being born of the Spirit is the crucial element of his discourse with Nicodemus. Here appears John's often quoted peroration that so eloquently summarizes the traditional Christology, "For God so loved the world that he gave his only Son,

[x] Jn 2:18–21. [y] Jn 8:28. [z] Jn 3:1–3. [a] Jn 3:4.

that whoever believes in him should not perish but have eternal life. For God sent the Son into the world, not to condemn the world, but that the world might be saved through him." [b]

At a later time in Jerusalem when the chief priests and Pharisees sent officers to arrest Jesus, they returned without having made the arrest, apparently because they were deeply impressed by Jesus' sayings and suspected that he was a prophet or the Christ. Nicodemus was among those present at the time of the officers' report, and he spoke briefly in Jesus' defense. The reply of the Pharisees to Nicodemus indicates the official Judean prejudice against Galileans, especially any Galilean claiming the status of a prophet: "Are you from Galilee too? Search and you will see that no prophet is to rise from Galilee." [c]

LIVING WATER AND THE BREAD OF LIFE

Returning to Galilee, Jesus passed through the district of Samaria. In his day the Jews were quite commonly contemptuous of Samaria and Samaritans, and in traveling between Judea and Galilee, they usually avoided Samaria by taking the longer route through Perea, east of the Jordan. The origin of the Jewish hostility towards Samaritans is lost to history, but that hostility was centuries old by the time of Jesus. It is commonly held that because the Samaritans were descended in part from foreign settlers and because their religion was a modified version of the Judean religion, they were generally regarded as heretical by the people of Judea and their descendants, the Jews.[13]

Jesus' meeting with the woman of Samaria and his later reception by the Samaritans was, in the Gospel of John, a providential surprise.

> The Samaritan woman said to him [Jesus], "How is it that you, a Jew, ask a drink of me, a woman of Samaria?" For Jews have no dealings with Samaritans. Jesus answered her, "If you knew the gift of God, and who it is that is saying to you, 'Give me a drink,' you would have

[b] Jn 3:16f. [c] Jn 7:52.

[13] The Samaritans are sometimes regarded as the earliest of the Jewish sects. Their temple at Mt. Gerizim was regarded by the Jews as heretical. The Samaritans of Jesus' time apparently accepted as scripture only the Pentateuch.

asked him, and he would have given you living water." The woman said to him, "Sir, you have nothing to draw with, and the well is deep; where do you get that living water?" . . . . Jesus said to her, ". . . whoever drinks of the water that I shall give him will never thirst; the water that I shall give him will become in him a spring of water welling up to eternal life." The woman said to him, "Sir, give me this water, that I may not thirst, nor come here to draw." [d]

In the Gospel of John, water conveys a spiritual-symbolic as well as a temporal-literal meaning. In this account of the woman's inability to comprehend Jesus' intention, to think beyond the immediate and physical, the author dramatically forces the reader to recognize a higher spiritual meaning. It is clear that John means that Jesus is the source of the spiritual water. All who drink the Spirit which he possesses will have eternal life. The "hour is coming, and now is, when the true worshipers will worship the Father in spirit and truth." [e] But in spite of this pronouncement, the woman, who apparently represents for John those who fail to recognize the true nature of Jesus, continues to misunderstand his meaning and fails to discern his true character. She declares, "I know that Messiah is coming . . . he will show us all things." At this point Jesus brings the episode to its climax, "I who speak to you am he." [f]

Contrasting in his discourses the symbolic-spiritual nature of true religion with the literal-temporal dimension of institutional religion, Jesus brought into focus the eternal nature of life in the Spirit. Indeed in John's Gospel, Jesus is God's Spirit which is eternal — unrestricted by time or place or form. Both Samaritans and Jews were in error in their religion, for "neither on this mountain [Mt. Gerizim] nor in Jerusalem will you worship the Father." [g]

For John the evangelist, Jesus is the living water and the bread of life. Jesus as the life-giving bread is the subject of John 6, which is apparently based on the Synoptic accounts of the feeding of the five thousand.[h] This is the only miracle recorded by all four gospels. John's account proceeds first on the temporal level,

[d] Jn 4:9–15. [e] Jn 4:23. [f] Jn 4:25f. [g] Jn 4:21.
[h] Mk 6:32–44; Mt 14:13–21; Lk 9:10–17.

where the circumstances lead up to a miracle of providing fish and bread for a large crowd assembled on "the other side of the Sea of Galilee."[i] When the people saw this miracle, they declared Jesus to be the prophet who was to come and were about to take him by force to declare him king, but he escaped and went into the mountain.

When evening came, the disciples crossed the sea to Capernaum, and as a dangerous storm arose, Jesus came to them walking on the sea and they reached land immediately. The crowd soon found Jesus and his disciples on the other side of the sea. Perceiving that their persistent effort to find him was for the miracle of food and not for the sign which was the true meaning of the miracle, Jesus said to them, "You seek me, not because you saw signs, but because you ate your fill of the loaves."[j] This was the occasion for the moving discourse on the bread of life. "Do not labor for the food which perishes, but for the food which endures to eternal life." Here the emphasis in John shifts from the physical to the symbolic-spiritual meaning of bread. "It was not Moses who gave you the bread from heaven; my Father gives you the true bread from heaven."[k] "I am the bread of life; he who comes to me shall not hunger, and he who believes in me shall never thirst." For the evangelist, Jesus is "the bread which came down from heaven," and "He who believes has eternal life."[l] Here as elsewhere it is obvious that the primary concern of the Fourth Gospel was not to provide an account of the events in Jesus' life but rather to provide a foundation in his teachings for the theology of the church of John's time.

THE ADULTEROUS WOMAN

Most scholars agree that the story of the adulterous woman does not belong to the original Gospel of John. Verses 7:53–8:11 are not found in the oldest manuscripts, and in manuscripts of later date they appear either after John 7:36, at the end of the Gospel, or after Luke 21:38. However, this story is consistent with others which express Jesus' attitude toward sinners and is not an arbitrary addition by the later church. The story also asso-

---

[i] Jn 6:1. [j] Jn 6:26. [k] Jn 6:27, 32. [l] Jn 6:35, 41, 47.

ciates judgment with the symbol of light, of seeing and belief —
major themes in John's Gospel. This point is made explicit in
9:39: "For judgment I came into this world, that those who do
not see may see, and that those who see may become blind." In
the story of the adulterous woman, scribes and Pharisees assume
the role of judges, but they are blind in their unbelief; they judge
only after the flesh. In contrast, Jesus' judgment illuminates the
mercy of God.

According to John, Jesus had gone to the Mount of Olives,
presumably to spend the night. The next morning he came to the
Temple and taught the people. The scribes and Pharisees brought
before him a woman who had been taken in adultery, saying,

> "Teacher, this woman has been caught in the act of adultery. Now in
> the law Moses commanded us to stone such. What do you say about
> her?" This they said to test him, that they might have some charge to
> bring against him. Jesus bent down and wrote with his finger on the
> ground. And as they continued to ask him, he stood up and said to
> them, "Let him who is without sin among you be the first to throw
> a stone at her." [m]

In John's account, those bringing the woman before Jesus were
not seeking advice or judgment but rather were trying to ensnare
him in a practical dilemma. According to the old law, both the man
and the woman caught in adultery were to be stoned. If Jesus had
explicitly upheld the old Mosaic Law, they might have charged
him with opposition to the Roman law. If he had said that she
should not die, he could have been accused of ignoring the Mosaic
Law. Jesus carefully avoided the entrapment. He wrote on the
ground. Although what he wrote can only be conjectured, according to a few early manuscripts, he wrote the sins of each of the
accusers. When he arose the woman's accusers had all departed.
Addressing her, he said, "Woman, where are they? Has no one
condemned you? . . . Neither do I condemn you; go, and do not
sin again." [n]

"Again Jesus spoke to them, saying, 'I am the light of the
world; he who follows me will not walk in darkness, but will have

---

[m] Jn 8:4–7. [n] Jn 8:10f.

the light of life.' " [o] Except perhaps for the words "life" and "truth" there is no more expressive word in John's vocabulary than the word "light." These three words, "life," "truth," and "light" are the great signatures of his Gospel.

GNOSTICISM

More than any other book of the New Testament, the Fourth Gospel exhibits the impact of Gnosticism on the foundations of Christian doctrine. John was clearly influenced by the gnostic religious ideas and attitudes that were widely diffused throughout the Graeco-Roman world of his time. Nowhere is this influence more evident than in the passages describing Jesus in terms of "life" and "light" [p] and in the extreme Johannine invectives against the Jews, where Jesus' opponents or enemies are called the offspring of the devil.[q] But notwithstanding gnostic influence, with Hellenistic ideas impacting on John's theology, the Fourth Gospel is today recognized as having a strong Jewish base. Its author was no doubt a hellenized Jewish Christian.

Gnosticism was a strange compound of oriental, Hellenistic, and probably Jewish mythology, theology, and cosmology that well into the third century, in various and subtle ways, entered into the religious thought and affected the religious and moral behavior of Christianity as well as pagan religion, the mystery cults, and to a lesser degree Judaism. The early Christian theologians of Alexandria, Clement and Origen, embraced gnostic elements in their theology, and under the influence especially of Marcion in the second century the infant church was seriously threatened by the spread of the gnostic heresy. The chief enemies of Gnosticism in the church of the second and third centuries were the theologians Irenaeus, Hippolytus, and Tertullian. Much of the current knowledge of early Gnosticism is known from their arguments against it. The so-called Nag Hammadi codices, a collection of gnostic religious texts translated from Greek to Coptic and dating from not later than the fourth century, were discovered in the Nile Valley in 1945 and added greatly to the knowledge of

[o] Jn 8:12. [p] Jn 8:12. [q] Jn 8:44.

Gnosticism.[14] The originals of some elements of the Nag Hammadi codices may date from as early as the first century. These texts have revealed far more diversity in early Christianity than historians had ordinarily supposed existed.

Gnosticism is a religion of salvation — salvation as release and escape from the evil, material world through the possession of revealed esoteric gnosis or knowledge.[15] Sometimes this escape involved ascetic discipline, usually the mediation of a saviour, but always the instrumentality of saving knowledge revealed from on high. Gnosticism was grounded in a Persian-type cosmic and moral dualism of spirit and matter, light and darkness, truth and lies, good and evil. The true Gnostic carried on an incessant war against the material world, a world which was evil by nature, the product of an evil creator. In its extreme form Christian Gnosticism attacked the Hebraic biblical religious tradition, declaring that the God of Genesis was the evil creator of the material world. The true Gnostics were the candidates for salvation, the spiritual beings or "pneumatics" who belonged to the Good God — that ultimate being whose realm is spirit and light, who is above all mundane reality. The children of Satan, the evil God, were the "hylics," material beings, ignorant of the true gnosis and destined for darkness and damnation. That the author of the Fourth Gospel was under gnostic influence is entirely evident.[16] But Gnosticism was burdened by a fantastic and complicated mythology, and

---

[14] See *The Nag Hammadi Library in English*, edited by James M. Robinson (New York, 1977), Elaine Pagels, *The Gnostic Gospels* (New York, 1981), and Kurt Rudolph, *Gnosis*, trans. by R. M. Wilson (San Francisco, 1983), 34–52.

[15] For scholarly discussions of Gnosticism, see especially Hans Jonas, *The Gnostic Religion* (Boston, 1963), and Rudolph, *Gnosis*. For a discussion of Gnosticism in early Christian thought, see also Robert M. Grant, *Gnosticism and Early Christianity*, rev. ed. (New York, 1966).

[16] The gnostic element in the Fourth Gospel is fully analyzed in Rudolf Bultmann, *Theology of the New Testament*, trans. by Kendrick Grobel (New York, 1955), Vol. II, Part III, and C. H. Dodd, *The Interpretation of the Fourth Gospel* (Cambridge, 1953), *passim*. Bultmann comments that "If the author's background was Judaism, as rather frequently occurring rabbinical turns of speech perhaps prove, it was, at any rate, not out of an orthodox but out of a gnosticizing Judaism that he came. . . . he lives within the sphere of Gnostic-dualistic thinking" (13f.). Dodd regards Gnosticism as a major element in the background and substance of the Fourth Gospel but is less inclined than Bultmann to treat the author as a "near-Christian gnostic."

the author's commitment to the historical Hebraic biblical tradition and to the basic principles of Judaism from which Christianity arose was strong enough to prevent his being fully dominated by gnostic myth and doctrine. Nevertheless, even such a thing as the intense polemic of Jesus against the unbelieving Jews that appears in John is in itself evidence of gnostic impact upon that Gospel.

HOSTILITY TOWARD THE JEWS

The opposite of the pneumatic assurance of salvation is the unbelief and perversity of "the Jews" who walk in darkness. Here John paralleled Mark's theme that Jesus' disciples, even those most intimate, including Peter, sometimes failed "to see," to discern Jesus' true identity and role. Matthew is inclined to play down this flaw of the disciples and transfer it to the Pharisees. In the Gospel of John it is "the Jews" who are lost in total and willful disbelief. John refers to the Jews in general more often than to the Sadducees or Pharisees.

This hostility toward Jews, which is far more evident in the Fourth Gospel than in the Synoptics, reaches its peak in Chapter 8. "You are from below, I am from above; you are of this world, I am not of this world." [r] However, as Jesus continued to describe himself as sent by "the Father," some Jews did believe and he promised them discipleship, "You will know the truth, and the truth will make you free." [s] "Knowing the truth" here is knowing the truth about Jesus — his divine nature and role. The freedom that comes from knowing the truth is freedom from unbelief and ignorance, freedom to experience the light of belief and eternal life. Then, Jesus continued, "I speak of what I have seen with my Father." [t] Other Jews present at that time, still thinking on the temporal, materialistic level, answered Jesus, "Abraham is our father." At this point the issue came to a dramatic climax in Jesus' bitterest denunciation: "You are of your father the devil, and your will is to do your father's desires." [u] According to the evangelist, the devil is the source of Jewish unbelief. He is a murderer and liar, and the reason the Jews do not hear the word of God is that they "are not of God" but rather of their father, the devil, and are

[r] Jn 8:23. [s] Jn 8:31f. [t] Jn 8:38. [u] Jn 8:39, 44.

totally incapable of belief. This extreme polemic followed the format of typical gnostic belief that distinguished the saved "pneumatics," the spiritual beings, from the condemned "hylics," the physical beings.

The bitter denunciation of the disbelievers is followed by the episode of the man blind from birth in which Jesus declares himself to be the "light of the world." Jesus' disciples asked about the man's condition, whether it was because of his sin or his parents' that he was born blind. Jesus answered neither, but rather that God's works might be manifest. Then Jesus declared, "As long as I am in the world, I am the light of the world." [v] He gave the blind man his sight and the Jews, true to their condition of disbelief, saw in the event only a violation of the sabbath. After further interrogation of the man who had received his sight and of his parents, the antagonists of Jesus declared that the man was "born in utter sin," and they cast him out.[w]

Possibly drawing on Mark's observation at the time of the feeding of the five thousand that the people "were like sheep without a shepherd," [x] if indeed he was acquainted with Mark's Gospel, John developed his own conception of Jesus as the Good Shepherd. Again, it is not John's primary purpose to simply describe important events in Jesus' ministry but rather to read meaning into his teachings and actions for the benefit of the church at least two generations after Jesus, when the Fourth Gospel was written, probably not earlier than 90 CE. Here the evangelist addressed the ongoing problem of Jewish-Christian relations that arose in the difficult period of reconstruction following the disastrous Jewish-Roman war. Gamaliel's reference in Acts 5:33–37 to what were probably two earlier abortive messianic movements, led by Theudas and Judas the Galilean, may refer to events which were alluded to in John's report of Jesus: "all who came before me are thieves and robbers; but the sheep did not heed them. I am the door; if any one enters by me, he will be saved, and will go in and out and find pasture." [y]

Jesus as shepherd is not like the hired man who tends the flock until he sees the wolf coming, who cares nothing for the

---

[v] Jn 9:5. [w] Jn 9:28, 34. [x] Mk 6:34. [y] Jn 10:8f.

sheep and abandons them to the wolves in order to find safety for himself. Jesus cares; he is the good shepherd who "lays down his life for the sheep." [z] Also, Jesus has other sheep, which will heed his voice. These are to be brought together "so there shall be one flock, one shepherd." [a] The other sheep were presumably the Gentiles.

THE RAISING OF LAZARUS

The raising of Lazarus, which is recorded only in the Gospel of John, is one of the major miracles toward which the image of Jesus as shepherd points. It is the miracle or sign which clearly establishes Jesus' uniqueness as the Son of God and the last and final sign leading up to his death on the cross. In the synoptic Gospels, the cleansing of the Temple was the crucial offense which fueled the final opposition leading to the arrest and execution of Jesus. But in the Gospel of John the raising of Lazarus was that decisive event.

The home of Lazarus was Bethany, a short distance east of Jerusalem. According to John's account, Lazarus died before Jesus arrived. His sisters, Mary and Martha, had asked Jesus to come, saying: "Lord, he whom you love is ill," [b] but Jesus delayed going to Bethany. John 11:4 explains why Jesus waited two days after Lazarus died: "This illness is not unto death; it is for the glory of God, so that the Son of God may be glorified by means of it."

Arriving at Bethany, Jesus and his disciples found that Lazarus had been in the tomb four days. Many were there to comfort the sisters in the loss of their brother. Upon hearing that Jesus was entering the village, Martha went to meet him and said, "Lord, if you had been here, my brother would not have died." Jesus said to her, "Your brother will rise again." But Martha, missing Jesus' meaning, replied, "I know that he will rise again in the resurrection at the last day." This was the occasion for Jesus' dramatic proclamation, which has been a source of comfort and hope to Christians throughout the centuries: "I am the resurrection and the life; he who believes in me, though he die, yet shall he live, and whoever lives and believes in me shall never die." [c]

[z] Jn 10:11. [a] Jn 10:16. [b] Jn 11:3. [c] Jn 11:21–26.

Clearly, the miracle of raising Lazarus from the dead appears in John to exhibit in a most dramatic way Jesus' power as the Son of God. Jesus has power over life and death, he is the giver of life. "When Jesus saw her [Mary] weeping, and the Jews who came with her also weeping, he was deeply moved in spirit and troubled; and he said, 'Where have you laid him?' They said to him, 'Lord, come and see.' Jesus wept." [d] Then Jesus prayed to the Father, " 'that they may believe that thou didst send me' . . . [then] he cried with a loud voice, 'Lazarus, come out.' [and] The dead man came out." [e]

Until the raising of Lazarus, according to John, the opposition at Jerusalem had come chiefly from the Pharisees. But from this time on, the chief priests, who were usually antagonistic to the Pharisees, joined hands with the Pharisees and through their combined influence in the Sanhedrin, they successfully opposed Jesus. They considered the public displays of enthusiastic support for Jesus, such as resulted from the miracle at Bethany, to be a serious danger to the Jewish people both politically and religiously. They no doubt believed that Jesus might be perceived by the Romans as a threat to law and order, a threat that could bring the wrath of Rome upon the Jewish nation and the destruction of their most holy place. Caiaphas, the high priest, addressing the council (Sanhedrin) as it debated the course to follow in view of this threat, made the historic judgment that "it is expedient for you that one man should die for the people, and that the whole nation should not perish." According to John, Caiaphas "did not say this of his own accord" but being high priest "he prophesied that Jesus should die for the nation, and not for the nation only, but to gather into one the children of God who are scattered abroad." [f] Caiaphas had uttered an oracle which neither he nor his fellow Jews could decipher correctly but which could have full meaning only for the Christian believers. Clearly in John's view the oracle of Caiaphas predicted the redemptive death and resurrection of Christ who is the good shepherd, the Door, the Gate to life. "So from that day on" wrote John, "they took counsel how to put him [Jesus] to

[d] Jn 11:33–35. [e] Jn 11:42–44. [f] Jn 11:50–52.

death." Therefore, John continued, he "no longer went about openly among the Jews." [g]

THE ARREST AND TRIAL

In its main outlines John's account of the arrest, trial, and crucifixion of Jesus is consonant with the Synoptics, but there are several important differences. Although there is no concrete evidence that John borrowed from the Synoptics, he may have had access to Mark and/or Luke or at least to a source that they held in common.[17] The triumphal entry into Jerusalem is described in all three of the Synoptics, but in John the crowds greeted him as the one who raised Lazarus. There is a "last supper" prior to the Passover, but no eucharistic ceremony of the bread and wine. Instead Jesus washes the feet of his disciples. In John there is no mention of prayer in Gethsemane, but he is arrested in the garden and arraigned before two high priests, not the Sanhedrin, before the trial by Pilate. There is no encounter with Herod Antipas. The "beloved disciple" is mentioned without name as one who was present at the "last supper," at the cross, and with Peter at the empty tomb. In John, responsibility for the crucifixion is placed squarely on "the Jews," since Pilate, who examined and questioned him, found him innocent. Nevertheless, Pilate had Jesus scourged. Pilate would have released Jesus but for the insistence of the chief priests and the clamor of the crowd that he be executed because "he has made himself the Son of God." [h] [18]

In John, the last days in Jerusalem were occasions for extensive discourses by Jesus to his disciples and others on the meaning of his life and death and on the promise of salvation to those who believe and accept him. Jesus admonishes his listeners to follow him and promises that "when I am lifted up from the earth, [I] will draw all men to myself." [i] The gnostic elements in these

[g] Jn 11:53f. [h] Jn 19:7. [i] Jn 12:32.

[17] On the background and possible origins of John's information, see Rudolf Bultmann, *The Gospel of John*, trans. by G. R. Beasley-Murray et al. (Philadelphia, 1971), and C. K. Barrett, *The Gospel according to St. John* (London, 1978).

[18] For comparisons and contrasts among the several Gospels in their treatment of the trial and crucifixion, see Joseph B. Tyson, *The New Testament and Early Christianity* (New York and London, 1984), 258–70.

Jesus in the Gospel of John

discourses are especially prominent — the references to "him who sent me," the judgment against "this world" and the "ruler of the world," the devil, and the identification of Jesus as the "light" that has come into the world.ʲ Even the washing of the feet enacted a sermon symbolizing Jesus' relation to his disciples and their proper relation to one another.

After Judas left the supper to perpetrate the betrayal, there is in John one of the longest discourses in the New Testament, the eloquent sermon on Jesus as the way, the truth, and the life, which uses various symbols to reiterate the promise of salvation. "Let not your hearts be troubled; believe in God, believe also in me. In my Father's house are many rooms; if it were not so, would I have told you that I go to prepare a place for you?" ᵏ Also the promise that "I will come again and will take you to myself, that where I am you may be also." ˡ To the request of Philip that he show them the Father, Jesus replied, "He who has seen me has seen the Father, . . . I am in the Father and the Father in me." ᵐ And the promise that the Father will send another Counselor, the Spirit of truth, the Holy Spirit who proceeds from the Father. Certainly much of the substance of the Christian religion, including Christological doctrine, is set forth in this sermon, which closed with a prayer, acknowledging that the hour had come, that his mission to bring eternal life was completed, and pleading that his disciples and all who believed in him would be kept from "the evil one" ⁿ and sanctified in the truth.

In the garden across the Kidron, Judas came with soldiers and officers from the chief priests and the Pharisees and arrested Jesus. In John Peter resisted and was told to put up his sword, and in John Peter also denied Christ three times as in the Synoptics. After questioning by Annas and Caiaphas about his disciples and teachings, Jesus was arraigned before Pilate in the Praetorium.[19]

John's account of the trial before Pilate is if anything even more emphatic in placing the responsibility for the crucifixion on the Jewish leaders, for he lays greater stress on the presumed

---

ʲ Jn 12:31, 44, 46. ᵏ Jn 14:1f. ˡ Jn 14:3. ᵐ Jn 14:9f. ⁿ Jn 17:15.

[19] Annas, the father-in-law of the high priest Caiaphas, had been deposed as high priest by the Roman authorities in 15 CE.

efforts of Pilate to set Jesus free than do the Synoptics. Pilate's question of Jesus, "What is truth?" was in response to Jesus' statement, "Every one who is of the truth hears my voice," º a clear expression of a gnostic claim that those who belong to the supreme God are marked for salvation. Such a concept was no doubt confusing to the Roman Procurator, as was Jesus' statement "My kingship is not of this world." ᴾ

THE CRUCIFIXION

John's account of the crucifixion often parallels that of Mark.[20] But in John's Gospel Jesus carried his cross to Golgotha, and Mary the mother of Jesus, her sister, and "the disciple whom he loved" were present at the cross. Jesus consigned his mother's care to the disciple and, after receiving the hyssop of vinegar, he said, "It is finished," and died with apparent calm. In both Mark and John there was the title King of the Jews required by Pilate, and the division of Jesus' clothes by the soldiers. But unlike the Synoptic accounts, in John there was no darkness, no earthquake, and no crying aloud to God, "Why hast thou forsaken me?" The account of the soldier piercing Jesus' side, which flowed with blood and water, appears only in John. The author may have included it, as some historians have speculated, to emphasize the fact that Jesus had a human body of flesh and blood and that in accordance with the will of God he truly suffered and died, a fact which early Christian docetists denied in their adoption of gnostic ideas with respect to the redeemer. It was this strong emphasis on the humanness as well as divineness of Jesus that radically distinguished the author of the Fourth Gospel from typical Christian gnostics. The real death of Jesus was important for John's theology, for the death of Jesus meant life for humankind. This concern of the author confirms the statement of the Prologue that the Word became flesh. The question of the humanity as well as divinity of

º Jn 18:37f.   ᴾ Jn 18:36.

[20] Some scholars, for example C. K. Barrett, have held that John's version of the crucifixion is based on Mark. Others, for example C. H. Dodd, arguing especially on the ground of language differences, have insisted that it is an independent account.

Jesus was already a major controversy when the Gospel was written and was to become the center of great contention in the early church, separating the docetists and Gnostics from the central body of Christians, who held that Jesus was at the same time both human and divine. This position became a central doctrine of the church, and those who opposed it were declared heretical.

THE RESURRECTION APPEARANCES

The Johannine account of the resurrection appearances of Jesus, now the risen Christ, has much in common with the synoptists' but apparently is also based on an independent tradition. John stresses the fact of a bodily resurrection, that the real body of Jesus was laid in the tomb and rose. The physicality of the resurrection is attested by the empty tomb which Peter and the disciple whom Jesus loved entered, the showing of the wounds to Thomas, the doubter, and the eating of the fish with the disciples by the Sea of Tiberias in Galilee after the miraculous catch of fish. But notwithstanding this identification of the resurrected being with the human Jesus, the Gospel dramatically sets forth the spiritual nature of the risen Christ, who warns Mary when she recognizes him at the tomb, "Do not hold me, for I have not yet ascended to the Father . . . ,"[q] and the apparent capacity of Jesus to enter the closed room in his meetings with the disciples.[r] [21]

Clearly a dominant theme of John, expressed in the account of Thomas's doubting, is that faith is of greater power and worth than actually seeing; "Blessed are those who have not seen and yet believe."[s] And it is evident that although the Gospel emphasizes the pastoral leadership of Peter, who three times assured Jesus of his love, the disciple "whom Jesus loved" is intended to receive special attention from the reader. He raced with Peter to the empty tomb, was the second person to enter the tomb, and recognized Jesus on the shore of Tiberias.[t] The final chapter intimates that this disciple might not die until the return of Jesus.[u]

[q] Jn 20:17. [r] Jn 20:26. [s] Jn 20:29. [t] Jn 21:7. [u] Jn 21:20–23.

[21] The Synoptics do not place Mary at the tomb. For an analysis of the possible meanings of the resurrection appearances, see Barrett, *John*, 560–88.

In the opinion of some scholars, the Epilogue or final chapter of John (chapter 21) was not an integral part of the original redaction of the Fourth Gospel,[22] which instead ended with the impressive final statement of chapter 20:

> Now Jesus did many other signs in the presence of the disciples, which are not written in this book; but these are written that you may believe that Jesus is the Christ, the Son of God, and that believing you may have life in his name.

In support of this, it is sometimes argued that the disciples would not have returned to their trade as fishermen, as described in Chapter 21, after being commissioned by Jesus to go into the world, with the message of salvation and having received the Holy Spirit. " 'Peace be with you. As the Father has sent me, even so I send you.' And when he had said this, he breathed on them, and said to them, 'Receive the Holy Spirit....' "[v]

---

[v] Jn 20:21f.

[22] See Raymond E. Brown, *The Gospel according to John* (New York, 1970), 1077–82.

Part II

PAUL, PAULISM, AND THE EARLY CHURCH

CHAPTER 12

Paul and His Letters

Paul occupies a central place in the history of Christian thought and in the Christian canon, the New Testament. Of the twenty-seven documents which comprise the New Testament, ten were either written by Paul or in his name. His first letter to the Thessalonians is probably the earliest document in the New Testament collection. All of his letters were written earlier than the Gospels. Of great significance, moreover, is the probability that Paul and Paulinism stand behind the writing of other major works of the canon. Some scholars hold that the synoptic Gospels, the epistles of James, Hebrews, 1 and 2 Timothy and Titus, and the Gospel of John all contain allusions to Pauline concepts and interpretations or to Deutero-Pauline doctrines, which are ideas expressed in epistles traditionally assigned to Paul but whose authenticity of authorship is now seriously questioned.[1]

PETER AND PAUL

Aside from Jesus, Peter and Paul are the most prominent persons in New Testament literature. Rather early in the development of Christianity they came to represent two different and at times conflicting doctrinal positions. During the later years of the first century, there were strong efforts to reconcile these divergent positions and thereby unify the faith, efforts which may be seen even in the synoptic Gospels. The hostility toward Peter expressed in the Gospel of Mark on the occasion of the Confession at Caesarea Philippi, for instance, was greatly tempered in the Gospel of

---

[1] S. Sandmel, *The Genius of Paul, a Study in History* (New York, 1970), 208, goes so far as to claim that "except for Revelation, every writing in the New Testament is by Paul, or attributed to Paul, or deals with issues and problems created for the Church by reason of Paul's tremendous contribution."

Matthew by elimination of the verb "rebuke" in describing Jesus' response to Peter.[2] In Matthew's account of the Confession, Peter became in effect the successor to Christ as head of the Christian church — "upon this rock." In Luke's second book, Acts of the Apostles, Peter became a major transitional figure standing between the "Judaizers," the Jewish Christians in Jerusalem with their strong commitment to the Law and works, and the Hellenistic and mystical tendencies emphasizing the doctrine of grace that characterized the Pauline writings.

LUKE AND PAUL

Paul died ca. 60–64, several years before the end of the Jewish-Roman war which resulted in the destruction of Jerusalem and the Temple. The Jews and their institutions, especially in Jerusalem, were decimated by the war, and consequently the Christian community, which was presumably established in Jerusalem under the leadership of James, the brother of Jesus, faced possible extinction. Apparently prior to the siege of Jerusalem some Jewish Christians fled north across the Jordan to Pella and into the rugged hills of the upper Galilee.[3] Although some may have returned to Jerusalem, the most viable alternative for the Christians after the war, considering the destruction and the occupation by the Roman military, was to gather in Galilee where they might survive as a community of faith awaiting Christ's imminent return. Communities of Christians were planted in Capernaum and Remmon and across the Jordan in Cochuba.

It was probably during this critical post-war period that Paul's letters were collected and the Pauline doctrines of grace and salvation through Christ became prominent in Christian thought. Paul's eschatology and doctrine of the Spirit were preserved and pro-

---

[2] This rebuke by Jesus is omitted from Luke's Gospel. Cf. Mark 8:32f. with Matthew 16:22f. The view that Mark's Gospel contains an anti-Petrine interpretation is supported by Sandmel. It is Sandmel's view that Matthew's revitalization of Peter's status as successor to Jesus and chief among the apostles was intended to neutralize the pro-Pauline bias in Mark. Sandmel is probably correct that one major effort of Luke in Acts of the Apostles was to synthesize the Petrine and Pauline traditions into a continuous, unified account. Sandmel, 165–92.

[3] Eusebius, *Ecclesiastical History III*, 5:3, trans. by Kirsopp Lake, Loeb Classical Library (Cambridge, Massachusetts, Harvard University Press, 1926), 380.

moted in the Gospel of Mark. Luke's writings, especially Acts of the Apostles, show how the Spirit, which was present in Jesus during his ministry, entered the church on the occasion of Pentecost with power to convert and transform the gentile world. Paul became the central figure in the account of this conversion. The Pauline documents which often are not considered to be the authentic work of the Apostle — 2 Thessalonians, Colossians, and Ephesians — were written and added to the original Pauline collection. Ephesians was perhaps intended as a cover letter for the entire Pauline corpus.[4]

Several of Paul's religious teachings were apparently opposed by some Christians in the last quarter of the first century as leading toward anarchy. For those chiefly concerned about order, succession, and authority in the structure of the Christian church, Paul's ideas were unacceptable. S. Sandmel is probably correct in holding that Acts of the Apostles and other New Testament documents, the Epistle of James and the Gospel of Matthew, for example, were in large measure responses to Paulinism, intended to correct and neutralize the individualistic emphasis and mystical tendencies in Paul's doctrine of the Spirit, the imminent aspect of his eschatology, and the trend toward antinomianism in his pronouncements on freedom from the Law.

Christianity seems to have developed through several phases during the first century: (1) The Jewish Christianity in Jerusalem prior to the Jewish-Roman war was probably dynastic or family in format. (2) The early gentile Christianity showed gnostic and montanist-spirit tendencies, which were probably based upon Paul. (3) Mark's proposal in the period of reconstruction following the war was for a new beginning on the basis of Paul's doctrine of the spirit, including a devaluation of Peter and the Judaistic-Christian faith. (4) Matthew's Gospel was a reinstatement of Peter as the successor to Jesus and head of the church. (5) Finally, Luke's synthesis of the Pauline and Petrine traditions in Acts of the Apos-

---

[4] E. J. Goodspeed, making use of the opinions of earlier scholars, Julicher and Weiss, is largely responsible for the formulation of the thesis that Ephesians was written by a disciple of Paul as an introduction to or a cover letter for the Pauline letters. See Edgar J. Goodspeed, *An Introduction To The New Testament* (Chicago, 1946), 222ff.

tles became the church's official account of Christian origins and its own development.[5]

ACTS OF THE APOSTLES AND PAUL'S MINISTRY

Because of the abundance of extant primary materials on Paul and his teachings, it is often assumed that an account of his ministry should be simple to construct. On the surface this assumption might seem justified, for the letters should be reliable and productive sources — personal and in at least one case intimate correspondence. However, there have been many diverse and sometimes conflicting interpretations of Paul, his life and teachings. Some of these have been flawed, mainly because the traditional accounts of Paul have depended almost entirely on the narrative of his life given in the Acts of the Apostles: that Paul was a Jew named Saul, who was born in Tarsus in Cilicia and was educated at the feet of Gamaliel; that he persecuted the Christian community; that after his conversion on the road to Damascus,[a] he engaged in three great missionary journeys and was finally arrested at Jerusalem and sent to Rome for trial.

The problem with this well known account from Acts is that several of its most important elements are not substantiated from Paul's own writings.[6] For example, the pattern of the three missionary journeys in Acts is not found in his letters, and in some important respects the chronology followed in Acts does not agree with the data provided in the letters, particularly in Galatians and the Corinthian epistles.

Other important differences are evident: In Acts of the Apostles the unique status of the Jerusalem church is emphasized. Here Paul is represented as accountable to the leadership in Jerusalem, a base of operations and center for the Christian communities.

---

[a] Acts 22:3–8.

[5] On these phases in Christian development, see S. Sandmel, 183–86.

[6] For a discussion of the primary sources on Paul and the status of Acts of the Apostles as a source, see Günther Bornkamm, *Paul*, trans. by D. M. G. Stalker (New York, 1971), xiv–xxi. Also, John Knox, "Acts and the Pauline Letter Corpus," and Hans Conzelmann, "Luke's Place in the Development of Early Christianity" in L. E. Keck and J. L. Martyn, eds., *Studies in Luke-Acts* (Philadelphia, 1980).

However, according to Paul's letters, Ephesus, not Jerusalem, seems to have been the headquarters for much of his ministry. On several occasions he went to Jerusalem but primarily to confer with the leadership there. The authority of the Twelve over the entire Christian movement is also asserted in the Acts account, and Paul is represented as submissive to the Jerusalem council. However, on the witness of Paul's own letters, he was not submissive, nor did he consider his authority inferior to that of the Jerusalem council.[7]

Today Acts is almost universally accepted by scholars as a second volume written by the author of the Gospel of Luke, the two volumes being frequently referred to as Luke-Acts. Studies of Luke's Gospel have shown that its author selected and arranged his sources, edited the details, and ordered events in accord with his own religious interests. This fact provides the key for understanding Luke's second volume, that it is to be interpreted in light of his overall concern to tell the story of Christianity; that God's spirit, which was in Jesus, came to the Christian church with great power and that the expansion of Christianity was straightforward and inevitable, a natural development toward the fulfillment of God's plan. In Luke's account of the expansion of the Christian church, Paul and Peter were the central figures in initiating the transformation of Christianity from a Jewish sect to a major religion in the Roman world.[8]

Paul lived during a critical time for the infant church; his letters speak of much internal conflict and strife. He felt strongly

---

[7] John Knox argues persuasively that Luke, the author of Luke-Acts, must have known of the letters of Paul, despite the fact that Paul's letters are not mentioned in Acts nor is Paul mentioned as a letter writer. Knox assumes that Luke deliberately omitted reference to the Pauline letters because they were being misunderstood and misinterpreted by Gnostic Christian writers. See John Knox, "Acts and the Pauline Letter Corpus," *Studies in Luke-Acts*, eds. Leander E. Keck and J. Louis Martyn (Nashville, 1966), 279–87.

[8] Martin Hengel argues for the basic importance of Acts as a source on Paul. He warns that "without the account written by Luke, incomplete, fragmentary and misleading though it may be, we would not only find it almost impossible to put Paul and his work in a chronological and geographical setting; we would still be largely in the dark about the development of Paul's great mission around the Aegean and the events that led up to it, and about his concern to go to Rome and to Spain (Rom 15:22–29)." *Acts and the History of Earliest Christianity*, trans. by John Bowden (Philadelphia, 1980), 38.

about rival factions developing among Corinthian Christians and about the Judaizers, presumably Jewish Christians from Jerusalem who were undermining his efforts in Galatia. According to his letters, decisions important to the church were pending. The precarious condition of the Christian congregations, Paul's relation to them, and the threat posed to the unity of the early church by its internal disputes — all of which appear so clearly in Paul's letters — seem to have been intentionally glossed over in Acts. This book was apparently written in retrospect, some time after Paul had faced the crucial issues of his day.

In Acts Paul's doctrine of the Spirit ("in Christ Jesus," "in the Spirit") is brought to a prominent position in the Christian gospel.[b] In Acts, Luke adopted a modified Pauline position on the coming of the Spirit and speaking in tongues. To the Corinthians Paul had exclaimed, "I would rather speak five words with my mind, in order to instruct others, than ten thousand words in a tongue."[c] Considering Paul's attitude toward tongues, Luke may have converted the mystical Pentecostal tongues-of-fire experience into a miracle of understanding in which the gentiles from foreign lands heard in their own languages the message of the apostles. This interpretation of the coming of the Spirit and tongues became the guideline for the church later on in its struggle with Montanist Christians. However, Luke's dependence on Paul was never total, for he seems to have rejected some of Paul's views and modified others. For example, Luke apparently had serious reservations about Paul's claim to be an apostle, probably because this claim was founded on a personal vision of the Christ. The "Coming of the Spirit" at Pentecost, according to Luke, was not to individual persons as in the case of Paul but rather to the apostles as members of an official body. Apparently Luke wanted to provide controls for developing the structure of the church by formalizing and regularizing the coming of the Spirit as well as the procedure for selecting replacements in the apostolic council.

In the early church the "Twelve" seem to have been regarded primarily as missionaries, who were to bear witness to the resurrection of Jesus. In this early period (ca. 35–44 CE), it is difficult

[b] Rom 8:1, 9f.; 2 Cor 5:17; 13:5; Gal 2:20.   [c] 1 Cor 14:19.

to establish primacy in the church for one of the three claimants for succession: the family of Jesus for whom Davidic descent was basic; the prophets, whose claim to succession was derived through the power of the Holy Spirit; and the apostles, whose credentials rested upon the fact that they walked and talked with Jesus. In Acts the trend is toward the recognition of a formal, authoritative body, "the Apostles," whose status and role were enhanced and formalized as an apostolic council. Luke shows Paul accepting the preeminence of the Jerusalem Council led by James, the brother of Jesus, and Peter.

PAUL'S JEWISH ENVIRONMENT

Certainly environmental factors play a major role in the development of a person's perceptions, presuppositions, ideas, and attitudes. Nowhere is this more evident than in Paul's early intellectual and spiritual nurturing in the Jewish culture and religion. The Jewish heritage into which Paul was inducted through his home, synagogue, and community was clearly the chief factor conditioning his attitudes and beliefs even after his conversion to Christianity.

Little is known of Paul's childhood and youth. According to his letter to the Philippians, he was a circumcised Jew "of the people of Israel, of the tribe of Benjamin, a Hebrew born of Hebrews; as to the law a Pharisee." [d] [9] However, it is known from both Acts and his own letters that Paul was a Jew of the Diaspora. First century Judaism was not a unified system of beliefs and practices. The accounts by Philo and Josephus of the religious and political parties and sects in their day, recent archaeological studies, and the knowledge that has issued from the discovery of ancient documents such as the Essene scriptures, the Dead Sea Scrolls, indicate that even in Palestine Judaism was not a simple monolithic faith and culture. Religious ideas and moral ideals

[d] Phil 3:5f.

[9] Although Paul's own account of his birth and education has in general been accepted by most historians, both Jewish and Christian, it is occasionally challenged. The Jewish scholar Hyam Maccoby in *The Myth Maker: Paul and the Invention of Christianity* (New York, 1986) has argued that Paul was a convert to Judaism and was *not* a Pharisee. Maccoby holds that Jesus *was* a Pharisee.

were involved inextricably with political, economic, and regional interests and traditions. There were Messianic movements expecting the end of history, zealous revolutionaries yearning for rebellion against Rome, purist-separatist movements, as the Essenes, protesting against the controlling Jewish parties in Jerusalem. Others accommodated their Judaism to Greek ideas, Hellenistic culture, and Roman power.

But while there was such variety in Palestinian Judaism, there was equal diversity in the Judaism of the Diaspora, with Jewish communities extending from Rome to Babylon and Egypt. The impact of foreign cultures, especially Greek, produced types of Jewish faith that deviated from Palestinian norms. In the late nineteenth century the historian Adolf Harnack wrote in *History of Dogma*, "The Judaism of the diaspora was long since surrounded by a retinue of half-bred Grecian brethren, for whom the particular and national forms of the Old Testament religion were hardly existent." [10] But W. D. Davies, writing in 1964, insisted that the evidence has mounted that it is impossible to distinguish definitively between Diaspora and Palestinian Judaism.[11] According to S. Sandmel, Paul "was a Greek Jew," but this "does not asperse Paul's loyalty and allegiance to Judaism . . . . It means simply that the content of his Judaism, like that of other Greek Jews, had undergone a subtle, but radical shift." [12]

Tarsus, Paul's native city, was in his day a cosmopolitan center of commerce and culture. It was an old city, thoroughly Hellenized, and from at least the time of Antiochus IV supported a substantial Jewish population. The Roman proconsul Pompey made it the capital of the province of Cilicia in 66 BCE, and after the death of Julius Caesar, Mark Antony granted Roman citizenship to its free inhabitants, an endowment later honored by the emperor Augustus. Apparently this was the basis of Paul's claim to citizenship that in his later years entitled him to a hearing

---

[10] A. Harnack, *Outlines of the History of Dogma*, 1893 (Boston, 1957), 22f. For the impact of Hellenistic Judaism on Christianity, see also Joseph Klausner, *From Jesus to Paul* (New York, 1945).

[11] *Paul and Rabbinic Judaism* (London, 1979), chap. 1.

[12] S. Sandmel, 9, 15.

before Nero. That Tarsus was a center of philosophical thought is well known. The geographer Strabo, an older contemporary of Jesus, mentioned its philosophical schools, favorably comparing them to both Athens and Alexandria.[13] Stoic and Epicurean philosophy flourished there and Platonic influences of the kind that generally pervaded the intellectual life of the Hellenistic world.

Although educated no doubt in the Jewish community of Tarsus, Paul may have been influenced as well by the northern Judaism of Galilee. Jerome refers to a rumor that Paul's family was originally from the village of Gischala in Galilee.[14] The German scholar Adolf Deissmann, responding to this brief note in Jerome, raised an interesting question, "Jesus and Paul — were they actually 'fellow-countrymen'?"[15] More evidence would be required to answer this question definitively, but if Paul's family was from Gischala, north of Galilee, he might well have shared with Jesus the Jewish religious tradition which emphasized the power of the Spirit, a heritage from Moses, Samuel, and Elijah. This tradition became a foundation element of the Christian religion.

Apparently Paul was also trained in the Pharisaic tradition as a student of the celebrated Rabbi Gamaliel I.[16] He had been taught from childhood to cherish the Torah as the standard for Jewish belief and practice, and in his later years he may have been preparing to become a rabbi. In all likelihood he was conditioned to hold himself aloof from alien culture and religious concepts notwithstanding the subtle influences from his Greek intellectual and cultural environment. These factors in Paul's background not only shaped the Judaism to which he gave his early allegiance but undoubtedly gave form to his later religious attitudes and theological doctrines as a Christian.

---

[13] Strabo, *Geography*, XIV, v, 13 (Loeb edition, 347).

[14] Jerome, *Epistle to Philemon*, 23–24.

[15] G. A. Deissmann, *Paul, A Study in Social and Religious History*, trans. by William E. Wilson, 2nd ed. (New York, 1927), 90f.

[16] Acts 22:3. Some scholars have questioned the reliability of the reference to Gamaliel, while others point out that Paul handles the scriptures in the rabbinic manner of Hillel. Hyam Maccoby, in *The Myth Maker* (New York, 1986), chap. 6, argues that Paul could not have been a student of Gamaliel.

Although his conversion to Christianity was a turning away from some basic commitments to Judaism, even as a Christian and as the chief creator of Christian theology Paul did not abandon his fundamental allegiance to the Jewish religious tradition. His religion as a believer in Christ became a religion of grace rather than law, but he remained committed to the monotheistic foundations of Judaism and to the moral principles of the Hebrew prophets. His reverence for Moses and the Hebrew patriarchs, Abraham and Jacob, and his devotion to the Hebrew scriptures were typically Jewish. He understood and shared the popular eschatological expectations of his time. Christianity was for him the consummation of Judaism, the continuation of God's chosen lineage until the end of the age. Christ crucified and risen was the fulfillment of the promise.

PAUL'S HELLENISTIC ENVIRONMENT

No doubt even as a youth Paul was concerned with the differences between the religious beliefs and practices of his home and synagogue and those of his Gentile neighbors with their temples and multiple gods. Even if he deliberately avoided contacts with non-Jewish practice and thought, in Tarsus he could not have failed to acquire considerable knowledge of gentile ways and ideas. His own writings reveal his effective usage of the common Greek dialect, the Koine, the language of the New Testament and chief bearer of Hellenistic culture. It is significant, moreover, that the Septuagint, the Greek translation of the Old Testament, was the scripture from which Paul quoted. This was typical of a Hellenistic Jew of the Diaspora. Greek and Roman architecture, sculpture, and religious art and symbols were elements of the environment in which he was nurtured. Much of the life-style of the Hellenistic cities was Greek in character. The theater, the stadium games, even the names of many Jews, expressed Greek habit, interests, and values. Notwithstanding his commitment to Judaism, Paul must have been strongly influenced by religious beliefs and practices of the gentile world in which he lived, both before and after his conversion to Christianity.

Three elements of Hellenistic thought and practice are of particular importance for any analysis of the religious concepts of Paul: Graeco-Roman Stoicism, which in this period was a major philosophical movement; the Oriental mystery cults that were increasingly important, especially in the eastern part of the empire; and the Gnosticism which pervaded much Hellenistic religion. To what extent these movements affected Paul's religious attitudes and beliefs has long been a matter of scholarly dispute. If they influenced him, questions remain about whether he borrowed directly from Stoic literature, for instance, or simply imbibed Stoic ideas from the philosophical atmosphere in which he lived; whether the similarities between his teachings on salvation and some of the popular beliefs of the mystery religions were influenced by one or more of the prevalent mysteries or were simply additional evidence of what was becoming commonplace belief and practic relative to the ultimate destiny of the human soul. The extent to which Paul was influenced in the cosmic and psychological dimensions of his theology is a matter of debate, but that there were important gnostic facets of his thought is obvious.

STOICISM, THE MYSTERIES, AND GNOSTICISM

Whether Stoicism directly impacted Paul's thinking is conjectural. However, Tarsus, his early home, was an important center of Stoic learning and there are in Paul's writings interesting parallels with Stoic thought. For example, the presence of the divine in all creation, a basic concept of Stoic philosophy, is suggested in Paul's letter to the Romans.

> For what can be known about God is plain to them, because God has shown it to them. Ever since the creation of the world his invisible nature, namely, his eternal power and deity, has been clearly perceived in the things that have been made.[e]

This statement has overtones of typical Stoic metaphysics, but its context is anything but Stoic. And the idea of creation expressed here is Judaic rather than Stoic. In the past scholars have called attention to other phrases in Paul's letters that are similar

[e] Rom 1:19f.

to those of prominent Stoic writers. George P. Fisher, for instance, a major historian at the turn of the century, says, "We may reasonably assume a familiarity on the part of Paul with Stoic ideas and phrases, since Tarsus was a prominent seat of Stoic teaching. The quotation in Acts XVII.28, is from the hymn of Cleanthes, and from the Stoic-Poet, Aratus, who was connected with Tarsus." [17]

It is not possible to show that Paul consciously borrowed from Stoicism. But Stoic concepts and expressions were widely dispersed throughout the Hellenistic world and, despite his Jewish upbringing, Paul surely assimilated to his own thought much that had become common in the thought and expression of his time. There is, of course, another side to this coin. Considerable attention has been given to the possibility that Stoicism was influenced by both Judaism and Christianity. The pantheistic inclinations of Roman Stoicism, however, indicate that it differed fundamentally from both Jewish and Christian theism with their concept of God as creator of and therefore distinct from the world. Still scholars generally agree that Paul was influenced by Stoicism in his literary style, as in his use of the so-called Stoic-Cynic diatribe.

The relation of Paul's religious teachings to the widespread mystery cults has long been a matter of study and dispute, and even today a definitive resolution is impossible. That similarities, if not identities, appearing in Paul's Christianity and in the chief mysteries suggest direct influence is obvious. But a careful examination casts serious doubt on the once common idea that Paul's early Hellenistic conditioning taken with his conversion revolt against Judaism produced a religion in the typical style of the Oriental mysteries.

[17] *The Beginnings of Christianity* (New York, 1891). The passage from Acts reads, "For 'In him we live and move and have our being'; as even some of your poets have said, 'For we are indeed his offspring.' " In his *The Mysticism of Paul the Apostle* (1931), 6–8, Albert Schweitzer questioned the authenticity of the attribution of this and other Stoic statements of Paul by the author of Acts. See chapter 1 on the distinctive character of Pauline mysticism. Schweitzer held that the Hellenization of Christianity came after Paul, with Ignatius and the Fourth Gospel, for example, though Paul's historically oriented "Christ-Mysticism" in a sense prepared Christianity for that Hellenization.

Although they were probably at the height of their influence a century or two later, the mysteries, which originated especially in Egypt, Persia, Syria, and Greece, were growing in strength and popularity in Paul's day, and it is unlikely that he entirely escaped their influence. Whether they were the cults of Cybele and Attis from Phrygia, of Astarte and Adonis from Syria, Isis and Osiris from Egypt, or the Persian Mithraism or the Greek Eleusinian religion, the vitality and popularity of the mysteries were grounded in the concern of the general urban masses of the empire for the salvation of the individual person, if not in this life at least in a blessed hereafter. In a world where the individual was burdened by totalitarian power, bureaucracy and military repression, even slavery, redemption from life's bondage was the dominant hope and substance of religion. The possibility, and indeed the reality, of personal immortality was found in identification with the dying and rising saviour gods of the mysteries, an identification achieved especially through the rituals of baptism or washing and a sacred meal.

The similarity of such central mystery beliefs to Paul's Christianity is obvious, and leading scholars of a few decades past argued persuasively that Paul, a Hellenized Jew of the Diaspora, had as a convert to Christianity transformed Christianity into a pagan mystery cult.[18] This simple explanation that resulted from the study of comparative religions has now been largely aban-

---

[18] The work of Richard Reitzenstein, Wilhelm Bousset, and others in studies of the history of religion provided a generation of scholars with historical data and arguments supporting this thesis. R. Reitzenstein, *Die Hellenistischen Mysterienreligonen* (Leipzig, 1927), and W. Bousset, *Kyrios Christos* (Göttingen, 1921). More recently the philosophers John Herman Randall, Jr., and Irwin Edman have insisted that Paul simply converted Christianity into a Hellenistic mystery cult: "Christianity, at the hands of Paul, became a mystical system of redemption, much like the cult of Isis, and the other sacramental or mystery religions of the day. Salvation is not forgiveness of sins, as it is for Jesus himself, but a transformation of human nature from the Flesh to the Spirit, from human to divine: it is literally a process of deification." J. H. Randall, *Hellenistic Ways of Deliverance and the Making of the Christian Synthesis* (New York, 1970), 154. In his *The Mind of Paul* (New York, 1935), 123, Edman held that Paul deserted Judaism in turning to Graeco-Roman religious culture in his treatment of Christianity as a mystery and insisted that if there is no connection between Paul's Christianity and the Hellenistic savior-cults, "we are faced with one of the most fantastic coincidences in religious history."

doned, or at least severely modified, by the increased understanding of ancient religion and reaction against interpretations of religious history commonly issuing from liberal scholarship. It has become evident that the major contacts of Christianity with mystery religions developed after Paul, especially in the second century, and linguistic studies have indicated that important accommodations to the language of the mysteries were probably made by Christian writers to facilitate understanding of their doctrines. Moreover, in recent studies, differences often count for more than similarities in considering causal influences.

While the surface similarities of the Christian and pagan mysteries are manifest, the differences are sometimes profound. The Hellenistic mysteries were grounded in myth and mythological deities; Paul's Christianity was grounded in temporal events and an authentic historical person. It is possible to overstate the differences in the area of Paul's emphasis on the moral life in contrast to the pagan mysteries, as some of these, as for instance Mithraism, generated more moral substance through their ritual and ceremony than is sometimes recognized.[19] In *The Mysticism of Paul the Apostle,* Albert Schweitzer defined the ground of Paul's religion of redemption as his "Christ-Mysticism," which, he insisted, was radically different from the "God-Mysticism" of the Hellenistic mysteries. Schweitzer argued that the religion of Paul, like that of Jesus, was rooted in Jewish eschatology rather than mystery religion. While affirming that in the second century Christianity was transformed into Hellenistic teaching due to the decline of the eschatological faith when Jesus failed to return, Schweitzer argued that "the Hellenization of Christianity does not come in with Paul, but only after him . . . . Paul was not the Hellenizer of Christianity. But in his eschatological mysticism of the Being-in-Christ he gave it a form in which it could be Hellenized." [20]

[19] The Jesuit scholar Hugo Rahner has argued, "Christianity is a mystery of revelation; it is a mystery of ethical law; it is a mystery of salvation by grace. And in these three points it contrasts sharply with Hellenistic mystery religion." "The Christian Mystery and the Pagan Mysteries" in Joseph Campbell, ed., *The Mysteries* (Princeton, 1955), 358.

[20] Albert Schweitzer, *The Mysticism of the Apostle Paul,* trans. by William Montgomery (New York, 1968), viii–ix. Chapter 1 of H. J. Schoeps's *Paul: The*

Schweitzer, who more effectively than any other scholar of this century insisted on the eschatological interpretation of the gospel, held fast to the thesis that Paul's doctrine issued not from Hellenistic thought but from Jewish eschatology. "Paulinism," he wrote, "in its essence . . . can be nothing else than an eschatological mysticism, expressing itself by the aid of Greek religious terminology." [21] However, today the rigorous distinction between Hellenistic and Palestinian Judaism, which Schweitzer assumed, is generally rejected by scholars of first-century Judaism and Christianity who have been influenced by recent archaeological findings and a reconsideration of earlier evidences. Some hold that the interaction of Greek and Jewish cultural elements from the time of Alexander's invasion in 332 BCE and especially after the Roman occupation in 63 BCE produced a culture that Schweitzer had ignored. Even if Paul is described as a Jewish "Rabbi become Christian," his Jewish religion was not free from Hellenisms.[22] Even Emil Schürer in his monumental work *The Jewish People in the Time of Jesus Christ,* first published toward the end of the last century, wrote that at the time of Jesus "the line of demarcation between [the literature of Palestinian Judaism and of Hellenistic Judaism] is of a somewhat fluctuating and indefinite character and . . . the designations applied to them are to be taken very much cum grano salis." [23]

Although Paul was by no means a Christian gnostic when compared to later gnostics in the church, his conception of the world being under the dominion of evil, his treatment of the spirit and the body, his doctrine of salvation by grace, and his doctrine

---

Theology of the Apostle in the Light of Jewish Religious History, trans. by Harold Knight (Philadelphia, 1961), is a useful discussion of the research on Paul and the Hellenization of Christianity. For a careful examination of the Hellenistic elements in Paul's religion, see Arthur Darby Nock, *Early Gentile Christianity and Its Hellenistic Background,* Part 3 (New York, 1964).

[21] See A. Schweitzer, *Paul and His Interpreters,* trans. by W. Montgomery, 1912 (New York, 1964), 241. Also, page 238: "The Apostle did not Hellenise Christianity. His conceptions are equally distinct from those of Greek philosophy and from those of the Mystery-religions."

[22] Davies, *Paul and Rabbinic Judaism,* 16.

[23] *The Literature of the Jewish People in the Time of Jesus* (New York, 1972), 1f.

of predestination echoed gnostic notions. These will be treated in the following chapter on Paul's theology.

PAUL'S CONVERSION

Paul's conception of salvation through Christ issued from his profound religious experience on the road to Damascus, which was crucial in changing him from a persecutor of the Christians to their most effective advocate and influential theologian. This experience was the ground of his faith and inspired his preaching, thinking, and writing through his remaining years. According to some interpreters, Paul's vision of Christ came to him as a "bolt from the sky," a supernatural "revelation" of the risen Lord. For others his conversion experience was the culmination and convergence of psychological factors which had produced strong internal conflicts in his religious beliefs, attitudes, and loyalties.[24] Thus Paul may have suffered severe psychological tension associated with his religious zeal.

Paul's Jewish home life and his strict formal training in the synagogue may have been difficult to reconcile with the Greek-pagan cultural values to which in all probability he was daily exposed. His own statements express the intense seriousness with which he embraced the religion of his people. He was zealous to observe the Law, perhaps more than most young Jewish men. "I advanced in Judaism beyond many of my own age among my people, so extremely zealous was I for the traditions of my fathers." [f] In the matter of righteousness under the Law, crucial to a practicing Jew, Paul felt blameless, for he had observed the tradition of his fathers to the letter.[g] Yet his consciousness of evil and the pressures of sinful desire were increased by the very prohibitions and restrictions which the Law enjoined. The Torah, Paul's hope for life, brought only keener awareness of the presence of sin, increased desire, and eventual death. "For sin, finding opportunity in the commandment, deceived me and by it killed me." [h] Thus Paul's early life under the Law was one of inner conflict and

[f] Gal 1:14. [g] Gal 3:6. [h] Rom 7:11.

[24] D. Riddle gives a somewhat speculative account of the psychological factors underlying Paul's conversion experience. See Donald Riddle, *Paul, Man of Conflict* (Nashville, 1940).

turmoil; his experience with the legal aspects of Judaism as he understood it was distressing. Only gradually did he realize the inadequacy of his inner striving under the Law, and the full and final recognition of this fact culminated in the conversion experience.

Paul's inner conflict seems to have reached a critical point during his contacts with the early Christian followers of the Way. Although the Christian movement began in Palestine among the disciples of Jesus, in Paul's time it was spreading among the Jews of the Diaspora, at least in Syria. Some members of this new sect, probably Hellenist converts, eliminated from their religion certain Jewish practices, among them circumcision. For most Jews this was a most grievous error, and for Paul, who appears to have been a Pharisaic missionary in the Diaspora, it was intolerable. The sensitiveness which had driven Paul to the point of fanaticism with respect to the Law now impelled him to act against the Christians.[25] But this only intensified his inner conflict, for apparently the followers of Jesus had a sense of security and freedom and of certain victory which sustained them in the face of danger and death. At least something like this picture of internal tension and conflict has often been held to explain Paul's conversion experience.[26]

Paul's own letters must be taken as the primary source in any discussion of his conversion. However, the traditional interpretation of his vision of Christ is based largely on Acts of the Apostles, where three references to the event are recorded.[i]

> But Saul, still breathing threats and murder against the disciples of the Lord, . . . approached Damascus, and suddenly a light from heaven flashed about him. And he fell to the ground and heard a voice saying to him, "Saul, Saul, why do you persecute me?" And he said, "Who

---

[i] Acts 9:1–9; 22:6–11; 26:12–18.

[25] See Bornkamm's arguments that Paul could not have been a persecutor of the Jerusalem Christians, as indicated in Acts 8:3, because they were practicing Jews, but rather that he persecuted the Christians of the Diaspora, who were not faithful to the Law. *Paul*, trans. by D. M. G. Stalker (London, 1971), chap. 2. Stephen, in whose persecution Paul was apparently implicated, was a Hellenized Jew.

[26] For a more traditional treatment of Paul's conversion experience, see *The Jerome Biblical Commentary*, 79:12–14. Here the vision on the Damascus road went beyond Judaism and Hellenistic "cultural roots," for it was a "revelation of Jesus" that "gave Paul an ineffable insight into 'the mystery of Christ' " (79:14).

are you, Lord?" And he said, "I am Jesus, whom you are persecuting; but rise and enter the city, and you will be told what you are to do." The men who were traveling with him stood speechless, hearing the voice but seeing no one.[j]

In all three accounts of the conversion in Acts, the vicinity of Damascus is mentioned as the location of the theophany. The word "light" is emphasized; "a great light from heaven suddenly shone about me."[k] In all accounts Paul heard a voice and in one the voice spoke to him "in the Hebrew language."[l] One discrepancy in the three accounts recorded in Acts is especially noticeable: In the first report (9:7) those who were traveling with Paul stood and heard the voice which spoke to him, but they saw no one. However, in the second account (26:14) they fell to the ground, and in the third account (22:9) his companions saw the light but did not hear the voice. Some scholars have interpreted the accounts of Paul's blindness and conversion in Acts as symbolic of the beginnings of Christianity: Paul, like the early Christians, had been blind in Judaism but had received spiritual illumination.

Paul's letters allude to the conversion experience. According to his own account the experience came without warning while he was actively persecuting Christians. A powerful light or illumination had a dramatic effect upon him. In the Acts accounts Paul fell to the ground, saw a great light from heaven, heard a voice, and his companions also either saw the light or heard the voice. But these details do not appear in Paul's own references to the experience.[m] However, one assertion is consistently maintained both in Acts and in the letters: Paul claims to have seen Jesus Christ. "Am I not an apostle? Have I not seen Jesus our Lord? Are not you my workmanship in the Lord? If to others I am not an apostle, at least I am to you."[n] He had not received his call from other men but God himself had revealed his son to him. "For I would have you know, brethren, that the gospel which was preached by me is not man's gospel. For I did not receive it from man, nor was I taught it, but it came through a revelation of Jesus Christ."[o]

---

[j] Acts 9:1, 3–7. [k] Acts 22:6. [l] Acts 26:14. [m] 1 Cor 9:1f.; 15:3–8; Gal 1:11–16.
[n] 1 Cor 9:1f. [o] Gal 1:11f.

The conversion experience was for Paul the basis for his authority; it made him a witness to the resurrected Christ and this qualified him as an apostle. Paul does not distinguish between the validity of his own experience and that of the other apostles. Peter and James the brother of Jesus were leaders of the Jerusalem church. But for Paul even their personal intimate relationship with Jesus carried no greater status than his own vision of the risen Christ.

> For I delivered to you as of first importance what I also received, that Christ died for our sins in accordance with the scriptures, that he was buried, that he was raised on the third day in accordance with the scriptures, and that he appeared to Cephas [Peter], then to the twelve.... Then he appeared to James, then to all the apostles. Last of all, as to one untimely born, he appeared also to me.... I worked harder than any of them, though it was not I, but the grace of God which is with me.[p]

Paul's letters make remarkably few references to Jesus and his teachings. There is no evidence that he had a serious interest in the Jesus who walked the pathways of Galilee, healed the sick, promised forgiveness for repentance, and proclaimed the imminent coming of God's Kingdom. His concern rather was with the crucified and risen Christ. Paul's faith in Christ was more than simply intellectual assent or belief. His conversion meant a total commitment to Christ and the gospel, for the fact of Christ's presence in his life was a powerful force. "I have been crucified with Christ; it is no longer I who live, but Christ who lives in me; and the life I now live in the flesh I live by faith in the Son of God, who loved me and gave himself for me." [q]

PAUL THE MISSIONARY

The dating of important events and the chronology of Paul's letters are controversial problems among historians of the New Testament. Scholars have commonly relied on Acts to provide the narrative framework for Paul's statements. However, Paul's letters provide more relevant information than is generally realized.

[p] 1 Cor 15:3–5, 7f., 10. [q] Gal 2:20.

Here it is possible to reconstruct from brief autobiographical statements a reliable sketch of Paul's missionary activities while relying on Acts only as a supplementary source.

Following his conversion experience Paul went into Arabia, the territory east and south of Syria. "I did not confer with flesh and blood, nor did I go up to Jerusalem to those who were apostles before me, but I went away into Arabia; and again I returned to Damascus." [r] Because of the meagerness of the reports, where precisely Paul went and what he did during the three-year period which followed is difficult to determine. He probably retired for a period to reflect on his theophany and conversion and the responsibilities which these imposed on him. Then he began his active proselytizing for the gospel in the cities of Arabia and Syria.

Paul's visits to Jerusalem were decisive events in determining his role in the life of the church. According to his own statements, after returning from Arabia he went to Jerusalem to visit and acquaint himself with the leaders of the Jewish Christian community.

> Then after three years I went up to Jerusalem to visit Cephas, and remained with him fifteen days. But I saw none of the other apostles except James the Lord's brother.[s]

After this brief visit he pursued missionary activities in the areas near his homeland, in Syria and Cilicia.[t] During the next eleven years (possibly fourteen), Paul expanded his field of activity. His independence and adventurousness, expressed in his desire to find new, untouched areas, led him eventually toward the West. Here he was so successful that in the accounts of his work Syria and Cilicia fade into the background. His center of activity shifted to the great cities of the west in Galatia, Macedonia, Greece, and the Roman province of Asia, where he evangelized and founded Christian fellowships among the Hellenistic Jews and Gentiles.

Paul's success was not without considerable opposition. When he was unable to handle critical problems in person he endeavored to resolve them in his letters, which were to become a rich deposit of faith for the Christian church and the chief foundation of its theology. In First Thessalonians, for example, he was concerned

[r] Gal 1:16f. [s] Gal 1:18f. [t] Gal 1:21.

with the small community which he had established at Thessalonica in Macedonia and wrote, probably from Athens or Corinth, to instruct and encourage the Christians there in the face of persecution. In the Graeco-Roman city of Corinth, he found immediate response to his message and a young, though immature Christian community was founded. Second Corinthians 6:14–7:1 is often accepted as a fragment of an early letter of Paul to this church written after he had arrived in Ephesus.

There are several theories concerning Paul's imprisonment and the writing of the so-called imprisonment letters, Philippians and Philemon. According to the traditional view, he was imprisoned only once — at Rome near the end of his life. Some scholars have held, however, that he was imprisoned earlier at Caesarea in Palestine.[27] Others allege that he was imprisoned earlier in Ephesus in the province of Asia on the Aegean coast. The evidence is inconclusive, but the latter thesis seems to present fewer difficulties than either of the other two. In 1 Corinthians Paul refers to a personal crisis in Ephesus:

> Why am I in peril every hour? I protest, brethren, by my pride in you which I have in Christ Jesus our Lord, I die every day! What do I gain if, humanly speaking, I fought with beasts at Ephesus?[u]

Other statements concerning afflictions in Asia also suggest Ephesus as the place of imprisonment from which Paul sent his letters to the churches at Philippi and Laodicea (the letter to Philemon).

Soon after his release from prison Paul made his second visit to Jerusalem, his so-called conference visit. His purpose was to resolve the important question of admitting non-Jews to fellowship in the churches. "Then after fourteen years I went up again to Jerusalem with Barnabas, taking Titus along with me. I went up by revelation, and I laid before them (but privately before those who were of repute) the gospel which I preach among the Gentiles."[v] That he was successful in presenting and defending his case seems evident from his own reference to the event. "And when they perceived the grace that was given to me, James and

---

[u] 1 Cor 15:30–32. [v] Gal 2:1f.

[27] This view depends entirely upon passages in Acts (Acts 23:35; 24:27).

Cephas and John, who were reputed to be pillars, gave to me and Barnabas the right hand of fellowship, that we should go to the Gentiles and they to the circumcised." [w]

The period which followed his return to the west, however, was probably the most trying of Paul's career. He was eager to cooperate with the Jewish Christian leaders in gathering an offering for the poor of Jerusalem and possibly to help overcome the tension between Jewish and Gentile Christians, but his desires were not easily attained.[x] Serious problems were developing in the young church at Corinth; internal dissension threatened to break the unity of the Christian community into rival factions, some professing to follow Paul, others Apollos, Cephas, or Christ.[y] Paul was distressed by the situation which certain groups had provoked, especially those of the Spirit (the Spiritualists or pneumatics), and wrote his long letter to the Corinthians (1 Corinthians) in which he attempted to establish rules for governing the gifts of the Spirit (speaking in tongues and prophecy), to revive their allegiance to his gospel, and to restore their unity. Confusion among the Corinthian Christians seemed imminent. For Paul, this was a critical situation, and in response he wrote two of the bitterest letters of his career: one to the church at Corinth (2 Cor. 10–13) and the other to the Galatians. Discipline and determination prevailed in the end, for Paul learned from his companion Titus that his harsh letter had taken effect. Rejoicing in the good news, he wrote again to Corinth but this time with the spirit of reconciliation and gratitude for their change of attitude (2 Cor. 1–9).[28]

The crisis period in Asia, as reflected in Galatians and 2 Corinthians 10–13, is significant for what it reveals about the chronology of Paul's missionary ventures. Both letters identify the height of the struggle which, according to the record, occurred "fourteen years" after Paul's conversion experience and his first visit to Jerusalem. Some difficulty arises at this point in determining whether the "three years" period mentioned in Galatians 1:18 should be included in the total "fourteen years" period. In any event, all of

[w] Gal 2:9. [x] Gal 2:10. [y] 1 Cor 1:10–17.

[28] See 2 Cor 1–9 (except the fragment from an earlier letter — 2 Cor 6:14–7:1).

the chronological data, including all of Paul's work in Galatia, Asia, Macedonia, and Greece and all of Paul's letters except 2 Corinthians 1–9, the letter to Phoebe (Rom. 16) and Romans 1–15, must fit into this eleven-to-fourteen-year period. Paul's statements about the crises which he faced are pertinent not only for what they reveal about the difficulties of the time but also for the pertinent chronological information they supply. One of these crises occurred when Jewish-Christians or Judaizers in Galatia sought to discredit Paul's teaching about freedom from the Law through faith in Christ.

Paul wrote his letters to the Galatians and to the Corinthians in order to resolve their conflicts. His success in both instances attests to the power of his written word.[z] With the problems largely resolved, he was free to turn his attention to other matters. In his letter to the Romans, he clearly expressed his desire to visit the church in Rome.[a] He had preached his gospel over an extensive area, "from Jerusalem and as far round as Illyricum," and he had ambitions to reach new areas yet untouched, possibly Spain, to build, but not on another's foundations.[b] He probably felt that his work was completed in the regions where he had already preached and established Christian congregations. Moreover, the field was too crowded for a man of his temperament. "But now, since I no longer have any room for work in these regions, and since I have longed for many years to come to you, I hope to see you in passing as I go to Spain, and to be sped on my journey there by you, once I have enjoyed your company for a little." [c]

But Paul had another obligation which required his attention: the collection for the poor at Jerusalem. For him, this was more than just a gift from one Christian group to another; this offering symbolized his longing for peace between the Jewish Christian and Hellenistic Christian churches. The collection was the basis for his agreement with the Jerusalem leaders and had been encouraged among the churches since his return from his conference visit.[d] At first he had hoped to send others with the gift to Jerusalem, but as the time arrived he realized that his own personal appearance before the Jerusalem community would be most effec-

[z] 1 Cor 1:10–13. [a] Rom 1:13. [b] Rom 15:19f. [c] Rom 15:23f. [d] Gal 2:10.

tive. Reconciliation and unity with the Jerusalem leaders were so important that he was willing to sacrifice his personal desires and face certain danger if not death in Jerusalem. "I appeal to you, brethren, by our Lord Jesus Christ and by the love of the Spirit, to strive together with me in your prayers to God on my behalf, that I may be delivered from the unbelievers in Judea, and that my service for Jerusalem may be acceptable to the saints." [e]

At this point the narrative that can be reconstructed from Paul's letters appears to end. It is continued, however, in the book of Acts, where Paul took the offering to Jerusalem. He was attacked by his opponents, arrested, imprisoned for two years, and eventually sent to Rome to be tried. His transfer to Rome was the result of his appeal on the basis of Roman citizenship.[f] The problem of assigning dates to these events is difficult. The date of Paul's final visit to Jerusalem and of the apparent termination of his active career is of central importance, but the date cannot be ascertained from evidence in his own letters. The book of Acts states that Paul was in prison during the change of administration between the procurator Felix and his successor Porcius Festus.[g] If one accepts this assertion, a date of 60–62 CE can be assigned to this imprisonment. His release at Caesarea and the long journey to Rome involving shipwreck at Malta must be accounted for. Since there is no scriptural record of Paul's death the historian must depend on the tradition preserved among the early church Fathers that Paul suffered execution in Rome during the reign of Nero. This may have occurred as late as 64 CE.

THE PAULINE LETTERS

Fourteen documents in the New Testament canon are traditionally attributed to Paul. However, many scholars maintain that the claim for Pauline authorship of some of these is not authentic. Few students of the New Testament now question the authenticity of seven of the letters: 1 Thessalonians, 1 and 2 Corinthians, Galatians, Philippians, Philemon, and Romans.[29] First Thessa-

---

[e] Rom 15:30f. [f] Acts 25:10–28:31. [g] Acts 24:27.

[29] See N. Perrin's assessment of this problem in *The New Testament, an Introduction* (New York, 1974), chapters 5 and 6. For a different resolution of the

lonians, Romans, Galatians, and 1 and 2 Corinthians make up what is known as the Pauline classics, documents so indisputably authentic to Paul that they provide the standards of internal evidence, ideas, vocabulary, and writing style against which the authenticity of other so-called Pauline writing is judged.

Many scholars seriously question Paul's authorship of 2 Thessalonians, Colossians, and Ephesians and conclude that they were written by followers of Paul who were inspired by him and wanted to bring to their writings the support and prestige of his name. These letters seem to reflect the interests of a later generation and are often classified as deutero-Pauline. None but the most conservative scholars would accept Hebrews or the pastoral letters, 1 and 2 Timothy and Titus, as authentically Pauline. These are generally assumed to have been composed well beyond Paul's time during the period of emerging Catholicism, probably in the early decades of the second century.

The chronology of the genuine letters is assumed by many students of Paul to be: 1 Thessalonians, Galatians, the Corinthian correspondence (including canonical 1 and 2 Corinthians), the imprisonment letters (Philippians and Philemon), and the letter to the Romans. If this ordering is in fact accurate, Paul's first letter to the Thessalonians is the earliest document in the New Testament, composed around 50 CE.

The letter to the Romans, the most important theological document in the Christian religion, will be discussed in the chapter on Paul's theology.

First Thessalonians

That 1 Thessalonians is an authentic letter of Paul has been almost universally accepted. Clement of Alexandria, Origen, Tertullian, and Irenaeus, all important ancient authorities, regarded it as genuine. The same opinion is shared by almost all modern scholars. The vocabulary and style seem to be thoroughly Pauline, and the chief Christological views expressed in the letter — as for example references to the *Parousia* in 4:15–5:11, where it is declared

---

question, see H. C. Kee, et al., *Understanding the New Testament*, 3rd ed. (Englewood Cliffs, NJ, 1973), Part II.

that God has raised up his son and that soon he will return to the earth — are consistent with the eschatological ideas found elsewhere in the Pauline classics.[30]

Moreover, it is commonly held that 1 Thessalonians has no interpolations and few textual corruptions. All elements fit neatly into Paul's period and his type of ministry; no unusually abrupt shifts in thought or style are evident in the letter. It was addressed to the church at Thessalonica in Macedonia (modern Salonika in Greece). This predominantly Gentile community, a free city, had been visited by Paul after his expulsion from Philippi. After a stay there of uncertain duration, Paul had continued on his way to Beroea and Athens and finally reached Corinth.[h] At Corinth in the winter or spring of 51 CE, Paul was reunited with his missionary co-workers, Philip, Silas, and Timothy.[i] Encouraged by the good news of their work, he composed this letter to the Thessalonians.

The purpose behind the composition of 1 Thessalonians was fourfold. The most obvious concern of Paul was the confusion among the converts about the *Parousia* and the physical resurrection.[j] Also, there was the influence of popular nature-cult religions, which were often without strong commitments to a genuinely moral deity. Paul preached a strict monotheism with a characteristic Jewish emphasis on morality. The third occasion for the letter, though not mentioned directly, seems to have been the suspicion, suggested in 2:3–3:13, that some in the church at Thessalonica regarded Paul as merely another mercenary street preacher. Finally, Paul found it necessary to encourage the Christians of Thessalonica to stand fast in the face of almost certain persecution.[k]

Galatians

Paul's letter to the Galatians, though brief, is one of the most significant writings in the New Testament. Its theological and moral concepts will be discussed in the chapter on Paul's theology. Historically, Galatians presents a primary account of Gentile Christian beginnings, for in defending his claim to be an apostle

[h] 1 Thes 2:1f., 17; 3:1. [i] 1 Thes 3:2, 6. [j] 1 Thes 4:13–18. [k] 1 Thes 5:1–11.

[30] Also, see 1 Thes 1:10; 2:19f.

of Christ, Paul reviews here his own background in Judaism and his early years as a Christian, including his first encounters with Peter and the apostles at Jerusalem. The theological importance of Galatians lies in the fact that it provides the earliest statement of Paul's Christology. Presumably his teaching and his authority had been under attack by conservative Jewish Christians from Jerusalem, who had been proselytizing among the churches which he had established earlier in Galatia. He apparently saw the need to clarify his own doctrinal position and to reaffirm his claim to authority as an apostle. As a religious document Galatians holds a unique position in the Pauline collection for it is written from the point of view of the emerging church. Until Paul's day, it had been assumed by many — Jews, Romans, and probably by some Jewish Christians as well — that the early Jewish Christian community (The Followers of the Way) was simply another of several splinter groups or sects of Judaism. Paul's account in Galatians of the pre-eminence of faith in his scheme of salvation and the place of the Law and the meaning of freedom in Christ clearly described Christianity as an independent religion.

Most scholars agree about questions of authorship and about the unity of Galatians. The letter stands in the canon essentially in the form given it by Paul. The date and audience to whom it was addressed are inconclusive. Some scholars speculate that it dates after Paul's so-called conference visit to Jerusalem, ca. 54–55 CE.

News had come to Paul while he was at Ephesus that there was great turmoil among the members of his churches in Galatia. Many were at the point of abandoning his new gospel of freedom from the Law in Christ and returning to a more distinctively Jewish faith. Antagonism toward Paul eventually grew so strong that he went to Jerusalem to lay the issue before Peter and the council. At Jerusalem, according to Acts, Paul's views and his authority as an apostle were vindicated, but the opposition continued. Some Jewish Christians persisted in their campaign to undermine Paul's position, his stand on the Law, particularly the Jewish practice of circumcision. Paul was profoundly disturbed by the crisis and wrote his letter to the Galatians, reiterating his claim to be an apostle of Christ and declaring the validity of a new foundation for salvation — "that a man is not justified by works of the law but through faith in Jesus Christ." [l] This principle, of course, was to become an essential element in the foundation of the Christian theology and religion.

The Corinthian Correspondence

Paul's letters to Corinth (including 1 and 2 canonical Corinthians) are a composite; this is a particularly accurate estimate of 2 Corinthians since it seems to include fragments of three, or possibly four, letters. First Corinthians is probably the best example of a genuine Pauline letter. Early Christian writers Clement of Rome, Polycarp, Irenaeus, Justin Martyr, and Tertullian attest to its authority. Some small parts of verses may include the insertion of marginal notes made by later scribes in order to smooth out or to supplement a particular text, but with relatively few exceptions the text of 1 Corinthians probably remains essentially as Paul wrote it.

The Greek city of Corinth was a thriving seaport located on the narrow isthmus connecting the Peloponnesus and the Greek mainland and had two harbors, one facing the Aegean Sea and the other the Adriatic. Because of this excellent geographical location, Corinth was a major center of commerce and attracted a cosmopolitan population from throughout the Roman empire. Archaeological excavations in the area have uncovered temples, baths, a large marketplace, and theaters. It was a city with a variety of religions and a reputation for vice and corruption, a city capable of producing the multiple problems concerning Paul in his Corinthian correspondence. Most of the Corinthian letters were probably written from Ephesus ca. 52–54.[m]

The events and circumstances which prompted the Corinthian letters can be reconstructed from internal evidence. Paul first visited Corinth and established a church there about 50–51. Acts recounts his activity there, particularly his trial before Gallio the Roman proconsul of Achaia.[n] He probably left for Syria to journey to Antioch shortly after his trial in the fall of 51 but returned

---

[l] Gal 2:16. [m] 1 Cor 16:1, 8, 19. [n] Acts 18:12–17.

later to Ephesus, where he remained for approximately two years.º During this visit, apparently between the summer of 52 and the fall of 54, he wrote 1 Corinthians. Sometime later he received word of serious difficulties within the Corinthian Christian community. In 1 Corinthians Paul alluded to a letter he had sent earlier charging the Corinthians to drive from their congregation the male members who were sexually immoral.ᵖ Second Corinthians 6:14–7:1 is believed by some scholars to be a fragment of that earlier letter. News of the failure of the attempt to reform the congregation was received from Chloe's people in Corinth,ᑫ perhaps conveyed to Paul by Stephanas, Fortunatus, and Achaicus.ʳ

In response to this apparent failure of his first letter, Paul wrote what is known as 1 Corinthians. In this letter he referred to several difficult internal problems confronting the church. Schism was perhaps the most threatening, for the Christians in Corinth were divided into contending factions, each claiming allegiance to their preferred teacher — some following Apollos, others loyal to Paul or to Cephas (Peter).ˢ One group, referred to as the Christ party, the *pneumatikoi* (the Spiritualists) claimed to have received superior gifts of the spirit. They believed themselves to be saved and, therefore, above the moral law. These persons, obviously gnostics, apparently were among the earliest identifiable Christian libertines. In response to this distressing situation, Paul rebuked the spirit-enthusiasts for their misguided loyalties and factionalism, their easy acceptance of immoral practices under the guise of their new-found freedom. He chided them for their boasting, self-deceit, and complaining against each other in the civil courts.ᵗ

Certain questions were conveyed to Paul in letters from the Corinthians concerning social practices: conduct in matters of marriage and celibacy,ᵘ whether or not to eat food offered to an idol,ᵛ and the meaning of rights and freedom.ʷ Paul also addressed the much misunderstood doctrine of the resurrection for Greek Christians totally unfamiliar with the doctrine. Paul's treatment of these practical matters and his great discourse on the true nature

---

º Acts 19:8–10. ᵖ 1 Cor 5:9–13. ᑫ 1 Cor 1:11. ʳ 1 Cor 16:17f.
ˢ 1 Cor 1:10–13; 3:3–7. ᵗ 1 Cor 6:1–8, 12–20. ᵘ 1 Cor 7:1–40. ᵛ 1 Cor 8:1–13.
ʷ 1 Cor 9:1–23.

of spiritual gifts has given 1 Corinthians a central place in the Christian canon.[x]

Paul had sent Timothy ahead to Corinth,[y] but apparently this effort to bring order out of the confusion among the Corinthian Christians was a failure. Paul himself then made a brief and stormy visit to Corinth in order to correct the problems which threatened the integrity of the Corinthian church, but he was rebuffed. His efforts (as implied in 2 Corinthians 2:1–11) were fruitless and unpleasant. As a result, Paul wrote his "harsh letter" (2 Cor. 10–13) alluded to in 2 Corinthians 2:3f., which was carried to Corinth by Titus.

Some time later Paul met Titus in Macedonia and learned from him that this harsh letter had been effective.[z] Paul then wrote his letter of reconciliation (2 Cor. 1–9, except the fragment of the first letter, 2 Cor. 6:14–7:1), an enthusiastic plea for forgiveness on both sides. On the basis of his expressed intention in 2 Corinthians 9:3f. and 13:1, Paul went to Corinth a third time, where presumably he found conditions within the church stabilized and in good order.

There are two issues in Paul's Corinthian letters which require some additional clarification: the rationale underlying Paul's stand on marriage and celibacy and the historically important implications of the spirit-enthusiasts' position on "spirit," "knowledge," and freedom. Clearly, the latter issue is the more significant in terms of the history of Christian thought. However, Paul's seemingly strange views on marriage need further explanation.

PAUL'S VIEWS ON MARRIAGE

Paul's comments on marriage arose in the context of questions which the Corinthians had directed to him, mentioned in 1 Corinthians 7, presumably about the status of the unmarried and widowed. "It is well" he wrote, "for them to remain single as I do. But if they cannot exercise self-control, they should marry. For it is better to marry than to be aflame with passion."[a] He continued, "I mean, brethren, the appointed time has grown very

---

[x] 1 Cor 12:1–14:40. [y] 1 Cor 4:17; 16:10f. [z] 2 Cor 7:5–16. [a] 1 Cor 7:8f.

short; from now on, let those who have wives live as though they had none." ᵇ

The key to Paul's position on marriage and on the status of the unmarried and widows is to be found in the imminent eschatology contained in his references to "the impending disaster," his insistence that the "appointed time has grown very short" and that the "form of this world is passing away." ᶜ The historian Michael Grant offers a somewhat different explanation of Paul's position. He maintains that some passages in Paul, 1 Corinthians 5:5, for example, show a "general contempt for the flesh and fleshly things" and suggests that this bias may explain his negative attitude toward marriage. Imminent eschatology, he argues, cannot be the only relevant consideration.[31] Nevertheless, the evidence suggests that Paul's counsel on this practical social issue was controlled by his conviction that the end of the age was very near and that Jesus the risen Lord would return soon. Imminent eschatology is implicit in his letter to the Thessalonians, which explains the order of events in the resurrection.

> For this we declare to you by the word of the Lord, that we who are alive, who are left until the coming of the Lord, shall not precede those who have fallen asleep. For the Lord himself will descend from heaven with a cry of command, . . . and with the sound of the trumpet of God. And the dead in Christ will rise first; then we who are alive, who are left, shall be caught up together with them in the clouds to meet the Lord in the air.ᵈ

Then Paul adds that as to the time and seasons, "For you yourselves know well that the day of the Lord will come like a thief in the night." They did not know the precise time when these events would take place, but it is amply clear that both the Thessalonians and Paul believed that they would occur within their own lifetimes.

Under the urgency of the imminent coming of the End the follower of Christ was expected to give full loyalty to Christ rather than to divide his or her loyalties and commitments with another person, as would be the case in marriage.ᵉ Widows, who presum-

---

ᵇ 1 Cor 7:29.   ᶜ 1 Cor 7:31.   ᵈ 1 Thes 4:15–17.   ᵉ 1 Cor 7:32–35.

[31] Michael Grant, *Saint Paul* (New York, 1982), 25, 28.

ably were without legal protection, constituted an especially difficult case for the church. In time their support was assumed to be a benevolent responsibility.[f]

GIFTS OF THE SPIRIT

Much of Paul's discourse on gifts of the Spirit is best understood in the context of his responses to the spirit-enthusiasts, whose views and practices were regarded by him as a major threat to the integrity of the Corinthian church. Evidently there were converts at Corinth who assumed that as Christians they enjoyed a privileged position based on their claim to possess the Spirit of Christ. They boasted of receiving special revelations of wisdom or knowledge beyond that given to other Christians. A precedent for this view of the Spirit was grounded in Old Testament accounts of God's Spirit coming upon Moses, Samuel, and Elijah to do miracles and to prophesy and to reveal the secret or hidden meaning of events. On the basis of such claims, these spirit-enthusiasts maintained that they were an elect group, that their newly found freedom in Christ meant freedom from the Law, that since they were of the Spirit, nothing done by the body could affect the status of their inner spiritual natures, such as eating food offered to idols or having sexual relations with prostitutes. However, for Paul freedom from the Law did not mean license to ignore or to flout the moral law. "Do you not know that your body is a temple of the Holy Spirit within you . . . . So glorify God in your body." [g]

Paul himself held a view of the Spirit which he undoubtedly taught to his gentile converts. This is evident in the fact that the expression, "in Christ" or "in the Lord," occurs many times in Paul's writings. According to A. Deissmann, "It is really the characteristic expression of his [Paul's] Christianity." Deissmann assumes that these mystical expressions were meant to be taken literally, that Paul thought of the Spirit-Christ as actually present in him "just as the air of life which we breathe is in us and fills us." [32] Some scholars are inclined to interpret Paul's expressions

---

[f] Acts 6:1. [g] 1 Cor 6:19f.

[32] See A. Deissmann, *Paul*, 140f., for a detailed treatment of Christ-mysticism in Paul. Also see A. Schweitzer's *The Mysticism of Paul the Apostle*.

"in Christ" and "Christ in me" metaphorically, evoking oneness or a unity of mind and purpose with Christ and not oneness in a literal mystical, ontological sense. In any event, Paul's problem was partially of his own making; his rather ambiguous doctrine of the Spirit had been misread and misunderstood by some of his converts in Corinth who were attracted to the more sophisticated, esoteric, and mystical aspects of his doctrine.[33]

Unlike the position of confirmed Gnostics, who held that the true spirit was possessed only by an elite, Paul held that the gospel of Christ was not founded on esoteric knowledge or wisdom reserved for a few. His own witness, he maintained, was not proclaimed "in lofty words or wisdom."[h] "Has not God made foolish the wisdom of the world?"[i] "Yet among the mature," he continued, "we do impart wisdom, although it is not a wisdom of this age or of the rulers of this age"; it is "a secret and hidden wisdom of God"[j] which is to be comprehended, spiritually discerned, interpreted, and taught through the Spirit of God.[k] Here Paul applied his doctrine of the Spirit to practical life in the church. The Spirit is not divisive. Of those who threaten to fractionalize the community into rival parties — "I belong to Paul" or "I belong to Christ" — he asks, "Is Christ divided?"[l] Then "you are still of the flesh. For while there is jealousy and strife among you, are you not of the flesh?"[m] According to Paul, "the unspiritual man," the natural man or man of the flesh, "does not receive the gifts of the Spirit of God."[n]

Paul's memorable and lengthy discourse on the gifts of the Spirit was delivered in such a context. Later Christians had great interest in Paul's doctrine, particularly the idea that Spirit preserved the unity of the church. This emphasis upon one Spirit, one body, and one doctrine became the format which guaranteed that unity. "For God is not a God of confusion but of peace."[o] Gifts of the Spirit may vary among individual members, but according to Paul all are inspired by one and the same Spirit and

[h] 1 Cor 2:1. [i] 1 Cor 1:20. [j] 1 Cor 2:6f. [k] 1 Cor 2:10–13. [l] 1 Cor 1:12f. [m] 1 Cor 3:3. [n] 1 Cor 2:14. [o] 1 Cor 14:33.

[33] The widespread influence in the Hellenistic world of various forms of Gnosticism no doubt affected the thought and attitude of the Corinthians and Paul. It certainly made massive inroads on Christianity in the next centuries.

though its manifestations are given to each person, they are "for the common good." ᵖ The gifts of the Spirit should not divide the membership — they are all of one body, each part adjusted by God to the whole so that "there may be no discord." ᵠ This principle was in fact employed by the early church as a strategy for social control, and it explains the historical connections between Paul and his disciples revealed in the so-called Deutero-Pauline period and later in the pastoral letters (1 and 2 Timothy and Titus) and in other Christian literature. Also, the influence of Paul's doctrine of the Spirit is possibly found in Luke-Acts and in the Gospel of John.

Paul admonished the members to seek the higher gifts, especially the most excellent gift — love or *agape*. "So faith, hope, love abide, these three; but the greatest of these is love." ʳ Perhaps no statement from scripture has elicited more attention and comment than this remarkably succinct definition and admonition. In this century intensive scholarly work about the religious context of Paul's teachings has given rise to careful distinctions between eros and agape, human love rooted in sensual experience and divine love.[34]

Glossolalia (speaking in tongues) had become a special problem for Paul. Apparently members of the Corinthian church were eager for manifestations of the Spirit and speaking in tongues was the most dramatic, spectacular, and mysterious of all of the experiences called spiritual. Left without restraint or control, subjective personal interpretations of living in the Spirit would have resulted in chaos in the church. Hence Paul's insistence that the higher gifts should edify the church: "He who speaks in a tongue edifies himself, but he who prophesies edifies the church." ˢ This was the rule which was to provide order and stability within the Christian community from Paul's time forward, "Let two or three prophets speak, and let the others weigh what is said." ᵗ "I would rather speak five words with my mind, in order to instruct others, than ten thousand words in a tongue." ᵘ

ᵖ 1 Cor 12:7. ᵠ 1 Cor 12:14–26. ʳ 1 Cor 13:13. ˢ 1 Cor 14:4. ᵗ 1 Cor 14:29. ᵘ 1Cor 14:19.

[34] The classic work is *Agape and Eros* by Anders Nygren, trans. by Philip S. Watson (New York, 1969).

THE LETTERS FROM PRISON

Reference was made earlier to a crisis in Ephesus and of the probability that Paul was imprisoned in Ephesus ca. 52–54 CE and that he wrote letters from there to the churches in Colossae, Laodicea, Philippi and to the person named Philemon.[35] Of these several letters only three are extant and in the canon: Philippians, Colossians, and Philemon. However, the authenticity of Pauline authorship of Colossians is questionable, which leaves Paul's letter to the Philippians and his private letter to Philemon to be considered.

Philippians

The letter to the Christians of Philippi in Macedonia, the first congregation established by Paul in Europe, exhibits a genuine Pauline vocabulary and style as judged by the standard provided in the Pauline classics, Galatians, 1 Corinthians, and Romans. Also, early church fathers Clement of Rome, Ignatius, and Polycarp all supported the judgment of authenticity. Some scholars have argued that the canonical letter to the Philippians is a composite made up of fragments from at least three letters: (1) 4:10–20; (2) 1:1–3:1, and (3) 3:2–4:9.[36] This conclusion is supported by Polycarp, who in his own letter to the Philippians referred to other letters which Paul had written to them.

In 4:10–20 Paul expresses his joy for the gift he had received from the Philippians through Epaphroditus. He recounts for them how in the beginning they alone had entered into partnership with him on the matter of his material support. Now that he has received the gift he is fully supplied and is gratified by their loyal devotion.

In part two Paul speaks of the joy he receives from his strong personal relationship with the Philippians, and he writes with great warmth about their affection for him. He is torn by his desire to be with Christ, but his longing for his friends at Philippi who need his assistance finally prevails. He urges them to stand

---

[35] See G. Bornkamm's discussion of the imprisonment in his chapter on Ephesus. G. Bornkamm, *Paul*, 80–84. Michael Grant argues that these letters and others were written during Paul's imprisonment in Rome. M. Grant, *Saint Paul*, 4.

[36] The contents of the remnants of three letters are sketched in Perrin, *New Testament*, 105f.

firm in the faith, loving one another and having a common care for the unity of their beliefs. Paul is not completely certain of his own fate, but he hopes to send Timothy to assist them.

Assuming the composite structure of Philippians, in the third letter Paul's tone changes markedly. He rails against the Judaizers, those Christians who regard circumcision under the Law as essential for salvation. "Look out for the dogs," "Look out for those who mutilate the flesh." [v] In this connection Paul recites his own credentials as a Jew, an Israelite of the tribe of Benjamin and with respect to the Law a Pharisee. But all such assets he has written off as non-essential baggage. Having accepted Christ, Paul claims no righteousness of his own, no legal rectitude. He urges them to keep to his way of thinking, to accept him as their example and model. They are his beloved friends, his joy and his crown.

Philippians is a highly personal letter or collection of letters. However, it does contain references to some of Paul's basic doctrinal views. His view of the imminent end appears in the context of his exhortations to his friends at Philippi to encourage one another and study the faith. He writes of "The Day of Jesus Christ" [w] "the Lord is at hand." [x] He also explains the significance of life in Christ,

> ... Who, though he was in the form of God, did not count equality with God a thing to be grasped, but emptied himself, taking the form of a servant, being born in the likeness of men. And being found in human form he humbled himself and became obedient unto death, even death on a cross. Therefore God has highly exalted him and bestowed on him the name which is above every name, that at the name of Jesus every knee should bow, in heaven and on earth and under the earth, and every tongue confess that Jesus Christ is Lord, to the glory of God the Father.[y]

This passage is clearly one of the most important in the Pauline corpus. It has been cited by churchmen and theologians over the ages in support of the Christian doctrine of the incarnation of Christ. According to A. Deissmann, these words are "a confession of the primitive apostolic cult, made by Paul, the prisoner, in order

[v] Phil 3:2. [w] Phil 1:6, 10; 2:16. [x] Phil 4:5. [y] Phil 2:6–11.

to rally his fellow-worshippers of Jesus Christ around the object of their cult."[37] This was Paul's confession of Jesus Christ as the pre-existent Lord (Kyrios). Nevertheless, Paul's primary interest here was pastoral, not theological. He was concerned for the unity and integrity of the members at Philippi — that as disciples of Christ they be as humble and obedient as Christ, the suffering servant.

Philemon

Philemon is the only example in the Pauline collection of an intimate, private letter. It is a personal note containing an appeal to a fellow worker, Philemon, a leading member of the Christian community at Colossae, in behalf of his slave Onesimus. This letter was not intended to be doctrinal; nor was it written as a tract on the Christian attitude toward slavery.

Onesimus had run away from his master. Presumably he hid in Ephesus but was discovered and arrested. In prison he met Paul and was converted to the Christian gospel. Punishment for runaway slaves under Roman law was severe, and Paul endeavored to bring about a reconciliation between Philemon and his slave. He hoped to convince Philemon that brotherly feeling founded upon the love of Christ transcends the legal distinctions between masters and their slaves. He appealed to Philemon to take Onesimus back as a brother in Christ and as a substitute for Paul himself.

It has been observed, perhaps correctly, that "Paul at his best belongs not to theology, but to religion."[38] In this letter Paul is clearly manifest as a man of religion. His primary concern was with Philemon and Onesimus as real living persons. Sometimes his attacks on opponents were harsh and his language coarse, but in the letter to Philemon Paul's genuine concern for the man and the depth of his compassion and affection are revealed.

---

[37] A. Deissmann refers to this passage as Paul's "Kyriosconfession," which Deissmann claims "can be understood only by the pious simplicity of silent devotion." A. Diessmann, *Paul*, 194.

[38] Ibid., 6.

CHAPTER 13

The Theology of Paul

Without the apostle Paul, the Christian religious movement might well have died in its infancy and the world's history since the first century would have been radically different. The Christian faith was grounded on the person of Jesus and his proclamation of the Kingdom of God, and the church as a community and institution was founded on the belief in his resurrection and the hope and expectation of his return. However much it may have flourished under the leadership in Jerusalem of James, the brother of Jesus, Jewish Christianity with its devotion to the Temple, synagogue, and the Law, seems to have effectively disappeared from history before the close of the first century. It was the Gentile or Hellenistic Christianity, firmly established through the missionary efforts especially of Paul, that survived to become the mainstream of historical Christianity, not only of the Catholic Church but of the major heretical movements — Montanism, Marcionism, Nestorianism, and Arianism.[1]

PAUL AS THEOLOGIAN

While Paul's powerful personality and missionary zeal were major factors in establishing and preserving the early church, his faith in the risen Christ as the hope and salvation of the human soul became the foundation of Christian theology. Major theologians, both Catholic and Protestant, from Augustine to Luther to Karl Barth have grounded their theology in Paul. Evangelical

---

[1] The Coptic Christianity of Egypt, which eventually extended to Nubia and Ethiopia and sent missionaries to Europe, the British Isles, and Arabia, was according to tradition originally established by St. Mark, the reputed author of the Gospel of Mark. See Eusebius, *Ecclesiastical History*, Bk. II, ch. XVI. See Aziz Atiya, *A History of Eastern Christianity* (London, 1968), for an extended account of the origins and history of Coptic Christianity.

The Theology of Paul

Christians of all persuasions have followed his admonition in committing themselves to Christ.

Paul's theology is neither systematic nor entirely consistent, although it displays a general logical coherence. Romans is easily the most influential theological document in Christian literature, but even it has the character of occasional writing which marks all of Paul's epistles. They were composed for specific occasions, often advising on particular problems or engaging in vigorous admonition. Paul's emphasis on salvation by faith rather than works, for instance, the central thrust of his religion and theology, was at times expressed in the heat of polemic against the "Judaizing" Christians, those who insisted on adherence to the Jewish Law, especially the requirement of circumcision. Moreover, his theological ideas were grounded in his personal religious and moral experience, the experience of an intensely passionate and committed man who was subject to changing moods and affected by changing circumstance. They were not the issue of a dispassionate institution, the product of councils, or, as far as is known, even of considered dialogue and discussion. Paul's theology, therefore, is not an intricately structured system of ideas nor is it free from contradiction. Its appeal is more to the sentiments of morality and religion than to the reflections of the disinterested intellect.[2]

Nevertheless, there is a singleness of purpose and meaning which characterizes Paul's writing: salvation comes through the risen Christ, with him and in him the converted soul dies to sin and, justified by God's grace, rises again to the glory of eternal

---

[2] The Cambridge historian Michael Grant has written that "Paul's mind, despite its great strength, remained undisciplined, paying scant attention to the niceties of rational coherence. The Letters are vividly varied and lively, but unrounded, unarranged and muddled, making their points not by any orderly procedure but by a series of hammer-blow contrasts and antitheses. Paul is far too impulsive and enthusiastic to standardize his terms or arrange his material. He is often ambiguous — with results that have reverberated down the centuries. And he commits flagrant self-contradictions, which caused Augustine, among many others, the deepest anxiety." *Saint Paul* (New York, 1982), 6. A contrary estimate of Paul is given by Albert Schweitzer in his *The Mysticism of Paul the Apostle*, 139: "And how totally wrong those are who refuse to admit that Paul was a logical thinker, and proclaim as the highest outcome of their wisdom the discovery that he has no system!" Schweitzer's criticism was directed at Adolf Deissmann's characterizations of Paul in his *St. Paul*, Eng. trans. (1912).

life. This Christocentric conviction of salvation ruled his life as a passionate missionary and became not only the main foundation of traditional Christian theology but the chief moving power of the Christian religion.

The foundation of Paul's thought and feelings is found in Romans 7. Here Paul provides his account of the human predicament, derived from analysis of his own existential dilemma:

> I do not understand my own actions. For I do not do what I want, but I do the very thing I hate. Now if I do what I do not want, I agree that the law is good. So then it is no longer I that do it, but sin which dwells within me. For I know that nothing good dwells within me, that is, in my flesh. I can will what is right, but I cannot do it. For I do not do the good I want, but the evil I do not want is what I do. Now if I do what I do not want, it is no longer I that do it, but sin which dwells within me.
>
> So I find it to be a law that when I want to do right, evil lies close at hand. For I delight in the law of God, in my inmost self, but I see in my members another law at war with the law of my mind and making me captive to the law of sin which dwells in my members.[a]

In response to this desperate plight, Paul exclaims, "Wretched man that I am! Who will deliver me from this body of death?" and concludes with his own resolution, "Thanks be to God through Jesus Christ our Lord! So then, I of myself serve the law of God with my mind, but with my flesh I serve the law of sin."[b]

Paul's theology, his beliefs about God and Christ, are the outcome of his assessments about his own predicament as a person. From this assessment he generalized about the dilemma of all humanity, that all were created in God's image with God's image written upon their hearts, but that all had fallen under the power of sin. In this respect, Jews were no better off than the Gentiles; none were excused.[c]

REDEMPTION AND THE MESSIANIC FAITH

The concept and experience of religion as salvation or redemption were not unknown in ancient Judaism. Indeed, the hope of redemption was a central element in the religious life of the Jewish

---

[a] Rom 7:15–23. [b] Rom 7:24f. [c] Rom 1:20; 2:1, 12–16.

The Theology of Paul

people, and it may be justifiably assumed that it was this Jewish expectation of eventual deliverance that was the foundation of Paul's Christ-centered faith. Moreover, Jewish faith was not only faith in redemption, but redemption through an atonement that would overcome estrangement from God, the result of the nation's sins. This was, in effect, the messianic hope that both consoled and inflamed the Jewish people of the first century, the masses of whom labored under the heavy hand of Rome.

The Jewish hope for redemption through atonement was as old as the earliest accounts of the Exodus from Egypt, and in the sixth century BCE it became a foundation for a profound philosophy of history relating to the chosen-people concept in the Suffering Servant songs of Deutero-Isaiah. In some of the world's most sublime poetry, the suffering of Israel was described as an atoning power that would reconcile not only Israel but also the entire human race with God.[3]

> I will give you as a light to the nations,
> that my salvation may reach to the end of the earth.[d]

The followers of Jesus, ever anxious to see him and their faith in him as the fulfillment of ancient expectations, not surprisingly recognized him as the object of the poet's prophecy:

> Surely he has borne our griefs
> and carried our sorrows;
> yet we esteemed him stricken,
> smitten by God, and afflicted.
> But he was wounded for our transgressions,
> he was bruised for our iniquities;
> upon him was the chastisement that made us whole,
> and with his stripes we are healed.
> All we like sheep have gone astray;
> we have turned every one to his own way;
> and the Lord has laid on him
> the iniquity of us all.[e]

---

[d] Is 49:6. [e] Is 53:4–6.

[3] For an analysis of the redemption message of Second Isaiah and its universalistic character, see especially Robert H. Pfeiffer, *Introduction to the Old Testament* (New York, 1948), 470–80. Pfeiffer regards the people of Israel as the Servant and treats the Second Isaiah as apocalyptic rather than typically prophetic.

The message of redemption that ran through the entire prophetic religious tradition was for the most part a promise of eventual redemption of the nation and of the world through the nation. To be God's agent in atonement was the role of the chosen people. They were chosen to bear vicariously a burden for mankind, the burden of sin and punishment. The prophetic message centered often on the eventual restoration of the Davidic kingdom, a restoration made possible by the leadership of God's anointed one, a Messiah, an authentic hero who would overcome the enemies of Israel and lead his people in bringing blessings to themselves and through them to the world. This anointed one was not a divine being, for such a notion would compromise the monotheism which from at least the sixth century was the very foundation of Judaism, but a leader with the natural and even supernatural endowments requisite to the great task of redeeming the people of God. Or the Messiah was the Jewish people personified as a group, or a faithful saving remnant of Israel.

The apocalypse of Daniel gave expression to an alternative, non-prophetic, non-historical conception of the Messiah as a preexistent being who would descend from the clouds of heaven to establish the Kingdom of God. While both conceptions of the Messiah existed in first-century Jewish thought, and in the Gospels themselves — the historical, horizontal Davidic and the apocalyptic, vertical "from above" — Paul held the latter view, the apocalyptic.[4] For Paul Christ was not a figure in the upward historical movement of the Jewish religion, one destined by lineage to usher in the Kingdom. He was the Son of God sent from above to die and be resurrected. And his resurrection was the gospel of salvation. For Paul everything was tied to the resurrection. As he said in 1 Corinthians: "If Christ has not been raised . . . your faith is in vain."[f] The Messiah was not the mighty one of Israel to lead the chosen people into an era of national greatness, of peace and good

---

[f] 1 Cor 15:14.

[4] For a discussion of the Davidic and apocalyptic concepts of the Messiah, see Leo Baeck, *Judaism and Christianity*, trans. by Walter Kaufmann (Philadelphia, 1958), chap. 3. See also Joseph Klausner, *The Messianic Idea in Israel*, trans. by W. F. Stinespring (London, 1956), especially the appendix, "The Jewish and the Christian Messiah," 519–31.

will for the world. He was the Son of God who had by his vicarious suffering atoned for the sins of mankind and by his resurrection overcome death and brought salvation for those who believed in him as their savior.

PAUL'S CONCEPTION OF SIN

The central role which sin plays in Christian theology, especially in western Christianity, is due primarily to the Apostle Paul. Not exclusively, because the long tradition of hope for redemption, even the redemption of the nation, was the hope for salvation from a condition which resulted from sin, the sins of the people. Jesus, for whom sin was not the central issue, nevertheless called for repentance, the repentance which would bring forgiveness. But for Paul the sin of the individual person is central. It is sin that estranges a person from God, that alienates him from the source of his being. But for Paul it is not a matter of repentance and forgiveness. The salvation of everlasting life for the individual is possible only through atonement for sin. That atonement can come only as an intervention of divine power.

As Christian theology developed, especially in the west under the influence of St. Augustine, 354–430, a distinction was made between *actual* sin, the sin committed by a person, and *original* sin, the condition and predicament of the human being in estrangement and alienation from God.[5] The common view was, and is, that a person is not sinful because he sins; rather he sins because he is sinful. Paul does not employ the term *original* sin, and the concept of original sin is not clearly developed in his letters, but the Christian doctrine of original sin, though complex in its origins, is to a considerable extent Pauline in source. Christian theologians before Augustine who contributed to the concept of original sin seem not to have grounded their views directly on Paul's

---

[5] The Roman Catholic concept of original sin as the loss, because of Adam's sin, of the supernatural gift of sanctifying grace can be found in the decrees of the Council of Trent, First Session, 1546. The standard Lutheran position is found in the Augsburg Confession, Art. II, 1530, and the Formula of Concord, Art. I, 1584. The Calvinist doctrine is best seen in the Westminster Confession of Faith, chap. VI, 1647. These creeds are readily available in *The Creeds of Christendom*, 3 vols., by Philip Schaff (1877); 6th ed. (Grand Rapids, 1977).

pronouncements, but Paul's almost obsessive consciousness of sin as central to the definition of man and description of the human predicament certainly predisposed Christian theology to such a belief.[6] Sin and death, Paul insisted, came into the world as a consequence of Adam's sin, his willful opposition to God. Expiation for universal sin and victory of mankind over death through resurrection requires the atoning power of Jesus Christ, whose vicarious suffering and death and resurrection are the sole justification of man to God. "Justification" for Paul was a juridical term, apparently intended to mean "to pronounce just," or "righteous," the free gift from God to those who have faith in Christ. "Therefore, since we are justified by faith, we have peace with God through our Lord Jesus Christ."[g] In his most influential statement, Paul wrote to the Christians in Rome:

> We also rejoice in God through our Lord Jesus Christ, through whom we have now received our reconciliation. . . . Sin came into the world through one man and death through sin, and so death spread to all men because all men sinned.[h]

That the Fall of man required salvation through the sacrificial suffering of a chosen servant was firmly established in Paul's Jewish background and was not the product of his Hellenistic or Greek learning and experience. Nor was it necessary for Paul to derive the ingredients of his doctrine from non-Jewish Gnostic influences, even though mythologies of an original fall were common in the Gnosticism of Paul's time. The account of the Fall in Genesis 3 was an early attempt to explain the origin of sin and death. Its setting in the Jahvist history, perhaps early in the ninth century, gives it a universal rather than nationalistic meaning. But the Hebrew religion was in a comparatively primitive state when the Garden of Eden myth and narrative originated, and the Fall

[g] Rom 5:1. [h] Rom 5:11f.

[6] For an analysis of the concept of original sin, see Frederick R. Tennant, *The Concept of Sin* (Cambridge, 1912), *Philosophical Theology*, 2 vols. (Cambridge, 1928–30), and *The Sources of the Doctrines of the Fall and Original Sin* (Cambridge, 1903; New York, 1968). *Man as Sinner*, by Mary Frances Thelan (New York, 1946), treats the concept of sin in contemporary theology. For a discussion of Paul and original sin, see *The Jerome Biblical Commentary* (Englewood Cliffs, 1968), 53: 53–57.

in those stories can hardly be regarded as a theological concept. It was to achieve theological status at a later time and eventually became a major determinant of religion and morals. Perhaps in part because of its artistry as well as its relevance to human experience, the Fall idea, which is found in many cultures, has been a useful receptacle for theological and philosophical analysis. In his *Systematic Theology*, the existentialist theologian Paul Tillich, in discussing his view that "existence is estranged from essence," wrote:

> The symbol of "the Fall" is a decisive part of the Christian tradition. Although usually associated with the biblical story of the "Fall of Adam," its meaning transcends the myth of Adam's Fall and has universal anthropological significance. . . . Theology must clearly and unambiguously represent "the Fall" as a symbol for the human situation universally, not as the story of an event that happened "once upon a time." [7]

Reinhold Niebuhr expressed the universality of the meaning of the Fall in his Gifford Lectures:

> When the Fall is made an event in history rather than a symbol of an aspect of every historical movement in the life of man, the relation of evil to goodness in that moment is obscured.[8]

Notwithstanding its emphasis on sin, and its probable impact on Paul, the Hebrew Bible does not contain the idea of "original sin" as a condition of human nature, and as a clearly defined concept, it is probably not to be found in pre-Christian Judaism. That Judaism of the intertestamental period cultivated the ingredients of a doctrine of original sin is evidenced, however, in apocalyptic and pseudepigraphical literature as well as in certain rabbinical writings.[9] But a formulated doctrine probably does not appear in

---

[7] Paul Tillich, *Systematic Theology* (Chicago, 1957), 2:29.

[8] Reinhold Neibuhr, *The Nature and Destiny of Man* (New York, 1953), 1:269.

[9] The classic analysis of the original sin problem in early Jewish literature is F. R. Tennant's *The Sources of The Doctrines of The Fall and Original Sin* (New York, 1903, 1968), chaps. 5–10. See also Solomon Schlechter, *Aspects of Rabbinic Theology* (New York, 1901, 1972), chaps. 14–18.

Judaism until late in the first century, CE, in the apocryphal book of II Esdras (IV Ezra), written by a Palestinian Jewish author addressing the Almighty. Ezra, like Job, complained bitterly that sin and death afflicted the covenant people.

> And thou didst lead him [Adam] into the garden which thy right hand had planted before the earth appeared. And thou didst lay upon him one commandment of thine; but he transgressed it, and immediately thou didst appoint death for him and for his descendants. (3:6f.)

And again,

> For the first Adam, burdened with an evil heart, transgressed and was overcome, as were also all who were descended from him. Thus the disease became permanent; the law was in the people's heart along with the evil root, but what was good departed, and the evil remained. (3:21f.)

The Book of II Esdras (IV Ezra) as it appears in its final redaction has suffered Christian additions in the first two and the last two chapters, but the third chapter, from which the above passages come, is authentically Jewish.[10] The position of II Esdras on sin and its attitude toward the Law have similarities to Paul, but the eschatological elements of the book have much in common with the Revelation to John. In his monumental work published early in this century, *The Sources of the Doctrines of the Fall and Original Sin*, F. R. Tennant found elemental ingredients of the Fall–Original Sin doctrine in Ecclesiasticus, where, for instance, in 25:24, Ben Sira says, "From a woman sin had its beginning, and because of her we all die." Though Tennant did not ascribe a theological doctrine of original sin to Ecclesiasticus, there being no corruption of human nature in the Fall, he did agree that here was the first clear affirmation in Hebrew literature that the Fall in Genesis was the cause of death.[11]

---

[10] Cf. the commentaries on IV Ezra in R. H. Charles, *The Pseudepigrapha of the Old Testament* (London, 1913, 1968), Vol. 2 of *The Apocrypha and Pseudepigrapha of the Old Testament*, and Robert H. Pfeiffer, *History of New Testament Times with an Introduction to the Apocrypha* (New York, 1949), 81–86.

[11] "Ben Sira supplies evidence that, in his day at least, the way was being prepared for such an interpretation of the Paradise-story as eventually led to the doctrine of Original Sin." F. R. Tennant, *The Sources of the Doctrines of the Fall and Original Sin*, 121. The authorship of Ecclesiasticus is usually assigned to the early part of the second century BCE.

The Theology of Paul

The apocryphal Wisdom of Solomon, probably produced by an Alexandrian Jew in the latter part of the first century BCE, contained elements of a concept of original sin but did not yield an explicit statement comparable to the Christian doctrine which was to achieve full-blown status in Augustine's dispute with Pelagianism.[12]

Jewish literature of the period is replete with references to the Fall. That death was a consequence of the Fall was clearly a common Jewish belief by the first century CE. But the notion that the sin of Adam was transmitted universally to his posterity and resulted in the alienation of the human race from God did not appear until II Esdras and the Pauline epistles. The Epistle to the Romans probably antedated II Esdras by several decades, although there is no evidence that Esdras was influenced by Paul's doctrine. The original sin doctrine in Christianity, however much it may have been influenced by Hellenistic and Gnostic currents of thought, seems thus to have come from the same basically Jewish intellectual and religious milieu which independently produced the Esdras doctrine.

This is not to deny the general truth of Gilbert Murray's description of the ancient world, both non-Jewish and Jewish, in which Christianity arose in a period in cultural history characterized by a "failure of nerve." The original sin doctrine, though probably Jewish in origin, was in his view a culminating expression of that failure, which characterized both Jewish and Gentile culture. Murray described it as a

> rise of asceticism, of mysticism, in a sense, of pessimism; a loss of self-confidence, of hope in this life and of faith in normal human effort; a despair of patient inquiry, a cry for infallible revelation; an indifference to the welfare of the state, a conversion of the soul to God. It is an atmosphere in which the aim of the good man is not so much to live justly, to help the society to which he belongs and enjoy the

---

[12] Referring to the Canaanites the Wisdom of Solomon says:
> Though thou wast not unaware that their origin was
>   evil and their wickedness inborn,
> and that their way of thinking would never change.
> For they were an accursed race from the beginning (12:10f.).

But here there was no attribution of sin or evil to the generality of mankind, since the Canaanites were regarded as under the curse of Canaan (Gn 9:25).

esteem of his fellow creatures; but rather, by means of a burning faith, by contempt for the world and its standards, by ecstasy, suffering, and martyrdom, to be granted pardon for his unspeakable unworthiness, his immeasurable sins. There is an intensifying of certain spiritual emotions; an increase of sensitiveness, a failure of nerve.[13]

This "failure of nerve" contrasts vividly not only with the rational philosophic and scientific temper of Greek thought of the earlier Hellenic period but as well with the life-affirming qualities of the traditional Hebraic religion with its prophetic foundations. Judaism and probably early Jewish Christianity were less susceptible to the failure of nerve than was Gentile Christianity with its greater openness to Hellenistic influences. Whatever the causes, the religion which was to become mainstream Christianity was grounded through Paul's theology in a negative assessment of the human predicament if not actually of human nature, a condition of sin and death from which the individual could not extricate himself. Only by God's grace, by a free and unmerited gift, was salvation possible.

MATTER, BODY, AND SIN

It is difficult to know precisely what Paul intended in his use of the Greek terms *soma, psyche,* and *pneuma. Psyche* appears in Paul where it means "life," "soul," or "person." The basic meaning of the Greek term *pneuma* is "wind," which over time came to be associated with the respiratory process "breath" and eventually to express that which was regarded as vital life — "Spirit." [1]

The Greek terms *soma* (body) and *psyche* (soul) were used early to express a dualistic conception of man — the body being understood as the prison of the divine, immortal soul. According to Orphic-Dionysian mythology, for example, "the body is a tomb." Releasing the soul from the body (its person) was the central feature of this cult's beliefs about salvation. But for other Greeks, including Aristotle, *psyche* referred to the principle of life, being a biological term which simply differentiated living organisms from

---

[1] 1 Thes 5:23.

[13] Gilbert Murray, *Five Stages of Greek Religion* (London, 1935), 123.

dead objects and marked the capacity for self-activity in living things.

According to C. H. Dodd, *soma* is the more comprehensive and significant term in Paul's vocabulary and refers to the individual entity, the totality of a person, including the *psyche* understood as the non-physical aspects of a person. *Soma* (body) thus designates the principle of individuality in Paul and "refers to the pure organic form which subsists through all changes of material particles" not to "the structure of bone, flesh and blood to which we give the name of body." [14]

Many scholars assume that Paul being a Jew, albeit a Hellenistic Jew, held a more traditional Jewish–Old Testament view emphasizing the unitary nature of a human being. This view is close in some respects to that of Aristotle for whom "soul" represented the individual person as a totality and not an independent entity merely joined with the body until death. Similarly, in the Hebrew-Jewish view, persons were understood as animated bodies, not incarnated souls. Persons do not *have* souls which at death escape the body; persons *are* living souls which perish at death and which, in the views of some, are destined to be revived at some future time.

Paul's writings are not always explicit or consistent in his conception of the nature of actual sin. Scholars have differed about whether his treatment of sin came mainly from traditional Hebraic or more contemporary Hellenistic influences. On the surface elements of both seem evident. Certainly Paul's references to Adam and the Fall exhibit his Jewish roots in this matter, and his distinction between the flesh and the spirit suggests Greek influences. The British scholar W. D. Davies has argued convincingly that despite the Hellenistic elements in his views, Paul's treatment of

---

[14] C. H. Dodd, *The Meaning of Paul For Today* (New York, 1957), 58. For Paul the promise of resurrection applies to the body (soma) but not to flesh (sarx). In his view man's flesh cannot enter into the Kingdom of God, but man as body (soma) has the promise of resurrection into eternal life (1 Cor 15:50). New Testament scholar John Robinson adds by way of interpretation that in Paul's thought the terms *sarx* and *soma* do not delineate two *parts* of a man's make-up, one mortal and the other not. Each, he maintains, "stands for the whole man differently regarded — man as wholly perishable, man as wholly destined for God." John A. T. Robinson, *The Body, A Study in Pauline Theology* (Chicago, 1952), 31, n. 1.

sin came mainly from his Jewish experience and education, but it is to the Jewish tradition by way of rabbinical theology and practice that one must look to find the basis of his position, not directly to the Pentateuch and the Prophets.[15]

It is especially Paul's emphasis on the distinction between spirit and flesh that has resulted in the argument that his doctrine of sin is Hellenistic. On the whole, the Hebraic-Judaic attitude toward the material world, including the human body and its functions, was traditionally positive, while the Greek position, expressed especially through the Orphic religion and the Platonic philosophical tradition, was at times negative in the extreme. In Plato's metaphysics, immaterial form was at the top of the ontological hierarchy, and formless matter was at the bottom, the lowest level of reality. Plato was probably atypical in his own time, but his dualistic theory of reality laid foundations for the denigration of matter that became common in the Hellenistic philosophies and religions after his time. Thus the Jews by the time of Jesus and Paul had developed a definite belief in the resurrection of the body, but the Greeks with their anti-material bias were quite commonly committed to belief in the immortality of the spirit or soul.[16] Paul's negative regard for the body and matter can probably be taken as an indication of gnostic influence upon his beliefs and attitudes.

The word "flesh" in Paul no doubt referred to more than the physical body, its drives and appetites, though it certainly referred to these. Sex was an important factor in his derisive attitude toward flesh, but it was not as central in his moral admonitions as it became later in St. Augustine, where the sin of Adam in the Garden was tied to the sexual act. For Paul, the spirit might be willing even when the flesh is weak. But "flesh" probably meant for Paul whatever attaches to the selfishness and self-centeredness

---

[15] W. D. Davies, *Paul and Rabbinic Judaism*, 3rd ed. (London, 1970), chap. 2.

[16] For Plato the body was not evil in a moral sense but was a source of moral evil. It was a severe impediment to the soul in its quest for the good, which involved wisdom and knowledge. Death was good because the soul was immortal and in death it achieved release from the body. On the immortality of the soul in Plato, see the Phaedrus and the Phaedo.

of the person. Sin was not simply something that issued from the bodily nature but was whatever destroyed the free and positive exercise of the spirit. "Flesh" referred to material, worldly desires, to whatever tyrannizes human spirituality and freedom.

The actual commission of sin is, for Paul as for the general Judeo-Christian tradition, a transgression of the law and will of God. But Paul also refers to sin almost as if it were a transcendent, though probably impersonal, power. In Romans, for instance, he says that all men are "under the power of sin." [j] Here sin seems almost to be an objective "power" that has humanity in its dominion. Christ as the savior redeemed men from their sin and overthrew Sin as a power. It is important to remember that for Paul man is not sinful because he commits sins. Rather he commits sins because he is sinful. His reference to Sin as a controlling power over the human will is at best ambiguous, and it is probably not possible to fully identify its origins in his thought. It may have simply followed from his intense moral consciousness. Certainly its deepest roots were in his Jewish experience and rabbinical education, which were in his time subject to Greek and gnostic influences. Sin as an objective power or powers conceived in mythological terms had a rather rich but ambiguous history in the Judaism of the pre-Christian era. Sometimes sin was personalized and tied to the popular folk demonology common in the Jewish world.

LETTER TO THE ROMANS

Paul's letter to the Christian congregation in Rome was probably written from Corinth between 54 and 58 CE and was intended to introduce him to a religious community where he was not personally known. In anticipation of extending his ministry as far west as Spain, Paul reflected intensively on his conception of salvation through Jesus Christ, setting forth his mature thought that was eventually to have a decisive influence on the foundations of Christianity. This letter was not directed to specific problems of the Roman congregation, which probably included many Jewish Christians as well as gentiles, and it is not laced with polemic

---

[j] Rom 3:9.

against the Judaizers in the style of some of the earlier letters. It is concerned especially with the universality of sin, the condition of the human soul resulting from the Fall, and the way to salvation.[17]

Romans may have influenced 1 Peter, Hebrews, and James, and from at least the time of Clement of Rome, bishop at the close of the first century CE, it received attention from the church fathers. Its great influence was due especially to its impact on Origen and St. Augustine, as also on Aquinas, Luther, Calvin, and most recently Karl Barth.[18] Its chief influence on the course of Christian theology was due especially to its impact on St. Augustine (354–430), whose work was to become the chief single determinant of Christian doctrine from the fifth century to the present.

In its early passages (1:18–2:29), Romans confirms the universality of sin. In the light of the Gospel it is clear that all mankind is in sin. Sin invades the life of the gentiles with their heathen vices and idolatry and the life of the Jews in their failure to keep the Law. The Jews received the Law of God through Moses, but the gentiles had it written on their hearts. "When Gentiles who have not the law do by nature what the law requires, they are a law to themselves, even though they do not have the law. They show that what the law requires is written on their hearts." [k] But notwithstanding the good which they do, all have sinned, both Jew and gentile. "All who have sinned without the law will also perish without the law, and all who have sinned under the law will be judged by the law. For it is not the hearers of the law who are righteous before God, but the doers of the law who will be justified." [l] That a person is a Jew does not entitle him to more consideration in God's judgment than a gentile. "There will be tribulation and distress for every human being who does evil, the Jew first and also the Greek. . . . For God shows no partiality." [m]

---

[k] Rom 2:14f. [l] Rom 2:12f. [m] Rom 2:9, 11.

[17] Paul's authorship of Romans is rarely seriously questioned, but there are possible problems with the composition of the letter. The doxology, 16:25–27, may not have been a part of the original letter, as its style is not consonant with the letter as a whole and in the early texts it appears in various places and is sometimes omitted. Also, 16:1–23 may have originally been a separate letter, while verse 24 is definitely a later addition to the text.

[18] For the impact of Romans on twentieth-century theology, see especially Karl Barth's *The Epistle to the Romans*, English trans. by Edwyn C. Hoskyns (London, 1933), and H. R. Mackintosh, *Types of Modern Theology* (London, 1937), chap. 8.

The very existence of the Law, Paul held, brings consciousness and recognition of sin. His own vain attempt to live by the Law brought him to the realization that salvation through works, through the strict observance of the ceremonial and moral Law, is impossible. "Yet, if it had not been for the law, I should not have known sin. I should not have known what it is to covet if the law had not said, 'You shall not covet.' " [n] He had been saved, that is, justified, not by his commitment and devotion to the Law but by an act of God's grace, by salvation freely given in the absence of deserving merit.

PAUL, THE LAW, AND FAITH

Paul's attitude toward the Law has been a matter of continuing scholarly controversy. The simple and extreme view that as a Christian he completely abandoned or abrogated the Law is no doubt unwarranted. But his criticism of the Law's effect on man and his insistence that it was now superseded by the Gospel was so revolutionary and radical that since his time he has often been regarded as an arch-apostate from Judaism. Having failed in his efforts to live according to the Law, he came to believe that the Law cannot deliver either Jews or gentiles from the power of sin. In this judgment on the Law, Paul departed radically from established Jewish tradition, which held that by full observance of the Law the evil of the world and the sin of the individual could be overcome. Whether it was Paul's conversion to Christianity that brought him to this critique of the Law or his disenchantment with the saving power of the Law that brought him to Christianity is still a matter of scholarly debate.[19]

According to Paul, the Law, which often means for him the Prophets as well as the Pentateuch, imparts to the sinner a knowledge of his sinfulness, but despite every effort to overcome the power of sin and achieve righteousness, the sinner remains in bondage to sin until liberated by God through Jesus Christ. Salva-

---

[n] Rom 7:7.

[19] Samuel Sandmel in his *The Genius of Paul* (New York, 1958), 28, argues that "it is not his Christian convictions which raise the Law as a problem for him, but rather it is his problem with the Law that brings him ultimately to his Christian convictions."

tion comes not by works but by the grace of God through faith in the resurrected Christ. This faith is not an intellectual commitment, a simple belief that Jesus has been resurrected as the Christ and is the savior, but rather is a mystical participation in the dying and rising of Christ. The dying in baptism and rising in the resurrection of Christ brings not simply assurance of salvation but actual deliverance from sin and death. It is an act of God in accepting the sinner who does not merit salvation:

> For I through the law died to the law, that I might live to God. I have been crucified with Christ; it is no longer I who live, but Christ who lives in me; and the life I now live in the flesh I live by faith in the Son of God, who loved me and gave himself for me. I do not nullify the grace of God; for if justification were through the law, then Christ died to no purpose.º

The death of the man of faith in the waters of baptism is death to sin, and his resurrection is to a new life, the life to God in Jesus Christ.ᵖ [20]

The classic work on Paul's conception of faith as mystical participation in Christ is Albert Schweitzer's *The Mysticism of Paul the Apostle*. Perhaps more than any other scholar, Schweitzer has emphasized the distinctive character of Pauline mysticism, that the "being-in-Christ" is not a "being-in-God." It is a "Christ-mysticism" not a "God-mysticism." In contrast with those who have regarded Paul's mysticism as Hellenistic, Schweitzer insists that it has Jewish origins and follows from eschatological problems resulting from the delay of the Parousia and its meaning for redemption. Paul's

> paradoxical assertion that those who are in Christ are only in outward appearance natural men, and are to be considered as having in reality already died and risen again, is irrefutable, once the two-fold fact of the dying and rising again of Jesus has been given the place of importance in the eschatological expectation which it actually possesses for eschatological thought.[21]

º Gal 2:19–21.   ᵖ Rom 6:11.

[20] Paul's reference in 2 Corinthians to the mystical experience of a man caught up into the third heaven, Paradise, is generally regarded as pertaining to himself (12:1–5).

[21] Albert Schweitzer, *The Mysticism of Paul the Apostle*, trans. by William Montgomery (London, 1931; New York, 1968), 139f.

Paul, who endured great and varied suffering as a missionary, interpreted suffering as akin to dying. Suffering for Christ was a dying with Christ. The possession of the Spirit was living again in the resurrection. We are, he wrote, "heirs of God and fellow heirs with Christ, provided we suffer with him in order that we may also be glorified with him."[q] That suffering has power to overcome sin was a well-established belief in the Judaic tradition, most notably in the Suffering Servant songs of Isaiah[r] but also in the Jewish apocalyptic book *The Psalms of Solomon*:

> For the Lord spareth His pious ones, And blotteth out their errors by His chastening. (XIII:10)

and,

> If the righteous endureth in all these [trials], he shall receive mercy from the Lord (XVI:15).[22]

The atoning power of suffering was to become a major element of Christian doctrine. Because Christ suffered for our sins, or, in some extreme interpretations, took on himself the sins of the world, our sins became his sins and he suffered death for them. Since, according to Paul, death followed from sin, the overcoming of sin in Christ's suffering, death, and resurrection was an overcoming of death itself. This seems to have been a death of the soul as well as the body, a concept not fully developed in Paul's extant letters. Paul said of himself in 2 Corinthians, after an account of the beatings, hardships, and dangers that he had endured, "For the sake of Christ, then, I am content with weaknesses, insults, hardships, persecutions, and calamities; for when I am weak, then I am strong."[s]

FREEDOM AND MORAL RESPONSIBILITY

Paul's letter to the Galatians, which condemned as apostasy the teaching that Christians were subject to the Mosaic law, has

---

[q] Rom 8:17. [r] Is 53. [s] 2 Cor 12:10.

[22] The pseudepigraphic Psalms of Solomon were probably composed during the first century BCE. R. H. Charles, et al., eds., *Apocrypha and Pseudepigrapha of the Old Testament in English*, Vol. 2, *Pseudepigrapha* (Oxford, At the Clarendon Press, 1913), 645, 647. The atonement for sin through a ritual sacrifice was a commonplace in Jewish life. See, for instance, the description of the sin offering for the Day of Atonement set forth in Leviticus 16:1–28.

often been considered a declaration of freedom. It celebrated the freedom that comes through faith in Jesus Christ, the faith that brings a release of the spirit and the realization of salvation.

> Now before faith came, we were confined under the law, kept under restraint until faith should be revealed. So that the law was our custodian until Christ came, that we might be justified by faith. But now that faith has come, we are no longer under a custodian; for in Jesus Christ you are all sons of God, through faith.[t]

And again:

> Formerly, when you did not know God, you were in bondage to beings that by nature are no gods; but now that you have come to know God, or rather to be known by God, how can you turn back again to the weak and beggarly elemental spirits, whose slaves you want to be once more?[u] [23]

An obvious but crucial question that issues from Paul's theology of salvation by grace, where God through Jesus Christ justifies the sinner who is redeemed by his faith but can do nothing to merit the gift of salvation, concerns the moral responsibility of the person thus justified. Those who have died and risen in mystical unity with Christ are in Christ, or Christ is in them. In gnostic terms, not at all foreign to Paul and his teachings, they are the pneumatics, the spiritual beings. They are the elect to salvation, no longer subject to the Law. They are free and in a sense already know salvation. Does this mean that they are released from all moral obligation and responsibility? This is a problem which Paul himself encountered in his own converts. Moral licentiousness has not been uncommon among those convinced of their own deification.

Paul's reply, set forth in his forceful letter to the Galatians, declared that the freedom which issues from faith is a freedom which abjures the "flesh" and pursues the life of the Spirit which

---

[t] Gal 3:23–26. [u] Gal 4:8f.

[23] The "elemental spirits," an expression which appears elsewhere in Paul's letters, probably refers to the control of human beings by astral powers, an indication of Paul's confrontation with astrology, and perhaps also to regulations of the Law governing religious observances.

is a moral life at the highest level. Here he should speak for himself:

> For you were called to freedom, brethren; only do not use your freedom as an opportunity for the flesh, but through love be servants of one another. For the whole law is fulfilled in one word, "You shall love your neighbor as yourself." But if you bite and devour one another take heed that you are not consumed by one another.
> But I say, walk by the Spirit, and do not gratify the desires of the flesh. For the desires of the flesh are against the Spirit, and the desires of the Spirit are against the flesh; for these are opposed to each other, to prevent you from doing what you would. But if you are led by the Spirit you are not under the law. Now the works of the flesh are plain: fornication, impurity, licentiousness, idolatry, sorcery, enmity, strife, jealousy, anger, selfishness, dissension, party spirit, envy, drunkenness, carousing, and the like. I warn you, as I warned you before, that those who do such things shall not inherit the kingdom of God. But the fruit of the Spirit is love, joy, peace, patience, kindness, goodness, faithfulness, gentleness, self-control; against such there is no law. And those who belong to Christ Jesus have crucified the flesh with its passions and desires.
> If we live by the Spirit, let us also walk by the Spirit. Let us have no self-conceit, no provoking of one another, no envy of one another.[v]

Whether Paul's ethics is logically consonant with his theology may be questioned, but clearly in declaring freedom from the Law he had no intention of allowing a decline in the moral life of the individual or the society. Quite the opposite. The life of the Spirit was fulfilled in the genuine love of God and love of one another. "For he who sows to his own flesh will from the flesh reap corruption; but he who sows to the Spirit will from the Spirit reap eternal life." [w]

ELECTION AND PREDESTINATION

The concept of divine election, of having been selected by God, is found running through much of the Hebrew scriptures, especially in the form of the belief that the descendants of Abraham through Jacob (Israel) are a "chosen people." Just what they were chosen for is not always entirely clear. But that there was a cove-

[v] Gal 5:13–26. [w] Gal 6:8.

nant of God with Israel and that he revealed himself and his word to Israel through Moses and the prophets was firmly established in the faith of the Jews long before the beginning of Christianity:

> You shall be holy to me; for I the Lord am holy, and have separated you from the peoples, that you should be mine.[x]

and

> Now therefore, if you will obey my voice and keep my covenant, you shall be my own possession among all peoples; for all the earth is mine, and you shall be to me a kingdom of priests and a holy nation.[y]

The covenant of God with Israel as variously depicted in the Pentateuch was, of course, God's election of a people, the nation of Israel. It was not a promise or guarantee of individual salvation. Both the religion and morality of the Hebrews in the early period were communal in character. But in the sixth century BCE, Jeremiah, the prophet of individualism, declared a new covenant, a concept that was to play an important role in the Christian philosophy of history and theology, that centered on the individual person:

> Behold, the days are coming, says the Lord, when I will make a new covenant with the house of Israel and the house of Judah, not like the covenant which I made with their fathers when I took them by the hand to bring them out of the land of Egypt, my covenant which they broke. . . . I will put my law within them, and I will write it upon their hearts; and I will be their God, and they shall be my people.[z]

But Jeremiah's "new covenant" or new testament did not refer to an election for the salvation of the individual soul in a hereafter; rather it was a grounding of the old communal covenant in the religious experience and conviction of the individual. The covenant of individual salvation was to appear later in the proclamation of election in the Gospels and Paul, but even there it was not divorced from the Old Testament promise to Israel, a promise which God would not break. For Paul, the Israel of the covenant became the Christian church, the Israel of the Spirit. Those who were the authentic saints, those who confessed Christ and accepted

---

[x] Lv 20:26. [y] Ex 19:5f. [z] Jer 31:31–33.

The Theology of Paul

him as their savior and died and arose with him in baptism, were the elect of God appointed to a salvation they could not earn under the Law through meritorious works.

The concept of the elect appears several times in the synoptic Gospels. In Matthew: "For false Christs and false prophets will arise and show great signs and wonders, so as to lead astray, if possible, even the elect." [a] In Mark: "And if the Lord had not shortened the days, no human being would be saved; but for the sake of the elect, whom he chose, he shortened the days." [b] In Luke: "And will not God vindicate his elect, who cry to him day and night?" [c] In John the same concept appears in the sermon on the bread of life: "All that the Father gives me will come to me; and him who comes to me I will not cast out." [d]

In Luke's Book of Acts, as in Paul's letters, the belief in election was more clearly an affirmation of predestination, or at least foreordination. Acts 13:48, referring to believing gentiles in Antioch who were converts of Paul and Barnabas, reads: "And when the Gentiles heard this [that salvation might come to the gentiles], they were glad and glorified the word of God; and as many as were ordained to eternal life believed."

In the earliest of the letters, Paul addressed the Thessalonians by describing their faithfulness as a mark of their election: "For we know, brethren loved by God, that he has chosen you; for our gospel came to you not only in word, but also in power and in the Holy Spirit and with full conviction." [e] The same idea appears in 2 Thessalonians, "But we are bound to give thanks to God always for you, brethren beloved by the Lord, because God chose you from the beginning to be saved, through sanctification by the Spirit and belief in the truth." [f]

In his letter to the Romans, Paul explicitly interpreted election as predestination:

> We know that in everything God works for good with those who love him, who are called according to his purpose. For those whom he foreknew he also predestined to be conformed to the image of his Son. . . . And those whom he called he also justified; and those whom he justified he also glorified.[g]

[a] Mt 24:24. [b] Mk 13:20. [c] Lk 18:7. [d] Jn 6:37. [e] 1 Thes 1:4f. [f] 2 Thes 2:13.
[g] Rom 8:28–30.

But Paul obviously had the problem of God's apparent departure from his ancient covenant with Israel in now extending election to the gentiles. In Romans he faced this issue,[h] reminding his readers that God said to Moses, "I will have mercy on whom I have mercy, and I will have compassion on whom I have compassion,"[i] and insisting that in this God was not unjust. The chosen people of Israel, he declared, had fallen in disobedience and therefore had lost the blessing.

> What shall we say, then? That Gentiles who did not pursue righteousness have attained it, that is, righteousness through faith; but that Israel who pursued the righteousness which is based on law did not succeed in fulfilling that law. Why? Because they did not pursue it through faith, but as if it were based on works.[j]

But God has not abandoned his chosen people, and the rejection of Israel is not final. After the "full number of the Gentiles come in," all Israel will be saved.[k] Some Israelites will be brought to Christ through jealousy of the Gentiles.[l] And there is the "saving remnant," similar to the faithful remnant in the time of Elijah, who had not worshipped Baal.[m]

Somewhat like his teachings regarding original sin, Paul's treatment of election as predestination is more or less rudimentary and not clearly defined as a theological concept. Though he laid the foundations of the idea for Christian theology, the doctrines as they were developed later, especially by Augustine, Luther, and Calvin, should not be read back into Paul's letters. But it is clear that for Paul, even though he had rescued the Christian church from oblivion as a Jewish sect, the Christian religion was not genuinely universal. Only those who were designated by God would come to Christ in faith and know salvation.

For Paul, real salvation was eschatological; salvation was to be realized at the end of the age.[24] In his view justification or

---

[h] Rom 9–11. [i] Rom 9:15; Ex 33:19. [j] Rom 9:30–32. [k] Rom 11:25f.
[l] Rom 11:13f. [m] 1 Kgs 19:10–18.

[24] The term "eschatology" from the Greek words *eschaton* (end) and *logeia* (teaching) means the teaching about the end of history. In theological terms it has come to mean "teaching about the last things." "Apocalyptic" is a form of eschatology. See the discussion of apocalyptic in chap. 14.

The Theology of Paul

acquittal would provide only a foretaste of salvation in this life; reconciliation and atonement would be achieved only at the final end. For Paul all Christians were to live in hope of the fulfillment of this promise.

PAUL'S ESCHATOLOGY

There was strong precedent in Jewish apocalyptic literature for the belief in imminent eschatology, which was a central feature of the early Christian faith. There is little doubt, for example, that John the Baptist was an apocalyptist or that Jesus himself believed that the coming of God's Kingdom was near. Indeed, Jesus probably went with his followers from Galilee to Jerusalem to prepare the Jewish nation for the coming of God's Messiah.

Paul's theology preserves the essential format of popular Jewish apocalypticism, but he added a very important Christian belief — the doctrine of the Parousia (the Second Coming), which would bring the resurrection. He held the view that Jesus was the long expected Messiah (the Christ) and that his return as the supernatural Savior of the world was imminent. Paul declared that on the day of his return the resurrected Christ would usher in God's kingdom and mark the beginning of the general resurrection of the righteous dead. From Paul's time on the entire apostolic church looked to the Parousia as the great day of triumph.

Paul expected that a personal, visible appearance of the risen Lord would herald the events of the last day. That day, he declared, would come like a thief in the night.[n] Although the precise time was not known, Paul was certain that it would occur in his own time.[o] In 1 Thessalonians he writes,

> For this we declare to you by the word of the Lord, that we who are alive, who are left until the coming of the Lord, shall not precede those who have fallen asleep. . . . And the dead in Christ will rise first; then we who are alive, who are left, shall be caught up together with them in the clouds to meet the Lord in the air. (4:15–17)

The mystical expression "in Christ" that was basic to Paul's proclamation of the new life in the Spirit did not fully capture the

---

[n] 1 Thes 5:1f. [o] 1 Thes 4:17.

meaning of salvation. Mystical experiences gained through faith only served to guarantee the salvation that was to come on that future day of the messianic kingdom.

Paul addressed the question of the resurrection directly when it was raised by the skeptics among his converts at Corinth.[p] Apparently, some were doubting the validity of his teaching about resurrection. According to Paul, the resurrection is God's singular act of salvation in human history. Christ was the unique person who made resurrection possible for mankind in general.[q] Through his death and resurrection to new life, death was finally defeated and destroyed. And how are the dead raised? What kind of bodies will they have?[r] According to Paul in 1 Corinthians they are raised as spiritual bodies. Flesh and blood, physical bodies, could not inherit new life in the Kingdom.[s] To enter the Kingdom they must have bodies of spirit as Christ had. As spirit bodies they will retain their separateness as persons. Paul's doctrine of the resurrection thus retained for Christianity the principle of individuality; the idea of new life for individual persons in immortality.

Imminent eschatology was a troublesome doctrine for the early church after Paul's day. Second generation Christians needed an explanation of the delay of the Parousia, and an interpretation was attempted in the New Testament document 2 Peter, which explained "that with the Lord one day is as a thousand years, and a thousand years as one day."[t] This declaration represented a dramatic change in the Christian calendar of last events, a postponement of the Second Coming, declaring the time of the end to be indefinite, in the future yet always near. Every generation of Christians was bound to conclude that it lived in the latter days, committed to the expectation of Jesus' imminent second coming.

Modern scholarship too has confronted the dilemma which this doctrine of eschatology posed for the Christian church. The existentialist theologian Rudolf Bultmann attempted to preserve the relevance of New Testament claims about Christ as savior by de-mythologizing or de-literalizing the setting (the world view)

[p] 1 Cor 15:12. [q] 1 Cor 15:20–23. [r] 1 Cor 15:35. [s] 1 Cor 15:44f. [t] 2 Pt 3:8.

of the first century Christian writers.[25] Bultmann advanced an interpretation of Paul's literal pronouncements about the resurrection and the End as future historical events. He realized that the first-century view of the world, the literal ways in which the myths of the age were perceived, was archaic and obsolete and that the relevance of the Christian proclamation about Christ (the kerygma) would be lost if Christians were obliged to accept as literal and historical the mythical categories in which it was packaged. Accordingly, he reinterpreted the kerygma by insisting that the key events — the Resurrection and Second Coming — really were mythical images which point out the way in which God encounters man in the world. For Bultmann, the purpose of myth was not to present an objective picture of the world as it is, but to express man's experiential understanding of himself in the world. Thus myth should not be interpreted cosmologically but rather anthropologically or existentially. In this way the traditional Christian claims become meaningful to modern man. Such an interpretation may contribute to the preservation of the Christian faith, but there can be no doubt that Paul himself lived in the expectation that these events, the Parousia and the Resurrection, were literally to take place in historical time, and this meant during his own lifetime.

---

[25] Vol. 1 of Bultmann's major work *Theology of the New Testament*, trans. by Kendrick Grobel (New York, 1951), treats Paul's theology. The discussion of Johannine theology is in vol. 2. See also Bultmann's *Jesus Christ and Mythology* (New York, 1958) and *Kerygma and Myth*, ed. by H. W. Bartsch (New York, 1961). Also, see Norman Perrin, *The Promise of Bultmann* (New York, 1969).

CHAPTER 14

The Tradition of Paul

Three major religious traditions grounded in three different conceptions of the way to salvation can be distinguished in the early years of the Christian movement. These can be identified as (1) the Jewish Christian tradition, (2) the tradition of Paul, and (3) the tradition of John. These early Christian traditions are the subjects of this and the following two chapters. Because Paul's letters are the earliest extant documents of the New Testament, the Pauline tradition is treated first, followed by the Johannine, and finally by the Jewish Christian.

In all three traditions the Christians were committed fully to the ethical monotheism that defined the Jewish religion and set it apart from the mainstream of religions in the Hellenistic-Roman world in which Christianity originated. Christians accepted the Hebrew scriptures, Torah and Prophets, as their sacred literature, and were united in their faith in the resurrected Christ as their savior. Each of the three traditions claimed apostolic support for its authority and expressed its title to authenticity by the literature it produced under the names of the appropriate apostles. Notwithstanding their common elements, this literature, which was eventually included in the New Testament canon, quite clearly exhibits the differences that characterized these early Christian movements.

The Jewish Christian tradition was rooted in the beliefs and practices of the earliest followers of Jesus in Jerusalem after the gathering at Pentecost. Under the leadership of Peter and James, they were devoted to the accepted Jewish beliefs and practices. They were Jews by birth or conversion who apparently had no inclination to separate from mainstream Judaism. They lived by the Jewish Law, insisted on circumcision and the dietary regulations, observed the sabbath and the other holy days of the Jewish calendar, accepted the Temple and its ritual, and participated in the synagogue. Their eschatological expectations differed from those of other Jewish sects of their time because of their belief that the Messiah had come, that he was not a national leader but a savior of souls, that he had died and risen and would come again in triumph to usher in the Kingdom of God.

This original form of Jewish Christianity, centered in Jerusalem under the leadership of Peter, the apostle of Jesus, and James, a brother of Jesus, can be traced at least to the destruction of Jerusalem by the Romans in 70 CE, although both Peter and James had been executed before that time.[1] Thereafter the history is clouded, and though there are evidences of the continuation of the sect into at least the second century, Jewish Christianity lost its central importance in Christian history as the Hellenistic, gentile forms of religion became Christianity's mainstream.[2]

The canonical literature bearing the names of Peter and James, the First and Second Letters of Peter and the Letter of James, expresses the emergence of the church as an institution and belongs to a somewhat later period. However, at least some facets of the religious tradition of the early Jewish Christians are identifiable in that literature. The claim of these writings to apostolic authority was tied, of course, to the leadership of Peter and James, Peter by virtue of his status as one of the original apostles and James because of his close family relationship to Jesus. To the documents bearing these names, which in all probability are pseudonymous, can be added the Letter of Jude. The literature of this tradition exhibits in some degree the early beginnings of the Catholic ecclesiastical movement in the second century as well as perhaps some reaction against the strong Pauline bias favoring salvation by faith and grace only. But before the letters attributed

---

[1] According to Josephus (*Antiquities*, XX, 9), James was put to death by the Jewish Sanhedrin in 61. According to tradition, Peter was executed by crucifixion in Rome during a persecution by Nero, possibly in 64.

[2] The Ebionites, poor men, a sect east of the Jordan in the early centuries, have been regarded by some scholars as a continuation of the original Jerusalem Christians. An ancient Jewish Christian sect in Syria, called Nazarenes by some early Christian writers, has sometimes, as by Adolf Harnack, been identified with the Ebionites. Both Ebionites and Nazarenes kept close to the Jewish Law.

to Peter and James appeared, the authentic letters of Paul had been composed and the movement of Hellenistic Christianity was well under way.

The mainstream of early Hellenistic Christianity, the second tradition, was the tradition of Paul, the Christianity of grace through faith alone rather than salvation by obedience to the Law. This religion at first did not cut its ties to Judaism, but it moved away from Judaism nevertheless, abandoning Jewish orthodoxy and eventually becoming a separate religion while still preserving and nourishing its Jewish roots. What can be called the tradition of Paul is given literary expression not only in the New Testament letters written by Paul, but as well by those written in the name of Paul.

The third tradition identifiable in New Testament literature is associated with the name of John. The Johannine literature includes not only the Fourth Gospel but also the three letters of John and the Apocalypse, the Revelation to John. The question of the authorship of these books is discussed elsewhere. It is sufficient here to point out that the early Christian religious tradition which claimed authority from the John alleged to be an apostle of Jesus exhibited a strong emphasis on mystic experience. It was the "way of Spirit." It was committed as well to intense eschatological expectation and faith.

AUTHORSHIP OF THE PAULINE LITERATURE

Many scholars assume that 2 Thessalonians, Colossians, and Ephesians were not written by Paul but rather by disciples of Paul.[3] Written in Paul's name, these documents, sometimes referred to as Deutero-Pauline, involve subtle differences in emphasis and concern that reflect a time after Paul, presumably the period of reconstruction following the Jewish-Roman war, perhaps 80–95 CE.

Literature from yet a later period, called Pseudo-Pauline, includes the so-called Pastoral Letters, 1 and 2 Timothy and Titus and the Letter to the Hebrews. Although these documents all

---

[3] See Norman Perrin, *The New Testament, An Introduction* (New York, 1974); S. Sandmel, *The Genius of Paul* (New York, 1970); G. Bornkamm, *Paul*, trans. by D. M. G. Stalker (New York, 1971); Howard Clark Kee, *Understanding the New Testament*, 4th ed. (New Jersey, 1983).

purport to be Pauline, the claim for their authenticity based on internal and external evidences is substantially weaker than that of the Deutero-Pauline literature. The Pseudo-Pauline writers employed the name of Paul primarily as a strategy for confronting gnostic-like schismatics who threatened anarchy within the church. Here the open-ended and somewhat ambiguous character of Paul's original emphasis upon grace and faith, his insistence on freedom from the Law, and his imminent eschatology are compromised. This is done by attributing to Paul the development of a sophisticated Christology which unifies Christianity and makes all competitors, Jewish and Gnostic, irrelevant and describes Paul as a churchman whose primary concern was the unity and centralization of institutional Christianity. This interpretation of the Pseudo-Pauline writings assumes that the authors were responding to historical circumstances relating to the survival of Christianity and that their faith determined what Paul meant, how he was to be understood, and how and where his teachings applied.[4]

THE DEUTERO-PAULINE LITERATURE

Second Thessalonians

Second Thessalonians is very much like 1 Thessalonians; it is throughout Paul-like in style and structure. Yet there are significant doctrinal differences between the two documents. The cardinal emphasis in 1 Thessalonians is Paul's imminent eschatology. In this letter he speaks of the Parousia, the coming of Jesus as the risen Christ, the apocalyptic redeemer and judge, an event which Paul expects to take place in his own lifetime.

The imminent aspect of Paul's expectation about the coming of the heavenly Christ is effectively neutralized in 2 Thessalonians. N. Perrin maintains that 2 Thessalonians is "so like 1 Thessalonians and yet so different that it must be an imitation of 1 Thessalonians written to meet a later situation."[5] This later situation was the delay of the Parousia; Christ had not returned and some

---

[4] This is in part the view advanced and effectively defended by S. Sandmel in *The Genius of Paul*. See especially his chapter 6 entitled "Paul and Other New Testament Writings," 163ff.

[5] Perrin, *New Testament*, 119.

explanation to the Christians of a new generation was needed. The time table for the coming is changed in 2 Thessalonians; certain events involving the "son of perdition" must first take place before the End. The Day of the Lord's coming cannot take place before the final rebellion against God, when the man of lawlessness "takes his seat in the temple of God, proclaiming himself to be God." [a] Then that man, Satan, will be revealed and destroyed by the Lord Jesus at his coming. And all who refuse the truth will perish. According to the writer, God will send upon these "a strong delusion, to make them believe what is false, so that all may be condemned who did not believe the truth but had pleasure in unrighteousness." [b]

Those scholars are probably correct who detect in this new interpretation of the Parousia a threat of persecution. Before the end Christians must expect a time of persecution. Those who persevere in the truth will be rewarded at the Coming and the Judgment and their persecutors will themselves be judged and persecuted. As Perrin pointed out, this expectation of things to come is similar in tone to that expressed in the Revelation to John, which was composed at the end of the first Christian century.[c][6] Another more subtle suggestion of a developing Christology is the enrichment in 2 Thessalonians of the attributes and status of Christ.[d]

Colossians

The question of the authorship of Colossians is more complicated. Arguments for authenticity or for pseudonymity based upon style and vocabulary are not persuasive. As Perrin and others have pointed out, twenty-five words in Colossians are not found in any of the Pauline classics and thirty-four are not found anywhere else in the New Testament canon.[7] But such a word count is not conclusive, for Paul may have used these specific terms precisely because they were required for his discussion of the dilemma confronting him in the church at Colossae.

---

[a] 2 Thes 2:3f. [b] 2 Thes 2:11f. [c] Rv 16:5–7; 19:2. [d] 1 Thes 3:11, 13; 2 Thes 2:16.

[6] Ibid., 120.

[7] Ibid., 121.

The real case against the authenticity of this document is based on the number of concepts not found in the earlier Pauline letters. For example, the Christology contained in the following hymn to Christ is similar to the Logos doctrine in the prologue of the Gospel of John, which was written considerably later than Paul.

> He is the image of the invisible God, the first-born of all creation; for in him all things were created, in heaven and on earth, visible and invisible, . . . all things were created through him and for him. He is before all things, and in him all things hold together. He is the head of the body, the church; he is the beginning, the first-born from the dead, that in everything he might be pre-eminent. For in him all the fulness of God was pleased to dwell, and through him to reconcile to himself all things, whether on earth or in heaven, making peace by the blood of his cross.[e]

Obviously, this is a more sophisticated, speculative Christology than appears in the clearly authentic writings of Paul. Here Christ is the image of the invisible God. His primacy is asserted over all created things. He is not merely the first-born but the first born of all creation. He is before and superior to all created things, including the angels and the elemental spirits of the universe.

In Colossians 1:24–29 the Christian faith appears more like a mystery religion than in the earlier literature. The theme about "God's secret" is similar in some respects to the secrecy motif of the Gospel of Mark and to the notion of the "power of darkness" in Luke's account of the cosmic struggle between Christ and Satan.[f] However, Colossians emphasizes that the secret is Christ himself; in him lie hidden all "wisdom" and "knowledge," and because of him all gnostic or gnostic-like speculations are made irrelevant and useless. Apparently the author employed gnostic terminology to convince the Colossians that the best gnostic insights are to be found already in Christian claims about Christ.[g]

The special problem at Colossae seems to have been the introduction into the congregation of an early form of Gnosticism. Reference in Colossians 2:16 to questions about food and drink or "to a festival or a new moon or a sabbath" suggests that a Jewish form of Gnosticism may have been involved. The Colossians were

---

[e] Col 1:15–20. [f] Mk 4:10ff.; Lk 22:53. [g] Col 2:2f.

blending Jewish-Gnostic and Hellenistic-Christian ideas, some of which undoubtedly were from Paul. This form of Gnosticism included beliefs about "the elemental spirits of the universe," possibly as intermediaries between heaven and earth, the practices of self-abasement, and the worship of angels.[h] The statement about taking one's stand on visions in Colossians 2:18 probably refers to the special experience claimed by the Gnostics as essential for salvation. The author warns the Colossians that for Christians "these are only a shadow of what is to come; but the substance [the solid reality] belongs to Christ."[i] Christ has authority over all of the principalities and powers of the universe; on "that cross" he discarded them like an unneeded garment. The author reminds the Colossians that they have died to the elemental spirits; therefore they should set their minds on and "seek the things that are above, where Christ is, seated at the right hand of God."[j]

Also Colossians shows some trends toward the making of the institutional church. Perrin characterized these as steps from the earlier letters of Paul to the Pastorals, to 1 Peter and the literature of the emerging Catholic institutions.[8] One of the evidences for this development involves the use of the term "minister" in Colossians. Paul uses the same Greek term in his letter to the Romans and in the Corinthian correspondence, where (except for 2 Corinthians 3:6) the Revised Standard Version translates it as "servant."[9] "Minister" in Colossians suggests a more formal usage, the designation of an office (as in 1 Timothy), "you will be a good minister of Christ Jesus."[k]

Another evidence of the non-Pauline character of Colossians is the distinction between the body, the church, and Christ as "the head of the body." Such elaboration of Christ's nature, even more pronounced in Ephesians, is not found in the authentic letters of Paul.[l] In 1 Corinthians, for example, Christians are "the body of Christ" and just as the "members of the body . . . are one body, so it is with Christ."[m] Also the term "church" in Colossians seems

[h] Col 2:8, 18. [i] Col 2:17. [j] Col 3:1. [k] 1 Tm 4:6. [l] Col 1:18; Eph 5:23.
[m] 1 Cor 12:12, 27.

[8] Ibid., 122f.
[9] The Greek term *diakonos* appears in Col 1:7, 23, 25. In Rom 15:8 and in 1 Cor 3:5; 2 Cor 6:4; 11:23 the term is rendered as "servant."

to mean the entire Christian community in the sense of the Universal Church rather than a local congregation as in the earlier letters of Paul.

In addition, the meaning of baptism and circumcision and their inter-relationship have been modified in Colossians 2:11f. The author tells the Colossians that Christians are circumcised not in the literal, physical sense but by being divested of their lower natures in baptism. This is Christ's way of circumcision. They were "buried with him in baptism" and "raised with him through faith in the working of God." [n] It would seem that when Colossians was written the Jewish ritual of circumcision as a sign of the covenant had been replaced by the Christian ritual of baptism. This point is not entirely clear, but the close proximity of the two terms "circumcision" and "baptism" in this passage supports this thesis. This interpretation correlates well with Jesus' justification for his own baptism in the Gospel of Matthew: "Let it be so now; for thus it is fitting for us to fulfil all righteousness." [o] This account of Jesus' baptism and Jesus' words provides the model and the justification of baptism for all Christians. The earlier tendency to explicitly reject Jewish legal requirements seems to have been replaced in Colossians by a strategy of correction and appropriation, as in this substitution of baptism for circumcision.

Ephesians

Ephesians and Colossians both purport to have been written by Paul from prison, as were the authentic letters of imprisonment, Philippians and Philemon. Of the three documents classified as Deutero-Pauline — 2 Thessalonians, Colossians, and Ephesians — Ephesians is the least likely to be the work of Paul.

Actually Ephesians is not a letter at all, despite its epistolary opening and blessing at the end. The contents of the document do not address a particular situation as do Paul's authentic letters. The letter format of this treatise probably was invented by Paul's disciples to lend his authority to the document. The phrase "at Ephesus," which is intended to specify the audience, does not

---

[n] Col 2:11f. [o] Mt 3:15.

appear in the oldest manuscripts.[10] Also, the reference in Ephesians 3:5 to "holy apostles and prophets" having revelations "by the Spirit" and to the church being "built upon the foundation of the apostles and prophets" (2:20), seems out of character with Paul's assessments of the status and function of apostles as stated in Galatians and elsewhere.

The place of Ephesians in the Pauline collection poses an intriguing set of questions. As scholars have correctly observed, Ephesians contains a summary of Pauline ideas and doctrines drawn from almost every one of the Pauline letters, yet nothing essential to Paul's thought would be lost if Ephesians had not been written. This raises the question of the special function and significance of this document. Presumably, from the canonizers' point of view it makes some distinctive contribution. What was it? A thesis restated by E. J. Goodspeed in 1937 but modified here by the significance of the impact of the Jewish-Roman war (66–70 CE) suggests one plausible resolution.[11]

In Goodspeed's opinion, following the period of the Pauline letters, after the fifties and early sixties, interest in Paul waned. The circumstances of Christian life had changed dramatically and Paul's letters, because they really were letters in every sense of the word, had become dated. According to Goodspeed, "Second-generation Christianity needed to be reminded of the great religious values it had inherited." [12] The Jewish-Roman war probably resulted in the near collapse of Jewish Christianity in Jerusalem and Judea. In the period of reconstruction after the war, problems of Christian identity needed to be resolved. These included the problem of Christianity's relation to Judaism and to the Law and its relation to new religious movements in the gentile world, to Greek philosophic thought, and to the threat of persecution in the Roman world. A special problem was the rise of gnostic-like sects within the church which threatened its unity.

Paul's letters and teachings are revived in Ephesians by followers of the Pauline tradition. Followers were no doubt respon-

---

[10] Markus Barth, *Ephesians* (Garden City, New York, 1974), 67.

[11] Edgar J. Goodspeed, *An Introduction to the New Testament* (Chicago, 1937), 222ff.

[12] Goodspeed, *Introduction*, 227.

sible as well for collecting and publishing the entire Pauline corpus. Onesimus, the slave in Paul's letter to Philemon, may have become the bishop of Ephesus, the person most responsible. Some scholars have argued that Ephesians appeared first as an introduction for the Pauline collection, that it was written and placed first among the documents to be circulated among second generation Christians to remind them of the values of their religious tradition. Goodspeed says, "Ephesians is a great rhapsody on the worth of the Christian salvation. Like Hebrews it belongs to an age when men needed to reflect on the worth of their faith." [13]

Ephesians was evidently designed to show that the Christian tradition was a unity, that it had been an established tradition since the earliest times of the church and that Paul's letters, though initially directed toward the solution of specific local problems, set forth the essentials of that unity. Ephesians should be regarded as a summary of Paul's insights presented to the entire church as a foundation of faith and a guide in matters of belief and practice.[14]

Of central importance in Ephesians was the commitment to preserve the unity and integrity of the institutional church. The church was considered to be a crucial feature of God's plan, but its unity was threatened by the rise of cult-like groups within the main body. It is not by accident that Ephesians, concerned with the church as an institution, echoes approximately three-fifths of Colossians and that much of the material found in Ephesians relates to the gnostic problem. To counter the appeal of such groups, the author of Ephesians attempted to show that the Christian gospel, including the idea of the church, is eternal, "true," and unchanged since the beginning. "Before the foundation of the world" the Christians were destined to be "sons through Jesus Christ." [p] God elevated Christ to "sit at his right hand . . . far above all rule and authority" in all ages. God made him "head over all things for the church." [q] The author informed the Christians at Ephesus that they were fellow citizens with the saints and

[p] Eph 1:4f. [q] Eph 1:20–22.

[13] Ibid., 226.

[14] According to M. Grant, it is in Ephesians "that there appears a particularly well developed sense of the Universal Church, one, holy, catholic and apostolic." M. Grant, *Saint Paul*, 143.

members of God's household. This household was "built upon the foundation of the apostles and prophets" with Christ as the "cornerstone." ʳ

According to Ephesians, Christ is the head of the church, but the church itself has come to have a special status as the body through which Christ and the Holy Spirit function. Here the expression "Christ and the church" is significant.ˢ In the author's counsel about marriage, showing how Christian partners in marriage should regard one another, the church and Christ provide the model. "As the church is subject to Christ, so let wives also be subject in everything to their husbands. Husbands, love your wives, as Christ loved the church. . . . For no man ever hates his own flesh, but nourishes and cherishes it, as Christ does the church." ᵗ This, the author says, is a profound mystery which for him contains a truth about Christ and the church but it also applies to love between husbands and wives.ᵘ

In Ephesians 4:11 the author uses Paul in 1 Corinthians 12 in order to establish the need for unity in the church. According to Ephesians the gifts that some should be apostles, some prophets, some evangelists, etc., were precisely "for the work of ministry, for building up the body of Christ." ᵛ These are no longer the gifts of the spirit to individual Christians as in 1 Corinthians, but gifts understood as official positions within the structure of the institution of the church. The rationale behind this notion of gifts for the sake of creating a unity in the church is clear, that "we all attain to the unity of the faith . . . that we may no longer be children, tossed to and fro and carried about with every wind of doctrine, by the cunning of men." ʷ "There is one body and one Spirit, just as you were called to the one hope that belongs to your call, one Lord, one faith, one baptism, one God and Father of us all." ˣ

THE PSEUDO-PAULINE LITERATURE

The Pastorals: 1 and 2 Timothy and Titus

The so-called Pastoral letters include three literary compositions supposedly written by Paul as instructions to two of his lead-

ʳ Eph 2:19f. ˢ Eph 5:32. ᵗ Eph 5:24f., 29. ᵘ Eph 5:32f. ᵛ Eph 4:12.
ʷ Eph 4:13f. ˣ Eph 4:4–6.

ing disciples, Timothy and Titus.[15] These are probably not genuine letters but rather three treatises which form a corpus intended for use in instructing church leaders or officials. All three may have been written by the same person. Many scholars regard the opening and closing of each document, which provide both the setting and the occasion, as literary fictions employed to claim Pauline authorship and to give the appearance of genuine letters.

The Pastorals were quoted by Irenaeus ca. 185 CE, but Marcion (ca. 140 CE), a strong and enthusiastic devotee of Paul, did not include them in his collection of Pauline writings, a collection which was to have an important influence on the formation of the Christian canon. Marcion's omission of the Pastorals probably indicates either that they were not available to him or that he did not regard them as authentic.

One of the strongest reservations regarding Pauline authorship of the Pastorals rests on differences in vocabulary and style. There is a significant absence of Pauline terms. Also, these documents have the smooth flow and continuity of thoughtfully prepared treatises rather than the energy of thought and vividness of expression characteristic of the authentic letters of Paul. Moreover, the Pastorals seem to depart from Paul's teaching as well as refer to developments in the ecclesiastical order which occurred after his time. Paul's emphasis on the Parousia, for example, and the new life in the Spirit, "putting on Christ,"[y] are absent from the Pastorals. The Spirit has now become something conferred by the laying on of hands by officials of the church.[z] Moreover, the major concern of these documents is no longer the missionary work fundamental to Paul's interests but rather the ecclesiastical system, including prescriptions for the qualifications for bishops and deacons.[a]

The date of the Pastorals is uncertain.[16] The first established reference to 1 Timothy appears in Polycarp's letter to the Philip-

[y] Rom 13:14; Gal 3:27. [z] 1 Tm 5:22. [a] 1 Tm 3:1–13.

[15] The term *pastoral* suggests the major focus of these letters, that they are addressed to Christian ministers (pastors) and are primarily concerned with their qualifications and duties.

[16] A range of dates from ca. 90 to 150 CE has been suggested. E. J. Goodspeed held that the Pastorals came from the middle of the second century; N. Perrin settles

pians, but the dating of Polycarp's letter is controversial. There seems to be no other reference to the Pastorals until the middle of the second century. That they were written after Paul's time is indicated by the system of beliefs and formal organization of the church which they describe. Also, the description of the activity of false teachers corresponds to the views and practices of the Gnostics of the second century as described by Tertullian and Irenaeus.[b] This evidence indicates that the letters were probably written ca. 125 CE.

The principal objectives of the Pastorals were to instruct those who aspired to church offices about church affairs and the correct order of worship — "how one ought to behave in the household of God" [c] — and also to strengthen the doctrines of the church against the threat of heresy. These ends were to be accomplished through a rigid Christian discipline involving the establishment of rules of conduct and the rejection of all false teaching and speculation. The ministers were to guard their trust through a wise selection of qualified assistants and through personal example.

Goodspeed maintains that the Pastorals were directed against the Marcionite and gnostic sects. They were attributed to Paul partly in order to counter the uses of Paul's writings by Marcion, an influential gnostic Christian leader, and his followers around 140 CE. Especially at issue was Marcion's repudiation of the Hebrew canon as the basic scripture of the church.[17] Several passages are identified by Goodspeed as possible allusions to Marcion: "There is one God," 1 Timothy 2:5; "All scripture is inspired by God," 2 Timothy 3:16; "Avoid the . . . contradictions of what is falsely called knowledge," 1 Timothy 6:20. Goodspeed holds that "contradictions" in this passage is a reference to Marcion's own work, entitled *The Antitheses*. By naming Paul as the author of these letters, Paul himself is made to disclaim Marcion's major positions. In this way, according to Goodspeed, Paul is recovered "for standard Christianity." [18]

[b] 1 Tm 1:4; 4:1–3, 7f.   [c] 1 Tm 3:15.

for a date around 125 CE. See E. J. Goodspeed, *Introduction*, 343; N. Perrin, *The New Testament*, 265.

[17] Goodspeed, *Introduction*, 336.

[18] Goodspeed, *Introduction*, 338f.

The Tradition of Paul

In the introduction to 1 Timothy, the author attacks the doctrine of false teachers; he urges Timothy to direct certain persons "not to teach any different doctrine," to avoid wasting their time "with myths and endless genealogies" which promote vain and aimless speculations.[d] Undoubtedly, these are references to some form of Gnosticism, presumably of Jewish origin. This is suggested in 1 Timothy 1:7–9 where the question of the Law arises; also in the letter to Titus where reference is made to "deceivers, especially the circumcision party."[e] Here the author charges Titus to rebuke those who give "heed to Jewish myths" and urges him to insist upon the avoidance of "stupid controversies, genealogies, dissensions, and quarrels over the law."[f]

In 1 Timothy the author refers to these myths as contradictions "falsely called knowledge."[g] He cautions also against those apparently non-Jewish groups who require ascetic practices and are unduly involved with training the body. He is concerned "that in later times some will depart from the faith by giving heed to deceitful spirits and doctrines of demons, . . . who forbid marriage and enjoin abstinence from foods. . . ."[h] More about false doctrine appears in 2 Timothy, where it is reported that some are teaching the resurrection has already taken place.[i]

In the Pastorals, especially in 2 Timothy, Paul is represented as prophesying times of stress before "the last days."[j] He predicts a time of persecution when "people will not endure sound teaching" but "will turn away from listening to the truth and wander into myths."[k] Threats of schism, dissension, and heresy from within and threats of persecution from without permeate the Pastorals. There is a great need for unity, for order and organization in the institution of the church. Church offices are named — Bishops and Deacons — and strong emphasis is placed upon the qualities required of those who aspire to these offices. According to Titus, it is essential that they be models of integrity, of true fidelity, and of sound faith.[l] In 1 Timothy a modest lifestyle is required of a candidate: that he be "the husband of one wife," no lover of money, a good manager of his own household,

[d] 1 Tm 1:3f. [e] Ti 1:10. [f] Ti 1:14; 3:9. [g] 1 Tm 6:20. [h] 1 Tm 4:1, 3. [i] 2 Tm 2:18. [j] 2 Tm 3:1. [k] 2 Tm 4:3f. [l] Ti 2:1–10.

and not a recent convert. He must "be well thought of by outsiders" and "not addicted to much wine." [m]

On the matter of church order, candidates for the positions of deacon and bishop are instructed concerning the place of women, that they live modestly and "learn in silence with all submissiveness." [n] Special consideration is to be given to "real widows." [o] None should be enrolled who is under sixty years of age or who has been married more than once.[p] This is probably the earliest reference to an ecclesiastical order of widows, an order well established by the third century.[19] The church is to assume the burden of the "real" widows; others, presumably, are to be cared for by their relatives.[q]

In the Pastoral polemic against false teachings, the term "faith" is used in a distinctive way. In Paul's letters, "faith" referred to one's personal relationship to God, to an attitude of complete trust in God with "promise" and "hope" as allied and supporting sentiments. In the Pastorals, "faith" seems to be a synonym for loyalty to the revealed doctrines of the church. The expressions "sincere faith" and "disowned the faith" in 1 Timothy[r] and in 2 Timothy, "Follow the pattern of the sound words which you have heard from me, in the faith," and "kept the faith" [s] display this new meaning as do such expressions appearing in Titus as "a common faith" and being "sound in the faith." [t] [20] The trend here is toward "faith in" the apostolic tradition, a notion central to Christian literature in the period of emerging Catholicism.

Hebrews

It is extremely difficult to assign with accuracy the time, place, and audience for the Letter to the Hebrews. Only the closing passage of the document, which contains references to Timothy and "those who come from Italy," [u] resembles a genuine Pauline letter.

[m] 1 Tm 3:2–8. [n] 1 Tm 2:11. [o] 1 Tm 5:3, 5. [p] 1 Tm 5:9. [q] 1 Tm 5:8.
[r] 1 Tm 1:5; 5:8. [s] 2 Tm 1:13; 4:7. [t] Ti 1:4, 13; 2:2. [u] Heb 13:23f.

[19] Care of widows was regarded by the Jews as an obligation (Ex 22:22; Dt 24:17–21). According to Acts 6:1, the early Christian community assumed this responsibility.

[20] Note the use of such expressions as: "The saying is sure" in 1 Tm 1:15; 3:1; 4:9; 2 Tm 2:11; and Ti 3:8.

Some scholars suggest that chapter 13, the final chapter, was probably an addition made by a later writer who endeavored to make Hebrews resemble authentic Pauline letters and that the original ended at 12:29.[21] The transition from the body of the letter to the personal note beginning in chapter 13 with its Pauline-like exhortations, the reference to Timothy, and the mention of an intended visit seems to have been contrived.

Hebrews was not ascribed to Paul until after the second century CE and then only by the Alexandrian school. It was not accepted as canonical by the western church until the middle of the fourth century.[22] The internal evidence against Pauline authorship is even more conclusive. Few if any of the characteristics of Paul's authentic writings are evident in this document. For example, there is no mention of the doctrine of a Second Coming, which is so prominent in Paul. The polished sentence construction in this writing is unlike that found in Paul's letters. It is a widely held opinion that Hebrews is composed in the purest Greek of any book in the New Testament. Though it is generally referred to as an epistle, it contains no salutation, no statement of reason for writing, and does not mention the author's name or the person or persons addressed. Tertullian and Novatian considered it to be the work of Barnabas, but Augustine in his later years declared that its author was anonymous. Other early, prominent Christian leaders have been suggested as its author, including the Alexandrian Apollos. On the basis of available evidence, it seems probable that the author, whose name remains unknown, was a Hellenistic Jewish Christian, probably influenced by the views of the Alexandrian school, a man of considerable literary training and familiar with both the Old Testament and the teachings of Paul.[23]

Most arguments concerning the date of Hebrews are inconclusive. First Clement makes clear use of the writing and thereby

---

[21] For a discussion of the problems of the introduction to Hebrews, its authorship, date, audience, etc., see M. S. Enslin, *Christian Beginnings* (New York, 1938), 308–16; E. G. Goodspeed, *Introduction*, 253–64; N. Perrin, *The New Testament*, 137–41 and W. G. Kümmel, *Introduction to the New Testament* (Rev. Ed.), trans. by Howard Clark Kee (New York, 1973), 388–403.

[22] Simon J. Kistemaker, *New Testament Commentary: Exposition of the Epistle to the Hebrews* (Grand Rapids, Michigan, 1984), 7f.

[23] See, for instance, M. S. Enslin, *Christian Beginnings*, 311–15.

establishes the latest date possible for its composition. Those critics who maintain that 1 Clement refers to a persecution by Domitian conclude that the date for Hebrews must be placed ca. 85–90 CE.[24] That the book may have been written late in the first century is supported by the reference to "former days,"[v] the rebuke of the readers for their complacency,[w] and the absence of any mention of the Parousia.

One of the most troublesome problems in Hebrews concerns audience. The title "to the Hebrews" was probably added to the original document at a later date in order to give the book the status and authority of a Pauline letter. Those critics are probably correct who contend that Hebrews was written for Hellenistic Jewish Christians, possibly those in Rome who had become complacent about their loyalty to Christian beliefs and values and were in danger of losing the faith under the threat of Roman persecution.[25]

The use of Old Testament literature in Hebrews is distinctive.[26] Figures of the temple (the tabernacle), priest and priesthood, sacrifice, law, and covenant—all drawn from the formative Mosaic period — are represented as types or copies of the heavenly prototype. The author's strategy was to establish the superiority of Christianity to the ancient Hebrew faith by contrasting the old and temporary covenant and priesthood with the new, eternal priesthood and covenant of Christ.

Much of Hebrews is in the form of proclamations about Christ, his supreme status, and his role as the great high priest. He is superior to Moses and the prophets; through him God sent his final word.[x] His priesthood is of heavenly origin and is superior to the Levitical, which is temporal only, a copy and shadow of the real priesthood. The revelation of Christ is superior to all revelations given in ancient times. In days of old, God spoke "to our

---

[v] Heb 10:32. [w] Heb 5:11ff. [x] Heb 3:3.

[24] Since Clement in 96 CE quotes from Hebrews, N. Perrin holds that the date for Hebrews is near the time of the composition of Luke-Acts, 85–90 CE. See Perrin, *The New Testament*, 137.

[25] Ibid., 138.

[26] The author frequently refers to Old Testament passages, especially from the Psalms: e.g., Heb 1:7–13 (Ps 45:6f.; 104:4; 102:25–27; 110:1); Heb 2:6–8 (Ps 8:4–6); Heb 3:7–11 (Ps 95:7–11); Heb 10:5–7 (Ps 40:6–8).

fathers by the prophets; but in these last days he has spoken to us by a Son." [y] Christ is greater than the angels who pay him homage and whose role it is to serve his purpose and minister to those who are heirs of salvation. He founded the heavens and earth in the beginning and now sits upon a throne with God forever.[z] Therefore, the author of Hebrews warns, the neglect of the salvation offered by Christ is a far more serious offense than failure to heed what the angels had declared earlier.[a]

It is probable that for some Hellenistic Christians the humanity of Christ had become an issue; they could not understand or accept the necessity for Christ's humanity in the person of Jesus. The author explains, therefore, that Christ was for a little while made "lower than the angels," that he partook of the nature of man, sharing man's struggles, sufferings and temptations, in order to destroy the power of death, and that he tasted death for everyone.[b]

In Hebrews, Christ and his priesthood supersede everything which came before in the heroic era of Genesis and Exodus. This is the dominant theme of a major section of the book. Christ is greater than Moses. Moses was faithful only as a servant in God's house, but Christ was faithful over God's house as a Son.[c] Christ is the great high priest after the order of Melchizedek, king of Salem to whom Abraham paid a tenth. Levi, in the family of Abraham, also paid tithes to Melchizedek.[d] This account from Genesis is cited as an example of the lesser honoring the greater and proclaims the superiority of the Melchizedek priesthood over the Levitical and, therefore, Christ's absolute supremacy. He is a high priest, "not according to a legal requirement concerning bodily descent but by the power of an indestructible life." [e] His priesthood is eternal, not dependent, as in the case of earthly priests, upon credentials involving lineage or genealogy. In Hebrews Christ supersedes both prophets and priests, but clearly the developing typology emphasizes the priest and the priestly institutions of religion. According to Hebrews Christianity has a high priest who ministers in "the sanctuary and the true tent." [f] The Tabernacle or tent of meeting in Moses' day was but a shadow of

---

[y] Heb 1:1f. [z] Heb 1:5–14. [a] Heb 2:1–3. [b] Heb 2:5–9, 14–18. [c] Heb 3:1–6.
[d] Heb 5:8–10; 6:19f.; 7:1–17. [e] Heb 7:15f. [f] Heb 8:1f.

the heavenly and perfect sanctuary.^g Christ as High Priest entered into the Holy Place, offered his own blood to replace all sacrifices, and thereby secured "an eternal redemption." ^h

In the background of Hebrews the threat of persecution hangs heavily over the Christian community in Rome. The author's immediate objective apparently is to bring the full weight of the Christian proclamation and tradition about Christ and salvation upon those Christians threatened by persecution and to strengthen their faith and preserve the integrity of the religious community. On the one hand he exhorts them to remain steadfast in the faith and warns that the consequences of apostasy are fearful. These are the "last days"; ^i there is no second chance. Here he insists that "it is impossible to restore again to repentance those who have once been enlightened, who have tasted the heavenly gift, and have become partakers of the Holy Spirit, . . . if they then commit apostasy, since they crucify the Son of God." ^j Judgment and fire await those who sin deliberately after they know the truth. "It is a fearful thing to fall into the hands of the living God." ^k

On the more positive side, Hebrews speaks of hope and things to come. The final Christian goal is captured in the author's vision of a "heavenly Jerusalem." They seek the city which is to come, "the city of the living God." ^l The author encourages the Christians to "hold fast the confession of our hope without wavering." ^m They are heirs of the promise which God made with an oath. Jesus himself has become "the surety of a better covenant." ^n

In the context of his proclamation about the promise and better covenant, the author develops one of his best known themes — the need for faith and hope. For the writer faith is the acceptance of an unseen order of reality beyond this world. "Now faith is the assurance of things hoped for, the conviction of things not seen." ^o This combination of faith, hope, and the promise of a more certain covenant is the key to the author's interpretation of biblical history. He cites many examples of heroes from the Israelite community of the past, notably Enoch, Noah, Abraham, and Moses, who did mighty deeds by the power of faith.^p "We

^g Heb 8:5. ^h Heb 9:12–14. ^i Heb 1:2; 10:25. ^j Heb 6:4, 6. ^k Heb 10:26f., 31.
^l Heb 12:22. ^m Heb 10:23. ^n Heb 6:17; 7:22. ^o Heb 11:1. ^p Heb 11:4–31.

are," he said, addressing the Jewish Christians, "surrounded by so great a cloud of witnesses." ^q Yet all of these, he explains, "though well attested by their faith, did not receive what was promised, since God had foreseen something better for us, that apart from us they should not be made perfect." ^r The ancients only saw dimly; they lived in anticipation of Christ's day. But for the unknown author of Hebrews, Christ and Christianity represented the perfection of God's plan.

In trying times endurance becomes a high virtue. In Hebrews Christ is proclaimed as the perfect example of courage in the face of death, of steadfastness to the very end; he is the model of the Christian martyr, "the pioneer" of salvation, made perfect through suffering.^s Thus, a rationale for persecution and suffering is provided. Persecution is God's way of chastening and testing his children. "It is for discipline that you have to endure," Hebrews explains. God is treating the followers of Christ as sons, and "what son is there whom his father does not discipline?" To be left without discipline is to be treated indifferently as an illegitimate child.^t God disciplines his children for their own good. For the moment it seems painful but in the end it will yield the peaceful fruit to those well trained. They will enter into God's rest and "share his holiness." ^u This is the ultimate goal, the fulfillment of the promise.

---

^q Heb 12:1. ^r Heb 11:39f. ^s Heb 2:10. ^t Heb 12:7f. ^u Heb 12:10f.

CHAPTER 15

The Tradition of John

The Johannine literary tradition includes the Gospel of John, the First, Second, and Third Letters of John, and The Revelation to John, sometimes referred to as the Apocalypse. Traditionally the authorship of all of these has been assigned to John, presumably John the son of Zebedee, one of the apostles of Jesus. Since the time of Justin Martyr, the view that John wrote all five documents has been widely held but by no means universally accepted. There is little internal evidence to support this claim.[1] Reference in Papias that "John the divine and James his brother were killed by Jews" and the possible allusion to the martyrdom of James and John in Mark's Gospel (10:38f.), tend to confirm the fact that their deaths took place before 70 CE, too early for the Johannine authors. Moreover, the great differences in style, vocabulary, and viewpoint evident among these five documents severely undermine the case for their common authorship.

The question of the authorship of the "John" literature is still far from settled. Why were all five writings regarded from ancient times as Johannine? Or why was the name "John" ascribed to two documents so glaringly different as John's Gospel and The Revelation to John? There may have been three, possibly four, different persons involved in these writings. It is likely, though not certain, that the anonymous person who authored the Fourth Gospel also wrote 1 John. A second person referred to by that name, called John "the Elder," wrote 2 and probably 3 John, and a third was the author of the Apocalypse.[2] But it is not the name "John"

---

[1] See the discussion of the problem of authorship of the Johannine documents in Morton Scott Enslin, *Christian Beginnings* (New York, 1938), 343–50, 357–72.

[2] Kümmel holds the view that all three documents, 1, 2, and 3 John, were written by the same person and dated ca. 90–110 CE. See W. G. Kümmel, *Introduction to the New Testament* (New York, 1973), 434–45, 450f.

but rather the doctrine of the Spirit that best identifies these writings as the Johannine tradition.[3] The close connection between "the Spirit" in John's Gospel and the spirit of prophecy in The Revelation to John relates both documents to the same school of thought.[4] Apocalyptic prophecy was common among the Jews from the time of the Maccabees and was strong among the early Jewish Christians. Christian apocalyptic literature was laced with futuristic predictions of the last day, the "uncovering" or disclosure of events at the end of the age, the coming of the heavenly Christ, and the overthrow of the antichrist. These eschatological themes appear in the Johannine letters but in the Revelation to John are so vividly detailed that they have had a lasting impact on Christian imagery, myth, theology, and religion.

APOCALYPTICISM AND THE APOCALYPSE

Christianity began as an eschatological movement. For approximately a century following the crucifixion and resurrection it retained much of its enthusiasm for the doctrines of the Parousia, the second coming of Jesus, and the imminent end of the age. Christian eschatology had its origin in that Jewish apocalyptic eschatology which developed in the post-exilic era under Persian, Egyptian, and Hellenistic influence. That apocalyptic was a flourishing Jewish religious literary genre in Palestine at the time of Jesus is evident from a study of the Dead Sea Scrolls.[5] The Essenes,

---

First John is usually included among the General or Catholic Epistles. Eventually it may have had general use in the church, but originally it was probably a tract or letter intended to address a specific historical problem — the threat which gnostic Christian groups posed for the unity of the church.

[3] Howard Kee's view is similar. He holds that the key to the Johannine writings is not merely the name of John but rather the authority of the spirit. See Howard Clark Kee, *Understanding the New Testament*, 4th ed. (New Jersey, 1983), 351.

[4] In the opinion of N. Perrin there was a Johannine "school," probably at Ephesus, and The Revelation to John does not "have a claim to a place in the 'Johannine corpus.'" Perrin points out that the existence of a Johannine school is "extremely likely . . . in the cultural conditions of the first century." There is precedent for the establishment of such institutions among the Jews; Rabbi Shammai and Rabbi Hillel are both known to have gathered disciples together and founded schools. See N. Perrin, *The New Testament*, 221, 249f.

[5] According to Norman Golb the "discoveries at Qūmran and Masada pointed to a much wider phenomenon of manuscript concealment in the Judean Desert dur-

the people of the Scrolls, were Jews who regarded themselves as faithful to the tradition of the Law and the prophets and sought a purification of the faith and ritual, but they looked for the end when God would break through into human history to destroy evil and usher in the Golden Age of truth, light, and saving knowledge.[6]

> The earth cries aloud at the ruin
> which has been wrought in the world;
> all its sentient beings shout;
> all who are upon it go mad
> and melt in utter ruin.
> For God thunders with the noise of his might,
> and his holy dwelling re-echoes with his glorious truth;
> the host of heaven utter their voice;
> the external foundations melt and shake;
> and the war of the mighty ones of heaven
> rushes about in the world and turns not back
> until the full end decreed forever;
> and there is nothing like it.[7]

From its beginning early Jewish Christianity was a messianic-apocalyptic movement begun by John the Baptist and after his execution led by Jesus of Nazareth. The apocalyptic anticipation of the imminent end of the age, with Jesus as the supernatural Son of Man and agent of the transformation, was a distinctive feature of the Jewish Christian community in Jerusalem and was as well a dominant feature in Paul's writings and in the beliefs of the Hellenistic Christians to whom he ministered.[8]

That the primitive Christians adopted but modified Jewish apocalyptic themes is evident from a comparison of first-century

---

ing the period of the war with Rome . . . . that these manuscripts stem not merely from sectarians but from first-century Palestinian Jews in general . . . they show that much of the Jewish society already at the beginning of the first century was in spiritual turmoil and doctrinally divided among itself." See Norman Golb, "Who Hid the Dead Sea Scrolls?" in *Biblical Archaeologist* 48 (June 1985), 2:79, 81.

[6] See especially Millar Burrows, *The Dead Sea Scrolls* (New York, 1955), chap. 12, and Theodor H. Gaster, *The Dead Sea Scrolls* (Garden City, 1976).

[7] From *The Thanksgiving Psalms*, iii, trans. by Millar Burrows, from Burrows, op. cit., 405.

[8] Paul's expectations of the cataclysmic end of the age are clearly discernible in 1 Thessalonians 4:13–17 and in 1 Corinthians 15:12–58.

Jewish and Christian apocalyptic writings. Apocalyptic is a special form of eschatology, the teaching concerning the end of things.[9] Eschatology generally presents an optimistic view of the ultimate end of history — that history is under the control of the deity, that whatever its direction there will eventually be an ideal end, a golden age or the coming of God's Kingdom. Details of the End are generally missing in eschatological writings; the end is distantly future and is usually left undefined and vague. The movement of history toward that future goal may be gradual or evolutionary.

Apocalyptic is a form of eschatology in which the events of the end of the age are detailed, often vividly portrayed in symbolic imagery. The end is sharply defined by the impact of divine or supernatural intervention in human history. In the apocalyptic vision the end comes about in a series of cataclysmic events. Apocalyptic is revolutionary rather than evolutionary.

The theology of Jewish apocalyptic is often called crisis theology because it often issued from tragic historical situations, as, for example, the persecution of the Jews by the Syrian Greeks under Antiochus IV. In the face of terrible persecution it seemed as if all of God's promises were about to be reversed by political and military events. The apocalypse that issued from the Syrian persecution was the Book of Daniel, which affirmed God's goodness and power in the face of the most catastrophic defeats by projecting the promises of fulfillment across history to the end of the age. On that day God would intervene in the course of history and fulfill his purposes for his people.

Jewish apocalyptic writings generally contain certain formal features. First is the use of a pseudonym in place of the author's own name. The name of some great historical personage is attached to the document to gain the authority of that person and to guarantee acceptance. Second, the substance of the author's message is found in revelations received usually in visions, sometimes in dreams. His apocalypse is presented as a vision describing critical events taking place in the author's own time as the fulfillment of

---

[9] See the discussion of apocalypticism in early Christianity in Norman Perrin, *The New Testament*, 65–85.

past prophecy. The accounts do not clearly identify by name the countries or persons involved but instead make use of images and symbols. Finally, and most important, such visions of God guarantee the outcome of human history.[10] The parable of Enoch on the future lot of the wicked and the righteous is an excellent example of the Jewish apocalyptic form.

> The words of the blessing of Enoch, wherewith he blessed the elect [and] righteous who will be living in the day of tribulation, when all the wicked [and godless] are to be removed. And he took up his parable and said — Enoch a righteous man, whose eyes were opened by God, saw the vision of the Holy One in the heavens, [which] the angels showed me, and from them I heard everything, and from them I understood as I saw, but not for this generation, but for a remote one which is to come.[11]

Jewish apocalyptic also features model heros and martyrs, those who persevered in the faith even at the cost of their lives. Eleazar and the seven sons in IV Maccabees and Daniel are cases in point. Messianism is a significant feature of some Jewish apocalyptic documents. The Messiah, one anointed by God as his agent, would appear at the Last Day to bring about the events leading to the fulfillment of the divine promises, the rewarding of the righteous and the punishment of the ungodly.

Apocalyptic became a primary literary-faith response to crises in history among Jewish writers from ca. 200 BCE to 134 CE.

---

[10] See R. H. Charles, *Translation of Early Documents*, series 1, *Palestinian Jewish Texts, The Book of Enoch* (London, 1960), 31.

It appears that the term "apocrypha" was originally applied to books which were believed to be so sacred that their truths were kept secret from the general populace and were available only to the inner circle of the most pious believers. Such books were often apocalyptic in both substance and form. The fourteen books of the so-called Old Testament Apocrypha were included in the Septuagint, the ancient Greek translation of the Hebrew Bible, but were not included in the Hebrew canon established in the first century. Most of them, however, were translated by St. Jerome in the fourth century and are in the Vulgate, the official Catholic Latin Bible. Protestants generally have followed the Jewish practice of omitting them from the canon. The title "pseudepigrapha," falsely inscribed, usually refers to the collection of non-canonical Jewish writings not in the Apocrypha, produced between 200 BCE and 200 CE, bearing the names of ancient worthies such as Adam and Enoch, and purporting to contain truths revealed especially to the earliest of Israelite patriarchs.

[11] *The Book of Enoch* 1:1–2, trans. by R. H. Charles.

Prophecy was an important element in this apocalyptic frame but not in the sense understood by Amos, Hosea, or Micah of the eighth century BCE, prophets who spoke forth for God on crucial matters which Israel encountered in their own time. Rather, apocalyptic prophecy was foretelling events of the future. For the apocalyptic prophets the experience of God was not primarily hearing, as in the case of the classical prophets, but rather a "seeing," as in a vision or dream, the events of the end of the age. Also, apocalyptic was a national eschatology, bringing hope for the nation's future, for political as well as religious redemption.

The Christian response to crisis in the first century was not primarily apocalyptic and therefore Christian apocalyptic writings are relatively few. The Revelation or Apocalypse of John is the only Jewish type apocalyptic book in the New Testament canon. However, the canon includes the so-called "little apocalypse" of Mark 13, a notable example of apocalyptic writings and important for the Christian faith.[12]

The characteristic form of the Christian apocalyptic is shown in Mark's apocalyptic sermon.

> And when you hear of wars and rumors of wars, do not be alarmed; this must take place, but the end is not yet. For nation will rise against nation, . . . there will be earthquakes in various places, . . .
> But in those days, after that tribulation, the sun will be darkened, and the moon will not give its light, and the stars will be falling from heaven, . . .
> And then they will see the Son of man coming in clouds with great power and glory. And then he will send out the angels, and gather his elect . . . . (13:7f., 24–27)

Undoubtedly, the Christian form and content of apocalyptic prophecy were based on such books as Daniel in the Old Testament and the Book of Enoch in the Pseudepigrapha:

> I saw the night visions,
> and behold, with the clouds of heaven there came one like a son of man,

---

[12] Other Christian apocalyptic documents are to be found in *The New Testament Apocrypha*. The Apocalypses of Peter, of Paul, and of Thomas are the major examples.

> and he came to the Ancient of Days and was presented before him.
> And to him was given dominion and glory and kingdom,
> that all peoples, nations, and languages should serve him;
> his dominion is an everlasting dominion, which shall not pass away.... (Dan. 7:13f.)[13]

> And there I saw One, who had a head of days,
> And His head was white like wool,
> And with Him was another being whose countenance had the appearance of a man, ...
> And I asked the angel who went with me and showed me all the hidden things, concerning that Son of Man, who he was, and whence he was, [and] why he went with the Head of Days?
> And he answered and said unto me:
> This is the Son of Man who hath righteousness, ...
> And who revealeth all the treasures of that which is hidden.
> (The Book of Enoch, XLVI, 1–3)[14]

The idea of prophetic prediction within the frame of apocalyptic is an essential aspect of earliest Christian thought dating back to possibly before Paul. There were at least three different ways of establishing the authority of one's credentials as a prophet and apostle: being a descendant of David (dynastic Christianity); as a personal witness (the apostolic way); or having the gift of God's spirit of prophecy (the prophetic, charismatic way).

Dynastic Christianity was Jewish and eschatological. The restoration of the Davidic kingdom and the expectation of the imminent coming of God's Messiah were at the heart of the Jewish Christian proclamation. Apparently James, "the brother of the Lord," was head of the Jewish Christian community in Jerusalem for a time. His leading role in settling the circumcision issue, for instance, is well documented in Acts of the Apostles.[a]

Both apostolic and prophetic credentials are discussed by Paul. His claim to be an apostle differs from that of Peter and the other apostles in that his calling was by a special revelation of the risen Christ. Peter's claim was his personal witness of Jesus' words and deeds during his mortal ministry.

---

[a] Acts 15:13–21.

[13] This is from the Septuagint (the Greek) translation.

[14] R. H. Charles, *The Book of Enoch* 46, L-3 (London, 1960), 63f.

The Tradition of John

Prophecy as a gift of the Spirit was an important part of Paul's teaching. In 1 Thessalonians Paul instructs the congregation, "Do not quench the Spirit, do not despise prophesying." [b] In 1 Corinthians he speaks of "prophetic powers," and in his pronouncements about the gifts of the Spirit, he speaks of the need to pursue the spiritual gifts, especially prophecy.[c] In Paul's day, glossolalia, speaking in tongues, as a gift of the Spirit was a strong feature of church worship but prophecy was probably seen as less threatening to the order and stability of the church. Paul admonished the congregation at Corinth to seek the gift of prophecy for the edification of the church rather than to speak in tongues. "How shall I benefit you unless I bring you some revelation or knowledge or prophecy or teaching?"[d] As a recommendation for church order he says, "Let two or three prophets speak . . . you can all prophesy one by one."[e]

In the Acts of the Apostles there are several references to the activity of prophets and to prophecy. Although the book of Acts in its present form was probably written ca. 80–90 CE, it may have included materials from an older stratum of the Palestinian tradition, material about Christian prophets, who presumably had considerable influence on the earliest Christian communities. Such a prophet, Agabus, is reported to have come down from Jerusalem to Antioch. He foretold "by the Spirit" that there would be a great famine, which, according to the author, took place in the days of Claudius.[f] Later, Agabus is reported to have prophesied the imprisonment of Paul.[g] Also, the author of Acts says that "in the church at Antioch there were prophets and teachers."[h] These were prophets on the model of the Books of Samuel and Kings, called the "Former Prophets," which include such charismatic figures as Samuel, Elijah, and Elisha, seers and visionaries through whom the Spirit worked powerful miracles of healing in ancient Israel.

It is interesting in this connection that in the Acts account, David is referred to as prophet rather than as king. And the Psalms are credited to David as prophetic utterances:

> Brethren, the scripture had to be fulfilled, which the Holy Spirit spoke beforehand by the mouth of David, concerning Judas.[i]

[b] 1 Thes 5:19f. [c] 1 Cor 13:2; 14:1–3. [d] 1 Cor 14:3–6. [e] 1 Cor 14:29, 31.
[f] Acts 11:27. [g] Acts 21:10f. [h] Acts 13:1. [i] Acts 1:16; 2:25, 30; 4:25f.

Then, the author quotes portions of Psalm 69:25 and 109:8, which contain the original prophecy. According to the scholar Philipp Vielhauer,

> These observations compel us to conclude that Palestinian Christianity had a strongly pneumatic colouring and that the prophets must have had a considerable significance in the leading of the Palestinian church.[15]

Apocalyptic writing was a major influence upon the Jews in the two centuries before the birth of Jesus and continued through the tumultuous years of the Jewish-Roman war and the Bar Kokhba revolution ca. 133–135 CE. Apocalyptic literature flourished as the main inspiration for revolt in this period. After the failure of the Kokhba uprising, the appeal of apocalypticism declined markedly as Judaism sought to stabilize itself upon the foundation of the Torah, the rabbi, and the synagogue. Of all the apocalyptic literature produced in the Jewish world, only the book of Daniel was finally canonized in the Jewish scripture (the Tanak), and then as a part of the Kethubim or Hagiographa rather than the Prophets.

But in the Christian experience, the failure of the Parousia, conflict with non-Christian Jews, and the urgent need to come to terms with the Roman government inclined some Christians toward apocalypticism. Also, itinerant prophets and visionaries, many of whom were suspected of being gnostic and/or libertine in their teachings, were an obstacle to the developing organization of the church. Prophets were too individualistic, too free, too volatile to serve as the main support of the church institution. Caution about the status of wandering prophets is reflected in the Didache; considerable space is devoted in one part of the Didache, the manual of Church Order, to developing guidelines identifying genuine and false prophets.

> However, not everybody making ecstatic utterances is a prophet, but only if he behaves like the Lord. It is by their conduct that the false

---

[15] Edgar Hennecke, *New Testament Apocrypha*, ed. by Wilhelm Schneemelcher, English translation by R. M. L. Wilson, Vol. 2, *Writings Relating to the Apostles, Apocalypses and Related Subjects* (Philadelphia, 1964), 606.

prophet and the [true] prophet can be distinguished. For instance, if a prophet marks out a table in the Spirit, he must not eat from it. If he does he is a false prophet.[16]

By the end of the first quarter of the second century, as the need for unity and stability increased, prophets and prophecy lost their initial significance in the church and prophets and teachers were gradually relegated to lesser roles.

1 JOHN

First John is structured more like a theological tract or sermon than a letter. The epistolary frame, including a salutation and a formal ending, is not present. Yet, as R. H. Fuller perhaps correctly points out, in content it is a letter. In 1 John a specific historical situation is identifiable in which the theological concerns probably related to the event are so important that they substitute for the usual form of a letter.

The occasion for the writing of 1 John was the defection of an important, perhaps fairly large and influential group of Christians from the main body of the church. Their separation was especially threatening because it was led by false teachers who came from within the church. They denied the divinity of the historical person, Jesus, that he was the Christ, the Son of God. Apparently, their beliefs about Jesus Christ were similar to those of that form of Gnosticism called Docetism which differentiated between the human Jesus and the heavenly Christ, proclaiming that the supernatural and divine Christ had come upon Jesus at his baptism and remained with him only a brief time until his crucifixion. First John was written ca. 90–110 CE to establish for orthodox Christians in Asia Minor the claim that Christianity was the true gnosis and to affirm the foundation of that claim, that Jesus was in fact the heavenly Christ and that their salvation did ultimately depend

---

[16] Didache 11:8f. The *Didache* or *Teaching* is made up of two parts: a code of Christian morals presented as the way of life versus the way of death and a manual of Church Order. Dating the Didache is difficult. It may have been edited ca. 150 CE. The part from which this quote was taken, the manual of Church Order, is presumed to have come originally from Syria, perhaps from the city of Antioch. See Cyril C. Richardson, ed., *Early Christian Fathers*, Vol. 1 (New York, 1970), 161–66, 176–77.

upon his life, his actual suffering, and the actual shedding of his blood upon the cross.

The concern about the "false teachers" in 1 John did not simply refer to the Jewish denial that Jesus was the Messiah but rather to the denial that Jesus Christ had come "in the flesh." [j] This teaching is similar to that of the Docetists or "Seemists" alluded to in Ignatius' letter to the Ephesians, the Trallians, and Smyrnaeans in Asia Minor (ca. 117 CE).[17]

> What good does anyone do me by praising me and reviling my Lord by refusing to acknowledge that he carried around the flesh? . . . Let no one be misled: Heavenly beings, the splendor of angels, and principalities, visible and invisible, if they fail to believe in Christ's blood, they too are doomed. (Smyrnaeans)

and again in the letter to the Trallians,

> Be deaf, then, to any talk that ignores Jesus Christ, of David's lineage, of Mary; who was really born, ate, and drank; was really persecuted under Pontius Pilate; was really crucified and died in the sight of heaven and earth and underworld. He was really raised from the dead, for his Father raised him, . . .
>
> And if, as some atheists (I mean unbelievers) say, his suffering was a sham (it's really *they* who are a sham), why, then, am I a prisoner? Why do I want to fight with wild beasts? In that case I shall die to no purpose. (Trallians)

According to the Docetist view, Christ did not die on the cross. The human Jesus suffered and died; the heavenly Christ only seemed to die. Such a "Seemist" view is shown in the *Acts of John*, a New Testament Apocryphal source presumed to have been written by a person named Leucius Charinus, who was supposedly a disciple of John,[18]

> Sometimes when I meant to touch him I encountered a material, solid body; but at other times again when I felt him, his substance was

---

[j] 1 Jn 4:2.

[17] Cyril C. Richardson, *Early Christian Fathers*, 1:100, 114.

[18] That the author, Leucius, was a disciple of John is highly questionable. The earliest attestation of the *Acts of John* is its mention by Eusebius (HE III.25.6). The document probably came from Asia Minor. It was never strongly regarded as authentic to John and was better known by the fourth century as part of the Manichaean corpus of Acts literature. See Edgar Hennecke, *New Testament Apocrypha*, Introduction, 188–206; on the texts, 227, 232–34.

immaterial and incorporeal, and as if it did not exist at all . . . And I often wished, as I walked with him, to see his footprint in the earth, whether it appeared — for I saw him raising himself from the earth — and I never saw it.[19]

On the mystery of the cross, the Acts of John says,

> And I saw the Lord himself above the Cross, having no shape but only a kind of voice; yet not that voice which we knew, but one that was sweet and gentle . . . which said to me, "John, there must (be) one man (to) hear these things from me; for I need one who is ready to hear. This Cross of Light is sometimes called Logos by me for your sakes, sometimes mind, sometimes Jesus, sometimes Christ, sometimes a door, sometimes a way . . . and so (it is called) for men's sake . . .
> But this is not that wooden Cross which you shall see when you go down from here; nor am I the (man) who is on the Cross, . . . Therefore ignore the many and despise those who are outside the mystery; . . .
> So then I have suffered none of those things which they will say of me; even that suffering which I showed to you and to the rest in my dance, I will that it be called a mystery.[20]

First John begins with a declaration of the fundamentals of the Christian faith: that the "word of life," "the eternal life which was with the Father . . . was made manifest" to them so that they might have fellowship with each other and "with the Father and with his Son Jesus Christ." [k] If they claim to have fellowship with him but "walk in darkness," their lives are a lie. But if they "walk in the light, as he is in the light," the blood of Jesus cleanses them from all their sins.[l]

Such key expressions as "from the beginning," "the word of life," "the eternal life," "the life was made manifest," and especially the prominence of "the Spirit" are similar to the gnostically inclined christological language and thought of the Fourth Gospel. The emphasis is upon "life," upon light as contrasted with darkness, the truth versus the lie, and upon the claim to "know"— which means to "love" — rather than to hate. The expression

---

[k] 1 Jn 1:1–3. [l] 1 Jn 1:6f.

[19] E. Hennecke, *New Testament Apocrypha*, Vol. 2, 227, *Acts of John*, 93.

[20] Ibid., Vol. 2, 133f., *Acts of John*, 98–101.

"abides in him" occurs frequently: "Every one who commits sin is guilty of lawlessness"; "No one born of God commits sin; for God's nature abides in him." [m] "All who keep his commandments abide in him, and he in them. And by this we know that he abides in us, by the Spirit which he has given us." [n] References to the anointing which they received "from him" and "as his anointing teaches you" probably are intended to reinforce the Johannine doctrine of the Spirit.[o]

First John repeatedly emphasizes the enormity of the sin of those who deny the humanity of Christ and the importance of *knowing* the truth.

> I am writing this to you so that you may not sin; but if any one does sin, we have an advocate with the Father . . . he is the expiation for our sins . . . also for the sins of the whole world.[p]

"If we say we have no sin, we deceive ourselves. . . . If we say we have not sinned, we make him a liar." [q] By implication the author makes it clear that the Christian schismatics are denying that they sin and by doing so place themselves beyond redemption. The charge against them rests upon their claim to "know" God despite behavior inconsistent with God's commandments; they claim to live "in the light" yet they hate their brothers.[r] According to 1 John, only "he who loves his brother abides in the light," he who hates his brother is blinded by the darkness.[s]

The claim to have unique spiritual experiences and to "know" God led to a form of moral libertinism in which the traditional Christian sense of duty to one's brother became irrelevant. John warns these heretics that they should not believe every spirit but should test the spirits to see whether they come from God; for, he declares, "many false prophets have gone out into the world." [t] But "We are of God. Whoever knows God listens to us. . . . By this we know the spirit of truth and the spirit of error. Beloved, let us love one another; for love is of God, and he who loves is born of God and knows God. . . . for God is love." [u] According to 1 John, there is a key for knowing the spirit of God: "every spirit which confesses that Jesus Christ has come in the flesh is of

[m] 1 Jn 3:4, 9. [n] 1 Jn 3:24. [o] 1 Jn 2:27. [p] 1 Jn 2:1f. [q] 1 Jn 1:8, 10.
[r] 1 Jn 2:3f., 9. [s] 1 Jn 2:10f. [t] 1 Jn 4:1. [u] 1 Jn 4:6–8.

God, and every spirit which does not confess Jesus is not of God." [21] This is the spirit of antichrist, which they knew was already in the world.[v]

The threat posed by the Christian schismatics is described in apocalyptic terms within an apocalyptic frame: "the world passes away." The "antichrist is coming, so now many antichrists have come; therefore we know that it is the last hour." [w] "They [presumably the Docetist Christians] went out from us, but they were not of us." Here, the author attempts to explain the defection "that it might be plain that they all are not of us." [x] "Who is the liar," he asks, "but he who denies that Jesus is the Christ? This is the antichrist, he who denies the Father and the Son. No one who denies the Son has the Father." [y] For the author, such denial is the most deadly of sins.

Such a discussion may be an early Christian attempt to distinguish between two classes of sins. In 1 John 5 the author advises that if any sees his brother committing "what is not a mortal sin," he should ask and God would give life to those "whose sin is not mortal." He adds, "There is sin which is mortal; I do not say that one is to pray for that." [z] The implication seems to be that there is sin for which God will grant no forgiveness. Probably, it is the sin committed by the Docetist Christians who had at one time fully embraced the faith given by the Spirit. They had denied the witness of the Spirit and rejected the doctrines of resurrection and the efficacy of the atoning blood of Christ, beliefs at the heart of the Christian gospel.

R. H. Fuller and others are certainly correct that 1 John 5:7 is an addition from a later date. Fuller claims that this is "the

---

[v] 1 Jn 4:2f. [w] 1 Jn 2:17f. [x] 1 Jn 2:19. [y] 1 Jn 2:22f. [z] 1 Jn 5:16f.

[21] As Enslin pointed out, the notion that Jesus was neither born nor subject to suffering or death constituted a serious problem for early orthodox Christians. This is made clear in the Gospels. For example, in Matthew's account of the empty tomb the women "took hold of his feet" (28:9); also, the resurrected Christ says to his disciples in Luke 24:39, 42f., "see my hands and my feet, that it is I myself; handle me, and see; for a spirit has not flesh and bones as you see I have," and asks for food, "They gave him a piece of broiled fish and he . . . ate before them." See Enslin, *Christian Beginnings*, 345f.

In the early Christian church, preserving the humanity of Jesus Christ was an issue of highest importance; today the chief issue is the divinity of Christ.

clearest statement of the doctrine of the Trinity [found] anywhere in the N.T." [22] However, its Christology seems consistent with the content and emphasis of the Johannine literature.

> And the Spirit is the witness, because the Spirit is the truth. There are three witnesses, the Spirit, the water, and the blood; and these three agree.... He who believes in the Son of God has the testimony in himself.... And this is the testimony, that God gave us eternal life, and this life is in his Son. He who has the Son has life; he who has not the Son of God has not life.[a]

2 JOHN AND 3 JOHN

Second and 3 John have the form of private letters. Both purport to have been written by John, called "the Elder." Whether or not they were written by the same person is not clear, but they no doubt came from the same Johannine school. According to the text, 2 John was written "to the elect lady and her children,"[b] but this is probably a figurative designation for a particular Christian congregation. Third John was written to an individual person named Gaius, presumably a convert of the Elder.[c] Kümmel dates these two documents about the same time as 1 John, ca. 90–110 CE; Enslin dates 3 John somewhat later.[23]

The purpose of the two letters seems to be different. Second John was composed as a warning to a particular congregation against false teachers who reject the doctrine of the incarnation of Christ. For the author, they are deceivers, the antichrist, as the Docetist Christians were called in 1 John. Much of the content of this brief letter is related to belief in Christ's humanity, which the author regards as "the truth which abides in us."[d] As in 1 John, he does not claim to write a new commandment but one they "have had from the beginning, that we love one another." Love, he claims, is a crucial aspect of the Christian gospel. "This is love, that we follow his commandments."[e] He warns against

---

[a] 1 Jn 5:6–8, 10–12. [b] 2 Jn 1:1. [c] 3 Jn 1:1. [d] 2 Jn 1:2. [e] 2 Jn 1:5f.

[22] Fuller holds that 1 John 5:7 is a later insertion. The fact that it occurs in none of the Greek manuscripts earlier than the fourteenth century, in no early Christian Fathers, and in no Old Latin texts seems conclusive. R. H. Fuller, *A Critical Introduction to the New Testament*, 182.

[23] See Kümmel, 450f. Also, see Enslin, 350.

the deceivers who refuse to acknowledge the coming of Jesus Christ in the flesh and the implications of that doctrine.[f] Such persons do "not have God."[g] At this point, the author's hostility toward his opposition seems to overcome his commitment to love — "Do not receive him" who does not bring this doctrine, "for he who greets him shares his wicked work."[h]

Third John was written to Gaius personally rather than to a local congregation. The Elder seems to have had a close relationship with Gaius and his congregation, whom he refers to as "my children."[i] He commends Gaius for the hospitality he extended to visiting "brethren" who are strangers. Probably, they were a group of preachers sent by the Elder and led by Demetrius. He learns from them upon their return of Gaius' kind assistance in fitting them for their journey. This was an act of special importance since they could not accept aid from the heathen. The Elder applauds the action of Gaius and recommends it to other Christians, that they "may be fellow workers in the truth."[j]

Diotrephes, apparently the leader of the congregation to which Gaius belongs, does not accept the Elder as his superior authority and has a different attitude toward itinerant evangelists. He not only refuses to welcome them but excludes those who accept them from the church.[k] The suspicion of heresy probably is at issue here as well. It would seem that the evil the Elder cautions against in 3 John is precisely the lack of love represented in Diotrephes' refusal to accept his fellow Christians. In 3 John the author emphasizes the importance of "love" and of truth. He speaks of "love in the truth," of workers "in the truth," and the fact that he who does good "is of God."[l]

Third John seems to correct the overzealous reaction of Christians like Diotrephes who interpreted the advice of 2 John against greeting heretics too broadly and rejected Christian evangelists with suspected sympathy for the Docetist heresy. To such Christians, the Elder warns that in denying love to their fellow Christians, they are not the children of God.

[f] 2 Jn 1:7. [g] 2 Jn 1:9. [h] 2 Jn 1:10f. [i] 3 Jn 1:4. [j] 3 Jn 1:8. [k] 3 Jn 1:10.
[l] 3 Jn 1:1, 3f., 6, 8, 11.

THE REVELATION TO JOHN

The authorship of the Revelation to John has long been argued by New Testament scholars. The conservative tradition holds that the document was written by John, son of Zebedee, a leading apostle of Jesus who supposedly authored the Fourth Gospel and the three letters of John as well. However, the internal evidence does not support this conclusion. Though the author of Revelation does refer to himself as John several times, once as a servant of Jesus, and once as "your brother" in Jesus,[m] he nowhere suggests that he is an apostle nor does he indicate that he was ever present with Jesus. The great differences in style, vocabulary, ideas and point of view among these so-called Johannine documents throw serious doubt on this tradition.[24] Though the identity of the author remains unknown, the Apocalypse does reveal some of the author's characteristics. For example, he probably was a Jewish Christian from Asia Minor. His familiarity with the condition of the churches in Asia Minor and his feeling of responsibility toward them suggests this. That he was a Jewish Christian is indicated by his familiarity with the Jewish scriptures and the materials of the Old Testament Apocrypha.[25]

The dating of the Revelation is problematic. Some scholars have maintained that the entire book was written before the fall of Jerusalem in 70 CE. The reign of Vespasian following the Jewish war has been suggested as another possibility. However, it seems most likely that the book was produced during the final years of Domitian's reign near the end of the first century (ca. 96 CE).[26] This view conforms with both the tradition established by Irenaeus (ca. 180) and the internal evidence of the Revelation itself. The author's reference to the two beasts in chapter 13, which reflects his hatred for the Roman empire and the imperial cultus, and his comment on the condition of the seven churches in chapters 2 and 3 seem to substantiate this judgment.

---

[m] Rv 1:1, 4, 9; 22:8.

[24] See Kümmel, *Introduction*, 462.

[25] Ibid., 472.

[26] See Enslin, *Christian Beginnings*, 366.

Some interpreters maintain that "the letters" (chapter 2 and 3) were never sent independently of the main body of the book nor were they intended only for the seven churches. According to this view the number seven was probably intended to represent the whole of Christianity.[27] However, the view that the author originally intended the letters to be read in the several churches in the Roman province of Asia has merit. The Revelation probably was written in response to a specific historical situation, the threat of Roman persecution of the churches in this area. The threat, at least in the mind of the author, was immediate and serious.

In the prologue, 1:1–3, John provides the authentication for his apocalypse: the message of his book, entrusted by God to Jesus Christ, had been revealed to him through a heavenly angel. John's concern is to place the immediate circumstances in proper perspective to show through visions of the future that the present historical situation is only the final phase of the larger cosmic struggle between the forces of God and Satan.

Following the introduction and the recitation of the Christian witness,[n] the author describes the circumstances leading up to his vision. He had been exiled to the island of Patmos because he had persisted in preaching God's word. On the Lord's day John, "in the Spirit," heard a voice like a trumpet which charged him to write to the seven churches what he was about to see.[o] When he turned to identify the person of the voice, he saw seven standing lamps of gold and among them "one like a son of man,"[p] whom he describes in terms markedly similar to the son of man figure in the books of Ezekiel and Daniel.[28]

In Ezekiel and Daniel the person like the son of man is not identified; the imaginative and symbolic description in each of these books only indicates what that person is *like*. Similarly, symbolic imagery is employed in John's description of the supernatural figure — that his hair was "white as white wool"; "his eyes were like a flame of fire"; "his feet were like burnished bronze"; "his

---

[n] Rv 1:4–8. [o] Rv 1:10f. [p] Rv 1:12f.

[27] Ibid., 21, 358.

[28] Observe the use of the expression "son of man" in Ezekiel 2:1, 3, 8; 3:1, etc. Also, Daniel 7:13; 8:17.

voice was like the sound of many waters"; and "his face was like the sun." [q] But John identifies this symbolically described messianic figure as Jesus Christ, the Son of man. This is made clear when Christ speaks to John, "I am the first and the last, and the living one; ... I have the keys of Death and Hades. Now write what you see, what is and what is to take place hereafter." Then Christ identifies the seven churches who are to receive the seven letters.[r]

Certain patterns of expression are discernible in John's seven letters. Each is addressed to an angel, presumably the guardian angel of each Christian community. The author concludes each letter with the cryptic comment, "He who has an ear, let him hear what the Spirit says to the churches." [s] Apparently communication by or through the Spirit is the key to his instructions. Finally he repeats in several places the complaint that "I have this against you" or "I have a few things against you." [t]

The main body of the Apocalypse (4:1–22:19) is made up of the seven cycles of visions. Howard Kee in his *Understanding the New Testament* describes the cycles: an introduction to the sevenfold prophecy (4:1–5:14) followed by John's description of the seven cycles—seven seals (6:1–8:1), seven trumpets (8:2–11:15), seven visions of the kingdom of the dragon (11:16–13:18), seven visions of the coming of the Son of man (14:1–20), seven bowls (15:1–16:21), seven visions of the fall of Babylon (17:1–19:10), and seven visions of the End (19:11–21:4).[29]

Did John intend these as a series of events in a chronological order? The usual scholarly approach has been to locate a chronological sequence for the visions. Others have followed the suggestion that the visions are intended to be repetitious, that is, they are different visions or portrayals of the final events. Such repetitions emphasize the meaning and significance of the events, not primarily the order, leading up to the End and assure that under God's direction they will take place.

The apocalyptic cycles begin with a vision of the throne of God.[u] A voice directed John "to come up hither" and be shown

---

[q] Rv 1:14–16. [r] Rv 1:17–20. [s] Rv 2:7, 11, 17, 29; 3:6, 13, 22. [t] Rv 2:4, 14, 20.
[u] Rv 4:1–11.

[29] Kee, 446f.

The Tradition of John

what must take place. "At once," he said, "I was in the Spirit" and stood before the throne of God. The emphasis here on God's holiness is reminiscent of the prophet Isaiah's pronouncements in his temple vision.ᵛ That the author is familiar with Jewish apocalyptic imagery is evident.

Thus the stage is set for the heavenly Christ (the Lamb of God) to assume his central role. John saw in the right hand of one seated on the throne a scroll which was sealed with seven seals. None was able to meet the criterion of worthiness and open the scroll; then one of the twenty-four elders said, "The Lion of the tribe of Judah, the Root of David, has conquered . . . he can open the scroll." ʷ Thus Jesus Christ, the Lamb, was introduced into the cosmic drama.

The seven seals are to be opened to disclose the secrets (the mysteries) of the future, to portray the imminent destruction of the world. The first four of the seven seals, represented by horses of different colors, symbolize the ways in which destruction is to be carried out. These are similar to Zechariah's vision of the future.[30] The fifth seal represents the slaughter of the martyrs who cry out for vengeance.ˣ They are given a white robe and told to rest until the tally of their brethren who are to be slain should be complete. The sixth seal involves tremendous cosmic upheavals: a great earthquake will occur, the sun will become black, the full moon will become like blood, and the stars will fall from the heavens.ʸ At this point, before the situation worsens, there is to be a pause to set apart the faithful so that they will be protected from the chaos to follow. This involves the sealing of the one hundred and forty-four thousand, the perfect number.ᶻ [31]

How is one to understand such a grandiose projection of future events? Some Christians in all ages since the canonization of this document have attempted to apply it literally and have assumed that the end of the age described by John was imminent and relevant to their own time. But clearly this is not what John had in

---

ᵛ Is 6:1–3.   ʷ Rv 5:5.   ˣ Rv 6:9–11.   ʸ Rv 6:12–17.   ᶻ Rv 7:1–8.

[30] Zechariah 1:8; 6:1–3. The format is similar to that reported in Mark's apocalypse (13:7f.).

[31] Some scholars think these passages allude to the return of the lost ten tribes. See 2 Esdras 13:39–50.

mind. His prophecy of future events was not intended for Christians at all times and places. Christians in John's time faced a specific historical crisis. Roman officials were suspicious of those Christians in Asia Minor whose opposition to the emperor cult was interpreted as a sign of disloyalty to the state. Given the historical context of such suspicion, charges of sedition, and threats of execution, symbols and cryptic comments usefully concealed pertinent information (the names of persons and peoples) from the Roman officials who were likely to take action against the Christians. At the same time, such symbols communicated important information to those of the elect who were most vulnerable.

An important use of mystical symbols can be found in the second series of judgments (8:7–15:8). There appeared a great portent in heaven — a woman "clothed with the sun" and having "a crown of twelve stars"[a] (probably representing Israel). The dragon in this episode, identified as Satan "the deceiver of the whole world," was eventually "thrown down to the earth" and his angels with him.[b] This is probably an allusion to the story of Adam and Eve and the paradise story in Genesis. For Christians the serpent in the Genesis account was Satan or the Devil.[c] According to John, the dragon or Satan, furious with the woman, went off to war against her offspring (those who keep their testimony of Jesus).[d]

Another instance of the use of mystical symbols is John's vision of the two beasts. According to John, the number of the second beast represents a man's name and the numerical value of its letters is "six hundred and sixty-six."[e] The number may represent either the priesthood of the imperial cult or one of the Roman emperors. The number was arrived at by adding the numerical value of the letters in the name of the emperor spelled in Hebrew. Although the person of the number cannot be identified with certainty, the intent of the cryptic number is clear; it points to the Roman emperors who claimed to be divine. Domitian seems to be the most likely candidate. He was thought by some in his time to be the reincarnation of Nero.

The Revelation builds in intensity and volume in chapters 17 and 18. Here John is carried away in the Spirit into a wilderness where

[a] Rv 12:1. [b] Rv 12:9. [c] Gn 3:1–5, 14. [d] Rv 12:17. [e] Rv 13:17f.

he sees the future fall of Babylon. "Babylon" is employed as a mystical symbol referring to Rome. The fact that in the vision the woman sits on "seven mountains" or hills seems to confirm this conclusion.[f] The phrase "Fallen is Babylon the great!" reminds one of Zephaniah's rejoicing over the destruction of the ancient city of Nineveh.[g]

The finale of the Revelation begins with chapter 19:11 when John "saw heaven opened." An angel with the key to the bottomless pit comes down from heaven, seizes the dragon, and chains him up for a thousand years.[h] Those who had been beheaded for the sake of their testimony to Jesus are resurrected and reign with Christ for the thousand years.[i] The rest of the dead are not to be brought to life again until the millennial reign is ended. "This," John says, "is the first resurrection."[j]

At the end of the thousand years, Satan is released. He gathers the hosts of Gog and Magog and lays seige to the camp of God's people. But, John says, fire comes down from heaven and consumes them. Then the dead are judged by the books which are opened. The sea, Death, and Hades give up their dead and each person is judged on the record of his deeds.[k]

The final two chapters of the Revelation portray the coming of the new and everlasting kingdom. "Then I saw a new heaven and a new earth; . . . And I saw the holy city, new Jerusalem, coming down out of heaven from God."[l] The number twelve is of special importance in John's description of the city; it has twelve gates for the twelve foundations and on these are the names "of the twelve apostles of the Lamb." Of importance to the author is the fact that he saw no temple in the city.[m]

The metaphors of living water and the river of the water of life are similar to themes found in the Gospel of John. According to the Revelation, a river will flow from the throne of God through the middle of the street of the holy city. On either side of the street, trees of life grow with their twelve kinds of fruit yielding twelve crops of fruit.[n] The apocalyptic-prophetic vision ends with the theme of light: night shall be no more, and they need no sun or light of lamp in the city of God, for God will be their light forever.[o] The author

---

[f] Rv 17:9. [g] Rv 18:2f., 10, 21; Zeph 2:13–15; 3:1–4. [h] Rv 20:1–3. [i] Rv 20:4.
[j] Rv 20:5. [k] Rv 20:7–15. [l] Rv 21:1f. [m] Rv 21:12–14. [n] Rv 22:1f. [o] Rv 22:5.

concludes that these things shown to John by God's angel "must soon take place.... For the time is near." This warning of the imminent end of the age is repeated. "Surely I am coming soon." [p]

Many Christians over the centuries have been troubled that the Revelation to John is so heavily concerned with punishment and destruction. So relentless is the author's pursuit of the wicked and so fierce is his picture of their destruction that at certain points in the vision he feels compelled to set the faithful apart that they may be protected from the wrath to come.

How is one to account for John's bitterness and resentment, his pleas for vengeance, his seemingly over-riding passion for judgment and punishment? Clearly the Revelation is the response of a person under extreme pressure. In these circumstances one is able to understand the bitter tone of John's fury but surely not to approve it. It is important that the author's intention to give courage to those Christians who were under the immediate threat of death be taken into account. By means of apocalyptic-prophetic imagery, John sought to overcome the meaninglessness of their suffering and death by projecting Christian promises of fulfillment and hope to the end of the age. These promises were secured through martyrdom interpreted as a baptism of fire.

Other important trends in Christian thought are discernible in the Revelation: The visions came to John as he was carried away by or "in the Spirit." The Spirit then is the vehicle of the vision. The connection between Spirit and prophecy (the Spirit of prophecy) is a significant doctrinal development. The place and function of angels is also made clear; they are mediators between God and Christ and the prophets in this world. God in the Revelation is wholly transcendent, the creator of the universe with absolute power and total omniscience. Judgment, punishment, and destruction describe him. Except for immanence suggested in the image of the Lamb, Christ has become a transcendent figure like the Father, judging and punishing the wicked. Finally the Revelation to John points the way toward a more distinctive Christian literary genre, the martyrology, and the cult of the martyrs which developed in the second century.

[p] Rv 22:6, 20.

CHAPTER 16

The Jewish Christian Tradition

Usually the letters in the Christian canon are divided into two groups: (1) the genuine Pauline epistles and the deutero-Pauline letters, the Pastorals and Hebrews, and (2) James, 1 Peter, Jude, 2 Peter and 1, 2, 3 John. The latter group are often referred to as the "Catholic" or "General" epistles because they were supposedly written to the church in general rather than to a particular Christian community or congregation or to an individual.

James, 1 Peter, Jude, and 2 Peter can be grouped together as constituting the Jewish-Christian tradition of the canon. Among these four writings, 1 Peter and James were perhaps the most influential. They bear two of the most illustrious names in early Christian history.

1 Peter

Most scholars agree that the evidence against the authenticity of 1 Peter as a letter by the apostle Peter is convincing, yet the letter claims the authority of Peter and some critics believe that he may have written it. However, internal evidence reveals a significant similarity of religious concepts with those in Paul's letters, particularly Romans. For example, Paul's phrase "in Christ" is used three times (1 Pet. 3:16; 5:10, 14); also, the structure of the letter — salutation, thanksgiving, and benediction — is similar to that of Paul's letters. To account for this similarity, those who hold that the letter is authentic to Peter suggest that Peter had an amanuensis, either Barnabas or Silvanus, to whom he dictated the letter. The Pauline characteristics of the letter can be attributed to Silvanus, as he had been early associated with Paul.

But even this indirect connection with Paul is improbable. Although Silvanus was apparently associated with Paul there is no evidence to indicate that he had been the companion of Peter.

It is also unlikely that Peter, who was generally regarded as chief among Jesus' disciples, would have relied so heavily upon Paul's ideas. Moreover, Peter was a Galilean fisherman who probably knew very little Greek. In contrast, 1 Peter was written in scholarly Greek, included quotations from the Septuagint, and displayed a style and a vocabulary of classical terms such as might be expected from the pen of one who had command of the Greek Koine. According to Papias, Peter was so unfamiliar with Greek that he required an interpreter.

It is more likely that 1 Peter was written by an unknown Christian from the church in Rome. That he was from Rome seems apparent from the words "she who is at Babylon," [a] in all probability a reference to Rome.[1]

First Peter seems to have been written at a date later than Paul although the writing does reveal affinity with Paul and Paulinism; the language of 1:5, 22; and 2:13f., 16f. closely parallels passages in Paul's letters to the Romans and the Galatians.[b] That it was not written later than 150 CE is indicated by Polycarp's clear use of it in his letter to the Philippians.[2] The exhortation to "tend the flock of God that is your charge . . . not for shameful gain but eagerly, not as domineering over those in your charge" [c] suggests an ecclesiastical organization not found in the earliest Christian communities. Most conclusively, however, the correspondence between Pliny, the governor of Bithynia, and Trajan, the emperor of Rome (ca. 111 CE), indicates that the Christians of the provinces of Asia Minor were to be executed if discovered.[3] Though apparently written for all Christians, 1 Peter had particular meaning for the gentile Christians of Bithynia and other provinces of

---

[a] 1 Pt 5:13. [b] Gal 3:23; 5:13; Rom 7:23; 12:9f.; 13:1–4. [c] 1 Pt 5:2f.

[1] That "Babylon" was a symbol for Rome is suggested by its use in Jewish apocalyptic literature and in The Revelation to John 14:8; 16:19; 17:5; 18:2, 10, 21. See *The Jerome Biblical Commentary* for a summary of the arguments for and against the Petrine authorship and about the date and place of composition. J. A. Fitzmyer argues that the letter was written by Peter from Rome ca. 64 CE.

[2] See Polycarp's letter to the Philippians 1:3; 8:1; 10:2.

[3] This is referred to in Pliny's Letter to the Emperor Trajan and Trajan's response. See Howard Clark Kee, *The Origins of Christianity, Sources and Documents* (Englewood Cliffs, New Jersey, 1973), 51–53.

Asia Minor given such threat of persecution.[d] If the apostle Peter was the author, the letter would be dated around 64 CE, since Peter's execution supposedly took place in Rome under Nero. But a more probable date for the letter is 95 to 115 CE.[4]

Employing the epistolary form of the Pauline letters, the author writes to the "exiles of the dispersion," Christian converts living in the Roman provinces of Asia Minor: Pontus, Galatia, Cappadocia, Asia, and Bithynia. The expression "exiles of the dispersion" may have been a metaphor for these Christians as the new Israel scattered among the nations as ancient Israel had been in exile centuries earlier. In any event the author writes under the pseudonym of Peter, "an apostle of Jesus Christ," and addresses them as "chosen and destined by God." [e] The letter form is repeated in the conclusion.[f] Here brief reference is made to Silvanus and Mark. Apparently, 1 Peter is the basis of the tradition that a close historical connection existed between Peter and Mark and between Mark's Gospel and Peter.

New converts are reminded that they should expect to suffer "various trials" in order for the genuineness of their faith to be "tested by fire." [g] Because persecution is to be understood as a test of faith they should rejoice that they have been "born anew" to a living faith and to an inheritance "kept in heaven." The author assures them that the outcome of persevering in faith will be the salvation of their souls.[h] Even the prophets of ancient times prophesied of the grace which was to be theirs. These prophets, the author insists, were serving not themselves or the people of ancient Israel but those Christians to whom this letter was addressed. Even the angels longed to see the things they have been privileged to see fulfilled in their own time.[i]

One can see in these passages the development of a tradition of suffering. The models are Christ, Paul, and Peter. Christ is the supreme model; he suffered for those who believe in him, leaving them "an example." And since he suffered in the flesh for them, they should "arm themselves with the same thought," living their

---

[d] 1 Pt 1:1, 6. [e] 1 Pt 1:1f. [f] 1 Pt 5:12–14. [g] 1 Pt 1:6f. [h] 1 Pt 1:9. [i] 1 Pt 1:10–12.

[4] See Morton Scott Enslin, *Christian Beginnings* (New York, 1938), 325f.

lives by the will of God.ʲ Peter and Paul are examples of those early Christian heroes who, being perfect in their obedience to Christ, accepted their suffering with courage, humility, and joy, and persevered in faith to the end just as Christ had done.

The author proclaims to the Christians in Asia Minor that they were ransomed with the blood of Christ, that Christ was "destined before the foundation of the world but was made manifest at the end of the times" for their sake.ᵏ They are God's people who have been "born anew to a living hope" through Christ's resurrection. In the promise of salvation, he says, they have cause to rejoice.ˡ [5] Christ is the foundation of a new life and a new hope. He is the cornerstone, but a living stone that will cause men to stumble because they disobey the word.ᵐ They are urged to be holy in their conduct, setting their hope on the grace that is coming to them. Hence the author makes a special appeal to scripture, "You shall be holy, for I am holy." ⁿ [6]

Continuing this theme, the author exclaims that they are "a chosen race, a royal priesthood, a holy nation, God's own people." ᵒ But even as God's own people, they are to regard themselves as exiles and aliens among the Gentiles.ᵖ According to 1 Peter, this world is temporary and soon to pass away. In the interim, Christians are to live in the world but look to the next, the spiritual world, for the fulfillment of their hopes and aspirations. The other world is their real home; it is their goal and destiny. Undoubtedly, this image of the other world as the reality is for the author the basis of an interim ethics rather than an ethics for living in this world.

A kind of interim or "meanwhile" standard of morality seems to follow from this other-world emphasis, an ethics based on the supremacy of God's authority. Christians must honor all men, even the emperor, and they are to *fear* God. "One is approved if, mindful of God, he endures pain while suffering unjustly." ᑫ

ʲ 1 Pt 2:21; 4:1f. ᵏ 1 Pt 1:18–20. ˡ 1 Pt 1:3, 6. ᵐ 1 Pt 2:4–8. ⁿ 1 Pt 1:13–16. ᵒ 1 Pt 2:9. ᵖ 1 Pt 1:1, 17; 2:11. ᑫ 1 Pt 2:19.

[5] This appeal to "rejoice" in a time of trial is reminiscent of Paul's pronouncements from prison on "love," "joy," and "rejoicing" (Phil 1:4; 2:1; 3:1; 4:1, 10).

[6] This passage is based on Leviticus 11:44f.

If one does right and suffers for it patiently, he has God's approval, and suffering for righteousness brings a blessing. Resting their case on God and Christ, they are to "live as free men" and allow nothing to terrify them.[r] They are to maintain good conduct among the gentiles, but more important they are to be subject to human institutions; servants must obey their masters and women should be reverent and modest, "of a gentle and quiet spirit." [s] There is no program for social or political action in 1 Peter, although there is an exhortation for harmony and unity. Nowhere in scripture is there a more impressive catalogue of personal moral virtues descriptive of a holy people. Here in the New Testament is a flowering of the Judaic genius for moral religion. Baptism brings new life in the grace of Christ, but redemption requires purity of soul through obedience to truth and love of one another. The author and the Christians he addresses live in anticipation of the End of the age. This is the time and the place of their exile, but the End is near.[t]

Some scholars believe that much of the exhortation material in 1 Peter is taken from the formal instruction of new converts at the rite of baptism.[7] It is possible that a portion of the liturgical formula of baptism is present in 1 Peter in 1:23; "you have been born anew, not of perishable seed but of imperishable, through the living and abiding word of God." Emphasizing the importance of the formula, the author added that the word "is the good news which was preached to you." [u] Also, 1 Peter makes note of Christ's preaching to the spirits in prison who disobeyed in Noah's day.[8] The reference to Noah's ark and the flood, emphasizing that a few were saved "through water," is employed as typology, for "baptism, which corresponds to this, now saves you." [v] Presumably

---

[r] 1 Pt 2:16; 3:6. [s] 1 Pt 2:13, 18; 3:1–7. [t] 1 Pt 1:17; 4:7. [u] 1 Pt 1:25. [v] 1 Pt 3:20f.

[7] Perrin refers to 1 Peter as a "baptism homily." Norman Perrin, *The New Testament: An Introduction* (New York, 1973), 257f. Kümmel and others maintain that baptism is not the central point of 1 Peter, that references and allusions to baptism are used in support of the main theme, which is the necessity for the strengthening of Christians for suffering. W. G. Kümmel, *Introduction to the New Testament*, rev. ed., trans. by H. C. Kee (New York: Abingdon Press, 1973), 421.

[8] The reference to "the spirits in prison" (1 Pt 3:19) is probably related to the myth of "the sons of God" in Genesis 6:1–7, whose descendants were the *Nephilim* or giants (Gn 6:4) believed to have introduced evil into the world before the flood.

baptism saves as the Flood saved Noah and his descendants. Baptism in the time of 1 Peter obviously had become established as the basic church ritual.

James

Questions about the authorship, date, purpose, and audience of the letter of James are among the most difficult in New Testament literature. A few scholars contend, primarily on the basis of the opening lines, that it is a letter from James, the brother of Jesus. If their judgment was correct, this is clearly one of the earliest letters in the New Testament. Apparently Origen, writing in the third century, was the first to arrive at this conclusion; he seems to have identified the author of the document as Jesus' brother. Those who hold this view on authorship usually argue that the substance of James and parts of the synoptic Gospels, especially Matthew, are sufficiently similar to support the view that James preserves some of the original sayings of Jesus.

Many scholars, however, especially non-Catholics, have rejected this conclusion and the early date it would require.[9] James the brother of Jesus apparently died about 62 CE. It seems improbable that a document written by so prominent a figure as James, leader of the early Christian community in Jerusalem, would have remained unknown for almost two centuries. Equally important is the fact that James is written in scholarly Greek of a quality second only to Hebrews in the Christian canon. It seems unlikely that James, the brother of Jesus, would have written in such fluent Greek. The excellence of the Greek, the vocabulary, and its similarity to the Greek diatribe, suggests to some scholars that the author of James probably was a Jewish-Hellenistic Christian who used the name "James" as a pseudonym.[10] Others have argued that the lack of teaching in the document which is specifically Christian tells against authorship by James. Some insist that if James was the author, the Jewish legalism of the Jerusalem church

---

[9] R. H. Fuller and W. G. Kümmel are among those who reject this conclusion. Kümmel discusses the various persons in New Testament literature named "James" and details the arguments for and against Jamesian authorship. Kümmel, *Introduction*, 411–13.

[10] Kümmel, *Introduction*, 412.

would be evident. Certainly the document does not appear to have been written in the context of the intense Judaizing controversy between Paul and Jerusalem.

Dating this document depends on the question of authorship, which clearly is problematic. The fact that Origen assumed it to be earlier than his own time excludes the possibility of placing it much later than 150 CE. The author's apparent use of 1 Peter and his familiarity with some letters in the Pauline corpus indicate a date early in the second century, perhaps around 125. According to Kümmel, the date "cannot be determined more exactly than toward the end of the first century." [11]

Various locations have been suggested as the place of the writing of James, including Rome, Syria, and Galilee. It purports to be a letter written by James to a number of scattered groups of Jewish Christians, "to the twelve tribes in the Dispersion." [w] Aside from this greeting, there seems to be no clearly recognizable historical occasion or situation which would explain its composition. The original was probably a sermon or homily consisting primarily of moral exhortations on a range of important Christian values. Even so this in itself would not explain or account for the inclusion of this document in the canon. Here the literary talent of the author, the excellence of his expressions in the Greek language, his rhetorical skill and persuasiveness must be taken into consideration. Undoubtedly, these explain its inspirational and faith-promoting quality and why it was later canonized for general use in the church.

Still N. Perrin's comment that James "has no discernible structure" — that it "simply moves from theme to theme as the mind of the homilist takes him" — is hardly justified.[12] This sermon-letter does have a focal point: a demand for moral conscience and moral action. James is committed to the moral religion rooted

---

[w] Jas 1:1.

[11] According to R. H. Fuller, "James" is the only one of the New Testament authors who "refers to the local Christian congregation as a 'synagogue' " (2:2). This, he concludes, indicates rather clearly that the author is a Jewish Christian. R. H. Fuller, *A Critical Introduction to the New Testament* (London: Duckworth, 1966), 152.

[12] N. Perrin, *Introduction*, 256.

in the teachings of Jesus and the Hebrew-Jewish prophets and grounded in the expectation of the judgment to come.[13] The author's instructions — on apathy, insincerity, arrogance, libertinism, the condition of the rich and the poor, faith and works, and on human passion and unfaithfulness — can be brought together as features of this emphasis.

The appeal in James goes back to the foundations of the Christian religion. "Religion that is pure and undefiled before God and the Father is this: to visit orphans and widows in their affliction, and to keep oneself unstained from the world."[x] This definition contains the heart of the prophetic theme found in Jesus and in the prophets Amos, Micah, and Isaiah, and in the Hebrew Law — social justice. Clearly, it is the writer's intention to reaffirm the centrality of morality as preparation for the day of judgment.

The letter indicates that some Christians had become indifferent to the moral requirements of the proclamation about Christ and salvation and had apparently taken the position that the doctrine of grace, of faith in Christ alone, based upon Paul's thought, guarantees salvation and freedom from the Law. In the author's view, this minimizes the importance of the moral law in the Christian proclamation. Undoubtedly the author believed that such Christians had substituted the externals of religion, the performance of ritual and profession of correct belief, for the authentic religion of love. But for James, the actual doing of God's will was essential; merely hearing the word and observing the institutional forms and apparatus were not sufficient. The thesis of James is clear: "But be doers of the word, and not hearers only, deceiving yourselves. . . . He who looks into the perfect law, the law of liberty, and perseveres, being no hearer that forgets but a doer that acts, he shall be blessed in his doing."[y]

It is at this point that the writer of James insists that religion must find expression in conduct. His statement which follows is one of the best known in the Christian scriptures: "What does it

---

[x] Jas 1:27. [y] Jas 1:22, 25.

[13] Kee is probably correct that the ethical code in James is based on the apocalyptic theme (the threat of punishment). H. C. Kee, *Understanding the New Testament*, 387.

profit, my brethren, if a man says he has faith but has not works? Can his faith save him? . . . So faith by itself, if it has no works, is dead." [z] To strengthen his instruction on faith and works, the author provides examples from the Old Testament: Abraham was justified by works when he offered his son Isaac as a sacrifice; in this instance faith was active along with Abraham's works.[a] The same was true of Rahab when she aided the messengers from Joshua and sent them out of Jericho by a different route.[b] The analogy and summary of the relation of faith and works is widely quoted in the Christian churches, "For as the body apart from the spirit is dead, so faith apart from works is dead." [c]

One of the major problems in James is its relation to Paul with its commitment to moral religion, its treatment of the doctrine of justification, and the relation of faith to works. Martin Luther, whose doctrine was intensely Pauline in the matter of salvation by faith, was strongly opposed to the Epistle of James. It has often been held in low esteem by very conservative modern Protestants. R. H. Fuller's explanation has merit: "Faith" in James has "the characteristic sub-apostolic sense, i.e., propositional faith." [14] But "faith" is also closely connected to the moral virtues — steadfastness, patience, perseverence.

Much of the polemic of James is directed against boastful and pretentious Christians who claimed to possess superior wisdom. Some of these (the libertines) advocated freedom from the Law and used Paul as their primary source. James's purpose was more to combat corrupt Paulinism than to oppose Paul's doctrine. Moreover, it may be that the claim to special wisdom was related to the office of Teacher in the church. It seems likely that some were seeking the prestige of office to promote their own doctrines. According to James, they who teach are to be strictly judged.[d]

---

[z] Jas 2:14, 17. [a] Jas 2:21f. [b] Jas 2:25. [c] Jas 2:26. [d] Jas 3:1.

[14] Fuller, *Introduction*, 154. Martin Luther's attack on the value of James is well known: "the epistle of St. James is an epistle full of straw, because it contains nothing evangelical . . . because in direct opposition to St. Paul . . . it ascribes justification to works . . . . not once does it give Christians any instruction or reminder of the passion, resurrection, or Spirit of Christ." "Preface to the New Testament"; "Preface to the Epistles of St. James and St. Jude," in John Dillenberger, ed., *Martin Luther, Selections From His Writings* (New York, 1961), 19, 35.

"Who is wise and understanding among you?" he asks, and warns them against jealousy and selfish ambition.ᵉ The wisdom of the jealous and selfish is "earthly, unspiritual, devilish." ᶠ In contrast, the wisdom from above is "pure, . . . without uncertainty or insincerity." ᵍ The author exhorts his "brethren" to call upon God for wisdom:

> If any of you lacks wisdom, let him ask of God. . . . But let him ask in faith, with no doubting, for he who doubts is like a wave of the sea that is driven and tossed by the wind. For that person must not suppose that a double-minded man, unstable in all his ways, will receive anything from the Lord.ʰ

The author concludes that inordinate desires and passion lead to unfaithfulness and aggressive acts against one another.

> Is it not your passions that are at war in your members? You desire and do not have; so you kill. And you covet and cannot obtain; so you fight and wage war. . . . You ask and do not receive, because you ask wrongly, to spend it on your passions.ⁱ

Clearly this author is concerned that this generation of Christians no longer lives under the expectation of the imminent end of the age and consequently ignores the urgency of doing God's will. He declares, "you do not know about tomorrow. What is your life? For you are a mist that appears for a little time and then vanishes." ʲ All boasting, he maintains, is arrogance. Instead, they should place their trust in the Lord's will.

Apparently the church in James's day had begun to take note of members who favored those of wealth over the poor. For James no partiality could exist among the faithful. God has chosen the "poor in the world to be rich in faith and heirs of the kingdom." ᵏ Here as throughout the document the appeal is to the moral law, particularly the new word from Christ in Matthew's Gospel, "You shall love your neighbor as yourself." ˡ

The threat of persecution and suffering provides the background for this writing. However, no imminent crises are referred to. Rather, a general deterioration of morality prompts the author to

---

ᵉ Jas 3:13. ᶠ Jas 3:15. ᵍ Jas 3:17. ʰ Jas 1:5–8. ⁱ Jas 4:1–3. ʲ Jas 4:14. ᵏ Jas 2:5.
ˡ Jas 2:8; Lv 19:18.

call for steadfastness in faith, perseverence, and loyalty to the church.

The Old Testament prophets and Job are cited by James as examples of patience and perseverance in time of great stress. They possessed the Christian virtues he hopes to instill in his readers, who are exhorted to see that the church provides for uncertainties in their future. If anyone is sick, the elders may be called to anoint him with oil. If any has sinned, prayer and confession will bring forgiveness.[m]

Jude and 2 Peter

The originals of Jude and 2 Peter were probably polemical tracts revised as letters to imitate the Pauline format. They purport to have been written by Simon Peter, the chief apostle of Jesus, and by Jude, the brother of Jesus mentioned in the Gospels of Mark and Matthew. Obviously, the names "Peter" and "Jude" are used here as pseudonyms. In Jude the author identifies himself as a "brother of James" but does not identify himself as the brother of Jesus. Presumably, he knows the doctrine of virgin birth; Jesus could not have had any real brothers and sisters.[15]

The precise date for these documents remains problematic. Ecclesiastical and doctrinal developments, including evidence of the centrality of the baptism ritual, reference to "love feasts," the failure of the Parousia, and the emergence of Gnosticism as a major threat to the unity of the church suggest a date around the middle of the second century. Such concerns would preclude the possibility of their having originated in the time of the historical persons Peter and Jude. Since 2 Peter seems to have borrowed a significant portion of the 25 verses of Jude, Jude was probably written at a slightly earlier date than 2 Peter.[16]

Jude and 2 Peter together reflect a period of severe stress in Christian history. They describe a church facing great internal turmoil created by false, greedy, and licentious teachers and reacting

[m] Jas 5:15f.

[15] See Mk 6:3; Mt 13:55.

[16] Second Peter 2:1–22 repeats much of Jude 3–13. See Bo Reicke, *The Epistles of James, Peter, and Jude* (Garden City, New York, 1964), 189f.

defensively to threats to its security. Jude and 2 Peter represent two different but related appeals to authority in early Jewish Christianity. While Jude claims to be a "brother of James" and therefore, presumably, one of the brothers of Jesus,ⁿ the author of 2 Peter identifies himself as "Simon Peter, a servant and apostle of Jesus Christ." °

Heresy and rebelliousness are related issues in Jude and 2 Peter. The heretical teachers threatening the congregations were probably Gnostics and gnostic-like Christians. In some congregations a majority of the members may have been gnostics in their religious beliefs. It appears that some were libertines who may have engaged in sensual practices in their rituals. Others, referred to as scoffers and doubters, were perhaps gnostic skeptics who rejected some of the standard doctrines of the church such as the resurrection and the Parousia. They may have opposed the literal beliefs of the tradition and replaced them with myth or symbolism more palatable to Hellenistic Christians.

Jude

Jude's approach is direct and personal; he appeals to his readers as his "Beloved" and to the salvation which they and he have in common. He exhorts them "to contend for the faith" which was entrusted to them and about which they had been "once for all" fully informed.ᵖ Clearly, in these passages "faith" has a different meaning than for Paul. Here, faith, "once for all" delivered to them as a trust, refers to belief in the apostolic tradition, which had become established in the church.[17] Faith requires believing in and accepting this tradition as God's word and rule for living.

According to Jude, some ungodly persons had secretly gained admission to the Christian community,ᵠ persons designated in the scripture as doomed for destruction. Remember, he says, the pre-

---

ⁿ Jude 1. ° 2 Pt 1:1. ᵖ Jude 3. ᵠ Jude 4.

[17] Kümmel, commenting on the meaning of faith in Jude, concludes that faith "once for all delivered to the saints" (3) is an early Catholic concept of faith. See Kümmel, 426f. Martin Luther regarded Jude as dependent on 2 Peter. It is "an excerpt from, or copy of, the second epistle of St. Peter" and not to be "among the canonical books that lay the foundation of faith." "Preface to the Epistles of St. James and St. Jude."

dictions of the apostles who said that in the last days there would be skeptics who followed their own passions.ʳ The author's judgment about the severity of this problem is indicated by the harshness of his attack: He calls the intruders "loudmouthed boasters, flattering people to gain advantage" who set up division within the community.ˢ Others he calls "waterless clouds," "fruitless trees," "wandering stars" and "malcontents, following their own passions." ᵗ They are devoid of the Spirit; they "pervert the grace of our God...and deny our only Master and Lord, Jesus Christ." ᵘ

The apocalyptic tradition is strong in Jude and 2 Peter. Apocalyptic texts, of course, were popular and widely read by both Jews and Christians throughout the first and second centuries. Apocalyptic prediction was effective in strengthening the faith of the members and preserving the unity of the church by demonstrating through biblical references that God's plan is eternal and no changes have occurred in the tradition. Every detail of the present and future is known to God, and much has already been revealed through his prophets. Thus the difficult and sometimes unfortunate events in Christian history up to their time — the skepticism and apathy, heresy, rebellion against authority, and even the participation in libertine-sexual practices — were known to God in advance and predicted in the scriptures. Jude includes as scripture certain texts from the Jewish Apocrypha and Pseudepigrapha. Second Peter seems to have intentionally omitted all references to apocalyptic works which were not included in the Christian canon. This difference is an important clue to understanding the development of the Christian canon.

The apocalyptic passages in Jude emphasize a final judgment day and the certainty of God's punishment.[18] He refers to angels, who "did not keep their own position but left their proper dwelling" and were kept "in eternal chains in the nether gloom until the judgment of the great day." ᵛ This motif of fallen angels was probably borrowed from the book of Enoch, a major Jewish apoc-

---

ʳ Jude 17f. ˢ Jude 16. ᵗ Jude 12f., 16. ᵘ Jude 4, 19. ᵛ Jude 6.

[18] A similar emphasis upon judgment and punishment is to be found in The Revelation to John.

alyptic writing. Jude says of Enoch that he prophesied of the Lord's coming to execute judgment on all of the ungodly.[w]

The writer reminds his "beloved" of disbelief and rebellion against authority in ancient times when God's punishment was certain and severe, how the cities of Sodom and Gomorrah were punished with eternal fire because the people indulged in unnatural lusts, and how those who rebelled in Moses' day were destroyed by God's punishment. All such disbelievers and rebels "walk in the way of Cain . . . and perish in Korah's rebellion." [x]

2 Peter

Second Peter purports to have been written as a testament of the chief apostle, Simon Peter.[19] However, the content and style indicate that it was written well beyond the time of Peter and Paul and in fact may be the latest writing in the Christian canon, possibly as late as 150 CE. It was written to defend Peter's teaching against the interpretations of Paul made by some Christians. The author takes care to show that his intention is only to remind his readers of essential beliefs, for they already know the tradition and are well grounded in its truths. Expecting death in the near future, he leaves his own testament, that they (the apostles) were not deceived when they told them of the power of Jesus Christ.[y] They were eye witnesses of Christ's majesty and heard the voice of the Almighty proclaim (following the wording of Matthew): "This is my beloved Son, with whom I am well pleased." [z] Undoubtedly, this personal witness, testifying to the Transfiguration reported in the synoptic Gospels, was intended to support the authority of the apostolic tradition.

Second Peter emphatically insists on the surety of the prophetic word concerning the day of judgment and the certainty of the punishment of the ungodly. The author claims that Christians "have the prophetic word" and warns them to pay attention to this until the final day of judgment.[a] Prophecy is not a matter of personal interpretation. The ancient Hebrews had false prophets and teachers among them. He cites evidence from the Old Testa-

---

[w] Jude 14f. [x] Jude 11. [y] 2 Pt 1:12–15. [z] 2 Pt 1:16f.; Mt 17:5. [a] 2 Pt 1:19.

[19] This is the view of Kümmel and others. See W. G. Kümmel, *Introduction*, 430.

ment of God's punishment of the ungodly, who promise freedom but are themselves slaves of corruption.[b]

It has also been suggested that perhaps two brief letters (2 Peter 1:1–2:22 and 3:1–18) may have been combined in canonical 2 Peter.[20] Scoffers were saying, "Where is the promise of his coming? . . . all things have continued as they were from the beginning of creation."[c] Clearly, this is an acknowledgment of the delay of the Parousia. Evidently, large numbers of Christians were troubled by what must have been seen as a failure of the Second Coming.

The author's explanation of the delay in the Parousia is significant for the study of the history of Christian doctrines. He contends that God's chronology or time table is different from man's, "With the Lord one day is as a thousand years, and a thousand years as one day."[d] However, the author insists, "The Lord is not slow about his promise as some count slowness." Rather God is patient in order for all to come to repentance and be saved. But the "day of the Lord will come like a thief [that is, unexpected], and then the heavens will pass away with a loud noise" and the earth will be consumed by fire.[e] Thus, in 2 Peter the doctrine of the Parousia means especially the day of judgment and the destruction of the ungodly.

The author's relationship to Paul is very important for understanding not only 2 Peter but all the documents purporting to represent the views of the apostle Peter and other writings from the Jewish Christian tradition — James, Jude and 1 Peter. Second Peter speaks of "our beloved brother Paul" but significantly adds, "there are some things in them [his letters] hard to understand."[f] Undoubtedly, this comment refers to the ambiguities found in some of Paul's writings, for example, his teaching about freedom. Perhaps the author wanted to correct an errant Paulinism which the "ignorant and unstable twist to their own destruction." He cautions them to beware lest they be carried away by the word of lawless men and lose their own stability.[g]

[b] 2 Pt 2:1–10. [c] 2 Pt 3:3f. [d] 2 Pt 3:8. [e] 2 Pt 3:9f. [f] 2 Pt 3:15f. [g] 2 Pt 3:16f.

[20] Bo Reicke, *Epistles*, 173, holds that 2 Peter 3:1 is an allusion to 1 Peter. Fuller, *Introduction*, 162. W. G. Kümmel also seems to take this view for granted. Kümmel, 430.

CHAPTER 17

The Formation of the New Testament Canon

The Christian canon,[1] the New Testament, was not formed immediately after the death of Jesus and his disciples. In the early years of the church the living apostles with their oral traditions were the bridge between Jesus and his followers, who expecting his imminent return did not depend on the written word. When the New Testament books were written, perhaps because of geographical as well as chronological distance, they had a long history which began with the original documents, the autographs, and extended to their eventual canonization. They were used in the various early church communities for over a half century before they were collected, edited, and finally adopted by the emerging church as authoritative and binding. The writing had extended over at least fifty years, and their canonization was a gradual process from at least the last quarter of the first century to the end of the second century.

Two major crises helped to shape the canon to its present form. First, the threat and fact of persecution resulted in the development of a strong martyr theme in the Christian literature of the first three centuries. Second, schism within the church produced a diversity of Christian thought about God, Christ, and man.

Precedent for accepting certain select writings as holy scripture, inspired by God, was already well established in the Jewish cultural and religious tradition. The Pentateuch, the so-called five books of Moses or books of the Law, was probably recognized as

[1] "Canon" derives from the Greek noun *kanon* which refers to the straightness of a rod. It refers to those documents which are accepted as the standard of faith, the norms for the religion, the guide to what is considered sacred and authoritative. To regard the New Testament collection of documents as "scripture" means to hold them as canon, normative for belief and practice. The Latin theologian Tertullian appears to have been the first writer to have used the term "New Testament" about 200. See A. F. J. Klijn, *An Introduction to the New Testament* (Leiden, 1967), 178.

sacred scripture and thus normative for Jewish belief and practice as early as 400 BCE.[2] The prophetic books, the Prophets, and historical writings regarded as prophetic were apparently regarded as divinely inspired at least as early as 200 BCE. The third part of the Jewish scripture, the Hagiographa or the Writings as it was later designated in the Talmud, was not included in the canonical writings until sometime between 90 and 100 CE, when a Jewish synod at Jamnia recognized a tripartite canon. Whether this recognition was an official action is a matter of some disagreement among competent scholars. But the Jewish historian Josephus, writing after the destruction of Jerusalem in 70 CE (probably about 90 CE) in his essay "Against Apion," described Jewish religious literature by referring to the five books of Moses, thirteen prophetic books, and four books of hymns and precepts, all of which he regarded as divine.[3]

It is possible to identify several early Jewish "canons" in addition to those of Josephus and Jamnia. The "Qumran canon" was reclaimed from the books and fragments of the so-called Dead Sea Scrolls, and an "Alexandrian canon," which is believed to have been the basis of the Greek Septuagint, included several apocryphal books accepted by the Catholic church but not regarded as canonical in Judaism or Protestantism.

THE TORAH AND THE PROPHETS AS THE ORIGINAL CHRISTIAN CANON

Only the Law and the Prophets were considered sacred scripture by Jesus and the early Christian community in Jerusalem. Christians referred to the "Old Testament" probably to contrast the old covenant between God and the Hebrews with the new covenant which they believed was established by God through Jesus Christ.

The earliest Palestinian Christians, who were believing, practicing Jews, quite naturally regarded the Jewish scripture as sacred

---

[2] On the canonization of the Old Testament, see "Canonical and Non-Canonical" in the *Cambridge History of the Bible*, 1: 113–159, *From the Beginnings to Jerome*, ed. by P. R. Ackroyd and C. F. Evans (Cambridge, 1970), and "The Canon of the Old Testament" in *The Jerome Biblical Commentary* (Englewood Cliffs, 1968), 518–24.

[3] Flavius Josephus, *Against Apion*, I:8.

literature. That they did is evident from countless references to it in their writings, especially in the books that were eventually to become the accepted Christian canon. The traditional biblical idea of covenant as a contract or agreement between God and Israel, involving Israel's faith in God and his promises of Israel's destiny as a nation, became for the Christians the historic foundation of the new covenant. The prophet Jeremiah had looked forward to a new covenant saying, "I will put my law within them, and I will write it upon their hearts."[a] In his Second Letter to the Corinthians, Paul had referred to the veil of the "old covenant," which can be removed only through Christ.[b] And the anonymous letter to the Hebrews contains an extended discussion of the fulfillment of Jeremiah's prophecy of the new covenant, interpreted as a covenant based on the Gospel of Christ. The first covenant was declared obsolete but under the new covenant, declared the Lord,

> I will be their God, and they shall be my people. And they shall not teach every one his fellow or every one his brother, saying, "Know the Lord," for all shall know me, from the least of them to the greatest.[c]

For Christians Jesus' new Word given from the Mount eventually became the foundation of the new Covenant, set forth in the literature known as the New Testament.

In the period following the Jewish-Roman war and the destruction of Jerusalem, Jewish Christians became increasingly estranged from mainstream Jews. Their differences and enmities multiplied until, with the conversion of diaspora Jews and gentiles, the Christian community became less a Jewish sect and more a distinct religion. But Christianity remained moored to its Jewish foundations despite the efforts of some, especially the gnostic Christians, to uproot it. For the author of the Gospel of Matthew, writing probably about 80–90 CE, the new religion was to build on Jesus Christ as the new Word or Revelation from God. In the Epistle of Barnabas, written about 130 CE, the question of Christian independence from the Jewish religion was at a new level. Barnabas held that the Jews had lost the promise under the old covenant.

[a] Jer 31:33. [b] 2 Cor 3:14. [c] Heb 8:10f.

That promise, according to Barnabas, pointed to Jesus for its fulfillment, "Learn then, my children, . . . that Abraham, the first who enjoined circumcision, [was] looking forward in spirit to Jesus."[4] In his dialogue with the fictitious Jewish character Trypho, Justin Martyr referred to certain items in "your Scriptures" then added, "or rather not yours, but ours."[5] Clearly, by this time (ca. 150 CE) Christian writers had appropriated the Jewish scripture, at least the Torah and Prophets, as their own.

As many scholars have pointed out, the process of appropriation of the Old Testament was made easier through the Christian adoption of the Greek translation, the Septuagint, as a sacred book. This volume is referred to as the LXX because of the tradition, undoubtedly erroneous, that seventy (or seventy-two) elders translated it from the Hebrew. The Septuagint was translated over a period of years, beginning around the middle of the third century BCE, especially for the Jewish colonies in Egypt. It was widely used in the Diaspora, where Greek was the most common written language. It was the Bible of the Alexandrian Jewish philosopher Philo and apparently was the Bible of Paul and the Greek-speaking Christian communities of the first century.

Philo Judaeus of Alexandria (c. 20 BCE–c. 40 CE), a Jew educated in Platonic and Stoic thought as well as in the Mosaic Law and tradition, vigorously advanced the thesis that the Hebrew scripture was consonant with important elements of Platonic and Stoic philosophy, the dominant intellectual forces of his time. To effect a synthesis of Plato and Moses, of Greek philosophy and Hebrew religion, as well as to better understand the scriptures, Philo enlisted the technique of allegorical interpretation, which was already popular in Greek rhetoric and Stoic literature. Allegorical interpretation assumes that important meanings lie hidden in the literal accounts of places, persons, and events, meanings too profound or dangerous to expose to the unsophisticated and literal-minded. In treating Genesis 2:10, for instance, Philo iden-

---

[4] "The Epistle of Barnabas," chap. 9 in A. Roberts and J. Donaldson, eds., *Ante-Nicene Fathers* (Grand Rapids, Michigan, 1956), 1:142.

[5] "Justin's Dialogue with Trypho," chap. 29, in Roberts and Donaldson, eds., *The Ante-Nicene Fathers*, 1:208f.

tified the four rivers that came from Eden as the cardinal Greek virtues of prudence, courage, self-mastery, and justice.[6] He interpreted the event of the burning bush in Exodus as the suffering of those Israelites who were treated unjustly. As the bush was not consumed, so "the sufferers would not be destroyed by their aggressors." He described the angel as a "symbol of God's providence."[7] Philo's allegorical method probably affected the Christian interpretation of the Hebrew Bible. Christian writers commonly assumed that the Old Testament contained numerous passages in which hidden meanings referred to the coming of Jesus Christ. The Alexandrian Christian theologian Origen (185–254 CE), for instance, who was influenced by the Philonic school, provided clear examples of this method of interpretation when he admonished his readers to look for the soul and the spirit of the scripture, urging them to go beyond the literal letter of the word to the higher, divine meaning.[8]

PAUL'S LETTERS AND THE BIRTH OF THE NEW TESTAMENT CANON

The missionary character of the early Christian movement was an important factor in the development of the canon. During the first century Christian missionaries were active throughout Asia Minor and Greece, making converts and establishing churches or congregations. These missionaries assumed responsibility for the communities of newly converted Christians and wrote letters to them for their edification and guidance. Paul, clearly the most prominent among the early evangelists, being separated from his congregations much of the time, wrote to them in response to their

---

[6] "Allegorical Interpretation of Genesis," Bk. I, 63. This entire treatise clearly exhibits the attempt of Philo to achieve a synthesis of Platonism and the Hebrew scriptures through the use of allegory.

[7] Philo Judaeus, "The Life of Moses," I, 65–70. English trans. by F. H. Colson, in *Philo*, Vol. 6 (1935) of *Loeb Classical Library*. On the employment of allegorical exegesis by the rabbis and Philo and the influence of allegory on Paul and other New Testament writers, see H. A. Wolfson, *The Philosophy of the Church Fathers*, Vol. 1, *Faith, Trinity, Incarnation* (Cambridge, 1956), Chap. 2.

[8] See Origen, *De Principiis*, Bk. IV, Ch. 1, 11, in Alexander Roberts and James Donaldson, eds., and Frederick Crombie, trans., *Ante-Nicene Christian Library* (Edinburgh, 1871), 10:299–303.

questions, advising them on important issues, clarifying principles of belief and practice, and at times admonishing them for their behavior. There are no grounds for supposing, however, that Paul expected his letters to become the core of a new collection of sacred writings. His primary concern was the specific problems of the congregations which he had established. Nevertheless, some of his later disciples valued his letters enough to preserve and distribute them to other congregations. Eventually they found their way throughout much of the church. Clement of Rome (ca. 96 CE), for example, writing to the church at Corinth almost forty years after Paul, reproached the Corinthian Christians for their factiousness and dissent and urged them to "Pick up the letter of the blessed apostle Paul. What was the primary thing he wrote to you? . . . To be sure, under the Spirit's guidance, he wrote to you about himself and Cephas and Apollos, because even then you had formed cliques." [9] In his letter to the church at Ephesus, Ignatius (ca. 98–117 CE) spoke highly of Paul; "You have been initiated into the [Christian] mysteries with Paul, a real saint and martyr, who deserves to be congratulated. When I come to meet God may I follow in his footsteps, who in all his letters mentions your union with Christ Jesus." [10] These passages are evidence that thirty or forty years beyond the time of Paul, leaders in the Christian community were consulting his writings on matters of church practice and belief. It is unlikely that by this time Paul's letters had anything like the status of inspired scripture. Nevertheless, they were highly prized for their instructional and devotional value and eventually were collected to form a Pauline literary corpus that became a basic element of the Christian canon.

The New Testament document 2 Peter, probably written well into the second century, contains the clearest early witness to the beginnings of a Christian canon. It refers to Paul and to Paul's letters but also alludes to "other scriptures." [d] The author knows

---

[d] 2 Pt 3:15f.

[9] "The Letter of the Church of Rome to the Church of Corinth, commonly called Clement's First Letter," 47:1–3, trans. and edited by C. C. Richardson, *Early Christian Fathers*, 65.

[10] "The Letters of Ignatius: Ephesians," 12:2, trans. and edited by C. C. Richardson, *Early Christian Fathers*, 91.

of the synoptic tradition about the event of Jesus' Transfiguration.[e] This seems to suggest that from the earliest stages of the development of the canon there began to emerge a two-part tradition about Jesus: the apostolic tradition about the risen Christ founded upon the vision of Paul and the tradition about Jesus' glorification in the synoptic Gospels.

THE GOSPELS

The tradition of the Gospels developed gradually. Probably in the beginning this tradition, reporting the sayings of Jesus and describing his miracles and especially his passion, was transmitted orally. Indeed, some early Christian leaders preferred the oral tradition, a living witness, to the written word. Papias,[11] reported in the writings of the early church historian Eusebius, exhibits such a view:

> But if I met with anyone who had been a follower of the elders anywhere, I made it a point to inquire what were the declarations of the elders. What was said by Andrew, Peter or Philip. What by Thomas, James, John, Matthew, or any other of the disciples of our Lord . . . for I do not think that I derived so much benefit from books as from the living voice of those that still survive.[12]

At first the Gospels probably were circulated without the titles which attributed authorship to Mark, Matthew, and Luke. Ignatius wrote to the church at Philadelphia, "To my mind it is Jesus Christ who is the original documents. The inviolable archives are his cross and death and his resurrection and the faith that came by him." [13] The emphasis in Ignatius and later in Irenaeus was upon the one Gospel of Jesus Christ; the individual Gospels of Mark, Matthew and Luke were regarded as aspects or forms of the one Gospel. Also, it is likely that during this early stage each church had its own particular Gospel. Some scholars, for example, hold

[e] 2 Pt 1:16–18.

[11] Papias was bishop in Hierapolis in Asia Minor ca. 130 CE.

[12] Eusebius, *Ecclesiastical History*, Bk. 3, Chap. 39. Eusebius, the bishop of Caesarea in Palestine (ca. 315–340), is often called the "Father of Church History."

[13] "The Letters of Ignatius: Philadelphians," 8:2, trans. and edited by C. C. Richardson, *Early Christian Fathers*, 110.

the view that Mark came from the church at Rome and Matthew from Antioch and that for a time there was no disposition to bring these writings together. As each Gospel gained in reputation, copies were circulated for more general use in the various churches. Later collections were made and titles added, probably for the purpose of distinguishing the various Gospels.

Concern for unity among the churches was undoubtedly a major factor accounting for collecting the four Gospels into one literary tradition. Gathering the various Gospels into a unity was part of an attempt to eliminate the prejudice against one or other of the Gospels and thus remove a potentially divisive factor in the church. This was especially important in the acceptance of the Gospel of John. Initially, there seems to have been considerable resistance in the West to the Fourth Gospel, in part because it was fundamentally different in character from the synoptic Gospels and from the oral tradition concerning Jesus which the churches in the West had inherited. The inclusion of John's Gospel in the collection of four probably gained for it a wider circulation and eventually a general acceptance beyond the eastern churches. M. Werner in his work on the development of Christian dogma holds that it was the peculiar theological character of John's Gospel — its gnostic-like interpretation of Paul's thought — which many early Christians found objectionable. But it was the affinity of John's spiritual-sacramental doctrine of salvation to the Logos-Christology which ultimately led to the popularity of John and to its high place in the canon.[14] It is significant that Clement of Alexandria ascribed to John's Gospel a spiritual quality and a higher status than he attributed to the synoptic Gospels, which he regarded as portraits of the physical-temporal Christ. Of John's special place in the canon, he writes, "But John, the last of all, seeing that what was corporeal was set forth in the Gospels, on the entreaty of his intimate friends, and inspired by the Spirit, composed a spiritual Gospel." [15]

[14] Martin Werner, *The Formation of Christian Dogma*. Trans. by S. G. F. Brandon (New York, 1957), 62f.

[15] Fragments from Clement of Alexandria, the *Hypotyposes*, in Eusebius, *Ecclesiastical History*, Bk. 6, 14, in A. Roberts and J. Donaldson, eds., *The Ante-Nicene Fathers. Fathers of the Second Century* (Grand Rapids, Michigan, 1956), 2:580.

The earliest references to one of the four Gospels as scripture comes from an anonymous Christian sermon dated in the middle of the second century known as Clement's Second Letter to the Corinthians. The reference to "another Scripture" quotes from either Matthew 9:13 or Mark 2:17, "I did not come to call the righteous but sinners," and shows that he accepted a Christian Gospel as scripture.[16] Justin, who was martyred in Rome ca. 167 CE, elaborated on proper Christian worship and in doing so recommended reading from the "memoirs composed by them [the Apostles], which are called Gospels."[17] From this passage we learn that the Gospels, which originally were apparently circulated anonymously, were in Justin's time claiming apostolic authorship and authority.

PERSECUTION AND MARTYRDOM

There can be no doubt that persecution was a critical problem for the early church.[18] The early Christian community, a minority group unpopular in the Roman empire, was from its beginning faced with dangers of both persecution and legal prosecution. Survival by conformity to state demands and the threat of eventual failure as an autonomous religious community was one of the most critical issues confronting the early church.[19]

---

[16] "An Anonymous Sermon, Commonly Called Clement's Second Letter to the Corinthians," 2:4, trans. and edited by C. C. Richardson, *Early Christian Fathers*, 194. Eusebius mentions a second letter ascribed to Clement, which he rejected as unauthentic.

[17] "The First Apology of Justin," 66, 67, trans. and edited by C. C. Richardson, *Early Christian Fathers*, 286f.

[18] W. R. Farmer refers to the New Testament as a martyr's canon of scripture. The martyr tradition, he points out, traced through Origen, Hippolytus and Irenaeus, was exemplified in the martyrdom of Polycarp and Ignatius, and presumably included from the earlier period the models of martyrdom, Steven, Peter, and Paul and, most perfect of all, the martyrdom of Jesus. His conclusion is probably correct. Although persecution and Christian martyrdom do not answer fully the question of the origin of the canon, they do partially explain why the New Testament canon took the shape it did. William R. Farmer and Dennis M. Farkasfalvy, *The Formation of the New Testament Canon, An Ecumenical Approach* (New York, 1983), 39–41.

[19] For a detailed discussion of the factors — religious, social and economic — which account for the conflict between the church and the Roman Empire in the first three centuries, see W. H. C. Frend, *Martyrdom and Persecution in the Early Church* (Oxford, 1965).

According to Christian tradition, the church survived ten persecutions. Only a few of these appear to have been organized attempts by the Roman state to eradicate the entire Christian community.[20] Opposition to Christians usually amounted to severe public disapproval, but at times it was organized prosecution. The state claimed to have a legal basis for discrimination, since Roman law declared religious cults under certain circumstances to be illegal. Christians were often suspected of atheism because they refused to use images in their worship and rituals. They were sometimes accused of practicing sexual immoralities and cannibalism in the name of religion. Most important, because they refused homage to the emperor, a basic civic duty in the state religion, and because they objected to military service, they were considered unpatriotic and seditious. Also, extreme ascetics were despised as religious fanatics.

The Roman government attempted periodically to enforce its demands upon an unyielding and expanding Christian minority, and Christian leaders in turn sought to control the responses of their followers, to firm up their loyalty and devotion to Christian values even at the cost of their lives. These circumstances account for the emergence of the literature of the martyr, the martyrology, which became a popular Christian literary type in the second and third centuries.

The martyr motif began as early as the composition of the Gospels. Jesus' dignity during his trial and his composure on the cross are salient features of martyrology. These elements of the passion story as related especially in Mark suggest that Mark shaped his account as a martyrology. The passion and resurrection narratives were apparently meant to be the focal point of Mark's Gospel, for they constitute more than half of the total work.

Martyr interest, however, is not confined to the Gospel of Mark. The other Gospels, especially John, contain characteristic martyr elements. Jesus' voluntary death, the attention given to

---

[20] Apparently only the Roman emperors Decius (249–251), Valerian (253–260), and Diocletian (284–305) undertook action against Christians on this general scale. Earlier uprisings occurring in the reigns of Nero (54–68), Domitian (81–96), and Trajan (98–117), though terrible for many Christians, were local and not prolonged.

Peter's denial and grief, and the predictions of persecution are all elements of martyrdom. The pastoral letters,[f] 1 Peter,[g] the Revelation to John,[h] and Hebrews[i] all seem to be consciously concerned with persecution and the possibility of martyrdom. Stephen, probably the second great martyr proto-type, conforms to the pattern set by Jesus. The account of Stephen's death in Acts of the Apostles was probably intended to fix the form and to be a prime example of a Christian martyrology. The act of martyrdom was assumed to be in full accord with the Gospels, meaning that it conformed to the pattern set by Jesus as recorded in the passion narratives. He was the supreme exemplar of religious commitment and faith and loyalty even to death.

The promise of special rewards was a principal motivation for martyrdom. Martyrs were guaranteed forgiveness of sins and resurrection and promised special blessings of position and privilege in the life to come. They were placed in the apostolic line of succession to receive visions and prophetic gifts of the Spirit. They were even described as great athletes participating in contests like those performed in the Greco-Roman stadium, with the Holy Spirit as their trainer. It is not surprising, therefore, that a cult of Christian martyrs arose in the middle of the second century. Martyrs were venerated as heroes. Various parts of their bodies — bones, hair, blood, and clothing — were often made the centerpiece of Christian worship. These relics were believed by many Christians to possess magical powers.

A sizable body of martyr literature emerged during this period.[21] Unfortunately, the attitudes of many would-be martyrs became psychopathic. Voluntary martyrdom became such a problem that some of the early fathers, noting the alarming trend, strongly advised against it. It is to the credit of the Christian leadership that while the persecution-martyr theme was prominent in the literature of the New Testament, none of several major martyrologies was finally canonized.

[f] 1 Tm 6:12f; 2 Tm 2:11–13; 3:10–12; 4:7f. [g] 1 Pt 3:14; 4:12–16. [h] Rv 6:9; 7:13f. [i] Heb 2:10; 6:12; 12:7–11.

[21] For a translation and brief analysis of twenty-eight of the most important texts of the martyr literature, see Herbert Musurillo, *The Acts of the Christian Martyrs; Introduction, Texts and Translations* (Oxford, 1972).

SCHISM IN THE CHURCH

Threats from within the Christian church as well as from outside contributed significantly to the establishment of the canon. These were especially threats of heresy, of schism, and anarchy. The emergence of Montanist and Gnostic Christian sects was a major factor in this development. Montanism, one of the earliest schismatic heresies in the ancient church, began in Phrygia in Asia Minor in the middle of the second century, presumably near where Paul had established his congregations at Colossae and Laodicea. It took its name from its founder, Montanus, a former priest of the cult of Cybele who had converted to Christianity.

The historian of Christian theology J. Pelikan holds that the growing secularization within the church and the rigidity of its polity and institutional form account for the birth of the Montanist movement. The early Christian's hope for salvation based on the doctrine of an imminent eschatology had declined and with it the sense of need for extraordinary operations of the Holy Spirit.[22]

The Montanist Christians sought to restore to the church the miraculous gifts of the Spirit, especially the gift of prophecy. In accord with this, Montanus and other charismatic leaders, including the prophetesses, Maximilla and Priscilla, made extravagant claims that they possessed Christ's spirit and received special revelations and visions. That they reached an extreme state of heresy is evidenced by their claim to be at one with the Father, the Son, and the Paraclete. This kind of charismatic prophecy seriously threatened the stability of the church. Combined with the Montanist belief in the imminent end of the age and in the doctrine of the Second Coming, this undermined the church's institutional movement toward order and guarantees of continuity.[23]

As Pelikan has pointed out, it was impossible for the church to repudiate outright the Montanists' emphasis on the gift of the spirit of prophecy. Yet if orderly development of the church was to proceed, firm guidelines about claims to the operations of the

---

[22] See, for example, Jaroslav Pelikan, *The Christian Tradition; A History of the Development of Doctrine* (Chicago, 1971), 1:98f.

[23] For details of Montanist history, doctrines, and practices, see Philip Schaff, *History of the Christian Church. Ante-Nicene Christianity A.D. 100–325* (Grand Rapids, Michigan, 1950), 2:417–27.

Spirit were required. The church turned to its historical past, to its tradition, and particularly to apostolicity for the solution to this problem. The apostolic canon of sacred literature as well as the apostolic creed and apostolic episcopacy were adopted as the final standards of orthodoxy.[24]

MARCION

The development of the Christian canon is often dated from the literary collection made by the Christian gnostic Marcion (d. ca. 160). Although the movement toward the rudiments of a canon was already underway well before Marcion's time, he deserves special attention as a central figure in advancing the process of canonization.[25] Indeed some scholars have suggested that the idea of the New Testament as distinct from the Old may have come from Marcion's rejection of Jewish scripture.

Marcion, the son of a bishop in Pontus, a Roman province in northern Asia Minor, went to Rome ca. 140 CE, where he undertook to restore the original gospel of Christ based on the teachings of Paul. He was firmly convinced that Paul's letters contained the essentials of the Christian Gospel — love, the spirit, and salvation by grace — which he believed had been overlooked and diminished in the doctrines and preachments of his time, resulting in a reversion toward Jewish legalism.

The view that Marcion's determination to sever Christianity from its ancestral roots in Judaism and from the Old Testament was the result of the disastrous outcome of the Bar Kokhba rebellion in 135 CE has some merit. Many Jews, including the celebrated Rabbi Akiba, believed that Bar Kokhba was the long-

---

[24] J. Pelikan, op. cit., 105–107.

[25] Some scholars, notably Adolf Harnack, have considered Marcion to be a major force in determining the make-up of the Christian canon. Others have regarded the thrust toward canonization as a gradual movement that antedated Marcion. See "The History of the Text and Canon of the New Testament to Jerome," by C. S. C. Williams, in *The West From the Fathers to the Reformation*, Vol. 2 of *The Cambridge History of the Bible* (Cambridge, 1969). See also Farmer and Farkasfalvy, *The Formation of the New Testament Canon*, and Hans von Copenhausen, *The Formation of the Christian Bible*, trans. by G. A. Baker (Philadelphia, 1972), 148–67. Von Copenhausen says, referring to Marcion, "whatever the facts, the first Christian canon remains his peculiar and unique creation, one in which neither churchman nor gnostic anticipated him" (p. 148).

awaited Jewish Messiah. This claim and the ensuing rebellion undoubtedly raised important questions in the minds of thinking Christians concerning their own claims about Jesus as the Christ. The emperor Hadrian executed the rabbis who supported the rebellion, and all Jews were banished from Judea. The Roman city of Aelia Capitolina, built on the site of the old Jerusalem, was officially declared off-limits to Jews. As William Farmer has pointed out, not since the war of 66–70 CE culminating in the dismantling of the Jewish state had the Gospel of Paul been so clearly and convincingly vindicated. Marcion probably went to Rome supposing that both Judaism and Jewish Christianity were finished. The Christian church must now break completely with its Jewish roots and establish itself solely on the basis of a relationship to God and Christ as understood and proclaimed by Paul.[26]

Marcion objected to the practice of Christian leaders who regarded the Hebrew Bible as sacred scripture for the followers of Jesus. Influenced by Paul's writings, he rejected the Jewish commitment to Torah, with its emphasis on Law, which based salvation on works and merit. He found the conceptions of deity in the historical books of the Old Testament, where Yahweh often appears as a vengeful and tribal warlord, inconsistent with Christ's loving and merciful God. These Hebraic conceptions, Marcion believed, lacked the essential attributes of a redeeming, savior God: goodness, mercy, omniscience, and impartiality in his judgment on mankind.

Marcion held that the God of grace and love was unknown in the world until Christ brought God's free gift of salvation for all humanity. For him Christ was the son of God, but his view of Christ was docetist: Christ never received a body of flesh but only "seemed" or "appeared" to have a bodily form. Marcion's position was based on a Gnostic view that the earth was created by an inferior deity from evil matter.[27] According to Marcion man had

[26] Farmer and Farkasfalvy *The Formation of the New Testament Canon*, 61–63.

[27] Some scholars have argued that Marcion was not a thoroughgoing Gnostic but borrowed some Gnostic themes to advance the Christian gospel of love. That Marcion's teaching omitted the mythological doctrines of the gnostics about the aeons and the mysteries of salvation seems to support this contention. His salvation was by faith alone, as in Paul, not by gnosis (knowledge) gained by secret rites available to a privileged few.

to be saved from his condition of bondage or entanglement in the evil materiality of the real world. Salvation was the release of man's spiritual nature from the material body, the flesh. He rejected belief in the resurrection of the body and apparently assumed that his doctrine was entirely consistent with Paul's emphasis upon the Spirit and salvation as release from the body of flesh. Like Paul, Marcion held that salvation comes through faith, not by esoteric knowledge as with the Gnostics or works as with the Jews and Jewish Christians.

Having rejected the Old Testament as scripture, Marcion replaced it with his own collection of Christian writings, which included a revised and corrected edition of Luke's Gospel[28] and the ten epistles of Paul. This collection included only the now canonical Pauline and deutero-Pauline letters. The Pastorals were not included, presumably because Marcion did not recognize them as authentic to Paul. His entire approach to salvation was affected by Paul's doctrine of faith and grace. Marcion also included in his collection a volume of his own, the *Antitheses*. This book is no longer extant, but Marcion's view can be reconstructed from Tertullian's work, which contains his refutation of Marcion's doctrines which he regarded as heretical.

ACTS OF THE APOSTLES

It is thought by some scholars that the opposition generated by Marcion's elimination of the Hebrew Bible was a determining factor in the elevation of the Christian writings to the status of sacred literature comparable to the Old Testament. Marcion's attempt to establish a Christian canon posed a serious threat to leading Christians in Rome, who felt compelled to set their own standards on what should and should not be accepted as holy scripture. N. Perrin suggests that many orthodox Christian leaders rejected Marcion's views as heretical but nevertheless adopted his division of the Christian scriptures as "gospel" and "apostle."[29]

[28] Marcion's version of Luke's Gospel omitted the story of Jesus' miraculous birth.

[29] This division, Perrin claims, "became as traditional for Christians as that of the division of the Jewish scriptures into 'law,' 'prophets,' and 'writings.' " Norman Perrin, *The New Testament, An Introduction* (New York, 1974), 331.

Presumably, then, it was the Christian community in Rome which first contended for adding other Gospels and other letters to Luke and the letters of Paul.

Those scholars may be correct who hold that this was the first occasion for including the Pastoral Letters as Pauline. Probably they were included as authentic to Paul because they expressed an emerging institutional interest in Paul as a churchman, a position which countered the primary emphasis of Marcion's interpretation of Paul as a Gnostic-type Christian. Because of this threat the church felt compelled to interpret Paul through the medium of the Pastoral Letters. This meant, as M. Werner points out, that in the church's interpretation, the real Paul was to become partially concealed behind the Pastoral Letters. So, also, the synoptic Gospels were eclipsed behind the Gospel of John, which was a product of the new theological perspective emerging in the post-apostolic period.[30] Further, it is the contention of several scholars that Acts of the Apostles came into prominence among Christian documents at this point in the second century as the bridge between Paul and the Jerusalem apostles. It was written specifically to show that harmony existed among all of the early apostles and to establish the fact that Paul himself acknowledged the authority of the apostles of the Jerusalem church. Acts is also the link which established the unity among the four Gospels and the Pauline letters as well as between Paul and the General or Catholic Epistles purportedly written by Jesus' other disciples — Peter, James, and John.

Undoubtedly Farmer is correct that while the four Gospels represent the apostolic witness to the death and resurrection of Christ, they did not do justice to the full importance of the apostolic tradition in the church's account of its origins. This was the contribution of the Acts of the Apostles.[31] Acts explained how the gospel, which began with Jesus and his disciples, was perpetuated in Paul's proclamation about Christ. It established the historical connection between Gospel and apostle and accomplished the unity of the

---

[30] See Martin Werner, *Formation of Christian Dogma*, 61–63.

[31] See W. R. Farmer's discussion of "The Conceptual Importance of Luke-Acts" in Farmer and Farkasfalvy, *Formation of the New Testament Canon*, 48f., 56–58. See also M. Werner, 64.

church's tradition. Irenaeus, Bishop of Lyon (c. 130–202), more than any other church father accorded Acts of the Apostles a central position in the canon. Irenaeus was committed to Peter as represented in his speeches in Acts and to Paul as interpreted in Acts and in the Pastoral Letters, which he believed to be Pauline.

In *Against Heresies*, Irenaeus vigorously promoted the unity of the Gospels against heretical Christian groups who favored one or other of the Gospels. For example, the Ebionites used only the Gospel of Matthew, Marcion left out portions of the Gospel of Luke, and Gnostic Christians misused the Gospels of Mark and John in order to demonstrate their own doctrinal positions. For Irenaeus, "The Gospels could not possibly be either more or less in number than they are." He argued that since there were four zones in the world and four general covenants given to mankind, there must be four forms of the one Gospel. Since this was so, those Christian groups were foolish, even audacious, who changed the pattern of the Gospel and presented either more or less than the four Gospels. In his mind the four Gospels were *one* Gospel of Christ.[32] With Irenaeus, the acceptance of the four-fold Gospel to head the list of New Testament books became a fact. Probably at this point it became necessary for the first time to separate Luke's Gospel from his second volume, Acts of the Apostles. Thereafter, Acts was placed between the Gospels and Paul to unite the four Gospels with all of the apostolic writings, including Paul and the General or Catholic Letters.

Irenaeus was responding to the need for unity and a single Gospel within the Christian community. Eventually, such impetus toward unity led to the concept of a Christian canon separate from the Jewish scripture. It led also to the Roman church's determination to include other documents than those in Marcion's collection and yet to set limits which would exclude Gnostic additions to the body of Christian literature. The claim to apostolic authorship and authority emerged as the test of orthodoxy for documents designated as sacred literature. Irenaeus was the key figure in the development of the apostolic tradition. He maintained that the

---

[32] Irenaeus, *Against Heresies*, Bk. 3, chap. 11:7f., trans. and edited by C. C. Richardson, *Early Christian Fathers*, 381–83.

gospel was first preached by the apostles of Jesus, then later by God's will handed down "in Writing" as the foundation of faith. According to Irenaeus, each writer-apostle was perfect in knowledge through the Holy Spirit. Thus, each of the four Gospels was equal in its possession of the word of God.

> So Matthew among the Hebrews issued a Writing of the gospel in their own tongue, while Peter and Paul were preaching the gospel at Rome and founding the Church. After their decease Mark, the disciple and interpreter of Peter, also handed down to us in writing what Peter had preached. Then Luke, the follower of Paul, recorded in a book the gospel as it was preached by him. Finally John, the disciple of the Lord, . . . himself published the Gospel, while he was residing at Ephesus in Asia. All of these handed down to us that there is one God . . . and one Christ the Son of God.[33]

The tradition of apostolic writings and their truths regarding God and Christ, which had come down from the apostles, was found in every church. But significantly Irenaeus cited the church at Rome as the primary example in the preservation of that tradition. Irenaeus referred to it as "that very great, oldest, and well-known Church, founded and established at Rome" by Peter and Paul, whose faith had come down through the succession of bishops. The church at Rome was pre-eminent among all the churches, since "the apostolic tradition is preserved in it by those from everywhere." [34] For Irenaeus the issue of apostolicity went beyond merely determining the historical authenticity of particular documents bearing the names of Peter, James, and John. The Holy Spirit directed the church in its judgments about which books were apostolic. Ultimately, Irenaeus held, the tradition handed down is sufficient even without the writings of the apostles. He recited the case of many barbarian converts who have "salvation written in their hearts by the Spirit without paper and ink." [35]

---

[33] Ibid., 370.

[34] Ibid., 372.

[35] Ibid., 371–75. According to D. M. Farkasfalvy, it was Irenaeus' doctrine of the Church which settled the issue of apostolicity, that in the last analysis it was the Holy Spirit which guided the Church "to pass correct judgment about the documents of faith." Farmer and Farkasfalvy, *The Formation of the New Testament Canon*, 159f.

THE APOCRYPHAL WRITINGS AND THE TRADITIONAL CANON

Three observations seem relevant at this point: First, the church produced the literature of the New Testament, not the reverse, that the New Testament produced the church. The church did not grow out of a literary movement, notwithstanding the importance of the literature to its integrity, strength, and growth. Second, there was nothing inevitable about the shape that the New Testament eventually assumed. The canon might have developed in a variety of ways, depending upon varying circumstances. Adolf Harnack suggests, for instance, that there may have been as many as seven different hypothetical constructs which could have led to a different collection and arrangement of sacred writings.[36] Third, there were many more documents produced in the church than were finally included in the canon. Oscar Cullmann's comment that "generally speaking, the New Testament canon was not formed by addition, as some may think, but by *elimination*" is an apt description of what occurred.[37] Besides letters and apocalypses, a number of Gospels were written in the first two centuries which were never canonized. While complete copies are no longer extant, some are available in fragmentary form. Among the most important are the Gospels of the Ebionites, the Hebrews, the Egyptians, the Nazaraeans, and a Gospel of Peter. Although exact dating is problematical, many are of the opinion that these were produced during the first half of the second century. Among these "apocryphal" writings are some deserving not only study but actual use as religious documents. Still there is general agreement that the eventual canonization of the present New Testament, bypassing a wealth of extant early literature, is evidence of the good judgment of the Christian congregations and their leaders.

The Gospel of Peter dates from the middle of the second century. The Gospel of Thomas, now available among the Nag Hammadi documents discovered in 1945, dates from ca. 140 CE

---

[36] Adolf Von Harnack, *The Origin of the New Testament*, trans. by J. R. Wilkinson (London, 1925), 168–78.

[37] Oscar Cullmann, *The New Testament*, trans. by Dennis Pardee (Philadelphia, 1968). This small but informative book should be read in its entirety.

The Formation of the New Testament Canon 419

and contains a collection of the sayings of Jesus believed to be founded upon an earlier source. The Gospel of the Ebionites is apparently an abridged form of the Gospel of Matthew. It was used by Jewish Christians, called "Ebionites," who maintained that Jesus' sonship was established at the coming of God's Spirit at his baptism. They rejected the doctrine of the virgin birth. The Gospel of the Nazaraeans, also apparently based in part on Matthew's Gospel, was reported to have been circulated among some Syrian Jewish Christian churches.[38] The Gospels of Thomas and Peter reflect a gnostic influence that exceeds that found in the four canonical Gospels, even the strong gnostic element in the Fourth Gospel.

Although acceptance of the present four Gospels seems to have been undisputed by the latter half of the second century, other gospels continued to be used to some extent in various Christian communities. Clement of Alexandria, for example, indicated that the gospels of the Hebrews and the Egyptians enjoyed limited popularity in several churches in his day (ca. 200).

By the middle of the second century many letters, sermons, and treatises of the early church fathers as well as Gospels were regarded as worthy of special use in the church. The eventual verdict, however, denied them canonical status. Known since the seventeenth century as the Apostolic Fathers, these writings include documents from Rome, from Asia Minor, and Egypt. First Clement (ca. 95) and a Christian apocalypse called the Shepherd of Hermas were sent from the church at Rome. The seven letters of Ignatius, bishop of Antioch, a letter to the Philippians from Polycarp, bishop of Smyrna ca. 120, and a document called the Martyrdom of Polycarp were sent from the church at Smyrna in Asia Minor. The Epistle of Barnabas, so-called Second Clement, one of the earliest examples of a Christian sermon, and the Didache, a manual of instruction sometimes referred to as the

---

[38] For a discussion of the Jewish and Jewish Christian sects — the Ebionites and Nazarenes (or Nazorenes) and Naasanes — see A. Harnack, *History of Dogma*, trans. 3rd German edition by N. Buchanan (New York, 1958), 1:287–310. See also Walter Bauer, *Orthodoxy and Heresy in Earliest Christianity*, ed. by R. A. Kraft and Gerhard Krodel, trans. by team from the Philadelphia Seminar on Christian Origins (Philadelphia, 1971).

Teaching of the Twelve Apostles, came from Alexandria in Egypt. Some of these documents were undoubtedly serious competitors for adoption as holy scripture. The Didache, the Epistle of Barnabas, and 1 Clement, for example, seem to have been accepted by Clement of Alexandria as deserving at least quasi-canonical status.

THE COLLECTIONS

The situation with respect to canonization apparently remained somewhat fluid until the last quarter of the second century. But even after that there was no general agreement among all of the churches as to just which documents were inspired and therefore to be regarded as sacred. At this time three classes of documents had come into view: First, those which made up much of the present canon, the four Gospels, Acts, and the thirteen letters claiming Pauline authorship. Second, some documents or books whose authority at first was challenged but were later accepted into the canon — Hebrews, James, 2 and 3 John, Jude and 2 Peter. Some scholars are inclined to place 1 Peter and 1 John and perhaps the Revelation to John in this second category. The third class included documents which initially had garnered favored status but which were finally recommended for reading but rejected from the canon. Among these were those referred to by M. S. Enslin as the "more fluid": the Gospel of Peter, the Revelation of Peter, the Shepherd of Hermas, Barnabas, 1 Clement, and 2 Clement.[39]

In response to the challenge of orthodoxy primarily from Marcion and the Christian gnostics, the church at Rome declared that twenty-two books were binding upon faith and were the authorized guide to Christian worship. These were to be the authority in all doctrinal controversies. The earliest extant list of New Testament writings, known as the Muratorion canon, was published by Ludovico Muratori in 1740. This list, usually dated from the late second century, is a significant indicator of what was regarded as canonical by the Roman church of that period. It included all of the books of the present New Testament except James, 1 Peter, 2 Peter, Hebrews, and 3 John. Included in the canon were the Apocalypse of Peter and the Wisdom of Solomon.

[39] M. S. Enslin, *Christian Beginnings* (New York, 1956), 469.

The Shepherd of Hermas was rejected as too recent. The Muratorion canon is believed by some scholars to have been the work of Hippolytus (c. 170–c. 236). Thus for all practical purposes it would seem that the church had at least an unofficial canon by approximately the end of the second century. Yet even beyond that time the situation was not completely stabilized. Later, Clement of Alexandria (c. 150–c. 215) considered Hebrews to be a part of the Pauline writings. Also, he included the letters of Barnabas and Clement of Rome, the Shepherd of Hermas, the Apocalypse of Peter, and a document called the Preaching of Peter, which is no longer extant. Clement's collection of sacred writings may have included as many as thirty books. The status of Hebrews, the Revelation to John, James, 2 Peter, Jude, and 3 John was not finally settled until the time of Constantine in the fourth century (306–337).

Athanasius, bishop of Alexandria (c. 296–373), listed in an Easter Letter the authoritative writings of both the Old and the New Testaments. His list of Christian documents agrees with the twenty-seven today included in the New Testament. "These," he said, "are fountains of salvation.... In these alone is proclaimed the doctrine of godliness. Let no man add to these, neither let him take aught from these." [40] This position was dogmatized by the council at Carthage held in 419 CE: "besides the Canonical Scriptures nothing be read in church under the name of divine Scripture." [41]

The Council of Chalcedon (451 CE) was a pivotal event in the history of the canon. The decisions of this council represent for at least a majority of Christian churches in the West the closing of the canon. However, the diversity with respect to the names and the number of the New Testament books which prevailed in the pre-Constantine era was continued among the non-Chalcedon churches. For example, the Syrian Christian Church, which used

---

[40] See Athanasius' Festal Letters, xxxix, written for Easter 367 CE in P. Schaff and H. Wace, eds., *Nicene and Post-Nicene Fathers of the Christian Church*, Second Series (Grand Rapids, Michigan, 1953), 4:551f.

[41] From "The Code of Canons of the African Church," Canon xxiv, in P. Schaff and H. Wace, eds., *Nicene and Post-Nicene Fathers of the Christian Church*, Second Series (Grand Rapids, Michigan, 1956), 14:453.

the Peshitta, a 5th century Syriac version of the New Testament, included only twenty-two books; the Revelation to John, 2 Peter, 2 and 3 John, and Jude were not included.

Even as late as the Protestant Reformation in the sixteenth century the canonical authority of some books was still in question. Erasmus, for example, raised questions about the status of Hebrews, the Revelation to John, and 3 John. The reformers raised questions about the canonicity of certain books and favored grading the level of divine inspiration of the books included in the canon. Martin Luther, for instance, had serious reservations about the inclusion of the Letter of James in the canon and concluded that Hebrews, Jude, and the Revelation were of secondary importance. In 1546 the Council of Trent settled the issue for the Roman church. After naming the books as they are now found in the established Old Testament and New Testament (and several Old Testament apocryphal books), the Decree Concerning the Canonical Scriptures reads,

> But if any one receive not, as sacred and canonical, the said books [of both Old and New Testaments, including much of the Old Testament apocrypha] entire with all their parts, as they have been used to be read in the Catholic Church, and as they are contained in the old Latin vulgate edition; . . . let him be anathema.[42]

The decisions of Trent on the New Testament canon were based primarily on traditional usage in the churches. Whether or not this forecloses the possibility of additions to the canon, resulting, for instance, from the discovery of a heretofore unknown authentic Pauline letter, is a matter of discussion among Catholic authorities.

---

[42] Philip Schaff, *The Creeds of Christendom*, Vol. 2, *The Greek and Latin Creeds* (Grand Rapids, 1977), 82.

Postscript

The Bible can be read in a variety of ways. There can be little argument concerning its uses for liturgical and devotional purposes. There is no question that sacred literature is sometimes essential to religious ceremony and ritual or that millions of devout persons find consolation, spiritual uplift, and moral courage in reading the scriptures. But too often they are employed to support religious prejudices and established theological beliefs or simply to confirm new and sometimes highly speculative ideas. The Bible is all too infrequently read in the interest of learning what its authors in fact wrote and to understand what they meant by what they wrote.

The problem of establishing reliable texts and ensuring competent translations respecting the language usages of the readers, the textual or "lower criticism," is a task for expert scholarship. Determining the meaning of the text, the so-called "higher criticism," is equally a task for experts, as it requires up-to-date and sophisticated linguistic, literary, historical, and archaeological analysis.

Certainly the effort to understand the New Testament is a never-ending task involving the commitment and untiring work of genuinely competent scholars. No one person or group of persons can be presumed to have the last word in a matter of this kind. Every scholar must interpret the text from some standpoint and must run the risk of error, but there is reason for believing that genuine gains in understanding are being made. There will always be differences due to presupposition, method, access to knowledge, principles of interpretation, and perhaps temperament. But all who treasure the Bible owe a lasting debt of gratitude to those scholars who literally expend their lives in an effort to achieve that understanding.

APPENDIX I
Important Versions of the Bible

The Septuagint

The Septuagint or LXX was a Greek version of the Hebrew scriptures begun early in the third century BCE during the reign of the Greek ruler of Egypt, Ptolemy II Philadelphus. The process of translation may have extended into the first century CE. This translation was made presumably for the use of Jews and Jewish converts in the Diaspora and was of major importance for Christianity since it was the version employed by the Diaspora Christians and most of the writers of the New Testament books. It was first printed in Venice in 1518. Approximately 1,800 manuscripts of the LXX on parchment or papyrus are now extant. Manuscript remains prior to 100 CE are fragmentary. The Vatican library has the most important and earliest — fourth century — manuscript, the *Codex Vaticanus*, which includes almost all of the Old Testament and much of the Apocrypha. Other important but incomplete manuscripts, the *Codex Sinaiticus*, fourth century, and *Codex Alexandrinus*, fifth century, are in the British Museum.

The Vulgate

The most important translation of the Bible into Latin, the Vulgate, was the work of Jerome (ca. 342–420) in the late fourth century. His work of editing and translating was begun in the 380s. Because there was considerable confusion among the various Latin versions of the scriptures, Jerome was involved in both editing and translating. He was a man of massive scholarship, and although he employed the Greek LXX and other Latin translations in his work, his translation of the Old Testament was based on his knowledge of Hebrew. As in the case of the Old Testament, Jerome employed Old Latin versions of New Testament books but corrected them from Greek manuscripts. The first printed edition of the Vulgate was the Gutenberg Bible, 1452–55.

The Vulgate, which had been commissioned by Pope Damasus, was declared official Bible of the Roman Catholic church by the Council of Trent in 1546. The holy Synod "ordains and declares, that the said old and vulgate edition, which, by the lengthened usage of so many ages, has been approved of in the Church, be, in public lectures, disputations, sermons, and expositions, held as authentic; and that no one is to dare, or presume to reject it under any pretext whatever."

Luther's Bible

The High German Lutheran Bible which included the Apocrypha was published at Wittenberg in 1534. Martin Luther had begun the transla-

Appendix I

tion in 1522, translating the New Testament from Greek and the Old Testament from Hebrew. Because of his illness, friends of Luther assisted in translating the apocryphal books, employing especially the LXX and the Vulgate. Luther's insistence on grounding Christianity firmly in the Bible impelled him not only to make the sacred books available in the vernacular but also to employ the most reliable documentary sources available. An earlier German translation published in 1466 was simply made from the Vulgate.

Tyndale's Bible

William Tyndale translated from both Hebrew and Greek against difficult official opposition in England. Proficient in Greek and perhaps to a lesser degree in Hebrew, Tyndale was assisted by both the LXX and Vulgate as well as Luther's New Testament translation. Because of persecution from conservative factions, Tyndale's New Testament was published in Worms in 1526, with a final revision in 1535. Only parts of the Old Testament were completed and published. Tyndale's translation, the first to be published in English, was an important source for the King James Version.

English Versions Between Tyndale and the King James

After the publication of Tyndale's testament, several English translations appeared. The Coverdale Bible (1535) was not translated from the ancient Hebrew and Greek sources, but it depended heavily on the Vulgate, Tyndale, and Luther's Bible. The Great Bible (1539) like the Coverdale, depended, among others, on Tyndale's translation and the Geneva Bible translated in Geneva by Protestant scholars under John Knox, the Scottish Puritan, and published in full in 1560. The Bishop's Bible was published in 1568. The main Catholic English version, the Reims-Douai Bible — New Testament published in 1582 at Reims and Old Testament in 1609–10 at Douai — was based primarily on the Vulgate, in keeping with the admonition of the Council of Trent. It countered Protestant versions considered to be erroneous by the Catholic church.

Authorized Version (King James)

In 1604 James I of England appointed a commission to revise the widely used Bishop's Bible. The revision, done at Oxford, Cambridge, and Westminster and published in 1611, depended heavily on earlier versions, especially the Geneva and Reims-Douai, and did not have access to the ancient and more authentic texts. It replaced the Bishop's Bible in official usage and gradually, especially because of the quality of its language, superseded the Geneva in popular acceptance.

Revised Versions

Changes in English language usage, the availability of more authentic textual materials, and improved knowledge of the biblical languages and style resulted in the Revised Version, the work of British Protestant scholars with American consultation. The New Testament was published in 1881, the Old Testament in 1884, and the Apocrypha in 1895. An American version adapted to American language usage was published in 1901.

Revised Standard Version

Under authorization from the National Council of Churches, the Revised Standard Version was produced by committees of American scholars who had the advantage of the most advanced knowledge of the languages and literary styles, and the most recent text discoveries. This version, which preserved much of the linguistic and stylistic character of the Authorized Version, has been vigorously opposed by many conservatives but is widely employed by biblical scholars. The New Testament was published in 1946, the Old Testament in 1952, and the Apocrypha in 1957.

Other Recent English Versions

Among the many other versions in recent decades intended to update both scholarship and English usage have been the New English Bible, published in England, the New Testament in 1961, the Old Testament and Apocrypha in 1970; and the Jerusalem Bible, a Catholic translation with a useful new format which was originally done in French but was translated into English from the ancient texts and published in English in 1966. A publication of the Bible in 1845–53 by D. Leeser was popular among American Jews. In 1892 a new translation was planned under auspices of the Jewish Publication Society, but it was not until 1917 that a complete translation of the Massoretic Text was published. A new translation was projected in 1955, and the Torah was published in 1962.

APPENDIX II

Historical Events from the Exodus to the New Testament

ca. 1280 BCE	*Exodus* from Egypt — Moses and the Sinai Covenant
1250–1200	Invasion of Canaan — Joshua
1200–1050	The League of Hebrew Tribes — The Judges
1020– 922	*The United Monarchy*
1020–1000	Saul, Samuel
1000– 961	David — Consolidation of the Kingdom; conquest of Jerusalem
961– 922	Solomon — The First Temple, disruption of the Kingdom
922– 587	*The Divided Monarchy*
922– 721	*Israel* — The Northern Kingdom; Elijah, Elisha, Hosea
721	Assyrian conquest
922– 587	*Judah* — The Southern Kingdom; Amos, Micah, I Isaiah, Jeremiah, Habakkuk
587	Babylonian conquest, fall of Jerusalem
587– 539	Babylonian Exile — Ezekiel, II Isaiah
539	Persian conquest — fall of Babylon
539– 331	*The Persian Period*
	Edict of Cyrus the Great
	Return from Exile
516	Second Temple — Haggai, Zechariah
ca. 400	Canonization of the Pentateuch — Ezra, Nehemiah
332– 31	Conquest by Alexander the Great
331– 167	*The Greek Period*
331– 323	Rule by Alexander
323– 198	Rule by Ptolemies (Egyptian Greeks)
198– 167	Rule by Seleucids (Syrian Greeks)
167– 63	*Hasmonean Rule* — An Independent State
168	Maccabaean revolt
165	Rededication of the Temple
	Rise of the Pharisees and Sadducees; Essenes at Qumran
63	Conquest by the Romans
	The Roman Period
63	Roman general Pompey captures Jerusalem; Antipater, adviser to the High Priest, becomes ruler of Judea, 63–43, succeeded by his sons Herod and Phasael

[427]

	48	Julius Caesar defeats Pompey
	44	Assassination of Caesar
	42	Marc Antony and Octavianus divide Roman Empire between East and West
	40	Parthians invade and conquer Judea
	37	Herod the Great, with Roman assistance, recaptures Jerusalem and Judea
	37– 4	Herod governs Judea under Roman rule;
	31	Octavianus defeats Marc Antony; end of Roman civil war
	27 BCE– 14 CE	Octavianus (Augustus) first emperor of united Roman Empire
		Philo Judaeus, ca. 12 BCE–50 CE
ca.	4 BCE	Death of Herod; birth of Jesus
		Herod's successors:
	4 BCE– 6 CE	Herod Archelaus (Judea, Idumea, Samaria)
	39	Herod Antipas (Galilee and Perea)
	34	Herod Philip (East of Galilee)

APPENDIX III

An Early Christian Chronology

	Events in Early Christian History	Roman Emperors	Roman Administrators of Judea (procurators)
27 BCE–14 CE		Octavianus (Augustus) First ruler of the Roman Empire	
4 BCE	Death of Herod Birth of Jesus		
1 CE			Coponius, 6–9 Ambibulus, 9–12 Annius Rufinis, 12–15
20		Tiberius, 14–37	Valerius Gratus, 15–26
	John the Baptist, ca. 27–29 Jesus' Ministry, ca. 29–30		Pontius Pilate, 26–36
30	Crucifixion of Jesus, ca. 30 Early Jewish Christianity in Jerusalem; Peter and James the brother of Jesus; the "Q" tradition; early Gentile Christianity in Antioch		Marcellus, 36–37
	Paul's Conversion, ca. 33	Gaius (Caligula), 37–41	Marullus, 37–41(?)
40	Herod Agrippa I, 37–44 Persecution of the "Followers of the Way"; execution of James the disciple and imprisonment of Peter	Claudius, 41–54 (banishment of Jews from Rome)	Cuspius Fadus, 44–46 Tiberius Alexander, 46–48
50	Gamaliel d. ca. 50		Ventidius Cumanus, 48–52
	Paul's letters, ca. 50–88 Herod Agrippa II, 53–86(?)	Nero, 54–68	Antonius Felix ca. 52–60(?)
60	Paul in Rome; his execution ca. 60–64		Porcius Festus 60–62(?)

	Events in Early Christian History	Roman Emperors	Roman Administrators of Judea (procurators)
	Execution of James (Jesus' brother), 62		Lucceius(?) Albinus 62–64
66–70	Jewish–Roman War; Josephus (ca. 37–92)		Gessius Florus 64–66
	Flight of Christians to Pella, 66		
		Galba, Otho and Vitellius, 68	
70	Destruction of Jerusalem and the Second Temple	Vespasian, 69–79 (Judea transferred from a Procuratorial to an Imperial Province)	
	Fall of Masada, 73		
70–110	Period of Reconstruction, Judaism & Christianity		
	Writing of Mark, ca. 70		
	Founding of Jewish Academy at Jabneh (Jamniah), ca. 80	Titus, 79–81	
80	Development of a doctrine of the church — New Israel and a New Covenant	Domitian, 81–96	
	The Gospel of Matthew, ca. 80–90		
90	Collection of the Pauline letters; writing of Luke–Acts, ca. 85–95		
	The Gospel of John, ca. 90–100	Nerva, 96–98	
	Closing of the Jewish Canon at Jabneh, ca. 90		
100–135 CE	The Emerging Church — Adjustment to Roman Rule	Trajan, 98–117	
	Diasporan Jews revolt against Rome, 114–17		
	Martyrdom of Ignatius, 117		
	Bar Kokhba Messianic uprising; Judea devastated, 132–35	Hadrian, 117–38	
	2 Peter, probably latest document in Christian canon, ca. 135–50		

APPENDIX IV

Major Non-Canonical Christian Writings, 95–430 CE

A. Early Church Fathers

ca. 95 CE	Clement of Rome	*1 Clement*
110–117	Ignatius	Six letters to the Churches: *Ephesus, Magnesia, Tralles, Rome, Philadelphia, Smyrna*
		To *Polycarp* (bishop of Smyrna)
ca. 70–156	Polycarp	To the *Philippians*
100–110		*Didache* (also known as the "Teaching of the Twelve Apostles")
130	Written from Alexandria	*Epistle of Barnabas*
144	Marcion	Collects Paul's epistles (excluding Pastoral letters)
150	Tatian	*Diatessaron* — a synthesis of the 4 Gospels
ca. 165	Justin called the Martyr	*Apology*
		Dialogue with Trypho
ca. 150	Anonymous	*2 Clement* (called *Clement's Second Letter to the Corinthians*), a Christian sermon
150–155	Tertullian	*Against Marcion*
ca. 200	Irenaeus	*Against Heresies*
200–213	Clement of Alexandria	*Exhortation to the Heathen*
		The Address
		The Instructor
		Miscellanies
184–254	Origen	*On Prayer*
		Against Celsus
		On First Principles
		Hexapla (the compiler)
170–235	Hippolytus	*Refutation of All Heresies*
260–340	Eusebius of Caesarea	*Church History* (10 vols.)
342–420	Jerome	*The Vulgate Translation*
		Dialogue Against Pelagians
354–430	Augustine	*Confessions*
		City of God

B. Early Non-Canonical Gospels

Gospel of the Ebionites	Early second century Jewish Christian gospel thought to be an abridged form of the Gospel of Matthew; seven fragments are in Epiphanes, *Against Heresies* 30, 13–22.
Gospel of the Hebrews	Early second century. Probably from Egypt, written for Greek-speaking Jewish Christians.
Gospel of the Egyptians	Early second century. Quoted in 2 Clement and in Clement of Alexandria; shows gnostic influence.
Gospel of the Naassenes	Gnostic gospel, quoted in Hippolytus' *Refutation of All Heresies*, Book 5; considered heretical by Hippolytus.
Gospel of the Nazaraeans	Early second century. Apparently used by Syrian Jewish Christians; probably from an Aramaic translation of the Greek Gospel of Matthew.
Gospel of Peter	Middle to late second century. Shows gnostic influence; contains an unusual account of Jesus' resurrection.
Coptic Gospel of Thomas	Written ca. 140 CE. Found at Nag Hammadi in Egypt near the Nile River; a collection of Jesus' secret sayings strongly influenced by Gnosticism.
Gospel of Philip	Second half of the third century. Written and used by gnostic Christians; on gnostic sacramental theology and practice.
Infancy Gospel of Thomas	Written ca. 150 CE. Contains popular legends and miracle stories about Jesus from five to ten years of age.

Selected Readings

Many of the readings suggested here relate to several of the subject categories listed. The titles are given only once, however, under the heading where their relevance is most evident.

A few of these books were written in the early part of this century and a very limited number in the nineteenth century. These have been included because they are classics in their fields which have had a large impact on subsequent scholarship — works such as those by David Strauss, Johannes Weiss, Albert Schweitzer, and George Foot Moore. Included also, of course, are ancient writers such as Josephus, Philo, and Eusebius.

Most of the readings have been published during the remarkably productive era of New Testament scholarship from the Second World War to the present. They represent the recent and contemporary work of major scholars in the exposition and analysis of numerous critical problems in the study of the New Testament. They are readily available in English, and wherever possible, the dates of publication given are for the most recent editions or printings.

A. Historical Background

Avi-Yonah, Michael, ed. *The Herodian Period.* New Brunswick: Rutgers University Press, 1975.

Bright, John. *A History of Israel.* 2d ed. Philadelphia: Westminster Press, 1972.

Bultmann, Rudolf. *Primitive Christianity in Its Contemporary Setting.* Trans. by R. H. Fuller. New York: Meridian Books, 1956.

Epstein, Isidore. *Judaism; A Historical Presentation.* Baltimore: Penguin Books, 1959.

Grant, Michael. *The Jews in the Roman World.* New York: Dorset Press, 1984.

Jagersma, Henk. *A History of Israel from Alexander the Great to Bar Kochba.* Trans. by John Bowden. Philadelphia: Fortress Press, 1986.

Jeremias, Joachim. *Jerusalem in the Time of Jesus.* Trans. by F. H. Cave and C. H. Cave. Philadelphia: Fortress Press, 1975.

Josephus, Flavius. *Antiquities of the Jews.* Books I–IV, V–VIII trans. by H. St. J. Thackeray. Books IX–XI, XII–XIV, XV–XVII trans. by Ralph Marcus. Books XVIII–XX trans. by H. Feldman. Cambridge: Harvard University Press, 1930; rpt. ed., 1976–81.

———. *The Jewish War.* Trans. by G. A. Williamson; rev. ed. by E. Mary Smallwood. New York: Penguin Books, 1981.

Neusner, Jacob. *Judaism in the Beginning of Christianity.* Philadelphia: Fortress Press, 1984.

Noth, Martin. *The History of Israel.* 2d ed. Trans. from the German by P. R. Ackroyd. New York: Harper & Row, 1960.

Pfeiffer, Robert H. *History of New Testament Times; With an Introduction to the Apocrypha.* New York: Harper & Brothers, 1949.

Russell, D. S. *The Jews from Alexander to Herod.* Oxford: Oxford University Press, 1978.

Safrai, S., and M. Stern. *The Jewish People in the First Century.* 2 vols. Philadelphia: Fortress Press, 1974–76.

Sandmel, Samuel. *Herod: Profile of a Tyrant.* Philadelphia: Lippincott, 1967.

Schalit, Abraham, ed. *The Hellenistic Age: Political History of Jewish Palestine from 332 BCE to 67 CE.* New Brunswick, NJ: Rutgers University Press, 1972.

Schürer, Emil. *The History of the Jewish People in the Age of Jesus Christ*, Vol. 1. Rev. and ed. by G. Vermes and Fergus Miller. Edinburgh: T. & T. Clark, 1973.

Smallwood, E. Mary. *The Jews Under Roman Rule; From Pompey to Diocletian.* Leiden: E. J. Brill, 1976.

Zeitlin, Solomon. *The Rise and Fall of the Judaean State.* Vol. 1: 372–37 BCE; vol. 2: 37 BCE–66 CE; vol. 3: 66 CE–120 CE. Philadelphia: Jewish Publication Society of America, 1962–78.

B. General Introduction to the New Testament

Bruce, F. F. *New Testament History.* Garden City, NY: Doubleday, 1972.

Davies, W. D. *Invitation to the New Testament.* Garden City, NY: Doubleday, 1969.

Fuller, Reginald H. *A Critical Introduction to the New Testament.* London: Duckworth, 1966.

Grant, Robert M. *A Historical Introduction to the New Testament*. New York: Harper & Row, 1963.
Harvey, A. E. *The New English Bible Companion to the New Testament*. Cambridge: Oxford University Press and Cambridge University Press, 1979.
Kee, Howard C., F. Young, and K. Forelich. *Understanding the New Testament*. 4th ed. Englewood Cliffs, NJ: Prentice-Hall, 1983.
Koester, Helmut. *History and Literature of Early Christianity*. Philadelphia: Fortress Press, 1982.
Kümmel, Werner G. *Introduction to the New Testament*. Rev. ed. Trans. by H. C. Koe. New York: Abingdon Press, 1973.
Marxen, Willi. *Introduction to the New Testament*. Trans. by G. Buswell. Philadelphia: Fortress Press, 1968.
Perrin, Norman, and Dennis C. Duling. *The New Testament: An Introduction*. 2d ed. New York: Harcourt Brace Jovanovich, 1982.

C. The Jewish Religion in the Time of Jesus

Baeck, Leo. *The Pharisees and Other Essays*. New York: Schocken Books, 1947; rpt., 1966.
Danby, Herbert. *The Mishnah*. London: Oxford University Press, 1967.
Edersheim, Alfred. *The Temple; Its Ministry and Services*. Grand Rapids, MI: Wm. B. Eerdmans, 1982. (Rpt. of an early classic.)
Finkelstein, Louis. *The Pharisees: The Sociological Background of Their Faith*. Philadelphia: The Jewish Publication Society of America, 1962.
———, ed. *The Jews: Their History*. New York: Schocken Books, 1977.
Herford, R. Travers. *The Pharisees*. Boston: Beacon Press, 1962.
———. *Talmud and Apocrypha*. New York: KTAV Publishing House, 1971.
Moore, George Foot. *Judaism in the First Centuries of the Christian Era: The Age of the Tannaim*, vol. 2. New York: Schocken Books, 1975. (Recent ed. of a classic book.)
Neusner, J. *The Rabbinic Tradition About the Pharisees Before 70*. 3 vols. Leiden: E. J. Brill, 1971.
Schürer, Emil. *The Literature of the Jewish People in the Time of Jesus*. Ed. by Nahum N. Glatzer. New York: Schocken Books, 1972. (Recent ed. of an early classic.)
Stone, Michael E., ed. *Jewish Writings of the Second Temple Period*. Assen: Van Gorcum; Philadelphia: Fortress Press, 1984.

D. Jesus and the Jews

Brandon, S. G. F. *Jesus and the Zealots: A Study of the Political Factor in Primitive Christianity.* Manchester: Manchester University Press, 1967; New York: Charles Scribner, 1968.

Charlesworth, James H. *Jesus Within Judaism; New Light from Exciting Archaeological Discoveries.* New York: Doubleday, 1988.

Klausner, Joseph. *Jesus of Nazareth.* Translated by Herbert Danby. New York: Menorah, 1979.

Vermes, Geza. *Jesus the Jew.* Philadelphia: Fortress Press, 1981.

―――――. *Jesus and the World of Judaism.* London: SCM Press, 1986.

E. Jesus and His Teachings

Bornkamm, Günther. *Jesus of Nazareth.* Trans. by Irene McLuskey and Fraser McLuskey with James M. Robinson. London: Hodder & Stoughton, 1960; New York: Harper & Row, 1975.

Brown, Raymond E. *The Birth of the Messiah.* New York: Image Books, 1979.

Davies, W. D. *The Sermon on the Mount.* Cambridge: Cambridge University Press, 1966.

Dodd, Charles H. *The Founder of Christianity.* New York: Macmillan, 1970.

―――――. *The Parables of the Kingdom.* Rev. ed. New York: Charles Scribner's Sons, 1961.

Enslin, Morton S. *The Prophet from Nazareth.* New York: Schocken Books, 1968.

Goguel, Maurice. *The Life of Jesus.* Trans. by Olive Wyon. New York: Macmillan, 1949.

Jeremias, Joachim. *The Parables of Jesus.* 6th ed. Trans. by S. H. Hooks. New York: Charles Scribner's Sons, 1963.

―――――. *The Sermon on the Mount.* Trans. by N. Perrin. Philadelphia: Fortress Press, 1963.

Kelber, Werner H. *The Kingdom in Mark: A New Place and a New Time.* Philadelphia: Fortress Press, 1974.

Manson, T. W. *The Sayings of Jesus.* London: SCM Press, 1961.

Perrin, Norman. *The Kingdom of God in the Teachings of Jesus.* London: SCM Press, 1963.

Saunders, Ernest W. *Jesus in the Gospels.* Englewood Cliffs, NJ: Prentice-Hall, 1967.

Schweitzer, Albert. *The Quest of the Historical Jesus*. Trans. by W. Montgomery, with a new introduction by James M. Robinson. New York: Macmillan, 1964. (Recent ed. of an old classic.)

Smith, Morton. *Jesus the Magician*. San Francisco: Harper & Row, 1981.

Strauss, David F. *The Life of Jesus Critically Examined*. First German ed., 1835. Trans. from the 4th ed. by George Eliot. Ed. by Peter C. Hodgson. Philadelphia: Fortress Press, 1972.

Tödt, H. E. *The Son of Man in the Synoptic Tradition*. Trans. by Dorothea M. Barton. Philadelphia: Westminster Press, 1965.

Weiss, Johannes. *Jesus' Proclamation of the Kingdom of God*. Trans. and ed. by Richard H. Hiers and David L. Holland. Philadelphia: Fortress Press, 1971. (Recent ed. of an old classic.)

F. The Synoptic Gospels

Bornkamm, Günther, Gerhard Barth, and H. J. Held. *Tradition and Interpretation in Matthew*. Philadelphia: Westminster Press, 1963.

Caird, G. B. *The Gospel of Saint Luke*. Baltimore: Penguin Books, 1963; rpt. ed., 1975.

Conzelmann, H. *The Theology of St. Luke*. Trans. by H. Buswell. New York: Harper & Row, 1960.

Fenton, John C. *The Gospel of St. Matthew*. Baltimore: Penguin Books, 1963; rpt. ed., 1976.

Grant, Michael. *Jesus: An Historian's Review of the Gospels*. New York: Charles Scribner's Sons, 1977.

Kee, Howard C. *Jesus in History: An Approach to the Study of the Gospels*. 2d ed. New York: Harcourt Brace Jovanovich, 1977.

Kelber, Werner H. *Mark's Story of Jesus*. Philadelphia: Fortress Press, 1979.

Nineham, D. E. *St. Mark*. Westminster Pelican Commentaries. Philadelphia: Westminster Press, 1978.

Stendahl, Krister. *The School of St. Matthew*. Philadelphia: Fortress Press, 1968.

Taylor, Vincent. *The Gospel According to St. Mark*. London: Macmillan, 1952.

Throckmorton, Burton H., Jr., ed. *Gospel Parallels: A Synopsis of the First Three Gospels*. 4th ed. rev. Nashville: Thomas Nelson, 1979.

G. The Gospel of John

Barrett, Charles K. *The Gospel of John and Judaism*. Trans. by D. M. Smith. Philadelphia: Fortress Press, 1975.

———. *The Gospel According to St. John*. 2d ed. New York: Westminster John Knox, 1978.
Bultmann, Rudolf. *The Gospel of John: A Commentary*. Trans. by G. R. Beasley-Murray et al. Philadelphia: Westminster Press, 1971.
Charlesworth, James H., ed. *John and Qumran*. London: Geoffrey Chapman, 1972.
Colwell, E. C., and E. Titus. *The Gospel of the Spirit; A Study in the Fourth Gospel*. New York: Harper & Brothers, 1953.
Dodd, C. H. *The Interpretation of the Fourth Gospel*. Cambridge: Cambridge University Press, 1953.
Martyn, J. L. *History and Theology in the Fourth Gospel*. 2d ed. Nashville: Abingdon Press, 1979.
Smith, D. M. *The Composition and Order of the Fourth Gospel*. New Haven: Yale University Press, 1965.
Titus, Eric L. *The Message of the Fourth Gospel*. New York: Abingdon Press, 1957.

H. The Trial, Crucifixion, and Resurrection

Fuller, R. H. *The Formation of the Resurrection Narratives*. New York: Macmillan, 1971.
Kelber, Werner, ed. *The Passion in Mark*. Philadelphia: Fortress Press, 1976.
Marxen, Willi. *The Resurrection of Jesus of Nazareth*. Philadelphia: Fortress Press, 1970.
Perrin, N. *The Resurrection According to Matthew, Mark, and Luke*. Philadelphia: Fortress Press, 1977.
Winter, Paul. *On the Trial of Jesus*. Berlin: Walter de Gruyter, 1961.
Zeitlin, Solomon. *Who Crucified Jesus?* 2d ed. New York: Harper & Row, 1947.

I. Hellenism, Judaism, and Christianity

Atiya, Aziz S. *A History of Eastern Christianity*. London: Methuen, 1968; rpt. ed., Millwood, NY: Kraus Reprints, 1980.
Baeck, Leo. *The Essence of Judaism*. New York: Schocken Books, 1948.
———. *Judaism and Christianity*. Trans. by Walter Kaufmann. New York: Harper & Row, 1966.
Bréhier, Emile. *The Hellenistic and Roman Age*. Trans. by Wade Baskin. Chicago: University of Chicago Press, 1965.
Buber, Martin. *Two Types of Faith*. Trans. by Norman P. Goldhawk. New York: Harper & Row, 1961.

Bultmann, Rudolf. *Primitive Christianity in Its Contemporary Setting*. Trans. by R. H. Fuller. New York: Meridian Books, The World Publishing Company, 1956.

Chadwick, Henry. *The Early Church*. Harmondsworth: Penguin Books, 1975.

Clemen, Carl. *Primitive Christianity and Its Non-Jewish Sources*. Trans. by R. G. Nisbet. Edinburgh: T. & T. Clark, 1912.

Cochrane, Charles Norris. *Christianity and Classical Culture*. New York: Oxford University Press, 1957.

Daniélou, Jean. *A History of Early Christian Doctrine Before the Council of Nicaea*. 3 vols. Trans. by John A. Baker. Vol. 2, *Gospel Message and Hellenistic Culture*. London: Darton, Longman, and Todd; Philadelphia: Westminster Press, 1973.

Daube, David. *The New Testament and Rabbinic Judaism*. London: Athlone Press, University of London, 1956.

Eliade, Mircea. *A History of Religious Ideas*. Vol. 2, *From Gautama Buddha to the Triumph of Christianity*. Trans. by W. R. Trask. Chicago: University of Chicago Press, 1982.

Glatzer, Nahum N., ed. *The Essential Philo*. New York: Schocken Books, 1971.

Grant, Frederick C., ed. *Hellenistic Religions*. New York: Liberal Arts Press, 1953.

Hatch, Edwin. *The Influence of Greek Ideas on Christianity*. New York: Harper & Bros., 1957. (Rpt. of an old classic.)

Hengel, Martin. *Judaism and Hellenism*. Trans. by John Bowden. 2 vols. London: SCM Press, 1974; 1-vol. ed., 1981.

Jaeger, Werner. *Early Christianity and Greek Paideia*. Oxford: Oxford University Press, 1961.

Koester, Helmut. *History, Culture, and Religion of the Hellenistic Age*. Trans. by Helmut Koester. Philadelphia: Fortress Press, 1982.

Long, A. A., and D. N. Sedley. *The Hellenistic Philosophers*. Vol. 1. Cambridge: Cambridge University Press, 1987.

Nock, Arthur Darby. *Early Gentile Christianity and Its Hellenistic Background*. New York: Harper & Row, 1964.

Peters, F. E. *The Harvest of Hellenism*. New York: Simon & Schuster, 1970.

Rivkin, Ellis. *The Shaping of Jewish History*. New York: Charles Scribner's Sons, 1971.

Sandmel, Samuel. *The First Christian Century in Judaism and Christianity*. New York: Oxford University Press, 1969.

———. *Judaism and Christian Beginnings*. New York: Oxford University Press, 1978, 1980.

———. *Philo of Alexandria: An Introduction*. New York and Oxford: Oxford University Press, 1979.

Tarn, W. W. *Hellenistic Civilization*. Rev. ed. New York: New American Library, 1952, 1961.

Tcherikover, Victor. *Hellenistic Civilization and the Jews*. Trans. by S. Applebaum. New York: Atheneum, 1970.

Wolfson, Harry A. *Philo: Foundations of Religious Philosophy in Judaism, Christianity, and Islam*. 3d ed., rev. 2 vols. Cambridge: Harvard University Press, 1962.

J. Paul and His Theology

Bornkamm, Günther. *Paul*. Trans. by D. M. G. Stalker. New York: Harper & Row, 1971.

Davies, W. D. *Jewish and Pauline Studies*. Philadelphia: Fortress Press, 1984.

———. *Paul and Rabbinic Judaism*. London: SPCK, 1979.

Grant, Michael. *Saint Paul*. New York: Crossroad, 1982.

Maccoby, Hyam. *The Mythmaker*. New York: Harper & Row, 1986.

Sanders, E. P. *Paul and Palestinian Judaism*. Philadelphia: Fortress Press, 1983.

Sandmel, Samuel. *The Genius of Paul; A Study in History*. New York: Schocken Books, 1970.

Schoeps, H. J. *Paul: The Theology of the Apostle in the Light of Jewish Religious History*. Trans. by Harold Knight. Philadelphia: Westminster Press, 1961.

Schweitzer, Albert. *The Mysticism of Paul the Apostle*. Trans. by William Montgomery. New York: Seabury Press, 1968. (Recent ed. of an old classic.)

Ziesler, John A. *Pauline Christianity*. Oxford: Oxford University Press, 1983.

K. The Early Church and Its Theology

Bauer, Walter. *Orthodoxy and Heresy in Earliest Christianity*. Trans. by a team of scholars and ed. by R. A. Kraft and G. Krodel. Philadelphia: Fortress Press, 1971.

Bultmann, Rudolf. *Theology of the New Testament*. Trans. by Kendrick Grobel. 2 vols. London: SCM Press, vol. 1, 1952; vol. 2, 1955.

Cullmann, Oscar. *Christ and Time.* Rev. ed. Trans. by Floyd V. Filson. London: SCM Press, 1967.

———. *Solution in History.* Trans. by Sidney G. Sowers. London: SCM Press, 1967.

Eusebius, Pamphilus. *Ecclesiastical History.* Trans. by Christian Frederick Cruse. Grand Rapids: Baker Book House, 1976. (Recent pub. of an old classic.)

Frend, W. H. C. *The Rise of Christianity.* Philadelphia: Fortress Press, 1984.

Goguel, Maurice. *Jesus and the Origins of Christianity.* Trans. by Olive Wyon. New York: Macmillan, 1933; ppb. ed., New York: Harper, 1960.

———. *The Primitive Church.* Trans. by H. C. Snape. London: George Allen & Unwin, 1964.

Kelly, J. N. D. *Early Christian Doctrines.* London: Adam and Charles Black, 1968.

———. *Early Christian Creeds.* 3d ed. New York: Longman, 1985.

Koester, Helmut. *History and Literature of Early Christianity.* Trans. by Helmut Koester. Philadelphia: Fortress Press, 1982.

Lietzmann, Hans. *A History of the Early Church.* Vol. 1. Trans. by Bertram L. Woolf. Cleveland: Meridian Books, World Publishing Co., 1937.

MacMullen, Ramsay. *Christianizing the Roman Empire.* New Haven and London: Yale University Press, 1984.

Meeks, Wayne A. *The First Urban Christians.* New Haven: Yale University Press, 1983.

Moule, C. F. D. *The Origin of Christology.* Cambridge: Cambridge University Press, 1978.

Pelikan, Jaroslav. *The Christian Tradition: A History of the Development of Doctrine.* Vol. 1, *The Emergence of the Catholic Tradition, 100–600.* Chicago: University of Chicago Press, 1971.

Schillebeeckx, Edward. *Jesus: An Experiment in Christology.* Trans. by Hubert Hoskins. New York: Vintage, 1981.

Tennant, F. R. *The Sources of the Doctrines of the Fall and Original Sin.* New York: Schocken Books, 1968.

Weiss, Johannes. *Earliest Christianity: A History of the Period A.D. 30–150.* 2 vols. Trans. by F. C. Grant and others. New York: Harper Torchbooks, 1959. (Rpt. of an early classic.)

Wolfson, Harry Austryn. *The Philosophy of the Church Fathers.* Vol. 1, *Faith, Trinity, Incarnation.* Cambridge: Harvard University Press, 1956.

L. Apocrypha, Apocalypse, and Eschatology

Charles, R. H. *The Apocrypha and Pseudepigrapha of the Old Testament.* 2 vols. Oxford: The Clarendon Press, 1913, 1965–68. (Rpt. of a standard work.)

———. *A Critical History of the Doctrine of a Future Life in Israel, in Judaism, and in Christianity.* London: Adam and Charles Black, 1899. (An old classic.)

Charlesworth, James H., ed. *The Old Testament Pseudepigrapha.* 2 vols. Garden City, NY: Doubleday, 1983, 1985.

———. *The Old Testament Pseudepigrapha and the New Testament.* Cambridge: Cambridge University Press, 1986.

James, M. R. *The Apocryphal New Testament.* Oxford: The Clarendon Press, 1953.

Klausner, Joseph. *The Messianic Idea in Israel.* Trans. from the Third Hebrew Edition by W. F. Stinespring. London: George Allen & Unwin, 1956.

Otto, R. *The Kingdom of God and the Son of Man.* Rev. ed. Trans. by F. V. Filson and B. Lee-Woolf. London: Butterworth, 1943.

Rowley, H. H. *The Relevance of Apocalyptic.* Rev. ed. New York: Association Press, 1964.

Schneemelcher, E., ed. *New Testament Apocrypha.* Vol. 1, *The Gospels.* Trans. and ed. by R. M. Wilson. Philadelphia: Westminster Press, 1963.

Schweitzer, Albert. *The Mystery of the Kingdom of God.* Trans. by W. Lowrie. New York: Schocken Books, 1964.

Silver, Abba Hillel. *A History of Messianic Speculation in Israel.* Boston: Beacon Press, 1927, 1959.

Stone, Michael E., ed. *Jewish Writings of the Second Temple Period.* Philadelphia: Fortress Press; Assen: Van Gorcum, 1984.

Wilder, A. *Eschatology and Ethics in the Teaching of Jesus.* Rev. ed. New York: Harper & Row, 1950.

M. The Dead Sea Scriptures

Burrows, Millar. *Burrows on the Dead Sea Scrolls.* Includes *The Dead Sea Scrolls* and *More Light on the Dead Sea Scrolls.* Grand Rapids, MI: Baker Book House, 1978.

Cross, Frank M., Jr. *The Ancient Library of Qumran and Modern Biblical Studies.* 2d ed. Grand Rapids, MI: Baker Book House, 1980.

Gaster, Theodor H. *The Dead Sea Scriptures.* 2d ed. Garden City, NY: Anchor Press/Doubleday, 1976.

Rabin, Chaim. *Qumran Studies.* New York: Schocken Books, 1975.

Vermes, Geza. *The Dead Sea Scrolls: Qumran in Perspective*. Cleveland: William Collins & World Publishing Co., 1978.

Yadin, Yigael. *The Temple Scroll: The Hidden Law of the Dead Sea Sect*. New York: Random House, 1985.

N. Gnosticism and Christianity

Grant, Robert M. *Gnosticism and Early Christianity*. New York: Harper & Row, 1959, 1966.

Hedrick, Charles W., and Robert Hodgson, Jr., eds. *Nag Hammadi, Gnosticism, and Early Christianity*. Peabody, MA: Hendrickson, 1986.

Jonas, Hans. *The Gnostic Religion*. 2d ed., rev. Boston: Beacon Press, 1958, 1967.

Pagels, Elaine. *The Gnostic Gospels*. New York: Vintage Random House, 1981.

Robinson, James M., gen. ed. *The Nag Hammadi Library; In English*. Trans. by Members of the Coptic Gnostic Library Project of the Institute for Antiquity and Christianity, Claremont, CA. 3d ed., rev. San Francisco: Harper & Row, 1988.

Rudolph, Kurt. *Gnosis*. Trans. by Robert M. Wilson. San Francisco: Harper & Row, 1983.

O. Mystery Religions

Angus, Samuel. *The Mystery Religions*. New York: Dover Publications, 1975.

Campbell, Joseph, ed. *The Mysteries*. Princeton: Princeton University Press, 1978.

Cumont, Franz. *Oriental Religions in Roman Paganism*. Authorized trans. New York: Dover Publications, 1956.

Ferguson, John. *The Religions of the Roman Empire*. London: Thames and Hudson, 1982.

Meyer, Marvin W., ed. *The Ancient Mysteries: A Source Book*. San Francisco: Harper & Row, 1987.

Reitzenstein, Richard. *Hellenistic Mystery Religions: Their Basic Ideas and Significance*. Trans. by J. E. Steely. Pittsburgh: Pickwick Press, 1978.

P. Materials for the Study of the New Testament

Austin, M. M. *The Hellenistic World from Alexander to the Roman Conquest: A Selection of Ancient Sources in Translation*. Cambridge: Cambridge University Press, 1981.

Barrett, Charles K., ed. *The New Testament Background: Selected Documents*. New York: Macmillan, 1957.

Beare, Francis W. *The Earliest Records of Jesus*. New York: Abingdon Press, 1962.

Bruce, F. F. *Jesus and Christian Origins Outside the New Testament*. Grand Rapids, MI: Wm. B. Eerdmans, 1977.

Bultmann, Rudolf. *History of the Synoptic Tradition*. Trans. by John Marsh. New York: Harper & Row, 1963.

Cartlidge, David R., and David L. Dungan, eds. *Documents for the Study of the Gospels*. Philadelphia: Fortress Press, 1980.

Edwards, R. A. *A Theology of "Q": Eschatology, Prophecy, and Wisdom*. Philadelphia: Fortress Press, 1976.

Hengel, Martin. *Acts and the History of Earliest Christianity*. Trans. by John Bowden. Philadelphia: Fortress Press, 1980.

Keck, L. E., and J. L. Martyn, eds. *Studies in Luke–Acts*. Rpt. ed. Philadelphia: Fortress Press, 1980.

Metzger, Bruce M. *The Text of the New Testament; Its Transmission, Corruption, and Restoration*. New York: Oxford University Press, 1964. 2d ed., 1968.

Stevenson, J., ed. *A New Eusebius: Documents Illustrating the History of the Church to AD 337*. Rev. by W. H. C. Frend. London: SPCK, 1987.

Q. Critical Studies

Bultmann, Rudolf. *Jesus Christ and Mythology*. New York: Charles Scribner's Sons, 1958.

―――, and Five Critics. *Kerygma and Myth*. Ed. by Hans W. Bartsch. New York: Harper & Row, 1961.

Dibelius, Martin. *From Tradition to Gospel*. Trans. from the 2d rev. ed. by Bertrom L. Wolff. New York: Charles Scribner's Sons, 1935.

Fuller, R. H. *Interpreting the Miracles*. Philadelphia: Westminster Press, 1963.

Gast, Frederick. "Synoptic Problem." In *The Jerome Biblical Commentary*. Ed. by J. A. Fitzmyer and R. E. Brown. Vol. 2. Englewood Cliffs, NJ: Prentice-Hall, 1968.

Harnack, Adolf. *What Is Christianity?* Trans. by T. B. Saunders. New York: Harper & Row, 1957.

Jaspers, Karl, and Rudolf Bultmann. *Myth and Christianity*. New York: Noonday Press, 1966.

Kselman, John S. "Modern New Testament Criticism." In *The Jerome Biblical Commentary*. Ed. by J. A. Fitzmyer and R. E. Brown. Vol. 2. Englewood Cliffs, NJ: Prentice-Hall, 1968.

McKnight, Edgar V. *What Is Form Criticism?* Philadelphia: Fortress Press, 1969.

Ogden, Schubert M. *Christ Without Myth: A Study Based on the Theology of Rudolf Bultmann.* Dallas: Southern Methodist University Press, 1979; rpt. ed., 1985.

Perrin, Norman. *What Is Redaction Criticism?* Philadelphia: Fortress Press, 1969.

R. Formation of the Canon

Ackroyd, P. R., and C. F. Evans, eds. *The Cambridge History of the Bible.* Vol. 1, *From the Beginnings to Jerome.* Cambridge: Cambridge University Press, 1970, 1980.

Farmer, William R., and Denis M. Farkasfalvy. *The Formation of the New Testament Canon.* Ramsay, NJ: Paulist Press, 1983.

Grant, Robert M. *The Formation of the New Testament.* New York: Harper & Row, 1965.

Moule, C. F. D. *The Birth of the New Testament.* 3d ed., rev. San Francisco: Harper & Row, 1982.

Turro, James C., and Raymond E. Brown. "Canonicity." In *The Jerome Biblical Commentary.* Ed. by J. A. Fitzmyer and R. E. Brown. Vol. 2. Englewood Cliffs, NJ: Prentice-Hall, 1968.

von Campenhausen, Hans. *The Formation of the Christian Bible.* Philadelphia: Fortress Press, 1977.

S. Commentaries

The Encyclopedia of Religion. 16 vols. Mircea Eliade, editor-in-chief. New York: Macmillan, 1987.

The Interpreter's Bible. 12 vols. Ed. by George A. Buttrick. New York and Nashville: Abingdon Press, 1951.

The Interpreter's One-Volume Commentary on the Bible. Ed. by Charles M. Laymon. Nashville and New York: Abingdon Press, 1971.

The Jerome Biblical Commentary. Ed. by J. A. Fitzmyer and R. E. Brown. Englewood Cliffs, NJ: Prentice-Hall, 1968.

Léon Dufour, Xavier. *Dictionary of the New Testament.* Trans. by Terrence Prendergast. San Francisco: Harper & Row, 1983.

The Oxford Dictionary of the Christian Church. Ed. by F. L. Cross and E. A. Livingstone. London: Oxford University Press, 1974.

Peak's Commentary on the Bible. 1 vol. Ed. by M. Black and H. H. Rowley. London and New York: Nelson & Sons, 1962.

T. Bible Atlases

Aharoni, Yohanan, and Michael Avi-Yonah. *The Macmillan Bible Atlas*. 2d ed. New York: Macmillan, 1977.

Karmon, Y. *Israel: A Regional Geography*. New York: John Wiley & Sons, 1971.

May, Herbert G., ed. *Oxford Bible Atlas*. Revised for the 3d ed. by John Day. New York: Oxford University Press, 1984.

Pritchard, James B., gen. ed. *The Harper Atlas of the Bible*. San Francisco and New York: Harper & Row, 1987.

Index

A

Aaron, 117, 170

Aaronides, 170n. 27

Abraham: in the Baptist's denunciation, 54; as first Hebrew patriarch, 148; as representing Israel, 160; in Jesus' discussion of resurrection, 202; in Jewish claims to be God's elect, 268, 335; Paul's reverence for, 288; as first to enjoin circumcision, 403

Acts of the Apostles: Luke's Gospel in, 44, 174; fulfillment of promise in, 47; the Twelve in, 118; world set against Jesus in, 231; Paul in, 282–83, 294–98, 302; the Spirit in, 312; foreordination in, 337; prophets and prophecy in, 369; and development of canon, 414–16

Adam, 45, 322–28, 382

Adonis, cult of, 291

Adultery: Jesus on, 86, 187–89

Aelia Capitolina, 413

Agabus, early Christian prophet, 369

Agape: defined, 87–88, 88n. 18. *See also* Love

Akiba, Rabbi, 29, 412

Alexander, son of Herod the Great, 22

Alexander the Great, Macedonian king, 17, 18, 127; and Greek influence on Jewish culture, 128, 292–93

Am-ha-aretz (the common people), 117, 122

Amos, first classical Hebrew prophet, 169, 367; as a model, 170; Jesus in tradition of, 173, 249; in James, 392

Andrew, brother of Simon Peter, 71, 121, 259

Angels: in the Apocalypse, 384; fallen, 397

Annas, ex-high priest: and arrest of Jesus, 273n. 19

Annunciation: of births of Jesus and John, 5–7

Antichrist: in apocalyptic, 375

Antioch, capital of Seleucids, 19, 229

Antiochus III the Great, Seleucid (Syrian Greek) king, 19

Antiochus IV Epiphanes, Seleucid (Syrian Greek) king, 19, 365

Antipater, Roman governor of Judea, 21

Antonia Fortress, 233–34

Apocalyptic: of Mark, 40, 209–11, 367; of Essenes, 59–60; Jesus and, 65n. 21, 186; opposition to, 186; among early Christians, 208–11, 241; in Paul, 339–41; in Johannine literature, 363–71; described, 365; in Daniel, 365; structure and purpose of Jewish, 365–67; apocalyptic prophecy, 367–69; and Apocalypse of John, 378–84; effect of, on Christians, 397. *See also* Eschatology

Apocrypha: Messiah in, 29; defined, 366n. 10; and Pseudepigrapha in Jude, 397–98

Apocryphal Gospels: as sources on Jesus, 248

Apollos, leader of Corinthian faction, 300, 307, 357, 405

Apostasy: penalty for, 360

Apostles: failure of, to understand Jesus, 40–41, 91, 95, 141–44, 151, 192–93, 192n. 22; calling of, 71, 71n. 33, 117–22; instructions to, 123–24; ambitions of, 192–93; and resurrection report, 244–47; calling of, in Fourth Gospel, 259; Paul as, 284, 296–97, 305–6; in early church, 285; Jerusalem conference of, with Paul, 299–300. *See also* Acts of the Apostles

Aramaic Semitic, language of Jesus' home, 13

Aratus, Stoic poet, 290

Archelaus, son and successor of Herod, 22n. 32
Aristobulus, son of Herod the Great, 22
Aristobulus II, rival of Hyrcanus II, 21
Aristotle: Logos in, 252–53; *psyche* in, 326–27
Asceticism: warning against, 355
Astarte, cult of, 291
Astrology: and the Magi, 8–9, 8n. 10; and Paul, 334n. 23
Atonement: Paul on, 321–22; and sin and suffering, 333, 333n. 22
Attis, cult of, 291
Augustine, Bishop of Hippo: influence of Paul on, 316; influence of, in Christian theology, 321; original sin in, 325; importance of flesh and sex in, 328; influence of Romans on, 330; doctrines of election and predestination in, 338; on authenticity of Hebrews, 357
Augustus, first Roman emperor, 3, 21, 23
Authority: for disciples, 130–31, 130n. 41; of Peter, 145–46; of Jesus, 153–54, 167; in post-exilic Judaism, 170; Jesus questioned on, 199; of Jesus' family, 246; of Paul, 296–97; of apostles, 368, 398

B

Baptism: in Judaism, 56–57, 59; of Jesus, 57–60; of Essenes, 60; in Fourth Gospel, 255; of the Spirit, 258; replaces circumcision, 349; as basic ritual, 389–90
Baptist. *See* John the Baptist
Baptists (sect), 7n. 7
Barabbas, 232–33
Barnabas, 299–300; with Paul, 337; as reputed author of Hebrews, 357; and Peter, 385
Barnabas, Epistle of, 402–3, 419–21
Bar Kokhba, Simon, revolutionist, 29, 209n. 21; apocalyptic influence on, 370; influence of, on Marcion, 412
Bar Kokhba Revolt, 29, 209n. 21
Bartholomew, disciple of Jesus, 120
Bartimaeus, blind man of Jericho, 193
Benedictus, song-prophecy, 7

Benjamin: tribe of, 285, 314
Bethany: home of Martha and Mary, 175; Jesus' ascension from, 246; home of Lazarus, 270
Bethlehem, city of David, 4, 11, 12
Bethsaida: blind man healed at, 143
Beth-zatha: impotent man healed at, 90n. 22
Bread of life: as symbol in Fourth Gospel, 263–64; discourse on, 264

C

Caesarea Maritima, Roman capital of Palestine, 22n. 28, 229
Caesarea Philippi, 63, 150, 165, 168, 172, 192; rebuilt by Herod Philip, 23n. 33; confession at, 40, 58n. 11
Caiaphas, high priest: and Jesus' arraignment, 215, 224, 229, 271, 273
Cana: miracle at, 49, 259
Canon, Jewish: at Jamnia, 43n. 17, 84n. 10; Jewish Christian, 385
Capernaum: synagogues in, 25, 67; as center of Jesus' activity, 70, 76; healing in, 93, 106–7, 138; early Christian community at, 280
Celibacy: Jesus on, 188–89
Children: Jesus and, 189
Chloe: people of, 307
Christ: Jesus as, purpose of Synoptics, 37; as savior, 78; divine–human controversy concerning, 78; resurrected Savior-Christ, 153; evangelists' confession of, 169; and David, 203; rejection of, and anti-Semitism, 223–24; question of high priest concerning, 226–27, 227n. 24; as logos, 252; as spirit, 257–58; in Paul's religion, 288; Paul's testimony of, 297; Paul on incarnation of, 314–15; and the End, 345–46; and the Church, 351; as high priest, 358–59; as exemplar, 361; as judge, 384, 398. *See also* Logos; Messiah; Passion; Son of God; Son of Man
Christianity: relation of, to Judaism, 37; estrangement of, from Jews, 42n. 16, 186–87, 260, 260n. 12; as universal religion, 45; Jewish, 342–43

Index

Christology: in Colossians, 347; in Hebrews, 359–60; in 1 John, 373, 376

Church: in Luke, 47; perspectives of early, 154–55; and universalism, 157; and Jesus' ministry, 174; qualification for membership in, 206; and destruction of Jerusalem, 208–9; and delayed Parousia, 242; and disciples, 246; and history, 251; and Gnosticism, 266–68, 281; opposition of, to docetism, 275; division in early, 279; Peter and Paul and, 279–80, 280n. 2; in Galilee after Jewish war, 280; conflict in, 281, 283–84, 301–2; as independent religion, 305; Jewish Christianity lost to history, 316, 343; early religious traditions of, 342; literature on emergence of, 343–45; and Christ, 348–49, 352; and gnostic sects, 350; post-war relation of, to Judaism, 350; as institution, 351–54; and women, 356; as superior to ancient faith, 358–59

Circumcision: and Christian converts, 295; and Hellenistic Christians, 305; and Judaizers, 314; replaced by baptism, 349

Citadel: built by Herod, 22n. 29

Claudia, wife of Pontius Pilate, 228

Claudius, Roman emperor, 50

Clement of Alexandria, second-century theologian: on memoirs of Peter, 39n. 13; in John's Gospel, 255, 407; on 1 Thess., 303; influence of, on the canon, 419–21

Clement of Rome, bishop of Rome, 51; gnostic influences on, 266; on the Pauline letters, 313, 405, 408n. 16

Cleopatra, last of the Ptolemies, 22n. 31

Colossae, 313, 346–49

Colossians: authorship of, 303

Constantine, Roman emperor, 4, 235

Corban: Jesus on, 139, 139n. 11

Corinth, 299, 304, 306–12

Corinthians: letters of Paul to, 299–312, 340

Covenant: at Sinai, 23–24; and Messianic hope, 28–29; Exodus-Sinai, compared with David-Zion, 66–67; Jesus and, 84–85; new, 247; Jesus as surety for, 360; in 1 Peter, 387

Crucifixion: as Roman mode of execution, 234–35; catastrophes following, 239; burial of Jesus after, 239–40; in Fourth Gospel, 274–75. *See also* Passion

Cybele, cult of, 291, 411

D

Damascus, 20, 91, 128; Paul's vision on the road to, 294–96

Daniel, Book of, 210, 167; Messiah predicted in, 29, 37, 320; Son of Man in, 162–63, 166, 379; in early Christian church, 166–67; desecration of Temple predicted in, 210; messianic figure in, 320; apocalyptic prophecy in, 365–67; canonized, 370

David, 61, 67, 80, 119; and Messiah concept, 28–29, 41, 63, 146, 159; Jesus as son of, 160, 193, 195, 203, 208, 285; Jesus rejects model of, 230; in Paul's Christology, 320; and dynastic Christianity, 368; in Acts, 369; in Revelation to John, 381

Dead Sea Scrolls, 28, 285, 363, 401. *See also* Essenes; Qumran

Death: and sin in Paul, 322, 324–26; and resurrection, 333, 340; Christ and, 359

Decapolis, allied Greek cities, 70, 91, 128

Decius, Roman emperor, 409n. 20

Defilement: Jesus and Pharisees on, 138–40

Demetrius, Christian preacher in 3 John, 377

De-mythologizing: Bultmann's, 340–41

Deutero-Isaiah: suffering servant in, 46, 160–61, 231, 319, 333; and Jesus, 68, 172, 198; Messiah concept in, 163, 167; entry into Jerusalem predicted by, 195; in James, 392. *See also* Suffering Servant

Deuteronomy, 62, 156, 180, 201–2; Moses in, 171, 187–88, 257

Devil (Satan): tempts Jesus, 60–63; and power of Jesus, 92, 111–12; to be cast out, 178n. 7; in Judas, 215; in passion events, 223; and Jewish rejection of Christ, 223–24; in Gnosticism, 266–

67; at the End, 346; in cosmic struggle, 379; in Apocalypse, 382; and millennium, 383

Diaspora: in Mediterranean world, 18–19; and Temple, 197; Judaism in, 285–86; Hellenism in, 288; spread of Christianity in, 295; Septuagint in, 403

Didache, manual of church order, 370–71, 371n. 16

Dietary law: in Torah-tradition, 27

Diocletian, Roman emperor, 409n. 20

Diotrephes, congregation leader in 3 John, 377

Discipleship: conditions of, 124–26; in the Kingdom, 130–31, 189; and persecution, 147; and religious commitment, 190; test of, 213

Dives: in parable of the Rich Man and Lazarus, 182

Divorce: Jesus on, 86; in early Church, 86. *See also* Marriage

Docetism: and Gnosticism on Jesus, 275; opposition to, in Fourth Gospel, 275; in early Church, 371–73; as sin, 375, 375n. 21; in 3 John, 377

Domitian, Roman emperor, 358, 378, 382; persecutes Christians, 409n. 20

E

Ebionites, early Jewish Christians, 343n. 2, 416, 418

Ecclesiasticus: portrait of Elijah in, 148; prophet of fire in, 257n. 9; doctrine of sin in, 324

Eleazar, hero in 4 Maccabees, 366

Election. *See* Predestination

Eleusinian religion, 291

Eliezer, Rabbi: on the Law, 85n. 12

Elijah: and Phoenician baalism, 117; at Mt. Carmel, 171; prophesies in Malachi, 53; imbued with Spirit, 60n. 16, 94, 169, 250, 287, 310; at Transfiguration, 44, 147–50, 172; at the Confession, 145, 168; and power of the Spirit, 173; aids a non-Jewish widow, 69; to prepare for Messiah, 238, 238n. 47

Elisha: in northern tradition, 66, 169, 369; heals Syrian leper, 69; leads prophets, 94; Spirit in, 173

Elizabeth, mother of the Baptist, 6, 7

Emmaus, 169, 244–45, 246–47

Enoch, 103, 166, 167, 360; parable of, 366–67; prophesies the Lord's coming, 397–98

Enoch, Book of: Son of Man in, 162–63

Epaphroditus: in Phil., 313

Ephesians, Deutero-Pauline letter, 303; authorship of, 344, 349–52

Ephesus: as Paul's headquarters, 283, 305, 307, 313

Epicureanism, 287

Eschatology: and Messianic hope 28–29, 32n. 4, 59; and Kingdom, 166; and apocalyptic religion, 186; and resurrection, 246; in Mark, 250; in Paul's religion, 288, 292–93, 309, 314, 332, 339–41; in Johannine tradition, 363–71; described, 365; in Revelation to John, 378–84; in 1 Peter, 389. *See also* Apocalyptic

2 Esdras, apocryphal Book of, 324–25

Essenes, Jewish sect at Qumran, 28, 59, 115, 117, 286, 363–64; destroyed, 36, 42, 208; the Baptist and, 55; ablutions and, 57; Manual of Discipline of, 87; as the faithful remnant, 98; scriptures of, 285

Eusebius, church historian, 39n. 13, 50, 406

Eve, 382

Evil. *See* Sin; Sinners

Exile: reconstruction after the, 170

Exorcism: in Capernaum synagogue, 71; of Satan and evil spirits, 74–75; Jesus and, 74n. 37, 75; of demoniac, 92; G. Vermes on, 129; of evil spirit from boy, 150

Ezekiel, Book of: "Son of Man" passages in, 162, 164, 379

Ezra: and the Scribes, 108–9; and the Pharisaic movement, 113

F

Failure of nerve: Gilbert Murray on, 325–26

Index

Faith: salvation through, 306; Paul's emphasis on, 317, 319, 331–32; salvation and, 331–33; and freedom, 333–34, 344; conceptions of, 356; in Hebrews, 360–61; and works, 393; and opposition to Paulism, 393; as belief, 396

Fall, the: in Paul, 318, 322–26; universality of meaning of, 323; in Judaism, 323–25; and death, 324–25; and sin and salvation, 330. *See also* Sin

False doctrine: warning against, 355

Feeding the Four and Five Thousand: meaning of, interpreted, 134–36

Felix, procurator at Paul's imprisonment, 302

First Rebellion. *See* Jewish–Roman War

Forgiveness: by Jesus, 77, 110; by others, 131–32; in parable of unmerciful servant, 131–32; of adulterous woman, 264–65; in James, 395

Freedom: and faith, 333–34; and moral responsibility, 334–35

G

Gabriel: appears to Mary, 6, 11

Gadara, city in the Decapolis, 91, 128

Gaius, convert of the Elder in 3 John, 376, 377

Galatia, 298, 301; Paul combats Judaizers in, 284, 305

Galatians: Paul's letter to, 298, 301; and crisis in Asia, 300–1, 304–6; on faith and the law, 331–32; on freedom, 334–35

Galileans: love of independence of, 12–13; rebellion of, 13; and Judeans, 65–67, 171, 171n. 28, 185–86; prophetic spirit of, 171; opposition to, 66, 262

Galilee, northern district of Palestine, 63, 65

Galilee, Sea of (also Lake of Gennesaret, Sea of Tiberias), 65; storm on, 91

Gallio, proconsul who tried Paul, 306

Gamaliel I, Rabbi, 13n. 18, 269, 282, 287

Genealogy of Jesus: in Luke and Matthew, 7–8

Gentiles: Jesus and, 106–7, 126–28; Jesus' instruction to Twelve concerning, 123; Jesus' opposition to, 157–58; Jesus' description of, 193; as other sheep, 270

Gerasa, city in the Decapolis, 91, 128

Gerizim, Mount of, sacred mountain of Samaritans, 263

Gethsemane, 46, 219–21; and Passion, 220–21; Jesus' prayer in, 221; arrest of Jesus in, 221–23; in John, 272–73

Gischala, possible birthplace of Paul, 287

Gnosticism: defined 253, 266; in Paul and Fourth Gospel, 253, 266; influence of, 266–68; and author of Fourth Gospel, 267, 267n. 16; in last discourses of Jesus, 272–73; in truth, 274; and John, 274–75; in early gentile Christianity, 281; in Hellenistic religion, 289, 311, 322, 345; and Paul, 293, 322; and the fall, 322; and Paul's attitude toward body, 328; in Colossians, 347–48; inspires sects in church, 350–51, 354; in Pastorals, 355; and defection of gnostics, 371–73; and heretical teachers, 395–96, 411; in Marcion, 413–14

Godfearers: defined, 107

Golgotha, place of execution and burial, 214, 235, 235n. 39, 236–39

Gomorrah, Hebrew city, 124, 398

Good Shepherd: Jesus as, 270

Gospels: character of four, 34; purposes of authors of, 34; trustworthiness of, 34; background and purpose of Synoptics, 37–38

Grace: Paul on, 317–18; and failure of nerve, 325–26; salvation by, in Paul, 331–32, 343–44

Great Commandments: Jesus' quotation of, 202–3

H

Hades, in Parable of the Rich Man and Lazarus, 182–83

Hadrian, Roman emperor: and Bar Kokhba Revolt, 29, 209n. 21; banishes Jews from Judea, 413

Hagiographa, Jewish canon, 163, 370; canonized at Jamnia, 401

Hasidism: and Pharisees, 113n. 13. *See also* Pharisees

Hasmonean dynasty, 3, 20–21, 28, 115, 230. *See also* Maccabees

Hebrews, Letter to the: authorship of, 356–57; Christ as high priest in, 358–61

Helena, mother of Constantine, 235

Hellenism: in Paul's environment, 288–89; elements of, in Judaism, 293

Heraclitus: and "logos" in philosophic thought, 252

Herod Antipas, son of Herod the Great, 22, 66; and John the Baptist, 108, 111, 126, 133, 135; interrogates Jesus, 230–32

Herod Archelaus, son of Herod the Great, 22–23

Herod the Great, 4, 21; as builder, 35, 196, 144, 233–34

Herodians, supporters of Herod, 120, 126; attempts of, to discredit Jesus, 199–200

Herodias, former wife of Herod Philip, 133; marries Herod Antipas, 108

Herodium, fortress built by Herod the Great, 22n. 28; 35

Herod Philip, son of Herod the Great, 22, 23, 144

Hillel, Jewish sage, 43n. 17

Hippolytus, Christian theologian, 266; and the Muratorion Canon, 421

Holiness: in 1 Peter, 388

Hosea, 8th-century prophet, 249; in Luke's nativity story, 9; enjoins love of God, 88; opposes sacrifice, 120

Hylics: in Gnosticism, 269

Hyrcanus II, Hasmonean prince, 21

I

Ignatius, Bishop of Antioch, 51, 419; attests authenticity of Phil., 313; rejects Docetist teachings, 372; on canonization of Paul's letters, 405; on one gospel, 406

Immortality. *See* Resurrection; Salvation

Interim morality: among Jewish Christians, 388

Irenaeus, Bishop of Lyon: on the relation of Paul and Luke, 45n. 20; on the Fourth Gospel, 48; as enemy of Gnosticism, 266; attests authenticity of 1 Thess., 1 Cor., 303, 306; quoted in the Pastorals, 353; on one gospel, 406; and canonization of Acts, 416; on gospel writers, 417

Isaac, Hebrew patriarch, 148, 393

Isaiah: Jesus and, 71, 95, 249; on faithful remnant, 98, 115; on spiritual blindness, 103; messianic prediction in, 108; pronounces oracle against Tyre and Sidon, 127; as classical prophet, 169, 170, 173

Israel: identified with Christians, 43, 84, 84n. 9

J

Jacob, 148, 202, 288, 335

Jairus: in Jesus' miracle, 92–93

James, disciple of Jesus, 71; "son of thunder," 121; at the Transfiguration, 147; requests promise of high position, 192; with Jesus on Mount of Olives, 208; at Gethsemane, 221; in John, 259; in Galatians, 299–300; in Papias, 362

James, Book of, 390; in Jewish Christian tradition, 385, 399; conduct and faith in, 392–93; and Paul, 393; threat of persecution in, 394, 417

James the Just, brother of Jesus and Jude, 40, 51, 121, 396; as leader in Jerusalem, 280, 316, 343, 368; as head of Jerusalem Council, 285, 297

Jamnia (Jabneh), 42, 84n. 10, 401

Jeremiah, 160, 196, 198; in the prophetic tradition, 169–70, 173, 249; and new covenant, 336, 402

Jericho, 175, 193

Jesus (in the Synoptics): birth and early life of, 6–7, 10–11, 13–15, 15n. 23; wisdom of, 15–16, 30; and Judaism, 37, 68–70; in Mark, 38–41; in Matthew, 41–44; in Luke, 44–48; in John, 48–50; baptism of, 57–60; temptation of, 61–63; proclaims the Kingdom, 63–65; first disciples of, 70–72; in Capernaum, 71; fame of, and opposition to, 73, 77, 185–86; as supreme teacher, 78–88; exorcises, heals, and raises the dead, 74–77, 88–95; and parables of the Kingdom, 95–103; and the Baptist's inquiry, 107–8; on sin and sinners, 110; rejection of, by family, 111–12, 125; calls the Twelve, 117–22; on the Sabbath, 119–20; gives Sermon to the Twelve, 123–26; journeys to Phoenicia, 126–27; journeys to Decapolis, 128; and miracle of Feeding the Five Thousand, 134–36; and miracle of Walking on the Sea, 137; discourse of, on bread, 141–43; and confession at Caesarea Philippi, 63, 144–46; Transfiguration of, 147–48; Messianic consciousness of 152–55; as Son of God, 158–59; as Son of David, 159–60; as Suffering Servant, 160–61; as Son of Man, 161–66; as prophet, 167–70; parochialism and universalism of, 155–58; as a magician, 155n. 2; on Moses, Elijah, and the Spirit, 171–73; parables of, 176–84; on marriage and divorce, 187–89; on true discipleship and wealth, 189–92; entry into Jerusalem of, 195; and confrontation in the Temple, 195–99; authority of, 199–207; apocalyptic sermon and parables of, 207–13; Last Supper, betrayal, and arrest of, 214–23; trials of, 224–33; crucifixion, death, and burial of, 233–40; resurrection accounts of, 240–46

Jesus (in Gospel of John): coming of the Spirit upon, 255–58; signs of authority of, 259; miracles of, 259–64, 270–71; hostility toward Jews of, 268–69; arrest, trial, and crucifixion of, 272–75; resurrection of, 275–76

Jesus Christ (in Paul and the early church): spirit of, in the church, 283; family of, 285; James, the brother of, 297, 316; and doctrine of Second Coming, 309, 345–46; on the resurrection, 328; humanity of person of, 359; Christian eschatology and, 363–64; on apocalypticism and the Parousia, 370; divinity of, 371; and Docetist heresy, 377; Revelation to John entrusted to, 379; as Son of Man, 380; original teachings of, in James, 392; as fulfillment of the covenant in Barnabas, 403; as prototype of the martyr, 409–10

Jewish religion: in Jesus' time, 23–25; effect of First Rebellion on, 36; distortions of, by evangelists, 109, 140–41, 186; diversity in, 285–86. *See also* Oral Law; Pharisees; Sadducees; Torah

Jewish–Roman War, 114, 143, 225; relation of, to Judaism and Christianity, 35–37; in Mark, 39–40, 241

Jezebel, wife of King Ahab, 94, 117, 171

Joanna, wife of a steward of Antipas, 111

Job: suffering of the innocent in, 160; complaint of, 324

John, Gospel of: difference of, from Synoptics, 33–34, 48–50; authorship of, 48; conception of Jesus in, 47–50, 262–64; nature and purpose of, 252, 269; logos conception in, 254; doctrine of the Spirit in, 255–57; miracles as signs in, 259–62; and Gnosticism, 266–67; hostility toward Jews in, 268–69

John, Letters of: tradition of, 362; and defection of Christians and Docetist teachers, 371–72, 374

John, Revelation to (or Apocalypse of), 367, 379; authorship of, 378; mystical symbols in, 382; the Spirit and vision in, 384

John, son of Zebedee, disciple of Jesus, 71; brother of James, 93, 121; at the Confession, 147; in Samaria, 172; requests high position, 192; on Mount of Olives, 208; at Gethsemane, 221; call of (in John's Gospel), 259; in Galatians, 299; tradition of, 342, 362–84

John the Baptist: in nativity story of Luke, 6, 7; as messianic figure, 29, 54; problem of relation of, to Christianity, 37; relation of, to Jesus, 53, 53n. 1, 58n. 12, 134; ministry and message of, 53–54; and Essenes, 55; and Herod, 54n. 5, 133; treatment of, in Gospels, 55; baptizes Jesus, 57–60; inquiry of, concerning Jesus, 106–8; as Messiah, 108n. 5; Pharisaic interest in, 109; and disciples, 121; arrest of, 134; execution of, 126, 133–34, 133n. 2; Jesus as follower of, 134, 248; as Elijah, 150; authority of baptism by, 199; relation of, to Jesus in Fourth Gospel,

255–56; identity of, 256–57; and messianic movement, 339, 364
John the Elder, author of John 2 and 3, 376; against false teachers, 376–77
John Mark. *See* Mark
Jonah: the sign of, 141
Jonathan: revolts against Antiochus IV, 20
Joseph, father of Jesus, 4, 9–10, 68
Joseph of Arimathea, 239–40
Josephus: as primary source on Zealots, 13n. 18; on Sadducees and Pharisees, 26, 113, 139; refers to Jesus as Christ, 50; on the Baptist, 54n. 5, 108, 133; as governor of Galilee, 66; against Apion, 401
Judaizers: in conflict with Paul, 46, 284; Jewish Christians and, 280, 305; in Scriptures, 314, 317
Judas, son of James, disciple of Jesus, 120, 122
Judas the Galilean: revolts against Rome, 12–13, 116, 116n. 20, 269
Judas Iscariot: Satan in, 215n. 3; character of, 216–17; theories on betrayal by, 216–17; and arrest of Jesus, 221–22; and betrayal in John, 273
Jude, Letter of, 343, 396, 397–98
Judgment, Day of: as warning, 398–99
Julius Caesar, Roman general, 21
Justinian, Roman emperor, 5
Justin Martyr: on memoirs of Peter, 39n. 13; attests to authenticity of 1 Cor., 306; dialogue of, with Trypho, 403; killed, 408

K

Kerygma: Bultmann on, 341. *See also* Christ; Kingdom of God
Kingdom of God (Kingdom of Heaven): and messianic movement, 28–29, 32n. 4; Mark on, 40–41; in Baptist's message, 53–55, 59; Essenes on, 59–60; Jesus' proclamation of, 63–65; meaning of, 64–65; early Christian views of, 64–65; proclamation of, in Nazareth, 69–70, 69nn. 27, 29; appeal of proclamation of, 74; in Sermon on Mount, 80; and miracles, 91; in parables, 98–102; relationships in, 112; values in, 112; in instruction to Twelve, 123–24, 125; receive, as child, 130–32, 189; and feeding the multitude, 136; Pharisees' doubts concerning, 142; Jesus' concern with, 152; and Son of Man, 166; final proclamation of, 174–75; commitment to, 176; imminence of, 184–85; sacrifice for, 191; and service, 193; proclamation of, at Jerusalem, 195
Kings, Book of, 169

L

"L": as source for Luke, 32–33, 58, 175
Laodicea: Paul's letter to, 299, 313
Last Supper: and feeding of multitude, 134–36; reference to Son of Man in, 165; and Passover, 217–19; as table-fellowship, 218; in Fourth Gospel, 272–73
Law, Mosaic: traditions of, 3; and Sinai covenant, 23–24; affected by First Rebellion, 36; Jesus on, 84–85, 88, 156, 202; Pharisees' criticism of Jesus and, 138–39; Paul and, 294–95, 301, 331–32. *See also* Oral Law; Pentateuch; Torah
Lazarus, 49, 255; raising of, 90n. 22, 92, 270–71; in parable, 182–83
Lebanon, 65, 127
Legalism: importance of, in Jewish religion, 27–28. *See also* Oral Law; Torah
Leucius Charinus, author of Acts of John, 372
Levi, disciple of Jesus, 72, 119–20
Levites, 29; in parable of Good Samaritan, 180; with priests in the Temple, 200, 220; question Jesus, 256
Leviticus, Book of, 76, 156; regarding neighbor, 180, 203, 227
Light: and Gnosticism, 253; of the world, 265–66, 269; in Paul's conversion, 295–96; Jesus on, 373; in the Apocalypse, 383
Logos: in prologue to John, 248, 252–54; in Greek thought, 252–53; in Philo, 253–54; as principle of reason, 252–53; as Jesus and Christ, 253; as pre-existent Christ, 254

Index

Love (Eros and Agape): Jesus on, 87–88; in Judaism, 88, 88n. 18; in Paul, 312, 335; as God, 374; in 3 John, 377; in James, 392, 394

Luke, Gospel of: nativity story in, 4–9; on Jesus in the Temple, 14–15; "L" as special source for, 32–33, 58; "Q" as source for, 32–33; relation of, to Acts, 44; special section of, 45; conception of Jesus in, 46; relation of, to Paul, 45n. 20; on John the Baptist, 53; Sermon on the Plain in, 79; on divorce, 86; Feeding the Five Thousand in, 134; Transfiguration in, 147–49; Son of Man in, 164–65; Spirit as leading theme of, 172; Jesus at home of Martha and Mary in, 175; arrest of Jesus in, 222–23; complaint against Jesus in, 229; Jesus sent to Herod in, 230–31; role of women in, 235, 244; Jesus' utterance from the cross in, 236; Christian doctrine of resurrection in, 247; Spirit and divine plan in, 251; Baptist as Elijah to come in, 256; and Acts of the Apostles, 280, 283; Pentecost in, 284; Marcion's edition of, 414; in Irenaeus, 417. *See also* Synoptic Gospels; Synoptic Problem

Luke–Acts. *See* Acts of the Apostles

Luther, Martin: grounds theology in Paul, 316; influence of Romans on, 330; Paul's doctrine of election in, 338; rejection of James by, 422

M

"M," as source for Matthew, 32–33

Maccabaean Revolt, 19–20, 113, 113n. 13. *See also* Jewish–Roman War

Maccabaeus, Judas: revolt of, against Antiochus IV, 20; believed to be Messiah, 28

1 Maccabees, Book of: records Jewish massacre, 26–27

Machaerus, Herod's fortress, 35, 108, 108n. 4

Magi, wise men, 5, 8n. 10

Magnificat, song of Mary, 7

Malachi, 53, 148, 172

Marc Antony, 21, 234, 286

Marcion, 266; heresy of, 316, 420; as devotee of Paul, 353–54; and development of the canon, 412–14, 413n. 27

Marcionism: and Jewish Scriptures, 413–14; concept of God, Christ, and salvation in, 413–14; canon of, 414; reaction against, 414. *See also* Marcion

Mark, Gospel of: as source on Jesus, 31; authorship of, 38–39; on destruction of Jerusalem, 39; on Jesus and Judaism, 39n. 34; apocalyptic sermon in, 40; Peter's confession in, 40–41, 144–46; on the Baptist, 54; the baptism in, 57; calling of the four in, 71; Levi in, 72; on healings and exorcisms, 74; on divorce, 86, 89; rebuking the storm in, 91; healing of demoniac in, 92; failure to "see" in, 95; as favorable to Pharisees, 109; Jesus misunderstood by family in, 111; execution of Baptist in, 133; on Feeding the Five Thousand, 134, 136; Walking on the Sea in, 137; disciples' blindness in, 141–42, 144; on disciples' failure to understand, 192; on Jesus' self-consciousness, 158–60; Son of Man in, 161, 164; on Elijah Spirit in Jesus, 172; on healing of blind Bartimaeus, 193; on entry into Jerusalem, 195; on Jesus in the Temple, 197; on the Great Commandments, 202; the Last Supper in, 217–19; on Gethsemane, 219–21; arrest and trial of Jesus in, 221–33; crucifixion in, 233–39; burial and resurrection in, 239–43

Marriage (and Divorce): Jesus' dispute with Pharisees on, 187–89; Shammai and Hillel on, 187n. 11; Jesus' confrontation with Sadducees on, 201–2; Paul on, 308–9

Martha, friend of Jesus, 175, 180–81, 270–71

Martyrdom: in Apocalypse, 384; influence of, on New Testament canon, 409–10; literature of, 410

Mary, friend of Jesus, 216, 275

Mary Magdalene, 111, 240, 240n. 51, 275

Mary, mother of James, 240, 240n. 51

Mary, mother of Jesus, 6–7, 274

Masada, 22n. 28, 35, 35n. 9, 57

Mattathias: and Maccabaean Revolt, 19–20

Matthew, Gospel of: nativity story in, 4–7; Jesus' genealogy in, 7–8; massacre of infants and flight into Egypt in, 9–10; on Herod's cruelty, 22; date and structure of, 41–44; new Law in, 44; on baptism of Jesus, 57–58; on temptation of Jesus, 60–62; Kingdom of Heaven in, 64; Sermon on the Mount in, 78–88; on Jairus' daughter, 93; parables of Kingdom in, 97–102; parables as puzzles in, 103; on healing of centurion's servant, 107; on Feeding the Five Thousand, 134–35; on Walking on the Sea, 137; on Pharisees, 140; on Transfiguration, 147; on Jesus' parochialism, 157; on Jesus' self-consciousness, 159, 164–65; on divorce and celibacy, 188–89; on Jesus' entry into Jerusalem, 195; on taxes, 200; passion narrative in, 215; fulfillment of prophecy in, 216; Last Supper in, 218–19; on Gethsemane, 220; on Peter's denial, 224; on Jesus' arraignment, 224–25; on Pilate and Barabbas, 232–33; Jesus on the cross in, 236; on fulfillment of scripture, 237n. 43; resurrection appearances in, 242; on postponement of Parousia, 243; Christianity on a new foundation in, 251; on Jesus as New Word from God, 402. *See also* Synoptic Gospels; Synoptic Problem

Maximilla, Montanist prophetess, 411

Messiah: Jesus as, in Matthew, 8–9; Peter's conception of, 41; Mark's conception of, 41; Gospel writers' conviction concerning, 61n. 18; Jesus' refusal of Davidic Messiahship, 63, 144; as savior, 78; John the Baptist as, 108, 108n. 5; proclamation of Jesus as, 127, 135, 135n. 4; confession of Jesus as, 137; apostles' confession of, 145–46; defined, 145; Peter's confession of, 145–47; conception of, in Deutero-Isaiah and Daniel, 163; Jesus' claim as, 152, 165; proclamation of, at Jerusalem, 195; to suffer and die, 147, 245; Jesus identified as, 263; Davidic and Apocalyptic concepts of, 320; Paul's view of, 320–21; early church tradition of, 343. *See also* Christ; Jesus

Messianic hope: in Judaism and Christianity, 5, 319, 339; and the covenant, 28–29; and conceptions of Messiah, 28–29, 29n. 40; after First Rebellion, 37, 135; Sadducees and Pharisees on, 142–43

Micah, 367; in Matthew, 125; Jesus in tradition of, 173; in James, 392

Millennium: in Apocalypse, 383

Miracles: problem of, 75; nature of, 88–89; Jewish belief in, 89; types of, 90; and early church, 89–91; David Hume on, 90n. 21; Joseph Klausner on, 90n. 21; as signs, 91, 93; and restoration of life, 92–94; of Centurion's Slave, 106–7; of daughter of Syro-Phoenician woman, 127–28; in Decapolis, 128; saliva in, 129; of Walking on Sea, 137; of Loaves, 137; of restoring sight, 143–44; as evidence of Jesus' power, 154; of healing blind Bartimaeus, 193; of cursing fig tree, 197–98; at Cana, 259–60; of Feeding Five Thousand, 263–64; of raising of Lazarus, 271

Mishnah, the Oral Law, 43. *See also* Oral Law; Talmud

Mithraism, mystery religion, 291–92

Monotheism: in prophetic religion, 24; in early Christian tradition, 342

Montanism, 281, 284, 316, 411–12

Montanus, priest of Cybele, 411

Morality: Christian, based on prophets, 391–92; as central to religion, 393; in religion and conduct, 392–93

Mosaic Law. *See* Law, Mosaic; Torah

Moses, 187–88, 201; Jesus one like, 41, 195, 251; epiphany of, 44; as source of Israel's faith, 94; and Essenes, 115–16; in Transfiguration, 147–49, 172; authority of, 170–71; the Seventy and, 178–79; and resurrection, 202; and bread from heaven, 264; power of the Spirit in, 287; Paul's reverence for, 288; covenant revealed through, 336; in Romans, 338; in Hebrews, 359; in Josephus, 401; in Philo, 403

Moses, Books of, 25, 84, 400. *See also* Torah

Index

Mount of Olives, 207–8, 219–20
Mount Sinai, 94
Muratori, Ludovico, 420
Mystery religions: and Paul, 290–92; described, 291, 291n. 18; compared with Christianity, 292; in Colossians, 347
Mystical symbols: in Apocalypse, 382
Mysticism: in Paul, 332, 339–40; in Johannine tradition, 344

N

Naaman the leper, 69
Nag Hammadi: Gnostic Christian texts at, 104n. 42, 266–67, 418
Nain: widow's son at, 93, 106, 168
Nathanael, disciple of Jesus, 120–21
Nazaraeans: apocryphal Gospel of, 418
Nazarenes, Jewish Christian sect, 343n. 2
Nazareth, 11–12, 67, 70, 168
Nero, Roman emperor, 35, 50, 121, 302, 387, 409n. 20
New Testament Apocrypha; non-canonical writings, 418–20
New Testament Canon: crises shaping, 400; Jewish precedent for, 401–2; Hebrew scriptures as original Christian, 402; Paul's letters in, 404–6; Gospels in, 406–8; influence of persecution on, 408–9; influence of martyrdom on, 409–10; influence of Marcion on, 412–14, 420–21; Irenaeus and, 416–17; apostolic tradition and, 416–17; decisions of councils concerning, 421–22
Nicodemus, 240, 260–62
Nicodemus, Gospel of, 15n. 22
Noah, 389–90
Non-biblical Christian sources, 51–52, 52n. 27
Non-canonical gospels: on Jesus' infancy, 15n. 22
Non-Christian sources: Roman writers, 50; Josephus, 50–51, 51n. 26
Novatian: on Hebrews, 357

O

Oaths: Jesus on, 86
Octavianus. *See* Augustus
Omar, Caliph, 22n. 30
Onesimus: in Philemon, 315; bishop of Ephesus, 351
Oral Law: described 26–28; and Pharisees and Sadducees, 26–28, 114, 138–39; Sabbath regulations in, 26–27; dietary regulations in, 27; after First Rebellion, 36, 43; and Talmud, 114n. 15. *See also* Talmud
Origen, third-century theologian, 45n. 20; gnosticism in, 266; impact of Romans on, 330; on authorship of James, 390–91; influence of Philo on, 404

P

Palestine: successive conquests of, 16–19; Greek influence on, 16–19
Papias of Hierapolis, 38, 48, 362, 386, 406
Parables: defined, 95–96; of the Sower, 96–97; of the Weeds, 97–98; of the Seed Growing Secretly, 99; of the Mustard Seed, 99–100; of the Leaven, 100; of the Net, 101; of the Treasure and the Pearl, 102; as Secret Sayings, 102–5; of the Unmerciful Servant, 131; *of Luke:* the Unjust Steward, 176; the Servant's Wages, 177; the Rich Fool and Great Banquet, 177; the Friend at Midnight and Unjust Judge, 177–78; the Good Samaritan, 179; the Lost Sheep and Lost Coin, 181; the Two Sons, 181; the Rich Man and Lazarus, 182–83; the Ten Lepers, 183; the Pharisee and the Tax Collector, 184; *in the Temple:* the Two Sons, 204; the Wicked Tenants, 204; the Marriage Feast, 205; *apocalyptic:* the Ten Maidens, 211; the Talents, 212; the Last Judgment, 213
Paraclete: Father, Son, and, 411
Parousia: delay of, 37, 241–43, 370, 399; and false prophets, 40; Mark's faith in, 41; Luke on, 46–47; as Christ's return, 210–11; God's plan for, 246; in Paul, 303–4, 332, 339–41; in Deutero-Pauline literature, 345–46; as absent from Pastorals, 353; in Jude and 2 Peter, 395, 399
Passion: Jesus' announcement of, 146, 165, 191–92; synoptists on, 147; sec-

ond prediction of, 151; Jesus' expectation of, 192; God's plan for, 223, 246; narratives of, 214–15; and prophetic scriptures, 222; on Golgotha, 235, 235n. 39, 239–40. *See also* Crucifixion; Gethsemane; Trial of Jesus

Passover, 135, 260; pilgrimage to Jerusalem for, 14, 195; and Procurator, 23; after First Rebellion, 36; Last Supper and, 215–18

Patmos, 379

Paul: source on 282–83; letter of, to church at Colossae, 313; importance of, 316–17; on sin and death, 323–26; on faith and the Law, 331–33, 351; on 1 Thess., 31; Luke's relation to, 46, 281; imminent eschatology in, 47; in Polycarp, 51; on cup and remembrance in 1 Cor., 219; Christian theology grounded in, 248; background of, 285–94; experience of Christ of, 294–97; as evangelist, 297–302; authentic letters of, 303–8; on marriage, 308–9; on the Spirit, 310–12; letters of, from prison, 313–15; faith and theology of, 316–20; on sin, 321–29; letter of, to the Romans, 329–33; on meaning of freedom, 333–35; doctrine of election of, 335–39; eschatology of, 339–41; and Deutero-Pauline letters, 345–52; and the Pastorals, 352–56; and Hebrews, 356–57; apocalyptic prediction in, 368–69; in 1 Peter, 385; as model of suffering, 387–88; and James, 393; Jude compared with, 396; and the canon, 403–4; in Clement of Rome, 405; apostolic tradition founded on, 406; as basis of Marcion's canon, 412–14

Paulism: documents opposing influence of, 281; and authenticity of Pauline letters, 302–3; and Deutero-Pauline documents, 303; and Pauline tradition, 344; opposition to, 398

Pella, city in the Decapolis, 42n. 16, 128, 280

Pentateuch, 41, 84, 87, 400; as authority after Exile, 170–71. *See also* Torah

Pentecost, 155, 342; Luke on, 47; the Spirit and, 47, 174, 246, 251, 281, 284

Persecution: to be expected by disciples, 193; at the End, 209; Roman, 360, 386–87; justification of, 361; threat of, in Apocalypse, 379, 384; and New Testament canon, 408–10

Peshitta, 422

Peter: memoirs of, 38, 39n. 13; as leader of Christianity in Jerusalem, 40; view of Messiah of, 41, 192; confession of, at Caesarea Philippi, 63, 145; denial of Jesus by, 66n. 24, 220, 225; conversion of, 71; Mark's hostility toward, 143; as holding key of ecclesiastical authority, 146; and Transfiguration, 147, 149; on discipleship, 191; on Mount of Olives, 208; at Gethsemane, 221; at trial, 224; at the tomb, 244; as transitional figure, 246, 283; calling of, 259; failure of, to "see," 268; with John, 272–73; as successor to Christ, 280; leads Jerusalem church, 285, 297, 342–43

Peter, Books of, 385–88, 395

Pharisees, 26, 54, 66–67, 72–73, 95; increased influence of, after First Rebellion, 36, 42; and Jesus, 109–10; and the Baptist, 109; and Scribes, 108–9; distortions concerning, in Gospels 109–10, 140–41; and Torah, 113, 113nn. 13, 14, 114; influence of, at time of Jesus, 115; hostility of, 118–20; investigate Jesus, 138–41; Jesus' discourse on, 142–43; opposition of, to apocalyptic religion, 186; confrontation with, in Temple, 199–200; increase in influence of, 201; agree with Jesus, 203; Jesus' attack on, 206–7; opposition of, to chief priests, 271. *See also* Rabbis

Philemon, 313, 315, 351

Philip, disciple of Jesus, 121, 259, 273

Philip, missionary with Paul, 304

Philip. *See* Herod Philip

Philippians: Paul's letter from prison to, 313–15

Philo Judaeus, 229; "logos" in, 253; influence of, on Christian thought, 254n. 3, 285, 403–4

Phinehas: and Zealot heritage, 116–17

Phoebe: Paul's letter to, 301

Index

Pilate, Pontius, Roman procurator, 50; and Jesus' trial, 228–33, 272–74

Plato: "logos" in, 252; metaphysics of, 328; in Philo, 403

Pliny the Younger: on Christians, 50, 386

Pneumatics: in Gnosticism, 269; in Corinth, 300, 307–8; and threat of spirit-enthusiasts, 310; and morality, 334

Polycarp, 51; on Paul's Corinthian letters, 306; on Phil., 313; on 1 Tim., 353–54; letter of, to the Philippians, 386; and the canon, 419

Pompey, Gnaeus, 3, 20–21

Predestination (and Election): and chosen people, 335–36; and new covenant, 336; of nation and individual, 336; in Acts, 337; in Gospels, 337; in Paul's letters, 337–39

Priesthood: in Hebrews, 358–59

Priests: Temple ritual of, 24–25; effect of Jewish rebellion on, 36; after Exile, 170; caste of (Aaronides), 170n. 27; decline of influence of, 201; opposition of, to Jesus, 271–72

Priscilla, Montanist prophetess, 411

Prophets, 84, 88, 156; moral religion and monotheism of, 24; Christian, 40; false, 46; defined, 167–68; Jesus as, 167–73; after the Exile, 170–71; and prophecy in early church, 369–71

Psalms, Book of, 83, 203, 214, 238

Pseudepigrapha, 29, 59n. 14, 367–68

Ptolemaic empire, 18–19

Q

"Q" (Quelle): as source for Matthew and Luke, 32, 32n. 4, 33, 175

Quirinius, Syrian governor, 4, 12

Qumran, 28, 57. *See also* Dead Sea Scrolls; Essenes

R

Rabbis: in post-war period, 43, 43n. 17

Rahab: in James, 393

Ransom: Jesus as, 193, 193n. 24, 388

Redemption. *See* Salvation

Repentance: for sin, 131–32; Jesus and, 321

Resurrection: Jesus' announcement to disciples of, 146, 151; meaning of, questioned, 150; Jesus' messianic consciousness and, 165; Jesus quotes Hebrew Scriptures on, 202; as the Way, 239; of Jesus, 241, 242n. 54, 244–46; Jesus as, 270; in John, 275; in Paul, 307, 309, 320–21, 332–33, 339–41; in Apocalypse, 383. *See also* Passion

Revelation: in apocalyptic literature, 365; in Apocalypse, 378–84

Romans, Letter to, 303, 318, 329–31; on sin and salvation, 322, 330–35; on election and predestination, 337–38

Rome: conquest of Jerusalem by, 20; Jewish rebellion against, 35, 35nn. 8, 9; Christian relations with, 107; taxes of, 129, 200; Jesus as threat to, 271; persecution by, 358; in Apocalypse, 382–83

S

Sabbath: observance of, 26; and Oral Law, 26; and Seleucid massacre, 26–27; made for man, 199, 155, 164

Sacrifice: ritual of, in Judaism, 56

Sadducees, 26, 67, 69, 139, 223, 226; decline of, after First Rebellion, 36, 42; origin and doctrine of, 114–16; confrontation of, with Jesus, 141; Jesus' discourse on, 141–43; opposition of, to apocalyptic religion, 186; as instigators of Jesus' arrest, 199–201; on marriage and resurrection, 201–2; as Jesus' opponents, 228

Salome, 240

Salvation (and Redemption): by God's will, 190–91; and wealth, 190–91; in Gnosticism, 267, 269; in last discourses of Jesus, 272–73; Paul's conception of, 294; grace and, 317–22; eschatological, 338–41; and suffering, 387

Samaritans: in Jesus' instruction to the Twelve, 123; Jewish animosity toward, 179–80, 262, 262n. 13; origin of, 179; in parable of Good Samaritan, 179–80; women at well, 262–63

460 Index

Samuel, 60n. 16, 66; in the northern tradition, 94; power of God's Spirit in, 169, 287; as precedent for Spirit in Paul, 310; as model for Christian prophets, 369

Samuel, Book of, 169

Sanhedrin: after First Rebellion, 36, 42; and Sadducees, 115; authority of, 199; and trial of Jesus, 225–30; against Jesus, 271

Satan. *See* Devil

Saul, 60n. 16, 65, 74, 169

Saul. *See* Paul

Scribes: influence of, 36, 109n. 6; and Pharisees, 42, 84, 108–9; opposition of, to Jesus, 119, 138–39, 181, 199

"Seemists," Docetist heretics, 372

Sepphoris, in Galilee, 12

Septuagint: use of, by early Christians, 163, 167, 403; and Jewish Alexandrian canon, 401

Sermons of Jesus: Sermon on the Mount, 42, 45, 64, 78–88; Sermon on the Plain, 78–79, 79nn. 1, 3, 80n. 5, 106; Beatitudes, 80–83

Seventy, 45; origin of, 178; to proclaim gospel, 178–79

Sex: as sin in Paul and Augustine, 328

Shammai, early Jewish rabbi, 43n. 17

Shema, 227

Sidon, Phoenician city, 126–27

Signs: Jesus' opposition to, 141; miracles in Fourth Gospel as, 255, 259–60; Book of, in Fourth Gospel, 259; raising of Lazarus as final, 270

Silas: with Paul and Timothy, 304

Siloam: healing of blind man at, 91

Silvanus, secretary of Paul, 385, 387

Simon, son of Mattathias, 20

Simon the Pharisee, 109–10

Simon the Zealot, disciple of Jesus, 120, 122

Sin (and Evil): Paul's consciousness of, 294, 317–18; as alienation from God, 321; actual and original, 321; Paul and original, 321–26; origin of Paul's views on, 327–28; and flesh in Paul, 328–29; as objective and personal, 329; universality of, 330; and the Law, 330–31; and resurrection, 332; of denying Christ, 374. *See also* Fall

Sinners, 117; and ritual law, 127n. 37; in parables, 181–82, 184

Sodom, Hebrew city, 124, 398

Soferim. *See* Scribes

Solomon: ancient temple of, 24, 196; Messiah of lineage of, 29; hope of, for restoration of kingdom, 80

Son of David: Jesus as, 159–60, 167, 203

Son of God: Jesus as, 15, 59, 152, 158–59; in Judaism, 158; in Christian view, 167, 169; in testimony of the Baptist, 258; in Fourth Gospel, 261–62; glorification of, 270; and trial of Jesus, 272

Son of Man, 77, 158, 210–11, 213; and messianic age, 28; salvation and, 39, 364; and passion of Jesus, 146; and Transfiguration, 149–50; passion of, 151; Jesus' consciousness of, 152; Jesus' statements on, 161–66; Hebrew scriptures on, 161–63; as individual versus Israel, 162–63; as generic designation, 164; as agent of salvation, 167; in Daniel and Enoch, 367–68; in Revelation to John, 380

Son of Perdition: in Pauline tradition, 346

Soul (and Body): in Greek and Hebrew-Jewish thought, 326–27; Paul on, 328–29; immortality of, in Greek thought, 328–29

Speaking in tongues: Paul on, 312, 369

Spirit: in Luke, 47; and the church, 47; in Gospel of John, 50; and John's baptism, 54; at baptism of Jesus, 58, 58nn. 11, 13, 59, 258; and Jesus in wilderness, 60, 60n. 16; and miracles, 91; in gospel concept of prophets, 172; and Jesus, 172–73, 246–47, 260–63, 276; summary of, in Synoptics, 250; as central in Fourth Gospel, 255–57; as mediator between heaven and earth, 257; Paul's doctrine of, 284; in Galilee, 287; Paul on gifts of, 310–12; and love, 315; -bodies, 340; in Johannine literature, 363, 373–74; and prophecy, 369; and Trinity, 376; in Apocalypse, 380

Stephen, 58, 410

Stoicism: and Paul 287, 289–90; in Philo, 403

Suetonius, Roman historian, 50

Suffering Servant, 46, 68, 172, 198, 319, 392; as Messiah, 29; in Judaism, 160–67; Jesus as, 158, 160–62, 231; and sin and atonement, 333; tradition of, 387–88. *See also* Deutero-Isaiah

Sukkot: and Transfiguration, 147–49; meaning of, 148n. 23

Susanna, 111

Synagogue: as center of worship and education, 3, 13–14, 25; origin of, 25n. 34; after First Rebellion, 36, 42–43; ritual purification in, 57, 57nn. 9, 10; and Pharisees, 115

Synoptic Gospels: purposes of, 34, 37, 247–48, 250; historical background of, 36–37; as source of data on historical Jesus, 248–51; Jesus' message in, 249; Jesus' proclamation of the Kingdom in, 250. *See also* Luke; Mark; Matthew; Synoptic Problem

Synoptic Problem: relation of Matthew, Mark, and Luke as, 31–33, 32nn. 3, 4, 33n. 5. *See also* Synoptic Gospels

T

Table-fellowship: in Judaism and Christianity, 117, 218; and Last Supper, 218–19. *See also* Last Supper

Tacitus, Cornelius, Roman historian, 50

Talmud, 51n. 26, 57n. 9, 89, 401; and Oral Law, 43, 114n. 15; and messianism, 186

TANAK, the Hebrew scriptures, 4n. 1, 370; canon defined, 36

Tarsus, Gentile city, 282, 286, 287, 289

Temple: sacrificial rites in, 3, 56–57; rededication of, 20; and feast of Hanukkah, 20n. 27; and covenant, 24–25; destruction of, by Romans, 24, 35; effect of destruction of, 36; and Jesus, 38–39; history of, 196; Jesus' cleansing of, 196–200; Jesus prophesies destruction of, 207–8; cleansing of, in Fourth Gospel, 260–61

Temptation of Jesus: synoptic accounts of, 60–63

Tertullian, Latin theologian: on relation of Paul and Luke, 45n. 20; against Gnosticism, 266; on 1 Thess., 303; on 1 Cor., 306; on Hebrews, 357; and term "New Testament," 400n. 1

Thaddaeus, disciple of Jesus, 120

Theophilus, 44

1 Thessalonians: earliest New Testament book, 31, 279, 303–4, 339

2 Thessalonians, 345–46

Thessalonica, in Macedonia, 299

Theudas, messianist, 269

Thomas, Didymos Judas, 104–5. *See also* Thomas, Gospel of

Thomas, Gospel of, 15n. 22, 104–5, 418–19

Tiberius Caesar, Roman emperor, 50–51, 228

Timothy, Letters to, 344, 352–56

Timothy, missionary with Paul, 304, 308, 314

Titus, Letters to, 353, 355–56

Titus, missionary with Paul, 299–300, 308

Titus, son of emperor Vespasian, 35

Torah (Pentateuch), 14, 80, 109, 116, 139, 294, 305–6, 314, 317, 330–31; described, 25–26, 26n. 37; Sadducees and Pharisees and, 26, 113–14. *See also* Law, Mosaic

Trajan, Roman emperor, 50, 386, 409n. 20

Transfiguration: in Synoptics, 38, 165; meaning of, in Matthew, 44; in Luke, 58n. 11; and Jesus' identity, 137; appearance of Moses and Elijah, 147–49

Trial of Jesus: Jesus before high priest and Sanhedrin, 224–26; question of Jesus' guilt, 227–28; Jesus before Herod, 230–31; charges before Pilate, 229–30; trial as fulfillment of prophecy, 231; release of Barabbas, 232–33; Pilate's sentence, 233, 272–74. *See also* Passion

Trinity: doctrine of, 375–76

Trypho: Justin's dialogue with, 403

Twelve: calling of, 118–19, 122; instructions to, 123; meaning of discipleship for, 124–26; and unity of the church,

143; Peter as leader of, 146; in Son of Man passages, 165; desert Jesus, 250; as apostles, 284; as apostolic council, 285

Tyre, Gentile city, 74, 127, 157

U

Universalism: in Jesus' teaching, 127–28; Jesus and, 155–58; Jesus' parochialism and, 155–58; following resurrection, 243, 245–46; in the church, 251; and election, 338; and church universal, 351n. 14

V

Valerian, Roman emperor, 409n. 20

Vespasian, Roman emperor, 35, 378

W

Water: as spiritual symbol, 263; in Apocalypse, 383; and saving, 389

Wisdom: as mēmrā in origin of logos, 254; as from God, 394

Women: Jesus anointed by, 110; identification of Mary of Magdala, 111n. 10; Jesus and, 110–11; the Syro-Phoenician, 127–28; at the crucifixion, 235, 235n. 40; at Jesus' burial, 240; at the tomb, 240–41; at the cross, 274; in the church, 356, 389

Word of God: salvation through, 389

Z

Zacchaeus: and Jesus at Jericho, 194

Zealots: Galilee rebellion of, 13n. 18; at Masada, 35; and Christians, 36; and Jewish rebellion, 42, 63; in Josephus, 66, 116n. 19; beliefs of, 116; Judas Iscariot as, 217

Zechariah, father of the Baptist, 6, 7

Zechariah, prophet, 195, 216, 381

Zephaniah, prophet, 383

Zion: in David-Zion covenant, 67; in Isaiah, 195

Toward Understanding the New Testament

Jacket design by Scott Knudsen

Book design and typography by Donald M. Henriksen
in Intertype Garamond

Printed by Publishers Press
on Warren Sebago Antique Cream

Bound by Mountain States Bindery
in Holliston Roxite B
with French Speckletone endpapers